SIXTH EDITION

EDUCATIONAL RESEARCH

FUNDAMENTALS *for the* CONSUMER

James H. McMillan
Virginia Commonwealth University

Boston Columbus Indianapolis New York San Francisco Upper Saddle River Amsterdam
Cape Town Dubai London Madrid Milan Munich Paris Montreal Toronto Delhi
Mexico City Sao Paulo Sydney Hong Kong Seoul Singapore Taipei Tokyo

Vice President/Publisher: Kevin Davis
Series Editorial Assistant: Matthew Buchholz
Marketing Manager: Joanna Sabella
Production Editor: Karen Mason
Editorial Production Service: Jouve/TexTech International
Manufacturing Manager: Megan Cochran
Electronic Composition: Jouve/TexTech International
Art Director: Linda Knowles
Cover Administrator: Jenny Hart

Library of Congress Cataloging-in-Publication Data

McMillan, James H.
Educational research : fundamentals for the consumer / James H. McMillan.—6th ed.
p. cm.
ISBN-13: 978-0-13-259647-3
ISBN-10: 0-13-259647-4
1. Education—Research. I. Title.
LB1028.M365 2012
370.7'2—dc22

2011000761

Printed in the United States of America

10 9 8 7 EBM 15 14

www.pearsonhighered.com

ISBN-10: 0-13-259647-4
ISBN-13: 978-0-13-259647-3

To Janice, Jon, and Ryann

About the Author

James H. McMillan is Professor of Education in the School of Education at Virginia Commonwealth University, Chair of the Department of Foundations of Education, and Director of the Metropolitan Educational Research Consortium. He obtained his doctorate from Northwestern University and masters from Michigan State University. Dr. McMillan has also published *Research in Education: Evidence-Based Inquiry; Understanding and Evaluating Educational Research*, and *Classroom Assessment: Principles and Practice for Effective Standards-Based Instruction* in addition to more than sixty journal articles. His current research interests include classroom assessment, grading, student motivation, and the impact of high-stakes testing on schools and students.

Contents

12 ACTION RESEARCH *with* LISA ABRAMS *342*

13 DISCUSSION *and* CONCLUSIONS *360*

14 *The INTELLIGENT* CONSUMER: PUTTING IT ALL TOGETHER *379*

To the Instructor

This edition of *Educational Research: Fundamentals for the Consumer* is primarily for consumers of educational research and those involved in conducting action research. Consumers locate, read, understand, critique, and then use the results of research to become more effective professionally and to make sound educational decisions. The book is designed to enable students to become *intelligent* consumers of educational research and to introduce its basic principles to those who may eventually be involved in research in their work. The book is intended for a one-semester or one-term course in educational research. It is best suited for advanced undergraduate and beginning graduate students in education, and it is ideal for students enrolled in extended teacher preparation programs for initial certification, which emphasize research on effective teaching and action research (teacher researchers). The examples and excerpts from published studies are drawn largely from research that students will find interesting and informative. There are now 165 excerpts from studies and different journals. The book is also appropriate for students in more traditional masters' programs, who will be consumers of educational research, and for students in related social sciences, who need to learn how to read and understand research.

The primary goal of this book is to educate students to be intelligent consumers. This is accomplished by promoting student understanding of the researcher's intent, the procedures, and the results. Students are then shown how to analyze and evaluate research, judging the usefulness of the findings for educational practice. More specifically, the book will help students to::

- Apply the principles of scientific inquiry to everyday problem solving and decision making.
- Develop a healthy skepticism about "studies" that purport to advance our knowledge.
- Understand the process of conceptualizing and conducting educational research.
- Understand strengths and weaknesses of different methodologies used in research.
- Be able to read, understand, critique, and use published reports of research.

- Understand the uncertain nature of knowledge about educational practice generated through research.
- Keep a balanced perspective about the relative contributions of research and professional judgment.
- Understand how to conduct action research.

These goals are reached with a concise presentation of principles for conducting research and criteria for evaluating its overall credibility. The style of the book is informal, the language is nontechnical, and no prerequisite courses in measurement or statistics are needed. Numerous illustrations and excerpts from actual studies are highlighted as examples to familiarize students with the style and format of published articles, and to introduce students to the language of research.

The sequence of topics has remained unchanged from the fifth edition. The book covers fundamental principles in the sequence found in the research process, beginning with research problems and ending with conclusions. The emphasis is on teaching students that all aspects of conducting and reporting research are important in judging the overall credibility of the findings, and how different parts of the research process are interrelated. The format of research articles is included in the first chapter to enable students to read published studies as early as possible in the course. My experience is that students need as much practice in reading and critiquing articles as possible.

Because good consumers know how to find helpful research, the chapter on reviewing literature includes skills in locating primary and secondary sources and in evaluating a review of literature section of an article. **New to this edition is an extensively revised chapter on reviewing literature that integrates the use of ERIC with the use of the Internet to locate research.** This provides hints, sites, and procedures that will make it easy for students to use ERIC and navigate the Internet.

The chapters on measurement are fairly extensive because of its important role in educational research. **This edition includes a review of standards-based assessment.** Basic statistical principles are presented first to enhance understanding. For example, students must know about correlation to understand reliability and validity.

The emphasis in the discussion of each methodology—descriptive, comparative, correlational, survey, experimental, single-subject, qualitative, and mixed-method, and action research—is on what to look for in evaluating the credibility of the design and procedures. **The chapter on experimental designs has been expanded to reflect the increased emphasis on doing field experiments initiated by the federal government, with a focus on quasi-experiments.**

The chapter on qualitative research has been expanded with added emphasis on data analysis. A conceptual introduction to inferential statistics is included to clarify the results sections of quantitative articles. **There is also new chapters on mixed-method designs and action research.** These chapters provide a more extensive discussion of mixed-method strategies and analyses than the previous edition and provides students with essential skills to conduct action research.

As in the previous editions, the chapters include aids to facilitate learning essential skills and knowledge. Learning objectives at the beginning of each chapter help students focus on key concepts and principles. Key research terms are highlighted in the margins to reinforce their importance, chapter summaries in the form of concept maps organize the material succinctly, and study questions allow students to check their knowledge. Throughout the book, special sections called Consumer Tips emphasize the skills needed to judge studies critically. Over 150 examples from more than 90 published articles are included in the form of direct excerpts or examples from actual research, most of which are new and updated. **Pedagogical aids** include Chapter Road Maps, Using Educational Research, and Author Reflections.

In summary, the sixth edition has been strengthened with the following:

- Updates of all chapters, examples, and references
- Many more excerpts from published research articles to illustrate concepts and research writing styles
- Addition of learning objectives for each chapter
- **New chapter** on mixed-method designs
- **New chapter** on action research
- Substantial revision and integration of Chapters 3 and 4 from the previous edition, reflecting current search processes enabled by the Internet
- More emphasis on electronic surveys
- Expanded and heavily revised and reorganized chapter on qualitative research, including methods for establishing credibility and critical studies
- New Review and Reflect sections midway through chapters to promote student understanding and retention
- More emphasis on mixed-method sampling procedures
- More diagrams and figures to aid student understanding

NEW! COURSESMART eTEXTBOOK AVAILABLE

CourseSmart is an exciting new choice for students looking to save money. As an alternative to purchasing the printed textbook, students can purchase an electronic version of the same content. With a CourseSmart eTextbook, students can search the text, make notes online, print out reading assignments that incorporate lecture notes, and bookmark important passages for later review. For more information, or to purchase access to the CourseSmart eTextbook, visit **www.coursesmart.com.**

SUPPLEMENTS

A full complement of supplements further enhance and strengthen the sixth edition.

MyEducationLab

Prepare with the Power of Practice MyEducationLab is an online learning tool that provides contextualized interactive exercises and other resources designed to help develop the knowledge and skills researchers need. All of the activities and exercises in MyEducationLab are built around essential learning outcomes. The Web site provides opportunities to both study course content and to practice the skills needed to understand and carry out research. For each topic covered in the course you will find most or all of the following features and resources:

Assignments and Activities Designed to enhance student understanding of concepts covered in class and save instructors preparation and grading time, these assignable exercises give students opportunities to apply class content to research scenarios. (Correct answers for these assignments are available to the instructor only under the Instructor Resource tab.)

Building Research Skills These exercises help students develop skills that are essential for understanding and carrying out research.

Study Plan A MyEducationLab Study Plan is a multiple choice assessment tied to learning outcomes, supported by study material. A well-designed Study Plan offers multiple opportunities to fully master required course content as identified by learning objectives:

- Learning outcomes identify the learning outcomes for the topic and give students targets to shoot for as they read and study.
- Multiple Choice Assessments assess mastery of the content. These assessments are mapped to learning outcomes, and students can take the multiple choice quiz as many times as they want. Not only do these quizzes provide overall scores for each outcome, but they also explain why responses to particular items are correct or incorrect.
- Study Material: Review, Practice and Enrichment give students a deeper understanding of what they do and do not know related to topic content. This material includes activities that include hints and feedback. Visit www.myeducationlab.com for a demonstration of this exciting new online teaching resource.

Instructor's Resource Manual

An **Instructor's Resource Manual,** including test questions and answers, additional exercises and activities, is available to adopters by contacting their local representative.

Power Point™ Presentation

A **PowerPoint™ presentation** is also available online to instructors by contacting their local representative.

ACKNOWLEDGMENTS

Numerous individuals have contributed much to this book. I am most grateful to my editor of the first two editions, Chris Jennison, for his support, encouragement, and needed recommendations; to my editor for the third edition, Art Pomponio; Arnis Burvikovs for the fifth edition; and this edition's editor, Paul Smith. I am also indebted to many students and instructors who provided feedback to me on my organization, writing, examples, and approach and materials.

The following reviewers of previous editions contributed constructive suggestions: Jean Swenk, National University; Anthony Truog, University of Wisconsin-Whitewater; Judith Kennison, Ithaca College; Beatrice Baldwin, Southeastern Louisiana University; Kaia Skaggs, Eastern Michigan University; Ayers D'Costa, Ohio State University; Tamera Murdock, University of Missouri at Kansas City; Andy Katayama, West Virginia University; John W. Sanders, Middle Tennessee State University; Anastasia Elder, Mississippi State University; Lisa Kirtman, California State University, Fullerton; William J. Murphy, Framingham State University; and Steven W. Neill, Emporia State University. I also appreciate feedback for the sixth edition from Keonya Booker, University of North Carolina at Charlotte; Patrick Dilley, Southern Illinois University, Carbondale; Catherine McCartney, Bemidji State University; Nancy Mansberger, Western Michigan University; and Pamela Murphy, Virginia Tech.

I am grateful to the staff at Pearson, especially Matthew Buchholz, who have been exemplary in their editing and production of the book.

Finally, Gwen Hipp, Angela Wetzel, and Jesse Senechal provided great editorial suggestions.

As this is being written, further ideas are germinating for possible changes in organization and content for the seventh edition. Please write with any suggestions. Your comments will be most helpful.

James H. McMillan
jmcmillan@vcu.edu

To the Student

It was not *too* long ago that I sat, somewhat nervously, in a university auditorium waiting for my first class in educational research. Perhaps you have had a similar experience. I distinctly remember thinking, given what I had heard about "research," that I needed to learn only enough to pass the course and would not have to worry about it again! It was another hurdle that I was forced to jump to graduate. I was not bad in mathematics, but my interest was in working with people, not numbers. I certainly never thought that I would someday teach and write about educational research. But something happened to me as I grudgingly struggled through the course. What I discovered was that research is a way of thinking, a tool that I could use to improve the work I do with other people and to enhance student learning. My hope is that this book can instill a similar disposition in you, providing knowledge, skills, and attitudes to improve your life and the welfare of others.

Although learning the content and skills needed to become an intelligent consumer of research is not easy, my experience in teaching hundreds of students is that you will improve yourself, professionally and otherwise, through your efforts. In the beginning, especially as you read published research articles, not everything will make sense. But as your experience in being an informed consumer increases, so will your understanding.

Good luck and best wishes, and please write to me or e-mail me if you have suggestions for improving the book.

James H. McMillan
jmcmillan@vcu.edu

Chapter 1

Introduction *to* Research *in* Education

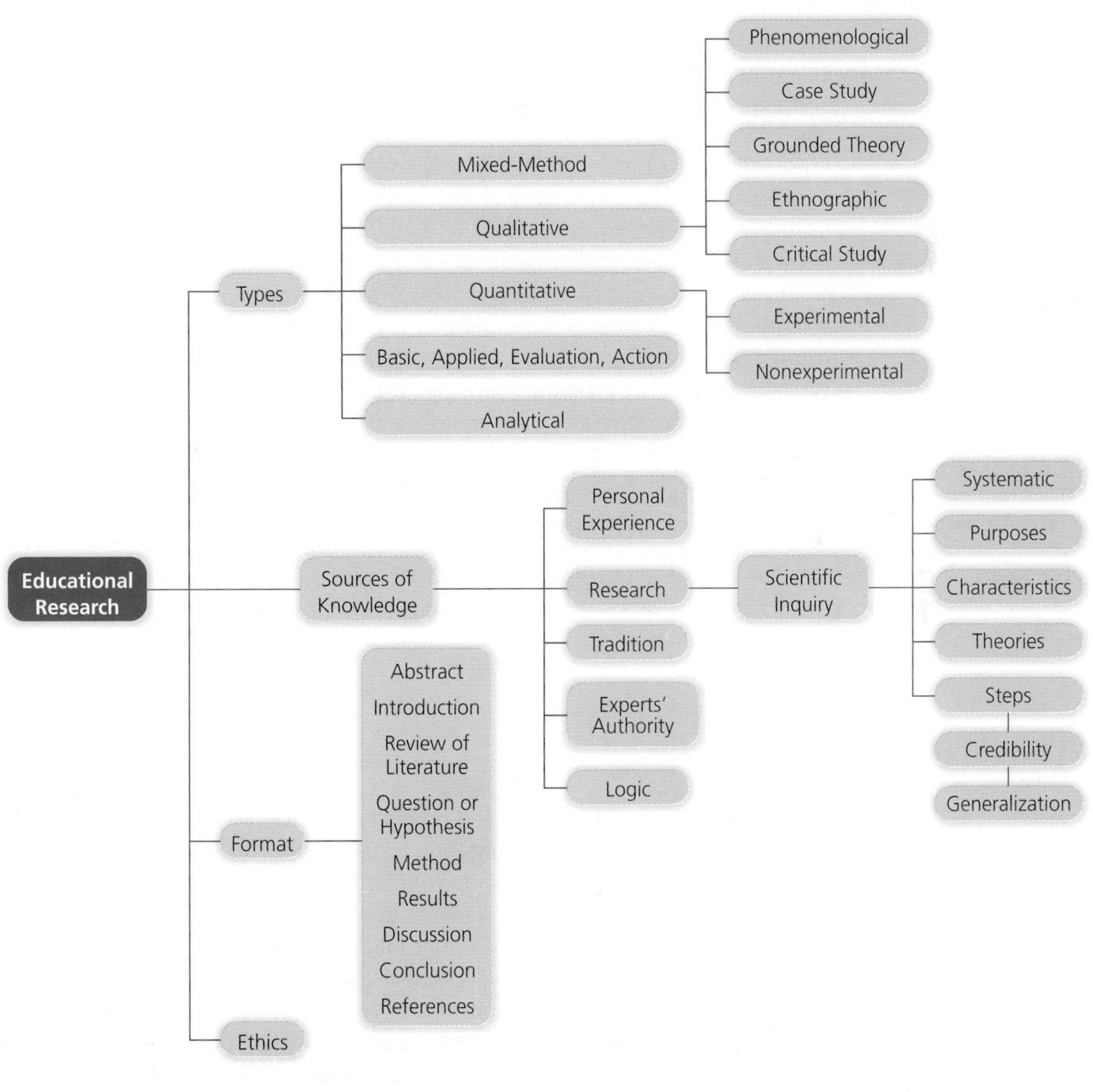

CHAPTER ROAD MAP

We begin our journey by considering different ways knowledge can be identified and constructed, with a special focus on how and why characteristics of scientific inquiry comprise the foundation for quality research. We then turn to overviews of different types of educational research and formats used with quantitative and qualitative studies, with two examples of published articles.

Chapter Outline	Learning Objectives
Why Research?	• Understand how research can make a positive difference.
Sources of Knowledge Personal Experience and Intuition Tradition Experts' Authority Logic Research	• Understand the limitations of various ways of knowing. • Understand the unique contributions of scientific inquiry to our knowledge of effective educational practices.
The Nature of Scientific Inquiry Purpose Principles	• Understand the steps of scientific inquiry.
Applying Systematic Inquiry to Education	• Apply principles of scientific inquiry to education.
Types of Educational Research Two Major Traditions: Quantitative and Qualitative Basic, Applied, Evaluation, and Action Research Research Ethics	• Become familiar with differences between quantitative and qualitative methods. • Identify and understand different types of research.
Article Format	• Become familiar with the format of research as reported in journal articles.

WHY RESEARCH?

This book is about helping you and others lead a richer, more satisfying life. That may seem like a strange beginning for a textbook like this, but I want to stress that there are good reasons for increasing your knowledge of research and the process of scientific inquiry. It is clear that research in education has made, and will continue to make, important contributions to our understanding of teaching and learning at all levels. Educators, like other professionals, need to read and interpret research to keep abreast of these contributions. However, the quality of educational research varies greatly, so it is essential that we are able to make informed judgments about the credibility and usefulness of the studies. Because education is a complex, situation-specific endeavor, we must each make these judgments in our own context.

A proper, balanced perspective on research will strengthen the judgments we make constantly in educational settings, and in that way touch the lives of many.

Furthermore, teachers and administrators are increasingly involved in conducting research in their own classrooms, schools, and districts. They have found that even informal, small-scale studies can provide new knowledge and insights to help improve student learning.

Finally, there is a renewed interest at the national level to use "evidence-based" findings to evaluate programs and policy. The trend is to use research whenever possible to make decisions about effectiveness and to determine "what works" in schools. The intent is to better connect research with practice. Here, then, is a list of the many benefits from conducting and disseminating research in education:

- Develops critical thinking and evaluation skills to examine arguments and claims made by others.
- Enables a more complete, more accurate understanding of educational research.
- Improves understanding of educational research reports in the media.
- Contributes to knowledge of best practice.
- Improves decision making.
- Informs educational policy.
- Improves educational practices.
- Fosters the ability to ask the right questions.

Author Reflection *Many of my students begin their study of research with hesitation and anxiety about the content. I tell them that's fine, that my job is to instill a positive attitude about research. Like my students, you may find that you actually like research. I tell my students if this happens (and I hope it will), it puts them in a special group. I hope you'll be a part of this special group as well!*

SOURCES *of* KNOWLEDGE

Judgments are based on knowing. We "know" something when it is accepted as true or valid, when we can be fairly certain of its consequences. For example, good teachers seem to "know" when they are losing the students' interest and need to change the method of instruction, when students need a strong rebuke or a soft reprimand, and how to phrase questions to elicit involvement from most students. How do these teachers obtain such knowledge? There are several ways, identified here as *sources of knowledge*. Each is important, and by examining them, we will be able to put research as a source of knowledge in perspective.

Personal Experience and Intuition

It has been said that there is no substitute for experience, whether it is your own or someone else's. In education we rightfully depend a great deal on direct experience to know what works. Professionals become effective through practice, and teaching is no exception. But imagine if experience was the *only* way to obtain knowledge, or if you were confined to your own experiences and those of friends. Not only would it be difficult to know where to begin, but it would also be difficult to know how to improve and how to handle new demands and situations. When research can be used to stimulate, inform, reinforce, challenge, and question our own experiences, the intuitive professional judgment that is absolutely essential for effective teaching and leadership is enhanced.

There are other limitations to using our personal experiences as sources of knowledge. Much of our knowledge from experience depends on what we have observed and how we have interpreted it. But as humans, we can and do make mistakes in our observations. Sometimes, because we bring our own biases to a situation, we fail to see things that are clearly evident, and we make inaccurate observations and interpretations. Finally, because we are personally involved with our own interpretations, we have a natural inclination to protect our self-esteem and ego, and consequently we may not be totally objective.

Tradition

Many things seem to be done right simply because they have always been done that way. Advice, rules, approaches to handling problems, and "right" and "wrong" answers are passed from year to year, from one group to another, as accepted truths. Tradition eliminates the need to search for new knowledge and understanding because we simply accept what has always been done as the best or right way. But reliance on tradition makes accepting new knowledge difficult and may mitigate our desire to question existing practices. For example, the tradition of a 180-day school year, with a summer vacation, in American public education makes it difficult to change to year-round schooling.

Experts' Authority

People we consider experts or authorities in a particular field are major sources of knowledge. An authority has experience or unique expertise in something and is able to provide insights and understanding that we are unable to see. We depend on such authorities, whether they are doctors, lawyers, professors, teachers, or plumbers, particularly in our specialized culture. But, like personal experience and tradition, authority can also hinder knowledge. Authorities can be wrong, and the public has a tendency to accept as fact what are actually opinions.

In fields such as education, where practice is heavily influenced by complex interactions among students, environments, and teachers, there is room for experts to disagree about what is known. Perhaps you have read one author who suggests one approach and another who suggests the opposite approach for the same situation or question. A good example is the evidence on the effectiveness of charter schools. During the year this book was revised, 2010, the effect of charter schools on student achievement was much debated. Some studies suggested that charter schools are more effective than traditional schools, but there was also research that showed little differential impact on achievement. Both sides of the argument were made by so-called experts and conducted by high-status centers, universities, and organizations. Also, the sheer number of authorities in education can be confusing. It is best to be able to analyze the suggestions of each authority and to make our own decisions.

Logic

Sometimes we can be convinced that something is true because a logical argument is made and defended. But logic is only as good as the facts that are used; logic by itself can't generate facts. There is a well-known saying that applies here—"garbage in, garbage out." Logic and reason are essential in conducting and reporting research, but these operations are done before and after a careful gathering of facts.

Research

In contrast to sources of knowledge that are primarily idiosyncratic, informal, and influenced heavily by subjective interpretations, **research** involves a systematic process of gathering, interpreting, and reporting information. Research is disciplined inquiry characterized by accepted principles to verify that a knowledge claim is reasonable. Defined in this way, research is not simply going to the library, gathering information on a topic, and doing a research paper. Rather, information is gathered directly from individuals, groups, documents, and other sources. **Educational research,** then, is systematic, disciplined inquiry applied to educational problems and questions.

Research: Systematic process of gathering and analyzing information.

Educational research: Disciplined inquiry applied to educational problems.

Research exhibits several characteristics that, together, distinguish it from other sources of knowledge:

1. *Objectivity* in observation, data collection, and reporting of results
2. *Control of personal bias* so that a researcher's personal prejudices, beliefs, desires, and attitudes do not influence the research and conclusions
3. *Precision* to provide detailed, specific definitions and descriptions
4. *Parsimony* to provide the least complicated explanation
5. *Tentative conclusions* that are open to change
6. *Verification* of findings through replication
7. *Openness to scrutiny* by others
8. *Logic*, inductive and/or deductive, to provide meaning

The NATURE *of* SCIENTIFIC INQUIRY

We expect scientists to use the **scientific** approach. It is easy to understand the usefulness of this approach in fields such as agriculture, medicine, engineering, biology, and the like, but is education or teaching a science? Without debating this question, the important point is that the scientific approach is a logical method of inquiry, not a body of knowledge. It is not tied to particular fields of study, to laboratory situations, or to men and women in white coats developing

Scientific: Systematic, testable, and objective.

complex theories. Consequently, we can study education in a *scientific manner*, even though education itself is not a science.

Purpose of Scientific Inquiry

The primary purpose of scientific inquiry is to explain natural phenomena and understand the underlying relationships and then, using this information, to predict and influence behavior. For example, we can use scientific inquiry to explain why some teachers appear to be more effective than others. The explanation leads to a knowledge base that novice teachers can use to become more effective.

Description provides fundamental knowledge about a phenomenon and is usually necessary before pursuing explanation and prediction. Accurate descriptions are essential to understanding explanations of events or people. For example, accurate descriptions of various teaching styles and student achievement are needed before the relationship between these two phenomena can be studied. Once these phenomena are adequately described, one may be predicted by knowledge of the other. This predictive power is very important because educators must constantly make predictive-type decisions (e.g., put Johnny in group A because he will do better with those children; admit a select group of students for a special program because they will benefit most; use cooperative teaching techniques because they will keep the students interested longer; advise against a particular occupation because the student will have difficulty passing the certification examination). Sometimes after describing phenomena, scientists control one to study its effect on the other. By controlling factors in experiments (discussed in detail in Chapter 8), researchers can determine whether one factor influences another.

In recent years, the idea that education can be studied "scientifically" has been strongly influenced by federal policy. Three significant developments include (1) the formation of the Institute of Education Sciences (IES) to provide leadership in expanding scientific knowledge and understanding of education; (2) formation of the What Works Clearinghouse to review studies for scientific rigor; and (3) publication of *Scientific Research in Education* (Shavelson & Towne, 2002). These influences have created unprecedented emphasis on the need for educational research to be "scientific" and policy and practice to be "evidence-based." This emphasis has focused researchers on what is meant by "scientific." Thus, the principles of scientific inquiry provide the foundation for conducting studies, regardless of the specific methodology used. These principles are in turn used in analyzing educational problems, making decisions, and designing, conducting, reporting, and evaluating studies.

Principles of Scientific Inquiry

Scientific inquiry, including educational research, is guided by six principles (National Research Council, 2002). While these principles are targeted to researchers, not consumers of research, they provide a set of guidelines that can be used to judge the quality and contribution of research. In concert with additional characteristics, these principles essentially constitute a set of norms that both researchers and consumers of research can employ to judge the quality of the research.

Scientific Principle 1: Pose Significant Questions That Can Be Investigated Empirically. This principle emphasizes two elements: (1) the need to identify important research questions that will have significant benefits once answered; and (2) the need for an "empirical" approach. An **empirical** study is one that gathers evidence (data) that is objective, evidence that is based on observation, measurement, or experience that can be replicated by others. It is based on concrete, physical evidence—what is seen, heard, or touched, using direct contact with what is being studied. Think of empirical as the opposite of theoretical, and objective as the opposite of subjective. The goal is to minimize the influence of subjectivity and bias so that there is little impact of a researcher's personal viewpoint, desires, or speculations.

Empirical: Evidence that is observable.

Scientific Principle 2: Link Research to Relevant Theory. In scientific research, generation and testing of theories are important for establishing a body of knowledge that will generalize widely. A **theory** can be defined as a set of propositions that explain the relationships among observed phenomena. Such general explanations of behavior can be used in many contexts and have more utility for a large number of people. For example, research on effective teaching has identified general teaching behaviors—such as close supervision, providing meaningful and timely feedback to students on their performance, and asking appropriate questions that keep students engaged—that are positively related to student achievement for most, if not all, teachers. It doesn't matter if the teacher has a fourth-grade class or a high school class, teaches French or science, or has honors or remedial students. The power of a theory to establish principles is what will advance our knowledge of effective teaching and educational interventions.

Theory: Explains relationships among phenomena.

Scientific Principle 3: Use Methods That Permit Direct Investigation of the Question. An important principle in conducting educational research is that the method used in the study should be the best one for the research question. There is no single method that always provides the best answers. Rather, method must be matched to question. Method is also influenced by the situation in which the research is conducted and access to information. For example, whereas experiments are often thought to be the best method for determining whether an educational intervention is successful, it is difficult to design such studies in schools. Scientific claims are strengthened when multiple methods are used.

Scientific Principle 4: Provide a Coherent, Explicit, and Evidence-Based Chain of Reasoning. Making scientific inferences, explanations, and conclusions requires a logical chain of reasoning that is coherent and persuasive. The chain includes links between the research question, pertinent literature, methods, findings, and conclusions. Inferences are strengthened when researchers identify limitations, uncertainty, possible bias, and errors. Descriptions of methods must include sufficient detail for others to review, critique, and analyze the study.

Scientific Principle 5: Replicate and Generalize Across Studies. Findings must be checked and validated, and subsequent studies need to determine if results generalize to a broader population and to other contexts. Access to data is needed for reanalysis.

Scientific Principle 6: Disclose Research to Encourage Professional Scrutiny, Critique and Peer Review. A hallmark of scientific inquiry is that studies are widely disseminated and subjected to review by peers. The information must be accessible and efforts must be made to publish results. This public, professional critique is needed so that the overall credibility of the findings is validated.

In 2008 the American Educational Research Association (AREA) convened an "expert working group" to formulate a definition of scientifically based research, using language that effectively translates scientific standards and principles into easily understood principles. This definition was written to clarify, from the perspective of AERA, fundamental principles of scientifically based research. This is what AERA came up with (retrieved January 18, 2010, from www.aera.net/uploadedFiles/Opportunities/DefinitionofScientificallyBasedResearch.pdf).

The term *principles of scientific research* means the use of rigorous, systematic, and objective methodologies to obtain reliable and valid knowledge. Specifically, such research requires:

A. development of a logical, evidence-based chain of reasoning;
B. methods appropriate to the questions posed;
C. observational or experimental designs and instruments that provide reliable and generalizable findings;
D. data and analysis adequate to support findings;
E. explication of procedures and results clearly and in detail, including specification of the population to which the findings can be generalized;
F. adherence to professional norms of peer review;
G. dissemination of findings to contribute to scientific knowledge; and
H. access to data for reanalysis, replication, and the opportunity to build on findings.

You can see that the AERA statement breaks out some of the more general principles from the National Research Council. It is interesting that the AERA definition does not emphasize the importance of questions and the need to link research to theory.

APPLYING SYSTEMATIC INQUIRY *to* EDUCATION

The purpose of research is to provide sound understanding and explanations that can become knowledge. The primary mode of inquiry employs a systematic series of steps to conduct the investigation. These steps are associated with questions that help us judge the quality of the research and, hence, the credibility of the results. The researcher's goal is to obtain credible answers to research questions by designing, conducting, and reporting data that others will view as trustworthy, that is, as reasonable results that make sense.

In its most simple form, research involves four steps:

Question ⟶ Method ⟶ Results ⟶ Conclusions

At the start is a question that needs to be answered, then there is some method of gathering and analyzing information. Based on the analysis and results, the researcher presents conclusions. For example, suppose you are interested in whether grading practices affect student motivation. The study could involve the four steps in the following manner:

Question ⟶	**Method** ⟶	**Results** ⟶	**Conclusions**
What is the effect of grading practices on student motivation?	Teacher and student surveys	More frequent grades, greater student motivation	Training teachers to grade more frequently may increase student motivation.

Once the question is established a method is selected. This involves identifying who will provide data, the instruments used to collect data, and procedures for gathering data and/or administering interventions. Results are determined by some kind of data analysis. Based on these results, the method, and previous studies, conclusions are drawn from interpretations of the results. This forms an expanded version of the four steps to show that choice of method and data analyses can affect the conclusions (see Figure 1.1). That is, depending on the nature of the subjects who are studied, the instruments, and the procedures, different conclusions can be reached for the same question. So in the example above, how motivation is measured could make a big difference (e.g., is motivation based on student self-efficacy or level of interest, or both?). The conclusion is also limited to the nature of the sample (e.g., fourth- and fifth-graders).

The expanded number of steps in Figure 1.1 shows how researchers actually go about planning and then conducting research. Each step in the process is important and contributes to the overall credibility and usefulness of the research. This book is organized around these steps and questions to provide you with the knowledge and skills you will need to make sound overall judgments about the credibility and usefulness of various studies. We will elaborate the steps and questions introduced in later chapters, but it is helpful to understand the nature of the entire process from the beginning.

In the first step, the investigator faces an obstacle to effective decision making or understanding, or identifies a general idea or question that warrants further thought. The next step, reviewing previous research on the topic, involves finding relevant research, analyzing it, and relating it to the initial question.

Next, the researcher formulates a specific research hypothesis or question. The hypothesis is an informed guess about the answer to the research question,

FIGURE 1.1 **Steps in the research process.**

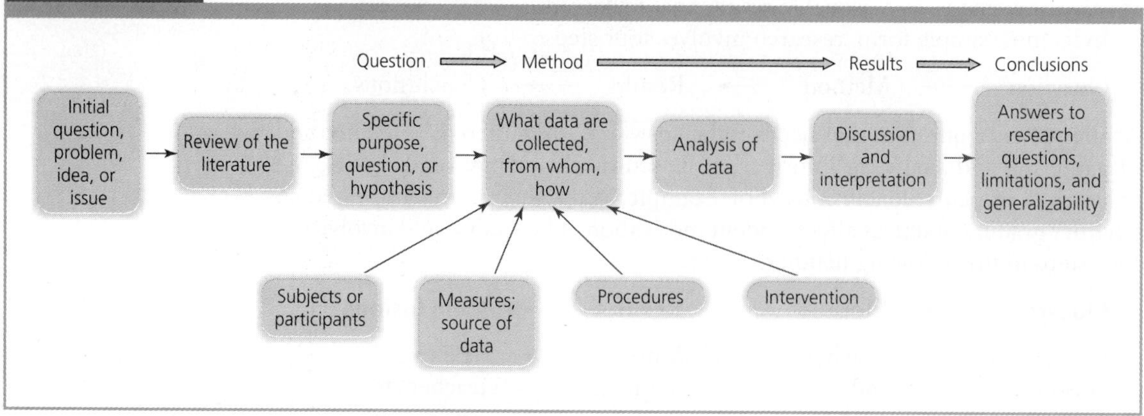

a hunch based on related literature and professional judgment. A question is warranted when the nature of the original idea or problem does not lend itself to a hypothesis. In research that follows an interpretive/constructivist approach, there may be only a general research problem or statement.

The design of the study is based on what will be an adequate test of the hypothesis or what will answer the question. It includes subjects, measures, procedures, and interventions. A carefully designed study is structured so that the explanation provided is the most credible one. Here the researcher must address "rival" explanations, often a result of faulty methodology, that may mitigate the credibility of the explanation offered.

The credibility of the results builds on previous aspects of the study, focusing on the reasonableness of the results in light of previous research and the extent to which alternative explanations are eliminated. The evaluation of the conclusions, in turn, also builds on previous credible judgments. Finally, judgments are made on the **generalizability** of the research, that is, whether the findings and explanations are useful in other situations and with other subjects, times, procedures, and measures. In other words, can the conclusions be generalized to other people in other contexts? This is an important concern for educational research because educators are interested in applying the results to particular groups and circumstances.

Generalizability: Use of results in other situations with other individuals.

Both the National Research Council and AERA emphasize the importance of a *chain of reasoning* as essential to scientific inquiry. This principle is illustrated in Figure 1.2. What is shown is that each step of scientific inquiry is connected to others. A "chain" with "links" is established, with a weakness in any link sufficient to break the soundness of the study. Keep this illustration in mind—all steps in research are important, and when a strong and reasonable chain is established, the credibility and usefulness of the conclusions are enhanced.

Review and Reflect *What are the major tenets of scientific inquiry? What are the key components of how educational research is defined? What are the advantages of gathering knowledge using research compared to other ways of knowing? Think about how your understanding of effective education has been developed. Where does research fit with other ways of knowing?*

FIGURE 1.2 Chain of reasoning in scientific inquiry.

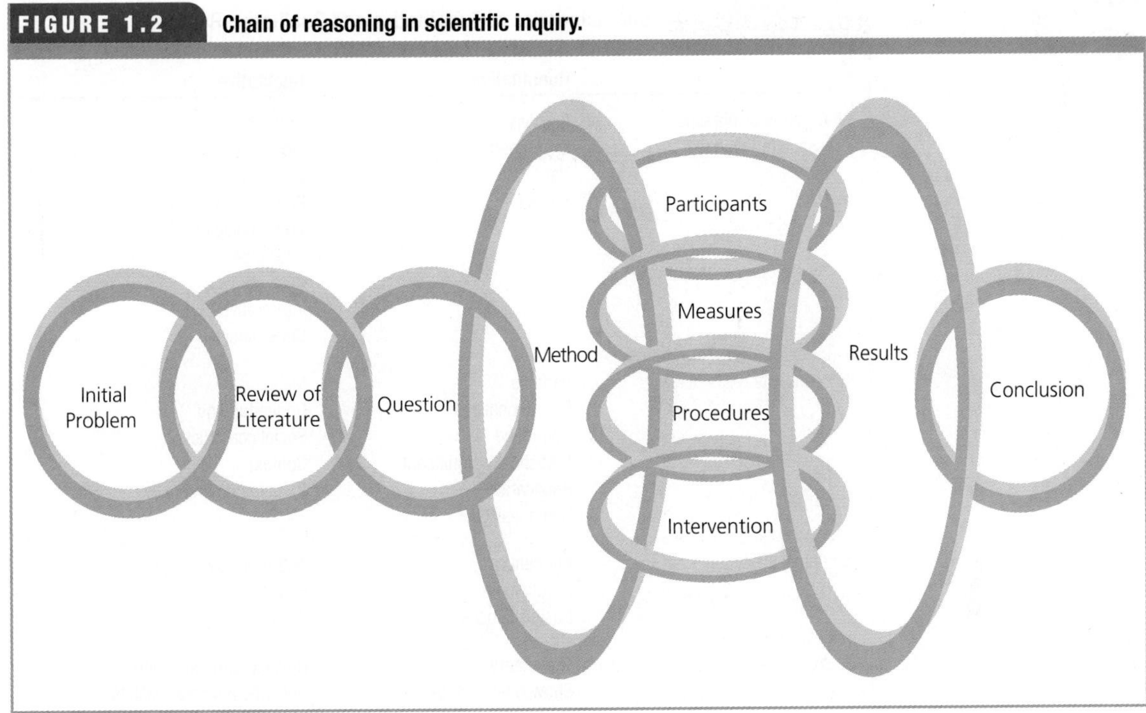

TYPES of EDUCATIONAL RESEARCH

Although all educational research is or should be conducted using systematic inquiry, there are different types of educational research. Indeed, it is common to discuss educational research in the context of one of these types because framing the discussion this way provides further information about the purpose and nature of the study. That is, it means more to say "experimental research" or "applied correlational research" than it does to simply say "research." We consider the major types of educational research in this section.

Educational research is often described as either *quantitative* or *qualitative* (or sometimes both in the same study). These terms refer to two different research traditions or paradigms, each with its own terminology, methods, assumptions, values, and techniques. For many decades most educational research was based on the **quantitative** tradition. This tradition assumes that phenomena should be studied objectively with the goal of obtaining a single true reality, or at least reality within known probabilities, with an emphasis on measurement, numerical data, control, and objectivity. It is based on a positivist or postpositivist view of the world. Until the mid-1970s the vast majority of studies in education were quantitative in nature. Today it is common to read studies that are qualitative, that have some qualitative features, or that use both approaches.

Quantitative: Emphasizes numbers, measurements, deductive logic, control, and experiments.

TABLE 1.1 Characteristics of Quantitative and Qualitative Research

	Quantitative	Qualitative
Other terms or phrases associated with the approach	Positivist Experimental Hard data Statistical	Naturalistic Field research Ethnographic Phenomenological Anthropological Ecological Case study Interpretive Constructivist
Key concepts	Variable Operationalized Controlled Statistically significant Replicated Hypothesized	Meaning Understanding Social construction Context Participant perspectives
Academic affiliation	Agriculture Psychology Basic sciences	Anthropology History Sociology
Goals	Test theory Show relationships Predict Statistically describe	Develop understanding Describe multiple realities Capture naturally occurring behavior Discover
Design	Structured Predetermined Specific Contrived	Emergent Evolving Flexible Natural Holistic

Qualitative: Emphasizes natural settings, understanding, verbal narratives, and flexible designs.

Mixed-method: Studies using both quantitative and qualitative methods.

Qualitative research stresses a phenomenological model in which multiple realities are rooted in the subjects' perceptions. A focus on understanding and meaning is based on verbal narratives and observations rather than numbers. Qualitative research often takes place in naturally occurring situations. It is based on an interpretive on structivist perspectives.

More recently, researchers have combined quantitative and qualitative approaches, resulting in **mixed-method** studies. These studies contain elements from both quantitative and qualitative traditions in an effort to better match research questions with appropriate methodology, and to use different methods to confirm and better understand more limited information that is gathered solely by either of the two major approaches.

Table 1.1 summarizes the major features of quantitative and qualitative traditions. Note the different terms that are used to refer to qualitative research. In the next section we examine different types of quantitative, qualitative,

TABLE 1.1 (Continued)

	Quantitative	Qualitative
Sample	Large Randomized	Small Purposeful
Data	One or few sources Measures/instruments Numbers Statistics	Multiple sources Verbal descriptions Field notes Observations Documents Photographs Narrative
Techniques or methods	One or few sources Experiments Quasi-experiments Structured observations Structured interviews Surveys Questionnaires	Multiple sources Observation Open-ended interviewing Review of documents and artifacts Direct data collection
Role of researcher	Distant Short-term Detached Uninvolved	Close Involved Trusting Evolving
Data analysis	Deductive Statistical	Interpretive Inductive Ongoing Search for themes Text analysis

Source: Adapted from Bogdan and Biklen, 2007; Creswell, 2009; and Johnson & Christensen, 2008.

mixed-methods *research designs*. Research design refers to the plan for carrying out a study.

Quantitative Research Designs

For quantitative research a major distinction is made between *nonexperimental* and *experimental* designs. In **nonexperimental research,** the investigator has no direct influence on what has been selected to be studied, either because it has already occurred or because it cannot be influenced. In other words, the investigator is unable to manipulate or control any factors or phenomena that may influence the participant's (subject's) behavior or performance. This characteristic has important implications for the conclusions that are drawn. It usually means that the study can only describe something or uncover relationships between two or more factors.

Nonexperimental research: No manipulation of factors that may influence subjects.

Nonexperimental quantitative studies can be classified as descriptive, comparative, correlational, or causal comparative. *Descriptive* research includes studies that provide simple information about the frequency or amount of something (e.g., How do high school counselors spend their time during the school day?). *Comparative* studies examine the differences between groups on a variable of interest (e.g., What is the difference between male and female self-concept scores? Do teachers in different grade levels have the same or different definitions of critical thinking?). *Correlational* studies investigate relationships among two or more variables (e.g., What is the relationship between physical conditioning and academic achievement? Is there a correlation between creativity and self-esteem?).

Causal-comparative research examines whether a naturally occurring "intervention" affects an outcome of interest, such as student performance. Ex post facto studies identify interventions that occurred in the past and subsequent responses in such a way that it may be possible to draw causal relationships between them (e.g., Do students who took typing in seventh grade have more positive attitudes in high school than students who did not take typing?).

Experimental research: Manipulation of factors that may influence subjects.

In **experimental research,** the investigators have control over one or more factors (variables) in the study that may influence the subjects' behavior. That is, they can manipulate a factor and then see what happens to the subjects' responses as a result. The purpose of manipulating a factor is to investigate its causal relationship with another factor. For example, investigators may be interested in studying the causal relationship between the amount of time devoted to a given subject, such as math, and achievement. They manipulate the former by having one group of children spend a small amount of time on the subject and a second group a large amount of time. If the children who spend more time studying math show higher achievement than the other children, then time devoted to studying may be causally related to achievement.

There are several types of experimental research, depending on specific design characteristics. A *true experimental* design is one in which subjects have been randomly assigned to different groups. A *quasi-experimental* design does not have random assignment. *Single-subject* designs use the ideas of an experiment with a single person or a few individuals.

Qualitative Research Designs

Unlike quantitative research, different types of qualitative research are not clearly distinguished by design characteristics. However, different purposes are identified with specific questions, data collection procedures, and analyses. The goal in a *phenomenological* study is to fully understand the essence of some phenomenon (e.g., What is essential for students to view teachers as caring?). This is usually accomplished with long, intensive individual interviews. An *ethnography* is a description and interpretation of a cultural or social group system (e.g., What is the effect of high-stakes testing on the climate of the school? How has high-stakes testing influenced teacher–principal interaction?). Ethnographers spend extensive time in the setting being studied and use observations, interviews, and other analyses to understand the nature of the culture. *Grounded theory* studies are conducted to generate or discover a theory or schema that relates to a particular environment (e.g., How do students with learning disabilities adapt to being in regular classrooms?). As in an ethnographic study, many different modes of gathering information are used. *Case studies* concern in-depth study of a single or a few programs, events, activities, groups, or other entities defined in terms of time and place (e.g., examining the culture of a particular magnet school). Again, multiple methods of data collection are used, including observations, interviews, and analyses of documents and reports. In *critical studies* the focus is on marginalized people, with investigations of injustice and inequity.

Mixed-Method Research Designs

Sometimes researchers use qualitative and/or analytical approaches and quantitative designs in the same study. By using multiple methods in a single study, the researcher is better able to match the approach to gathering and analyzing data with the research questions. The relative emphasis given to any particular method can vary widely. These studies can be primarily one method with a small contribution of another method, or can give the methods about the same weight. For example, it is typical in survey research to use sampling and closed-response type questions (quantitative) and also have some open-ended questions at the end that are analyzed qualitatively.

Analytical Research Designs

While most educational research can be classified as quantitative, qualitative, or mixed-method, there are some additional types that do not align well with these classifications. These can be called *analytical* studies. **Analytical research** is a mode of inquiry in which events, ideas, concepts, or artifacts are investigated by analyzing documents, records, recordings, and other media. Like qualitative studies (some researchers classify analytical studies, as described here, as qualitative), contextual information is very important to accurate interpretation of the data. In *historical analysis* there is a systematic gathering and criticism of documents, records, and artifacts to provide a description and interpretation of past events or persons. Both qualitative and quantitative data may be used in historical studies. *Legal analysis* focuses on selected laws and court decisions to examine how legal precedents influence educational practice. *Concept analysis* is concerned with implications and applications of the meaning and usage of educational concepts (e.g., high-stakes testing, performance assessment, and mainstreaming).

Analytical research: Historical, legal, or concept anaylsis.

Keeping these categories and examples in mind will help you understand important design characteristics of research. Use the decision tree in Figure 1.3 to identify different types of educational research. In the next section research is classified by the purpose or goal that is being pursued, regardless of methodology.

Author Reflection *Over the past two decades I have conducted many quantitative and qualitative studies. What have I learned about these methods as a result of these experiences? First, it is critical to match the reason for the research with the appropriate method. Method should always be determined by the purpose and the research question. Second, using each method*

FIGURE 1.3 A decision tree of educational research.

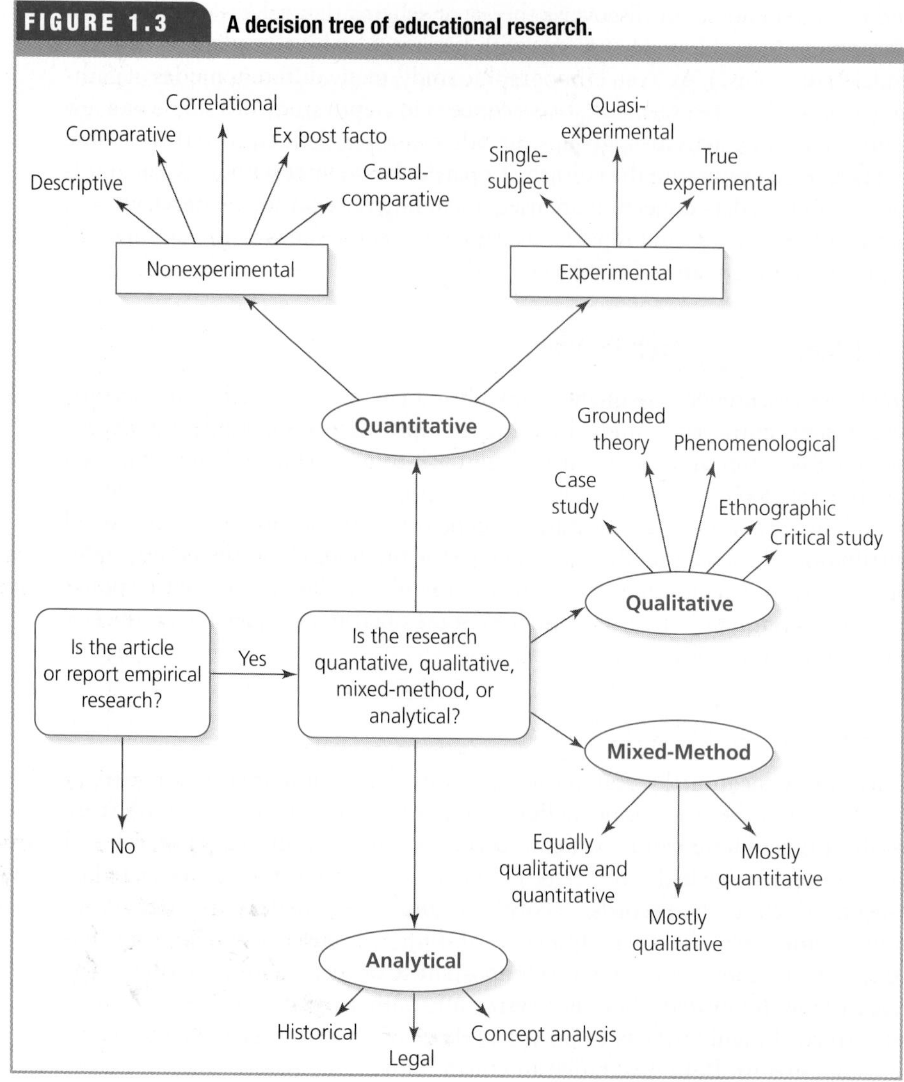

well is a challenge. Either can be used without appropriate rigor, which diminishes the usefulness of findings. Third, on balance, it seems that my qualitative studies have had more impact. I think this shows the importance of depth of understanding, regardless of the design. It is really important to engage in your topic with sufficient depth. Superficiality at any stage in the research process leads to less helpful results.

Basic, Applied, Evaluation, and Action Research

Basic research: Formulates and refines theories.

The purpose or goal of research is based on the use of the findings. The primary purpose of **basic research** (also called pure or fundamental research) is the development of theories. The goal of basic research is to understand and explain, to provide broad generalizations about how phenomena are related. It is not concerned with immediate application of the results to practical situations. Examples include studies of how the memory system works, language development, and social development. Few educational studies would be classified as basic, although educational researchers do conduct and use basic research.

The purpose of **applied research** is to test theories and other ideas in the context of naturally occurring educational settings. It is usually focused on a problem that needs to be solved to improve the practice of education. The results are immediately and directly relevant to educational decision making. To the extent that general theories are tested, the results may be generalized to many different educational settings. For example, based on theories of human memory developed through basic research, a new curriculum may be tested for improved retention of science concepts. Other examples of applied research in education are studies that compare different teaching styles, identify characteristics of effective schools, or examine the effect of lengthening the school day on student achievement.

Applied research: Improves practice and solves practical problems.

The goal of **action research** is to solve a specific classroom or school problem, improve practice, or help make a decision at a single local site. The intent is to improve practice immediately within one or a few classrooms or schools. Calhoun (1994) names three types of action research: individual teacher research, collaborative action research, and schoolwide action research. Teachers may act as researchers in action studies they have designed and carried out to improve practice in their classrooms. Administrators have used action research strategies for school renewal and other improvement efforts.

Action research: Investigates specific classroom problems.

Evaluation research is directed toward making decisions about the effectiveness or desirability of a program. The goal is to make judgments about alternatives in decision-making situations. In most cases evaluation research is focused on a specific location or type of program and involves judgments about such questions as: Which reading curriculum should be implemented? Did the new program work? Should the district build two small schools or one large school? What is the impact of increased technology on student and teacher knowledge and attitudes? Often, such questions require research methods that are unique to each situation. A summary of the major types of educational research, with additional examples, is provided in Table 1.2.

Evaluation research: Judgments for decision making.

Research Ethics

Before turning to the format of research articles, there is a very important topic related to conducting studies that you need to be aware of—ethics. Within the context of gathering data from subjects or using data in which subjects are identified, ethics are concerned with what is right or wrong, good or bad, or proper or improper. There has been extensive discussion of the ethics of research, much of it by established research organizations, though it is only touched on here. Researchers should follow established ethical guidelines, and if you do want to do any kind of study, even something within your own work context, you need to be aware of these guidelines. Organizations such as the American Educational

TABLE 1.2 Major Types of Educational Research*

Type	Purpose	Example
Quantitative	To describe phenomena numerically to answer specific questions or hypotheses.	The relationship between amount of homework and student achievement.
Qualitative	To provide rich narrative descriptions of phenomena that enhance understanding.	Observations of school renewal teams to understand the role of parents.
Mixed-Method	To study phenomena using both quantitative and qualitative methods.	From a randomly selected sample, use surveys and interviews to study at-risk students.
Nonexperimental	To describe, compare, and predict phenomena without actively manipulating factors that influence the phenomena.	Determine the relationship between socioeconomic status and student attitudes.
Experimental	To determine the causal relationship between two or more phenomena by direct manipulation of factors that influence the phenomena.	Determine which of two approaches to teaching science results in the highest student achievement.
Basic	To increase knowledge and understanding of phenomena.	Understand how feedback affects motivation or learning styles of adolescents.
Applied	To solve practical educational problems.	Determine the best approach for training teachers to use portfolios for classroom assessment.
Action	To improve practice in a school or classroom.	Determine which grouping procedure results in the highest achievement.
Evaluation	To make a decision about a program or activity.	Decide whether to keep or phase out a prekindergarten program.

*Note that some traits overlap among different types of research. For example, qualitative studies may contain numerical summaries of information.

Research Association (AERA) and the American Psychological Association (APA) have formal ethical guidelines for conducting research with humans, and you can visit their Websites for details (www.aera.net; www.apa.org). The ten basic aspects of most ethical concern are:

1. The primary investigator of a study is responsible for the ethical standards to which the study adheres.
2. The investigator should inform subjects of all aspects of the research that might influence their willingness to participate.
3. The investigator should be as open and honest with subjects as possible, which usually requires full disclosure. Sometimes deception is necessary and not unethical, in which case participants are usually debriefed after the study.
4. Subjects must be protected from physical and mental discomfort, harm, and danger. There should be minimal risk to those participating.

5. Often, informed consent must be obtained from the subjects prior to gathering data. In most studies of children, parental consent is required.
6. Subjects may discontinue participation at any time without penalty or risk.
7. Subjects should never be coerced to participate; participation must be voluntary.
8. Unless otherwise agreed to, data should be anonymous and/or confidential. Participant privacy should be protected.
9. For research conducted through an institution such as a university, approval for conducting the research should be obtained before data are collected. This often means obtaining permission from an internal review board (IRB) prior to data collection.
10. Potential benefits to a control group should be identified.

Universities may have specific ethical guidelines for conducting research with human subjects. An institutional review board (IRB) will need to approve studies in which there is interaction with or an intervention with humans. The IRB provides an independent judgment about the ethics of the research, and assures compliance with federal regulations. Each investigator needs to check carefully the requirements and protocols that have been established in his or her organization. Often the process of obtaining IRB approval can be time-consuming. Student projects may require approval. Even if IRB approval is not required, all researchers have a professional obligation to conduct studies with appropriate attention to ethical and legal guidelines.

Increasingly and significantly, local school districts also have formal procedures for conducting research with staff or students. This typically requires a proposal to conduct the research well before anticipated data collection. School districts may have their own ethical guidelines, and are also required to adhere to legal precedents that influence what data may be gathered and the role of parents in giving consent to use their children as participants.

EDUCATIONAL RESEARCH ARTICLE REPORT FORMAT

Every year millions of dollars are spent on educational research and millions more on related research in psychology, sociology, and other social sciences. Every year hundreds of articles and reports are published. One of the primary objectives of this book is to help you become an intelligent reader of these articles and reports. A research article report sets forth the research problem, what the researcher has done to collect data, how the data are analyzed and interpreted, and the conclusions. In other words, the article report is a summary of what was done, how it was done, why it was done, and what was discovered. Most articles, as well as research reports that are not articles, follow a standard format or organizational structure, as summarized in Figure 1.4, which show differences between quantitative and qualitative formats. These parts are discussed briefly and are then identified in published quantitative and qualitative articles.

FIGURE 1.4 Quantitative and qualitative research article report formats (adapted from Creswell, 2005).

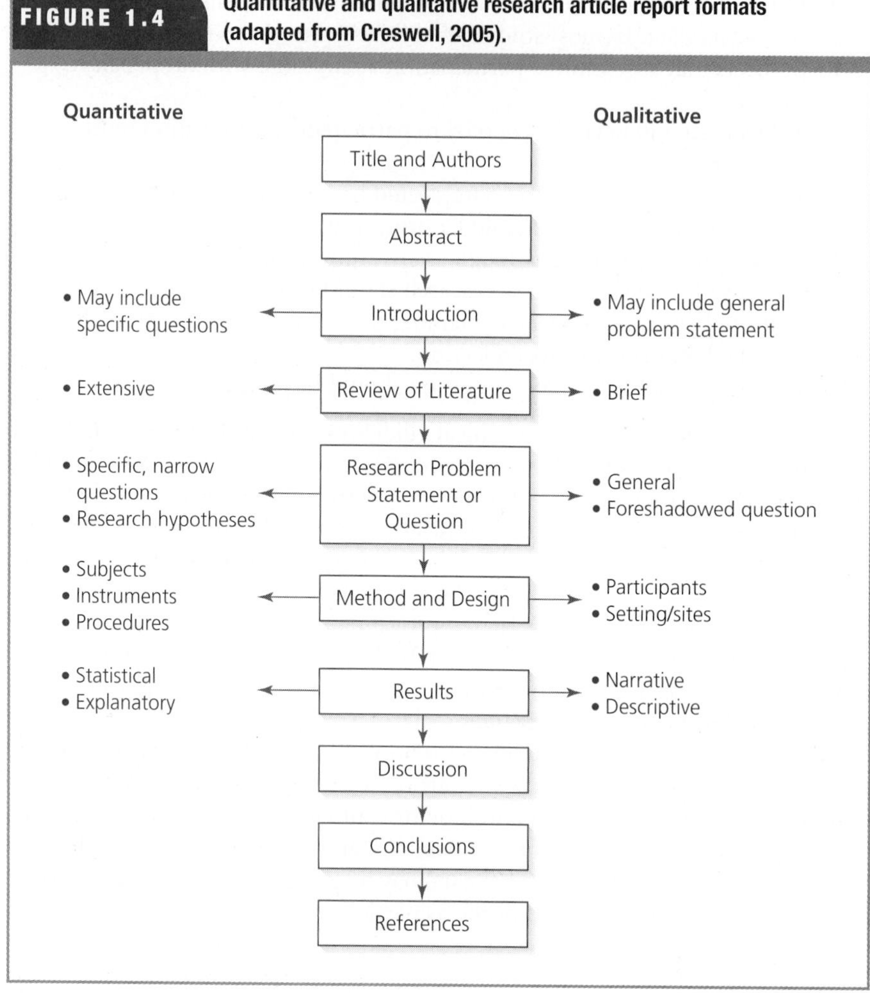

Title and Author(s)

The research article report typically begins with the title and name(s) of the author(s). The professional affiliation of the author(s) is provided in many reports and most published articles. This is the author's affiliation when the research was conducted, not necessarily his or her present affiliation. Good research article report titles tell the reader something about the major variables and type of subjects that are studied in less than 15 words.

Abstract

In many reports, especially journal articles, title and author are followed by an abstract. The abstract in journal articles is typically 50 to 150 words long and is often set in smaller type than or a different font from the rest of the article. The abstract is a brief summary of the entire study, including the problem, methods used, and major findings. The abstract will usually provide enough details to allow the reader to decide whether to read the entire report.

Introduction

The introductory section is usually one to several paragraphs in length, including a statement of the context for the research, the significance of the research, and the general or specific research problem investigated. The context provides background information relating the study to broader areas. It also indicates briefly the development of the research problem. The significance of the research is contained in a statement about how the results will be useful. It can be thought of as a justification for conducting the research. Almost all introductions include a statement that indicates the research problem of the study. This statement can be broad or specific, and sometimes both a broad and a more specific problem are included. The problem indicates as concisely and clearly as possible the focus of the study. Most general problems are stated near the beginning of the report, and more specific research questions, if any, just before the review of literature, but the level of specificity or location across articles and reports is inconsistent. In qualitative articles you will find a foreshadowed problem rather than specific questions.

Review of Literature

Although the introductory section may include some references to other research or literature, a more formal review of literature begins after the research problem is introduced. The review, typically several paragraphs long, summarizes and analyzes previous research on the same problem. A good review critiques the studies and shows how the findings relate to the problem being investigated.

Specific Research Question or Hypothesis

Often, but not always, in quantitative studies specific research questions or hypotheses follow the review of literature. The hypothesis usually follows the review of literature because it is based on what theories and previously completed related studies have found.

Method and Design

In this section the researchers indicate who was studied, how the information was obtained, and, in the case of an experiment, interventions or manipulations. The first part of the section usually describes the *subjects* (quantitative studies) or *participants* (quantitative and qualitative studies). These are individuals the researcher obtains information from to address the research problem. The report describes the characteristics of the subjects and indicates whether they have been selected from a larger group. The second section focuses on the instrumentation used to gather information from the subjects, including a description of the instruments and an evaluation of their reliability and validity. In some reports this section also describes how the instrument was administered; in others, this information is provided in the third section, procedures. The procedures section may also include a summary of how the data were collected and, in experimental studies, indicates how the interventions were carried out. The researchers may also discuss the design of the study and materials used, and they may indicate what precautions were taken to reduce bias or otherwise improve objectivity.

Results

In this section researchers describe how they analyzed the data, and they present the results. Tables and graphs may be used to summarize large amounts of data succinctly. This section should be an objective reporting of what was found, without interpretation or discussion.

Discussion

This is the section in which the investigators explain their results. The data are interpreted in light of other research and possible weaknesses in the methodology of the study.

Conclusions

Conclusions are summary statements that reflect the overall answers to the research questions or whether or not the research hypotheses are supported. The conclusion is an inference derived from the results, weaknesses in the study, and the relationship of the results to previous studies. Conclusions should be limited to what is directly supported by the findings and what is reasonable, given other research. Implications and recommendations are often included in this section, although investigators should be careful not to overgeneralize.

References

This is a listing of the sources cited in the report. The style of listing references will vary, the most common being APA. A bibliography includes sources that are not cited in the report but are used by the authors.

ANATOMY *of a* RESEARCH ARTICLE

The best way to become familiar with educational research is to read published articles. Becoming comfortable with the format and language will allow you to critique and evaluate research. Don't be too concerned about understanding *everything* you read. You are not expected to be an expert researcher or statistician. But if you don't read the studies, you can't be an intelligent consumer.

Article 1.1 is an example of a quantitative study. It illustrates the format you will find and points out other features of a research article.

ARTICLE 1.1 **Format and features of a journal research article.**

Gender, Achievement, and Perception Toward Science Activities[1]

Daniel P. Shepardson
Department of Curriculum & Instruction
Purdue University

Edward L. Pizzini
Science Education Center
The University of Iowa

Institutional affiliation when the study was conducted

The purpose of this study was to investigate the perception toward science activities and science achievement of boys and girls in middle school life science. Student perceptions toward science activities and achievement were measured in three different instructional treatments: textbook-worksheet, traditional laboratory, and Search, Solve, Create, Share (SSCS) problem solving. The results indicate no significant difference in student achievement by gender or science activities, and no significant difference in perception by gender. However, a significant difference ($p < .05$) was obtained for student perception by science activities. Follow-up comparisons suggested significant differences among SSCS problem solving and traditional laboratory and textbook- worksheet activities, with no difference between traditional laboratory and textbook-worksheet activities.

Abstract

The underrepresentation of women in scientific professions has become a national concern. This concern has resulted in a variety of studies designed to identify gender differences that may contribute to the dearth of females in the scientific pipeline (see Oakes, 1990). It has been proposed that the attitude of girls toward science is one factor that influences the decision of girls to participate in science, as well as their achievement in science. Important attributes of attitude formation, for girls, appear to be the perceived usefulness of the science being learned, confidence in learning and doing science, interest in people, and a liking of science (Oakes, 1990).

Introduction, background, and significance of the topic

Further, the learning situation can affect the attitude students develop toward science (Hofstein, Scherz, & Yager, 1986; Kulm, 1980; Talton & Simpson, 1987). Therefore, learning situations that are perceived positively by girls may contribute to their development of a positive attitude toward science, as well as improve achievement. The learning situation also influences the opportunity girls have to engage in learning science. Although there is evidence that boys benefit more from traditional instructional activities, whereas girls benefit more from cooperative and hands-on activities, the evidence is inconclusive (Oakes, 1990).

Kahle (1990) has stated that inquiry-oriented instruction has the potential of producing equitable outcomes in attitude and achievement, and Glaton (1981) has concluded that girls prefer inquiry-oriented instruction. Zimmerer and Bennett (1987) found that both eighth-grade boys and girls enjoy doing science experiments, but that boys were more enthusiastic than girls. Shymansky, Hedges, and Woodworth (1990) observed that inquiry-oriented instruction only improved the attitude of boys toward science, while Fleming and Malone (1983) found that boys had a more positive attitude

Review of literature to establish possible link between science class activities and attitudes

[1]Source: *School Science and Mathematics, 94* (4), April, 1994.

(continued)

ARTICLE 1.1 (continued)

toward science than girls at the elementary level, but that girls had a more positive attitude toward science at the middle school level. Finally, the National Assessment of Educational Progress (NAEP) indicates that boys tend to have a more positive attitude toward science than girls and that this trend has changed little over time (Mullis & Jenkins, 1988).

From an achievement perspective, the NAEP results indicate no difference between boys and girls at the knowledge level (knows everyday science facts), but that boys perform at higher proficiency levels than girls in middle school/junior high, suggesting a relationship between attitude and achievement (Mullis & Jenkins, 1988; Mullis, Dossey, Foertsch, Jones, & Gentile, 1991). However, Steinkamp and Maehr (1983) concluded that there is insufficient evidence to link gender differences in attitude toward science to science achievement.

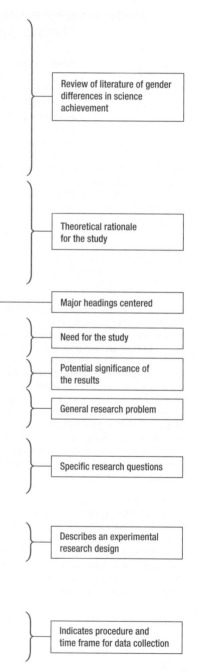

Review of literature of gender differences in science achievement

Because of the poor attitude toward science of both boys and girls, Yager and Penick (1986) have argued that science needs to be taught differently; that science needs to be taught dynamically, not as a static subject in textbooks. Exemplary science programs accentuate the dynamic teaching of science, emphasizing inquiry instruction, allowing students to pursue areas of personal interest (Reynolds et al., 1985). Exemplary science programs recognize that student attitude toward science arises from the success or failure students have with instructional materials (Penick & Krajcik, 1985).

Theoretical rationale for the study

Purpose

Major headings centered

Although studies have investigated student attitude toward science and achievement, few studies have attempted to investigate the underlying attributes of student attitude; that is, what it is about science that boys and girls like or dislike. The perception boys and girls have about science activities may contribute to the development of their attitude toward science, as well as influence achievement. Thus, the purpose of this study was to assess the perception toward science activities and science achievement of boys and girls in middle school life science. The specific questions of this study were:

Need for the study

Potential significance of the results

General research problem

1. Is there a difference in the perception boys and girls have of science activities?
2. Is there a difference in the science achievement of boys and girls exposed to different science activities?

Specific research questions

Method

The study involved a pretest/posttest design for student achievement and a posttest-only design for student perception toward science activities. Because students had different science experiences prior to the study, which colors their perception, and since we were only interested in their perception of the immediate science activities they were exposed to, the posttest-only design for student perception was considered appropriate. Gender was treated as an effect in both designs. The achievement pretest was administered 10 days prior to the study. The achievement posttest and perception questionnaire were administered immediately following the completion of the treatments, 20 days from the administration of the pretest.

Describes an experimental research design

Indicates procedure and time frame for data collection

Science Activities

Students were exposed to one of three science activities: textbook-worksheet, traditional laboratory, and problem solving. The problem-solving activities were considered representative of exemplary science. That is, they were inquiry oriented. The science activities were conducted in the context of a 10-day unit on simple plants, designed around the science content of a dominant middle school life science textbook (Weiss et al., 1989). Thus, each treatment was similar in content coverage and length of instruction, but differed in the nature of the science activities students completed. Each teacher maintained a teaching log, which was reviewed to insure consistency among teachers in the implementation of the treatments.

The textbook-worksheet treatment introduced students to science content through a combination of lecture and textbook reading. Students completed all textbook questions and publisher-based worksheets, which were designed to reinforce the content discussed during lecture and textbook reading. Worksheet activities consisted of puzzles/games and "dry" laboratory exercises. Answers to textbook questions and worksheets were discussed in whole-class situations to insure that all students received the "correct" answer.

Traditional laboratory activities were based on publisher materials, which according to Pizzini, Shepardson, and Abell (1991), emphasize verification or structured inquiry. Science content was presented to students prior to laboratory activities, through class lecture and textbook reading. Laboratory activities required students to follow predetermined procedures, collect and analyze data, and draw conclusions. Students worked together in small groups to complete the laboratory activities, and received an individual grade. Following the completion of the laboratory activities, teacher-led class discussion ensued. The purpose of class discussions was to insure that all students derived a similar conclusion from the laboratory activities.

Problem-solving activities revolved around the Search, Solve, Create, Share (SSCS) problem-solving model. SSCS activities involved students in identifying and refining their own problems in science, identifying potential solutions to their problems, developing and implementing their plan of action, preparing a means to communicate their problem and findings, and presenting their problem and findings to the class. To provide students with content background knowledge, a lecture and textbook reading session was conducted prior to student problem identification. SSCS involved students in collaborative group settings. For additional information on SSCS see Pizzini, Abell, and Shepardson (1988) and Pizzini, Shepardson, and Abell (1989).

Sample

The middle school (grades 7–8) students were taught in two different school districts by two different science teachers. Each teacher taught two classes within each treatment. The intact classes were randomly assigned to a treatment. Due to student absenteeism, only the achievement and perception scores for those students who completed the unit were analyzed. The number and gender of students in each treatment are displayed in Table 1. Students had not been exposed to SSCS problem-solving activities prior to the study. Thus, a potential novelty effect may exist.

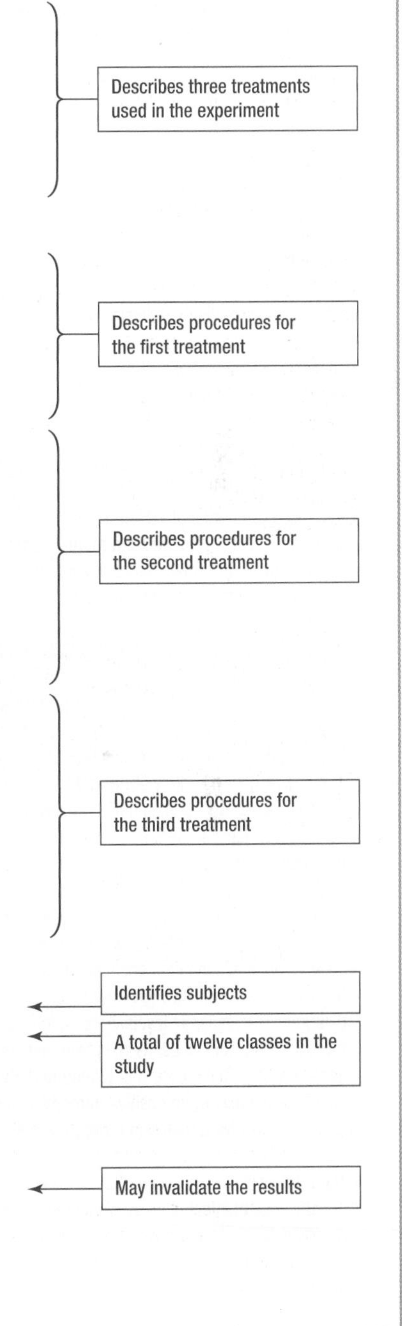

(continued)

ARTICLE 1.1 (continued)

Table 1.
Number of Students by Gender for Each Treatment

Treatment/Gender	*n*
Textbook-Worksheet Activities	
Girls	41
Boys	43
Total	84
Traditional Laboratory Activities	
Girls	41
Boys	47
Total	88
SSCS Problem-Solving Activities	
Girls	45
Boys	51
Total	96

n refers to number

Achievement Test and Perception Questionnaire

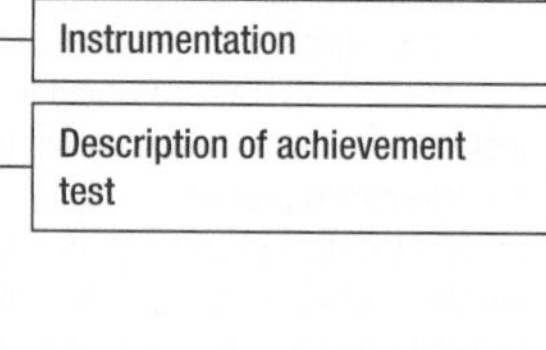

The pre- and post-achievement tests were identical, consisting of 30 items divided into three categories of 10 items each: textbook-based facts, processes, and application. Each item was of a multiple choice nature and weighted equally, providing a minimum achievement score of zero and a maximum achievement score of 30. Four science teachers and three university science educators deemed the achievement test to be content valid based on the textual information provided to all students. However, because of the nature of SSCS problem-solving activities (students determining their own learning within the content area), the achievement posttest may be negatively biased toward student performance. That is, the achievement posttest may not be content valid for the SSCS treatment. Reliability was determined by the KR20 procedure, using pretest scores. A reliability coefficient of $r = .43$ was obtained. The low reliability is likely attributed to the limited number of test items.

Questionable quality for this instrument

The perception questionnaire was designed to assess student perception toward science activities: student perception of involvement, learning usefulness, and personal enjoyment. The questionnaire was piloted in the prior academic year, under similar conditions. The questionnaire was refined based on teacher input, student responses, and item analysis. The questionnaire was designed to be brief to reduce resistance from students, which could influence the interpretation (Isaac & Michael, 1978). The questionnaire consisted of eight Likert Scale items. Each item contained five response levels: strongly agree, agree, undecided, disagree, and strongly disagree. The response levels were weighted according to their positive perception toward science activities, ranging from five (most positive) to one (least positive). Each response item score was totaled to derive an accumulative score. Thus, 40 would be the maximum positive perception score possible and 8 would be the minimum positive perception score possible. A reliability of $r = .84$ was obtained.

Description of perception questionnaire

Data Analysis

Because of intact classrooms, achievement and perception data were analyzed using an ANCOVA. Bonferroni t-tests were employed, where appropriate, as follow-up comparison tests. The pretest achievement scores served as the covariate in the achievement analysis by science activities and gender effect. Student perception was analyzed using the posttest achievement scores as the covariate and science activities and gender as the effect. Homogeneity of slope was analyzed and appears plausible for both achievement ($F_{2,262} = 0.18$, $p = .834$) and perception ($F_{2,262} = 1.51$, $p = .224$). All analyses were conducted using SYSTAT (Wilkinson, 1988).

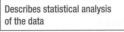

Describes statistical analysis of the data

Describes computer software used for data analysis

Results

The descriptive results are presented in Tables 2 (achievement) and 3 (perception). The ANCOVA results indicated no statistical difference in student achievement by gender or science activities (Table 4). The ANCOVA indicated a statistically significant difference in student perception toward science activities (Table 5). However, no statistical difference was indicated by gender.

Follow-up comparisons for student perception suggested significant differences among SSCS and traditional laboratory activities, $t_{1,182} = 20.53$, $p < .001$; and SSCS and textbook-worksheet activities, $t_{1,178} = 11.96$, $p = .001$. No significant differences between the traditional laboratory and textbook-worksheet activities were observed, $t_{1,170} = 2.14$, $p = .145$.

Shows that student perceptions toward the SSCS are more positive than toward traditional or textbook-worksheet activities

Table 2.

Descriptive Statistics for Achievement by Science Activities and Gender

	Pretest		Posttest	
Science Activities	M	SD	M	SD
Textbook-Worksheet				
Girls	8.71	3.33	11.73	3.96
Boys	7.84	3.12	11.09	3.15
Total	8.30	3.20	11.40	3.60
Traditional Laboratory				
Girls	7.42	3.06	12.34	3.90
Boys	7.36	3.33	11.66	3.70
Total	7.41	3.23	12.12	3.82
SSCS Problem Solving				
Girls	6.73	2.19	11.47	2.93
Boys	7.06	2.81	11.35	2.88
Total	6.94	2.51	11.44	2.90

M refers to mean
SD refers to standard deviation

Table 3.

Descriptive Statistics for Perception by Science Activities and Gender

Science Activities	M	SD
Textbook-Worksheet		
Girls	33.22	5.83
Boys	33.72	4.86
Total	33.50	5.30
Traditional Laboratory		
Girls	31.71	7.08
Boys	32.43	6.88
Total	32.10	6.90
SSCS Problem Solving		
Girls	36.13	6.25
Boys	36.77	6.13
Total	36.50	6.20

Table in American Psychological Association (APA) format

(continued)

ARTICLE 1.1 (continued)

Table 4.

ANCOVA for Achievement

Source	DF	SS	MS	*F*	*p*
Activities	2	8.93	4.49	0.55	.579
Gender	1	8.59	8.59	1.05	.305
Interaction	2	3.76	1.88	0.23	.794
Covariate	1	949.60	949.60		
Error	261	2127.00	8.15		

Table 5.

ANCOVA for Perception

Source	DF	SS	MS	*F*	*p*
Activities	2	938.63	469.32	12.12	.001
Gender	1	28.95	28.95	0.75	.388
Interaction	2	0.55	0.27	0.01	.99
Covariate	1	25.15	25.15		
Error	261	10108.89	38.73		

Discussion

This study provides a glimpse into middle school life science, contributing to our understanding of gender, achievement, and perception toward science activities. It appears that science activities in exemplary programs, like SSCS problem solving, do not impede the science achievement of boys and girls as they promote a more positive perception of science activities. Further, the results suggest that it is not the success or failure students have with the instructional materials (Penick & Krajcik, 1985), as determined by achievement, but the nature or context of the interactions with the instructional materials. However, this study was of a short duration, therefore, perhaps over longer periods such results would not be obtained.

From an achievement perspective, the results are consistent with the NAEP findings (Mullis & Jenkins, 1988; Mullis et al., 1991) that no proficiency difference exists between boys and girls in middle school science. However, caution is warranted in the interpretation of the achievement results of this study, because of the low reliability of the achievement test. Although Mullis and Jenkins (1988) alluded to the possibility of a positive relationship between attitude and proficiency, that relationship is not suggested here. It appears that a positive perception toward science activities is not an indicator of achievement, which is consistent with the findings of Steinkamp and Maehr (1983). That is, students may perceive the science activities (traditional laboratories and textbooks) engaged in as uninteresting, but their engagement in the activities is sufficient to promote achievement. Although Shymansky et al. (1990) noted a gender effect for attitude, no gender effect existed for student perception toward science activities. However, students (boys and girls) engaged in SSCS problem solving were more positive about the science activities than students engaged in traditional laboratory and textbook-based instruction. Thus, the nature of the instructional activities may be an underlying attribute of student attitude toward science, supporting the view of Hofstein et al. (1986) and Talton and Simpson (1987) that the nature of the activities affects student attitude. The results of this study support the notion that inquiry-oriented instruction has the potential for equitable outcomes (Kahle, 1990), and that girls (Galton, 1981)

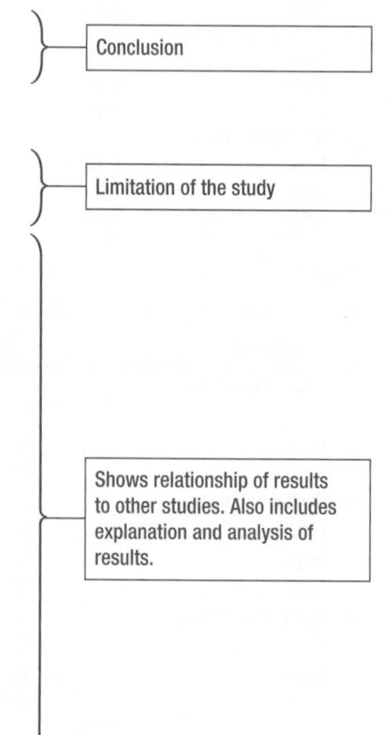
Conclusion
Limitation of the study
Shows relationship of results to other studies. Also includes explanation and analysis of results.

as well as boys prefer inquiry-oriented instruction. Although this study was of a short duration, the results suggest that when science is taught dynamically, student attitude toward science may be enhanced through positive student perception of science activities.

Restatement of conclusion

References

References in the American Psychological Association (APA) format

Fleming, M.L. & Malone, M.R. (1983). The relationship of student characteristics and student performance in science as viewed by meta-analysis research. *Journal of Research in Science Teaching, 20,* 481–495.

Glaton, M. (1981). Differential treatment of boy and girl pupils during science lessons. In A. Kelly (Ed.), *The missing half.* Manchester, England: Manchester University Press.

Hofstein, A., Scherz, Z., & Yager, R.E. (1986). What students say about science teaching, science teachers and science classes in Israel and the U.S. *Science Education, 70,* 21–30.

Isaac, S. & Michael, W.B. (1987). *Handbook in research and evaluation.* San Diego, CA: Edits Publishers.

Kahle, J.B. (1990). Why girls don't know. In M.B. Rowe (Ed.), *What research says to the science teacher,* (Vol. 6). Washington, DC: National Science Teachers Association.

Kulm, G. (1980). Research on mathematics attitude. In R.J. Shumway (Ed.), *Research in mathematics education.* Reston, VA: National Council of Teachers of Mathematics.

Mullis, I.S. & Jenkins, L.B. (1988). *The science report card elements of risk and recovery.* Princeton, NJ: Educational Testing Service.

Mullis, I.S., Dossey, J., Foertsch, M., Jones, L., & Gentile, C. (1991). *Trends in academic progress.* Washington, DC: Office of Educational Research and Inprovement, U.S. Department of Education.

Oakes, J. (1990). Opportunities, achievement, and choice: Women and minority students in science and mathematics. In C.B. Cazden (Ed.), *Review of Research in Education,* Washington, DC: American Educational Research Association.

Penick, J.E. & Krajcik, J. (1985). Middle school/junior high science: A synthesis and critique. In J. Penick & J. Krajcik (eds.), *Focus on excellence: Middle school/junior high science,* (Vol. 2, No. 2). Washington, DC: National Science Teachers Association.

Pizzini, E.L., Abell, S.K., & Shepardson, D.P. (1988). Rethinking thinking in the science classroom. *The Science Teacher, 55,* 22–25.

Pizzini, E.L., Shepardson, D.P., & Abell, S.K. (1989). A rationale for and the development of a problem solving model of instruction in science education. *Science Education, 73,* 523–534.

Pizzini, E.L., Shepardson, D.P., & Abell, S.K. (1991). The inquiry level of junior high activities: Implications to science teaching. *Journal of Research in Science Teaching, 28,* 111–121.

Reynolds, K.E., Pitotti, W.W., Rakow, S.J., Thompson, T., & Wohl, S.M. (1985). Excellence in middle/junior high school science. In J. Penick & J. Krajcik (Eds.), *Focus on excellence: Middle school/junior high science,* (Vol. 2, No. 2). Washington, DC: National Science Teachers Association.

Chapter in a book

Volume

Authors listed in order of relative contribution

Publisher

(continued)

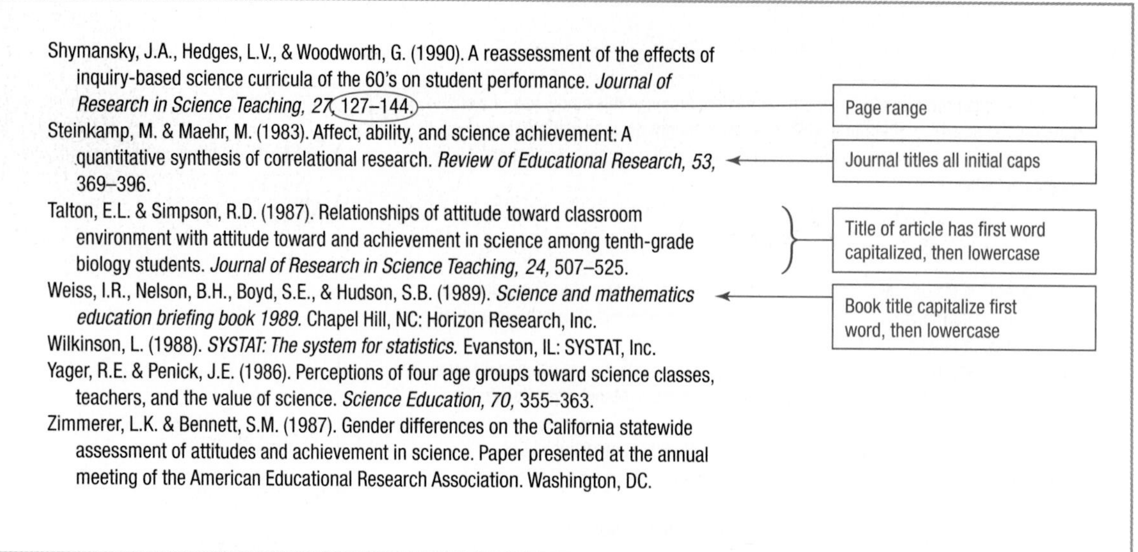

Shymansky, J.A., Hedges, L.V., & Woodworth, G. (1990). A reassessment of the effects of inquiry-based science curricula of the 60's on student performance. *Journal of Research in Science Teaching, 27,* 127–144.

Steinkamp, M. & Maehr, M. (1983). Affect, ability, and science achievement: A quantitative synthesis of correlational research. *Review of Educational Research, 53,* 369–396.

Talton, E.L. & Simpson, R.D. (1987). Relationships of attitude toward classroom environment with attitude toward and achievement in science among tenth-grade biology students. *Journal of Research in Science Teaching, 24,* 507–525.

Weiss, I.R., Nelson, B.H., Boyd, S.E., & Hudson, S.B. (1989). *Science and mathematics education briefing book 1989.* Chapel Hill, NC: Horizon Research, Inc.

Wilkinson, L. (1988). *SYSTAT: The system for statistics.* Evanston, IL: SYSTAT, Inc.

Yager, R.E. & Penick, J.E. (1986). Perceptions of four age groups toward science classes, teachers, and the value of science. *Science Education, 70,* 355–363.

Zimmerer, L.K. & Bennett, S.M. (1987). Gender differences on the California statewide assessment of attitudes and achievement in science. Paper presented at the annual meeting of the American Educational Research Association. Washington, DC.

STUDY QUESTIONS

1. What are some important ways in which educational knowledge is obtained? What are the strengths and weaknesses of different sources of knowledge?
2. How is a scientific approach to inquiry different from inquiry based on personal experience?
3. In what ways can explanation of educational phenomena improve teaching and learning?
4. In what ways can theories be useful in education? What are some limitations of theories?
5. What are the steps of scientific inquiry? Why are questions used as part of the overall framework?
6. What is necessary for a study to be judged "credible"?
7. What are the differences between qualitative, quantitative, and mixed-method approaches to research?
8. How can research you have read be classified as basic, applied, evaluation, or action research?
9. What is the essential difference between experimental and nonexperimental research?

Chapter 2

Research Problems, Variables, Questions, *and* Hypotheses

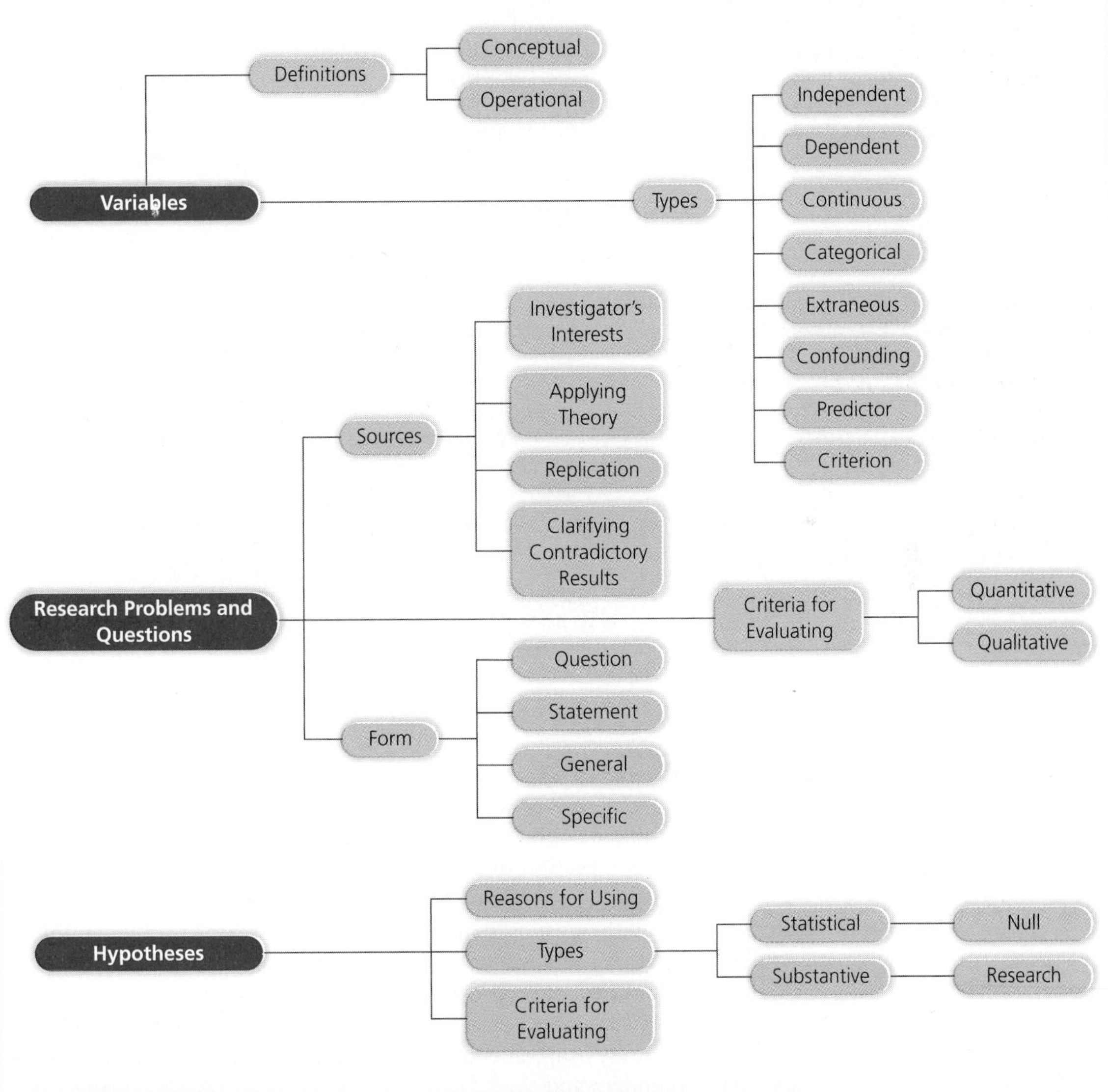

CHAPTER ROAD MAP

In this chapter we will discuss the first essential step in both conducting and understanding research: the research problem and/or question. We will see that all studies begin with a general research problem that is usually refined into more specific questions. We will also learn about variables and research hypotheses, important concepts in quantitative and mixed-method studies.

Chapter Outline	Learning Objectives
Research Problems and Questions Sources for Research Problems	• Understand the difference between general problems and more specific research questions. • Become familiar with how researchers come up with research problems and questions. • Write research problems for a personal area of interest.
Research Questions	• Know the components of good research questions. • Write research questions for a personal area of interest. • Know the difference between quantitative and qualitative research questions.
Quantitative Research Problems and Questions Variables Variable Definitions Types of Variables Hypotheses	• Apply criteria for evaluating quantitative research questions. • Understand the nature of variables. • Understand the difference between conceptual and operational definitions. • Understand the different types of variables used in quantitative studies. • Apply criteria for evaluating quantitative research questions. • Understand the nature and use of different types of hypotheses. • Understand the components of good hypotheses.
Qualitative Research Problems and Questions	• Understand the nature of qualitative research questions. • Apply criteria for evaluating qualitative research questions. • Understand the nature of the central phenomenon.

RESEARCH PROBLEMS *and* QUESTIONS

The research problem comprises one or more sentences that indicate(s) the goal, purpose, or overall direction of the study. It is generally found in the first paragraph of an article, often at the end of the paragraph, to provide an orientation to the reader about the proposed investigation. The research problem implies the possibility of empirical investigation. Usually, there is a controversy, issue, concern, or need identified. It provides a focus for the researcher and is an essential first step in the investigation. It also helps the reader decide quickly if the study is pertinent or interesting, and by providing an overview makes the research much easier to understand.

The research problem statement is typically rather general, with just enough information about the scope and purpose of the study to provide an initial understanding of the research. Often the problem is introduced using the following phrases, though there is no one correct or best way:

"The purpose of this study is to. . . ."
"The aim of the current investigation is to. . . ."
"In this study we investigated. . . ."
"The goal of the research was to. . . ."

Here are some examples of general research problems:

EXAMPLES 2.1–2.4 | Research Problem Statements

The purpose of this research is to study adolescent loneliness.

This research will investigate the social integration of adults with physical disabilities.

This study investigates the relationship between school culture and student achievement.

This research was designed to determine student perceptions of their high school experiences.

The research problem can also be stated as a question. Like problem statements, these tend to be general when located at the beginning of an article/report, prior to the review of literature. For example:

EXAMPLES 2.5–2.8 | Research Problem Questions

What is the relationship between school culture and student achievement?

Is there a difference in motivation between homogeneously and heterogeneously grouped students?

Do preschool teachers have different instructional styles?

What explains the high rate of teacher absenteeism?

It is important to distinguish the general research problem from more specific, focused statements and questions that communicate the nature of the study in greater detail. It should be noted that some researchers may use the term *research problem* as synonymous with a specific problem statement or question. Thus, you will find some variety in the form as well as in the location of the research problem in an article or report. In some articles the problem may be stated at the beginning in a general sense, with more specific questions later, while in other articles the research problem may be communicated only by more specific questions or statements. The nature of these more specific statements and questions depends on whether they are for quantitative or qualitative research (quantitative are specific, qualitative are general).

FIGURE 2.1 Components of research problems.

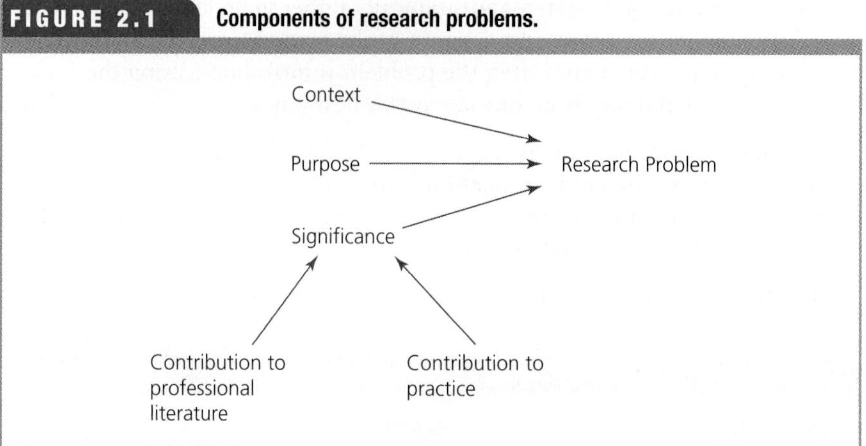

Research Problem Components

As illustrated in Figure 2.1, research problems consist of three components: context, significance, and purpose. Context explains the background or larger body of knowledge or subject. For example, a researcher might say, "There has been growing interest in the assessment literacy of beginning teachers," or "For the past decade researchers have investigated how classroom assessment practices affect student motivation," or "As a result of my experience in counseling pregnant high school girls, it has been clear that further study of their knowledge of prevention needs to be explored." Example 2.9 shows how context is described in an article.

EXAMPLE 2.9 | Context in Research Problem

In recent years there has been a growing concern regarding the current state of the educational system in the United States. For example, in comparison to other countries, high school students in the United States are falling behind students in other countries on various measures of academic achievement. . . . Given these concerns, one goal of this research was to examine the relative contributions of cognitive abilities to students' science achievement.

Source: O'Reilly, T., & McNamara, D. S. (2007). The impact of science knowledge, reading skill, and reading strategy knowledge on more traditional "high-stakes" measures of high school students' science achievement. *American Educational Research Journal, 44*(1), 161.

The purpose is a general statement of the goal of the study. The ubiquitous phrase, "The purpose of this study/investigation/research is to . . ." is used often. For example:

- The purpose of this study is to determine factors predicting high school dropout.

- The purpose of this investigation is to examine the relationship between student effort and attitudes.
- The purpose of this research is to understand beginning teachers' perspectives about having a mentor their first year.

Significance is the reason for the study. It is addressed by showing how the study will make a contribution to knowledge and/or practice. For basic and applied research, a case is made about how the results will enhance an existing body of knowledge or practice. For evaluation and action research, the focus is on practice. Example 2.10 shows how researchers indicate the significance of a study of school accountability and teacher motivation. In this case, there are contributions to both knowledge and practice, which is common with applied studies (note too that context is addressed).

EXAMPLE 2.10 | Research Problem Significance

This work attempts to move this larger body of research on school accountability policies forward by examining the influence of accountability policies on teacher motivation. . . . This empirical investigation of motivational theories in the SPS accountability context provides important insights into the motivation response of teachers to school accountability policies. . . . Understanding the factors that improve teacher motivation in low-performing schools . . . contributes to a broader knowledge based around improving teacher performance and, as a result, student performance.

Source: Finnigan, K. S., & Gross, B. (2007). Do accountability policy sanctions influence teacher motivation? Lessons from Chicago's low-performing schools. *American Educational Research Journal, 44*(3), 595.

Sources for Research Problems

How does a researcher come up with a good problem? Several sources are commonly used to begin the process of problem formulation, though this process may be a rather arduous and time-consuming task. Ideas that seem promising initially typically need revision as literature related to the idea is analyzed and implications for research design are clarified. Many researchers begin to identify a topic by reading current books and journals in their area and by talking with knowledgeable professionals about current problems or issues. Once a broad area of interest is identified, further reading usually leads to a more specific research problem. Additional factors influence the feasibility of the proposed study, such as cost, the ability and training of the investigator, and the availability of subjects.

Although there is no single strategy for identifying research problems that works best for all investigators, several sources have been useful for many.

Investigator's Interests and Experiences. Some of the best sources of ideas come from the interests and practical experiences of the investigator. A teacher encounters many problems and questions daily that may lead to researchable problems: concerns about teaching methods, grouping, classroom management, tests, individualization, grades, standardized test data. Administrators may face problems in scheduling, communicating with teachers, providing instructional leadership, generating public support, or handling serious discipline. University professors may see that student teachers are encountering difficulties that need to be resolved. In addition to personal experiences, each of us has interests and knowledge about our profession that can be the source of good problems. It may be a topic that we are curious about or have read about, or it may be a long-standing interest in certain areas.

Applying Theory. A common source for research problems is a theory that has implications for educational practice. One approach is to take a theory in a related area, such as psychology or sociology, and develop a problem that extends it to an educational setting. Examples include using theories of reinforcement, attitude development, information processing, and communication to generate research problems. In each case the theories suggest implications that can be further researched in educational settings. Another approach is to directly test, revise, or clarify an existing educational theory. Here the intent is to develop and change the theory rather than to test its implications.

Replication. An excellent type of study is one that replicates previous research with relatively minor changes. It may seem that replication would not add new knowledge, but in fact just the opposite is true. Progress in building a body of knowledge depends on a series of replications to verify and extend the initial findings. One of the weaknesses in educational research is that there have been too few replications. Gall, Gall, and Borg (2007) summarize five reasons for conducting replication studies:

1. *To check the findings of a major or milestone study.* Replications can confirm or disconfirm the validity of a study that produces new evidence or reports findings that challenge previous research or theory.

2. *To check the validity of research findings with different subjects.* Replications often use the same procedures but change the type of subjects used to see if the original findings hold for different subjects. For example, much of Kohlberg's initial research on moral development was with men. A good replication study would ascertain whether the findings hold for women as well. Studies that are originally limited in scope can justifiably be replicated to extend the findings to other people and conditions.

3. *To check trends or change over time.* Replications can be used effectively to see if initial findings hold over time. This type of replication is done with attitudes, values, achievement, and other areas where trend data are important. For instance, the National Assessment of Educational Progress (NAEP) has measured the performance of 9-, 13-, and 17-year-old school children in key subjects since 1969. Every two years similar questions are asked, which provides a useful assessment of changes in student performance over time.

4. *To check important findings using different methodologies.* It is possible that a research finding may be unduly influenced by the way a variable is measured. For example, there are many ways to measure critical thinking. A particular study may report a "significant" result using one way to measure critical thinking, but the result may be limited by the way it was measured. Thus, a useful replication would repeat the study but change the instrumentation. The same is true for procedures in a study. Research that replicates and changes what may be faulty methods, such as the way an intervention is administered or what the experimenter says to the subjects, may change the results. A related reason to replicate is to use different statistics to analyze the data.

5. *To develop more effective or efficient interventions.* With the recent emphasis on determining the success of educational interventions, designing research that fine-tunes an intervention is important to maximizing student achievement. Often interventions that have been investigated on a small scale or in laboratory settings are tested in less controlled settings.

Clarification of Contradictory Findings. There are seemingly contradictory findings on many topics in the literature. Some studies indicate one conclusion, and other studies investigating the same problem come to an opposite conclusion. These apparent contradictions present good sources for research problems. For instance, research on the effect of charter schools is mixed. Some studies indicate that students attending charter schools outperform students in regular schools whereas other studies conclude that it makes no difference in student achievement. Why are there contradictions? By examining the studies, discrepancies in methodology or populations may be found that suggest further research to explain the contradictions.

Author Reflection *Coming up with a good research problem statement or question is sometimes the hardest part of doing research. It requires time and energy to read literature and synthesize the information to know whether the problem or question is needed. Sometimes there can be a series of psychological ups and downs if what seems at first to be a good idea, upon further reading and reflection, turns out to be not so good after all. The process can take months. It took me about a year to come up with my dissertation research questions and only a few months to complete the study.*

QUANTITATIVE RESEARCH PROBLEM STATEMENTS *and* QUESTIONS

In quantitative research there is a need for clear, concise research problem statements and questions that unambiguously communicate what will be studied. One important aspect of the statement or question is to convey information about the *variables* that will be investigated. Understanding and using the term *variable* is fundamental to all quantitative studies. We will discuss variables in some detail now before turning to specific quantitative problem statements and questions.

Variables in Quantitative Research

Variable: A concept or characteristic that involves variations.

One of the most commonly used terms in quantitative research is *variable*. A **variable** is a label or name that represents a concept or characteristic. Concepts are nouns that stand for a class of objects, such as *tree, house, desk, teacher,* and *school.* A characteristic is a trait we use to describe someone, such as *tall, male, creative,* or *average.* Researchers use *variable* rather than *concept* or *characteristic* because most of what is studied varies, that is, involves variations that can be described numerically or categorically. Thus, a variable is a type of concept or characteristic that can take on different values or be divided into categories. For example, intelligence, achievement, social class, and cognitive style each involves a range of values, which is usually expressed numerically. However, some variables are better described as containing two or more categories, for example, male and female, cooperative versus individualized instruction, beginning teachers with or without student teaching experience.

Variables are composed of *attributes* or *levels*. An attribute is the value or category that makes up the variation. Thus, for example, the variable gender would have as attributes *female* and *male.* These categories may also be referred to as *levels*. For a variable such as learning style, the attributes or levels may be field-dependent and field-independent, or impulsive and reflective, depending on the conceptual definition. Here are some more examples of variables with corresponding attributes or levels:

Variable	Attributes or Levels
Socioeconomic Status	High, Middle, Low
Grade Level	Grades 7, 8, and 9; or Elementary, Middle, High School
SAT	Score from 200 to 800
Age	10–19, 20–29, 30+
Race	Caucasian, African American, Hispanic, Asian

Conceptual and Operational Definitions

A precise definition of each variable communicates clearly the researcher's intent and enhances the usefulness of the results. Vague definitions are difficult to interpret and usually lead to less meaningful results. Two types of definitions are commonly used in research, *conceptual* and *operational*. A **conceptual** (sometimes called *constitutive*) **definition** uses other words and concepts to describe the variable, as found in a dictionary. For example, *attitude* may be defined conceptually as "a predisposition to respond favorably or unfavorably toward a person, object, or event," and *value* may be defined as "the degree to which an event is perceived to be positive or negative." Conceptual definitions are important in communicating what is being investigated, but they may not indicate precisely what the variables mean. Another type of description, called an *operational definition*, is needed to provide this more precise meaning.

Conceptual definition: Uses words or concepts.

An **operational definition** indicates how the concept is measured or manipulated, that is, what "operations" are performed to measure or manipulate the variable. It is essential to understand operational definitions because researchers will use different ways of measuring or manipulating the same variable. Consequently,

Operational definition: Defines a concept by how it is measured or manipulated.

the meaning of the results depends on understanding the operational definition, not simply the more generic meaning implied by the conceptual definition. Suppose you are interested in learning about the relationship between parenting styles and children's loneliness. There are many definitions and ways of measuring both variables, and you would need to examine the questions asked and the way the responses were scored to know what a particular researcher means.

Consider the variable socioeconomic status (SES), in which the terms *high*, *middle*, and *low* often describe categories. These terms are meaningful only if you know the rules for classifying subjects as high, middle, or low. The same subject might be classified as high in one study and middle in another. Thus, to some extent, operational definitions are arbitrary and often are not explicitly stated. For example, if you are interested in knowing whether cooperative or individualized methods of teaching are most effective in promoting student achievement, knowing simply that a study of these two methods showed cooperative methods to be better is not sufficient. You need to know how the terms *cooperative*, *individualized*, and *achievement* are determined or measured.

Following are some examples of variables, with corresponding conceptual and operational definitions:

Variable	Conceptual Definition	Operational Definition
Self-concept	Characteristics used to describe oneself	Scores on the Coopersmith Self-Esteem Inventory
Intelligence	Ability to think abstractly	Scores on the Stanford-Binet
Teacher with-it-ness	Awareness of student involvement and behavior	Results of the Robinson Scale of teacher with-it-ness

Types of Variables

There are several types of variables in educational research. We will consider the most important: independent and dependent, extraneous and confounding, and continuous and categorical.

Independent variable: Precedes, influences, or predicts the dependent variable.

Dependent variable: Affected or predicted by the independent variable.

Independent and Dependent Variables. In much research, one variable precedes another, either logically or in time. The variable that comes first and influences or predicts is called the **independent variable.** The second variable, the one that is affected or predicted by the independent variable, is the **dependent variable.** In an experiment, at least one independent variable is the presumed cause of differences between groups on the dependent variable. The independent variable is the antecedent (intervention), the dependent variable is the consequence (outcome). Predictions are made from independent variables to dependent variables. When we say, "If *X*, then *Y*," *X* is the independent variable and *Y* is the dependent variable. When we control which students receive particular teaching methods (antecedent), we may see the effect on achievement (consequence). Teaching method is the independent variable; achievement is the dependent variable. In educational research, teacher behavior, methods of instruction, curriculum, individual characteristics of students, socioeconomic status, and peer group behaviors are common independent variables, and achievement, attitudes, values, self-concept, and social development are common dependent variables (these may also be independent variables, depending on the study).

In nonexperimental research, the independent variable cannot be manipulated or controlled by the investigator. Such variables may still be considered independent if they clearly precede the dependent variable, if they are used to create categories for comparison or are explanatory. For example, a study of the effect of school size (independent variable) on achievement (dependent variable) may locate and use large, medium, and small schools, although it cannot manipulate or alter the size of a particular school. However, it is clear that school size precedes achievement. In correlational studies, several nonmanipulated variables may be considered independent because they precede the dependent variable. For example, a school administrator may need to predict teaching effectiveness to hire the best teachers. Several variables are available for each candidate, including grade point average, supervisor's comments about student teaching, and an interview. If these variables are used to predict the outcome (effectiveness as a teacher), they are independent variables.

In some nonexperimental research, it is difficult to label variables as independent or dependent, particularly when one variable does not clearly precede the other. For instance, a study of the relationship between critical thinking and creativity may be conducted to show they are distinct, unrelated concepts. In this case neither is an independent or dependent variable; there are simply two variables in the study.

Nonexperimental, descriptive research may compare groups of subjects, and often the variable used to classify the groups is considered independent. For example, a descriptive study of the attitudes of school principals toward school financing might divide the principals into groups depending on the size and location of each school. Here attitudes would be the dependent variable and size and location of schools the independent variables.

A description of variables is shown in Example 2.11. In this study, student characteristics, school background, parent involvement, and school counselor aspirations were independent variables. Note that the term *categories* is used to refer to levels of different independent variables.

EXAMPLE 2.11 | Independent and Dependent Variables

The dependent variable in our study was student-counselor contact for college information [measured dichotomous—yes or no]. . . . The student variables in this study were race/ethnicity, gender, mother's educational level, socioeconomic status (SES), and 10th-grade achievement. . . . Race/ethnicity was made up of six categories (American Indian/Alaskan Native, Asian/Pacific Islander, Black or African American, Hispanic, multiracial, White). . . . The school background variables in this study were school setting, type of school, number of school counselors, school size, and percentage of students on free or reduced-price lunch. . . . four composite variables measured parent involvement. . . . Counselor postsecondary aspirations for students was a primary independent variable.

Source: Bryan, J., Holcomb-McCoy, C., Moore-Thomas, C., & Day-Vines, N. L. (2009). Who sees the school counselor college information? A national study. *Professional School Counseling, 12*(4), 285.

Extraneous Variables. An **extraneous variable** affects the dependent variable but is either unknown or not controlled by the researcher. Extraneous variables are conditions, events, features, or occurrences that influence the subjects in a particular group that are not part of the study and that may compromise the interpretation of the results. That is, they may provide an alternative explanation for the results—they "mess up" the study. Sometimes such factors are called *nuisance variables*.

Extraneous variable: Source of error affecting the results.

Confounding Variables. A **confounding variable** is one that varies systematically with the independent variable. For instance, suppose you find a study comparing two methods of teaching reading, a totally phonics approach and a combined phonics/whole language approach. Two classrooms are used in the study, one classroom implementing each approach. However, because different teachers are in each class, "teachers" is a confounding variable because the style, personality, and knowledge of each teacher are confounded with each approach to teaching and will affect reading scores (dependent variable). So if one group of students did score better than the other, you would not know if it was because of the method or the teacher. Think of confounding variables as having different values or degrees of influence in each group of subjects. Extraneous variables target a specific group. Throughout the rest of the book further types of extraneous and confounding variables will be identified, and examples will show how they affect the interpretation of research findings.

Confounding variable: Varies systematically with the independent variable.

Continuous and Categorical Variables. A **continuous variable** (or *measured variable*) can theoretically take on an infinite number of values within a given range of scores. In other words, the value of a continuous variable could be any point on a continuum. The values are rank-ordered, from small to large or low to high, to indicate the amount of some property or characteristic. Common continuous variables in educational research are achievement and aptitude test scores; self-concept; attitude and value measures; and height, weight, and age. A **categorical variable** is used to assign an object or person to a group (level) that is defined by having specified characteristics.

Continuous variable: Infinite values within a range.

Categorical variable: Groups defined by specific characteristics.

The most simple type of category has two groups (dichotomous), such as male/female, high/low, white/black, and morning/afternoon. Other categorical variables can have three or many more groups, for example, grade level, nationality, occupation, and religious preference. It is also common to use continuous scores to create categories. For instance, socioeconomic status is generally used as a continuous variable, but the scores can be grouped into categories such as high, middle, and low SES. Thus, the designation of a continuous or categorical variable may depend on how the researcher uses the scores. The same variable can be continuous in one study and categorical in another. Also, although most dependent variables are continuous, both independent and dependent variables can be either continuous or categorical. In nonexperimental studies that examine relationships, the independent, antecedent variable may be called a *predictor variable*, and the dependent variable, which is the outcome or result, may be termed a *criterion variable*.

FIGURE 2.2 Relationship of different types of variables.

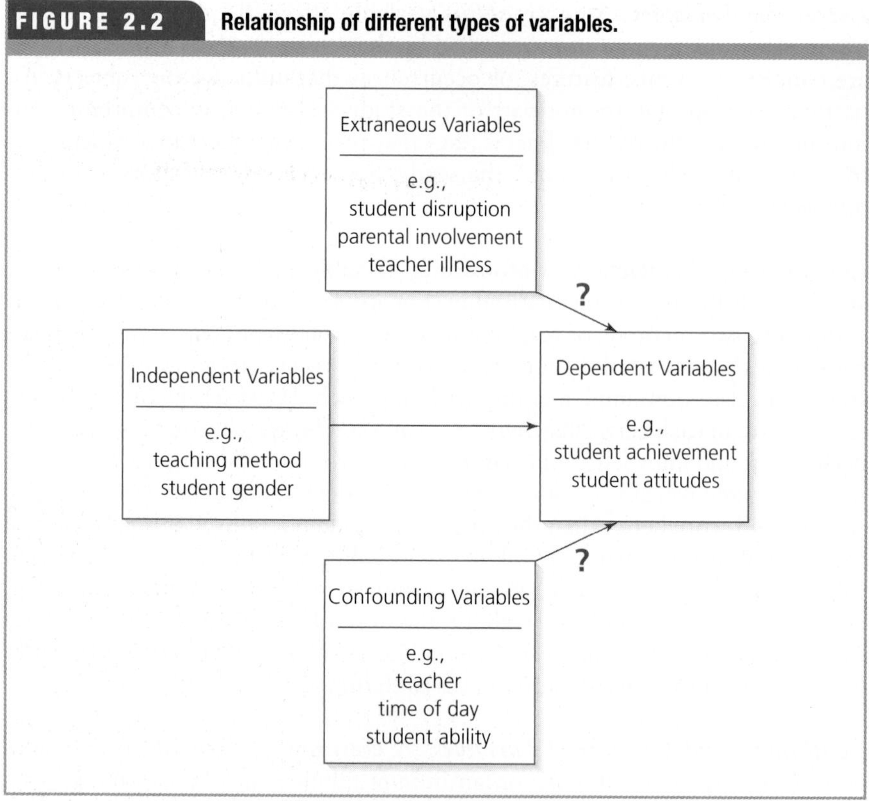

The relationship of independent, dependent, extraneous, and confounding variables is illustrated in Figure 2.2 in the context of an investigation on the effect of different science teaching methods on student achievement and attitudes.

Review and Reflect *Now is a good time to think about variables in your area of study. What are some examples of different kinds of variables that are typically studied in your area? Are some variables used as more than one type? Can you think of a study that would use the same variable as both an independent and dependent variable?*

Specific Research Problem Statements and Questions

We have already discussed general research problems as statements or questions that provide some indication of the direction of the research, a preview of what is to come. With these statements and questions you have a general idea of what will be studied, but for quantitative studies these statements may lack clarity, may contain ambiguous terms, and may not provide sufficient information. They are fine as a beginning statement of purpose, but they eventually need to be more focused.

At the other end of the specificity continuum are statements that contain more detail and information than is necessary. As a result, they are difficult to understand. An extreme example would be Example 2.12 on the following page:

EXAMPLE 2.12 | Research Problem That Is (Way) Too Specific

The purpose of this study is to investigate whether seventh- and eighth-grade male and female teachers who teach in a predominantly middle-class school in a western Michigan suburb who are identified by principal ratings and the Teacher Effectiveness Inventory, given in the fall semester by trained observers, will have students who, matched by ability when entering school in the fall, differ in the level of achievement in mathematics and language arts as measured by the Iowa Test of Basic Skills.

The majority of specific quantitative research problem statements are in the middle of the continuum. These statements contain sufficient detail and information in a sentence that is clear and succinct. The sentence may be in the form of a question or a statement. Following is an example of questions:

EXAMPLE 2.13 | Research Questions at Appropriate Levels of Specificity

In addition to the development of a knowledge test, the following questions were examined:

1. What are elementary teachers' beliefs about grade retention and do they differ by grade taught?
2. What factors influence teachers' decisions to retain students?

Source: Witmer, S. M., Hoffman, L. M., & Nottis, K. E. (2004), *Education, 125*, 178.

One of the reasons for using specific language in the research problem statement or question is to demonstrate that it is researchable. A researchable problem is one that can be answered with empirical procedures.

Table 2.1 includes quantitative research questions in both general and specific language to illustrate the difference between nonresearchable and researchable questions. The specific questions are good because they summarize several aspects of the study, including the type of research (experimental, relationship, or descriptive), independent and dependent variables, and characteristics of the subjects. Each of these will be considered in greater detail in discussing criteria for evaluating problem statements or questions.

CONSUMER TIPS: *Criteria for Evaluating Quantitative Research Problem Statements and Questions*

1. The problem should be researchable. A researchable problem is one that can be answered empirically by collecting and analyzing data. Problems that are concerned with value questions or philosophical ideas are not researchable in the sense that a specific question has a correct answer. There are many interesting questions in education that require value or ethical analyses, but to

TABLE 2.1 **Researchability of Quantitative Problems**

Nonresearchable	Researchable
Should we teach sex education in elementary schools?	What is the difference in knowledge and attitudes of fifth-graders taught sex education, compared to fifth-graders who are not taught sex education?
Do teachers need to have courses in test construction?	Will the classroom testing procedures used by teachers who take a course in test construction differ from those of teachers who have not had the course?
Should the school day be longer?	What is the relationship between length of the school day and SAT scores of high school students?
Should learning-disabled students be mainstreamed in English as well as in physical education?	What is the effect of mainstreaming fourth-grade learning-disabled students into English classes on the self-concept, attitudes, and achievement of all students?

be able to conduct research, the question must lend itself to the systematic process of gathering and analyzing data.

2. The problem/question should be important. The results of research need to have theoretical or practical importance. Theoretical importance is determined by the contribution of the study to existing knowledge. Are the results meaningfully related to what is already known? Do the results add new knowledge or change the way we understand phenomena? Practical importance suggests that the results will have immediate use in day-to-day activities or decisions.

3. The problem should indicate the type of research. The language used in the research problem should indicate whether the study involves a simple description, a comparison, a relationship, or a difference. A simple description is implied from such problems as these:

How many third-graders have computer experience?

What criteria are most important in placing children with autism spectrum disorder?

What are the social and personality characteristics of gifted children?

How do children react when parents separate?

A relationship study indicates how two or more variables may be related. For example, the following problems imply a relationship:

What is the relationship between achievement and self-concept?

Is there a relationship between effort in doing an assignment and attitudes about it?

Can leadership potential be predicted from high school grades, recommendations, and participation in extracurricular activities?

Research that compares categories of one or more independent variables can also be nonexperimental. For example:

> How do males and females differ in their attitudes toward freedom of the press?
>
> Are elementary school teachers different from secondary school teachers in assertiveness?
>
> What is the difference between sixth-, seventh-, and eighth-graders' self-concept of ability?

Some research problems imply more than a simple relationship or comparison. They suggest that one variable causes a change in another one. Here the intent of the research is to test a cause-and-effect relationship between the independent and dependent variables. This includes all experimental research and some types of nonexperimental research. Typically, differences are emphasized in the problem statement, and often the word *effect* is used. (Unfortunately, some relationship studies that are not causal still use the term *effect*, which may be misleading.) Here are some difference questions that imply cause-and-effect relationships:

> Will method A result in higher achievement than method B?
>
> Is there a difference in attitude between students having peer teaching, compared to students who have traditional instruction?
>
> What is the effect of small group instruction on the reading achievement of second-graders?

4. The problem statement/question should specify the sample. The sample is simply the people who the researcher investigated. A good research problem identifies, in a few words, the most important distinguishing characteristics of the sample. Too much detail about the participants will unnecessarily repeat the full description in the subjects section of the research report. Hence, the description of the population in the research problem should be concise yet informative. Here is a problem in which the description of the sample is too vague:

> Do children who practice with calculators achieve more than those who do not practice with calculators?

Here is the same problem with a description that is too specific:

> Do fourth-grade, low-SES, low-ability students from Carpenter Elementary School who practice with calculators achieve more than those who do not practice with calculators?

A good level of specificity would be this:

> Do low-ability, low-SES fourth-graders who practice with calculators achieve more than those who do not practice with calculators?

5. The problem statement/question should specify the variables. A good problem statement of a relatively simple study will name the variables and how they may be related in a single sentence. Often these will be independent and dependent variables. Variables are described, like the sample, with a moderate level of specificity. "A study of the effect of teacher workshops" is far too general; in fact there is no dependent variable at all. "A study of the effect of teacher workshops on teacher morale as measured by the Smith Morale and Attitude Scale" does provide a dependent variable, but provides more detail than necessary and still does not communicate much about the independent variable (workshop). Here the design of the study will contribute to the description of the independent variable. If two groups of teachers are being compared, one who attends the workshop and one who does not, a better, more informative problem would be: Is there a difference in the morale of teachers who attend a teacher workshop compared to teachers who do not attend? Here the independent variable is more than just named; it is described.

Research problems that are more complex because of having several independent and/or dependent variables may need to be stated in more than one sentence. The first sentence typically includes either the main variables or a general term to represent several variables. It is followed by one or more sentences that describe all the variables:

> The aim of this study is to investigate the relationship between measures of aptitude and attitudes toward college among high school students. The measures of aptitude include scores from the SRA and SAT, high school grade point average, and class rank. Attitudes toward college are assessed by the Canadian College Attitude Scale, which reports four subscale scores: motivation, academic versus social climate, reputation, and expectations for success.

This study involves four independent and four dependent variables, and it would be cumbersome to try to include all of them in one sentence.

6. The problem statement/question should be clear. The importance of a clear, concise research problem statement cannot be overemphasized. One purpose of the research problem statement is to communicate the purpose of the study, ensuring that the reader's understanding of the purpose is consistent with the researcher's. Also, a clear research problem reflects clear thinking by the researcher. A clear problem does not include ambiguous terms. Ambiguity occurs when different people, reading the same thing, derive different meanings from what is read. If a term or phrase can mean several things, it is ambiguous. Terms such as *effect*, *effective*, *achievement*, *aptitude*, *methods*, *curriculum*, and *students*, by themselves, are ambiguous or vague. They should be replaced or modified so that the meaning is clear. A vague statement such as "What is the effect of sex education?" needs much more specificity. What is meant by "effect" and "sex education"? What grade level is being studied? What type of study is it? A successful problem indicates unambiguously the what, who, and how of the research by using declarative sentences such as "The purpose of this study is to . . ." or questions such as "What is the relationship between . . ."; "Is there a difference between . . ."; "How do . . ."; and "What is . . ." Either type of sentence is acceptable, and you will find both in the literature.

Hypotheses

Hypotheses are educated "guesses" or tentative expectations about a correct solution to a problem, descriptions, possible relationships, or differences. In research, a hypothesis is typically the investigator's prediction or expectation of what the results will show. It is a conjectural statement of the researcher's expectations about how the variables in the study are related. In short, a hypothesis is a prediction that is made prior to data collection. (As we will see, this kind of hypothesis is usually referred to as a "research hypothesis.")

Hypotheses: Tentative predictions or expectations.

Why Researchers Use Hypotheses. Researchers use hypotheses in some quantitative studies because they serve a number of important purposes:

1. The hypothesis provides a focus that integrates information. Researchers often have hunches about predictions, based on experience, previous research, and the opinions of others. By forming a hypothesis, the researcher synthesizes the information to make the most accurate prediction possible. Usually, the researcher draws heavily on the related literature. If the hypothesis does not follow from or is not logically related to the previous literature, the importance or contribution of the research is questionable, and the overall credibility of the study is diminished.

2. The hypothesis is testable. It provides a statement of relationships that can be tested by gathering and analyzing data.

3. The hypothesis helps the investigator know what to do. The nature of the hypothesis directs the investigation by suggesting appropriate sampling, instrumentation, and procedures. It helps the researcher keep a focused, specific scope.

4. The hypothesis allows the investigator to confirm or disconfirm a theory. Hypotheses help advance knowledge by refuting, modifying, or supporting theories.

5. The hypothesis provides a framework for developing explanations that can be investigated scientifically. Explanations that are not contained in a hypothesis are metaphysical in nature and are not subject to scientific verification.

6. When supported, the hypothesis provides evidence of the predictive nature of the relationship between the variables. Knowledge of a tested, confirmed prediction is more powerful evidence than an unconfirmed, untested observation.

7. The hypothesis provides a useful framework for organizing and summarizing the results and conclusions of the research. It helps the reader understand the meaning and significance of the study.

Types of Hypotheses. There are two ways to classify hypotheses: whether the hypothesis is derived from inductive or deductive logic, and whether the hypothesis is stated as a *research* or *statistical* hypothesis.

An *inductive hypothesis* is formed from a researcher's observations of behavior. The observations are synthesized to form tentative explanations about how the behaviors are related to one another and to other variables such as teaching methods, curriculum materials, and teacher behavior. In fact, teachers provide a rich source for inductive hypotheses because they can use their experience and knowledge to formulate hypotheses that may explain observed relationships. A limitation of inductive hypotheses is that because they depend on local data and idiosyncratic observations, generalizations are often restricted and difficult to relate to a broader theory or established body of applied research.

Deductive hypotheses are derived from theory, and thus testing them contributes to a better understanding of the theory or its application. The findings are integrated with existing facts and theories, which helps build a meaningful body of knowledge. For example, the theory of positive reinforcement suggests that teachers should reward desirable behavior. This principle has generated a great amount of research based on deductive hypotheses. From the general theory we have built a larger knowledge base that includes the effects of intrinsic and extrinsic reinforcement, praise, tokens, immediate and delayed reinforcement, and self-reinforcement.

Research hypothesis: Statement of expected results.

Hypotheses are also classified as *research* or *statistical*. A **research hypothesis** is a conjectural, declarative statement of the results the investigator expects to find. Research hypotheses are sometimes referred to as working or substantive hypotheses. Most research hypotheses are directional, in which the nature of the expected difference or relationship is stated. That is, a specified group is expected to score higher or lower than other groups, or a relationship is positive or negative. For example, a research hypothesis for an experiment would be:

> Fifth-grade students participating in a computer-aided mathematics lesson will demonstrate higher achievement than students using a traditional paper-and-pencil lesson.

In a study of relationships the research hypothesis might be:

> There is a positive relationship between time on task and achievement.

A research hypothesis is used when the investigator anticipates the specific outcome of the study, for example, which group will score higher than the other, an increase or decrease in scores, a positive or negative relationship, more or less of something, and so forth. Here are some examples of research hypotheses from published studies:

EXAMPLES 2.14–2.15 | Published Research Hypotheses

We hypothesized that mastery goals would lead students to develop deep interests in particular domains and therefore pursue a reduced number of disciplines. . . . We also reasoned that mastery-approach goals for college courses in general could reflect a broad orientation toward learning. If this is the case, then mastery-approach goals might positively predict variety in students' course selections.

Source: Durik, A. M., Lovejoy, C. M., & Johnson, S. J. (2009). A longitudinal study of achievement goals for college in general: Predicting cumulative GPA and diversity in course selection. *Contemporary Educational Psychology, 34*, 115.

It is hypothesized that prior achievement will directly predict GPA because historically students' performance on standardized tests has been considered an optimal predictor of their subsequent success in school. Prior achievement is also expected to predict homework reports because high achieving high school students spend more time on their assignments than low achieving students. . . . In addition, high achieving students are hypothesized to form higher self-efficacy beliefs about their capability to learn on their own.

Source: Zimmerman, B. J., & Kitsantas, A. (2005). Homework practices and academic achievement: The mediating role of self-efficacy and perceived responsibility beliefs. *Contemporary Educational Psychology, 30,* 400.

EXAMPLE 2.16 | Research Hypotheses for Several Dependent Variables

The hypotheses guiding our research were as follows: Relative to students receiving traditional reading lessons, students assigned to PALS will (a) achieve higher reading comprehension scores on experimenter-developed and standardized test tasks; (b) be more effective in mastering tasks specific to the taught strategies; (c) report greater knowledge about the respective strategies; and (d) indicate a better understanding of activities characteristics of self-regulated reading.

Source: Sporer, N., & Brunstein, J. C. (2009). Fostering the reading comprehension of secondary students through peer-assisted learning: Effects on strategy knowledge, strategy use, and task performance. *Contemporary Educational Psychology 34,* 291.

Research hypotheses can also be nondirectional. The researcher believes there will be a difference or relationship, but is unsure about the nature of it; for example,

> There will be a difference in achievement when comparing individually tutored children to those receiving group tutoring.

Such nondirectional research hypotheses are not very common. Usually, either previous research or the experiences and intuition of the investigator suggest a direction.

The **statistical hypothesis** is a statement of a relationship or difference that can be tested statistically. Statistical hypotheses are usually stated in what is called the "null" form. A **null hypothesis** is a statement that there are no statistically significant differences or relationships. The null hypothesis is tested, based on the findings from the study, and results in either rejecting or failing to reject the null. The acceptance or nonacceptance of the null hypothesis provides support or no support for the research hypothesis. The statistical procedures used to test the null hypothesis are discussed in greater detail in Chapter 10. At this point it is important to understand that we do not test the research hypothesis itself; we "accept" it when the null hypothesis is rejected. We do it in this way because researchers do not prove true an expected result. Rather, they can tentatively

Statistical hypothesis: Statistical statement of possible results.

Null hypothesis: Statistical statement that no significant difference or relationship exists.

TABLE 2.2 Relationship of Research Problems, Research Hypotheses, and Null Hypotheses

Research Problem	Research Hypothesis	Null Hypothesis
What is the effect of a mainstreaming workshop on the attitude of teachers toward mainstreaming?	Teachers' attitudes toward mainstreaming will improve as a result of attending a workshop on mainstreaming.	There is no difference in teachers' attitudes toward mainstreaming measured before a workshop on mainstreaming, compared to their attitudes after the workshop.
Is there a relationship between teachers' attitudes toward the curriculum and student achievement?	There is a positive correlation between teachers' attitudes toward the curriculum and student achievement.	There is no correlation between teachers' attitudes toward the curriculum and student achievement.
Is there a difference in achievement between students who are given highly detailed written comments on their work, compared to students who are given grades only?	Students receiving highly detailed written comments on their work will show higher achievement than students given grades only.	There is no difference in achievement between students receiving highly detailed comments about their work, compared to students receiving grades only.

accept the research hypothesis when the statistical test shows that the null hypothesis, which is assumed to be true before the test, can be rejected.

Table 2.2 shows the relationship among research problems, research hypotheses, and null hypotheses. The investigator begins with a problem, forms a research hypothesis based on a review of literature and/or personal experiences, forms the null hypothesis, tests the null hypothesis, and accepts or rejects the research hypothesis. Often there will not be an explicit null hypothesis in an article or report; rather, it is usually implied in the statistical test. In some articles the research hypothesis is implied rather than explicitly stated.

Examples of research questions and hypotheses from a study of parents' teaching reading and mathematics to their children are illustrated in Example 2.17.

EXAMPLE 2.17 | Research Questions and Hypotheses

Research Question	Corresponding Research Hypotheses
Does mothers' and fathers' SES predict their teaching of reading and mathematics during kindergarten and Grade 1?	Mothers and fathers with low SES would show more teaching of reading and mathematics than those with higher SES.
Do mothers' and fathers' self-reported learning difficulties predict the extent to which they teach reading and mathematics to their children?	Mothers and fathers who had experienced learning difficulties end up teaching their children more reading and mathematics than those without learning difficulties.

Source: Silinskas, G., Leppanen, U., Aunola, K., Parrila, R., & Nurmi, J. (2010). Predictors of mothers' and fathers' teaching of reading and mathematics during kindergarten and Grade 1. *Learning and Instruction, 20,* 63–64.

CONSUMER TIPS: *Criteria for Evaluating Research Hypotheses*

1. The research hypothesis should be stated in declarative form. Because the research hypothesis is a possible explanation, it must be written in the form of a declarative sentence. A hypothesis cannot be stated in the form of a question.

2. The research hypothesis should be consistent with known facts, previous research, and theory. The research hypothesis should follow from other studies and established theories. In general, it should not contradict previous research but rather should build on related literature; the results should contribute to the established body of knowledge. It is best for the research hypothesis to follow the review of literature. The reader should be able to understand why a particular hypothesis is put forth.

3. The research hypothesis should follow from the research problem. It is confusing to use variables in the hypothesis that have not been identified by the research problem. A general problem may include several variables, and thus several research hypotheses may be used to indicate all of the anticipated relationships.

4. The research hypothesis should state the expected relationship between two or more variables. A hypothesis must have at least two variables and must indicate how the variables are related. A study that analyzes the relationship by a correlation coefficient will use the terms *positive relationship* or *negative relationship*. In a study that analyzes differences between groups, the relationship may be expressed as a difference (more or less, higher or lower). In either case, an expected relationship is stated. Most research hypotheses conjecture the relationship between two variables. It can be awkward and confusing to include more than two variables in one sentence, with the exception of studies that have several dependent variables and one independent variable (e.g., Students in the cooperative class will show more positive attitudes toward learning, higher achievement, and more prosocial behavior than students in the individualized class).

5. The research hypothesis should be testable. As pointed out previously, being testable means being verifiable; that is, data can be obtained to determine whether the hypothesis can be supported. It is a matter of measuring the variables in such a way that the hypothesis can be confirmed or not confirmed. Thus, the variables must be measurable, and the researcher must be able to obtain data that represent values of the variables. The researcher must therefore include operational definitions of the variables (not necessarily as part of the hypothesis statement, but perhaps following the hypothesis). Stated differently, the variables must be amenable to operational definitions that can be applied by using an instrument or observations to collect data. For example, the hypothesis "Children taking a unit on nutrition will be more healthy" is not testable because "more healthy" is difficult to operationalize and measure, and it would be almost impossible to attribute better health to the unit on nutrition.

6. The research hypothesis should be clear. Like the terminology used in research problems, words, phrases, and descriptions in the research hypothesis should be unambiguous. A clear hypothesis is easier for the reader to comprehend and easier for the researcher to test.

7. The research hypothesis should be concise. Consistent with criteria for research problems, hypotheses should be sufficiently detailed to communicate what is being tested and, at the same time, should be as succinct as possible. A concise hypothesis is easier to comprehend.

Review and Reflect *See if you can recall the criteria for evaluating research problems, questions, and hypotheses. Find an example of a study and see if you can identify the research questions and then evaluate them based on the criteria presented (those in the article in Chapter 1 would be one example). Write research questions and corresponding hypotheses, both research and null, given some variables from your area of study.*

QUALITATIVE RESEARCH PROBLEM STATEMENTS *and* QUESTIONS

In qualitative studies, researchers tend to use only general problem statements or questions (see Table 2.3). From the beginning, the logic and purpose of the questions are different from those of quantitative problems. As illustrated in the examples provided, qualitative problems tend to be much more open-ended, less specific, evolving rather than static, and process-oriented. These differences result in unique usage of terms and language. For example, it is common for qualitative problem statements to use words like *generate*, *understand*, and *explore*, rather than *relate*, *differ*, or *compare*. A qualitative question is neutral with respect to what will be learned through the study. There are no predictions or expected results.

Central phenomenon: Issue or process studied.

The first step in writing a qualitative problem statement or question is to identify the central phenomenon that is being studied. The **central phenomenon** is

TABLE 2.3 Differences Between Quantitative and Qualitative Research Problems

Quantitative	Qualitative
Specific	General
Closed	Open
Static	Evolving
Outcome oriented	Process oriented
Contains variables	Does not contain variables
Hypotheses	No hypotheses

an issue or process that is being investigated (Creswell, 2009). Issues would be such things as teenage alienation, teacher retention, or principal burnout. Processes could include the manner in which beginning teachers are inducted into the profession, how teachers integrate the demands of standardized high-stakes testing into their teaching, and the manner in which mainstreamed children are integrated into the regular classroom. The general research problem statement or question includes a single central phenomenon. Two or more phenomena are not compared or related, as would be done in a quantitative study (comparisons and relationships can emerge from the data, it's just that qualitative researchers don't go into the research with these already in mind). Here are some examples of general problem statements from published qualitative studies that have a clear central phenomenon.

EXAMPLES 2.18–2.22 | Qualitative Research Problem Statements and Questions

Our study aimed to investigate whether rural and suburban youth are as willing or able to articulate effective instructional and school improvement strategies as their urban counterparts . . . Furthermore, we wanted to see whether the perceptions of youth with disabilities regarding school improvement varied from those of their non-disabled peers.

Source: De Fur, S. H., & Korinek, L. (2010). Listening to student voices. *The Clearing House, 83* (1), 15.

This case study examines the complexity of enacting CRP [Culturally Relevant Pedagogy] with ethnic and language minorities . . . [and examines] the link between two mathematics teachers' beliefs, identities, and enactment of CRP with ELL high school students' interpretation of the mathematical task. The research questions that guided this case study were:

1. How do two mathematics teachers' beliefs and identity interact with their pedagogical decisions before and after implementation of CRP?
2. How did culture interact with predominately black ELL students' understanding, completion, and fidelity of the mathematical tasks?
3. How did the mathematical task adhere to the tenets of CRP?

Source: Leonard, J., Napp, C., & Adeleke, S. (2009). The complexities of culturally relevant pedagogy: A case study of two secondary mathematics teachers and their ESOL students. *The High School Journal, 93*(1), 5.

Our research was designed as a descriptive investigation of the joint effects of external and internal accountability on sustainable improvement and addressed the following general questions:

- How do schools adapt to external accountability standards?
- How do schools' structure and culture relate to their ability to make sense of and respond to external standards?
- How do perceived power relations affect local responses to state testing and accountability?

Source: Louis, K. S., Febey, K., & Schroeder, R. (2005). *Educational Evaluation and Policy Analysis, 27*(2) 181.

The study reported here was designed to address the issue [of] whether teacher education can make a difference in graduates' teaching competence. Specifically, we addressed the following research questions:

1. How does teaching competence develop over time?
2. What are the relative influences of teacher education programs and occupational socialization in schools on the development of teaching competence?
3. Which program characteristics are related to competence development?

Source: Brouwer, N., & Korthagen, F. (2005). Can teacher education make a difference? *American Educational Research Journal, 42*(1), 154.

The research questions were (a) What factors do students perceive to be contributing to their anxiety in learning statistics? (b) What instructional strategies do students feel helpful to lessen their statistics anxiety and to learn statistics effectively?"

Source: Pan, W., & Tang, M. (2005). Students' perceptions on factors of statistics anxiety and instructional strategies. *Journal of Instructional Psychology, 32*(3), p. 206.

It is important that the central phenomenon not be too general or too focused. If it is very general (e.g., a study on caring relationships or parental involvement), then it is not helpful in understanding the study. If it is too specific, as is acceptable for quantitative research questions, then the researchers may miss significant information because they are too narrowly focused.

It is common in qualitative studies to find that initial research problems are changed or that new research problems or questions are introduced as data are being collected. This flexibility is needed so that new ideas, based on data gathered, can be integrated and used to improve on initial problems or questions. There is essentially an interactive relationship between the problem and the data, each influencing the other. New research questions are often introduced *after* data have been gathered. The initial problems are often referred to as *foreshadowed.*

CONSUMER TIPS: *Criteria for Evaluating Qualitative Research Problem Statements and Questions*

1. The problem statement/question should not be too general or too specific. Research problem statements/questions that are too vague and general give the impression that the research is more like a fishing trip than systematic inquiry, while those that are too narrow are inconsistent with the reason for doing qualitative research. A middle ground is needed so that what is being investigated is clear, while at the same time not so specific that the researcher is unable to capture new and significant information when it arises.

2. The problem statement/question should be amenable to change as data are collected. It is important to write the initial problem statement/question so that it is somewhat open-ended and general. This allows for and encourages changes as the data are being collected. The continuing reformulation of a problem reflects the emergent design of the research. For example, beginning a study with a problem question like "What are the perceptions of students about tests for graduation?" would be more amenable to change than something like "What do students say about whether graduation tests are fair?"

3. The problem statement/question should not be biased with researcher assumptions or desired findings. In qualitative research the investigator's assumptions and biases must be considered in designing the study and interpreting the findings, but it is important to keep the central question as neutral as possible. All too often researchers want to gather data to "prove" something to be true, and this threat to good research is easily manifest in qualitative studies. Notice how a statement like the following suggests an assumption about what will be found: "The purpose of this study is to explore reasons college faculty give to explain a lack of multicultural awareness in their teaching." A better statement would be: "The purpose of the study is to explore multicultural awareness as reflected in teaching."

4. The problem statement/question should be written with "how" and "what" to keep the focus on description of phenomena. The most important goal of qualitative research is to be able to provide an in-depth description of the phenomenon that is studied. This goal is best achieved if the researcher focuses on what occurs and how it occurs, rather than why. If the focus is on why, there tends to be an emphasis on causal conclusions and relationships, not descriptions.

5. The problem should include the central phenomenon as well as an indication of the participants and the site in which the study is being conducted. Good qualitative research problem statements and questions contain three elements: the phenomenon being studied, the participants, and the research site or setting. Creswell (2009) suggests using the following script: "What is (*the central phenomenon*) for (*participants*) at (*research site*)?" (p. 131) An example would be "What is athletic participation like for seniors at James River High School?" This kind of statement is clear and concise and tells the reader quite a lot about what is being studied, who is being studied, and where the study takes place.

You may be wondering at this point about research problems, questions, and hypotheses for mixed-method studies. If you are—good! Essentially, the nature of the problems, questions, and hypotheses are matched to either the quantitative or qualitative part of the study. We will say more about these in Chapter 12.

STUDY QUESTIONS

1. What is the difference between a research problem and a research problem statement or question?
2. How is it possible for a research problem statement/question to be too specific?

3. What is the major difference between qualitative and quantitative research problem statements/ questions?
4. Under what circumstances would it be helpful to use research hypotheses?
5. What is the difference between research and null hypotheses?
6. What are some "original" examples of continuous and categorical variables?
7. Why is it important to have operational definitions of variables?
8. What is the difference between independent, dependent, extraneous, and confounding variables? How are they related?
9. Under what circumstances would it be difficult to identify separate independent and dependent variables?
10. Why is it important to indicate the central idea, participants, and site or setting in a qualitative research problem statement or question?
11. Why are qualitative research problem statements and questions tentative rather than fixed?
12. How are qualitative and quantitative research problem statements or questions different? In what way are they the same?

Chapter 3

Locating *and* Reviewing Related Literature

with ANGELA WETZEL

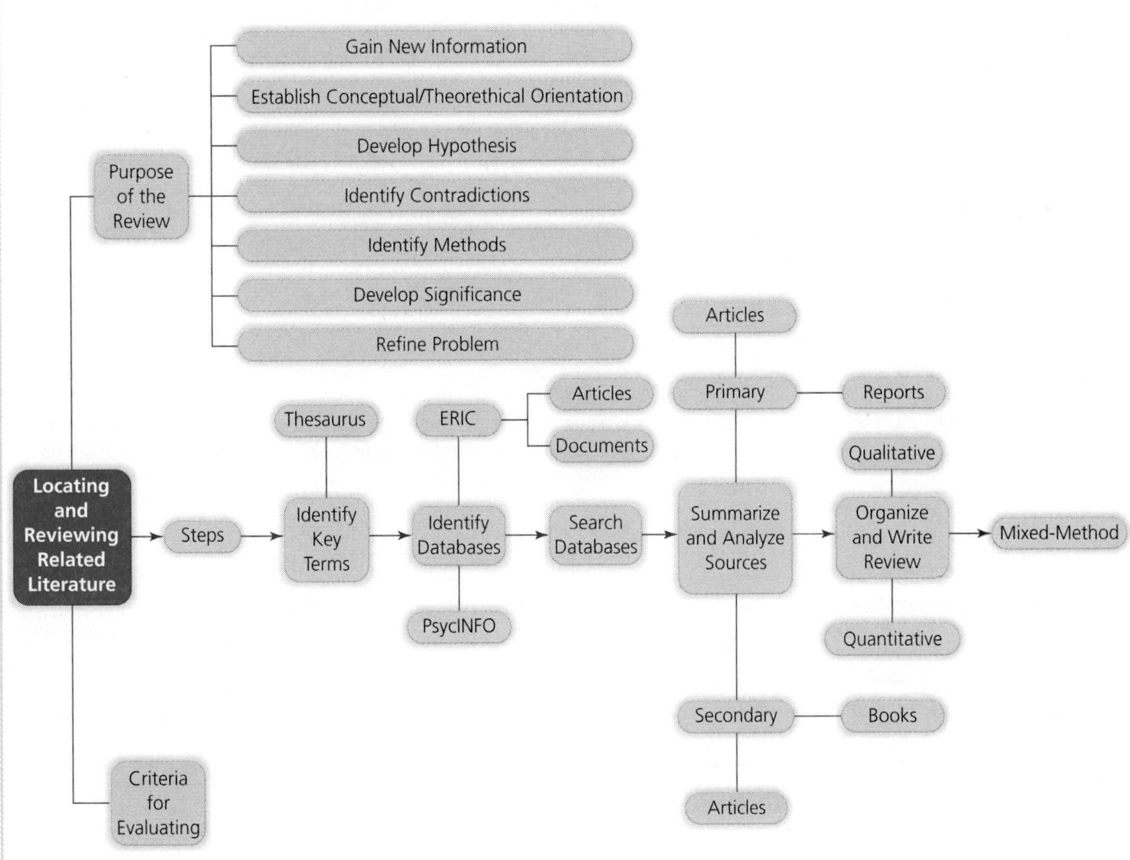

CHAPTER ROAD MAP

Once a research problem or general question has been identified, a review of the literature is needed for several reasons. In this chapter we begin by summarizing these reasons. We then turn our attention to procedures for conducting reviews. This will include both primary and secondary sources, each of which is important. Major differences between qualitative and quantitative reviews of literature are included. We conclude with suggestions for writing the review of literature section of a manuscript, article, or report.

Chapter Outline	Learning Objectives
Purpose of Reviewing Literature	• Understand the reasons researchers review related literature prior to designing and implementing their own investigation. • Know how the review of literature contributes to good research.
Steps in Conducting a Review of Literature	• Know and apply the sequence of steps that are taken to find literature that is related to the research problem.
Identify Key Terms	• Be able to search for and identify key terms to use in a search.
Identify Database	• Differentiate ERIC and PsycINFO from other databases.
Conduct Search	• Become thoroughly knowledgeable about ERIC. • Use ERIC to perform a literature search.
Use Primary Articles	• Understand the differences between primary and secondary sources.
Use of Internet	• Know the strengths and weaknesses of using the Internet to identify related literature.
Searching the Internet	• Understand the differences between subject directories, search engines, and metasearch engines.
Internet Communication Strategies	• Know how to use e-mail, blogging, social networking, and newsgroups.
Utilizing Known Locations	• Know about and access federal government websites, such as the Institute of Education Sciences, as well as association, organization, and university websites.
Internet Websites	• Become familiar with how to reference websites and how to evaluate the quality of the information that is accessed.
Writing a Review of Literature	• Be able to summarize, analyze, and relate literature to a proposed study. • Know the differences between writing a quantitative, qualitative, and mixed-method review of literature.
Evaluating a Review of Literature	• Understand and be able to apply criteria to the evaluation of a review of literature.

The PURPOSE *of* REVIEWING RELATED LITERATURE

Broadly stated, the purpose of the review is to relate previous research and theory to the problem under investigation. By showing how a current or proposed study compares to previous investigations, the research problem, as well as the methodology, can be placed in an appropriate context. Without a good review of literature, the researchers are less likely to use what have already been shown to be the most effective methods. From a consumer's viewpoint, knowing the purpose of the review will contribute to an overall evaluation of the credibility of the research, as well as indicate whether the nature of the review is closely targeted to the reader's needs. More specific purposes of reviewing literature include the following:

- Refining the research problem
- Establishing the conceptual or theoretical orientation
- Developing significance
- Identifying methodological limitations
- Identifying contradictory findings
- Developing research hypotheses
- Learning about new information

Refining the Research Problem

By reviewing related studies and discussions of research in that area, the investigator learns how others have defined the general problem in more specific ways. Ideas and examples are found that help delimit the problem, and concepts and variables are clarified as the researcher finds operational definitions.

The process of refining a research problem can be frustrating. Typically, an initial problem that seems to have merit needs to be changed as the researcher reviews previous studies in the area. A new problem is formulated, and often it, too, needs revision as further literature is reviewed. This process can be repeated many times.

Establishing the Conceptual or Theoretical Orientation

It is important to place an individual study within the context of a pertinent conceptual framework or theoretical orientation. This includes statements that identify, delimit, and define relevant scholarship in which the study is grounded—that summarize the intellectual tradition on which it is based. It should be clear if a new theory is being proposed or tested, or whether existing theory is being used to frame the research problem. This part of the review also establishes a logical link between the research questions and methodology.

Developing Significance

It is important for research to be significant or meaningful if it is to make a contribution to existing knowledge or practice. Within the context of previous knowledge from existing research, a researcher should link the proposed study to accumulated knowledge to indicate specifically how it will add to, expand, and build on this base. Previous studies will also help the researcher identify new directions worth pursuing and avoid unnecessary duplication. Furthermore, the researcher can interpret current results in terms of the findings from previous studies, making the conclusions more meaningful and enhancing the merit of the study.

Identifying Methodological Limitations

By learning about the specific methods other researchers have employed to select subjects, measure variables, and implement procedures, investigators can identify approaches that may be useful for their studies. Both successful and unsuccessful methods are usually found, and both help investigators identify new ideas and avoid past mistakes or difficulties. Often, methodological weaknesses can suggest a need for research to be replicated with improvements in specific methods, as shown in Example 3.1.

EXAMPLE 3.1 | Identifying Methodological Limitations

Furthermore, for a number of reasons, the existing research is limited in its applicability to the case of a universal mandate, with which all schools are required to change their curricular offerings and all students are required to take college preparatory classes: First, virtually all prior studies have suffered from some degree of selection bias; second, prior research has paid little attention to differential effects by ability; finally, the findings developed from data on national samples may not generalize to schools with chronic low performance and weak instructional capacity.

Source: Allensworth, E., Nomi, T., Montgomery, N., & Lee, V. (2009). College preparatory curriculum for all: Academic consequences of requiring algebra and English I for ninth graders in Chicago. *Educational Evaluation and Policy Analysis, 31*(4), 370.

Identifying Contradictory Findings

A review of the literature may uncover studies or theories that contradict one another. Researchers find this a fruitful area in which to conduct subsequent studies. Possible reasons for the contradiction, such as the use of different types of subjects, measures, or procedures, can be identified, and research can be designed to resolve the contradiction. Such studies provide significant contributions to knowledge.

EXAMPLE 3.2 | Identifying Contradictory Findings

Results of research on the effects of immediate feedback on anxiety during testing have not been consistent. Some researchers have found immediate feedback to be associated with decreases in anxiety. . . . On the other hand, researchers have also frequently observed increases in anxiety . . . as well as reductions in test performance.

Source: DiBattista, D., & Gosse, L. (2006). Test anxiety and the immediate feedback assessment technique. *Journal of Experimental Education, 74*(4), 313.

Developing Research Hypotheses

In quantitative research, a sound research hypothesis is usually based on a review of literature. Previous studies in related areas may suggest a specific result, and the hypothesis should be consistent with these studies. When there are few or no closely related studies, existing theories should be used to justify a particular hypothesis. Thus, the literature provides a basis for the hypothesis either by theory or by more specific facts established by previous studies. If educational studies or theories are not clearly related to the problem, the researcher should look to other fields of study, such as psychology, sociology, or communication. Often, theories in these fields can serve as the basis for the hypothesis. Example 3.3 illustrates how a research hypothesis is justified.

EXAMPLE 3.3 | Developing Research Hypotheses

We based our predictions about the number and nature of the dimensions underlying students' attributions on the work of Wimer and Kelley (1982) and Weiner (1979, 1985). First, as Wimer and Kelley note, "Researchers do not agree on a single set of attributional categories" (p. 1143). However, with few exceptions exploratory analyses of the structure of attribution have identified a locus of causality, or internal versus external, dimension (Meyer, 1980). . . . Although less consistently, several investigations have also revealed a "good-bad" dimension. . . . Wimer and Kelley (1982), for example, argue that attributors draw a major distinction between positive causes and negative causes, and term this the Good-Bad factor. . . . This view suggests that causes tend to be valenced: "good" causes increase the likelihood of success, whereas "bad" causes increase the likelihood of failure. We therefore expected to find evidence of both a locus of cause and a good-bad dimension in our analyses. . . . Second, we also predicted that the causes obtained would be hierarchically structured.

Source: Forsyth, D. R., Story, P., Kelley, K. N., & McMillan, J. H. (2008). What causes failure and success? Students' perceptions of their academic outcomes. *Social Psychology of Education, 12* (2), 161.

Learning About New Information

A review of literature almost always leads to new information and knowledge, either in the topic of interest or in unrelated areas. Often, while searching the literature for one topic, you will come across interesting and useful research in other areas. Through the review of literature, you will also learn about journals, books, and other sources that publish information in your field of study.

STEPS *to* REVIEW RELATED LITERATURE

One of the best ways to become an informed consumer of research is to be able to conduct a review of existing studies and evaluate them, and use your interpretations in your work, to solve problems, or conduct action research. You need to be able to find research before you can interpret and use it.

It is best to have someone orient you to the library, including the organization of reference materials and the computer software and databases used. Many libraries offer seminars or workshops to help students get started in research and some offer tutorials available through the library website. Often librarians will specialize in a particular discipline, so if available, seek out someone with experience in educational literature. Be comfortable seeking out resources and asking questions. Conducting a review of the literature for a new study could take 20 to 30 hours to complete. It is important to learn how to identify, locate, and access the best sources for your topic efficiently.

By following a set of sequential steps, you will increase the quality of the research reviewed and be able to locate the most appropriate studies more quickly (see Figure 3.1).

With the wealth of information available electronically, days of beginning the steps of a literature review with hard-copy books and journals have passed; it is now more effective to use a computerized database.

Step 1: Select a Topic and Key Terms

The first step in reviewing literature is to have some idea of the topic or subject in which you are interested. This could be rather general, like "What teaching methods are best for students with learning disabilities" or more specific, like the research questions and hypotheses discussed in Chapter 2. Identify the most important terms in the problem and then think about other terms that are closely related. You will then use these terms in computerized databases to find literature. For example, you may be interested in student motivation, and it would be wise to use related terms, such as *engagement*, *effort*, *persistence*, *intrinsic motivation*, and *self-efficacy*.

Once you have identified terms, you may want to jump right into a computerized database and see what literature comes up, or you may want to begin by refining your search terms. For most searches of educational literature, it is best to use a special thesaurus to help select the most appropriate key terms. You will want to use either the ERIC *Thesaurus* or the *Thesaurus of Psychological Index Terms* (accessed in the PsycINFO database with definitions and uses that are somewhat different than the ERIC *Thesaurus*). ERIC, the Education Resources Information Center, is your best friend when it comes to educational literature. ERIC

FIGURE 3.1 Steps to review related literature.

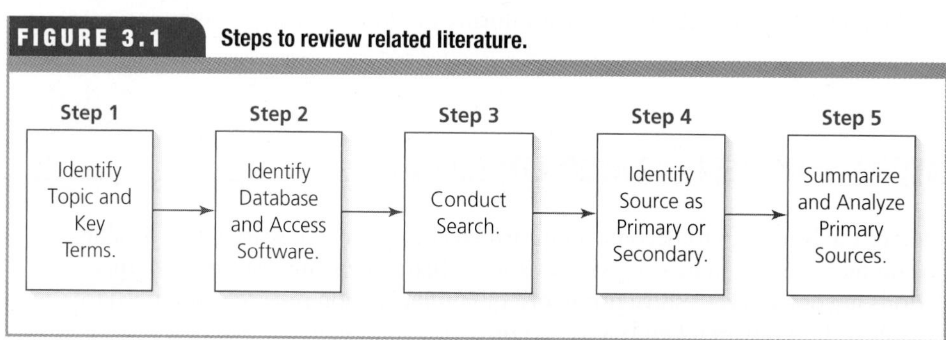
Step 1
Identify Topic and Key Terms.
Step 2
Identify Database and Access Software.
Step 3
Conduct Search.
Step 4
Identify Source as Primary or Secondary.
Step 5
Summarize and Analyze Primary Sources.

is a digital library of education-related resources. Although a hard copy of the *Thesaurus of ERIC Descriptors* could be used, the most recent and continually updated version is online (www.eric.ed.gov; other database vendors, such as EBSCO, use their own online format).

ERIC has a "controlled vocabulary" of terms called *descriptors*. Descriptors are used to organize and index database materials by subject. Each record is assigned several descriptors. The thesaurus also uses *keywords*. Keywords match words found in the indexed record, while descriptors locate records that may not contain the specific keyword. This means that if you use keywords for a search, you will locate many more records. For example, the keyword *cognitive style* identifies over 15,000 records, while as a descriptor about 2,000 records are identified.

You can search the ERIC *Thesaurus* by entering a specific term or phrase, or by browsing alphabetically or by category, to determine a match between how ERIC tends to define a term and your use of a term. A critical aspect of using terms is to understand that a given topic probably has general to narrow terms, as illustrated in Figure 3.2. When first beginning a search, it is best to use more general rather than more specific terms (e.g., categories rather than keywords). You can get an idea of the specificity of a term by pulling up the thesaurus record on it, as illustrated in Figure 3.3. The record shows other broader and narrower terms, as well as related terms. Suppose your topic is "the effect of using alternative assessment on student achievement." You enter "alternative assessment" in the thesaurus and it shows as in Figure 3.3. The results give you the definition ERIC has used. It is in the measurement category, with "evaluation" as a broader term and "performance based assessment" as a narrower term. Interestingly, "authentic assessment" is not a related term. For many this would be a type of alternative assessment. However, when *authentic assessment* is used as a keyword for an ERIC search, over 1,000 records are identified. This illustrates an important point in using key terms for your search: You must spend considerable time trying different searches with different terms, and you cannot assume that the way you think about and define terms is the same as the ERIC personnel who maintain the database. (In 2010, there was a nice two-minute video on the ERIC website to help identify the right terms.)

FIGURE 3.2 Specificity of ERIC descriptors.

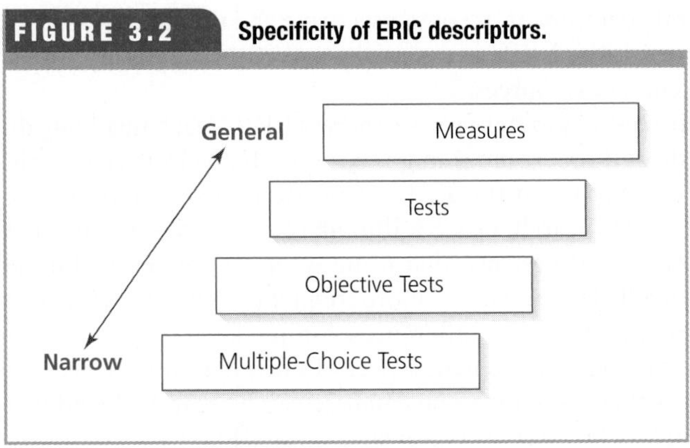

FIGURE 3.3 **Illustration of ERIC *Thesaurus* information.**

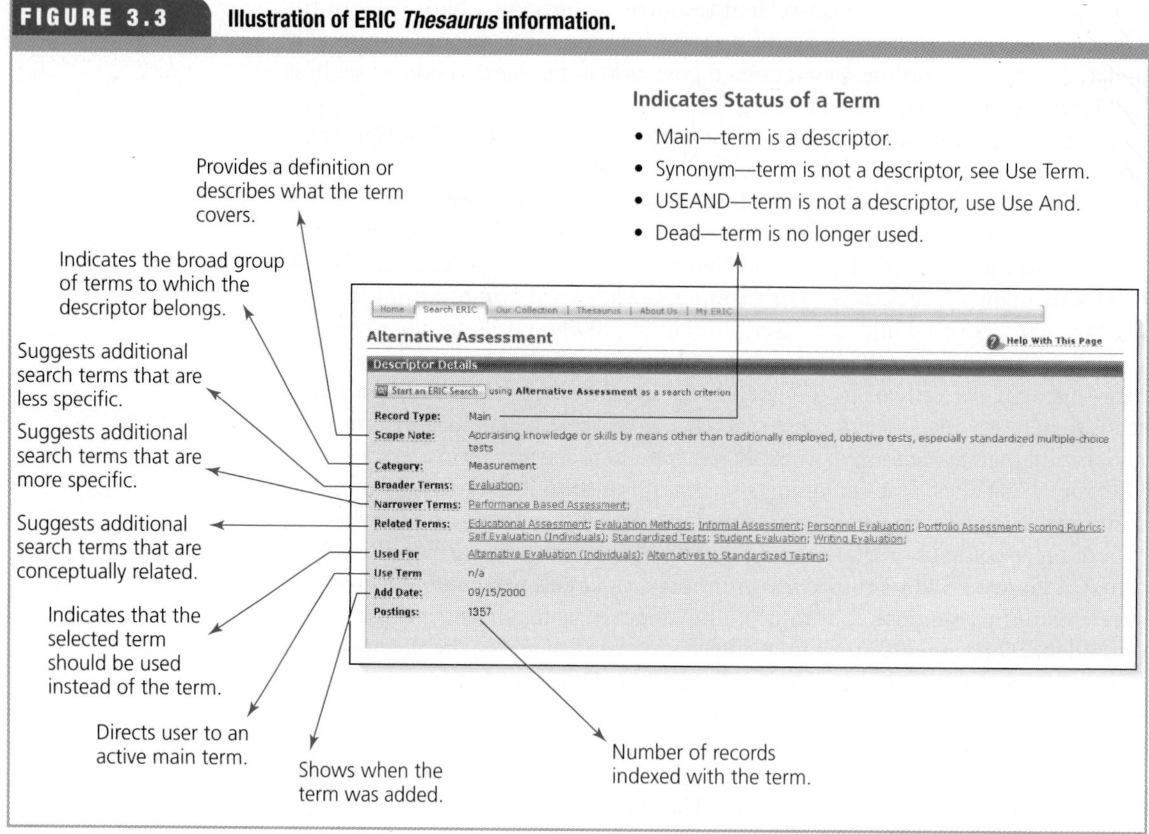

Step 2: Identify Database and Access Software

Equipped with a fairly focused set of key terms, you can use ERIC to identify articles and reports that can be reviewed in more detail to determine how helpful they will be for your literature review. ERIC is a database of resources sponsored by the federal government. It contains journal and nonjournal articles and reports obtained since 1966. ERIC is essentially a Web-based library for accessing historical and current resources.

There are several different ways to access ERIC, each involving different software. The most direct route is to go to the ERIC website (www.eric.ed.gov). In addition, you may reach the ERIC database by using another server such as EBSCOhost, FirstSearch, or CSA Illumina (Cambridge Scientific Abstracts).

It has been our experience that using www.eric.ed.gov will usually give you more hits since ERIC is updated more frequently, reflecting the most resources. It is not clear why there are differences. Simply keep this in mind and try more than one server. The convenient aspect of university library access points, such as EBSCO, is that more than one database can be searched, and it is easy to determine if an article or report is available online. The ERIC website and EBSCO allow you to save your searches and receive e-mail updates alerting you when new articles are available. (This feature is explained further in Step 3.) You will be able to access library resources and databases from home and, of course, be able to go directly to www.eric.ed.gov.

The PsycINFO database contains documents, articles, dissertations, and books in psychology and related disciplines, including education. This database is accessible online and contains over 2 million records covering 2,000 journals (98% are peer-reviewed). All university libraries provide access to PsycINFO. Individuals can use PsycINFO at a cost determined by time or number of records used.

One additional database used by many libraries is InfoTrac Onefile. This database has access to over 50 million articles, about half of which are available online and printed from your computer. This file combines scholarly and popular journals and magazines in all fields.

There are a number of other databases focused on topics within education, as well as databases in sociology, business, medicine, and other fields related to education. Consult your librarian for suggestions of databases that may help you locate other sources through a more specialized approach. We would be remiss not to mention the use of the Internet in locating specific sources. Google Scholar offers an efficient means of searching for specific articles, authors' names, and key terms with direct links to a full text if available through your university library. If you have a clear idea of what you are looking for, this is a valuable tool; however, a more comprehensive database, such as ERIC, will better serve your full literature review.

Step 3: Conduct Search

Although searches can be conducted in a number of different databases, we will limit our discussion of the literature search in education to ERIC and the Internet—the two most popular approaches in the field. First, we will describe the steps of searching in ERIC; the latter will be discussed in a separate section of this chapter dedicated to using the Internet.

The specific nature of the procedures to use to search ERIC depends on your server. Using the ERIC website as an example, you begin by typing in words that describe your topic in the Search box. It's usually best to click on Advanced Search and use that screen for your search. As illustrated in Figure 3.4, you have a number of options that can improve your search. The first decision with the Advanced Search screen is whether you want to limit your search to author, title, ERIC number, descriptor, or keywords (all fields), which is the default. These options appear when clicking on the box to the right with an arrow, along with some infrequently used options. You type the author, title, and so on in the box to the right. With Publication Date you can select documents appearing in specific years. It is often best to begin with the most recent five years. If you find too many documents, do another search limited to one year. If too few documents are identified, lengthen years to 10 or even more.

Author Reflection *Our experience in doing literature reviews is that the quality of studies has not changed appreciably for at least 20 years. Some topics were researched heavily many years ago with very good studies, so while it is important to use recent studies, don't ignore older research.*

FIGURE 3.4 Advanced search.

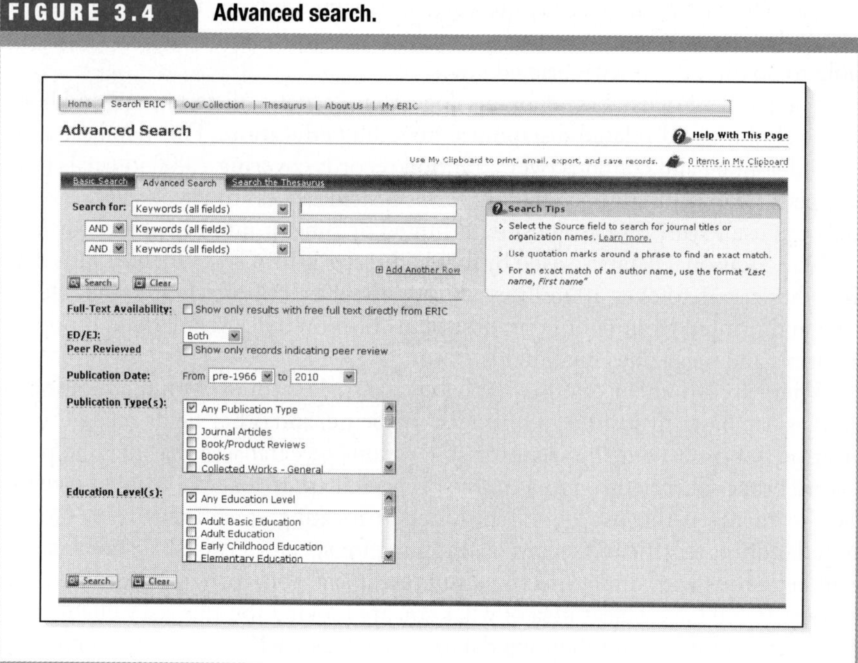

The next decision has to do with Publication Type(s). You have a large number of choices here, though typically only a few are relevant. Obviously, Any Publication Type encompasses all documents (even those not formally published in an article). You can select specific types of documents by checking as many as apply down the rather long list. Book/Product Reviews is excellent for identifying secondary sources. If you check Journal Article, only CIJE documents will be shown. Often the best search of primary sources uses Journal Articles and Reports/Research. The Tests/Questionnaires choice works well to find sources that use a particular measure.

Most students find that they need to tailor their search until they can identify a reasonable number of sources that appear to be closely related to their research problem. The most common way of limiting a search is to use the connector "and." Using *and* will reduce the search because the computer will look for entries that are categorized by all the descriptors or keywords indicated. For example, a search of *teaching styles* ***and*** *elementary* would produce fewer hits than using only one of these terms (*teaching styles* by itself would include elementary, middle, and high schools, as well as colleges and universities). If a third descriptor, say, *achievement*, is added, the search is further refined. This process of narrowing the search is illustrated in Figure 3.5, using Keywords, Any Education Level, Any Publication Type, and Publication Date years of 2005–2010. You can use either Sets (preferred) or Boolean logic (or, and) to construct a query. Put parentheses around sets, quotations around phrases, and commas between terms.

FIGURE 3.5 Narrowing an ERIC search.

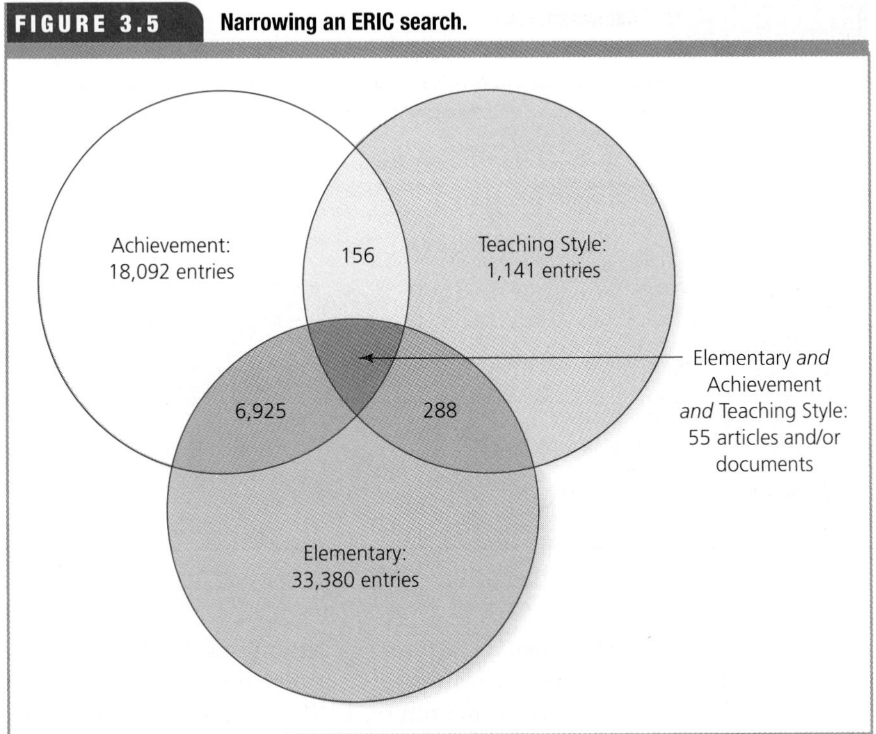

Once you construct a tailored search, you may wish to save the search, particularly when conducting ongoing research on a topic. The ERIC website and EBSCO host a joint system called My ERIC that allows you to save searches through both servers. To create a My ERIC account, select the My ERIC tab at the top of the screen, and choose Register to Use My Eric. An e-mail address is required. After logging into your account, you can save up to 10 searches and establish RSS feeds to alert you when new articles are added to the search. Ask your librarian if you need technical support.

When a topic is searched with www.eric.ed.gov, the user is presented with a list of articles and documents, summary information, and an abstract, as illustrated in Figure 3.6. This entry resulted from a search of "student motivation," completed in May 2010. From Figure 3.6 you will note that there is an ERIC number assigned to the entry. This number is permanent and will be the same for all servers. If the number begins with EJ, it is a journal article; if it begins with ED, it is a nonjournal document. Most journal articles have some kind of peer review, which tends to result in better quality than what you will find with nonjournal documents. But there are exceptions! Many journal articles, even with peer review, are not very credible, and many nonjournal documents are excellent. One advantage of searching nonjournal documents is that conference presentations are often included. Some of these presentations eventually become articles, but there may be a significant time lag between submission of a manuscript to a

FIGURE 3.6 ERIC search result.

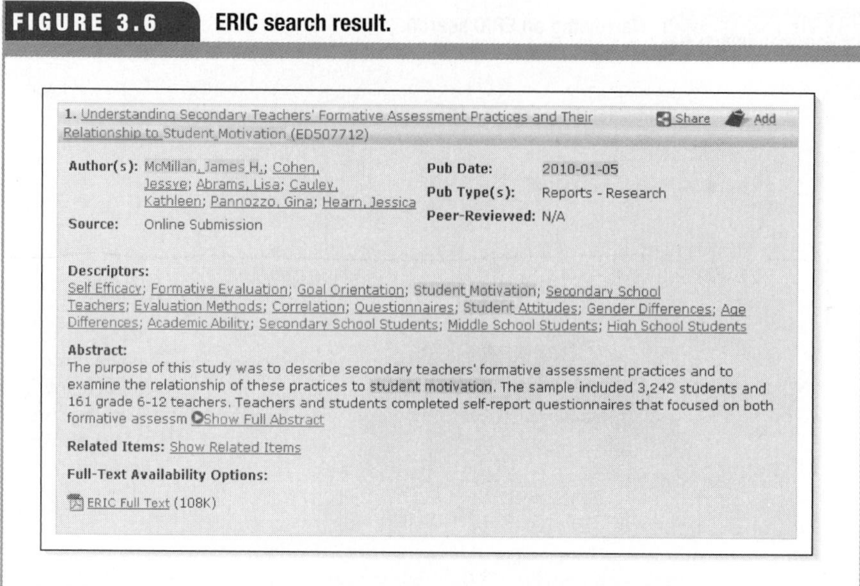

journal for publication and when the article appears in print. With this format (Figure 3.7) there is sufficient information to determine if it would be useful to locate the full article or report. In the future, ERIC will provide what it calls "Structured Abstracts" that, with predefined headings, will provide more specific information about the study design.

Once you have limited your search to a reasonable number of documents, for instance, between 5 and 20, you need to obtain the articles or reports to examine each one in greater detail to determine if they should be used in your review. Obtaining an actual article will depend on whether it is available online. Most journal articles are available on the Internet, or as hard copy in your library. You may need to use other libraries or interlibrary loan.

The typical process, then, involves taking a large number of possible documents and reducing that number down to the relatively few appropriate to your review. For example, you might begin a study on science and mathematics teaching strategies with some 12,000 hits; reduce that number by restricting your search to a few years; reduce it again by accessing only journal articles; locate those articles; and then, finally, pick 8 articles from among the 22 you obtained.

Step 4: Identify the Source as Primary or Secondary

As you review literature, you will come across many different types of articles and reports. This can seem confusing because there are hundreds of journals, agencies, and organizations publishing reports and sources on the Internet. A good first step is to identify sources as *primary* or *secondary*. A **primary source** is an original article or report in which researchers communicate directly to the reader the methods and results of their studies.

Primary source: Articles that report original research.

FIGURE 3.7 ERIC detailed search result.

Record Details

Full-Text Availability Options:

ERIC Full Text (108K)

Related Items: Show Related Items

Click on any of the links below to perform a new search

ERIC #:	ED507712
Title:	Understanding Secondary Teachers' Formative Assessment Practices and Their Relationship to Student Motivation
Authors:	McMillan, James H.; Cohen, Jessye; Abrams, Lisa; Cauley, Kathleen; Pannozzo, Gina; Hearn, Jessica
Descriptors:	Self Efficacy; Formative Evaluation; Goal Orientation; Student Motivation; Secondary School Teachers; Evaluation Methods; Correlation; Questionnaires; Student Attitudes; Gender Differences; Age Differences; Academic Ability; Secondary School Students; Middle School Students; High School Students
Source:	Online Submission
Peer-Reviewed:	N/A
Publisher:	N/A
Publication Date:	2010-01-05
Pages:	20
Pub Types:	Reports - Research
Abstract:	The purpose of this study was to describe secondary teachers' formative assessment practices and to examine the relationship of these practices to student motivation. The sample included 3,242 students and 161 grade 6-12 teachers. Teachers and students completed self-report questionnaires that focused on both formative assessment and motivation for a single class. Students referenced this single class, and teachers used the same class for their responses. This procedure was used to reflect the practices and effects of a single class rather than more generally for many classes. Results showed only moderate use of formative assessment practices, with little use of use of information to guide instruction or give students instructional correctives. The relationships between formative assessment practices and student motivation, using the classroom as the unit of analysis, showed small positive correlations. The relationship between students' goal orientation and teachers' formative practices was positive but nonsignificant. Student self-efficacy showed a statistically significant relationship with formative assessment as a whole. Student impressions of formative practice in their classroom were significantly related to student motivation. There were no differences for grade level, gender, subject taught, or student ability. Discussion of the results focuses on the significance of the findings, contribution to the literature, and recommendations for further research. (Contains 5 tables.)
Abstractor:	As Provided
Reference Count:	21
Note:	N/A
Identifiers:	Virginia
Record Type:	Non-Journal
Level:	N/A
Institutions:	N/A
Sponsors:	Metropolitan Educational Research Consortium, Richmond, VA.
ISBN:	N/A
ISSN:	N/A
Audiences:	N/A
Languages:	English
Education Level:	Grade 10; Grade 11; Grade 12; Grade 6; Grade 7; Grade 8; Grade 9; High Schools; Middle Schools; Secondary Education
Direct Link:	N/A

Secondary source: Summarizes, reviews, or discusses original research.

Secondary Sources. A **secondary source** is one that reviews, summarizes, or discusses primary research. The author(s) provide(s) information and analysis, but it is not a firsthand gathering of data.

In earlier editions of this book, I recommended that students begin a literature review by searching for appropriate secondary sources. Secondary sources are good to begin with because they provide an overview of the topic, often citing relevant research studies and important primary sources. Some examples of secondary sources are textbooks, scholarly books devoted to a particular topic, reviews of research in books or journals, yearbooks, encyclopedias, and hand books. When using secondary sources, you should be aware that because they combine the information from other secondary sources and actual studies, it is possible that the author did not accurately report the research. Furthermore, the review may be selective to support a particular point of view, or the author may have failed to locate important studies.

There are three main types of secondary sources:

1. **Professional Books.** Scholarly books are written on many topics for other researchers and professionals in the area; therefore, they often contain more details about the research. Textbooks are also secondary sources, providing a nontechnical overview of several topics within a particular field of study. Written for students, they may lack detail but offer general overviews and references.
2. **Encyclopedias.** Encyclopedias, with short summaries of other literature, are good sources during the initial stages of review. Here is a partial list of available encyclopedias:
   - *Encyclopedia of Adult Development*
   - *Encyclopedia of African American Education*
   - *Encyclopedia of Early Childhood Education*
   - *Encyclopedia of Higher Education*
   - *Encyclopedia of Special Education*
   - *Encyclopedia of School Psychology*
3. **Reviews, Yearbooks, and Handbooks.** A number of sources include comprehensive, up-to-date reviews on specific topics. Many of the reviews are in books or monographs that are published annually (i.e., Review of Research in Education), although different subjects are reviewed each year. Handbooks are more comprehensive than other secondary sources and more scholarly as the target audience is other professionals and students. They can serve as a helpful resource for identifying research theories, authors' names, background material, and keyword search terms relevant to your research topic. Here are a few examples of handbooks:
   - *Handbook of Educational Psychology*
   - *Handbook of Reading Research*
   - *Handbook of Research on Curriculum*
   - *Handbook of Research on Educational Administration*

- *Handbook of Research on Mathematics Teaching and Learning*
- *Handbook of Research on the Teaching of English*
- *Handbook of Research in Science Education*
- *Handbook of Research on Teaching*
- *Handbook of Research on School Supervision*

When searching for reviews in journals you may come across what is called a *meta-analysis*, a review that quantitatively synthesizes previous studies. A **meta analysis** is a procedure that uses statistical methods to systematically combine the results of a number of studies of the same problem. The studies are identified and the results from all the studies are used to arrive at an overall conclusion. Most meta-analyses reported in reputable journals are characterized by a comprehensive search of the literature and sound statistical procedures. Because there are many different ways of identifying the studies that comprise a meta-analysis, as well as different approaches to statistically combine them, it is necessary to examine the methodology to ensure credibility. However, because this type of review has only recently been published, there are some questions about its credibility. For example, what sense would it make if all studies, whether poorly conducted or well conducted, are included in the synthesis? (See Example 3.4 and 3.5.)

Meta-analysis: A quantitative review of previous studies.

EXAMPLES 3.4–3.5 | Meta-Analysis

Articles for this meta-analysis were identified using two methods. First, a computer literature search of PsycINFO and ERIC databases was conducted from 1980 to 2003. The descriptors included WM matched with dyslexia/reading disability/learning disability/LD. . . . The initial search yielded 75 studies . . . only 31 articles met the criteria for inclusion. . . . In the present meta-analysis 28 articles compared WM [Working Memory] performance of RD [Reading Disability] with that of skilled readers. . . . The 28 studies produced 208 effect sizes, for an average of 7 comparisons per study. The overall mean effect size across all studies was –0.81 ($SD = 0.92$). Based on Cohen's criteria, that is a large effect size that indicated that the over all mean performance of the RD group was almost one standard deviation below that of the normally achieving group."

Source: Swanson, H. L. (2005). Memory and learning disabilities: Historical perspective, current status, and future trends. *Thalamus, 23*(2), 37–38.

Studies were located through computerized databases (e.g., PsycINFO, ERIC, Medline) using subject terms such as *grade retention, grade repetition, grade failure, nonpromotion, transition classroom, flunked*, and other synonyms. Reference sections of recent review articles also were reviewed to identify relevant articles. . . . Of 199 studies that were identified and carefully evaluated as described above, a total of 22 studies met study inclusionary criteria. . . . The search produced 22 studies and 207 individual achievement outcomes.

Source: Allen, C. S., Chen, Q., Willson, V. L., & Hughes, J. N. (2009). Quality of research design moderates effects of grade retention on achievement: A Meta-analytic, multilevel analysis. *Educational Evaluation and Policy Analysis, 31*(4), 484–485.

Best-evidence synthesis: A review of quantitative and qualitative studies selected according to specified criteria.

You may also come across an alternative to a meta-analysis that is called a **best-evidence synthesis.** In this type of review both qualitative and quantitative research can be included. Clear criteria are used by the researchers to determine which of the studies merit inclusion. A best-evidence synthesis is shown in Example 3.6. Note that the term *narrative* is used to distinguish it from a meta-analysis.

EXAMPLE 3.6 Best Evidence (Narrative) Synthesis Review of Literature

In this paper, the authors provide an overview of the research literature on resiliency in adolescents. We explore the history of resiliency as it relates to the health and well-being of adolescents, identify common themes, provide a description of resilient youth, and introduce the developmental assets framework. To provide counselors with an increased understanding of the concept of resiliency as well as to encourage the application of resiliency to practice, a visual model is provided from which counselors can organize "resiliency" as a construct. The role of parents, families, schools, communities, and non-family adults are discussed with regard to asset development. Lastly, we examine developmental assets in relation to counseling practice, including how counselors can effectively incorporate the concept of resiliency into their professional practice in working with adolescents.

Source: Short, J. L., & Russell-Mayhew, S. (2009). What counselors need to know about resiliency in adolescents. *International Journal for the Advancement of Counseling, 31*(4), 215.

Primary sources are reported in a wide variety of journals. In fact, there are hundreds of journals, which differ greatly in quality. To understand these differences, consider how articles get published. The most common procedure is for the author(s) to write a manuscript that will be submitted to a journal for publication. If the format and topic of the article are appropriate, the editor will usually send the manuscript to two or three reviewers and/or associate or assistant editors to be evaluated. The evaluation is structured so that the reviewers, who are experts on the topic investigated, comment on the significance of the problem, methodology, data analysis, contribution of the findings and conclusions, and other criteria. Usually, the reviewers are asked to recommend that the manuscript be published as submitted, revised and resubmitted, or rejected. Rarely do they recommend to publish as submitted. The journal is said to be **refereed** if this procedure is followed. A **nonrefereed** journal does not use external reviewers to evaluate manuscripts.

Refereed: Sent to reviewers for an evaluation.

Nonrefereed: Not reviewed by outside experts.

The strength of the refereed process is that helpful suggestions from reviewers improve the quality of the manuscript. Most journals use a blind review process to control for reviewer bias. A blind review is one in which the names of the authors of the manuscript are omitted. Clearly, a blind review process is desirable and is usually employed by journals that have a reputation for publishing high-quality articles. In the "publish or perish" culture of higher education, it is more prestigious to be published in higher-quality journals. As a result, many more manuscripts are submitted than are actually accepted. Indeed, the rejection rate is often used, and justifiably so, as a barometer of quality.

Step 5: Summarize and Analyze Primary Source Information

Once you locate your primary sources, you will need to read them and summarize the information they contain. It is useful to have a strategy for recording notes on the articles as you read them. An efficient approach is to record your notes electronically or on index cards because after you have reviewed all the articles, the records or cards can be easily organized in different ways. Begin by reading the abstract of the article, if there is one, and the purpose or research problem. Then read the results and decide if it is worthwhile to read the article more carefully and take notes on it. Do not be too discouraged if some of the articles you locate are not useful. Part of the process of reviewing literature is to locate and read many more articles than you will eventually use.

After you decide to use the article, begin taking notes by writing or typing complete bibliographic information, preferably in the style you will use in writing; summarize the research problem as briefly as possible. Next, indicate in outline form the participants, instruments, and procedures used and then summarize the results and conclusions. Record interesting or insightful quotations; indicate any weaknesses or limitations in the methodology, analysis of the data, or conclusions; and indicate how the study may be related to your problem. You will find it useful to develop a code for indicating your overall judgment of the article. If you find it closely related to your problem and highly credible, you might give the article an A; if somewhat related and credible, a B; and so on. It will also help to develop a code that indicates the major focus of the study by topic or descriptor. For example, in reviewing studies on teacher awareness, you may find that some studies examine the effect of awareness on student achievement, some focus on strategies to improve awareness, and others emphasize different approaches to awareness depending on the type of students in the classroom. Each of these could have a code or notation on the card, such as "effect on ach.," "improv. awareness," and "approaches" to denote how they are different.

Author Reflection *One of the best sources for new articles can be found in the reference section of a primary source that is closely related to your study. Read the titles of the articles and other documents that the author(s) used. Though these will obviously be older, they are likely to very helpful. Finding other studies as much like yours as possible is more important than obtaining more recent sources that are less like yours.*

INTERNET SEARCHES

Strengths and Weaknesses of Using the Internet

The amount of information that is readily and quickly available on the Internet is unprecedented. Your challenge is to sift through hundreds, even thousands, of Web sources to find credible, helpful information. A careful consideration of the Internet's strengths and weaknesses will help you determine when and how to search the Internet for a specific topic. On the positive side, the Internet is particularly good at quickly delivering current and niche information, and it is

TABLE 3.1 Comparison of ERIC Database and Internet Sources

Source	Strengths	Weaknesses
ERIC	Controlled vocabulary 30+ year archive Reviewed for quality	Limited international coverage Abstracts instead of full-text articles At least 6 months behind current articles
Internet	Current information Full-text articles International coverage	No significant archive No search standards No quality control

conveniently accessed from almost anywhere. However, the Internet does not serve as an exhaustive source for searching educational literature. In addition, the Internet is not designed and organized for the educational researcher, nor are there uniform standards for accuracy and quality of the information.

One of the most difficult aspects of using the Internet for educational research is that, unlike databases such as ERIC, there is no standard controlled vocabulary that facilitates a search. In ERIC you can depend on the subject headings, descriptors, and keywords to target needed information. There is no comparable system in place for the Internet, and there is no universal thesaurus to consult to determine the best search terms. See Table 3.1 for a comparison of strengths and weaknesses of the Internet with ERIC.

Everything that you find in ERIC has been through some type of review process. Many journals in ERIC have an editorial staff of experts who judge the quality of the submissions. This does not mean that everything in ERIC is of high quality, but overall quality will be better than what is available from the Internet. Anyone (from a teenager to a respected scholar) can "publish" on the Internet. While there is an appealing democratic beauty to the Internet, it is crucial to evaluate the quality of Internet sources.

Even though ERIC offers a more comprehensive, better organized, and peer reviewed set of information about educational research, the Internet does have advantages. If a journal has an online version, you will be able to browse the most recent issues, issues that might take many months to appear in ERIC. Also, on-line journals will often contain the full text of each article, while some ERIC articles and documents are limited to abstracts. ERIC covers educational research and issues in the United States very well; the Internet offers a wider access to educational research from other countries. You will also find useful information on the Internet beyond journal articles and research reports, such as statistics, e-mail links to experts, governmental information, datasets, and discussion forums.

Fortunately, you are not limited in your research to either the Internet or journal databases like ERIC. In framing your research question, think about the type of information that each might offer. In turn, this will help with your searches in each source. For example, you would certainly want to know what the research on your topic has been for the past 10 years as well as in the past months. By combining the Internet with the research tools that were presented in earlier, you can capture a well-rounded and diverse portrait for your topic.

Internet Search Strategies

Before you start typing words into the first search engine that comes along, it is important to have a focused search strategy with a number of key terms and subject headings. Based on that search strategy, choose from an assortment of secondary finding tools, including subject directories and search engines. Once you have identified appropriate Internet search tools, pay attention to the various search options that each one offers, and construct your computer search accordingly. Finally, evaluate the sources that you find for their quality and relevance to your research question.

Each Internet search company (like Yahoo! or Google) compiles its own database of Internet sites. When you "search the Internet," you are really searching these databases. That is, your search does not go out onto the Web and look at every page in existence. In choosing an Internet search tool, you want to peer beyond the search screen and get some idea of the quality, content, organization, and scope of the data behind the scenes. The three primary types of Internet search utilities are *subject directories*, *search engines*, and *metasearch engines*. Understanding the differences between these will improve your Internet searching considerably.

Subject directory: Service that reviews and categorizes information.

Subject Directories. Internet **subject directories** are the "yellow pages" of the Internet in which you are able to browse through lists of Internet resources by topic. Typically, each topic is located within a hierarchy of subjects. For example, in a subject directory there may be a choice for "Education," then numerous choices under that subject, such as "Universities, K–12, Government, History," and so on. The advantage of subject directories is that the content has been reviewed and organized by a human! Subject directories rely on teams of editors who have knowledge of specific disciplines. Thus, under each category you will find a high degree of relevance and quality. Subject directories are often the quickest way to assemble a manageable list of Internet resources for a topic. Here are some research questions that would be especially good for a subject directory:

Where can I find a list of educational associations?
Where can I find the department of education from each state?
Where can I find a listing of online education journals?

Two of the largest subject directories, Yahoo! and Google, index more than 20 billion webpages. Some subject directories have partnered with search engines in order to increase their coverage. For example, if you use the search box in Yahoo!, there will be options to run the same search in any number of search engines. By clicking over to a search engine from Yahoo!, you will search a bigger set of data but will not have the advantage of Yahoo!'s organization. Often the best search strategy in a subject directory is to steer clear of the search box and use the categories. The search function of a subject directory is most useful when you are not sure what category to choose for a particular subject. For example, in Yahoo! it is somewhat difficult to find Montessori education, especially if you choose the education category "K–12." If you search Yahoo! for "Montessori education," you will find that it is listed in the education category of "Theory and Methods."

Search Engines

Search engine: Service that categorizes by automated indexing of key terms.

Search engines are large searchable databases of webpages. Whereas subject directories are assembled and organized by human editors, search engines are compiled in an automated fashion. Each search engine uses a "spider" or "robot" that trolls through the Web from hyperlink to hyperlink, capturing information from each page that it visits. Therefore, the content of each search engine is dependent on the characteristics of its spider:

- How many pages has it visited?
- How often does it visit each page?
- When it visits, how much of the webpage does it record?

This means that it is wise to try several search engines.

Since search engines index billions of webpages they offer a quick way to search for specific words that may appear in webpages. Here are some research questions that would be especially appropriate for a search engine:

Are there any webpages that cover standardized testing in the state of California?

Are there any webpages that deal with John Dewey's *Democracy in Education*?

Search Language. There is no standard search language that is consistent across all search engines. Some search engines understand logical connectors like "and," whereas others insist that you use a "+" before each word if you wish to limit your results to combined terms. Despite the lack of standards, there are several features that are common to most search engines. For example, even though some engines use "and" while others look for "+," the feature of combining more than one idea into a single search is available across all search engines. One of the best places to find out about each engine's search language is its online help page. It is advisable, even for seasoned Internet searchers, to periodically revisit the help pages of their favorite search engine. Google's searching tips are available at http://www.googleguide.com/. This site offers many tips to search more effectively and a guide that can be printed out from a pdf file (www.googleguide.com/print_gg.html). There is also a "cheat sheet," www.googleguide.com/cheatsheet.html, that offers examples for quick searches.

Special Search Features. Search engines continue to make advancements in the area of special search features. You will find these on the "advanced search" option within most search engines. Special search features help you construct very complex searches through the use of selecting various options from a menu. Special search features include the ability to limit your search by language, date, location, and media (such as audio or images).

From the search page in Yahoo!, select More and then Advanced Search. In Google, choose Google Advanced Search or Google Scholar by selecting More on the search page. Google also offers Google Alerts by selecting Even More under the More tab, a feature providing you with e-mail notifications of new search results related to your topic.

Relevancy. In addition to search options, it is helpful to be familiar with the retrieval algorithms of various search engines. **Retrieval algorithms** determine both how many pages each search retrieves as well as how the results of each search are ordered. The search algorithm is a mathematical formula that determines how many times and where your search terms appear in each document. For example, if you were searching for "cooperative learning," the webpages that appear at the top of your search results should be the most relevant. Perhaps these pages had both words as part of their title, whereas the webpages that appear at the very end of your search results might simply have the word "cooperative" somewhere in their text. If your results start to look less and less relevant, don't keep looking through the same list. Move on to a new search or a new search engine.

Retrieval algorithms: Number and order of documents.

Metasearch Engines

A **metasearch engine** submits your search to multiple search engines at the same time. Examples of metasearch engines include Dogpile, Clusty, and Metacrawler. Metasearch engines can be especially useful since studies have shown that each search engine includes pages that others do not. On the other hand, no single metasearch engine includes all of the major search engines. Also, you cannot take advantage of the specific search language or features that are native to each search engine. For this reason, it is best to use search engines for your complex Internet searching, and rely on metasearch engines for searches that are very simple, having only one or two words. With metasearch engines it is especially important to pay attention to relevancy, as you have less control over how each search engine interprets your metasearch query. Examples of good questions for a metasearch engine are:

Metasearch engine: Searches many engines at once.

Are there any sources that mention elementary school portfolio assessment?

Are there any sources that mention Jonathan Kozol?

Blurring the Line Between Search Engine and Search Directory

The line between search engine and search directory is often difficult to discern. Advanced search technology that makes it easier to find the information you need can mask the type of tool that you are using. In search engines, there will often be an associated directory listing. For example, when you use Google, your search will also be matched against the Open Directory project for categories that may be relevant to your search. Likewise in Yahoo!, if there are no matches in that directory, your search will get expanded to a subset of Google's database. Although these types of partnerships can improve searching, they can change from day to day. Many of the search engines and subject directories are, in the final analysis, businesses that are trying to be commercially successful.

Table 3.2 lists several subject directories and search engines that you will find useful in using the Internet to find educational research and other information on contemporary educational issues.

TABLE 3.2 Types and Examples of Internet Search Tools

Subject Directories	Web Address
The Internet Public Library	www.ipl.org
WWW Virtual Library	http://vlib.org
Yahoo!	www.yahoo.com
Education Subject Directories	
Education Index	www.educationindex.com
GEM: Gateway to Education Materials	http://thegateway.org
KidsClick	www.kidsclick.org
Educator's Reference Desk	www.eduref.org
Search Engines	
AllTheWeb	www.alltheweb.com
AltaVista	www.altavista.com
Google	www.google.com
Wisenut	www.wisenut.com
Ask	www.ask.com
Metasearch Engines	
Dogpile	www.dogpile.com
Fazzle	www.fazzle.com
Metacrawler	www.metacrawler.com

Beyond Web Pages: Scholarly Communication Strategies

Perhaps the most revolutionary aspect of the Internet is its ability to connect people with shared interests. This is especially powerful in highly technical and specific areas of study where geographical boundaries might otherwise hinder communication between a limited number of experts. For example, it might be hard to find a group of scholars in any one location who were all interested in the sociology of education. Through the Internet, however, scholars as well as practitioners are able to form groups and discuss various issues specific to their field of study. Through the use of e-mail, mailing lists, newsgroups, blogging, social networking, and conferencing, educational researchers have ready access to their peers and do not need to be isolated by location.

E-Mail and Social Networking. E-mail can be an especially valuable tool in conducting research. The speed and ease of e-mail communication allow you to find resources and "talk" to experts. Through e-mail it is possible to easily contact researchers, librarians, or institutions to get guidance on a specific research question. E-mail is also an excellent way to collaborate with colleagues on works in progress by sharing ideas, drafts, and files. You can locate experts on your topic by using Ask an Expert (www.askexpert.com) or the Directory of Educational Researchers and by searching university departments and schools of education that list faculty members and their research interests. Simply type in the name of the college or university in a search engine, go to the webpage of the appropriate school or department, and peruse the list of faculty, which usually includes e-mail addresses, or use the search feature on the university website.

One of the fastest-growing avenues for communication via the Internet is through social networking sites, such as Facebook. Social networking allows individuals to communicate individually and through participation in shared interest groups.

Newsgroups, E-Mail Discussion Groups, Blogs, and Listservs. On the Internet there are literally thousands of newsgroups, mailing lists, and listservs that cover every conceivable area of interest. Most Internet browsers, such as Netscape and Microsoft Internet Explorer, include a *news reader*, which allows you to read and post messages about various subjects to a newsgroup. A discussion group is similar to a newsgroup, except that the messages are transmitted as e-mail and are therefore available only to individuals who have subscribed to the mailing list. Blogs are a type of website most often administered by an individual providing commentary on a subject or issue. A listserv (registered trademark of www.Lsoft.com) is a specific type of software for managing e-mail lists.

There are many newsgroups and discussion groups that are very active in scholarly content and commentary. Through them, researchers can identify new viewpoints and new strategies for research as identified by others with similar interests. They are an excellent way to stay current in your area of interest.

Using Known Locations. The third method for doing effective literature reviews on the Internet is to access known sources, authorities, and experts. A good starting point for online research is a library website. Virtually all libraries have begun developing resource guides or directories of websites classified by subject in order to make the Internet more accessible and better arranged for their users. Many universities have resource guides for most academic subjects, that will be including one specific to education.

Researchers might investigate university and research center libraries that are known to be strong in the particular subject. Often the websites for these organizations include unique information and resources. For example, the University of Illinois has a strong collection of children's literature, so if you were interested in that area, it would make sense to contact the University of Illinois library to see what has been done there to organize the topic.

In addition to libraries, federal and state government websites are excellent sources. A good starting place is the U.S. Department of Education's website (discussed below). The department's page not only includes a great variety of primary data, but also hyperlinks to other government sites and related websites. Other known sources of information include websites for national associations and organizations, companies focusing on educational products, nonprofit organizations, newspapers, and online journals.

Federal Government. A good place for education professionals to begin their Internet research is at the U.S. Department of Education's website, www.ed.gov. This site contains current news and headlines, announcements about new projects, initiatives, related websites, and listings of the department's educational priorities and national objectives. It also includes budget information, policy issues, databases, funding opportunities, information on legislation that affects education, and websites for other departmental offices and contacts.

The Institute of Education Sciences (IES) is a particularly noteworthy part of the U.S. DOE. The IES maintains a prominent role in educational research by conducting, collecting, and distributing research studies and statistics. The IES website homepage includes links to current educational research news, grant opportunities, statistics, publications, and other federally supported centers. It publishes Education Research Notes, an electronic newsletter that summarizes ongoing IES programs.

The WWC reports on conclusions that can be drawn from rigorous experiments, and includes reasons why specific studies are not credible. A guided tour of the website is offered to help you search for reports, reviews, and practice guides.

Associations, Organizations, and University Websites. All larger professional associations and universities have a substantial Web presence. At each of these sites you can find useful information, such as lists of faculty, publications, resolutions, and links to other websites. By visiting these pages, you cannot only gain knowledge of educational research, but can also get a feel for the culture and activity of each organization.

The American Educational Research Association (AERA) is particularly relevant. AERA (www.aera.net) is comprised of divisions and special interest groups of all education areas (e.g., classroom assessment, teacher education, special education, mixed-method research). Researchers in these fields present their findings at a large conference each year, and there is electronic access to most of the papers that are presented. A particularly notable feature about AERA is that it is very inexpensive for graduate students who are not employed full time.

Author Reflection *Searching the Internet for educational research is now to the point where it actually makes sense to simply go online and try some things. There is so much out there that in all probability you will find something of value. It is especially helpful when searching for information on current issues and problems, even if much of what you find on these areas will be opinions, points of view, editorials, and positions, and not empirical studies. But to learn about contemporary topics quickly, the Internet is a great resource.*

CONSUMER TIPS: *How to Cite Internet Resources in Your References*

As with any research, it is important to document your sources so that other researchers can visit the same sites you have found. In addition to the author, title, publication date, and address, most citation formats encourage you to list the date that you accessed the site. Most educational research is documented in either *Chicago Manual of Style*/Turabian style or APA format. You can find the APA's official guideline for citing electronic sources in the *APA Style Manual* and on the APA webpage. Some examples of APA format follow:

EXAMPLES 3.7–3.11 | **APA Citations of Online Articles and Documents**

Journal Article

VandenBos, G., Knapp, S., & Doe, J. (2001). Role of reference elements in the selection of resources by psychology undergraduates. *Journal of Bibliographic Research,* 117–123. Retrieved October 13, 2001, from http://jbr.org/articles.html.

Multipage Document Created by Private Organization, No Date

Greater New Milford (Ct) Area Healthy Community 2000, Task Force on Teen and Adolescent Issues (n.d.). *Who has time for a family meal? You do!* Retrieved October 5, 2000, from http://www.familymealtime.org.

Chapter or Section in an Internet Document

Benton Foundation. (1998, July 7). Barriers to closing the gap. In *Losing ground bit by bit: Low-income communities in the information age* (chap. 2). Retrieved from http://www.benton.org/Library/Low-Income/two.html.

Electronic Copy of an Abstract Obtained from a Secondary Database

Fournier, M., de Ridder, D., & Bensing, J. (1999). Optimism and adaptation to multiple sclerosis: What does optimism mean? *Journal of Behavioral Medicine, 22,* 303–326. Abstract retrieved October 23, 2000, from PsycINFO database.

Electronic Version of U.S. Government Report Available by Search from GPO Access Database (on the Web)

U.S. General Accounting Office. (1997, February). Telemedicine: *Federal strategy is needed to guide investments* (Publication No. GAO/NSAID/HEHS-97-67). Retrieved September 15, 2000, from General Accounting Office Reports Online via GPO Access: http://www.access.gpo.gov/su_docs/aces/aces160.shtml?/gao/index.html.

CONSUMER TIPS: *Evaluating Information From the Internet*

Information obtained from the Internet can be an excellent complement to print research, but it can also be low quality, even deceptive and misleading. Researchers using the Internet need to critically evaluate resources found online just as they would evaluate information found in a library, government office, center report, or journal. Remember that in most cases there is no peer review of information. As a result, the quality of the information varies considerably. Some of what you find may be of high quality and credible, while other information may be biased to present a particular point of view or simply be of low quality. Your evaluation of Internet material will be strengthened by asking the following questions:

- Who is the author or publisher of the information?
- What is the author's reputation and what are the author's qualifications in the subject covered?
- Is the information objective or is there a noticeable bias?
- Are the facts or statistics verifiable?
- Is there a bibliography?
- Is the information current?

It is common when searching for contemporary topics to find center and nonprofit organization websites. Many of these organizations have a clear agenda that is promoted, so it is advisable to understand these points of view to detect bias and opinion rather than a more balanced, scholarly perspective. The key to evaluating any type of research is to carefully read and analyze the content. It is also helpful to find a variety of sources so that you can compare and contrast them in order to get a fully informed view of any subject.

WRITING *a* REVIEW *of* LITERATURE

The nature of the written review of literature will depend on whether the study is quantitative or qualitative. Quantitative reviews are often very detailed and found in the beginning sections of an article. Qualitative reviews, in contrast, tend to be brief in the beginning but more integrated throughout the whole of the article. Most literature reviews, particularly those found in quantitative research, approach the review by summarizing and analyzing individual studies. Some reviews are *thematic*, in which a topic is identified and discussed, without a detailed analysis of individual studies. Most qualitative reviews are thematic. Mixed-method studies reviews of literature tend to be consistent with the dominant approach (quantitative or qualitative). We will first examine the quantitative review.

Quantitative Reviews of Literature

Although reviews of literature can be organized in different ways, the most common approach is to group together studies that investigate similar topics or subtopics. This process is initiated by coding the studies as they are read; then the articles with the same code are put in one pile, those of another code in a second pile, and so forth. The different topics are then put in order, usually from articles related to the problem in a more general way first to articles specifically related to the problem. Within each topic it may be possible to organize the studies by date, with the most recent studies last. This arrangement gives you a sense of the development of the research over time. You should not organize your review by study or article, with each paragraph in the review dealing with a different study. Studies that are only generally related should be summarized briefly. If several of these studies have similar results, they should be grouped together; for example, "Several studies have found that teacher expectations are related to student achievement (Smith, 1978; Tyler, 1985; Wylie, 1983)." Most reviews select representative general studies; there is no attempt to do an exhaustive review of all studies. However, exhaustive reviews may be necessary for theses, dissertations, and other major projects.

The following steps will be useful for studies that are closely related to the problem:

Step 1 Provide a brief summary of the articles.

Step 2 Analyze the studies. The analysis is important because it suggests that you are not simply accepting the studies as credible; you are examining the methodology of the studies critically to make better judgments about the contribution of the results.

Step 3 State explicitly how the reviewed studies are related to the present research. A critical examination enables you to show the relationship of the proposed or current study to previous literature. This step is essential for the results to contribute to our knowledge. It also generates many good ideas that will improve subsequent research.

For a few studies, then, those that are closely related to the problem, the review should include three elements: a *summary* of the study reviewed, an *analysis* of the study, and a summary of how the study *relates* to the research problem. Example 3.12 is an example from a literature review that shows how the current study differs from previous studies.

EXAMPLE 3.12 | Showing How Current Study Differs From Previous Research

Although there are studies examining teacher efficacy after methods courses (Huinker & Madison, 1997) and after student teaching (Vinson, 1995), there is little research tracking the subject-matter-specific teacher efficacy of elementary preservice teachers throughout their preservice education (Tschannen-Moran et al., 1998).

Source: Utley, J., Bryant, R., & Moseley, C. (2005). Relationship between science and mathematics teaching efficacy of preservice elementary teachers. *School Science and Mathematics, 105*(2), 84.

This part of the review should not contain long quotations or use the same wording in discussing each study, for example, "A study by Brown (1987) indicated that . . ."; "A study by Smith (2000) indicated that . . ."; "A study by Jones (2001) showed that. . . ." Quotations in general should be used sparingly and only when a special or critical meaning could not be indicated by your own words. The researcher should use short sentences as well as transition sentences so there is a logical progression of ideas and sections. Many of these parameters are illustrated in Figure 3.8, which is an excerpt of a review of literature from a quantitative article (McMillan, 2001, p. 22).

The length of the review depends on the type of study, whether or not it is published, and the topic that is researched. The review of literature for an exploratory study may not be very long, whereas an exhaustive review in a thesis or dissertation can be as long as 30 or 40 typed pages. A lengthy review requires structuring with major and minor headings and periodic summaries.

Qualitative Reviews of Literature

Foreshadowed problems: Initial, general purpose of the study.

Rather than provide a detailed analysis of the literature prior to the methods section, the purpose of most qualitative reviews is to introduce the purpose and general or broad research questions. These questions provide a direction, but one that is purposefully general so that previous work does not limit, constrain, or predict what will be found. In this way, the review of literature is consistent with the discovery orientation and inductive approach of qualitative research. The statements or questions are often called **foreshadowed problems** or questions. The approach is to state a general purpose or question so that views of the participants will emerge. Thus, the initial review of literature in a qualitative study is often *preliminary* rather than complete. It provides conceptual frameworks by citing appropriate areas of scholarship and thinking from different perspectives, such as psychological or sociological. Together, the foreshadowed problems and conceptual frameworks are used to justify the need for a qualitative approach. Some qualitative researchers will not conduct an extensive review of the literature because they don't want what others have said about something to influence the openness that is needed or their own perspectives.

Once the qualitative study is under way and data are being collected, the researcher continues to read broadly in the literature. The additional literature reviewed enables the researcher to better understand what has been observed. The literature may provide meaningful analogies, a scholarly language to synthesize descriptions, or additional conceptual or theoretical frameworks to better understand and organize the findings. It helps the researcher to understand the complexities of what is observed and to illuminate subtle meanings and interpretations. Like good quantitative studies, the literature is integrated with the discussion and conclusion section of the article or report. At this point, additional new literature may be introduced to better explain and interpret the findings.

In qualitative studies there may or may not be a separate "literature review" section. Because of the format required by some journals, there may be a literature review header, but for a qualitative study the actual review will probably be different from what is provided for a quantitative study.

FIGURE 3.8 **Example of a review of literature for quantitative research.**

Summary of previous research

Cross and Frary (1996) and Cizek, Fitzgerald, Shawn, and Rachor (1996) report similar findings concerning the hodgepodge nature of assigning grades. Cizek et al. (1996) found that although almost all teachers used formal achievement measures in grading, other "achievement-related" factors such as attendance, ability, participation, demonstration of effort, and conduct were used by at least half of the teachers. Cross and Frary surveyed 310 middle and high school teachers of academic subjects in a single school district. A written survey was used to obtain descriptions of grading practices and opinions regarding assessment and grading. Consistent with Brookhart (1993), it was reported that 72% of the teachers raised the grades of low-ability students if they had demonstrated effort. One-fourth of the teachers indicated that they raised grades for high effort "fairly often." Almost 40% of the teachers indicated that student conduct and attitude were taken into consideration when assigning grades. Note that a very high percentage of teachers agreed that effort and conduct should be reported separately from achievement. More than half of the teachers reported that class participation was rated as having a moderate or strong influence on grades. In an earlier statewide study, Frary et al. (1993) used the same teacher survey that was used by Cross and Frary (1996), and obtained similar results. More than two-thirds of the teachers agreed or tended to agree that ability, effort, and improvement should be included in determining grades.

Another recent study, by Truog and Friedman (1996), further confirms the notion of the hodgepodge nature of grading. In their study, the written grading policies of 53 high school teachers were analyzed in relation to grading practices recommended by measurement specialists. In addition, a focus group was conducted with eight teachers to find out more about their reasoning behind their grading practices. They found that the written policies were consistent with the findings from earlier studies of teacher beliefs and practices. Nine percent of the teachers included ability as a factor in determining grades, 17% included attitude, 9% included effort, 43% included attendance, and 32% included student behavior.

Analysis of previous research

One of the limitations of current research on the grading practices of secondary teachers is that the studies do not differentiate grading practices by ability level of the classes. This may be important in examining such factors as effort and improvement, and may reveal patterns that exacerbate existing achievement differences among students with varying ability levels. For example, Alarso and Pigge (1993) reported that teachers believe essays provide better evidence of higher cognitive learning, and that students study harder for them. If it is demonstrated that higher-ability classes, such as honors and advanced placement classes, use more essays than basic classes, this may result in greater emphasis on thinking skills with higher-ability classes, while in lower-ability classes there would be more emphasis on rote memorization. Also, as with the research on assessment practices, most studies (e.g., Brookhart, 1991; Frary et al., 1993; Truog & Friedman, 1996) measure teacher beliefs, rather than actual practices or a reporting of what was actually used in a specific class.

Another limitation in the designs employed is that each of the factors used to assign grades has been considered separately. When put in the context of teaching, as pointed out by Stiggins, Frisbie, and Griswold (1989), it is more realistic to consider the joint effect of several factors. Only one study, Frary et al. (1993), reported an analysis of how factors were grouped into meaningful components for secondary teachers. In their study, teacher opinions about the desirability of different grading and assessment practices were examined together using a Likert scale. Their findings focused on teacher attitudes toward the desirability of certain practices, but did not investigate whether there were underlying dimensions associated with actual grading and assessment practices of teachers.

Relates previous research to current study

The present study used a large sample of secondary school teachers (grades 6–12) to describe assessment and grading practices in a way that addresses limitations cited from the previous research. The critical role of effort and other nonachievement factors in grading was examined, as was the way these different factors cluster together in describing teachers' practices. The study was designed to document differences in actual assessment and grading practices conducted for a specific class taught by each teacher across a range of classes representing different student ability levels. Four specific research questions were addressed:

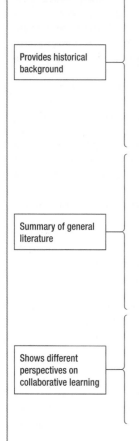

FIGURE 3.9 **Example of a review of literature for a qualitative study.**

Provides historical background

Research into children's behavior in groups and their productivity was pioneered at the University of Iowa's Child Welfare Research Station toward the end of the 1930s. Working under the direction of Kurt Lewin, an acclaimed experimental psychologist, graduate students Ronald Lippitt and Ralph White undertook a series of experiments in 1938 to investigate how children worked together in groups (Marrow, 1965). Participants chosen for the studies were 20 children who met after school to make papier maché masks and to engage in other play activities. The children were divided into three groups, two of which were directed by an adult; each child was rotated through each of the three groups. The results of the experiments proved remarkable. Researchers found that children in an autocratically led group seemed discontented, often aggressive, and lacking in initiative. Youngsters in groups without a leader experienced similar problems: members appeared frustrated, and much of the work remained unfinished. In marked contrast, children in groups organized with a democratic leader—someone who allowed the group to set its own agendas and priorities—appeared far more productive, socially satisfied, and demonstrated greater originality and independence in the work they completed.

Summary of general literature

Although the Iowa studies excited the educational community, the advent of World War II—and its aftermath—greatly interrupted research into how children behaved and learned in groups. Scholarly attention did not again turn toward efforts to understand children's behavior and learning in groups until the 1970s (Slavin, 1991). Since that time, researchers have come to agree that cooperative and collaborative learning are valuable components of classroom learning (Blumenfeld, Marx, Soloway, & Krajcik, 1996; Gamson, 1994; Kohn, 1991; Webb, Troper, & Fall, 1995), and children are often instructed to "work together" at school (Gamson, 1994; Patrick, 1994; Wood & Jones, 1994). Slavin (1991, p. 71) stated that cooperative learning has been promoted as a solution to "an astonishing array of educational problems" and has been endorsed as a learning strategy by numerous researchers (Burron, James, & Ambrosio, 1993; Wood & Jones, 1994) who have investigated its effects on student achievement (Slavin), as well as on the contexts and ways in which children work together in classrooms (Keedy & Drmacich, 1994).

Shows different perspectives on collaborative learning

Definitions for cooperative and collaborative learning, however, are contrary for different researchers and theorists. Vygotsky (1978), for example, viewed collaborative learning as part of a process leading to the social construction of knowledge. Other scholars (Kohn, 1992; Sapon-Shevin & Schniedewand, 1992) considered cooperative learning to be a form of critical pedagogy that moves classrooms and societies closer toward the ideal of social justice. Caplow and Kardash (1995) characterized collaborative learning as a process in which "knowledge is not transferred from expert to learner, but created and located in the learning environment" (p. 209). Others such as Burron, James, and Ambrosio (1993) and Ossont (1993) envisioned cooperative learning as a strategy to help students improve intellectual and social skills.

Figure 3.9 shows an example of the preliminary review of literature in a qualitative study.

Mixed-Method Reviews of Literature

In mixed-method studies the review of literature is usually presented in one section rather than having a separate review for the quantitative and qualitative sections. Though general reviews of literature in mixed-method studies typically are detailed and thorough, the review reflects the quantitative or qualitative emphasis of the study. With an exploratory study the review tends to be like those found in qualitative research, while explanatory research uses a review like those in a quantitative study. Because mixed-method studies are much less standardized than either quantitative or qualitative research, the literature review section is also less standardized. This means that with these types of studies you will likely encounter quite different approaches to the review.

CONSUMER TIPS: *Criteria for Evaluating the Review of Literature*

You should consider several criteria when reading and evaluating the review of literature section of research studies or reports. First, identify which part of the article is the review of literature. Sometimes the review has a separate heading, but often it does not. Be sure to differentiate between an introduction, which provides a general overview or background, and the review, which should hone in on empirical studies that are clearly related to the research problem. Once identified, scan the review to get an idea of the general structure and organization. When reading, highlight dates of references, places where findings from other studies are summarized, and analyses of the studies. In the margins of a copy of the article, you may find it helpful to write notes such as "sum" for summary and "an" for analysis, or even "+" to indicate places in the review that correspond to the criteria that follow. Finally, determine how well the review corresponds to these criteria. This can be recorded so that when you review the overall credibility of the researcher and the study, the quality of the review can be a part of this summary judgment.

1. The review of literature should adequately cover previous research on the topic. In reading research in an area with which you are familiar, you will be able to judge the scope of the review. Were important studies ignored? Does the number of studies in the review reflect research activity in that area? Often you will realize that there is far more research in an area than the review indicates. Do the authors of the article cite mainly their own research? Although it is sometimes quite appropriate for authors to use their own work as a major part of the review, it may also indicate investigator bias. If the authors limit their review to their own studies and do not include other related research, the credibility of the study could justifiably be questioned. Overall, then, you will typically have some sense of whether the review is sufficiently comprehensive. Based on length, a one- or two-paragraph review on a much studied topic for a quantitative study is probably too brief, while reviews that cover several journal pages are probably more than adequate.

2. The review of literature should cite actual findings from other studies. It is important for the review to be based on the empirical results of previous research, not on others' opinions about previous research or on the conclusions of previous research. To illustrate this point, consider the following example, 3.13, which is a review of literature citing results:

EXAMPLE 3.13 | Summarizing Results from Previous Studies

The lack of evidence concerning the effectiveness of state early education programs has been at issue as well. A meta-evaluation of state prekindergarten programs highlighted substantial issues in research designs, measures, and analytical methods of the evaluations conducted prior to the review, and the lack of evidence about the implementations and outcomes of the state programs (Gilliam & Zigler, 2001). However, the body of research has grown since this meta-evaluation, and the research shows that state prekindergarten programs can produce positive effects on short-term measures (Gormley & Gayer, 2005; Gromley, Gayer, Phillips, & Dawson, 2005; Henry et al., 2003) and are associated with higher levels of achievement in later years (Grissmer, Flanagan, Kawata, & Williamson, 2000).

Source: Henry, G. T., Gordon, C. S., & Rickman, D. K. (2006). Early education policy alternatives: Comparing quality and outcomes of head start and state prekindergarten. *Educational Evaluation and Policy Analysis, 28*(1), 78.

Notice how the next example (Example 3.14) focuses on conclusions:

EXAMPLE 3.14 | Summarizing Conclusions from Previous Studies

The effects of parents' and students' expectations for educational attainment are important in science achievement expectations (Miller & Brown, 1992). Student expectations affect student involvement in classroom learning or the effort that students apply to studying and, thus, ultimately affect achievement (Pintrich & Schrauben, 1992). The effect of track and curriculum on achievement is well documented (Oakes, 1985).

Source: Brookhart, S. M. (1998). Determinants of student effort on schoolwork and school-based achievement. *Journal of Educational Research, 91*(2), 203.

3. The review of literature should be up-to-date. The studies reviewed should include the most recent research on the topic. This does not mean that older studies are not relevant. Sometimes the best and most relevant research was conducted decades ago. You also need to consider that it may take a year or more to publish a study after it has been accepted for publication. But if you read a study published in 1999 and most of the citations are from work in the 1980s, the review is probably out of date. A quick glance at the references at the end of the study will provide you with a good idea of how contemporary the review is.

4. The review of literature should analyze as well as summarize previous studies. As noted, a good review interprets the quality of previous research. This analysis may be a critique of methodology or inappropriate generalizations, an indication of limitations of the study (e.g., to certain populations, instruments, or procedures), or a discussion of conflicting results. See how this is illustrated in Examples 3.15 and 3.16.

EXAMPLES 3.15–3.16 | Analysis of Previous Research

The research studies reviewed previously support the theoretical argument that combining reading and science is beneficial, suggesting that if students are provided time to read science texts and taught how to use reading strategies, they not only become more proficient readers, but also learn science content more effectively. . . . There are several limitations to these studies, however. First, with the exception of Gaskins et al. (1994), the studies all took place in the elementary setting. We have relatively little information about ways to infuse reading into secondary science and the impact of such systematic infusion on student learning. Second, these studies involve integrating science into the reading class, where the architect of classroom instruction is the reading teacher, who typically has specialized training in reading and provides instruction to the same group of students for almost the entire school day. This is different from integrating reading into the science class, where the architect of classroom instruction is the science teacher, who typically has little formal training in teaching reading and provides only one period of instruction to the same group of students in a school day. . . . Thus, it is important to know the extent to which reading can be infused into the middle grades and if such integration produces outcomes comparable to the studies conducted in the elementary school. We addressed this need by examining the effectiveness of an integrated reading—science middle school curriculum that featured the infusion of quality science trade books and explicit reading strategy instruction.

Source: Fang, Z., & Wei, Y. (2010). Improving middle school students' science literacy through reading infusion. *Journal of Educational Research, 103,* 264–265.

In addition to these cases, there is a rich research literature on the effect of ability grouping on racial segregation within schools (e.g., Darling-Hammond, 1985; Larkins & Oldham, 1976; Lucas & Berends, 2002; Meier, Stewart, & England, 1989; Mickelson, 2001; Oakes, 1985; 1990; Oakes & Guiton, 1995). While this literature has been extremely useful in highlighting the costs of ability grouping at the secondary level, it has not focused on measuring trends and patterns in within-school segregation as such. Rather, much of the work focuses specifically on the disproportionate placement of black students in low track classes within small samples of high schools. There are some important exceptions. For example, Mickelson (2001) documents racial segregation in all Charlotte, North Carolina, high schools by counting the number of "racially isolated classrooms," defined as classrooms where the percentage black (or white) deviates by a nontrivial amount from the percentage at the school level. However, this article does not compare the overall racial contact within Charlotte schools to that occurring across schools and does not explore trends over time or variation across grades in within-school segregation.

Source: (Conger, D. (2005). Within-school segregation in an urban school district. *Educational Evaluation and Policy Analysis, 27*(3), 226.

5. The review of literature should be organized logically by topic, not by author. A review that devotes one paragraph to each study usually fails to integrate and synthesize previous research. A well-done review is organized by topic. Typically, several studies may be mentioned together in the same paragraph, or may be cited together. For example, rather than using a separate paragraph to summarize and analyze each study, a good review might be something like the following shown in Example 3.17.

EXAMPLE 3.17 | Literature Review Organized by Topic

Decades of research have established that there are numerous types of parenting practices associated with positive school-related academic and social competencies. These practices include the following: (a) parental participation in school-related activities, such as monitoring homework and attending parent–teacher association meetings (Desimone, 1999; Keith et al., 1993; Steinberg, Lamborn, Dornbusch, & Darling, 1992); (b) parental encouragement of positive school behaviors (Atkinson & Forehand, 1979; Barth, 1979; Kelley, 1952; Schumaker, Hovell, & Sherman, 1977; Seginer, 1983); and (c) parental expectations for achievement and attainment (Ainley, Foreman, & Sheret, 1991; Fan & Chen, 2001; Scott-Jones, 1995; Seginer). For educators, promoting these practices presents an opportunity to help students achieve.

Source: Chen, W., & Gregory, A. (2010). Parental involvement as a protective factor during the transition to high school. *The Journal of Educational Research, 103,* 54.

6. The review of literature should briefly summarize minor studies and discuss major studies in detail. Minor studies are those that are related to one or two aspects of the study, or those that provide a general overview. Major studies are directly relevant to most aspects of the study or have important implications. A good review concentrates on major studies. It may be informative to mention minor studies, but the focus of the review should be on an analysis of the most closely related studies.

7. The review of major studies should relate previous studies explicitly to the research problem or methods. It is important to emphasize how the major studies relate to or contribute to the research problem or the methods of the current study. For example, the author might say, "These findings suggest that it is important to include gender as an independent variable in the study" or "This study adopts the methodology successfully used by Smith and Jones (1998)." It should be clear to the reader why a particular analysis or finding is important or helpful to the current study.

The following from a published study (Example 3.18) shows how the author effectively connected previous research to methodology:

EXAMPLE 3.18 | Explicitly Relating Previous Research to Methodology

The use of real-time observations has been an underutilized tool in the evaluation of school bullying, especially considering the important information such observations have provided about the environmental context and contributions of peers to the maintenance and cessation of bullying (e.g., Craig & Pepler, 1997; Hanish, Ryan, Martin, & Fabes, 2005). Without observations, most evaluations have been methodologically constrained by the difficulty of discriminating between changed perceptions measured via self-reports and actual behavior change. Objective evidence showing that schoolwide programs reduce bullying and victimization is therefore limited. Snyder et al. (2006) argued that observations are particularly well suited to intervention research because of blinding to intervention status and sensitivity to behavior change. Another benefit is that trained observers appear to differentiate between reactive aggression and the instrumental aggression typical of bullying better than other reporters (Card & Little, 2006). The current study makes use of both objective playground observations and subjective reports.

Source: Frey, K. S., Hirschstein, M. K., Edstrom, L. V., & Snell, J. L. (2009). Observed reductions in school bullying, nonbullying aggression, and destructive bystander behavior: a longitudinal evaluation). *Journal of Educational Psychology, 101*(2), 467.

8. The review of literature should provide a logical basis for the hypothesis. If there is a hypothesis, it should be based on the review of literature. This provides evidence that the hypothesis is based on reasonable logic supported by others, rather than on the researcher's whim. If the review of literature is unclear or provides conflicting predictions, the researcher may still state a hypothesis, though justification should be provided. Overall, there should be clear connections among the problem, review, and hypothesis.

9. The review of literature should establish a theoretical or conceptual framework for the problem. For basic and most applied research the review should provide the theoretical context for the study. A good theoretical context enhances the significance of the study and shows that the researcher is aware of the theory and has used it in framing the questions and methodology. Often, the theoretical framework is provided as a foundation for reviewing specific studies as illustrated by Examples 3.19 and 3.20.

EXAMPLES 3.19–3.20 | **Providing a Conceptual or Theoretical Framework**

The theoretical basis for the present work draws from Bronfenbrenner's bioecological model (Bronfenbrenner & Morris, 1998, 2006). This model considers four sources of influence on children's development: process, person, context, and time. . . . Proximal processes investigated herein refer to the reciprocal interactions between teachers and children; such interactions are hypothesized to be the primary mechanism by which children learn in classrooms. . . . Use of this framework to investigate teacher–child interactions may uncover the mechanisms through which teachers influence their students' development (Rutter & Maughan, 2002).

Source: Curby, T. W., Rimm-Kaufman, S. E., & Cameron, C. (2009). Teacher–child interactions and children's achievement trajectories across kindergarten and first grade. *Journal of Educational Psychology, 101*(4), 913.

Our investigation builds conceptually on the comparative state policy and politics literature, particularly theory and research on policy innovation and diffusion. Policy innovation and diffusion research draws on theories of U.S. federalism in viewing the 50 states both as individual policy actors and as agents of potential mutual influence within a larger social system (Dye, 1990). It holds that states adopt the policies they do in part because of their internal sociodemographic, economic, and political characteristics and in part because of their ability to influence one another's behavior.

Source: McLendon, M. K., Hearn, J. C., & Deaton, R. (2006). Called to account: Analyzing the origins and spread of state performance-accountability policies for higher education. *Educational Evaluation and Policy Analysis, 28*(1), 3.

10. The review of literature should help establish the significance of the research. The significance of a study is usually established by the nature of previous studies, which suggest that further research would be helpful or informative. However, be careful with studies you read that imply significance because of a "paucity of research" in an area. The significance of most investigations is based on what other, previous research has reported, not on the fact that few or no studies could be found on a topic.

Author Reflection *Writing a literature review is no easy task, so don't be surprised if it takes a while to write one. We find that it's best to use a large table and spread out summaries of different studies like a fan. That seems to help in the synthesis process, which is essential to being able to write a review that does much more than simply list what other studies have found. We also find it helpful to construct an outline before actually writing. You may find it necessary to step away for a few days and then come back. Finally, when you get in a writing mood, keep with it as long as you can.*

STUDY QUESTIONS

1. What are the major purposes of the review of literature?
2. How can the review help the researcher refine an initial research problem?
3. Why does previous research help to establish the credibility of the findings of a study?
4. Why are contradictory findings in previous research sometimes helpful?
5. How can the review improve proposed methodology?
6. What are the steps in conducting a review of literature?
7. What is the difference between a secondary and primary source?
8. What is a meta-analysis?
9. What is the procedure for identifying key terms?
10. What are the steps in finding articles using a database like ERIC?
11. What makes some journals better than others?
12. In what ways is searching the Internet different from searching a database such as ERIC?
13. What is the difference between using subject directories and search engines to locate information on the Web?
14. Why is the national Department of Education's website a good one to use when beginning a search?
15. What could you expect to obtain from a regional educational laboratory that you could not obtain from a national research center?
16. Take a few minutes to try different search strategies to locate information on a topic. Which strategy was most helpful? Which one was easiest? What did you learn about using different strategies?
17. What are the steps of writing a review of literature? How should the review be organized?
18. What is the difference between quantitative and qualitative literature reviews?
19. What are the criteria for evaluating a review of literature?

Chapter 4

Participants *and* Sampling

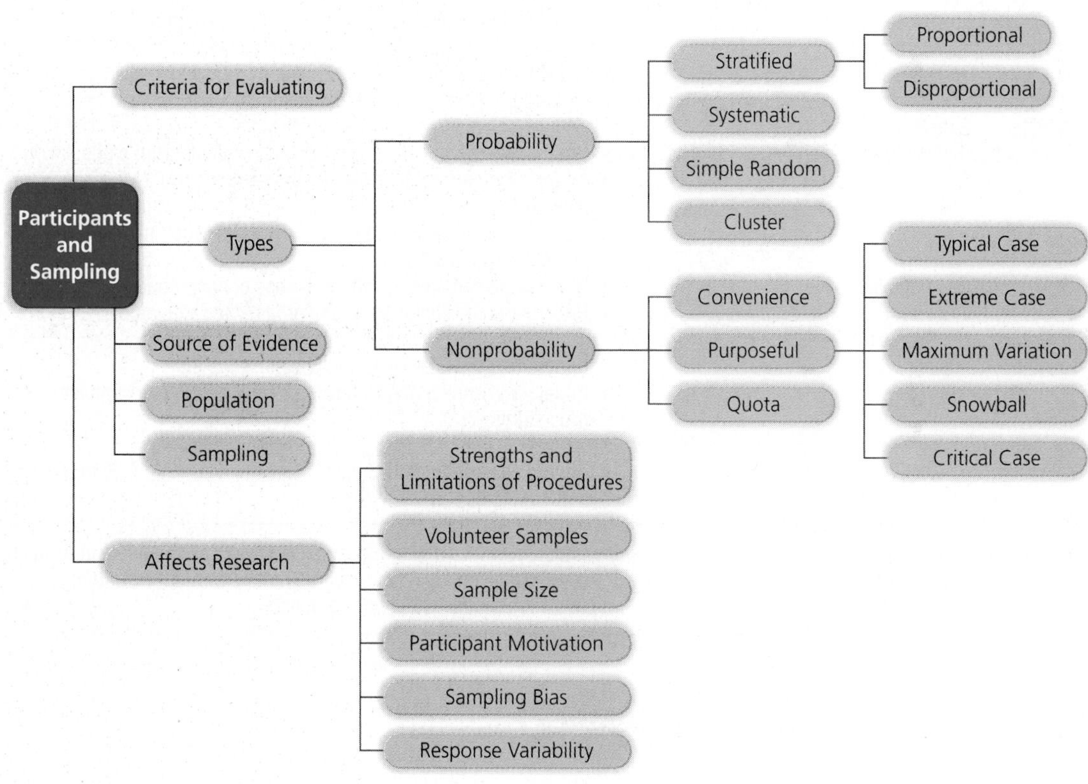

CHAPTER ROAD MAP

This chapter is divided into four major sections to help you understand the different ways researchers come up with participants (subjects) from whom data are collected. We will first review the common approaches taken for quantitative studies, then qualitative studies, and finally, mixed-method studies. We will then examine how sampling affects research.

As noted in Chapter 1, the first subsection of the methodology section usually describes the participants from whom data are collected. The manner in which participants are selected and their traits and characteristics have important implications for identifying factors that affect participant performance and for generalizing the results.

Chapter Outline	Learning Objectives
Sources of Evidence	• Know various sources of evidence from which data are gathered.
Participants and Samples	• Know what a sample is and how it is described in articles.
Quantitative Sampling Probability Sampling	• Understand the principles of selecting a sample from a population. • Understand and identify different procedures for drawing a random sample. • Know the advantages and disadvantages of different probability sampling procedures.
Nonprobability Sampling	• Understand and identify different types of nonprobability sampling • Understand the limitations of nonprobability samples
Qualitative Sampling	• Understand the reasons for purposeful sampling • Understand and identify different types of purposeful sampling procedures.
Mixed-Method Sampling	• Understand and identify different types of sampling used for mixed-method studies.
The Effects of Sampling	• Understand how volunteer samples, sample size, subject motivation, bias, response rate, and response variability affect research. • Apply criteria for evaluating sampling.

WHAT IS *a* PARTICIPANT *and a* SAMPLE?

Every empirical investigation collects data from someone or something (elements), what is often referred to as the *source of evidence* or *unit of study*. These terms refer to the individuals, groups, documents, sites, events, or other sources from which data are gathered. As we will see, it is critical to describe these sources and understand their effect on studies. The most common source of evidence is individuals, what is commonly called a *participant* or a *subject*.

Simply put, a **participant** (subject), is someone from whom data are collected. In experiments, for example, each person who receives the intervention and whose behavior is measured is considered a participant. The term *participant subject* may also identify individuals whose behavior, past or present, is used as data, without their involvement in some type of treatment or intervention. For instance, a researcher might use last year's fourth-grade test scores as data, and each fourth-grader included is considered a participant. In some quantitative studies the term *subjects* may be used rather than participants, though the meaning of the term is the same. The term *subject* is being replaced by *participant* and *source of data*. In qualitative research individuals are always identified as participants. Collectively, the group of subjects or participants from whom data are or have been collected is referred to as the *sample*.

Participant: Person from whom data are collected.

The **sample,** then, consists of the "element(s)" from which data are or have been obtained. Although the phrase "the sample included . . ." is used to indicate the characteristics of the individuals or events in the sample, the nature of the sampling procedure is usually described by one or more adjectives, such as *random* sampling, *purposive* sampling, or *stratified random* sampling. These types of sampling procedures are defined, with illustrations from actual studies, in the following section.

Sample: Group of participants from whom data are collected.

It is important for the researcher to identify, as specifically as possible, the sampling procedure rationale for using the procedure, and the characteristics of the sample used in the study (e.g., age gender, grade level, racel ethnicity). Here are two examples of good descriptions of samples.

EXAMPLES 4.1–4.2 | Descriptions of Samples

Participants included 26 male and 14 female students enrolled in 3rd-grade classes at an urban elementary school and classified with a learning disability in mathematics (MLD). . . . Participants were drawn from a larger sample from which children diagnosed with either attention-deficit/hyperactivity disorder or reading difficulties were not selected. . . . Selection criteria for participants required that WISC-III scores and WRAT-R reading and spelling standard scores fall within normal limits."

Source: Rosvic, G. M., Dihoff, R. E., Epstein, M. L., & Cook, M. L. (2006). Feedback facilitates the acquisition and retention of numerical fact series byelementary school students with mathematics learning disabilities. *The Psychological Record 56*(1), 39.

Students were enrolled in one of three kindergarten classes: 283 students (57.9%) attended half-day classes (157 half-day morning and 126 half-day afternoon) and 206 students (42.1%) attended full-day classes. Student ages ranged from 5 years 0 months to 6 years 6 months upon entering kindergarten; overall average age was 5 years 7 months. The total study included 208 girls (44.0%) and 265 boys (56.0%). The majority of students received no monetary assistance for lunch, which was based on parent income (89.0%, n = 424); 49 students (10.0%) received some assistance. Twenty-six students (5.3%) spoke a language at home other than

English. The majority of students (90.5%, n = 428) were Caucasian;31 students (6.3%) were Hispanic; and 14 students (2.8%) were African American, Native American, or Asian American. Those data reflect the community demographics within the school district."

Source: Wolgemuth, J. R., Cobb, R. B., Winokur, M. A., Leech, N., & Ellerby, D. (2006). Comparing longitudinal academic achievement of full-day and half-day kindergarten students. *The Journal of Educational Research 99*(5), 264.

TYPES *of* SAMPLING PROCEDURES *for* QUANTITATIVE STUDIES

The purpose of sampling in quantitative studies is to obtain a group of participants who will be representative of a larger group of individuals or who will provide targeted responses. The degree of representativeness and the quality of the information obtained are based on the sampling technique employed. In this section we will review types of sampling procedures that are most commonly used in quantitative studies.

Probability Sampling

Population: A larger group to whom results can be generalized.

Many quantitative studies need to generalize results to a well-defined larger group of individuals. This larger group of elements, whether individuals, objects, or events, is called the **population.** This group is also referred to as the *target population* or *universe.* The specification of the population begins with the research problem and review of literature, through which a population is described conceptually or in broad terms, for example, seventh-grade students, beginning teachers, principals, special education teachers, and so forth. A more specific definition is then needed, based on demographic characteristics. These characteristics are sometimes referred to as *delimiting* variables. For example, in a study of first-grade minority students, there are three delimiting characteristics: students, first grade (age), and minority.

It is important to distinguish the target population from the *survey population* or *sampling frame.* For example, in a study of beginning teachers, the target population may be beginning teachers across the United States, in all types of schools. The survey population may be a list of beginning public school teachers obtained from 40 states. Although the intent may be to generalize to all beginning teachers, the generalization in this case would be most accurately limited to beginning public school teachers in the 40 states.

Probability sampling: Known probability of selection from the population.

When investigating a large population, it is often impractical and usually unnecessary to measure all the elements in the population of interest. Typically, a relatively small number of subjects or cases is selected from the larger population. The goal is to select a sample that will adequately represent the population, so that what is described in the sample will also be approximately true of the population. The best procedure for selecting such a sample is to use **probability sampling,** a method of sampling in which the subjects are selected randomly in such a way that the researcher knows the probability of selecting each member of the population (remember—random *selection* is a type of sampling; random *assignment* is used for some experimental designs).

Random selection implies that each member of the population as a whole or of subgroups of the population has an equal chance of being selected. As long as the number of cases selected is large enough, it is likely that a small percentage of the population, represented by the sample, will provide an accurate description of the entire population. The steps taken in probability sampling are illustrated in Figures 4.1 and 4.2.

Note, however, that there is always some degree of error in sampling, and that error must be considered in interpreting the results. In probability sampling, this calculation can be made precisely with some statistical procedures. Consider a population of 1,000 third-graders, from which you will randomly select 5%, or 50, to estimate the attitudes of all the third-graders toward school. If the attitude score was 75 for the sample of 50 subjects, 75 can be used to estimate the value

FIGURE 4.1 Steps in probability sampling.

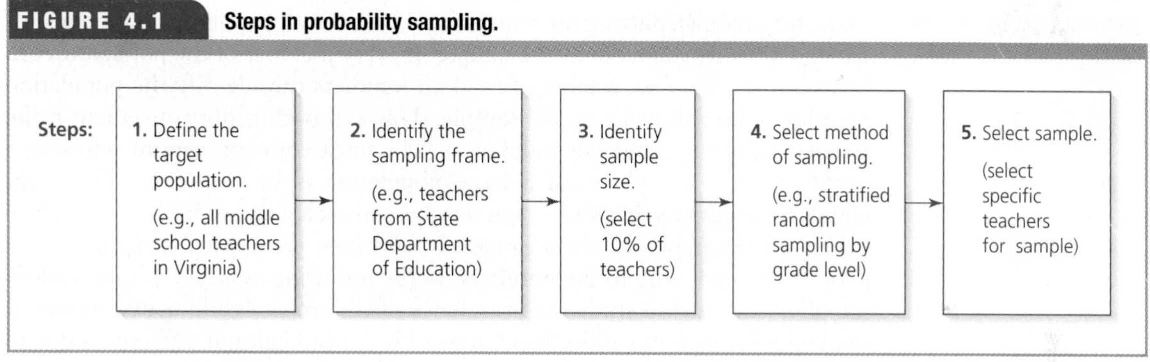

Steps:
1. Define the target population.
(e.g., all middle school teachers in Virginia)
2. Identify the sampling frame.
(e.g., teachers from State Department of Education)
3. Identify sample size.
(select 10% of teachers)
4. Select method of sampling.
(e.g., stratified random sampling by grade level)
5. Select sample.
(select specific teachers for sample)

FIGURE 4.2 Sampling and margin of error.

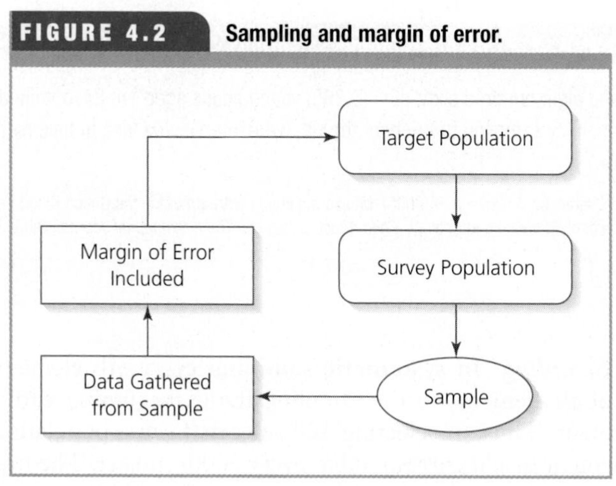

for the entire population of third-graders. However, if another sample of 50 students is selected, their score might be a little different, say,73. Which one is more correct? Since not all 1,000 students have been tested to obtain the result, we do not know for sure, but the results can be used to estimate the error in sampling. This is basically the technique that political polls follow when it is reported that the vote is 45% ± 3%. The plus or minus 3 is the estimate of error in sampling. For example, it is common to report what is called a *margin of error* in polling. The **margin of error** indicates an interval within which the true population value lies. In polling there is typically a 95% probability that the population value is within the interval. So for 45% ± 3, there is a 95% chance that when the entire population votes the result will be between 42 and 48.

Margin of error: Likely error in determining the result for the population.

There are many types of probability sampling procedures. You will most likely encounter four types in educational research: simple random, systematic, stratified, and cluster.

Simple random sampling: Each member of the population has the same probability of being selected.

Simple Random Sampling. In **simple random sampling** every member of the population has an equal and independent chance of being selected for the sample. This method is often used with a population that has a small number of cases, for example, putting the names or numbers of all population members in a hat and drawing some out as the sample. If every member of the population can be assigned a number, a table of random numbers can identify the population members who will make up the sample. This approach is not convenient if the population is large and not numbered. The most common way of selecting a simple random sample from a large population is by computer. There are computer programs that will assign numbers to each element in the population, generate the sample numbers randomly, and then print out the names of the people corresponding to the numbers. In the following example simple random sampling was used to study the prevalence of all forms of child maltreatment in the United Kingdom within the context of social and cultural differences due to social class, ethnicity, and region.

EXAMPLE 4.3 | Simple Random Sampling

Two thousand eight hundred sixty-nine (2,869) young adults aged 18–24, obtained by random probability sampling throughout the UK, were interviewed face to face by trained interviewers."

Source: May-Chahal, C., & Cawson, P. (2005). Measuring child maltreatment in the United Kingdom: A study of the prevalence of child abuse and neglect. *Child Abuse & Neglect: The International Journal, 29*(9), 969.

Systematic sampling: Every *n*th member of the population is selected.

Systematic Sampling. In **systematic sampling** every *n*th element is selected from a list of all elements in the sampling frame, beginning with a randomly selected element. Thus, in selecting 100 subjects from a population of 50,000, every *n*th element would correspond to every 500th subject. The first element is selected randomly. In this example that would be some number between 1 and 500. Suppose 240 was randomly selected as a starting point. The first subject chosen for the sample would be the 240th name on a list, the next subject would be the 740th, then the 1,240th, and so on until 100 subjects were selected.

An example of systematic sampling is illustrated in Figure 4.3. In this case there is a sampling frame of 80 students. The researcher needs a sample size of 10% (8 cases). This means that every 10th student will be selected from the list (80/8), beginning with a randomly selected number between 1 and 10.

There is a possible though uncommon weakness in systematic sampling if the list of cases in the population is arranged in a pattern so that only subjects with similar characteristics or who come from similar contexts are selected. For instance, if a list of fourth graders in a school division is arranged by classroom and students in the classrooms are listed from high to low ability, there is a cyclical pattern in the list (referred to as *periodicity*). If every *n*th subject selected corresponds to the pattern, the sample would represent only a certain level of ability and would not be representative of the population. Alphabetical lists do not usually create periodicity and are suitable for choosing subjects systematically.

Stratified sampling: Subjects are selected from strata or groups of the population.

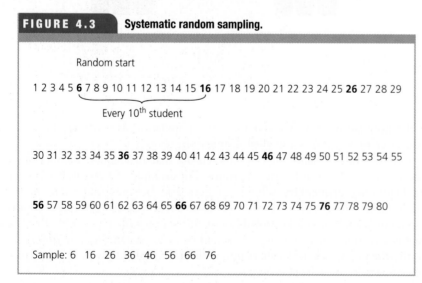

Stratified Sampling. **Stratified sampling** (*stratified random sampling*) is a modification of either simple random or systematic sampling in which the population is first divided into homogeneous subgroups. Next, subjects are selected from each subgroup, using simple random or systematic procedures, rather than from the population as a whole. The strata are the subgroups. In Figure 4.4 stratified random sampling is illustrated with male and female subgroups. Stratified sampling is used primarily for two reasons. First, as long as the subgroups are identified by a variable related to the dependent variable in the research (e.g., socioeconomic status in a study of achievement) and results in more homogeneous groups, the same-sized sample will be more representative

FIGURE 4.3 **Systematic random sampling.**

Random start

1 2 3 4 5 **6** 7 8 9 10 11 12 13 14 15 **16** 17 18 19 20 21 22 23 24 25 **26** 27 28 29

Every 10th student

30 31 32 33 34 35 **36** 37 38 39 40 41 42 43 44 45 **46** 47 48 49 50 51 52 53 54 55

56 57 58 59 60 61 62 63 64 65 **66** 67 68 69 70 71 72 73 74 75 **76** 77 78 79 80

Sample: 6 16 26 36 46 56 66 76

FIGURE 4.4 Stratified random sampling.

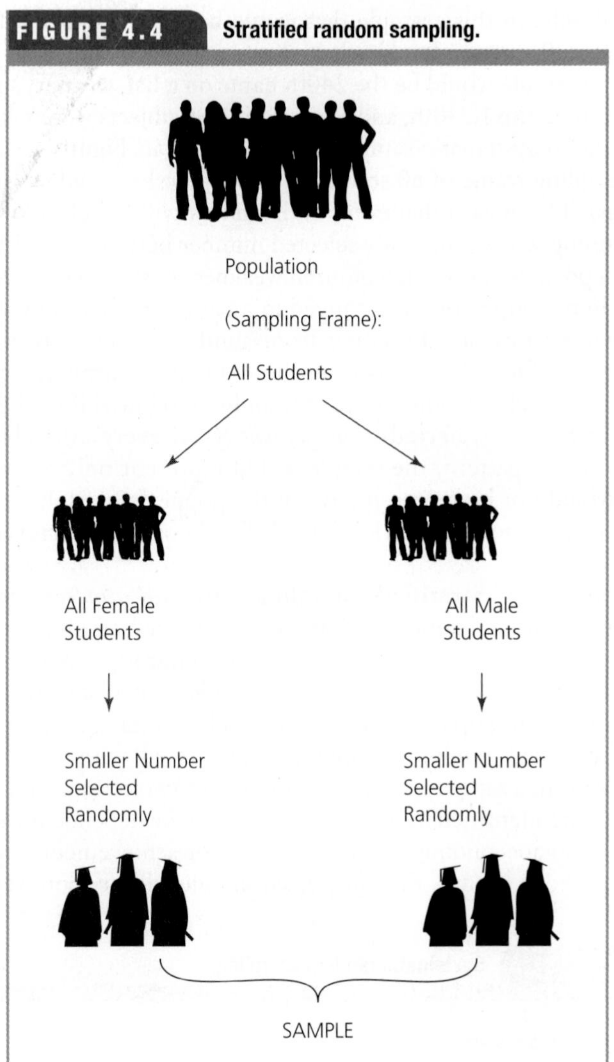

of the population than if taken from the population as a whole. This result reduces error and allows a smaller sample to be chosen.

Second, stratified sampling is used to ensure that an adequate number of subjects is selected from different subgroups. For example, if a researcher is studying beginning elementary school teachers and believes that there may be important differences between male and female teachers, using simple random or systematic sampling would probably not result in a sufficient number of male teachers to study the differences. It would be necessary in this situation first to stratify the population of teachers into male and female teachers and then to select subjects from each subgroup.

The samples can be selected using one of two methods. A **proportional stratified sample,** or *proportional allocation,* is used when the number of subjects selected from each stratum is based on the percentage of subjects in the population that have the characteristic used to form the stratum. That is, each strata is represented in the sample in the same proportion as represented in the population. Thus, if 20% of the population of 200 elementary teachers is male, 20% of the sample would also be male teachers. Proportional stratefied random sampling is illustrated in the following example:

Proportional stratified sample: Reflects proportion of stratum in population.

EXAMPLE 4.4 | Proportional Stratified Random Sampling

The participants in this study consisted of 2,100 adolescents. . . . Participants were chosen using a proportional stratified random sampling method. . . . The sample was first stratified in terms of participant's area of residence (urban or rural) and the type of institution (middle school, high school, or juvenile corrective institution). . . . The sample size was adjusted and allocated to ensure representativeness in terms of each stratification parameter.

Source: Kim, H. S., & Kim, H. S. (2008). The impact of family violence, family functioning, and parental partner dynamics on Korean juvenile delinquency. *Child Psychiatry and Human Development, 39,* 441–442.

Using proportional stratified sampling, however, does not always ensure that a sufficient number of subjects will be selected from each stratum. A second approach, referred to as **disproportional stratified sampling,** mitigates this problem by taking the same number of subjects from each stratum, regardless of the percentage of subjects from each stratum in the population. For instance, if only 10% of a population of 200 elementary teachers are male, a proportional sample of 40 would include only 4 male teachers. To study teacher gender, it would be better to include all 20 male teachers in the population for the sample and randomly select 20 female teachers. When disproportional sampling is used, the results of each stratum need to be weighted to estimate values for the population as a whole.

Disproportional stratified sample: Number of subjects in each strata does not reflect proportion in population.

In Example 4.5, disproportional stratified sampling is used with three levels of stratification.

EXAMPLE 4.5 | Disproportional Stratified Sampling

To obtain representative samples of all federal states, the sample was stratified by state and school type. Within each state and school type classification, random samples of schools were selected. Within each school, two seventh-grade classes were randomly sampled. In this way the final sample was reasonably representative of the different federal states.

Source: Marsh, H. W., Koller, O., & Baumert, J. (2001). Reunification of east and west German school systems: Longitudinal multilevel modeling study of the big-fish-little-pond effect on academic self-concept. *American Educational Research Journal, 35,* 332.

FIGURE 4.5 Example of disproportional stratified random sampling with two strata.

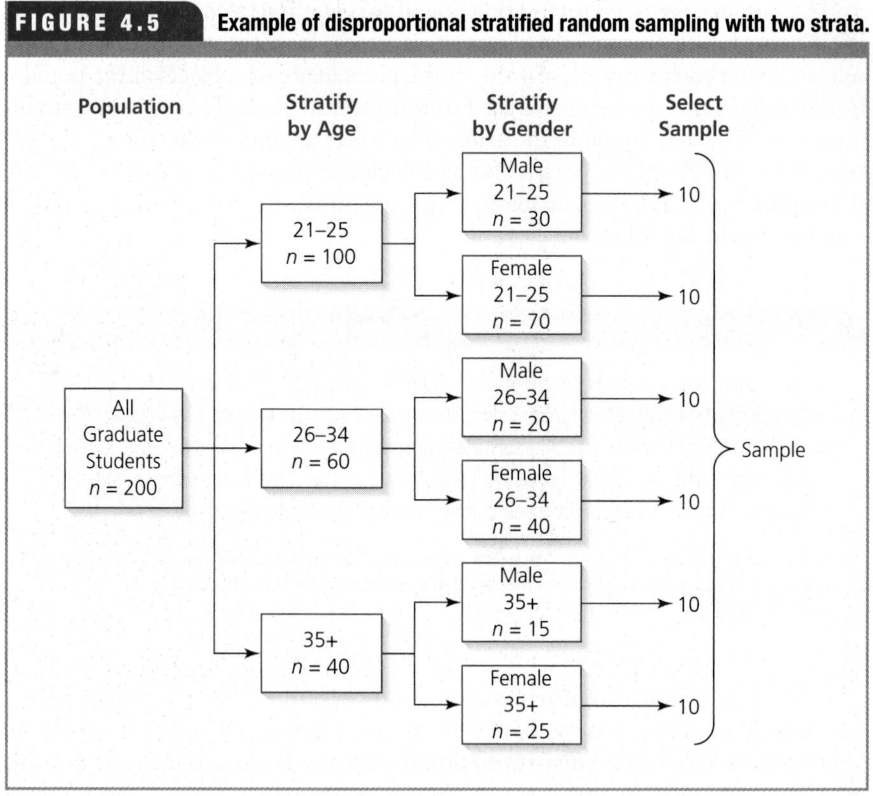

Disproportional stratified random sampling is further illustrated in Figure 4.5. In this example the population is divided first into three age groups, then by gender. Once the groups are stratified by gender, random samples are selected from each of the six subgroups.

Cluster sampling: Naturally occurring groups are selected.

Cluster Sampling. When it is impossible or impractical to sample individuals from the population as a whole, as when there is no exhaustive list of all the individuals, cluster sampling is used. **Cluster sampling** involves the random selection of naturally occurring groups or units (clusters) and then individuals from the chosen groups are used for the study. Examples of naturally occurring groups would be universities, schools, school districts, classrooms, city blocks, and households. For example, if a researcher was conducting a state survey on the television-viewing habits of middle school students, it would be cumbersome and difficult to select children at random from the state population of all middle-schoolers. A clustering procedure could be employed by first listing all the school districts in the state and then randomly selecting 30 school districts from the list. One middle school would then be selected from each district, and all students from each school, or a random sample of students, would be included in the survey. Although cluster sampling saves time and money, the results are less accurate than those based on other random sampling techniques.

Nonprobability Sampling

In many research designs it is either not feasible, unnecessary, or not desirable to obtain a probability sample. In these situations a *nonprobability* sample is used. A **nonprobability sample** is one in which the probability of including population elements is unknown. Usually, not every element in the population has a chance of being selected. It is also quite common for the population to be the same as the sample, in which case there is no immediate need to generalize to a larger population. In fact, much educational research reported in journals, especially experimental studies, uses a group of subjects that has not been selected from a larger population. Qualitative studies use nonprobability sampling exclusively.

Nonprobability sample: Probability of selection not known.

There are several types of nonprobability sampling procedures used in quantitative studies. We will consider the three types that are used most commonly: convenience, quota, and purposeful. Purposeful procedures will be summarized in the section on qualitative sampling procedures, though it is possible to use a purposeful sample in quantitative studies.

Convenience Sampling. A **convenience sample** is a group of subjects selected because of availability, for example, a class of a university professor who is conducting a study on college students, the classrooms of teachers who are enrolled in a graduate class, the schools of principals who are participating in a workshop, people who decide to go to the mall on Saturday, or people who respond to an advertisement for subjects. There is no precise way of generalizing from a convenience sample to a population. Also, the nature of the convenience sample may bias the results. For example, if the available sample for studying the impact of college is the group of alumni who return on alumni day, their responses would probably be quite different from those of all alumni. Similarly, research on effective teaching that depends on the participation of teachers in a particular geographic area, because they are available, may result in different findings than research done in other geographic areas.

Convenience sample: Nonprobability available sample.

Although we should be wary of convenience samples (sometimes these samples are negatively referred to as *accidental* or *haphazard*), often this is the only type of sampling possible, and the primary purpose of the research may not be to generalize but to better understand relationships that may exist. Suppose a researcher is investigating the relationship between creativity and intelligence, and the only available sample is a single elementary school. When the study is completed, the results indicate a moderate relationship: Children who have higher intelligence tend to be more creative than children with lower intelligence. Because there was no probability sampling, should we conclude that the results are not valid or credible? That decision seems extreme. It is more reasonable to interpret the results as valid for children similar to those studied. For example, if the children in the study are from a school that serves a low socioeconomic area, the results will be useful for children in similar schools but less useful for those from schools that serve a middle or high socioeconomic level. The decision is not to dismiss the findings but to limit them to the type of subjects in the sample. As more and more research accumulates with different convenience samples, the overall credibility of the results is enhanced.

Although it is uncommon for a researcher to state explicitly that a convenience sample was used, it will be obvious from the subjects subsection of the article. If some type of probability sampling procedure was used, it will be described. Thus, in the absence of such particulars you can assume that the sample was an available one. The following examples (Examples 4.6–4.7) are typical.

EXAMPLES 4.6–4.7 | Convenience Samples

Participants in this investigation were 482 undergraduate students. Student volunteers were solicited primarily from educational psychology and human developments courses at a large urban land-grant university in the mid-Atlantic United States.

Source: Buehl, M. M., & Alexander, P. A. (2005). Motivation and performance differences in students' domain-specific epistemological beliefs profiles. *American Educational Research Journal, 42*(4), 704.

Participants (*N* = 39) were adult graduate students attending a CACREP-accredited counselor training program at a comprehensive, regional university in Pennsylvania. Participants consisted of a nonprobability convenience sample of all students enrolled in one of two courses.

Source: Wilkerson, K., & Eschbach, L. (2009). Transformed school counseling: The impact of a graduate course on trainees' perceived readiness to develop comprehensive, data-driven programs. Professional School Counseling, 13(1), 4.

Quota sampling: Nonrandom sampling representative of a target population.

Quota Sampling. **Quota sampling** is used when the researcher is unable to take a probability sample but still wants a sample that is representative of the entire population. Different composite profiles of major groups in the population are identified, and then subjects are selected, nonrandomly, to represent each group. Thus, subjects are selected nonrandomly according to specific criteria. A type of quota sampling that is common in educational research is used to represent geographic areas or types of communities, such as urban, rural, and suburban. Typically, a state is divided into distinct geographic areas, and cases are selected to represent each area. As in availability and purposive sampling, there is a heavy reliance on the decisions of the researcher in selecting the sample, and appropriate caution should be used in interpreting the results.

Review and Reflect *One of the most important distinctions about quantitative sampling is the difference between sampling to generalize and sampling that may bias or otherwise seriously impact the findings. What are the major types of sampling used for generalizing to a population? Under what circumstances would it be best to use stratified random sampling? How can a convenience or available nonprobability sample be used to generalize the findings?*

TYPES *of* SAMPLING PROCEDURES *for* QUALITATIVE STUDIES

In qualitative studies participants are selected purposefully. That is, there is a reason or justification for why the sample of individuals or sites will provide the best information to address the research question. In **purposeful sampling** (sometimes referred to as *purposive, judgment,* or *judgmental* sampling), the researcher selects individuals or cases because they will be particularly informative about the topic. Based on the researcher's knowledge of the population, a judgment is made to include those cases that will be information-rich. These few cases are studied in depth. For example, in research on effective teaching, it may be most informative to observe "expert" or "master" teachers rather than all teachers. To study effective schools, it may be most informative to interview key personnel, such as the principal and teachers who have been employed in successful schools for a number of years. Sometimes researchers will be interested in *deviant* cases, selecting individuals who do not fit an established pattern. This approach can be used to establish a better understanding of more common traits.

Purposeful sampling: Selection of information-rich participants.

There are a number of different purposeful sampling procedures that qualitative researchers use to obtain "information-rich" individuals and sites. All of them use nonprobability sampling. The more common types are summarized here and in Table 4.1.

Criterion Sampling

With criterion (or *criteria*) sampling, the researcher selects participants on the basis of identified characteristics that will provide needed information. Often several criteria are used, as illustrated in Example 4.8, to ensure that participants have had sufficient experience with what is being studied. The criteria are determined prior to the selection of the participants. For example, a study of resilience

TABLE 4.1 Types of Purposeful Sampling Procedures

Sampling Procedure	Description
Criterion	Choosing individuals with certain important characteristics.
Typical case	Choosing individuals or sites that are representative of most others.
Extreme case	Choosing individuals or sites that are unusual or atypical.
Maximum variation	Choosing individuals or sites that represent extreme values of the phenomenon being studied.
Snowball	Selecting individuals based on recommendations of participants.
Critical case	Choosing a dramatic illustration of the phenomenon being studied.

among at-risk high school students may have been at risk of failure as one criteria and then doing well in school as a second criteria.

EXAMPLE 4.8 | Criterion Sampling

I made contact visits to screen volunteers according to predetermined criteria to determine if they qualified as participants (Seidman, 1991). The first criterion was attending Internet cafes regularly, at least twice a week, to ensure that the phenomenon was a part of the adolescent's lifeworld. The secondary criterion was having experiences of certain uses of computers that are indicative of educational use. . . . Those who referred to two or more items on the list of educational uses in their descriptions were considered qualified to participate in the study.

Source: Cilesiz, S. (2009). Educational computer use in leisure contexts: A phenomenological study of adolescents' experiences at internet cafes. *American Educational Research Journal, 46*(1), 242.

Typical Case Sampling

Typical case sampling: Selecting representative participants.

In **typical case sampling** (or *model instance* sampling) the researcher investigates a person, group, or site that is "typical" or "representative" of many. This kind of sampling requires sufficient knowledge about the important characteristics of the larger "population" of interest so that there is a reasonable definition of "typical." It is like sampling the "average" elementary teacher (one with several years of experience rather than a new teacher or one nearing retirement, and a woman). Note the criteria used to select the sample in Example 4.9 to identify the "typical" adult attending community college.

EXAMPLE 4.9 | Typical Case Sampling

Interviewees of these two community colleges were identified through a purposeful sampling strategy target to adults who (a) were at least 30 years of age, (b) were in good academic standing according to their institution's criteria, (c) were in a college transfer program, and (d) had completed at least 15 hours of academic coursework beyond developmental studies.

Source: Kasworm, C. (2004). Adult student identity in an intergenerational community college classroom. *Adult Education Quarterly, 56*(1), 6–7.

Extreme Case Sampling

Extreme case sampling: Selecting unique or atypical participants.

An extreme case is one that is unique or atypical, an outlier compared to most others in the category. In education, **extreme case sampling** is often used to identify unusually successful students or schools with the intent of studying them to learn why they perform so well. Another strategy is to identify a continuum of an important characteristic and then take samples at one end of that continuum.

In the following example, extreme case sampling is based on the significant role played by homework. The sample, Example 4.10, is at one end of a continuum of the importance of homework.

EXAMPLE 4.10 | Extreme Case Sampling

This student body was selected because homework played a major role in the curriculum and because it would provide a definitive test of the effects of this academic experience.

Source: Zimmerman, B. J., & Kitsantas, A. (2005). Homework practices and academic achievement: The mediating role of self-efficacy and perceived responsibility beliefs. *Contemporary Educational Psychology, 30*, 401.

Maximum Variation Sampling

In **maximum variation sampling** (or *maximum heterogenity sampling*) individuals, groups, or cases are selected to represent both ends of a continuum of values on a characteristic of interest. For example, if it is known that there are some teachers who never use zeros when grading and others who always use zeros, sampling from both extremes would provide for maximum variation. Or, suppose a researcher has a sample of schools differing on a measure of school climate. Schools scoring extremely high and schools scoring extremely low on school climate could be selected to understand how climate is formed and its impact on students.

Maximum variation sampling: Selecting participants to represent extreme cases.

Snowball Sampling

Occasionally, qualitative researchers are in a situation in which the sampling is carried out as data are being collected. In **snowball sampling** (also called *network sampling*), the researcher begins with a few participants and then asks them to nominate or recommend others who are known to have the profile, attributes, or characteristics desired. For example, a researcher could begin interviewing a few elementary school counselors known for using play therapy and then ask them to nominate other elementary school counselors they know who also use play therapy. This kind of sampling is especially useful when the researcher has only a limited pool of initial participants. A related kind of selection of cases, *opportunistic sampling*, also occurs after the study is under way and takes advantage of including participants who are identified as being rich in the information needed.

Snowball sampling: Selecting participants from recommendations of other participants.

Critical Case Sampling

Sometimes the phenomenon of interest is illustrated by individuals, groups, or sites in unique and dramatic ways. **Critical case sampling** is used in these situations as an opportunity to learn and understand. For instance, suppose a researcher was interested in how the implementation of a particular technology initiative—say, laptop computers for all students—was impacting teaching and learning. If a single school district could be identified that had such an initiative it would be considered a critical case (Example 4.11).

Critical case sampling: Selecting the most important participants to understand phenomena being studied.

EXAMPLE 4.11 | Critical Case Sampling

I selected Chicago Public Schools (CPS) and Oakland Unified School District (OUSD) in California, in part because both districts by the start of my data collection had begun to implement significant new small autonomous schools initiatives . . . as main strategies to improve school performance . . . in traditionally underserved neighborhoods. . . . Both districts received major implementation grants from the Bill and Melinda Gates Foundation. . . . I also selected CPS and OUSD because both district central offices organized around an implementation strategy that my conceptual framework suggested might be important to implementation; the creation of a new unit within the district.

Source: Honig, M. I. (2009). No small thing: School district central office bureaucracies and the implementation of new small autonomous schools initiatives. *American Educational Research Journal, 46*(2), 393.

TYPES *of* SAMPLING PROCEDURES *for* MIXED-METHOD STUDIES

The selection of participants for mixed-method research includes both probability/nonprobability methods used for quantitative studies and purposeful approaches from quantitative studies. Sometimes the quantitative and qualitative sampling procedures are completed with the matching phase of the study (e.g., using systematic sampling for the quantitative phase and purposeful for the qualitative phase). Some mixed-method studies use hybrid approaches in which quantitative and qualitative methods are combined (Teddlie & Yu, 2007). Four of these hybrids are summarized in the following. There are other combinations given the multiple ways mixed-method studies can be designed.

Stratified Purposeful Sampling

There are two variations of this kind of sampling. One is completed by first using the quantitative approach to stratifying a population, followed by purposeful sampling of a small number of cases from each stratum that are examined intensely. For example, graduate students could be stratified according to employment status into three groups—fully employed, employed part-time, and unemployed—and then individuals purposefully selected from each of these three groups for the qualitative part of the study. A second kind of stratified purposeful sampling occurs when the researcher first selects the purposeful sample, stratifies this group on a variable of importance, and then selects individuals from each of these groups.

Purposeful Random Sampling

This strategy combines random sampling with purposeful sampling. Typically, a random sample of a very small number of cases is selected from the population. This group of cases then becomes the purposeful sample. While there is a random selection procedure, the results are not intended to generalize to the population. Rather, it is an approach that improves the representativeness of the purposeful sample.

Concurrent Sampling

Concurrent mixed-method sampling is used when the sampling procedures for the quantitative and qualitative portions of the study are completed independently. Thus, probability sampling is used for the quantitative part of the study, and purposeful sampling is used for the qualitative part. Both sampling procedures are often used at about the same time (hence, *concurrent*). This allows for **triangulation**, in which different sources of information can be combined to address the same question. An example of a concurrent sampling design is illustrated in Example 4.12. In this study separate probability and purposeful samples are distinct but are combined in analysis, discussion, interpretation, and conclusions. Note how the researchers justify their samples in what are shared characteristics to add cohesiveness to the discussion.

Triangulation: Different sources addressing the same question.

EXAMPLE 4.12 | Concurrent Mixed-Method Sampling

We have pushed both data sources to be complementary in that they share three sample restrictions. First, both sources on children as they begin their formal schooling in kindergarten and first grade . . . focus on children who attend public schools in urban or suburban settings . . . focus on schools that enroll substantial proportions of children from low-income families. . . . We selected seven kindergarten classroom that fit several criteria. . . . We used quantitative data for this study from ECLS-K, a federally supported study that documents the educational status and progress of a nationally representative cohort of [a random sample of 24 students from 1,277 public and private schools]. . . .

Source: Halvorsen, A. L., Lee, V. E, & Andrade, F. H. (2009). A mixed-method study of teachers' attitudes about teacing in urban and low-income schools. *Urban Education, 44*(2), 188, 189, 195.

The sampling could also be done in a way that both probability and purposeful types are used jointly to result in a single sample, and that single sample participants are used in both the qualitative and quantitative parts of the study.

Multilevel Sampling

In this approach the researcher selects cases that are representative of different levels of aggregation that comprise the overall population. In education, levels include districts, schools, and classrooms. Appropriate sampling would be done for each level. This type of sampling is often called *nested* because classrooms are within schools and schools within districts.

HOW PARTICIPANTS *and* SAMPLING AFFECT RESEARCH

In reading and interpreting research, you need to be conscious of how the sampling procedures might have affected the results, and how the characteristics of the subjects affect the usefulness and the generalizability of the results. When evaluating the sampling used in a quantitative study, it is helpful to keep in mind the advantages and disadvantages of what has been used (see Table 4.2). That will allow you to better critique the effect of the sampling on the results and conclusions.

Volunteer Samples

A continuing problem in educational research, as well as in much social science research, is the use of volunteers as subjects. It is well documented that volunteers differ from nonvolunteers in important ways. Volunteers tend to be better educated, higher socioeconomically, more intelligent, more in need of social approval, more sociable, more unconventional, less authoritarian, and less conforming than nonvolunteers. Obviously, volunteer samples may respond differently than nonvolunteers because of these characteristics.

Volunteers are commonly used in research because the availability of subjects is often limited by time and resources. There have been thousands of studies with teachers who volunteer their classes for research. Much research on school-age children requires written permission from parents, and this necessity can result in a biased sample. Suppose a researcher needed parents' permission to study their involvement in the education of their children. Chances are good that parents who are relatively involved would be most likely to agree to be in the study, affecting a description of the nature of parental involvement for "all" students.

Sample Size

An important consideration in judging the credibility of research is the size of the sample. In most studies there are restrictions that limit the number of subjects, although it is difficult to know when the sample is too small. Most researchers use general rules of thumb in their studies, such as having at least 30 subjects for correlational research, and at least 15 subjects in each group for experimental research. However, in many educational studies conducted in the field, higher numbers of subjects are needed. In surveys that sample a large population, often a very small percentage of the population needs to be sampled, for example, less than 5% or even 1%. Of course, if the survey sample is too small, it is likely that the results obtained cannot characterize the population. Formal statistical techniques can be applied to determine the number of subjects needed, but in many educational studies these techniques are not used.

With purposeful sampling, the major criterion for using an adequate number of cases is the information provided. Since the purpose of the sampling is to provide in-depth information, sampling is considered complete when no new information is forthcoming from additional cases.

In educational research a major consideration with respect to sample size is the interpretation of findings that show no difference or relationships, particularly in studies that use small samples. For example, suppose you are studying the relationship between creativity and intelligence and, with a sample of 20 students, found that there was no relationship. Is it reasonable to conclude that in reality there is no relationship? Probably not, since a plausible reason for not finding a relationship is that such a small sample was used, and this limited what

TABLE 4.2 Strengths and Weaknesses of Sampling Methods

Method of Sampling	Strengths	Weaknesses
Probability		
Simple random	1. Usually representative of the population 2. Easy to analyze and interpret results 3. Easy to understand	1. Requires numbering each element in the population 2. Larger sampling error than in stratified sampling
Systematic	1. Same as above 2. Simplicity of drawing sample	1. Periodicity in list of population elements
Proportional stratified	1. 1, 2, and 3 of simple random 2. Allows subgroup comparisons 3. Usually more representative than simple random or systematic 4. Fewer subjects needed 5. Results represent population without weighting	1. Requires subgroup identification of each population element 2. Requires knowledge of the proportion of each subgroup in the population 3. May be costly and difficult to prepare lists of population elements in each subgroup.
Disproportional stratified	1. Same as above 2. Ensures adequate numbers of elements in each subgroup	1. Same as above 2. Requires proper weighting of subgroup to represent population 3. Less efficient for estimating population characteristics
Cluster	1. Low cost 2. Requires lists of elements 3. Efficient with large populations	1. Less accurate than simple random, systematic, or stratified 2. May be difficult to collect data from all elements in each cluster 3. Requires that each population element be assigned only one cluster
Nonprobability		
Convenience	1. Less costly 2. Less time-consuming 3. Ease of administration 4. Usually ensures high participation rate 5. Generalization possible to similar subjects	1. Difficult to generalize to other subjects 2. Less representative of an identified population 3. Results dependent on unique characteristics of the sample
Quota	1. Same as above 2. More representative of population than convenience or purposive	1. Same as above 2. Usually more time-consuming than convenience or purposive
Purposeful	1. 1, 2, 3, 4, and 5 of convenience 2. Adds credibility to qualitative research 3. Assures receipt of needed information	1. 1, 2, and 3 of convenience

was found. In addition to the small number of subjects, it is likely that there may not be many differences in either creativity or intelligence, and without such differences it is impossible to find that the two variables are related. That is, with a larger sample that has different creativity and intelligence scores, a relationship may exist. This problem, interpreting results that show no difference or relationship with small samples, is subtle but very important in educational research since so many studies have small samples. As we will see in Chapter 10, it is possible to misinterpret what is reported as a "significant" difference or relationship with a very large sample. Also, a sample that is not properly drawn from the population is misleading, no matter what the size.

Participant Motivation

Sometimes subjects will be motivated to respond in certain ways. Clues for this phenomenon will be found in the description of how the participants were selected. For example, if a researcher was interested in studying the effectiveness of computer simulations in teaching science, one approach would be to interview teachers who used computer simulations. The researcher might even want to select only those science teachers who had used the simulations for more than two years. It is not difficult to understand that the selected teachers, because they had been using the simulations, would be motivated to respond favorably toward them. The response would be consistent with the teachers' decision to use simulations. Psychology students may be motivated to give inaccurate responses in studies conducted by their psychology professor if they do not like the professor, or they may respond more favorably if they want to help a professor they like.

Sampling Bias

Sampling bias: Sampling error caused by the researcher.

In selecting a sample from a population, there is always some degree of sampling error. This error (which is expected and precisely estimated as part of probability sampling) is the discrepancy between the true value of a variable for the population and the value that is calculated from the sample. A different type of error is due to **sampling bias,** a type of sampling error that is often controlled or influenced by the researcher to result in misleading findings. The most obvious deliberate bias is selecting only those subjects who will respond in a particular way to support a point or result. For instance, if a researcher is measuring the values of college students and wants to show that the students are concerned about helping others and being involved in community service, bias would result if the researcher deliberately selected students in education or social work and ignored majors that might not be so altruistically oriented. Selecting friends or colleagues may also result in a biased sample. An even more flagrant type of bias occurs when a researcher discards some subjects because they have not responded as planned or keeps adding subjects until the desired result is obtained. Sampling bias also occurs nondeliberately, often because of inadequate knowledge of what is required to obtain an unbiased sample and the motivation to "prove" a desired result or point of view. In qualitative studies the researcher needs to be particularly careful about possible unintended bias if sampling changes during the study.

Bias can also result from selecting subjects from different populations and assigning them to different groups for an experiment or comparison. Suppose a researcher used graduate sociology students to receive a treatment in an experiment and graduate psychology students as a control group. Even if the samples were selected randomly from each population, differences in the populations, and consequently samples, in attitudes, values, knowledge, and other variables could explain why certain results were obtained.

When conducting a survey, the investigator typically sends questionnaires to a sample of individuals and tabulates the responses of those who return them. Often the percentage of the sample returning the questionnaire will be 50% to 60% or even lower. In this circumstance the sample is said to be *biased* in that the results may not be representative of the population. Thus, the nature of the results depends on the types of persons who respond, and generalizability to the target population is compromised. The specific effect of a biased sample on the results depends on the nature of the study. For example, a study of the relationship between educational level and occupational success would be likely to show only a small relationship if only those who are most successful respond. Without some subjects who are not successful in the sample, success cannot be accurately related to level of education.

Response Variability

An important goal in sampling in a quantitative study is to obtain subjects who will represent adequate variability on the measures that are used. Sufficient variability is needed so that differences and relationships can be detected. Thus, if you wanted to find a relationship between types of counseling techniques used and student depression, the sample would need to be selected so that there is a sufficient number of counselors using each type of technique, as well as students who have different degrees of depression.

USING EDUCATIONAL RESEARCH

Sometimes sampling can make all the difference when using educational research for policy. David Berliner, a noted educational psychologist, has argued that states emphasizing high-stakes testing fail to show gains on other measures of student achievement, such as on the SAT. Chester E. Finn, Jr., president of the Thomas B. Fordham Foundation, points out that the SAT is not taken by all students and therefore is not a good external measure, especially if state accountability efforts are focused on low-achieving schools. So the story may depend, in part, on the sample of students taking the test.

CONSUMER TIPS: *Criteria for Evaluating Subjects Sections of Reports and Sampling Procedures*

1. The participants in the study should be clearly described, and the description should be specific and detailed. Demographic characteristics, such as age, gender, socioeconomic status, ability, and grade level, should be indicated, as well as any unique characteristics, for example, gifted students, students enrolled in a psychology class, or volunteers.

2. The population should be clearly defined. It is especially important that a specific definition of the population be provided in studies using probability sampling. Vague descriptions, such as "retired workers" or "high-ability students," are inadequate. The characteristics of each stratum in a stratified sampling procedure should also be included.

3. The method of sampling should be clearly described. The specific type of sampling procedure, such as simple random, stratified, cluster, or convenience, should be explicitly indicated in sufficient detail to enable other researchers to replicate the study.

4. The response rate for survey studies should be clearly indicated. In addition, it is helpful to indicate procedures used to keep the response rate high, as well as an analysis of how nonrespondents compare to those who did respond to determine possible bias. With a low response rate there is a need to directly address possible limitations.

5. The selection of participants should be free of bias. The procedures and criteria for selecting participants should not result in systematic error. Bias is more likely when a researcher is "proving" something to be true, with convenience samples, and when volunteers are used as subjects.

6. Selection procedures should be appropriate for the problem being investigated. If the problem is to investigate science attitudes of middle school students, it would be inappropriate to use high school students as subjects. If the problem is to study the characteristics of effective teaching, the work of student teachers would probably not be very representative of effective teaching behaviors.

7. There should be an adequate number of participants. If the sample is selected from a population, the sample size must be large enough to represent the population accurately. There must also be a sufficient number of participants in each subgroup that is analyzed. Studies with small samples that report no differences or no relationships should be viewed with caution since a higher number or a better selection of subjects may result in meaningful differences or relationships. Studies that have a very large number of participants may report "significant" differences or relationships that are of little practical utility.

8. Qualitative studies should have informative and knowledgeable participants. Since the purpose of qualitative research is to understand a phenomenon in depth, it is important to select subjects that will provide the richest information. The researcher should indicate the criteria used to select subjects, the reasons why these particular individuals were selected, and the strategies used for selecting subjects during the study.

9. Sampling in mixed-method studies needs to clearly indicate samples used for both phases of the study. While in many cases the same sample is used for both the quantitative and qualitative parts of a mixed-method study, when there are different samples for each method, these sampling procedures need to have complete descriptions.

Author Reflection *I have found that the quality of research depends heavily on the nature of the sampling. The sources of data are critical, whether some kind of random sample is selected, a volunteer sample is used, or some kind of criteria are used to select participants in a qualitative study. This is because the responses of individuals depend heavily on who they are and what they have done. I have also found that some quantitative studies ignore individual differences when searching for overall group effects, and some qualitative studies place too much reliance on one or just a few individuals.*

STUDY QUESTIONS

1. What is a sample and a population?
2. Why is it important to define the population as specifically as possible?
3. What is the difference between probability and nonprobability sampling?
4. When should a researcher use stratified random sampling?
5. How is cluster sampling different from stratified sampling?
6. Why should readers of research be cautious of studies that use a convenience sample?
7. What are some strengths and weaknesses of various types of sampling?
8. How can volunteer participants cause bias in a study?
9. Why is sample size an important consideration in research that fails to find a significant difference or relationship?
10. In what ways can sampling be biased?
11. Give an example of a study that used both stratified and systematic sampling.
12. What is the difference between a convenience and a purposive sample?
13. What criteria should be used in judging the adequacy of a subjects section in a report or sampling procedure?

Chapter 5

Foundations of Educational Measurement

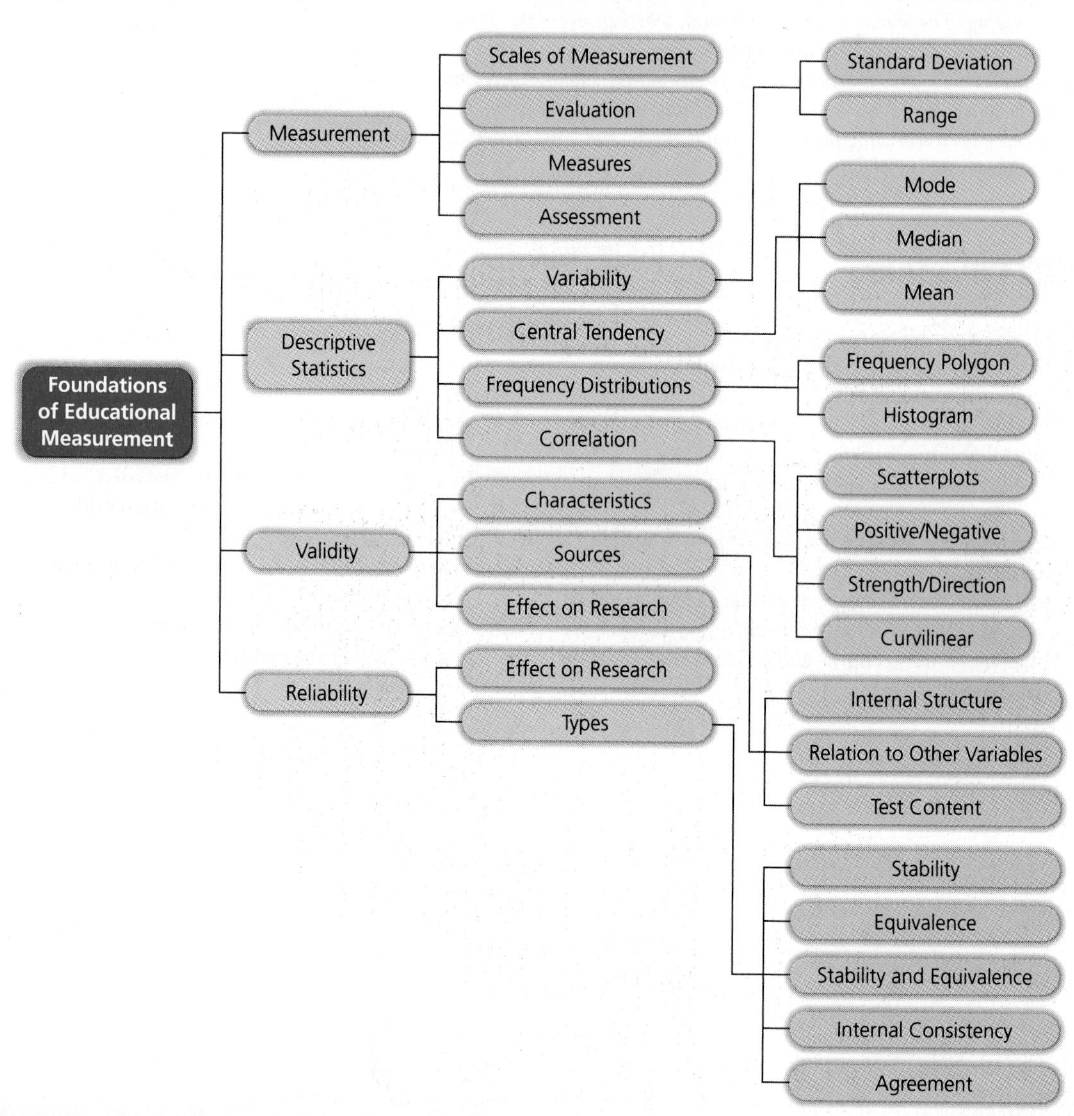

CHAPTER ROAD MAP

This is the first of two chapters that focus on gathering data primarily for quantitative and mixed-method research. Initially, we will review some fundamental principles of measurement and descriptive statistics, then look at validity and reliability as technical aspects that affect the quality of what is gathered.

Chapter Outline	Learning Objectives
Measurement	• Understand and differentiate between different scales of measurement. • Understand the differences between measurement, assessment, and evaluation.
Descriptive Statistics	
Frequency Distributions	• Understand different types of frequency distributions and how they are reported.
Measures of Central Tendency	• Understand the mean, median, and mode, and how these are used and reported.
Measures of Variability	• Understand principles of variability and why variability is important to research. • Understand standard deviation and how it is reported.
Correlation	• Understand and interpret scatterplots and correlation coefficients. • Distinguish between positive and negative correlations.
Test Validity	• Understand basic meaning of test validity and why this is important. • Identify different types of evidence for validity. • Understand how validity influences research results.
Test Reliability	• Understand the basic meaning of test reliability and why controlling error is important. • Identify different types of evidence for reliability and know when they should be used. • Understand how reliability influences research results.

INTRODUCTION *to* MEASUREMENT

What Is Measurement?

Measurement can be defined as the assignment of numbers to indicate different values of a variable; some researchers may also use it to refer to quantitative data collection. Measurement is used to determine how much of a trait, attribute, or characteristic an individual possesses. Numbers are used to describe and differentiate attributes or characteristics of a person, object, or event. **Measures** are specific techniques or instruments used for measurement and generally refer to quantitative devices. These are often tests and questionnaires that provide objective, quantifiable data. For example, a specific reading test may be used to provide measurement of reading ability.

Measurement: Assignment of numbers to differentiate values of a variable.

Measures: Instruments and techniques.

What Is Evaluation?

Evaluation: Decisions based on measurement.

Evaluation refers to procedures for collecting information and using the information to make decisions. In this sense evaluation uses the results of measurement in a particular way. Principles of measurement and specific instruments are part of evaluation, but other characteristics of research, such as sampling, design, and related literature, are also used to make decisions. For example, school districts routinely decide which textbooks will be adopted, a decision that may involve an evaluation of each potential textbook. Suppose teachers are surveyed for their opinions about the textbooks, and an instrument (the measure) is constructed to assess these opinions. This is measurement. The results of the survey are combined with other information, such as the cost of the textbooks, recommendations from a parent committee, and research on the effects of different modes of presenting information, to make decisions about the textbooks. The entire process is one of evaluation.

Evaluation is also used to compare performance with an objective or standard. In this sense student achievement may be evaluated by comparison to national norms or locally set standards of achievement (e.g., the dropout rate will be less than 4%; the number of high school students studying foreign languages will rise to 40%; the mean level of achievement of sixth-graders will be above the national mean). Other definitions of evaluation focus on professional judgment or a process in which a judgment is made about something. Such judgments may or may not involve measurement. The distinguishing aspect of evaluation is that data are interpreted and some kind of value is placed on the results.

What Is Assessment?

Assessment is a term that is used in a variety of ways. The shorter term, *assess*, is a synonym for measure. When researchers say they "assessed" something, they mean that they measured it. Sometimes *assessment* means "evaluation," and sometimes it refers to the more specific process of diagnosing of individual difficulties, such as assessing for learning disabilities. Some measurement specialists use assessment to refer to procedures used to obtain information about student performance. This is similar to how I have defined the term *measures*. In the context of classroom assessment, the term refers to the entire process of measurement, evaluation, and, finally, use of the information by teachers and students.

The Purpose of Measurement for Research

The purpose of measurement is to obtain information about the variables that are being studied. In education this includes variables such as intelligence, achievement, aptitude, classroom environment, attitudes, and values. Measurement is a critical component of quantitative research because it provides a systematic procedure for recording observations, performance, or other responses of subjects, and because it provides the basis for a quantitative summary of the results from many subjects. The information collected through measurement provides the basis for the results, conclusions, and significance of the research. Thus, if the measurement is not accurate and credible, the research is not credible. Simply put, good research must have sound measurement.

As noted in Chapter 2, there is a close relationship between the names and definitions of the variables being studied and the nature of their measurement. In practice, the variable is defined by how it is measured (operational definition), not by how it is labeled or given a constitutive definition by the researcher. This distinction is especially important for consumers of research who want to use the results. For example, if you were reading research on improving students' critical thinking, you would find that there are many ways to define and measure critical thinking. It would be important to read the instruments section of the research to determine the specific manner in which critical thinking was measured to see how well it matches the critical thinking you want to promote with your students. It would not be advisable to scan the results of various studies and employ the teaching methods that seem to be effective without examining the measures used to assess critical thinking.

Finally, measurement is a means by which we can differentiate different amounts of a trait. If a measure is correctly selected or developed, the results will show a good distribution of scores on the trait. Another way to think about this purpose is through the concept of variability, which is discussed later in this chapter. Essentially, measures need to provide sufficient variability, or spread, in the scores.

Scales of Measurement

Measurement requires that variables be differentiated. The nature of differentiation can vary, from a simple dichotomy, such as male/female, to more elaborate measures, such as aptitude tests. There are four basic ways that measures differ, depending on how much information is provided. These four categories are referred to as *scales of measurement.* Because the scales are arranged hierarchically on the basis of how much information is provided, they are often called levels of measurement. The scales are important for research because they help determine the nature of the measurement needed to answer research questions and help the researcher select the appropriate method of statistical analysis.

Nominal scale: Numbers assigned to categories.

The simplest scale of measurement is termed *nominal*, or *classificatory*. A **nominal scale** is one in which there are mutually exclusive categories, without any order implied. Mutually exclusive categories are those in which all observations assigned to the same category have a similar characteristic, and they differ on the basis of a specific characteristic from observations in other categories. Examples of nominal data in research are gender, race, type of school, and nature of community (e.g., rural, suburban, urban). Numbers are sometimes assigned arbitrarily to different categories for statistical purposes, without any value or order being placed on the categories. For example, male could be coded a "1" and female a "2." In fact, *nominal* means "to name," and in this sense the categories are named by different numbers.

In research the term *nominal* is also used to describe the nature of the data that are collected. Data are referred to as nominal if the researcher simply counts the number of instances, or frequency of observations, in each of two or more categories. Each of the following are examples: counting the number of male and female students; the number of fifth-, sixth-, and seventh-graders; the number of times a teacher uses different types of reinforcement; and the number of tenured and untenured teachers voting yes or no on a proposal to abolish tenure.

Ordinal scale: Numbers rank-ordered.

An **ordinal scale** is one in which the categories are rank-ordered. Each category can be compared to the others in terms of *less than* or *greater than*, but in an ordinal scale there is no indication of the magnitude of the differences. In other words, the categories are ordered but the degree of difference between the categories is not specified. A good example of an ordinal scale is the ranking of debate teams on their performance. The results show who is best, next best, and so forth, but not the magnitude of the difference between rankings, for instance, between first and second best. Ordinal scales are used extensively in educational research because many of the traits measured can be defined only in terms of order. Students are characterized as more mature, more serious, more ethical, more altruistic, more cooperative, more competitive, more creative, having greater ability, and so forth. Thus, the scores obtained from ordinal measurement can be interpreted to mean that one score is higher or lower than another, but the *degree of difference* between the scores is not known.

Interval scale: Equal intervals between numbers.

An **interval scale** is ordinal and has equal intervals between numbers. The characteristic of equal intervals allows us to compare directly one score to another in terms of the amount of difference. For instance, if John scores 90 on a test with an interval scale, June scores 80, and Tim scores 70, we know that the distance between Tim and John is twice the distance between John and June or between June and Tim. We also know that the distance between the scores of 50 and 60 is equal to the distance between 80 and 90.

Ratio scale: Numbers expressed as ratios.

A **ratio scale** is one in which ratios can be used in comparing and interpreting the scores. This use is possible if the trait being measured has a true zero point; that is, none of the trait is present. Height and weight are examples of ratio data because there is a true value for zero, which corresponds to no height or weight at all, and there are equal intervals between different heights and weights. We can say, for instance, that Fred, who weighs 150 pounds, is twice as heavy as Mary, who weighs 75 pounds. Few, if any, measures in educational research are ratio in nature.

Although identifying the scale of measurement of some variables is not always easy, it is important to distinguish between nominal and the other three levels. This is because the appropriateness of the statistical procedures depends on the scale of measurement for each variable. In fact, there are "assumptions" about the scale of measurement that must be met to calculate many statistical procedures. More about those in Chapter 9.

PRINCIPLES *of* DESCRIPTIVE STATISTICS *for* UNDERSTANDING MEASUREMENT

Since measurement involves the manipulation of numbers, basic principles of descriptive statistics are introduced now to help you understand subsequent principles of measurement presented in this chapter and in Chapter 6. We will also see that descriptive statistics, while relatively simple, are essential for understanding quantitative and mixed-method studies.

Statistics are mathematical procedures used to summarize and analyze data. In quantitative studies, the data are collected by the researchers, who apply statistical techniques to better understand the meaning of the numbers. In this sense, statistical procedures are applied after data collection to obtain the results of the study. **Descriptive statistics** transform a set of numbers into indices that summarize characteristics of a sample. Common descriptive statistics include the frequency of scores, percentages, mean, and standard deviation. These statistics communicate characteristics of the data as a whole and estimate the characteristics of the population. (The characteristics of a population are called *parameters* rather than statistics.)

Statistics: Procedures that summarize and analyze quantitative data.

Descriptive statistics: Summarizes a set of numbers.

Descriptive statistics also represent principles and are the basis for a vocabulary used in measurement. For instance, a *distribution* can be a statistical result from a study; it can also describe concepts related to measurement (e.g., "the distribution of scores from a norm-referenced test is normal").

TABLE 5.1 Example of a Frequency Table

Score	f	Score	f
28	2	21	1
27	3	20	2
26	3	19	3
25	4	18	3
24	3	17	1
23	3	16	3
22	3	15	2

Frequency Distributions

Suppose a researcher is interested in studying critical thinking with a class of eighth-graders. The researcher administers an instrument to measure critical thinking to 36 students and obtains the following scores, one for each student:

15 24 28 25 18 24 27 16 20 22 23 18
22 28 19 16 22 26 15 26 24 21 19 27
16 23 26 25 25 18 27 17 20 19 25 23

In this form it is difficult to understand how the students performed as a group or to have some idea of the number of students who obtained different scores. To understand the results, the researcher would first create a **frequency distribution,** which organizes ungrouped data by indicating the number of times (frequency) each score was obtained. The scores are typically rank-ordered from highest to lowest, and the frequency of each score is indicated. The simplest type of frequency distribution is a frequency table, in which the values of the scores and the frequencies are listed vertically. Table 5.1 shows a frequency table for the set of critical thinking scores above (*f* means frequency). Another way to present the frequencies is to construct a two-dimensional graph, in which the frequencies are indicated on the vertical dimension and the scores are indicated on the horizontal dimension. The number of students who obtained each score is then indicated in the graph. In this graphic form, the data can be presented as a *frequency polygon* or a *histogram.* A **frequency polygon,** illustrated in Figure 5.1 for the critical thinking scores, connects the observed frequencies with a line to show a picture of the distribution.

Frequency distribution: Indicates how often each score is obtained.

Frequency polygon: Graphic frequency distribution.

The shape of a distribution reveals some important characteristics of the scores: the most and least frequently occurring scores, whether the scores are bunched together or spread out, scores that may be isolated from the others, and

FIGURE 5.1 **Example of a frequency polygon.**

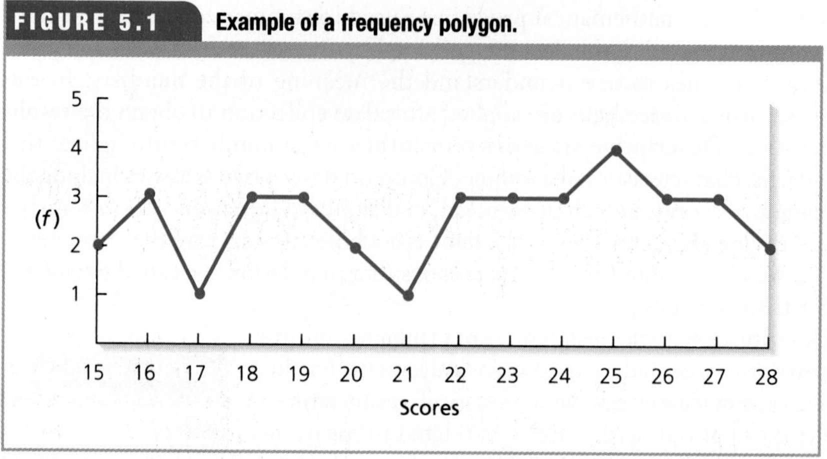

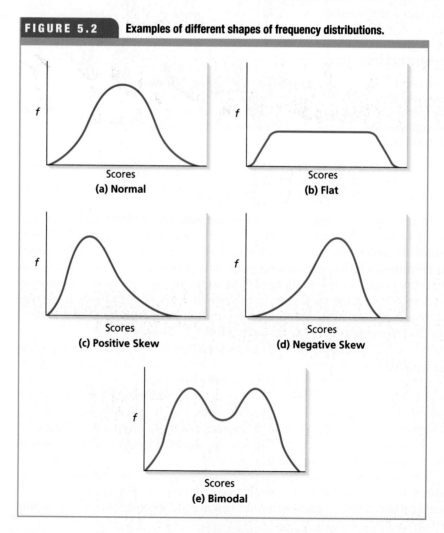

FIGURE 5.2 **Examples of different shapes of frequency distributions.**

f
Scores
(a) Normal

f
Scores
(b) Flat

f
Scores
(c) Positive Skew

f
Scores
(d) Negative Skew

f
Scores
(e) Bimodal

the general shape of the distribution. Figure 5.2 illustrates some common general shapes. The normal curve is perhaps most widely used. It is symmetrical and shaped like a cross-section of a bell. It tells us that the majority of scores tend to cluster around the middle, with the same number of scores above and below the middle point. Because the normal curve characterizes many naturally occurring phenomena and has standard properties, it is used extensively for research and statistical procedures. In a flat, or rectangular curve, the scores are widely spread out from the middle. Distributions that concentrate scores at the high or low end of the distribution are called *skewed*. In a **positively skewed** distribution, the scores are concentrated at the low end of the distribution; in a **negatively skewed** distribution, the majority of the scores are at the high end of the distribution. Actually, it is the mean that is either positively or negatively skewed, that is, either more positive or more negative than what is obtained with a normal curve.

Positively skewed: Large number of low scores; few very high scores.

Negatively skewed: Large number of high scores; few very low scores.

For example, in a study of administrators' salaries, the distribution would be positively skewed if most of the salaries were relatively low and a few of the salaries were very high. Negatively skewed distributions are common in mastery testing, where, typically, most of the students score high and a few students score low. Bimodal distributions are those that have two modes, as discussed below.

Frequency distributions are also important in identifying unusually high or low scores. Such scores, if they are very different from others, are *outliers*. **Outlier scores** are so atypical that their inclusion would distort the findings. Whenever researchers use quantitative data, they must look carefully for outliers and decide how to handle them. Sometimes outliers are bad data, perhaps because of a data entry error; sometimes they represent inaccurate responses. In both these cases it would be best to delete these scores. In Example 5.1, outlier scores were eliminated based on a specified set criterion.

Outlier scores: Scores that are very high or low in comparison to others.

EXAMPLE 5.1 | Outlier Scores

Preliminary analysis revealed five univariate outliers with *z* scores in excess of 3.20 (which Tabachnick & Fidell, 1996, indicates is a suitable threshold), and these cases were excluded from further analysis.

Source: Nussbaum, E. M., & Kardash, C. M. (2005). The effects of goal instructions and text on the generation of counterarguments during writing. *Journal of Educational Psychology, 97* (2), 160.

Author Reflection *There was a time when I thought that you had to include all your obtained scores, that ethically it was expected. I've learned that what you really want are accurate data. So, you should never include bad data in a study! Outliers are indicators of possible bad data, as are specific patterns of subject responses. Look and check data carefully. Bad data make for bad results and bad conclusions.*

FIGURE 5.3 Histogram of critical thinking scores.

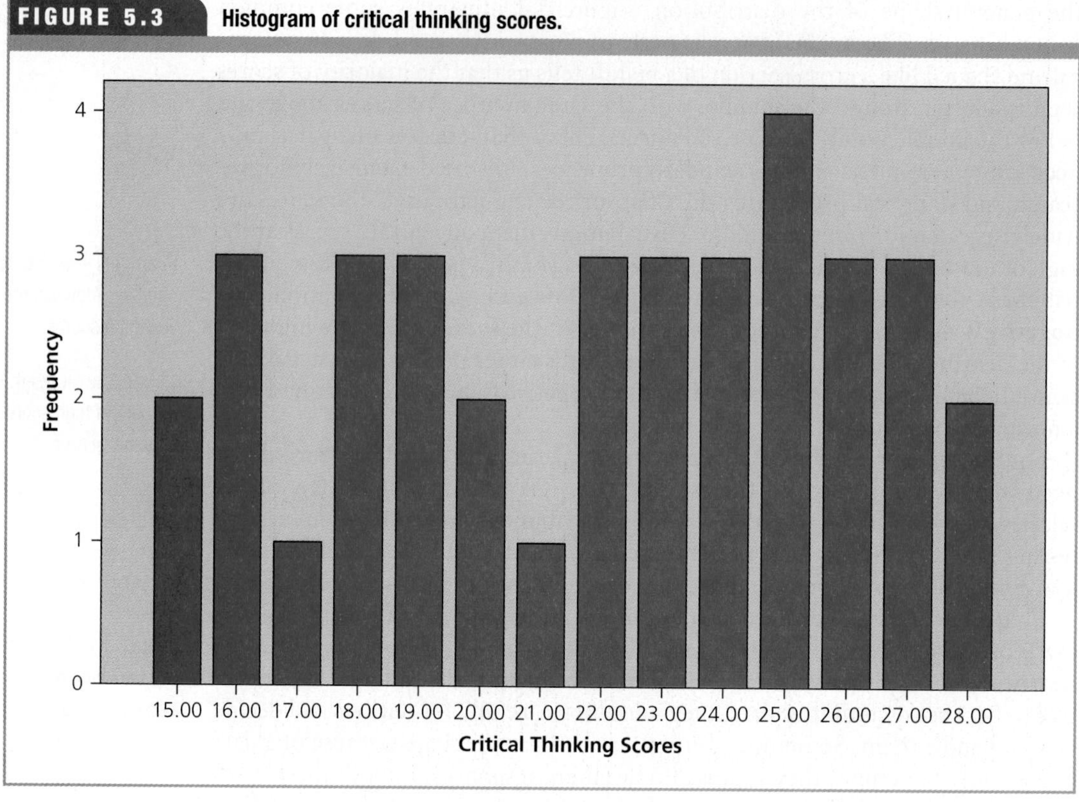

Histograms and Bar Charts

Histogram: Graph showing the number of scores.

Bar chart: Graph showing the number of cases.

Frequency data are often presented graphically in what are called *histograms* or *bar charts*. A **histogram** is a two-dimensional graph that uses vertical columns to show the frequency of each score (or score intervals). This is illustrated with our critical thinking data in Figure 5.3. A **bar chart** or graph also uses columns, but the ordering of the columns is arbitrary (i.e., nominal data). An example of this type of display of data would be to show how students at private colleges differ in their loan amounts to attend higher education compared to students in public colleges. Be warned, though, some researchers may use the terms *histograms* and *bar charts* interchangeably.

Measures of Central Tendency

Although it is useful to know the pattern of the scores as indicated by the frequency distribution, it is also important to be able to use a single score to characterize the set of scores. Measures of central tendency provide statistics that indicate the average or typical score in the distribution. There are three most commonly used measures of central tendency: mode, median, and mean.

Mode. The **mode** is simply the score in the distribution that occurs most frequently. It is a crude index of central tendency and is seldom used in research. Sometimes distributions have more than one most frequent score. Such distributions are bimodal, trimodal, or multimodal. These terms also describe a distribution that may technically have only one mode; for example, two scores in different parts of the distribution clearly occur more frequently than the rest in a bimodal distribution. There is no mode in distributions in which each score occurs the same number of times.

Mode: Score that occurs most frequently.

Median. The **median** is the middle score of the distribution, the point that divides a rank-ordered distribution into halves containing an equal number of scores. Thus, 50% of the scores lie below the median and 50% lie above the median. The median is unaffected by the values of the scores. This characteristic is an advantage when the distribution contains atypically large or small scores, such as measures of "average" income and the "average" cost of a new house. The median is symbolized by *Mdn* or *Md.*

Median: Score in the middle of the distribution.

In some studies the median score is used to split groups into two classifications or subgroups. In the following example, graduate students were divided into two groups based on an instrument that measured test anxiety.

EXAMPLE 5.2 | Median-Split Technique

The 61 students were allowed 10 minutes to complete the TAI (Spielberger, 1980) to assess their propensity toward test anxiety. TAI scores ranged from 28.0 to 49.0 with a median of 39.0 and a mean of 39.16. Using a median split, participants classified as high (i.e., above 39.0) or low (i.e., below 39.0) in text anxiety were assigned to either a high or low threat of evaluation section of the course.

Source: Hancock, D. R. (2001). Effects of test anxiety and evaluative threat on students' achievement and motivation. *The Journal of Educational Research, 94,* 286.

Mean. The **mean** is the arithmetic average of all the scores in the distribution. It is calculated by adding all the scores in the distribution and then dividing this sum by the number of scores. For example, if a distribution contains the scores 5, 7, 8, 10, 10, 12, 14, 15, 15, 17, the mean would be 11.3 ($5 + 7 + 8 + 10 + 10 + 12 + 14 + 15 + 15 + 17 = 113$; $113/10 = 11.3$). or for the distribution of critical thinking scores in Table 5.1, the mean is 21.92 (789/36). The mean is used extensively in research, usually symbolized by $\overline{x}$, or M for the sample mean and μ for the mean of the population. The mean may be misleading as a typical score in skewed distributions that contain extremely high or low scores because it is pulled toward the extreme scores. Thus, in a positively skewed distribution, such as personal income, the mean income is higher than the most typical income because some very high incomes are used in the calculation. In this case

Mean: Arithmetic average of all scores.

the median income is more typical. Conversely, in a negatively skewed distribution, the mean is lower than the median.

The mean is used extensively in reporting quantitative and mixed-method studies. An example that shows the use of both means and medians in describing characteristics of a sample is illustrated in Example 5.3.

EXAMPLE 5.3 | Use of Means and Medians

The mean age of participants was 42.4 years (SD = 11.0, Mdn = 41). . .the average student population was 1,209 (SD = 753.4, Mdn = 1,000), and the average number of school counselors employed in a school was 3.03 (SD = 1.94, Mdn = 3).

Source: Mason, E. C., & McMahom, H. G. (2009). Leadership practices of school counselors. *Professional School Counseling*, 13(2), 110.

Measures of Variability

Although a measure of central tendency is an excellent statistic of the most typical score in a distribution, to obtain a full description of the scores, we also need to know something about how they tend to cluster around the mean or median. Measures of variability show how spread out the distribution of scores is from the mean, or how much dispersion or scatter exists in the distribution. If there is a large degree of dispersion, that is, if the scores are very dissimilar, we say the distribution has a large or high variability, or variance. If the scores are very similar, there is a small degree of dispersion and a small variance.

The need for a measure of dispersion to describe a distribution is illustrated by comparing the different types of distributions in Figure 5.4. Distributions A

FIGURE 5.4 **Distributions with the same mean but different variability.**

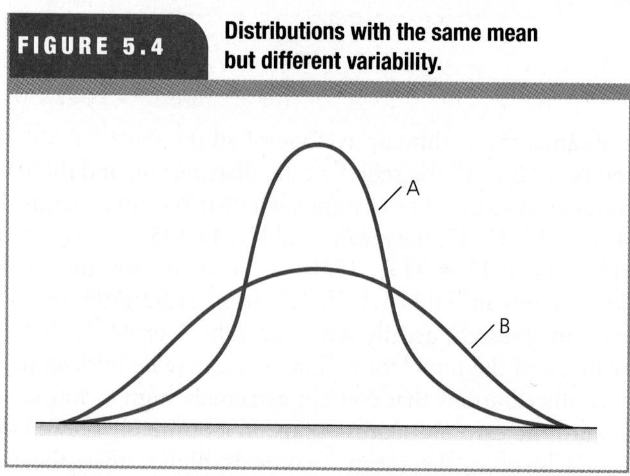

and B would have the same mean but represent different distributions. It is necessary to add a measure of variability to the mean to provide a more complete description. We will discuss two measures of variability, the range and the standard deviation, which provide more specific statistics than such general terms as *small*, *large*, *great*, or *little*.

Range. The **range** is simply the numerical difference between the highest and lowest scores in the distribution. It is calculated by subtracting the lowest score from the highest score. The range is a crude measure of dispersion because it is based on only two scores in the distribution, and it does not tell us anything about the degree of cluster. The range is particularly misleading in highly skewed distributions.

Range: Difference between the highest and lowest scores.

Standard Deviation. The measure of variability used most often in research is the **standard deviation,** a statistic that indicates the average distance of the scores from the mean of the distribution. It tells us, in other words, the "average" variability of the scores. It is determined by first calculating the distance of each score from the mean. These are the *deviation* scores, which tell us how much each score deviates, or differs, from the mean. Then the deviation scores are averaged to determine a number that is called the standard deviation. In one sense, then, the standard deviation can be thought of as the *"average" deviation.*

Standard deviation: Average distance of the scores from the mean.

For any set of scores, the standard deviation will be unique to the distribution of the scores. Thus, the standard deviation of one distribution may be .72; for another distribution, 16; and for yet another, 35. Once the standard deviation is computed, it is reported by indicating that 1 standard deviation equals a number; for example, 1 *SD* = 12.7, or 1 *SD* = 3.25. (Two other symbols are also used for standard deviation: *s*, which indicates the sample standard deviation, and the lowercase Greek letter sigma, σ, which indicates the population standard deviation.)

The standard deviation is particularly useful because of its relationship to the normal distribution. In a normal distribution, a specific percentage of scores falls within each standard deviation from the mean. For example, if the mean of a distribution is 40 and the standard deviation is 10, we know that about 34% of the scores of the distribution fall between 40 and 50. Similarly, we know that about 34% of the scores fall between 30 and 40. Thus, in normal distributions, regardless of the values of the scores, we know that about 68% of the scores fall between −1 and +1 *SD* (see Figure 5.5). Furthermore, we know that about 14% of the scores fall between +1 and +2 *SD* and between −1 and −2 *SD*, and that about 2% of the scores fall between +2 and +3 *SD* and between −2 and −3 *SD*. These properties of the normal curve and standard deviation, illustrated in Figure 5.5, allow researchers to compare distributions by knowing the standard deviations. Two distributions may have similar means, but if one has a standard deviation of 36 and the other 8, the former is far more variable. The square of the standard deviation is called the *variance*, though this term is also used more generally to mean dispersion or spread of scores.

FIGURE 5.5 Normal probability curve.

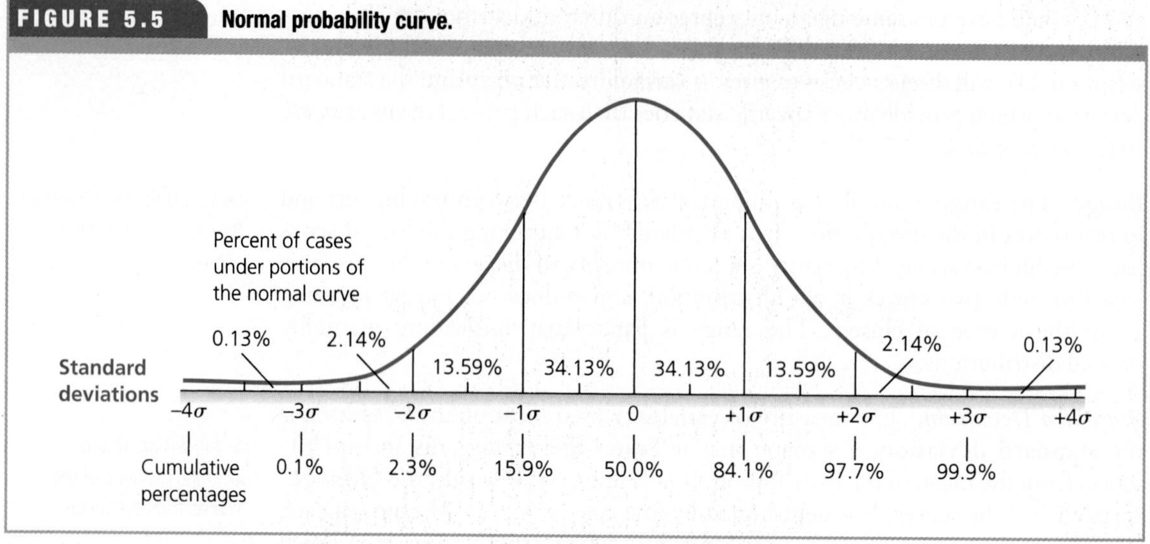

Percentile rank: Percentage of scores at or below a specified score.

Standard deviation is related to another important term in measurement, *percentile rank*. The **percentile rank** indicates the percentage of scores at or below a particular score. For example, if 17 is at the 64th percentile, 64% of the scores in the distribution are the same or lower than 17. In a normal distribution, a score at +1 *SD* is at the 84th percentile. In other words, 84% of the scores in a normal distribution are at or below +1 *SD*. Similarly, −1 *SD* is at the 16th percentile, +2*SD* is at the 98th percentile, and −2 *SD* is at the 2nd percentile (percentiles for the normal curve are indicated as cumulative percentages in Figure 5.5).

Correlation

Correlation: Measure of relationship between two or more quantitative variables.

Positive correlation: Increases in one variable accompanied by increases in the other variable.

A **correlation** is a measure of the relationship between two variables. A relationship means that the values of the variables vary together, that is, the value of one variable can be predicted by knowing the value of the other. For example, we would expect that there is a relationship between age and weight, that by knowing a person's age we can predict, in general, the person's weight. Thus, we can predict that most 10-year-olds weigh more than most 3-year-olds. In this case we have a **positive correlation,** in which an increase in one variable is accompanied by an increase in the other variable. This is also called a *direct* relationship. A positive correlation is illustrated graphically in the form of a *scatterplot* for age and weight in Figure 5.6. The values of each variable are rank-ordered, and the intersections of the two scores for each subject are plotted in the graph (see Figure 5.7). Scatterplots are useful in identifying scores that lie outside the overall pattern, such as point I in Figure 5.6, and indicate whether the relationship is linear or curvilinear. Correlation is indicated numerically by the correlation coefficient.

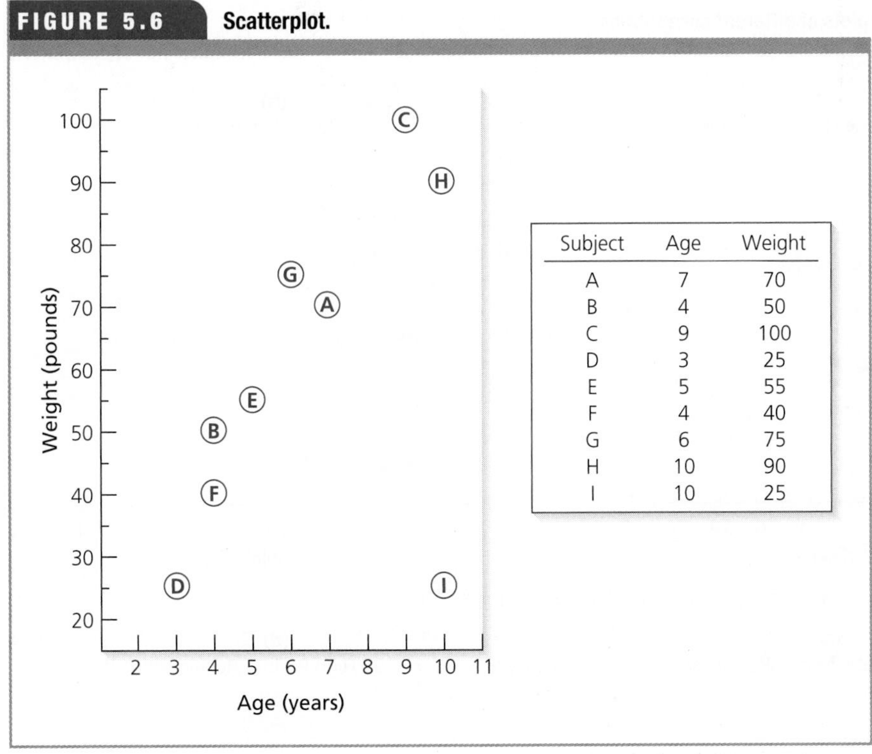

Subject	Age	Weight
A	7	70
B	4	50
C	9	100
D	3	25
E	5	55
F	4	40
G	6	75
H	10	90
I	10	25

FIGURE 5.6 Scatterplot.

Although there are several types of correlation coefficients, the one you will encounter most is the Pearson product moment coefficient. This type of correlation assumes a linear relationship between two interval or ordinal scale variables. Thus, if a scatterplot reveals that the correlation is curvilinear and the Pearson correlation coefficient is used, the calculated correlation will be less than the true relationship because of the assumption of linearity.

Correlation coefficient: Number between –1 and +1 that indicates the direction and strength of the relationship.

A **correlation coefficient,** or *bivariate* correlation, is a number between -1 and $+1$ that indicates the direction and strength of the relationship between two variables. The correlation coefficient is calculated by a formula and is reported as $r = .45$, $r = -.78$, $r = .03$, and so on. A positive correlation coefficient will have a positive value; for example, $r = .17$ or $r = .69$. The strength, or magnitude, of the relationship is the degree to which the variables are related. For a positive correlation the strength increases as the number increases. Hence, a correlation of .85 is stronger than a correlation of .53, which is stronger than .37. In general, correlations between .10 and .30 are referred to as small or low positive relationships, .40 to .60 as moderate positive relationships, and .70 and above as high positive relationships.

Negative correlation: Increases in one variable accompanied by decreases in the other variable.

A **negative correlation** indicates that as one variable increases, the other variable decreases. This is also referred to as an *inverse* relationship. Examples of negative correlations include the relationship between absenteeism and

FIGURE 5.7 Scatterplots of different correlations.

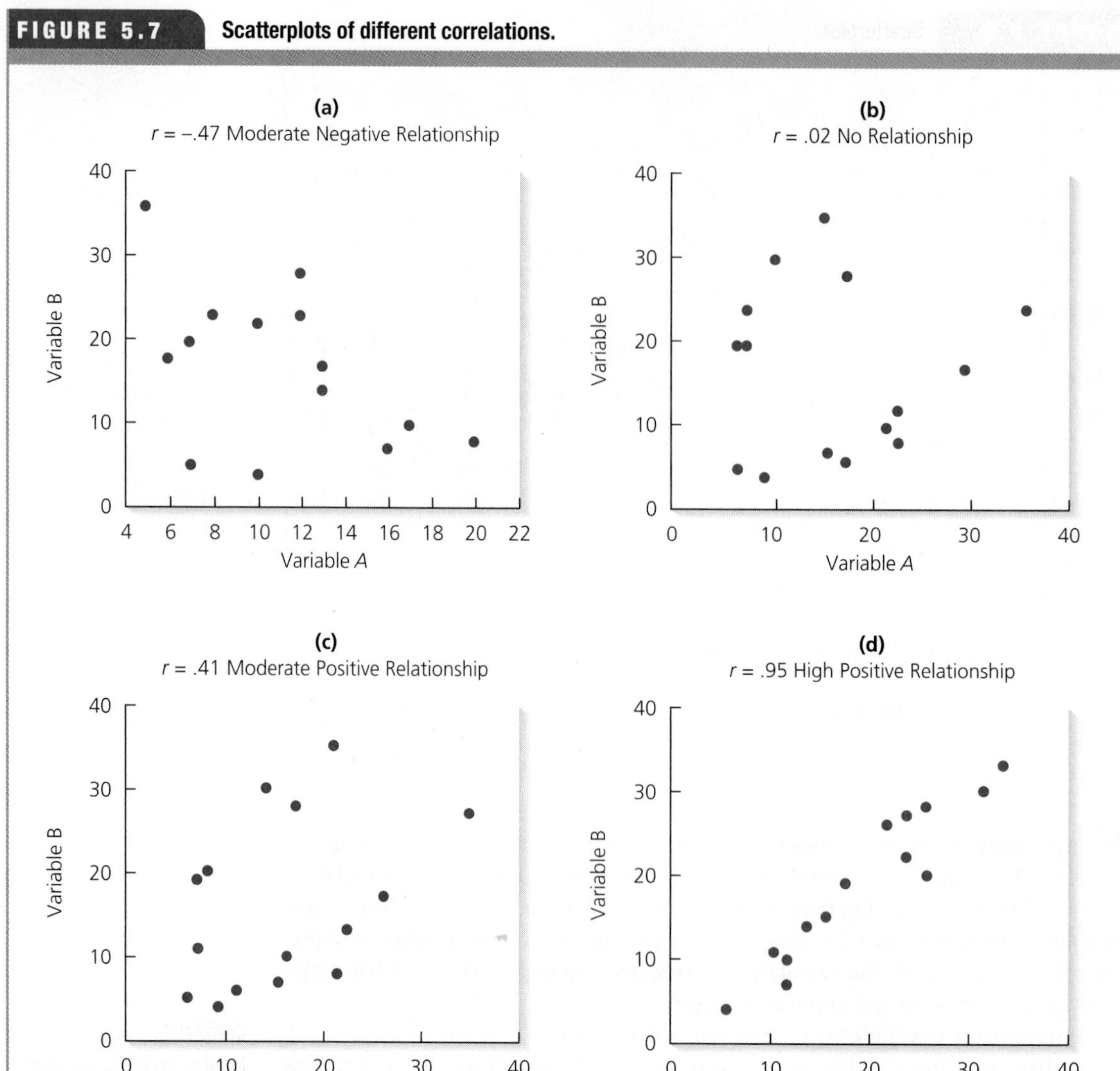

achievement and between amount of practice and number of errors in tennis. A negative correlation coefficient always has a negative sign (–). The strength of a negative relationship increases as the absolute value of the correlation increases. Thus, a correlation of −.75 is a stronger relationship than −.52. In other words, the strength of any relationship is independent of its direction. A correlation of −.63 indicates a stronger relationship than .35. Correlations between −.10 and

−.30 are considered small; between −.40 and −.60, moderate; and between −.70 and −1.0, high. Correlations between −.10 and .10 generally indicate no relationship.

Author Reflection *The more I learn about statistics the more I realize that simple descriptive indices such as mean and standard deviation are really important in understanding what numerical data tell us about something. These simple statistics not only form the foundation for other statistical procedures, they also give us the best direct measure. They are essential for appropriate interpretations.*

Review and Reflection *Now that we have covered basic descriptive statistics, it is helpful to consider them together in examples of datasets. Make a dataset that has 20 more or less random numbers between 1 and 10. Use that dataset to calculate the mean and median; prepare a frequency distribution and histogram. Estimate the variance of the scores by looking at the average deviation scores. Add a second set of random numbers for each member of your "sample" and show a scatterplot of the correlation.*

MEASUREMENT VALIDITY

It has been noted that the credibility of research depends on quality measurement. If the measurement is not sound, the results are not useful. In this section, we will discuss the first of two technical characteristics of measurement used to judge overall quality and appropriateness—validity. The second important characteristic, reliability, will be discussed in the next section.

What Is Validity?

Until recently, validity was defined as the degree to which an instrument measures what it says it measures or purports to measure. The emphasis was on judging the extent to which a test or questionnaire was valid. A more contemporary definition emphasizes the use of test results rather than the test itself: **Validity** is an overall evaluation of the extent to which theory and empirical evidence support interpretations that are implied in given uses of the scores. In other words, validity is a judgment of the appropriateness of a measure for the specific inferences or decisions that result from the scores generated by the measure. It is the *inference* that is valid or invalid, not the measure. The same instrument can be valid in one circumstance or for one use and invalid for another. For example, tests of beginning teacher competency may be valid for judging how much a prospective teacher knows and understands about classroom management, child development, learning, motivation, and curriculum, but it may be invalid as a predictor of teaching effectiveness. Similarly, most standardized achievement tests are not valid for evaluating the effectiveness of a specific curriculum in a specific school because the test was constructed to measure a broad range of curricula, not a specific one. Important characteristics of validity are summarized in Table 5.2.

Validity: The extent to which inferences are appropriate and meaningful.

TABLE 5.2 Characteristics of Validity

1. Validity refers to the *appropriateness* of the interpretation of the results, not to the procedure or measure itself. Saying "the validity of the test" is not as correct as saying "the validity of the inference."
2. Validity is a *matter of degree;* it does not exist on an all-or-none basis.
3. Validity is *specific* to some particular use or interpretation. No measure is valid for all uses or purposes. Each interpretation may have a different degree of validity.
4. Validity is a *unitary concept.* It is a single concept that is based on accumulating and integrating different types of evidence. There are not different types of validity.
5. Validity involves *an overall evaluative judgment.* Your professional judgment, given the evidence presented and the nature of the interpretation, is needed to determine the extent to which the inference is valid.

Source: Adapted from Miller, Linn, & Gronlund (2008).

Sources of Validity Evidence

Validity is established by presenting evidence that the inferences are appropriate. There are five major sources of evidence, each based on a different kind of logic and data: test content, internal structure, relations to other variables, response processes, and consequences of testing. Each source represents a different type of evidence. Under ideal conditions the nature of evidence used is consistent with the use of the results to provide support for the intended interpretation of the scores. Establishing sound validity involves an integration of information from these different types of evidence to show that the intended interpretation of the scores is appropriate and reasonable. We will consider the first three types of evidence since they are most closely related to conducting and reporting research.

Evidence based on test content: Representative sample of larger domain.

Evidence Based on Test Content. In general, **evidence based on test content** demonstrates the extent to which the sample of items or questions in the instrument is representative of some appropriate universe or domain of content or tasks. This type of evidence is usually accumulated by having experts examine the contents of the instrument and indicate the degree to which they measure predetermined criteria or objectives. Experts are also used to judge the relative criticality, or importance, of various parts of the instrument. For example, to gather evidence for a test of knowledge for prospective teachers, it is necessary to have experts examine the items and judge their representativeness (e.g., is a question about Piaget representative of what needs to be known about child development?) and whether the percentage of the test devoted to different topics is appropriate (e.g., 20% of the test is on classroom management, but maybe it should be 40%). Evidence based on test content is essential for achievement tests. Also, the domain or universe that is represented should be appropriate to the intended use of the results.

Unfortunately, evidence based on test content for validity is often not reported in research articles, usually because there is no systematic effort to obtain such evidence for locally devised instruments; when standardized instruments are used, the reader must refer to previous research, reviews of the instrument, or technical manuals.

EXAMPLES 5.4–5.6 | Content-Related Evidence for Validity

Content-related evidence for validity for the initial draft of 47 items was strengthened by asking 15 teachers to review the items for clarity and completeness of covering most, if not all, assessment and grading practices used.

Source: McMillan, J. H. (2001). Secondary teachers' classroom assessment and grading practices. *Educational Measurement: Issues and Practice, 20*(1), 23.

This assessment was reviewed by several experts in the field of early literacy to ensure that the content was accurate and research based. Each community-college instructor reviewed the assessment for content validity and alignment with the course syllabus. On the basis of their comments, revisions were made. . . . Results from this pilot were analyzed using item analysis to identify the best items for further analysis and inclusion in the assessment of teacher knowledge.

Source: Neuman, S. B., & Cunningham, L. (2009). The impact of professional development and coaching on early language and literacy instructional practices. *American Educational Research Journal,* 46(2), 544–545.

To support content validity, experts familiar with the purpose of the questionnaire examined the items and judged the extent to which they were adequate and representative for measuring relationships with supervising teachers. We included no items with less than 100 percent agreement from these individuals.

Source: Spooner, M., Flowers, C., Lambert, R., & Algozzine, B. (2008). Is more really better? Examining perceived benefits of an extended student teaching experience. *The Clearing House* 81(6), 265.

Evidence Based on Internal Structure. The *internal structure* of an instrument refers to how items are related to each other and how different parts of an instrument are related. **Evidence based on internal structure** is provided when the relationships between items and parts of the instrument are empirically consistent with the theory or intended use of the scores. Thus, if a measure of self-concept posits several "types" of self-concept (e.g., academic, social, athletic), then the items measuring the academic component should be strongly related to each other and not as highly related to the other components. In Example 5.7, the authors summarize data that support the internal structure of students' domain-specific (history and mathematics) epistemological beliefs (i.e.,

Evidence based on internal structure: Showing item relationships.

importance and certainty of knowledge). Data supported six distinct factors, and results were analyzed using these subscales.

EXAMPLE 5.7 | Evidence Based on Internal Structure

Confirmatory factor analyses of these data provided support for the domain specificity and multidimensionality of students' beliefs. . . . There were six distinct epistemological belief factors (three per domain) that represented students' beliefs with respect to the structure, stability, and source of knowledge of history and of mathematics.

Source: Buehl, M. M., & Alexander, P. A. (2005). Motivation and performance differences in students' domain-specific epistemological belief profiles. *American Educational Research Journal, 42*(4), 705.

Evidence Based on Relations to Other Variables. The most common way that validity of interpretations is established is by showing how scores from a given measure relate to similar as well as different traits. There are several ways this can be done. When scores from one instrument correlate highly with scores from another measure of the same trait, we have what is called *convergent* evidence. Convergent data are used as evidence of "construct validity," a term you may encounter in reading research. The term *construct validity* was used prior to the current categories of validity evidence. For example, scores from the Test of Early Reading Ability could be correlated to another measure of reading ability.

Discriminant evidence exists when the scores do not correlate highly with scores from an instrument that measures something different. Thus, we would expect that scores from a measure of self-concept would correlate highly with other measures of self-concept and show less correlation to related but different traits such as anxiety and academic performance.

Evidence based on relations to other variables: Showing relationships to external variables.

Another approach to gathering **evidence based on relations to other variables** pertains to the extent to which the test scores or measures predict performance on a criterion measure (test-criterion relationships). Two approaches are used to obtain test-criterion evidence: predictive and concurrent. With predictive evidence, the criterion is measured at a time in the future, after the instrument has been administered. The evidence pertains to how well the earlier measure can predict the criterion behavior or performance. For instance, in gathering evidence on a new measure to select applicants for leadership positions, the scores on the instrument would be correlated with future leadership behavior. If persons who scored low on the test turned out to be poor leaders and those who scored high were good leaders, predictive test-criterion evidence would be obtained. For example, in the following example from a published study on the mediating role of self-efficacy in the relationship between homework practices and achievement (Example 5.8), the authors correlated student self-reports of self-efficacy with teacher ratings of self-regulation gathered several weeks after the student self-reports.

EXAMPLE 5.8 | **Predictive Evidence Based on Relations to Other Variables**

To assess the predictive validity of the SELF [Self-Efficacy for Learning Form] . . . the English teacher for each grade level . . . was asked to rate each student's self-regulation of learning by a 12-point scale. . . . The teacher ratings were recorded at a later point during the semester after homework and self-belief measures were administered. . . . . The correlation between this teacher rating measure of self-regulation and the student self-efficacy for learning measure was .72, indicating a significant degree of predictive validity for the self-efficacy scale.

Source: Zimmerman, B. J., & Kitsantas, A. (2005). Homework practices and academic achievement: The mediating role of self-efficacy and perceived responsibility beliefs. *Contemporary Educational Psychology, 30*(4), 404.

Concurrent criterion-related evidence is established by correlating two measures of the same trait at about the same time. This type of evidence is illustrated in Example 5.9.

EXAMPLE 5.9 | **Concurrent Evidence Based on Relations to Other Variables**

The criterion-related or more specifically the concurrent validity of the UGAS and its three subscales was assessed by correlating them with the FSMAS and three of its subscales. A strong positive correlation ($r = .702$, $p < .001$) was found between the UGAS and the FSMAS. In addition, strong positive correlations were found on the corresponding confidence subscales ($r = .651$, $p < .001$), on the corresponding usefulness subscales ($r = .670$, $p < .001$), and between the enjoyment scale of the UGAS and the effectance motivation scale of the FSMAS ($r = .658$, $p < .001$).

Source: Utley, J. (2007). Construction and validity of geometry attitude scales. *School Science and Mathematics, 107*(3), 93.

Often researchers use several types of evidence for validity, which provides a stronger result than what is indicated with a single approach. Note how this is illustrated in the following study of resourcefulness and persistence in adult autonomous learning (Example 5.10).

EXAMPLE 5.10 | **Use of Several Types of Evidence for Validity**

Carr and Derrick's respective arguments supporting the validity of their respective instruments were based on the development of items with specific theoretical foundations (i.e., construct validity), a review by researchers whose work was pivotal to the development of these theories (i.e., face validity), and the results of principal components analyses performed to support the factor structure of each subscale (i.e., content validity).

Source: Ponton, M. K., Derrick, M. G., & Carr, P. B. (2005). The relationship between resourcefulness and persistence in adult autonomous learning. *Adult Education Quarterly, 55*(2), 119.

Effect of Validity on Research

Since validity implies proper use of the information that is gathered through measurement, it is necessary for both the investigators and consumers of the research to judge the degree of validity that is present, based on available evidence. In this sense, validity is a matter of degree and is not an all-or-none proposition. The investigators need to show that for the specific inferences they made in their study, there is evidence that validity exists. Consumers, however, may have their own uses in mind, and therefore need to base their own judgments on how they intend to use the results.

Does this suggest that evidence for validity must be established for each research situation and possible use? Such a requirement would add a considerable amount of data collection and analysis to each study. In practice, it is necessary to generalize from other studies and research that the intended interpretation and use are valid. This is one reason why established instruments, for which some evidence on validity has probably accumulated, usually provide more credible measurement. Some researchers mistakenly believe, however, that because an instrument is established, it is valid.

Locally devised instruments, with little or no history of use or reviews by others, need to be evaluated with more care. Typically, when researchers use new instruments, greater attention is paid to gathering evidence for validity, and this evidence is reported as part of the research. Consumers should be especially wary of research in which new instruments are used and evidence for validity is not presented. If an instrument has specific procedures for administration—for example, qualifications of the person who administers it, directions, and time frame—the results are valid only if these procedures have been followed. For instance, some instruments are appropriate for certain ages, but use with other ages would be invalid.

Validity should be established before the data to be analyzed in the research are collected. This is a major reason for a pilot test of the instrument and procedures for administering it. The evidence should be consistent with the use of the results. For example, if the results will be used to determine which students have mastered a body of knowledge, evidence based on test content is necessary. If a theory related to the development of cognitive style is being examined, evidence based on relations with other variables is needed.

Although validity is a key concept in research, you will find a great deal of variability in the amount of information given in articles and research reports. It is not uncommon to find that there is no mention of validity. However, the most credible and usable research is reported by investigators who understand the importance of validity, and explicitly address it.

MEASUREMENT RELIABILITY

An essential concept in understanding research is knowing that there is never a perfect indication of the trait, skill, knowledge, attitude, or whatever is being assessed. There is always error in measurement, and this error must be taken into consideration. It is not a question of whether error exists, only what type and how much. **Reliability** is the extent to which participant and/or rater scores are free from error. If a measure has high reliability, there is relatively little error in the scores, and if there is low reliability, there is a great amount of error.

Reliability: Consistency of scores.

Many factors contribute to the imperfect nature of measurement. Questions may be ambiguous, or students may not be trying hard, may be fatigued or sick, may be unfamiliar with the types of questions asked, or may simply guess incorrectly on many items. Sources of measurement error are listed in Table 5.3. Whatever the reasons, students will answer somewhat differently on one occasion than on another or on questions designed to measure the same thing. If possible, the researcher needs to indicate in specific, quantifiable terms the degree of error that exists.

Types of Reliability Estimates

An estimate of the amount of error in measurement is determined empirically through several types of procedures. As with validity, different types of evidence are used to indicate the error. These are called estimates of reliability. Each estimate measures certain kinds of errors. The estimates are reported in the form of a reliability coefficient, which is a correlation statistic that ranges between .00 and .99. If the correlation coefficient is high, say, .78 or .85, the reliability is said to be high or good. Correlation coefficients below .60 generally indicate inadequate or at least weak reliability.

Like validity, reliability is not a characteristic of a test or other instrument. Rather than saying "the reliability of the instrument was adequate," it would be more accurate to say, "the reliability of the scores was adequate."

TABLE 5.3 Sources of Measurement Error

Sources Associated with Test Construction and Administration	Sources Associated with the Subject
Observer differences	Test anxiety
Changes in scoring	Reactions to specific items
Changes in directions	Illness
Interrupted testing session	Motivation
Race of test administrator	Mood
When the test is taken	Fatigue
Sampling of items	Luck
Ambiguity in wording	Attitudes
Misunderstood directions	Test-taking skills (test wiseness)
Effect of heat, lighting, ventilation of room	Reading ability

We will consider five specific estimates of reliability: stability, equivalence, equivalence and stability, internal consistency, and agreement.

Stability: Measured by giving the same instrument twice.

Stability. A **stability** estimate of reliability is obtained by administering one measure to one group of individuals, waiting a specified period of time, and then readministering the same instrument to the same group. The correlation of the two sets of scores is then calculated. This type of estimate is also called *test-retest* reliability. What is being measured is the consistency of the subjects' performance over time. If the trait or skill that is being measured changes between the first and second administration, the correlation, and the reliability, will be low. Consequently, stability estimates should not be used with unstable traits such as mood, and when it is used, any changes that may have occurred between the administrations should be noted. The value of the correlation will also vary with the length of time between administrations. Other things being equal, a longer time interval will result in a lower correlation. It is therefore best to report the time interval with the correlation coefficient. On the other hand, if the interval is too short, subjects may remember their answers and simply reproduce them, making the reliability higher than it should be.

Stability estimates are used for many aptitude tests, tests in the psychomotor domain, and some achievement tests. As illustrated in the following example, stability estimates are written in a straightforward manner, so they are easy to identify.

EXAMPLE 5.11 | Stability Estimate of Reliability

Test-retest reliability: ASPeCT-DD total scores collected in October of 2007 were compared with scores collected in January of 2006 . . . for the school-based portion of the sample. Sixty-one of the 77 students for whom ASPeCT-DD scores were available in October of 2007 also had scores recorded in January of 2006. Approximately 56% of the 61 students rated in 2006 were rated by the same informant in 2007. The correlation between these two sets of scores was fair ($r = 0.56$), and significant at the $p < 0.01$ level (one-tailed).

Source: Woodard, C. (2009). Psychometric properties of the ASPeCT-DD: Measuring positive traits in persons with developmental disabilities. *Journal of Applied Research in Intellectual Disabilities, 22,* 438.

Equivalence: Correlation of two forms of the same test.

Equivalence. A measure of **equivalence** is obtained by administering two forms of the same test to one group of individuals and then correlating the scores from the two administrations. Each form of the test should be equivalent in content, mean, and standard deviation, although the specific questions are different. This type of reliability estimate is often used in research on achievement when both a pretest (Form A), given before a treatment, and a posttest (Form B), given after a treatment, are administered to show how much the achievement of the subjects changed. Rather than giving the same test twice, the researcher gives alternate but equal tests.

Equivalence and Stability. An **equivalence and stability** estimate is obtained by administering one form of an instrument and then a second form after a time interval to the same group of individuals. This method combines equivalence (alternate forms) with stability (time interval). Although this is the most stringent type of reliability estimate, it is seldom employed. It is especially useful when researchers are concerned with long-range prediction (the strength of stability) and need to generalize to a large domain of knowledge or aptitude (the strength of equivalence).

Equivalence and stability: Two forms given at different times.

Internal Consistency. **Internal consistency,** the most widely used estimate of reliability, indicates the degree to which subjects' answers to items measuring the same trait are consistent. Unlike the other estimates, only one form of an instrument is given once to one group of individuals. There are three common types of internal consistency estimates: *split-half, Kuder-Richardson,* and *Coefficient Alpha* (*Cronbach Alpha*). In split-half reliability the items in a test are divided into equal halves, and the scores of each person on the two halves are correlated for the reliability coefficient. The Kuder-Richardson method is used in tests for which there is a right and wrong answer to each item. It avoids problems of the split-half technique, such as deciding how to divide the test into equal halves, by calculating the average of all the correlations that could be obtained from all possible split-half estimates. This method is usually indicated as KR-20 or KR-21. The Coefficient Alpha method is similar to the KR-20 but is used with instruments that contain a range of possible answers for each item, such as agree-disagree, that constitute a scale rather than right/wrong scoring.

Internal consistency: Correlation of items measuring the same trait.

Internal consistency is used when the purpose of an instrument is to measure a single trait. To allow calculation of the correlation, several items must measure the same thing. Thus, in some instruments, it seems as if the same questions are being asked over and over. To have internal consistency, a general rule of thumb is that there must be at least three questions about the same thing. In instruments in which there are subscales or subtests, a separate measure of internal consistency should be reported for each subscale. Of all the estimates, internal consistency is easiest to obtain and usually gives the highest reliability.

As shown in the following examples, the accepted convention in reporting internal consistency is simply to state the type of method used and to indicate the correlations.

EXAMPLES 5.12–5.14 | Internal Consistency Estimate of Reliability

A three-part pre-tested instrument with 43 items was used to collect the research data. Section A with seven (7) items collected demographic data. This part of the instrument was designed by the researchers. Section B with 16 items consisted of a 6-point Likert-type attitude toward inclusive education scale (1SD, 2D, 3 Somewhat disagree, 4 Somewhat Agree, 5A, 6SA). This instrument was adopted from Wilczenski (1992). The alpha reliability for this scale was .86. . . . Section C contained the 21-item 4-point Likert-type concerns about inclusive education scale (1—Not at all concerned, 2—A little concerned, 3—Very concerned, 4—Extremely concerned). The scale's alpha reliability was 0.88.

Source: Bradshaw, L., & Mundia, L. (2006). Attitudes to and concerns about inclusive education: Bruneian inservice and preservice teachers. *International Journal of Special Education, 21*(1), 37.

We used Spence and Helreich's (1983) two-dimensional measure of achievement motivation to assess workmastery and competitiveness. Items to assess workmastery (14 items, e.g., "I prefer to work in situations that require a high level of skill," α = .81) and competitiveness (5 items, e.g., "I enjoy working in situations involving competition with others," = .71) were rated on a scale from 1 (*strongly disagree*) to 5 (*strongly agree*).

Source: Durik, A. M., Lovejoy, C. M., & Johnson, S. J. (2009). A longitudinal study of achievement goals for college in general: Predicting cumulative GPA and diversity in course selection. *Contemporary Educational Psychology, 34*, 115.

Cronbach's alpha was used to compute internal consistency reliability estimates for the pretest and posttest Value Scale and Difficulty Scale; these estimates ranged from 0.63 to 0.94. Table 3 displays the internal consistency reliability estimates for the pretest and posttest value and difficulty scales.

Table 3 Internal Consistency Reliability (Cronbach's alpha for pretest and posttest value and difficulty scales associated with attitudes and perceptions related to the integration of mathematics science, and technology education (n = 81))

Variables	Number of items	Cronbach's alpha
Pretest value scale	15	0.87
Posttest value scale	15	0.94
Pretest difficulty scale	3	0.65
Posttest difficulty scale	3	0.63

Source: Berlin, D. F., & White, A. L. (2010). Preservice mathematics and science teachers in an integrated techer proparation program for grades 7–12: A 3-year study of attitudes and perceptions related to integration. *International Journal of Science and Mathematics Education, 8*, 107.

Agreement. There are three situations in which some type of *coefficient of agreement* exists, expressed as either a correlation or as a percentage of agreement. The first situation concerns establishing the reliability of ratings. The usual procedure is to assess the extent to which different raters agree on what they observe or score. That is, when two or more raters independently observe the same behavior, will they record it in the same way? Will two raters scoring an essay give the same score? Typically, raters are trained until they reach a desired level of agreement. A statistic termed *kappa* is used to report the results, rather than a bivariate correlation.

EXAMPLE 5.15 | Interrater Reliability

There were four observers. They were all experienced researchers who were familiar with working in schools and able to explain the research and put teachers and pupils at their ease. The basic aim was to avoid passing judgments and to use the schedule as intended. All observers had initial training in which they were provided with an observation manual of categories, conventions, and procedures, as well as tips acquired during previous use. Conventions were discussed, and there was work on videotapes, accompanied by periodic checks of accuracy and understanding of how to use categories. This was followed by at least a day's observation in a class not involved in the study and then a follow-up training session to discuss field visits and iron out difficulties. . . . Reliability coefficients for the main sets of mutually exclusive categories were high. Setting; subject; teacher-child social setting, child role, teacher content; and child-to-teacher child contribution, child content, and not interaction all had reliability coefficients (kappas) greater than 0.80. Kappa for child-child content was 0.77.

Source: Blatchford, P., Bassett, P., & Brown, P. (2005). Teachers' and pupils' behavior in large and small classes: A systematic observation study of pupils aged 10 and 11 years. *Journal of Educational Psychology, 97*(3), 459.

The second situation involves an insufficient number of items on an instrument measuring a single trait to compute an internal consistency estimate. In this circumstance, the researcher can use a method similar to stability by giving the instrument to the same group of individuals twice. If there are only a few persons, say, 15 to 20, the researcher can compute the percentage of responses that are the same rather than a correlation coefficient. This alternative is common in studies in which a new instrument has been developed and there has not been an opportunity to use a large number of individuals in a pilot test.

EXAMPLES 5.16–5.17 | Agreement Estimate for Reliability

Interrater reliability was calculated across 20% of all live classroom observations, as two coders observed and independently rated the same children. Coders were within one point of each others' scores 87% of the time (with a range of 71–99%) across the nine inCLASS dimensions). . . . Intraclass correlations at the domain and dimension levels ranged from moderate to excellent (0.42–0.83; see Table 4 for details).

Source: Downer, J. T., Booren, L. M., Lima, O. K., Luckner, A. E., & Pianta, R. C. (2010). The Individualized Classroom Assessment Scoring System (inCLASS): Preliminary reliability and validity of a system for observing preschoolers' competence in classroom interactions. *Early Childhood Research Quarterly, 25*, 9.

Interrater agreement for the coding of the transcripts . . . was calculated by dividing the total number of agreements by the total number of agreements plus disagreements, and multiplying by 100, as well as by using Cohen's (1960) kappa value. The interrater agreement across the 19 categories was 88% (median = 86%, range = 67%–96%), Cohen's kappa was .86

(median = .84, range = .66–.95). . . . According to Fleiss's (1981) general benchmark, a kappa value between .40 and .75 can be interpreted as intermediate to good, and a value above .75 can be considered excellent.

Source: Veenman, S., Denessen, E., van den Akker, A., & vander Rijt, J. (2005). Effects of a cooperative learning program on the elaborations of students during help seeking and help giving. *American Educational Research Journal, 42*(1), 128–129.

Third, many achievement tests result in a skewed distribution of scores (e.g., criterion-referenced tests, discussed in Chapter 6). With highly skewed distributions it is difficult to obtain a high correlation, and thus, most estimates of reliability would be low. With these types of tests, a percentage of agreement is often used to show the number of individuals who would be classified in the same way on a second test as they were on the first. Generally, it is the consistency of the decision that would be made as a result of the test rather than the scores themselves that is used to estimate reliability.

These five methods for estimating reliability are compared in Table 5.4 according to three criteria—the number of forms of the instrument, when the instruments are administered to gather the evidence, and the type of statistic used to report reliability. For internal consistency only one form is given once; for stability the same form is given twice. Agreement estimates are done at one time but involve two or more raters.

Effect of Reliability on Research

As with validity, reliability is best established *before* the research is undertaken, and also reported for subject scores from the study. The type of reliability should be consistent with the use of the results. If you wish to use the results for prediction or selection for special programs, stability estimates of reliability are necessary. If you are interested in programs to change attitudes or values, internal consistency estimates are needed. Reliability should also be established with

TABLE 5.4 Procedures for Estimating Reliability[1]

	Time 1	Time 2
Stability	A	A
Equivalence	A B	
Equivalence and Stability	A	B
Internal Consistency	A	
Agreement	R1 R2	

[1]A and B refer to different forms of the same test; R1 and R2 refer to rater 1 and rater 2.

individuals who are similar to the subjects in the research. If previous studies report good reliability with middle school students and you intend to use the results with elementary school students, the reliability may not be adequate.

You will read some research in which reliability is not addressed, yet the results of the research show what are called "significant differences." This is an interesting situation in research because it is more difficult to find differences between groups with scores that have low reliability. It is as if the differences were observed despite what may have been low reliability. Of course, it is possible that the scores were reliable, even though no reliability estimates were reported. This situation is likely to occur in research in which the subjects are responding to questions so straightforward and simple that reliability is assumed. In much research, the participants report information such as age, sex, income, time spent studying, occupation, and other questions that are relatively straightforward. For these types of data, statistical estimates of reliability are generally not needed.

Several conditions affect reliability. One is the length of a test or questionnaire: A longer test is more reliable than a shorter one. Reliability is also a function of the heterogeneity of the group. It is greater for groups that are more heterogeneous on the trait that is being measured. Conversely, the more homogeneous the subjects, the lower the reliability. Reliability is also a function of the nature of the trait that is being measured. Some variables, such as most measures of achievement, have high reliabilities, whereas measures of personality have lower reliabilities. Consequently, a reliability of .80 or above is generally expected for achievement variables, whereas estimates of .65 are usually acceptable for measuring personality traits. By comparison, then, a personality instrument reporting a reliability coefficient of .90 would be judged excellent, and an achievement test with a reliability of .70 would be seen as weak. A much higher reliability is needed if the results will be used to make decisions about individuals. Studies of groups can tolerate a lower reliability, sometimes as low as .50 in exploratory research. Measures of young children are usually less reliable than those of older subjects.

To enhance reliability, it is best to establish standard conditions of data collection. All subjects should be given the same directions, have the same time frame in which to answer questions at the same time during the day, and so on. Error is often increased if different individuals administer the instruments. It is important to know if there are any unusual circumstances during data collection since these may affect reliability. The instrument needs to be appropriate in reading level and language to be reliable, and subjects must be properly motivated to answer the questions. In some research, it is difficult to get subjects to be serious, for instance, when students are asked to take achievement tests that have no implications for them. Reliability can also suffer when subjects are asked to complete several instruments over a long period of time. Usually, an hour is about all any of us can tolerate, and for younger children less than half an hour is the maximum. If several instruments are given at the same time, the order of their administration should not be the same for all subjects. Some subjects should answer one instrument first, and other subjects should answer the same instrument last. This is called *counterbalancing* the instruments.

Finally, reliability is a necessary condition for validity. That is, scores cannot be valid unless they are reliable. However, a reliable score is not necessarily valid.

You can obtain a very reliable score of the length of your big toe, but that would not be valid as an estimate of your intelligence!

Author Reflection *Measurement specialists have admonished researchers to use the language "the validity of the inferences and reliability of the* scores, *not the instruments," but with limited success. Most of the time there is wording such as "the reliability and validity of the test." I have been somewhat perplexed by this since the "new" definitions have been around for more than 25 years! I guess this shows that old habits die hard. So you may hear or read the "old" language, just interpret it with the "new" definitions.*

STUDY QUESTIONS

1. How is measurement different from evaluation and assessment?
2. Why is measurement important in determining the quality of educational research?
3. What is the purpose of different scales of measurement?
4. What is the difference between nominal and interval scales of measurement?
5. In what ways are descriptive statistics useful in research?
6. Give some examples of different types of frequency distributions.
7. What are the common shapes of frequency distributions?
8. What are the special properties of a normal distribution?
9. In what ways are the mode, median, and mean different?
10. Explain the concept of standard deviation. Why is it important for research?
11. What is the relationship between the standard deviation and percentile rank?
12. Why is a scatterplot important in examining relationships?
13. Give some examples of positive and negative correlations.
14. Define validity and reliability. How are they related?
15. What types of evidence are used for validity?
16. Describe some factors that should be considered when evaluating validity.
17. What are the types of evidence for reliability?
18. How is error in measurement related to reliability correlation coefficients?
19. In what ways can different factors affect reliability?

Chapter 6

Data Collection Techniques

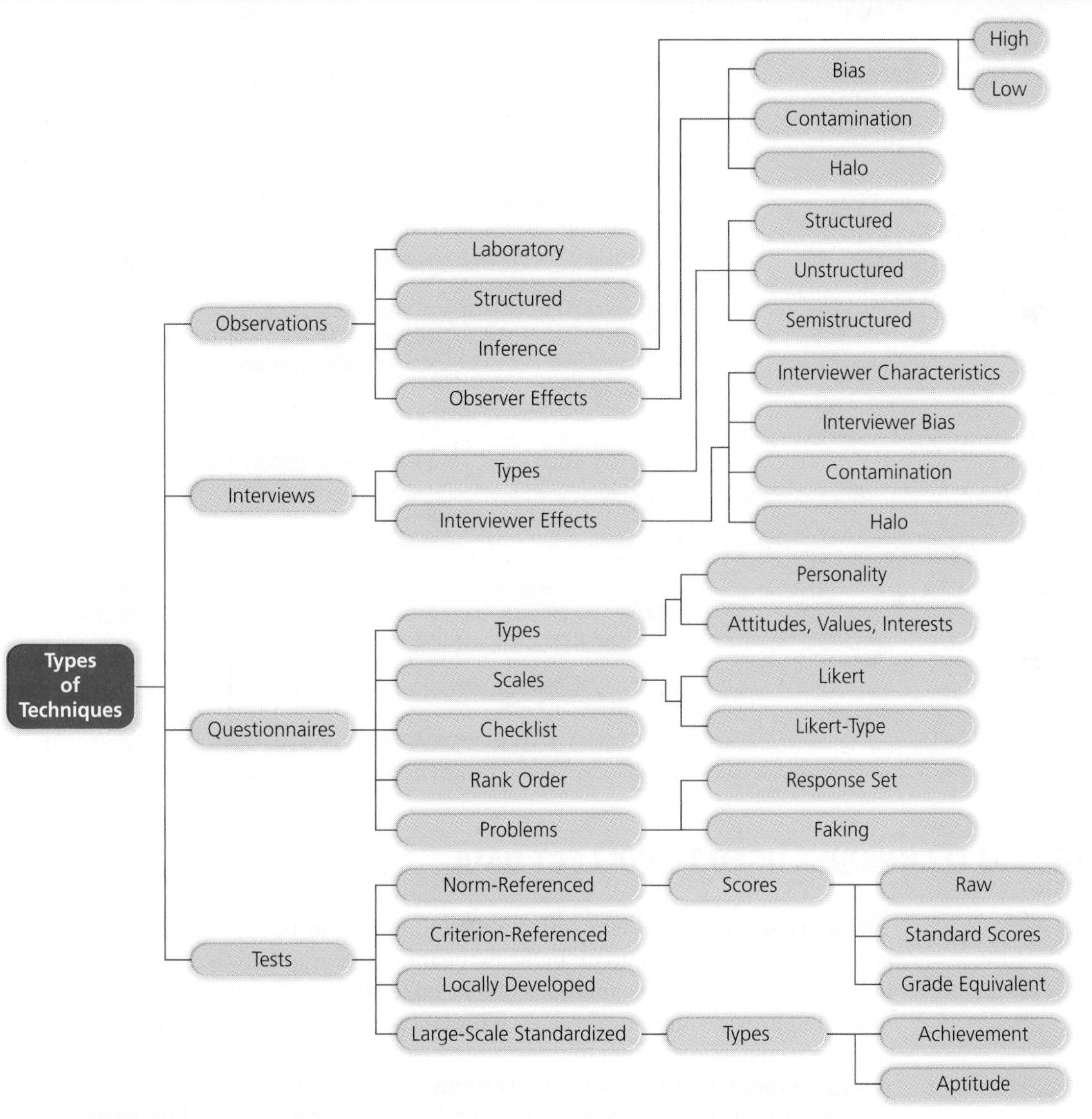

CHAPTER ROAD MAP

Researchers select from a large number of educational measures/instruments to gather data. The technique selected depends on the research problem, the advantages and disadvantages of each type, and practical constraints. As a consumer of research, it is important for you to understand the strengths and weaknesses of different approaches to data collection, how the results of different kinds of instruments should be interpreted, and how the nature of measurement influences results and conclusions.

Chapter Outline	Learning Objectives
Classifying Data Collection Techniques	• Recognize, recall, and distinguish among data assessment techniques.
Tests	
Norm and Criterion-Related (Standard-Based) Tests	• Distinguish between norm-referenced and criterion-referenced (standards-based) interpretations. • Understand the implications for research of using tests with different interpretation guidelines.
Standardized Tests	• Understand characteristics of standardized tests. • Understand strengths and weaknesses of using standardized tests. • Understand corresponding strengths and weaknesses of locally developed tests. • Know how to interpret scores reported from standardized tests.
Questionnaires	• Indentify different types of questionnaires according to what is assessed and format. • Know different types of response scales. • Understand how response set and faking can distort results.
Observations	• Distinguish between high-inference and low-inference observation. • Know how observer bias, contamination, demand characteristics, and the Halo effect may distort results.
Interviews	• Distinguish between structured, semi-structured, and unstructured questions. • Understand how the interviewer may affect participant responses.

CLASSIFYING TECHNIQUES USED TO COLLECT DATA

There are several ways data collection techniques can be classified. The most popular way is to differentiate by being quantitative or qualitative, as illustrated in Table 6.1. Quantitative methods of data collection are used to measure, document, and provide numerical values. This is accomplished by using objective and standardized data gathering for all research participants. Thus, we use tests, surveys, structured interviews and observations, and rating scales to measure and report quantitatively with statistics. Qualitative approaches are based on narrative and the multiple perspectives of the participants. The data gathering is relatively unstructured and often open-ended, though surveys, interviews, and observations

TABLE 6.1 Types of Quantitative and Qualitative Data Collection Techniques

Quantitative	Qualitative
Tests	Semi-structured and unstructured interviews
Questionnaires	Semi-structured and unstructured observations
Structured interviews	Artifact analysis
Structured observations	Document analysis
Secondary data analysis	
Performance-based assessments	

are still utilized, albeit in a different form from what is used for quantitative research. Mixed-method designs, as you no doubt now realize, use a combination of quantitative and qualitative data collection techniques.

Another important distinction is between *cognitive* and *noncognitive* measures. Cognitive measures focus on what a person knows or is able to do mentally. They include achievement and aptitude tests, measures of critical and creative thinking, and cognitive style. Noncognitive measures include personality, attitude, value, and interest inventories. These instruments require some degree of cognitive processing, but the emphasis is on affective, or emotional, "feelings" and intuitions.

A third major factor in distinguishing data collection techniques is whether the instrument is commercially developed (often referred to as "off the shelf") or developed locally by the researcher ("home grown"). Most commercially prepared instruments will have more extensive use, information on reliability and validity, and specific directions for administration and scoring. Locally developed instruments are often better suited to applied and action research but may lack technical indicators of quality.

A fourth important difference in educational measures is whether the subject is answering questions directly or the information is gathered without direct interaction with the subjects. Most tests, questionnaires, and interviews rely on information provided by the subjects. They are often called "self-report" instruments. Other measures, such as many observational ones, do not require subjects' responses to specific questions.

The first technique we'll examine in greater detail is cognitive tests. Given the current emphasis on accountability and high-stakes testing of student performance, beginning here is appropriate. Studies that include such test scores as dependent variables are ubiquitous.

TESTS

A **test** is an instrument that requires participants to complete a cognitive task by responding to a standard set of questions. The answers to the questions are summarized to obtain a numerical value that represents a cognitive characteristic

Test: Standard questions of cognitive knowledge or skills.

of the participants. All tests measure performance at the time the test is given. Tests differ in how the results are used, in their development, and in the types of evidence for validity and reliability that is established. The major differentiating characteristics are whether tests have norm- or criterion-referenced (standards-based) interpretations, whether they are measuring achievement or aptitude, and whether they are standardized or locally developed.

Norm- and Criterion-Referenced (Standards-Based) Interpretations

Norm-referenced: Interpretations that compare subjects with others.

A critical aspect of testing is the interpretation of the results. When a score is obtained, what does it convey? How do you interpret it? What does it mean, for example, when the average score is 70% correct? Measurement specialists have identified two approaches to interpretation to derive meaning from the scores: norm-referenced and criterion-referenced (standards-based). In **norm-referenced** interpretation, individual scores are compared to the scores of a well-defined norm (reference group) of others who have taken the same test. Ideally, the norm or reference group has the same characteristics, such as age and grade level, as the participants in the study. Performance is described as relative position (e.g., percentile rank). There is less emphasis on the absolute amount of knowledge or skill demonstrated. What matters most is the comparison group and the test's ability to distinguish between individuals on the trait being measured.

Because the purpose of a norm-referenced test is to differentiate between individuals, it is desirable to obtain a group distribution of scores that shows a high variance. It would be difficult to say much about relative standing if the scores were all about the same! To achieve high variability, the test items are typically moderately difficult. For instance, in many standardized achievement tests it is not uncommon for students around the middle of the distribution to answer only about 60% to 70% of the items correctly. Easy items, ones that most know the answer to, and very difficult items, ones that few can answer correctly, are used sparingly. The emphasis on items with moderate difficulty may affect what is covered on the test, which, in turn, would affect the interpretation of the results.

High variability is good when the researcher is looking for relationships between the test results and other variables. In fact, correlations are stronger if each variable has a large variation in the results. Many studies investigating relationships with achievement use norm-referenced tests because these types of tests are most likely to provide data that will show a large variance.

It is also necessary to attend carefully to the nature of the norm or reference group in interpreting the results. Proper interpretation requires knowing what the scores are being compared against. It is like being in a class with an instructor who grades on a curve (each student's grade depends on how others in the class did on the test). If the class contains mostly very bright, motivated students, you can learn a lot and still look bad by comparison! On the other hand, if you are in a class with students who have low ability and are unmotivated, you can look good even though you have not learned much. National standardized tests usually report national norms, so that the score is compared to students across the nation.

However, there are different ways of obtaining a "national" sample. Often, for instance, the norm group will contain a greater percentage of minority students than is actually present in the population to make sure each minority group is represented adequately. An accurate interpretation can be made only if the characteristics of the norm group are understood. Also, evidence of reliability and validity established with the norm group may be inappropriate for individuals not represented in the norm group.

The purpose of a **criterion-referenced** (standards-based) interpretation is to show how an individual compares to some established level of performance or skill. Here, the score is interpreted by comparison to a standard or criterion rather than to the scores of others. The result is usually reported either as a percentage of items answered correctly or as falling within categories such as *pass*, *proficient*, and *advanced*. Examples of criterion-referenced measurement include grading scales, such as 95 to 100 = A, 88 to 94 = B, and so on, and competency tests, in which the emphasis is on making sure that students know certain concepts and principles and have certain skills. An important characteristic of some tests with criterion-referenced interpretations is that the results show a highly negatively skewed distribution. This characteristic lessens variability, which may make it difficult to find relationships between the test results and other variables. With standards-based interpretations, professional judgment is used to set the passing or mastery score. There are many ways to make these professional judgments, with quite different results.

Criterion-referenced: Interpretations that compare subjects with a standard of performance.

The differences between norm- and criterion-referenced (standards-based) interpretations are summarized in Table 6.2.

Large-Scale Standardized Tests

A **standardized test** has uniform procedures for administration and scoring. Directions specify the procedures for giving the test, such as qualifications of the

Standardized test: A test with uniform procedures for administration and scoring.

TABLE 6.2 Characteristics of Criterion- (Standards-Based) and Norm-Referenced Interpretation

	Criterion-Referenced (Standards-Based)	Norm-Referenced
Purpose	To describe learning tasks that can and cannot be performed.	To discriminate between individuals; indicate relative standing.
Content Tested	A delimited domain tested by a relatively large number of items.	Typically, a large domain of tasks tested with relatively few items.
Item Difficulty	Items are matched to learning tasks; tend to be relatively easy.	Items are moderately difficult; omits very easy or difficult items.
Interpretation	Describes performance in relation to a clearly defined learning task.	Describes performance in relation to a clearly defined group.

Source: Adapted from Miller, Linn, & Gronlund, 2008.

person administering the test, time allowed to answer the questions, materials that can be used by the subjects, and other conditions. The scoring of responses is usually objective, with specific instructions for how to score that do not involve the tester's personal judgments. Scoring is typically a count of the number of items correct. Most standardized tests have been administered to a norming group, which is helpful in interpreting the results, and most are prepared commercially by experts in measurement. This means that careful attention has been given to technical aspects such as cultural bias, reliability, validity, clarity, and item analysis.

Large-scale standardized tests are intended to be used in a wide variety of settings; obviously, commercial test publishers want to sell as many tests as possible. The traits and skills measured are usually defined in broad, general terms. Consequently, the test may not be specific enough for use in a particular setting. For example, suppose a teacher is investigating the effect of different instructional methods on 11th-grade students' achievement in English. A standardized test of English (e.g., a test of national English standards) may be available but may not be consistent with the specific reading materials this teacher intends to use. In this case the standardized test would probably not be sensitive enough to the different materials to show positive results. Thus, a trade-off exists in using standardized tests for classroom-oriented research. Although there may be established technical qualities, the test may not focus directly on what is being studied.

Standards-based tests: Criterion-referenced test interpretation based on established standards.

Standards-Based Tests. In recent years there has been a trend toward accountability testing that is based on learning standards for students. These measures are often called **standards-based tests.** They are standardized achievement tests with criterion-referenced interpretations. As such, they are influenced both by what students learn in school and by what students learn at home and in the community. Students are typically judged to be "proficient" or "not proficient" on the basis of their scores on the tests. These tests are domain-referenced. A sample of content and skills is selected from a larger domain of standards. Because results from standards-based tests are very visible for both students and schools, there is now a tendency to use them in evaluating school programs and methods of instruction. This may be appropriate as long as inferences are limited to the domain that is tested, and as long as the influence of home and community is recognized.

These tests also have high stakes, often determining whether a student can be promoted to the next grade or can graduate from high school, whether schools can be accredited, and more recently for evaluating teachers. We know that in a high-stakes environment test score increases may, in part, reflect increased test-wiseness by students and other factors that cause test inflation rather than an increase in student knowledge and skills. Like other standardized tests, what is measured tends to be broad and general and may not be the best measure when research has targeted more specific dependent variables. For example, it would not be appropriate to use a high school end-of-course science test (one that covers the entire year) when an intervention in an experiment consists of a specific four-week unit.

Author Reflection *A great amount of research is now being conducted to relate student growth to teacher effectiveness by using value-added analyses. The idea is to use standards-based test scores to make conclusions about the quality of teaching over that period. That sounds like pretty good logic, except for one important reality—the student scores are affected by far more than what the teacher has done. There are influences such as the home environment, parents, siblings, peers, group dynamics in the classroom, and many other factors. Thus, the teacher will effect some achievement, but by no means all of it. Also, the teacher is influential in many other ways, on such traits as self-efficacy, attitudes, responsibility, and interpersonal skills. Considering these two well-known caveats, there are clear limitations in what student scores tell us about teacher effectiveness.*

Standardized Achievement Tests. A **standardized achievement test** is large-scale. It is commercially prepared, with the characteristics previously indicated, and measures present knowledge and skills of a sample of relevant content. The emphasis is on recent school learning—what has been learned by the student—measuring proficiency in one or more areas of knowledge.

Standardized achievement test: Tests content area knowledge or skill.

There are several types of standardized achievement tests. Some, diagnostic in nature, identify specific strengths and weaknesses in a particular discipline or area. Some measure achievement in a single subject, such as reading or mathematics. Survey batteries are achievement tests that survey a number of different subjects. Most standardized achievement tests are norm-referenced, although some are criterion-referenced. Some focus on recall and recognition of specific facts, concepts, and principles, and others measure skills and application of knowledge.

The type of achievement test selected (diagnostic, survey battery, etc.) depends on the purpose of the study. If the investigation is concerned with a single topic, a test that measures only that area would be preferable to a comprehensive battery of many topics. If the purpose is to compare schools on achievement, a norm-referenced achievement test would be best. Evaluations of overall school performance are best assessed with survey batteries. It is also important to select a test that has an appropriate degree of difficulty for the students. A test that is either too easy or too difficult will not have the variability needed to show relationships with other variables.

It is critical to evaluate evidence based on test content to establish validity when using an achievement test. This assessment should include judgments about the relevance of the test content to the selected curriculum. These judgments can be made by determining the degree of match between the test items and the curriculum being taught.

When existing standardized achievement tests do not match well with the purpose of the research, a locally developed test is needed. These are often called teacher-made, or informal, tests for examining classroom learning. There are important differences between large-scale standardized and locally developed achievement tests, as summarized in Table 6.3.

Standardized Aptitude Tests. A **standardized aptitude test** is a commercially prepared measure of knowledge or skills that is used to predict future performance. The difference between an achievement and an aptitude test is in the way

Standardized aptitude test: Predicts future performance.

TABLE 6.3 Characteristics of Large-Scale Standardized Tests and Informal, Locally Developed Tests[1]

	Large-Scale Standardized Tests	Informal, Local Tests
Relevance to research	Low	High
Technical quality	High	Low
Quality of test items	High	Low
Administration and scoring	Specific instructions	Flexible
Score interpretation	Compared to national norms	Limited to local context
Content tested	General	Specific to local context

[1]This table shows general trends. Some locally developed tests, for example, have high-quality items, and some standardized tests are highly relevant to the research.

the results are applied. The actual items can be very similar, especially in tests for young children. Often the terms *intelligence* and *ability* are used interchangeably with *aptitude*. Actually, *aptitude* is a more general term that refers to the predictive nature of the instrument. Intelligence tests measure a particular type of aptitude, which is defined by the content of each specific test. Intelligence usually means some indication of an individual's capacity to understand, process, and apply knowledge and skills in thinking or problem solving. It involves many different aptitudes.

Because of the negative connotation of intelligence tests, many publishers today use the terms *ability* or *academic aptitude* in naming the tests, for example, the Otis-Lennon School Ability Test and the Cognitive Abilities Test. The basic structure and content of these tests is much the same as when they were referred to as intelligence tests. Such tests are widely used in education and are useful in predicting performance on many tasks. Some tests, such as those just mentioned, are given to large groups of students; others, such as the Stanford-Binet and the Wechsler Scales, are given on an individual basis. For research, both individual and group tests are common, and, for both types, it is important that the person administering the test be properly qualified.

There are also a large number of aptitude tests that measure specific kinds of aptitudes, such as vocational, clerical, mechanical, critical thinking, and creative thinking skills, and the skills that are needed to be successful in law or medical school. A few aptitude tests are batteries that assess many aptitudes at once. For example, the Differential Aptitude Tests (DAT) measure eight aptitudes: verbal reasoning, numerical ability, abstract reasoning, clerical speed and accuracy, mechanical reasoning, spatial relations, spelling, and language use. These tests have been useful in predicting both scholastic and vocational success.

Because aptitude tests are concerned with predicting future behavior, it is important to establish predictive criterion-related evidence for validity. It is also best to have a stability estimate of reliability. These technical qualities are important in tests that are used to select individuals for special programs that attract a large pool of applicants. Almost all aptitude tests are standardized.

Scores from Norm-Referenced Interpretations

A characteristic of norm-referenced interpretation is that different types of scores are reported and used in research, each having unique characteristics. Two of the most common are *standard scores* and *grade equivalents.*

Standard Scores. Most publishers of standardized, norm-referenced tests report at least two types of scores. One is the actual number of items correct, the raw score, and another is calculated from these raw scores, the standard score. **Standard scores** are transformed raw scores that have a distribution in the same shape as the raw score distribution but with a different mean and standard deviation. The most basic standard score is called a linear z score. A z score has a mean of 0 and a standard deviation of 1. The formula is

Standard scores: Raw scores transformed to a standard scale.

$$z = \frac{\text{raw score} - \text{mean}}{\text{standard deviation}}$$

Every raw score can be transformed to a z score with known percentile ranks, as illustrated in Figure 6.1.

Many other derived standard scores are then calculated from z scores, such as SAT and IQ scores. When interpreting these types of standard scores, consider two important points. First, the unit of standard deviation is determined arbitrarily and does not reflect "real" differences between subjects. For instance, the SAT has a standard score mean of about 1,500 and a standard deviation equal to about 300. One subject may score 1,850 and another 1,890, but the 40-point difference is only in standard score units. In fact, the 40 points may represent a difference of

FIGURE 6.1 ***z* scores and percentile ranks.**

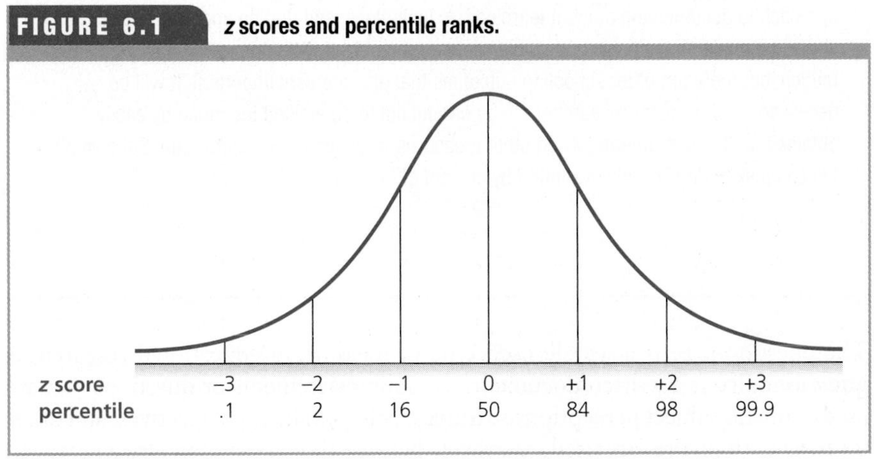

only a few correct answers. Second, in small distributions, and in any raw score distribution that is not normal, scores are sometimes "normalized," that is, forced into a normal distribution and reported as standard scores. This practice may distort the meaning of the scores. Despite these limitations, standard scores are often used in research because the data are in a form that can be used in statistical analyses of the results. Also, with standard scores, it is easier to compare groups who have taken different tests.

Grade equivalent: Norm-referenced grade-level performance.

Grade Equivalents. Grade equivalents (GEs) are a popular type of score for reporting achievement, even if they are often misinterpreted. A **grade equivalent** score indicates how an individual compares with others in a normative group in terms of grade level. For example, a student who scores 5.0 has achieved the median score for all beginning fifth-graders in the norm group. The score 3.2 is equivalent to the average score of third-graders in November. One limitation of GEs is in interpreting these in-between scores, 5.6, 2.3, and so on, since they are calculated as approximate, not exact, scores. Estimates are also made for grade levels beyond the norming group, although GEs are generally not used beyond the ninth grade because not all students take all subjects. Perhaps the most serious misinterpretation is the belief that a student who scores, say, 6.0, should be in the sixth grade, or knows as much as a sixth-grader. Grade determination is based on local school policy and the level of achievement of students in a particular school, whereas the GE is based on a national norm.

USING EDUCATIONAL RESEARCH

Over the last three decades qualitative research has surged. Now, with the federal-level emphasis on standards and accountability based on student achievement, there is a clear trend toward more objective standardized testing to determine the effectiveness of educational programs. This emphasis on large-scale, objective testing will influence the nature of dependent variables for many studies. What will be important is to recognize that any single approach to documenting student learning has limitations, and that no important decisions should be made on the basis of a single score. Standardized tests do provide important information, but there are other schooling outcomes that also are very important. It will be necessary, therefore, for researchers to be careful not to be enticed too much by easily obtained, visible instruments, when other measures would be more appropriate. Schooling is too complex to be narrowly evaluated by one set of measures.

QUESTIONNAIRES

Questionnaire: Solicits subject responses to written items.

The questionnaire is a widely used type of measure in educational research. A **questionnaire** is a written document containing statements or questions that are used to obtain subject perceptions, attitudes, beliefs, values, perspectives, and other traits. Questionnaires are used extensively because they provide an efficient way to obtain information about a wide range of research problems, from surveys of large populations to reactions of students to different instructional methods. Questionnaires can be used to assess different kinds of traits and can take several formats.

Personality Assessment

Personality assessment is tied to two traditions. One is closely linked to psychology and is used by trained counselors and clinicians. The other is used by teachers and researchers who typically have not had extensive psychological training.

Psychologists have been concerned with measuring personality for many decades. Although there are different definitions of personality, a common theme is that it involves the total individual—noncognitive, affective traits as well as cognitive characteristics. This holistic emphasis is evident in personality instruments that assess general adjustment, such as the Minnesota Multiphasic Personality Inventory (MMPI). The MMPI is a self-report questionnaire for adults aged 16 and above. Fourteen scales are reported, including paranoia, hysteria, social introversion, schizophrenia, and depression. Interpretation of the results of the MMPI requires a highly trained, skilled clinician.

Questionnaires related to personality that are used by teachers and educational researchers are not typically intended to identify psychopathology. Rather, they measure important individual traits related to learning and motivation, such as self-concept, cognitive style, and locus of control. The instruments are designed so that educators without clinical training can understand and use the results.

One personality trait that is studied extensively in educational research is self-concept. Self-concept, or self-image, can be defined as the way one characterizes oneself. It is a description formed by self-perceptions and beliefs. Although it is possible to measure a single, global self-concept, most questionnaires are designed to assess many different self-concepts, such as descriptions about the physical, social, academic, moral, and personal self. The items in the instruments require self-report perceptions.

Typically, short statements are presented that describe various aspects of self-concept. The subjects answer each item by indicating whether it is true for them, or whether they agree or disagree that the statement is like them. For example, subjects would be directed to answer yes or no or true or false to the following statements:

1. I have few friends.
2. I have happy parents.
3. I have a nice looking body.
4. I am good at schoolwork.
5. I make friends easily.
6. I get good grades.
7. I am happy in school.
8. I like my teachers.
9. I am confident of my athletic ability.

Often the scoring of the instruments indicates a positive or negative self-concept, an interpretation that has an evaluative component termed self-esteem.

It has to do with how subjects *feel about* their self-concepts. In the literature *self-concept* and *self-esteem* may be used interchangeably, so it is necessary to examine the nature of the items to understand what is being measured.

Another commonly assessed trait is self-efficacy. *Self-efficacy* is the judgment of the person's capabilities to undertake appropriate action that results in successful performance. With a strong self-efficacy, students are empowered to be more engaged and motivated to do well, and to persist in the face of difficulties. With low self-efficacy, students are more likely to avoid tasks with which they may not be successful and to give up more quickly. Self-report measures are used to assess self-efficacy and use items similar to these:

EXAMPLE 6.1 | Likert-Type Scale for Assessing Self-Efficacy

	Always	Almost always	Often	Some-times	Never/ Rarely
I am confident that I can complete most school work successfully.	A	AA	O	S	NR
Science is easy for me.	A	AA	O	S	NR
I am confident in my ability to do well in my English class.	A	AA	O	S	NR
No matter how hard I try, I have trouble with math.	A	AA	O	S	NR

Attitude, Value, and Interest Questionnaires

Attitudes, values, and interests are generally thought of as *noncognitive* or *affective* traits that indicate some degree of preference toward something. *Attitudes* are defined as predispositions to respond favorably or unfavorably to an object, group, or place. They reflect likes and dislikes and generally predict behavior. Like attitudes, interests are concerned with preferences. Both are related to favorable or unfavorable responses toward something. *Interests*, however, are feelings and beliefs about an activity rather than an object, concept, or person. Like attitudes and interests, *values* can be defined in a number of ways, so it is necessary to examine items in a value survey to know what is being measured.

Preferences are important in education because they influence motivation and goals, which in turn affect achievement. The most common measure of these preferences in educational research is through self-report questionnaires, in which students answer questions to indicate how they feel about something, what their beliefs are, or their self-perceived capability to perform well (self-efficacy).

When reading research that investigates attitudes, values, and interests, you will note that different types of items are used. We will consider three major types of items commonly used in questionnaires: scales, checklists, and ranked items.

Types of Scales

A **scale** is a series of gradations that describes something. The most typical format for a scaled item is following a question or statement with a scale of potential responses. Subjects indicate their attitudes or values by checking the place on the scale that best reflects their feelings and beliefs about the statement. The **Likert scale** (pronounced Li'kert) is the most widely used example. In a true Likert scale the statement includes a value or positive or negative direction, and the subject indicates agreement or disagreement with the statement:

Scale: Series of gradations.

Likert scale: Measures level of agreement to a statement.

It is very important to go to college.

strongly agree	agree	neither agree nor disagree	disagree	strongly disagree

Likert-*type* rating scales, which have a different form, begin with a neutral statement, and the direction or gradation is provided in the response options:

Mrs. Stadler's classroom management is:

outstanding	excellent	good	fair	poor

Likert-type scales are useful for measuring traits other than attitudes. Such measures are usually referred to as rating scales. Statements and response options can be selected for a wide variety of needs, as indicated in the following:

EXAMPLES 6.2–6.4 | Likert-Type Scales

How often does your principal visit your classroom?

every day	two or three days a week	once a week	once every two weeks	once a month

How often does your teacher give praise?

always	most of time	sometimes	rarely	never

How did you feel about your performance on the exam?

very satisfied	somewhat satisfied	somewhat dissatisfied	very dissatisfied

Note that the number of possible responses on a Likert-type scale is not always the same. There is usually a minimum of four options, and there can be as many as seven or eight. Some questions will have a middle option, and others will have an even number of options to "force" the subject to one side of the scale or the other. However, if a neutral or middle choice is not provided and this is the real attitude or belief of the subject, the subject will be forced to give an inaccurate response (or may choose not to respond at all).

A good example of a study in which I participated used Likert-type items to survey teachers about their grading and classroom assessment practices for a specific class and students about their motivation to be engaged in the class and to work for high grades. The purpose of the study was to determine relationships between teacher practices and student motivation. Some of the items for both the teacher and student surveys are illustrated in Examples 6.5 and 6.6. Both of the questionnaires used a 5-point scale. Sometimes a 3-point or 7-point scale is used, though rarely more than 7.

EXAMPLES 6.5–6.6 | Likert-Type Items

To what extent did you use the following grading and assessment practices *in the class you are currently teaching?*	**Not at All**	**Minimally**	**Some**	**Quite a Bit**	**Extensively**
19. feedback (written or verbal) on performance that was given privately to each student	1	2	3	4	5
20. specific, individualized feedback (written or verbal)	1	2	3	4	5
21. feedback (written or verbal) that contained suggestions for further learning	1	2	3	4	5
22. checklists to evaluate student work (**not** rubrics)	1	2	3	4	5
23. formative assessments (i.e., assessment given during instruction to check student learning; anecdotal or structured)	1	2	3	4	5
24. retakes of tests	1	2	3	4	5
25. assessments that measured student deep understanding (e.g., exploration, inquiry, and problem solving)	1	2	3	4	5
26. tests and other assessments of moderate difficulty	1	2	3	4	5

Directions: Carefully read each sentence and then rate ***how true*** each one is for you ***in this class.*** Circle the number next to each sentence that matches your answer. The number (1) stands for ***not at all true for me,*** (3) stands for ***somewhat true for me,*** and (5) stands for ***very true for me.***

	Not at All True for Me		**Somewhat True for Me**		**Very True for Me**
11. I'm certain I can understand the ideas taught in this class.	1	2	3	4	5
12. It's important to me that I learn a lot in this class.	1	2	3	4	5
13. It's important to me that other students in my class think I am good at my class work.	1	2	3	4	5
14. I **don't** want my teacher to think I know less than other students in class.	1	2	3	4	5
15. One of my goals is to gain a lot of new skills in this class.	1	2	3	4	5

Another type of scale is the **semantic differential,** which has adjective pairs that provide a series of scales. Each adjective acts as an end anchor, and the subject checks a point between each end anchor of each scale to indicate attitudes toward some person, concept, or idea. Although the true semantic differential uses the same set of adjective pairs in the three clusters, changing the object or concept that is being studied and changing the adjective pairs as appropriate are common in educational research.

Semantic differential: A 5-to 9-point scale with adjective pairs as end points.

An example of using a semantic differential for measuring the science attitudes of preservice teachers is illustrated in Example 6.7.

EXAMPLE 6.7 | Use of a Semantic Differential

The researchers developed a 20-item, five point semantic differential to measure attitudes and perceptions related to the concept of "mathematics, science, and technology education integration" using bipolar adjectives previously used in their research that had exhibited high internal consistency reliability (e.g., bad-good, boring-exciting, weak-strong, strange-familiar, hard-easy). Students responded to the series of bipolar adjectives by marking an X on one of five spaces to reflect their attitudes and perceptions.

Source: Berlin, D. F., & White, A. L. (2009). Preservice mathematics and science teachers in an integrated teacher preparation program for grades 7–12: A 3-year study of attitudes and perceptions related to integration. *International Journal of Science and Mathematics Education*, 8, 106.

A **checklist** provides the respondent with a number of options from which to choose. The checklist can require a choice of one of several alternatives, for example, Check one: The research topic I enjoy most is

Checklist: Provides a list of choices.

______ measurement
______ qualitative designs
______ quantitative designs
______ reviewing literature

Or, respondents can check as many as apply:

Check as many as apply. The topics in research that I find very useful are:

_______ measurement
_______ qualitative designs
_______ quantitative designs
_______ reviewing literature

Checklists are also used when asking participants to answer yes or no, or to check the category to which they belong. For example:

Are you a full-time student?

_______ Yes
_______ No

Check the appropriate category:

_______ single, never married
_______ married
_______ separated
_______ divorced
_______ widowed

Rank-ordered: Sequenced categories.

In a **rank-ordered** item the respondent is asked to place a limited number of categories into sequential order. The sequence could be based on importance, liking, degree of experience, or some other dimension. Asking subjects to rank-order may provide different results from those provided by a Likert item or semantic differential. For example, if a researcher is interested in determining the importance of different staff development topics, a Likert-type item format could be used. For each topic the teachers check or circle "critical," "very important," "important," or "not important." If most of the teachers check or circle "important" for each topic, then there is limited information about which of the topics should be given priority. However, if the teachers rank-order the topics by importance from 5 for most important to 1 for least important, an average rating can be found that will more likely identify which topic should be given priority.

Constructing Questionnaires

When researchers construct a survey or questionnaire, you can examine the steps they have taken to get a good idea of the quality and credibility of the instrument. These steps are illustrated in Figure 6.2.

The first step is to develop a sound rationale and justification. This depends on a thorough review of literature to determine if existing instruments are available or can be borrowed from. A constructed questionnaire is strengthened to the extent that theory and previous research support its development and use, providing a conceptual framework and theoretical foundation. Note in the following example how the researchers used previously reported research to provide a conceptual framework.

EXAMPLE 6.8 | Conceptual Framework for Developing an Instrument

I developed the LSPI using research conducted by Dunn and Dunn (1992), who classify individuals as analytical or global learners. Dunn and Dunn found that analytical learners are more successful when information is presented step-by-step in a cumulative, sequential pattern that builds toward a conceptual understanding. . . . Global learners have the opposite set of characteristics, learning more easily when they master a concept first and then concentrate on the details. . . . I developed an instrument to quickly assess these two major learning-style elements.

Source: Pitts, J. (2009). Identifying and using a teacher-friendly learning-styles instrument. *The Clearing House, 82*(5), 227–228.

FIGURE 6.2 **Steps in constructing questionnaires.**

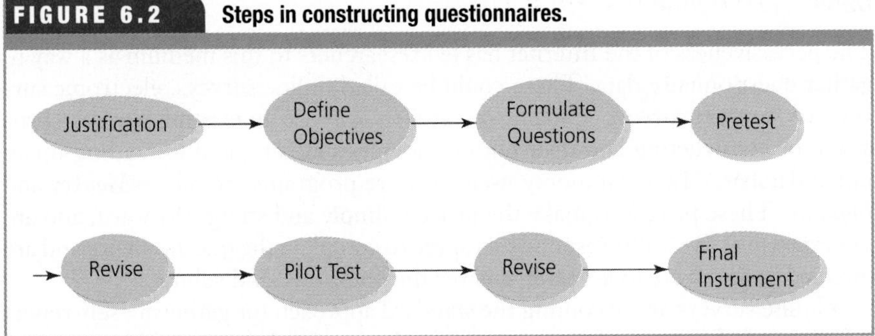

Justification is followed by identifying important objectives that will be achieved. There needs to be a clear link between the research questions and items, as well as a determination that the results will be meaningful. Once the objectives are determined, items and an appropriate scale are developed. These items are then pretested with individuals who are similar to those who will be used in the research. The purpose of the pretest is to obtain feedback on the clarity of the items and response scale. This step leads to revisions to result in an almost final form that can also be given to appropriate individuals to obtain more feedback and establish data for reliability and validity. Further revision is completed to result in the final instrument.

In evaluating locally developed instruments, examine what was used to come up with the questionnaire to determine if important steps have been skipped or seem inadequate. It is also helpful to inspect the items to determine whether it is likely that the results will be biased or misleading. Figure 6.3 illustrates what to check for in scrutinizing the items.

FIGURE 6.3 **Checklist of criteria for evaluating questionnaire items.**

- ✓ Are items short, simple, and clear?
- ✓ Are there any double-barreled questions?
- ✓ Does the response scale match the stem?
- ✓ Are respondents capable of providing answers?
- ✓ Are negatively worded items used sparingly, if at all?
- ✓ Are there biased items?
- ✓ Are there loaded or leading questions?
- ✓ Are there too many questions?

Online Questionnaires

The pervasiveness of the Internet has led researchers to this medium as a way to gather questionnaire data. These could be called online surveys, electronic surveys, or Internet surveys. Usually, researchers will use an existing software program for constructing and distributing the questionnaire, and for setting up an initial database. Two commonly used software programs are *SurveyMonkey* and *Inquisite*. These programs make the process simple and straightforward, and are not expensive. Typically, respondents agree to complete the questionnaire and are directed to a website to access it, answer the questions, and submit.

Online surveys are becoming the standard approach for gathering self-report information. Most people are familiar with them and comfortable answering their questions, and an electronic format saves money and time. The ability to easily create a database is an important feature. In general, online surveys are effective because they present questions clearly, can be used to enhance presentation, and are able to access distant populations. The main disadvantage is that respondents may be concerned about confidentiality and, as a result, give biased responses. It is also difficult to know if the person who responded is the targeted participant or someone else. More detail about online surveys is presented in the next chapter.

Problems in Measuring Noncognitive Traits

Compared to cognitive measures, such as achievement and aptitude tests, noncognitive instruments generally have lower reliability and less evidence for validity. One difficulty with noncognitive measurement is clearly defining what is being assessed. There are different definitions of terms such as *attitude*, *belief*, *value*, and *personality*. Thus, the same labels can be used, but what is being measured can be different. An "attitude" toward mathematics can mean one thing in one study and something different in another study. Consequently, when reading research that uses noncognitive instruments, it is important to examine the *operational* definition of the trait that is being measured, which is best accomplished by reading the actual items in the scale. The results are most meaningful in regard to the way in which the attitude or personality trait is measured, not by how the researcher labels or communicates the findings in titles or conclusions.

Response set: Tendency to respond in the same way.

Most noncognitive measures are susceptible to two sources of error: response set and faking. **Response set** is the tendency of the subject to respond in the same way, regardless of the content of the items, for example, always selecting the neutral category or the "strongly agree" category in a Likert scale or marking the favorable adjectives on a semantic differential. An especially troublesome type of response set is *social desirability*. This is the tendency to respond to the items in a way that is socially acceptable or desirable, regardless of the true or real attitudes or beliefs of the individual. For example, if a question asks students about their alcohol consumption, the responses may be influenced by what the students think is socially accepted. Or students may indicate an interest in attending college because that is more desirable socially than not attending college. Response set tends to be more prevalent on Likert-type inventories, with ambiguous items, and in situations in which the subjects are not motivated to give honest answers. In evaluating noncognitive instrumentation, it is best to look for techniques that lessen response set, such as forced-choice responses, short inventories, an approximately equal number of positively and negatively worded items, alternating positive and negative adjectives in the same column on a semantic differential, ensurance of anonymity, and motivation of subjects.

Faking: Deliberately inaccurate responses by subjects.

Faking occurs when subjects give deliberately inaccurate indications of their attitudes, personality, or interests. Faking is usually dependent on the purpose of the test and the consequences of the results. Sometimes it occurs if the researcher indicates that certain results will have positive consequences; sometimes subjects fake responses simply to please the researcher (which is why someone other than the researcher probably should administer the instrument). In other situations faking occurs because the results have important consequences for the individual, for example, to determine admission to college or selection for a management training program. Occasionally, subjects will fake to provide a more negative picture. Faking can be controlled by establishing good rapport with the subjects and proper motivation, by disguising the purpose of the instrument and research, and using a forced-choice format. There are also techniques to detect faking. Whatever the approach, it is best for the instrument to be pilot-tested with similar subjects to ensure that problems such as response set and faking are controlled as much as possible. If little or no attention is given to these problems, it is more likely that the responses will be invalid.

Review and Reflection *See if you can make a list of the four or five most important points to consider in evaluating whether a questionnaire is likely to give credible results. Do the same for the use of standards-based tests. What has been your own experience in taking surveys? Does your experience match the suggestions in the chapter?*

OBSERVATIONS

Tests and questionnaires are similar in that they rely on subjects' self-reports. Although self-reports are relatively economical and easy to obtain, they have limitations that may bias the results, such as response set, subject motivation, and faking. A second major type of data collection, which does not rely on self-reports, is the observational method. Although observational techniques also have limitations, they are more direct than self-reports. The observation of behavior as it occurs yields firsthand data without the contamination that may arise from tests, inventories, or other self-report instruments. Moreover, observation allows the description of behavior as it occurs naturally. Any kind of self-report introduces artificiality into the research. Observation of behavior in natural settings also allows the researcher to take into account important contextual factors that may influence the interpretation and use of the results. This is essential for qualitative studies.

There are several types of observational data-gathering techniques. Some observations are made in natural settings and others in controlled settings. Some observations may be guided by a general problem and there may be flexibility about what and who to observe, whereas other observations may be specific and highly structured. Observers may be detached from the subjects, even unknown, or they may essentially become subjects themselves. Quantitative observations are more controlled and systematic, and rely on numbers to summarize what has been observed. Qualitative approaches are much less controlled, allowing observers' hunches and judgments to determine the content and sequence of what is recorded. Either or both types of observations are used in some mixed-method studies. In this chapter we will focus on the more controlled, quantitative types of observation. Qualitative observations will be discussed in greater detail Chapter 10.

Inference

A major factor in observational research is the extent to which the person who is observing and recording the behavior makes inferences, or judgments, about what is seen or heard. Although there will always be some degree of inference, the amount can vary considerably. At one extreme, the observer may record specific, easily identified behaviors, such as "asks a question" or "wrote objectives on the board." These are called **low-inference** observations because the observer does not have to interpret what is seen. Either the behaviors are present or not, and the observer makes no judgment about their meaning. The recorded behaviors are then summarized and interpreted by someone else; the inference is made after all the data have been gathered. At the other extreme are observations that require the observer to make and record a judgment or interpretation. This approach, referred to as **high-inference** observation, requires the observer both to see relevant behaviors and to make inferences about their meaning. A common example of high-inference observation is that of a principal who, on the basis of a few visits to a classroom, rates a teacher as excellent, good, adequate, or poor on dimensions of teaching such as "classroom management" or "asking questions."

Low-inference: Involves little interpretation or judgment.

High-inference: Involves recording interpretations of judgments.

With low-inference observation the reliability is usually high, but in order to understand the results, you need to understand how the recorded behavior is translated. Translation can be a complex process and will involve some degree of arbitrary judgment, for example, how many times a teacher needs to give praise to be judged competent in praising students or how many student questions during a class period indicates acceptable student involvement. Critics of low-inference systems also point out that teaching and learning may not be understood by recording specific behaviors without putting them into context.

In high-inference observations the competency of the observer in making correct judgments is critical. Training high-inference observers is more difficult, and reliability is often lower, as compared to low-inference observation. With high-inference results, greater trust in the observer is needed. Thus, you should look for any factors that may bias a high-inference observer, such as the researcher also acting as the observer or observers knowing about the expected results of the study.

Some observations are in between the low- and high-inference extremes. One such approach is to make high-inference ratings and indicate the specific behaviors and contextual factors that led to the inference implied in the judgment.

The most structured observational techniques are found in controlled settings. A specified environment is created by the researcher and the observations are recorded during the study. A well-structured form or procedure identified before the study begins is used to record specific behaviors. Low-inference observations are made, and methods of summarizing and analyzing the observations are specified in advance. The emphasis is on objectivity and standardization.

Subjects in contrived settings may give biased responses because they know that they are in an "experiment" and are being observed. They may respond according to their interpretation of how they "should" respond, given the treatment they experience, or they may give answers they believe the researcher wants. These are called *demand characteristics.* Deception, in which the subjects are not told the real purpose of the study, is commonly used to reduce the effects of demand characteristics, but there are serious ethical problems with lying to subjects, even if they are debriefed after the study.

Most observational studies in education take place in the field, in schools and classrooms where behavior occurs naturally. From a quantitative perspective, the typical approach is to define the behaviors to be observed, identify a system of coding and recording them, train observers to use the system, and go to the school or other setting and make the observations. The intent is to measure the frequency and/or duration of predetermined behaviors.

The behaviors can be recorded in several ways. The most common approach is to indicate the number of times a behavior occurs during a specified time period. The observer has a list of behaviors that may be observed, and every time a behavior is seen, a tally is placed next to that behavior. Sometimes the observer will observe for a short time, such as 1 to 3 minutes, then record all the behaviors seen in that time; and sometimes the recording is done continuously. With high-inference instruments, the observer may not record anything for an hour or more.

Observer Effects

The observer is the key to observational research, and the quality of the results depends to a great extent on how the observer and the procedures for observing affect the subjects. In reading observational research, you should be aware of the following potential limitations.

Observer Bias. Bias is a type of error that occurs because of the background, expectations, or frame of reference of the observer. For example, if an observer of classroom management techniques has a predetermined idea that a particular approach is best, and the teacher who is observed does not use this style, the observer may have a tendency to bias the observations in a negative direction.

On the other hand, bias in a positive direction may occur when observers record the behavior of a style of management they believe to be most effective.

You should look for one of several procedures to reduce potential observer bias. First, there should be evidence that the observer has been trained and will provide reliable results. The evidence for training should be based on research done before the actual study is implemented. Second, if possible, two or more observers should independently observe at least some of the same behavior. Third, bias can also result because of prejudice toward certain races; toward one gender or the other; and toward other characteristics such as physical attractiveness, social class, and exceptionalities. In the following excerpt the researcher demonstrates her understanding of possible bias, using interobserver reliability to lessen this potentially problematic issue.

EXAMPLE 6.9 | Accounting for Observer Bias

I was aware that researcher bias would be a potential difficulty in my study and monitored flexibility and openness in the analysis of material. . . . In addition, my research supervisor re-coded some of the videos so that 36% of the total sample was reviewed to ensure reliability. Inter-observer reliability . . . was calculated using kappa, with high agreement (> 0.90) between observers.

Source: Anderson, C. (2006). Early communication strategies: Using video analysis to support teachers working with preverbal pupils. *British Journal of Special Education, 33*(3), 116.

Contamination: Knowledge of the study influences observer or interviewer.

Contamination. **Contamination** occurs when the observer has knowledge of one or more aspects of the study and this knowledge affects subsequent observations. One type of contamination results from knowledge of the study's hypothesis. If the observer knows which group is "expected" to do best, for example, he or she may unconsciously favor that group. Contamination also occurs if the same observer is assigned to more than one type of group. For example, if an observer begins with a group of "expert" teachers and then observes "poor" teachers, the second group will probably receive lower ratings than they deserve because of the comparison. Contamination is less likely to occur when specific behaviors are targeted for observation, when observers are trained, when the observers do not know about expected outcomes, and are not told which groups are experimental and control.

Halo effect: Specific ratings affected by initial impression.

Halo Effect. The **halo effect** occurs when an observer allows an initial impression about a person or group to influence subsequent observations. For example, an initial positive impression about a teacher, based on the way the teacher begins a class, may create an overall positive "halo" so that ratings of subsequent behaviors, such as questioning or monitoring of classroom activities, are higher than they should be. The halo effect is an inappropriate generalization about all aspects of the observation. It is suspected in ratings of different behaviors when all the ratings are the same, which results in a positive relationship between unrelated scales. The halo effect, like other sources of errors in observation, is reduced with adequate training.

INTERVIEWS

Interview: Oral questions and answers.

The **interview** is a form of data collection in which questions are asked orally and subjects' responses are recorded, either verbatim or summarized. There is direct verbal interaction between the interviewer and the respondent, which has both advantages and disadvantages compared to self-report tests, inventories, and questionnaires. By establishing a proper rapport with the subject, a skilled interviewer can enhance motivation and obtain information that might not otherwise have been offered. More accurate responses are obtained as the interviewer clarifies questions that the subject may have and follows up leads (probing). The interview allows for greater depth and richness of information. In face-to-face interviews, the interviewer can observe nonverbal responses and behaviors, which may indicate the need for further questioning to clarify verbal answers. The interview can be used with many types of persons, such as those who are illiterate or too young to read or write. The presence of an interviewer tends to reduce the number of "no answers" or neutral responses, and the interviewer can press for more complete answers when necessary. Compared to questionnaires, interviews usually achieve higher return rates; often as many as 90 or 95% of the subjects will agree to be interviewed.

One disadvantage of interviews is that because they are expensive and time-consuming compared with other methods of data collection, the sample size is often small. With small samples a high response rate is needed to avoid bias in the nature of the sample. The number of refusals to be interviewed, if greater than 20%, may seriously bias the results. The advantages of flexibility and the opportunity for probing and clarification allow for a certain degree of subjectivity in summarizing what is heard. This subjectivity may lead to biased interpretation of responses. These effects will be discussed in greater detail following a brief summary of different types of interview questions.

Like observations, interviews are used for quantitative, qualitative, and mixed-method studies. Here, we will be primarily concerned with interviews for quantitative and some mixed-method studies. More detail on qualitative interviewing will be covered in Chapter 10.

Types of Interview Questions

Structured questions: Subject chooses from responses provided.

There are three types of interview questions: structured, semistructured, and unstructured. **Structured questions** used for quantitative data collection give the subject choices from which an answer is selected. For example, in a study of student attitudes, the interviewer may ask, "How important is it to you to obtain high grades in school? Is it critical, very important, important, or not very important?" Structured questions are often used in telephone interviews, which for some purposes can provide data comparable to those obtained through personal interviews at much less cost.

Semistructured questions: Specific questions without predetermined response options.

Semistructured questions, which are used in both quantitative and qualitative studies, do not have predetermined, structured choices. Rather, the question is open-ended yet specific in intent, allowing individual responses. For instance, an interviewer may ask, "What are some things that teachers you like do best?" The question is reasonably objective, yet it allows for probing, follow-up, and clarification. It is the most common type of interview question in educational research.

Unstructured questions: Open-ended, general questions.

Unstructured questions, which are open-ended and broad, are a mainstay of qualitative research. The interviewer has a general goal in mind and asks questions relevant to this goal. Thus, there is some latitude in what is asked, and often somewhat different questions are used with each subject. The unstructured interview is difficult to conduct. It is highly subjective and requires considerable training and experience. Thus, in research that has employed unstructured questions, look carefully for evidence that the interviewer has the appropriate expertise to conduct the interview and then interpret the results.

Leading question: Encourages a certain answer.

Regardless of the type of interview, it is important that the questions are worded so that the subject is not led to a particular answer. A **leading question** biases the results by encouraging one answer from all the subjects. For example, if the interviewer asks, "Wouldn't you agree that Mrs. Jones is an excellent teacher?" the subjects are led toward a yes response.

Interviewer Effects

The ideal role of the interviewer is to act as a neutral medium through which information is transmitted. The interviewer should not have an effect on the results, except to make it possible for the subject to reveal information that otherwise would not have been known. However, because of the one-on-one nature of the interview, there are several potential sources of error. Like observers, interviewers must be careful that preexisting bias does not influence what they hear or record. Contamination can also occur if the interviewers have knowledge of facets of the study. With experiments they should not be aware of which subjects are receiving special interventions or whether certain results will have positive benefits. The halo effect can also occur with interviewers. Obviously, they need to be trained so that many of these potential sources of error will not arise. Interviewers also need to be trained to establish positive rapport with subjects.

There is some evidence that certain interviewer characteristics may influence the results of in-person interviews. For example, matching interviewers and subjects on demographic variables such as age, socioeconomic status, race, and gender may result in more valid results. Generally, most inhibition in responding occurs with persons of the same age but different gender. Interviewers should dress according to existing norms or in a fashion familiar to the respondents, not in such a way that the subjects sense that particular responses are desirable.

Additional error may occur from the way the in-person interview is conducted. It is important for the interviewer to be pleasant, friendly, and relaxed in establishing a relationship with the subject that is conducive to honest interchange and little inhibition. This result is often accomplished by beginning the interview with "small talk." Probing should be anticipated and planned for in the training of the interviewers, and specific types of probes should be identified for certain situations.

The manner in which the interviewer records responses may affect the results. At one extreme, a tape recorder can provide a verbatim record of the answers. The tapes can then be analyzed by different individuals to increase validity, as is typically done with qualitative research. This method is most useful with unstructured questions, which lend themselves to greater subjectivity on the part of the interviewer. However, the mere presence of a tape recorder may inhibit some subjects. At the other extreme, the interviewer can wait until the interview is over and then write notes that summarize the results. This procedure is more prone to error because it is easier for interview bias to affect what is remembered and recorded. To reduce this source of error, most interviewers take some notes during the interview. Typically, they write brief notes for each question during the interview that can be expanded after the interview is over. One way to increase reliability is to send a copy of the interviewer's notes to each subject and give them an opportunity to add or revise as necessary to increase accuracy.

A summary of problems faced by researchers using questionnaires, observations, and interviews for obtaining noncognitive information is provided in Table 6.4. Look for these problems when determining the quality of the measurement.

TABLE 6.4 Problems for Researchers Measuring Noncognitive Traits

Problems
Questionnaire
Multiple sources of error, especially over time.
Unclear definitions of the trait.
Response set, especially social desirability.
Faking; subject motivation to respond seriously and honestly.
Observation
High inference depends on quality of observers to make judgments; may be less reliable.
Low inference reliable but often too artificial.
Observer bias.
Contamination, especially if observer knows which group is experimental and which is control.
Halo effect.
Interview
Depends on skills of the interviewer.
Interviewer bias.
Low sample size.
Contamination.
Expensive and time-consuming.
No anonymity for subjects.
Halo effect.
Interviewer characteristics may influence subjects.
Procedure for recording responses may not be accurate or may influence subjects.

Author Reflection *Which method of collecting data is best? I have used all of the approaches in this chapter and have found that the richest, most relevant data come from well-done interviews. There is simply no substitute for engaging another person in a face-to-face setting. Yes, it is time-consuming, but the advantage of being able to probe and observe nonverbal communication is invaluable. There is something about direct personal interaction that is unique, even when determining what someone knows and can do from an achievement standpoint.*

My experience after being involved in many studies in which interviews were used to collect data is that respondents are very honest. This has been my experience with adults, children, and adolescents, whether tape-recorded or not. Generally, people want to be helpful, especially most education professionals. As long as you have the resources, interviewing is a great way to obtain great data.

SOURCES FOR LOCATING *and* EVALUATING EXISTING INSTRUMENTS

Literally thousands of instruments have been used in educational research over the past 50 years. When you read research, you will encounter many different measures. How will you know if they are providing valid and reliable information? As noted earlier, research is only as good as the measurement on which it is based. Consequently, it is best to be able to evaluate the instruments that were used by studying the information provided by the researchers in a report or article. Often, however, there is insufficient information in the article to make an informed judgment. In this case, a number of sources can be used to both identify and evaluate existing educational measures (see Table 6.5). Some of the sources summarize the instruments; others provide a critique as well.

TABLE 6.5 Sources of Information about Available Instruments

Source	Information Provided
Index to Tests Used in Educational Dissertations (Fabiano, 1989)	Describes tests and test populations used in dissertations from 1938 to 1980; keyed by title and selected descriptors.
ERIC	The ERIC database can be used to locate instruments in two ways. One approach is to find research articles and reports that include a measure of a construct that can be used as a keyword or descriptor in the search. Another good strategy is to go to the Advanced Search Web page, enter your keyword or descriptor, and then go to the Publication Type pull-down menu and click on "Tests/Questionnaires."
Test Link ETS Test Collection and Collection Database	Test Link is a database that contains descriptions of over 25,000 previously administered tests, surveys, and assessment tools that are contained in the ETS (Educational Testing Service) Test Collection. This library contains instruments collected from the early 1900s to the present, and it is the largest such compilation in the world. The database can be searched by author, title, topic, or date. Each record contains information about the test, including an abstract. Once identified, a test can be ordered from ETS. The collection also includes materials that accompany tests, such as administration guidelines, scoring procedures, and psychometric information.

TABLE 6.5 (Continued)

Source	Information Provided
Tests: A Comprehensive Reference for Assessments in Psychology, Education, and Business, 4th ed. (Maddox, 2002)	Provides a description of over 3,100 published tests, including purpose, cost, scoring, and publisher.
Test Critiques, Vols. 1–10 (Keyser & Sweetland, 1994)	Gives evaluations for widely used, newly published, and recently revised instruments in psychology, education, and business. Contains "user-oriented" information, including practical applications and uses, as well as technical aspects and a critique by a measurement specialist. The companion, *Test Critiques Compendium,* reviews major tests from *Test Critiques* in one volume.
Handbook of Family Measurement Techniques (Touliatos, Perlmutter, Straus, & Holden, 2001)	A three-volume set provides overviews and reviews of hundreds of instruments used to measure family variables.
Mental Measurements Yearbooks (MMYs) Buros Institute of Mental Measurements	Provides critical reviews of commercially available tests. References for most of the tests facilitate further research. The MMYs have been published periodically for 70 years. Each new MMY edition provides reviews of only new or revised tests. The MMY contains descriptions of newly released or revised instruments. Thus, if a test has not been revised recently, information could be obtained by consulting an earlier edition. The MMY evaluations are available on Test Reviews Online, also sponsored by the Buros Institute. Test Reviews Online is a subscription service that allows searching by title, purpose, publisher, acronym, author, and scores. The database contains nearly 4,000 commercially available tests.
Tests in Print (TIP)	Also published periodically by the Buros Institute. TIP provides a comprehensive index to the MMY by including brief descriptions of over 4,000 commercially available instruments, intended uses, and a reference list of professional literature about each instrument.
Handbook for Measurement and Evaluation in Early Childhood Education (Goodwin & Driscoll, 1980)	A comprehensive review of affective, cognitive, and psychomotor measures for young children.
Handbook of Research Design and Social Measurement, 6th ed. (Miller & Salkind, 2002)	Reviews and critiques popular social science measures.
Directory of Unpublished Experimental Mental Measures, Vol. 9 (Goldman & Mitchell, 2007)	Describes nearly 1,700 experimental mental measures that are not commercially available. Includes references, source, and purpose on topics ranging from educational adjustment and motivation to personality and perception.

In addition to these sources, an excellent way to obtain information about an instrument is to contact its developer. The developer may be able to send you a technical manual and may know about other researchers who have used the instrument. Technical manuals are almost always available for published tests.

Finally, you may want to try a computer search of journal articles that have up-to-date information on critical evaluations of validity and reliability and other studies that have used the instrument. In the ERIC database a proximity search is one alternative. In a proximity search terms that make up the name of the instrument, or related terms, are used to locate relevant articles. The database for *Psychological Abstracts*, PsycINFO, indexes major instruments by name.

CONSUMER TIPS: *Criteria for Evaluating Instrumentation*

1. **Evidence for validity should be stated clearly.** The researchers should address validity by explicitly indicating the type of evidence that is presented, the results of analyses that establish validity, and how the evidence supports the inferences that are made. For evidence that does not match well with the subjects or situation of the investigation, the researcher should indicate why it is reasonable to believe that the results are appropriate and useful. References should cite previous research that supports the validity of the inferences. It is best to collect evidence for validity in a pretest or pilot test.

2. **Evidence for reliability should be stated clearly.** The researchers should clearly indicate the reliability of all scores. The type of reliability estimate used should be indicated, and it should be consistent with the use of the results. Reliability should be established in a pretest or pilot test with subjects similar to those used in the research. High reliability is especially important for results that show no difference or no relationship.

3. **The instruments should be clearly described.** Sufficient information about the instrument should be given to enable the reader to understand how the subjects gave their responses. This information includes some idea of the type of item, which is often accomplished by providing examples. It is also necessary to indicate how the instrument is scored.

4. **The procedures for administering the instrument should be clearly described.** The reader needs to know when the instrument was given and the conditions of its administration. Who gave the instrument to the subjects? What did they know about the study? What were the subjects told before they answered the questions? Did anything unusual happen during the administration? Did the subjects understand the directions for completing the instrument? These questions are especially critical for standardized tests.

5. **Norms should be specified for norm-referenced interpretations.** The norms used to determine the results need to be clearly indicated. What is the nature of the norm group? Is it appropriate to the type of inferences that are made?

6. **Procedures for setting standards should be indicated for criterion-referenced (standards-based) interpretations.** It is necessary to know how the standards used to judge the results are set. Were experts consulted to verify the credibility of the standard? What is the difficulty level of the items in relation to the standard?

7. **The scores used in reporting results should be meaningful.** Often standard scores or some type of derived scores are used in reporting the results.

Whatever the scores, they should not distort the actual differences or relationships, either by inflating or deflating the apparent differences or relationships.

8. Measures of noncognitive traits should avoid problems of response set and faking. Researchers need to indicate how response set and faking are controlled for when measuring personality, attitudes, values, and interests. Special attention should be given to the manner in which the subjects are motivated.

9. Observers and interviewers should be trained. Researchers must show that the observers and interviewers in studies have been trained to avoid such problems as bias, contamination, and halo effect. Interviewers need to know how not to ask leading questions and how to probe effectively. Interobserver reliability should be indicated.

10. In high-inference observations the qualifications of the observers to make sound professional judgments should be indicated. With low-inference observations reliability is usually high, but if high-inference observations are used, the characteristics and training of the observer are more important and should be specified.

11. The effect of the interviewer or observer should be minimal. Examine the characteristics of the interviewers. Could these traits create any error in the nature of the responses obtained? Were appropriate steps taken to establish a proper rapport with the subjects? Any possible effects of the interviewer or observer on the subjects should be noted.

STUDY QUESTIONS

1. What are some ways of classifying educational measures?
2. What is the difference between "off-the-shelf" and "locally developed" tests?
3. What is the difference between criterion-referenced and norm-referenced interpretations?
4. Why are changes in scores and differences between groups difficult to obtain with many standardized tests?
5. What is the difference between standardized achievement tests and standardized aptitude tests?
6. Why are standard scores difficult to interpret?
7. Give some examples of different ways of measuring self-concept and attitudes.
8. What is the difference between Likert and Likert-type scales?
9. Identify factors that affect the measurement of noncognitive traits. How does each one affect the results?
10. What are the advantages of observations over self-reports?
11. Under what circumstances would it be better to use high-inference rather than low-inference observation?
12. In what ways are observer and interviewer effects the same?
13. Compare the interview with the questionnaire. What are the advantages and disadvantages of each?
14. Identify criteria for evaluating instrumentation. What would you look for when reading the instrumentation section of a research article?

Chapter 7

Nonexperimental Quantitative Research Designs

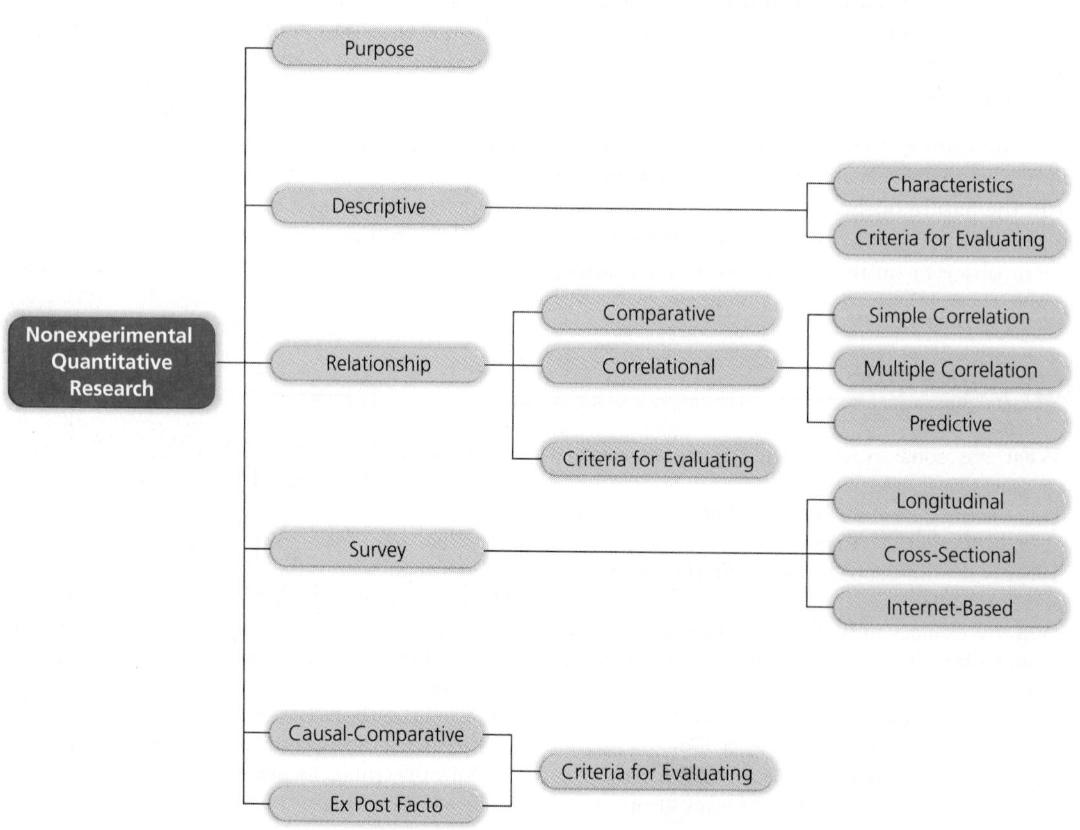

CHAPTER ROAD MAP

We now turn our attention to commonly employed quantitative research designs. **Research design** refers to the way information is gathered from subjects and, in the case of experimental research, the nature of the interventions. In this chapter we will consider four types of *nonexperimental* research designs: descriptive, comparative, correlational, and ex post facto. Identifying and understanding these designs will enable you to know what to look for and what to ask about research weaknesses, limitations, and mistakes.

Research design: How information is obtained.

Chapter Outline	Learning Objectives
Types of Nonexperimental Designs	• Know about and identify different types of nonexperimental designs.
Descriptive Designs	• Understand the importance of the sample and instrumentation for descriptive studies.
Researching Relationships	• Understand that relationships can be studied with either comparisons or correlations.
Comparative Studies	• Understand and apply criteria for evaluating studies that use comparative data. • Recognize possible limitations or shortcomings in comparative research.
Correlational Studies	• Understand and apply criteria for evaluating correlational findings. • Distinguish between bivariate and multiple correlation. • Be able to interpret a correlation matrix. • Understand why it is rare that causation or explanation can be inferred from correlational findings. • Understand the difference between statistical significance and practical significance in reporting correlational data.
Causal-Comparative Studies	• Understand the elements of a causal-comparative design. • Know the purpose, strengths, and weaknesses of causal-comparative studies. • Know the criteria for evaluating causal-comparative studies.
Ex Post Facto Studies	• Understand the elements of an ex post facto design. • Know the purpose, strengths, and weaknesses of ex post facto studies. • Know the criteria for evaluating ex post facto studies.
Survey Research	• Know the purpose of using surveys. • Know the steps used to create and administer surveys. • Understand the difference between cross-sectional and longitudinal survey research. • Know the strengths and weaknesses of electronic surveys.

The PURPOSE *of* NONEXPERIMENTAL RESEARCH

Whereas experimental research seeks to understand causal relationships by introducing an intervention, nonexperimental research essentially describes participants, traits, scores, and other characteristics without direct or active

TABLE 7.1 Purposes of Different Types of Nonexperimental Research Designs

Design	Purpose
Descriptive	To provide a description of a phenomenon.
Comparative	To compare values of two or more levels of an independent variable.
Correlational	To show how two variables are related using a correlation coefficient.
Predictive	To show how well one or more variables predicts something.
Causal-comparative	To suggest causal conclusions by comparing groups that receive naturally occurring interventions.
Ex post facto	To suggest causal conclusions by comparing groups that received different interventions in the past.

intervention. In this sense, nonexperimental studies investigate the current or past status of something. This general purpose leads to other reasons for nonexperimental designs, reasons based on relationships, comparisons, predictions, and explanations. While most nonexperimental research is not designed to suggest causal explanations, some studies target just this kind of finding. And many nonexperimental studies contain more than one purpose. A useful strategy to understand purpose is to identify which nonexperimental design is employed. These are summarized in Table 7.1 and considered in greater detail in separate parts of this chapter.

DESCRIPTIVE STUDIES

Characteristics of Descriptive Studies

A descriptive study simply describes a phenomenon. The description is usually in the form of statistics such as frequencies or percentages, averages, and sometimes variability. Often graphs and other visual images of the results are used. Descriptive research is particularly valuable when an area is first investigated. For example, there has been much research on the nature of classroom climate and its relationship to student attitudes and learning. A first step in this research was to describe adequately what is meant by "classroom climate," initially by a clear constitutive definition, then operationally with measures. Climate surveys, which assess characteristics such as how students talk and act toward one another, how they feel about the teacher and learning, and feelings of openness, acceptance, trust, respect, rejection, hostility, and cooperation, are used to understand classroom atmosphere. Once this understanding is achieved, various dimensions of climate can be related to student learning and teacher satisfaction, and ultimately climate can be controlled to examine causal relationships.

Suppose you read a study on the relationship between principals' leadership styles and teachers' attitudes. You should first look for an adequate description of *leadership styles* of principals and *attitudes* of teachers, since the usefulness of the results depends on credible descriptions. Much of the current emphasis on accountability in our schools is based on descriptive research, examining student outcomes such as current levels of proficiency or dropout rates. The following questions are the types investigated with descriptive research designs:

What do teachers think about magnet schools?
How often do students write papers?
What is the nature of the papers students are required to write?
What percentage of students score above 1100 on the SAT?
What forms of communication are used in the school district?
How often are higher-order questions used in the classroom?
What type of reinforcement does the teacher use?

Example 7.1 is a summary of a study about school counselors that was primarily descriptive in nature. We say primarily because this study also included some correlational analyses. This is not uncommon. Most nonexperimental studies contain more than one type of design element and purpose. Also, what is sometimes called "descriptive" by a researcher could mean correlational and comparative aspects as well.

EXAMPLE 7.1 | A Descriptive Nonexperimental Study

A survey was designed to comprehensively assess multiple aspects of school counselor job satisfaction and job-related frustration, as well as orientation with the comprehensive curriculum-based guidance program used in Arizona. . . . While the majority of respondents reported high levels of job satisfaction, the least satisfying aspects of their work involved working with district administrators. . . . and utilizing excessive time in providing system support. Respondents' greatest levels of satisfaction involved direct interaction and engagement with students.

Source: Kolodinsky, P., Draves, P., Schroder, V., Lindsey, C., & Zlatev, M. (2009). Reported levels of satisfaction and frustration by Arizona School counselors: A desire for greater connections with students in a data-driven era. *Professional School Counseling. 12*(3), 193.

CONSUMER TIPS: *Criteria for Evaluating Descriptive Studies*

1. Conclusions about relationships should be made with caution. An important limitation of descriptive studies is that relationship conclusions generally are not warranted. It is easy to make assumptions from simple descriptions about how two or more variables may be related, but such conclusions are unwarranted. For instance, suppose a study describes the types of questions students and teachers ask in a classroom and reports that teachers ask "low-level" questions and students do not ask questions at all. It would be tempting to conclude that there is a relationship between these variables—namely, the more teachers ask "low-level" questions, the fewer questions students ask. However, to address the question of relationship, teachers would also have to ask "high-level" questions.

2. Subjects and instrumentation should be well described. When evaluating descriptive research, you should pay particular attention to the subjects and the instrumentation. You should know whether the sample is made up of volunteers and whether the results would have been different if other subjects had been included. The instrumentation section should have documentation of validity and reliability, and the procedures for gathering the data need to be specified. You should know when the data were collected, by whom, and under what circumstances. For example, a description of what is occurring in a class may differ, depending on whether the observer is a teacher, principal, or parent.

Descriptive studies use simple descriptive statistics to report the findings. This includes percentages, means, standard deviations, rankings, and frequencies. This is illustrated in the manner in which results were reported for the study described in Example 7.2, which used both averages and percentages to report results.

EXAMPLE 7.2 | Using Averages and Percentages to Report Descriptive Results

Respondents reported spending an average of just under 37% of their time counseling students. . . . On average, school counselors reported spending 21.6% of their time working with teachers, just over 15% of their time responding to crises, 18.4 % of their time providing system support, and 12.1% of their time engaged in nonguidance activities. . . . In terms of reported job satisfaction, nearly 82% of surveyed school counselors reported that they were "mostly satisfied" or "satisfied almost all of the time". . . a majority (78.8%) were "mostly" or "almost all of the time" satisfied with their work with teachers.

Source: Kolodinsky, P., Draves, P., Schroder, V., Lindsey, C., & Zlatev, M. (2009). Reported levels of satisfaction and frustration by Arizona School counselors: A desire for greater connections with students in a data-driven era. *Professional School Counseling. 12*(3), 196.

RELATIONSHIPS *in* NONEXPERIMENTAL DESIGNS

Before we examine comparative and correlational designs, a word or two is needed on the nature of relationships among variables. All quantitative research that is not simply descriptive is interested in relationships (remember, some use "descriptive" as a category that includes correlational and comparative). A **relationship,** or *association*, is found when one variable varies systematically with another variable. Relationship is illustrated in Figure 7.1. Here the variables of interest are grade level and self-concept. You can see that a relationship exists

Relationship: Systematic variation between two variables.

FIGURE 7.1 Relationship between grade level and self-concept.

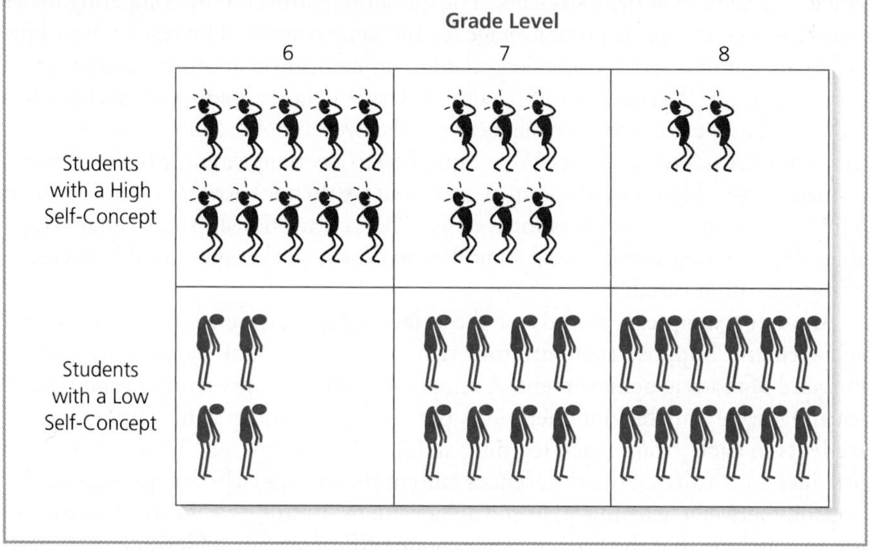

Grade Level

6 7 8

Students with a High Self-Concept

Students with a Low Self-Concept

between grade level and self-concept because there are progressively fewer students with a high self-concept as grade level increases. This example shows how relationship can be investigated by comparing different groups. In this case there is a negative relationship because as one variable increases (grade level), the other variable decreases (number of students with high self-concept). Relationships are also investigated with correlational designs.

Relationships are important in our understanding of teaching and learning for several reasons. First, relationships allow us to make a preliminary identification of possible causes of students' achievement, teachers' performance, principals' leadership, and other important educational outcomes. Second, relationships help us identify variables that may be investigated in experiments. Third, relationships allow us to predict the value of one variable from the value of other variables. Perhaps most important, the language of research is dominated by the term *relationship*. As a consumer of research, you need to be fully informed about what is meant by relationship and what relationship studies can and cannot tell us.

COMPARATIVE STUDIES

Characteristics of Comparative Studies

The purpose of comparative studies is to investigate the relationship of one variable to another by simply examining whether the value of the dependent variable(s) in one group is the same as or different from the value of the dependent variable(s) of other groups. In other words, a comparative study compares two or more groups on one or many variables. A simple example is a study of the relationship between gender and school grades. A sample of female students' grades could be compared to the grades of a sample of male students. The question is answered by comparing males to females on, say, grade point average for the same courses. The results show how differences in one variable, gender, relate to differences on another variable, grade point average. If the results show that females have a higher grade point average, this indicates that there is a relationship between the two variables. Notice, however, that this is not a *causal* relationship. We can predict, to a certain extent, whether females or males have a higher grade point average, but we do not know how being male or female affects or *causes* grade point average. That is, a relationship between two variables does not necessarily reveal an underlying cause or that one variable affects or changes another variable.

Another example is a study of the relationship between learning style and achievement. Suppose there are four types or categories of learning style and a measure of reading achievement. A sample of students representing each type of learning style can be obtained, and the average reading achievement of the students in each group (each learning style) can be compared. This method also provides a measure of the differences among the groups, which represent a relationship between learning style and achievement. In this case we must be careful not to conclude that the learning styles *caused* differences in achievement. At best, we can predict that students with a particular type of learning style will have higher or lower achievement. Learning style may affect or influence achievement, but our relationship study does not give us a good measure of cause and effect. This hypothetical study is diagrammed in Figure 7.2.

FIGURE 7.2 **Diagram of a relationship study examining group differences.**

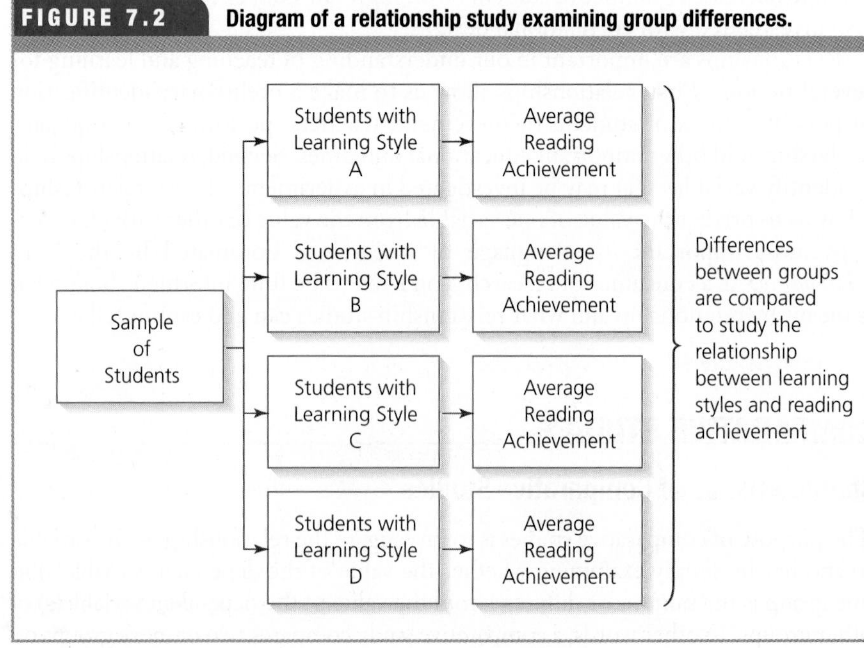

In the examples that follow, the first is a comparative study that determines the differences between men's and women's perceptions of bullying. In the second example, the study examines whether graduate students from a CACREP program have stronger counselor self-efficacy than graduates of non-CACREP programs (CACREP is an accrediting agency for school counseling programs).

EXAMPLES 7.3–7.4 | Comparative Research Designs

Do male and female teachers perceive bullying differently? To begin to answer this question, we compared the mean scores of men and women teachers on our measures of bullying. There were no significant differences between men ($n = 40$) and women ($n = 53$) on the two measures. For student bullying, men had a mean of 3.36 and women had a mean of 3.69 ($t = -.15$, ns) and for teacher protection, men had a mean of 3.62 and women 3.79 ($t = -.76$, ns).

Source: Smith, P. A., & Hoy, W. K. (2004). Teachers' perceptions of student bullying: A conceptual and empirical analysis. *Journal of School Leadership, 14*, 308.

This study was designed to investigate counseling self-efficacy of graduate students in counselor education programs to determine whether Bandura's (1986) self-efficacy theory applies. Specifically, we investigated the relationship between the training background of graduate students and counselor self-efficacy. . . . In other words, we examined whether students from CACREP-accredited and non-CACREP-accredited counselor training programs would demonstrate differences in counseling self-efficacy.

Source: Tang, M., Addison, K. D., LaSure-Bryant, D., Norman, R., O'Connell, W., & Stewart-Sicking, J. A. (2004). Factors that influence self-efficacy of counseling students: An exploratory study. *Counselor Education and Supervision, 44*, 73.

CONSUMER TIPS: *Criteria for Evaluating Comparative Studies*

1. Subjects, instrumentation, and procedures should be well described. As in descriptive studies, it is important for the researcher to clearly and completely describe the subjects, instruments used, and procedures for gathering the data. In comparative studies it is also important to know if subjects who are in different groups have unique characteristics that could better explain differences on the dependent variable than could be explained by the independent variable. For example, suppose a researcher drew a sample of first-grade students from one school and compared the students to second-graders from a different school on attitudes toward reading. Even if more positive attitudes were found for the second-graders, this result may have been because of differences between the student populations (e.g., one school serving a higher socioeconomic level, or one school being private, the other public) rather than grade level.

2. Identify the criteria for establishing different groups. It is important to know how the researcher formed the different groups that are compared. In some studies the criterion or procedure for forming the groups is self-evident, such as studies that compare males to females, but there are many studies in which the procedure is important to interpretation of the results. For example, suppose a study is designed to compare participation in athletics of low-ability students and high-ability students. How the researcher identifies "high ability" and "low ability" is important. What measure, if any, was used to assess ability? How were the groups formed? One approach would be to take all the students and divide them into two ability groups on the basis of the median ability score of the group as a whole. Or, the researcher could take the highest and lowest third or quartile of students. Another approach would be to establish groups by how the students compared with the national norms, rather than just themselves. You can see that several approaches are possible, and none of them are necessarily better or more correct than others.

3. Do not infer causation from comparative research designs. It is important not to infer that a causal relationship exists in a comparative study. The best that you can conclude with a comparative design is that a relationship exists or that there are significant differences between the groups, but it is not a *causal* relationship. This principle is easy to overlook because some comparative studies seem to logically establish a causal connection between the independent and dependent variables. For instance, suppose it is reported that students from private schools outscore students from public schools on measures of achievement. It is tempting to conclude that the reason, or cause, of the difference is the nature of the school (private or public). However, there are many other possible explanations, such as differences in parental involvement, socioeconomic status of students, curriculum used, and quality of teachers.

4. Graphic presentations should not distort the results. Since graphs are used frequently to present comparative results, you need to be careful in interpreting the resulting "picture." Graphs, whether histograms, pie charts, or frequency polygons, show an image of the results, and you are more likely to remember the image than the numbers that correspond to it. This is fine when the image is a reasonable representation of the numbers, but numbers can be manipulated in a graph to present different images. One type of disortion to look for is in the vertical dimensions of the graph. The size of the interval between different scores is set by the researcher, and this size greatly affects the resulting image. In fact, a crafty researcher can make fairly substantial differences appear quite small by decreasing the size of the intervals between scores or other measurement units. The researcher can also make small differences look large. For example, look at the two graphic presentations in Figure 7.3. Although each graph has summarized the same information about expenditures per pupil, the visual results are different because the size of the interval between each amount is much smaller in one graph than in the other. In Figure 7.4 you can see that, by changing the width of the bars, one bar can look more than twice as large as the other bar.

FIGURE 7.3 Current expenditures per pupil.

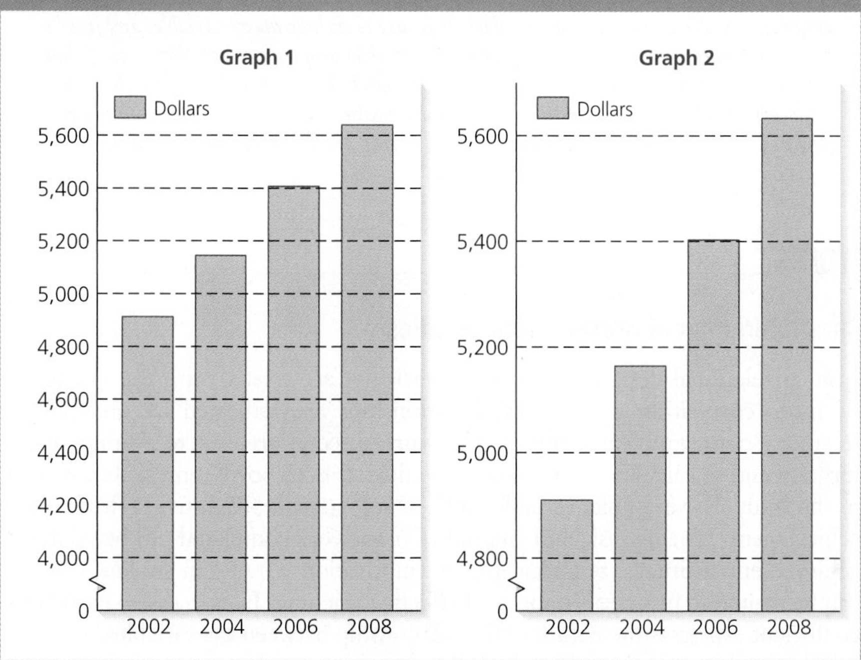

FIGURE 7.4 Distorted bar graph.

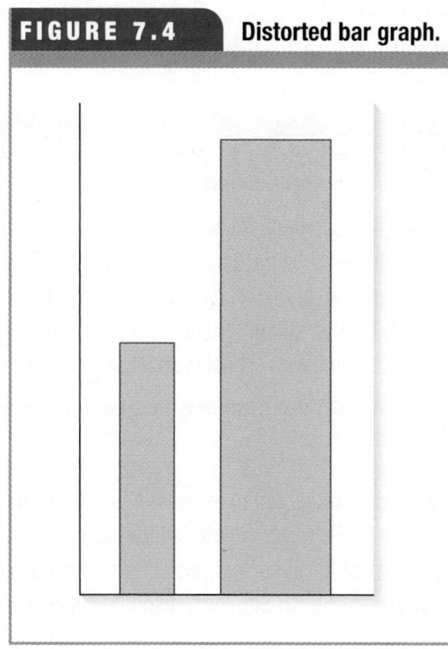

Author Reflection *Over the years I have seen many students conduct seemingly simple descriptive, comparative, or correlational studies and then become overwhelmed by the number of analyses, tables, and variables. It is easy to include many variables and just "a few more" questions on a survey. Often these variables or questions are "interesting" but not directly related to the main purpose of the research. Researchers learn more by focusing on a few variables or questions in depth than by measuring many variables with many questions and then spending arduous hours reporting and interpreting the results.*

CORRELATIONAL STUDIES

Characteristics of Correlational Studies

In a correlational design two or more variables are related with the use of one or more correlation coefficients. Relationships are indicated by obtaining at least two scores from each subject. The pairs of scores are used to produce a scattergram and to calculate a correlation coefficient. Each score represents a variable in the study. For example, variables such as self-concept, cognitive style, previous achievement, time on task, and amount of homework completed can be related to achievement, attitudes, self-concept, and motivation. Grades in student teaching can be related to principals' ratings of effective teaching. In each case a correlation coefficient expresses the nature of the relationship between the variables.

This is what was reported in the following two examples, Examples 7.5 and 7.6. The first examined the relationship between leadership practices and demographic characteristics; the second study measured correlations between the quality of school facilities, school climate, and student achievement.

EXAMPLES 7.5–7.6 | **Using Correlations to Report Nonexperimental Results**

Bivariate correlations (Pearson product-moment and Spearman's rank–order) were used to determine any relationships between school counselor demographics (gender, age, professional training, experience, and work setting) and leadership practices. . . . Negative relationships were indicated between leadership practices and graduate training . . . the year the most recent degree was obtained . . . and the number of school counselors employed in the school.

Source: Mason, E. C. M., & McMahon, H. G. (2009). Leadership practices of school counselors. *Professional School Counseling, 13*(2), 112.

Next, correlational analyses were conducted to examine the relationships between the variables. . . . The quality of school facilities was related to the School Climate Index ($r = 0.61$, $p < 0.01$). . . . The quality of school facilities was related to student achievement in English and mathematics ($r = 0.25$, $p < 0.05$). . . . Similarly, resource support was related to student achievement ($r = 0.31$, $p < 0.05$).

Source: Uline, C., & Tschannen-Moran, M. (2008). The walls speak: The interplay of quality facilities school climate, and student achievement. *Journal of Educational Administration, 46*(1), 65.

When highly reliable scores are used, correlations are stronger. Conversely, if reliability is low, correlations are weak. Consequently, the researcher should demonstrate evidence of reliability for the types of subjects in the study. It is also important for the instrument to provide a range of responses from a sufficient number of subjects. That is, the scores on the measures need to show good dispersion. If the scores are about the same on a variable, it is difficult to relate the variable to anything else. For example, if a study examines the relationship between ratings of teacher effectiveness and teaching style and all the teachers in the sample are rated as excellent, there would be no chance of finding a relationship. Similarly, it is difficult to find relationships between achievement of gifted students and other variables because of the lack of variability of achievement among these students.

Lack of variability can result when an instrument fails to differentiate along a continuum, or when the subjects are too homogeneous on one of the traits being measured. In either case, you will need to be careful in your interpretation of relationship studies that fail to find significant relationships. If there is a lack of variability, you will not know whether there really is no relationship or, because of a small range of responses, a particular study was unable to show the relationship.

There is also a limitation on finding significant relationships in a study that has a very large number of subjects and/or variables. Some researchers, using what is sometimes called the "shotgun" approach, measure a large number of variables with the hope that at least some of the many correlations that are calculated will be significant. However, in such studies some of the correlations will be statistically significant by chance alone, and without a theoretical or practical reason for inclusion, the results will be difficult to interpret. When thousands of subjects are used it is also possible to calculate statistically significant correlations that are actually quite small. Consequently, the relationship that is reported may be very small and of little value. We will discuss this limitation later in this chapter. Correlations studies strive to have at least 30 subjects.

Example 7.7 on page 186 shows how several simple correlations were reported in the form of a *correlation matrix*. Can you follow the narrative in this example? The statements come directly from the correlations in the table.

Prediction Studies

In a prediction study, correlation coefficients show how one variable can predict another. Whereas in a simple relationship study, both variables are measured at about the same time, a predictive study shows how one variable can predict what the value of a second variable will be at a later time. Predictions are made constantly in education. Teachers predict students' behavior. Principals predict teachers' behavior.

Suppose you are director of admissions at a selective university. You must choose a small number of students from the large pool of applicants. How should you select the students to be admitted? You decide to use some criteria to predict which students are most likely to succeed. Because one predictor is probably

EXAMPLE 7.7 | Correlation Matrix

Descriptive Statistics

Eighth grade. The overall classroom social environment construct was correlated positively with social efficacy with teachers ($r = .44$, $p < .001$), social efficacy with peers ($r = .18$, $p < .01$), academic efficacy ($r = .30$, $p < .001$), and self-regulated learning ($r = .20$, $p < .01$), and related negatively to disruptive behavior ($r = -.43$, $p < .001$). Means, standard deviations, and correlations among the four dimensions of the classroom social environment and the motivation and engagement indices measured in eighth grade are presented in Table 1. An expected pattern of correlations was found. Teacher support, promoting interaction, and promoting mutual respect were related positively to social efficacy with teachers and peers, academic efficacy, and self-regulated learning, and related negatively to disruptive behavior. Promoting performance goals was related negatively to social efficacy with teachers and peers, academic efficacy, and self-regulated learning, and related positively to disruptive behavior.

Table 1 Means, Standard Deviations, and Correlations Among Perceived Classroom Social Environment Variables and Student Motivation and Engagement In Eighth Grade, Gender, Race, and Prior Achievement

	1	2	3	4	5	6	7	8	9	10	11	12
1. Teacher support	—											
2. Promote interaction	.49	—										
3. Promote mutual respect	.60	.40	—									
4. Promote performance goals	−.41	−.14	−.39	—								
5. Social efficacy: teacher	.71	.47	.49	−.45	—							
6. Social efficacy: peers	.17	.15	.20	−.17	.30	—						
7. Academic efficacy	.35	.14	.46	−.29	.47	.42	—					
8. Disruptive behavior	−.41	−.16	−.35	.45	−.35	.04	−.18	—				
9. Self-regulated learning	.44	.25	.50	−.22	.41	.20	.50	−.38	—			
10. Gender[a]	.07	.15	.10	−.18	.11	.13	−.02	−.21	−.01	—		
11. Race[b]	.01	−.16	.16	−.05	−.05	.09	.31	−.02	.10	.06	—	
12. Prior achievement[c]	.21	.05	.06	−.31	.20	.11	.11	−.21	.00	.09	−.17	—
Mean	3.22	3.22	3.52	2.15	3.60	4.16	3.86	2.54	3.27	0.57	0.44	6.72
Standard deviation	1.05	1.07	1.11	0.97	1.01	0.77	0.92	1.14	0.82			3.56

Note: Correlations about .13 are significant at the $p < .05$ lavel.

[a]Gender is coded 0 = *male* and 1 = *female*.

[b]Race is coded 0 = *European American* and 1 = *African American*.

[c]Prior achievement is seventh grade math grades 0 = *F* through 13 = *A*+).

Source: Ryan, A. M., & Patrick, H. (2001). The classroom social environment and changes in adolescents' motivation and engagement during middle school. *American Educational Research Journal, 38*(2), 448–449.

previous achievement, you look at the high school grade point average (GPA) of each applicant. If it turns out to be correlated with college GPA, you have identified a variable that can be used to predict success in college. High school students with a high GPA are likely to have a higher college GPA than high school students with a low GPA. Since high school GPA precedes college GPA, it is called a **predictor variable.** College GPA would be termed the **criterion variable.**

Predictor variable: Predicts the criterion variable.

Criterion variable: The predicted dependent variable.

In a prediction study it is necessary to collect data on a group of subjects over some length of time. Data collection can be longitudinal, that is, first collecting predictor variable data, waiting a specified amount of time, and then obtaining criterion variable data. This approach for the preceding example would involve recording the GPA of high school students before they started college, then waiting, say, for a year and recording their first-year college GPA.

An example of this kind of study is illustrated in Example 7.8, which examines the predictive relationship between amount of leisure boredom and dropping out of high school. Another study (Example 7.9) also followed individuals over time, in this case to see if selected variables predicted achievement.

EXAMPLES 7.8–7.9 | Predictive Research

This prospective cohort study investigated whether leisure boredom predicts high school dropout. . . . The original cohort of grade 8 students ($n = 303$) was followed up twice at 2-year intervals. Of the 281 students at the second follow up, 149 (53%) students had dropped out of school. . . . Leisure boredom was a significant predictor of dropout.

Source: Wegner, L., Flisher, A. J., Chikobvu, P., Lombard, C., & King, G. (2008). Leisure boredom and high school dropout in Cape Town, South Africa. *Journal of Adolescence, 31*(3), 421.

This was a longitudinal, correlational study that was conducted in two phases. In the first phase (during students' first semester in college) students completed measures of achievement motivation and their general achievement goals for college. We obtained students' transcripts 2 years later.

Source: Diurik, A. M., Lovejoy, C. M., & Johnson, S. J. (2009). A longitudinal study of achievement goals for college in general: Predicting cumulative GPA and diversity in course selection. *Contemporary Educational Psychology, 34,* 116.

In some studies the predictive relationship is "tested" with another sample of subjects. The tested prediction (which will be lower than the original one), is the relationship that most closely indicates how well the predictor variable will predict the criterion variable with future groups of subjects.

A predictive study of student success in a gifted program is summarized in Example 7.10. The WISC-R, teachers' recommendations, grades, and achievement test scores were used as predictors, and the criterion variable was the degree of success in a gifted program. Notice in the method section how the authors indicate that one group of students is used to establish the predictive relationship and another group of students is used to "test" it.

EXAMPLE 7.10 | Predictive Research

This study was conducted in two phases. The initial phase of the study involved 120 elementary school students aged 6 through 11 years. These students had different degrees of success in a gifted program. . . . The second phase of the investigation involved random selection of an additional 41 subjects from the same gifted program. . . . In phase two, an attempt was made, using the results of phase one data, to predict those students who were known to have been either marginally or highly successful in the program.

Source: Lustberg, R. S., Motta, R., & Naccari, N. (1990). A model using the WISC-R to predict success in programs for gifted children. *Psychology in the Schools, 21*, 126–131.

Several factors influence the accuracy of the predictions. One, like simple correlations, is the reliability of the scores obtained from the predictor and criterion variables. Another factor is the length of time between the predictor and criterion variables. In most cases, predictions involving a short time span are more accurate than those involving a long time span because of the general principle that the correlation between two variables decreases as the amount of time between the variables increases; also, with more time there is a greater opportunity for other variables to influence the criterion variable, which would lower the accuracy. Finally, criterion variables, such as success in college, leadership, a successful marriage, and effective teaching, that are affected by many factors, are more difficult to predict than relatively simple criterion variables such as success in the next mathematics class.

In many situations predictions are most accurate if more than one predictor variable is used. For example, in predicting college GPA, several variables may be predictive, and by combining them, we can make more accurate decisions about who should be admitted. In studies in which several predictor variables are combined, a statistical procedure called **multiple regression analysis** provides a single index of the predictive power of all the predictor variables together. A **coefficient of multiple correlation,** symbolized by R, is the correlation of all the independent variables (predictor variables) to the dependent variable (criterion variable). A multiple correlation, then, correlates a combination of two or more variables; a *bivariate* correlation shows the relationship between only two variables. In interpreting multiple regression analysis, it is important to know about the correlations of the independent variables with one another. It is most desirable to have independent variables that are not correlated much with one another but highly correlated with the dependent variable. If the independent variables are highly correlated with one another, the predictive power of some of the variables may be masked.

Multiple regression analysis: Combines several predictor variables.

Coefficient of multiple correlation: The combined correlation of several predictor variables.

Researchers typically find that some of the independent variables are better predictors than others, and these are called *significant*. This is what the authors of the study in Example 7.11 report.

EXAMPLE 7.11 | Use of Multiple Regression in a Predictive Study

A series of regressions were conducted to predict students' achievement goals. . . . When the variables were used to predict mastery-approach goals, the overall model was significant. . . . Two significant univariate effects emerged. As predicted, workmastery positively predicted the adoption of mastery goals. . . . In contrast, competitiveness negatively predicted mastery goals.

Source: Diurik, A. M., Lovejoy, C. M., & Johnson, S. J. (2009). A longitudinal study of achievement goals for college in general: Predicting cumulative GPA and diversity in course selection. *Contemporary Educational Psychology, 34*, 116.

When a study examines a dependent variable that is dichotomous, for example pass/fail, a procedure called **logistic regression** is often used to explore the relationship between the explanatory or predictive variables and the outcome. (See Example 7.12.) This analysis is becoming popular in part because the results typically report something called the *odds ratio*. The odds ratio is an indication of the power of the independent variables in "odds" language. For instance, if a study was done to examine the relationship between course grades in different subjects and pass/fail of an English test, the result could be stated as: Students who obtain A or B on three of six courses are twice as likely to pass the test as students who receive a C or D.

Logistic regression: Combines several variables to predict a dichotomous outcome.

EXAMPLE 7.12 | Logistic Regression

Three separate forward logistic regressions were tested to determine which independent variables were predictors of school performance. . . . The data was screened for outlier cases and the existence of multicollinearity. . . . The 4th grade model correctly classified 84.4 percent of the cases, while the 8th and 10th grade models correctly classified 91.4 percent and 81.4 percent of the cases, respectively.

Source: Tajalli, H., & Opheim, C. (2004). Strategies for closing the gap: Predicting student performance in economically disadvantaged schools. *Educational Research Quarterly, 28*(4), 49.

CONSUMER TIPS: *Criteria for Evaluating Correlational Studies*

1. Causation should rarely be inferred from correlation. The most important principle in evaluating correlational research is that such analysis rarely infers causation. This is not as easy as it sounds, for many relationships based on correlations seem as if they *do* infer causation and many provide reasonable explanation. For example, if you find a positive predictive relationship between time on task and achievement, it is easy to conclude that increasing time on task will increase achievement. Although this *may* be true, it cannot be concluded from a correlational finding for two reasons. First, the direction of possible causation is not clear. That is, it may be that higher previous achievement causes students to be on task more. Second, other variables associated with time on task that are not included in the study may affect the relationship and may, in fact, be causally related. For instance, perhaps students who spend more time on task have a higher aptitude for learning, better motivation for learning, and more parental support than students who spend less time on task. Perhaps teachers interact differently with students who are on task compared with students who tend to be off task.

This principle is illustrated more clearly in a relationship between student achievement and per-pupil expenditures. Although a positive relationship exists, it would be a mistake to think that achievement can be affected simply by spending more money because many other variables also related to per-pupil expenditure, such as family background, are causes of student achievement.

As a final example of this important principle, consider the following "true" statement: There is a positive relationship between students' weight and reading achievement. Unbelievable, you think? Examine Figure 7.5. There is a positive relationship between the two factors because a third variable, age, is related to weight. Obviously, there is a positive relationship between age and reading achievement. If you were puzzled by the first conclusion, you were implying causation, which would lead to the conclusion that achievement could be improved by fattening up the students!

2. The *reported* correlation should not be higher or lower than the *actual* relationship. You need to be aware of factors that may spuriously increase or decrease a correlation. One factor is the nature of the sample from which the correlation is calculated. If the sample is more homogeneous on one of the variables than the population, the correlation will be lower than for the population as a whole. Conversely, if a sample is more heterogeneous on the variable than the population, the correlation will be higher than would be true for the population as a whole.

A second factor is the range of scores on the variables that are correlated. If the variability of scores on one variable is small, the correlation will be low. This is sometimes referred to as **restriction in range.** If the range is restricted, the variability is reduced, and without adequate variability the correlation will be low. Thus, in some research in which the range is restricted, the actual relationship is higher than that reported.

Restriction in range: A small range of variability.

A third factor relates to the reliability of the scores obtained of the correlated variables. As noted, correlations are directly related to reliability—the lower the reliability, the lower the correlation. A lowering of the correlation because of unreliability is called **attenuation** and is sometimes "corrected" statistically to show what the correlation would be if the measures were more reliable.

Attenuation: Lowering of correlation because of unreliable measures.

3. Practical significance should not be confused with statistical significance. Researchers use the word *significant* in two ways. In one sense, it refers to a statistical inference, which means the coefficient that is calculated is probably different from zero, that is, no relationship (Chapter 9 discusses this concept in greater detail). Thus, a researcher may report that "a correlation of .30 is significant." This type of phrase is associated *only* with the *statistical* meaning of significance. Another meaning of significance implies importance or meaningfulness

FIGURE 7.5 **Relationship between weight and reading achievement.**

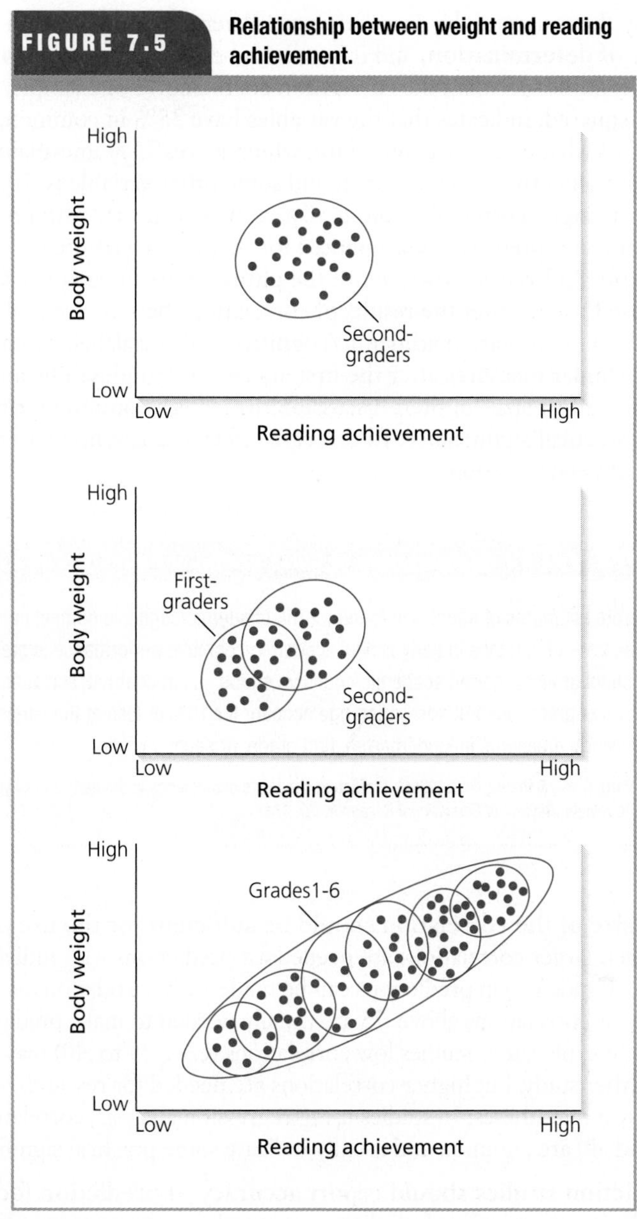

of the practical value of the correlation. This is a more subjective judgment, one that should be made by the reader of the research as well as by the researcher. One important principle of correlation needs to be considered in making this judgment. Because correlations are expressed as decimals, it is easy to confuse the coefficient with a percentage. However, the correlation coefficient is not an indication of the percentage of "sameness" between two variables. The extent to which the variables share common properties or characteristics is actually

Coefficient of determination: The square of the correlation coefficient.

indicated by the square of the correlation coefficient. This is called the **coefficient of determination,** and it is a much better indicator of practical or meaningful significance than the correlation coefficient. For example, a correlation of .50, squared, indicates that the variables have 25% in common, or 25% "explained" of what can be accounted for, which leaves 75% unexplained. Thus, if the correlation between achievement and some other variable is .70, which is regarded as a "high" correlation, about 50% of what can vary with respect to achievement is not predicted or accounted for by the correlation.

In Example 7.13 that follows, use of the phrase "percentage of variance predicted" is used to interpret the results of correlations between school readiness (preschool and kindergarten academic/cognitive and social/behavioral assessments) and similar measures after the first and second grades. The authors use the term "effect size" in their discussion, which is a common term when addressing practical significance. In this case effect size is synonymous with coefficient of determination.

EXAMPLE 7.13 | Interpretation of Correlation Coefficients

The moderate estimates of effect size found for the academic/cognitive domain indicate that, on average, 25% of variance in early school academic/cognitive performance is predicted from preschool or kindergarten academic/cognitive status. . . . In contrast, social/behavioral assessments at preschool or kindergarten age account for 10% or less of the variance in social/behavioral measures in kindergarten, first grade, or second grade.

Source: LaParo, K. M., & Pianta, R. C. (2000). Predicting children's competence in the early school years: A meta-analytic review. *Review of Educational Research, 70,* 474.

4. The size of the correlation should be sufficient for the use of the results. Much larger correlations are needed for predictions with individuals than with groups. Crude group predictions can be made with correlations as low as .40 to .60, whereas correlations above .75 are usually needed to make predictions for individuals. In exploratory studies low correlations (e.g., .25 to .40) may indicate a need for further study, but higher correlations are needed for research to confirm theories or test hypotheses. In studies using regression analysis, correlations between .20 and .40 are common and usually indicate some practical significance.

5. Prediction studies should report accuracy of prediction for new subjects. To use the results of prediction research, consumers must know the accuracy of the predicted relationship. This figure is found by testing a presumed predictive relationship with a new, different group of persons.

6. Procedures for collecting data should be clearly indicated. It is important for researchers to indicate, in detail, the procedures used to collect the data with which correlations are calculated because the procedures affect reliability. As previously noted, correlation coefficients are directly related to the reliability of the measures and the sampling of subjects.

7. Correlational studies that claim explanations should be examined for other influential factors. Correlational studies that imply causation or explanation need careful scrutiny for the influence of unaccounted for variables on the correlation. Such explanations are commonly found with multiple correlation studies. Typically, researchers claim that most known variables are used, resulting in the dependent variable being explained by differences in the independent variable. Such claims, however, are always tentative. Something not included could influence the relationship between the targeted independent variable and dependent variable, so the search for additional influential factors is essential.

Review and Reflect *Describe three principles that researchers should use to conduct a comparative or correlational study that will provide credible results. What are you most comfortable with: comparative or correlational designs? Give an example of a study that could be designed either way and use that information to justify which approach you think is best. There is no right answer here, simply a matter of preference.*

CAUSAL-COMPARATIVE *and* EX POST FACTO STUDIES

We have seen how correlations and differences between groups can be analyzed to examine relationships between variables. Although most nonexperimental, quantitative research designs explore simple or predictive relationships, some nonexperimental designs do investigate cause-and-effect relationships. We will look at two types of these designs that look very much like experimental studies: causal-comparative and ex post facto. There are also more complex correlational designs that are used to suggest causation. The most common of these used in educational research are *path analysis* and *structural equation modeling*.

USING EDUCATIONAL RESEARCH

With the growing importance of high-stakes testing for student promotion and graduation there has been a renewed interest in the relationship between teaching and student performance. One approach in studying this relationship is to use multiple regression analysis to determine if aspects of teaching, such as style or approach, correlate with student performance. Regression can use previous measures of student ability in the analysis to "control" for the effect of student differences prior to their classroom experiences. It would not make much sense, for example, to correlate teaching style with student achievement without accounting for student ability, socioeconomic status, absenteeism, and other variables that are related to performance.

Causal-Comparative Designs

The hallmark of an experiment is that the researcher has direct control of the intervention. In some situations there is an intervention *without* direct control. This kind of design may be called a *natural* experiment in the sense that something occurs differently for one group of participants compared to others. Though there is no direct control of the intervention, it is possible to monitor what occurs and measure outcomes that compare the groups. I choose to call these designs **causal-comparative** to distinguish them from experiments.

Causal-comparative: Nonexperimental studies designed to determine cause and effect.

Suppose you were interested in determining the impact of attending preschool on first-grade performance. The intervention, preschool, is the independent variable. You can't really control the intervention, but you can measure the extent to which it is implemented. A comparison group of children not attending preschool could be used in this design to investigate whether preschool results in greater first-grade achievement (dependent variable). The quality of the design depends on how well the comparison group is matched to the intervention group, and how well you can understand how the intervention may have caused an increase in achievement.

There are many types of "interventions" that can be studied using causal-comparative designs. For example, different approaches to mentoring beginning teachers, different curricula, staff development, different ways that principals evaluate teachers, group counseling compared to individual counseling, and inclusion of students with disabilities would lend themselves to investigation using a causal-comparative design because the researcher cannot control (manipulate) the program or strategy.

The obvious weakness of a causal-comparative study is lack of control. The researcher cannot control the independent variable or extraneous/confounding variables. If random assignment is possible, many of the extraneous/confounding variables can be accounted for, but there is still lack of control over the intervention and what occurs within in each group as the intervention is experienced. It is very important in these designs to choose comparison subjects who are as similar as possible in the intervention group. This is typically accomplished by matching or using homogeneous groups, and there are some statistical adjustments that can be used as well.

Ex Post Facto Studies

Ex post facto: Presumed cause that occurred in the past.

In **ex post facto** research the investigators decide whether one or more different preexisting conditions have caused subsequent differences when subjects who experienced one type of condition are compared to subjects who experienced a different condition (the phrase *ex post facto* means "after the fact").

Ex post facto designs are very much like causal-comparative designs. As in a causal-comparative study, typically an "intervention" and/or "comparison" group exist, and the results are analyzed with the same statistical procedures. Of course, in ex post facto research, there is no active manipulation of the independent variable because it has already occurred with two or more intact groups, but the comparison of group differences on the dependent variable is the same. In an ex post facto study, then, the researcher investigates an intervention that has already occurred, while in a causal-comparative design the researcher is able to monitor and observe the intervention as it occurs.

In conducting an ex post facto study, the researcher selects subjects who are as similar as possible except for the independent variable that is being investigated. For example, in a study of the effect of class size on achievement, the researcher needs to locate groups of subjects who are similar in all respects except whether they attended large or small classes. In making the final selection of the groups of subjects, the researcher must be aware of possible extraneous variables that make causal conclusions problematic. Thus, in a study of class size the only difference between students who attend small classes and those who attend large classes should be the size of the class, not such factors as socioeconomic status, quality of teachers, teaching methods, curriculum, student ability, and student motivation. That is, if the students in all the small classes had more ability, better teachers, or higher motivation, these factors could affect achievement in addition to, or in spite of, class size.

In Example 7.14 the researchers use an ex post facto design to study the extent to which a specific freshman year course is responsible for increased student retention and academic success. Students enrolled in the course over three years are compared to similar, matched students who did not enroll in the course. Note how the authors use the terms "experimental" and "control groups" to describe their design, even though there is no direct manipulation that technically means it is not an experiment. Student records were used to compare students who took the course to other students who did not take the course (different conditions) in previous years.

EXAMPLE 7.14 | Ex Post Facto Design

The institution's Office of Admissions and Records generated individual reports . . . that contained the entry information for first-year students . . . enrolled in each section of the freshman-year experience. . . . In order to match students in the control group . . . student data on all of the pertinent class lists were coded to show the specific combination of courses in which an individual student was enrolled during his or her first semester on campus. Once the final sample of students in the experimental and control groups was identified, the completion rate for the first academic year . . . [and] the percent of general education courses completed were determined by reviewing each student's transcript. . . . Findings from the ex post facto investigation were based on the academic characteristics for the experimental group ($n = 431$) and the control group ($n = 431$).

Source: Sidle, M. W., & McReynolds, J. (2009). The freshman year experience: Student retention and student success. *NASPA Journal, 46*(3), 436.

CONSUMER TIPS: *Criteria for Evaluating Causal-Comparative and Ex Post Facto Studies*

1. The primary purpose of the research should be to investigate causal relationships when an experiment is not possible. The experiment is the best method for studying cause-and-effect relationships, so causal-comparative studies should only be used when it is not possible or feasible to conduct an experiment. There should be sufficient evidence in prior research to indicate that relationships exist between the variables and that it is appropriate to study causal relationships. Without existing empirical evidence of relationships, a strong theoretical rationale is needed.

2. **The presumed causal condition should have already occurred in an ex post facto study.** It is essential for the condition represented by the independent variable to have occurred before data are collected on or recorded for the dependent variable. The "intervention" must have already taken place for a study to be classified as ex post facto.

3. **Potential extraneous variables should be recognized and considered.** It is crucial for the researcher to show the reader that potential extraneous variables have been considered. Because existing groups are usually used in the comparison, these variables usually consist of differences in characteristics of the subjects, but other factors may also be related. It is incumbent on the researcher to present evidence that the groups being compared differ only on the dependent variable. Failure to do so suggests that the groups have not been carefully selected to avoid the influence of extraneous variables.

4. **Differences between groups being compared should be controlled.** When it is clear that there are measurable differences between groups being compared, researchers must use appropriate procedures to control their effect. Matching subjects is one procedure; statistical techniques can also be used.

5. **Causal conclusions should be made with caution.** Even when all potential extraneous variables have been controlled, which is rare, it is best to accept *with caution* results that seem to suggest a causal relationship. Researchers should indicate possible limitations and frame the finding as "suggesting" a causal relationship. In almost all causal-comparative studies, there will be sufficient reason to be tentative in concluding cause-and-effect relationships.

USING SURVEYS *in* NONEXPERIMENTAL RESEARCH

Survey research has evolved over the years to become a popular method of collecting data for nonexperimental designs. In a survey, the investigator selects a group of respondents, collects information, and then analyzes the information to answer the research questions. The group of subjects is usually selected from a larger population through some type of probability sampling, which allows accurate inferences about a large population from a small sample. In other surveys an entire population is included.

Surveys are used frequently in business, government, public health, politics, psychology, sociology, and transportation, as well as in education. In addition to being descriptive, surveys are also used to investigate relationships between variables, with a comparative or correlational design.

Survey research is popular because of versatility, efficiency, and generalizability. Surveys are versatile in being able to address a wide range of problems or questions, especially when the purpose is to describe the attitudes, perspectives, and beliefs of the respondents, and can be conducted with written questionnaires or with interviews. Relative to interviews, written surveys are less costly than phone interviews or personal interviews when there is a large number of respondents. An important value of survey research is that sampling from a population can be used to result in fairly accurate generalizable conclusions about the larger population. National polls of political preference or voting intentions, which may include 1,200 to 1,500 adults, are accurate indicators of the nation or state as a whole.

In designing a survey, the researcher should complete the following steps:

1. Define the purpose and objectives. List each pertinent objective or research question that will be addressed and only collect information that has a direct bearing on the objectives or questions. Researchers should refrain from asking questions that "would be nice or interesting to know about," or questions whose results are analyzed before identifying how the data will be used.

2. Identify resources needed and target population. It is necessary to calculate the cost of preparing, printing and mailing if not electronic, and analyzing surveys, and to know the nature of the target population. These parameters help knowing whether the survey is too long and the needed size of the sample.

3. Choose an appropriate survey method. Surveys are either paper- or Web-based written questionnaires, telephone interviews, or personal interviews. Each method has advantages and disadvantages. The most important advantages of the written survey are that many questions can be asked, respondents can be assured of anonymity, lower cost, and the ability to reach a fairly large sample. Interviews are used when a need exists to have a very high response rate; when there is a need to probe, particularly with nonverbal feedback; when many open-ended questions exist; and when there are just a few questions.

4. Word questions carefully. Questions should be clear, understandable, and unbiased. To accomplish these goals, the questions should:

- Use everyday, common terms and avoid jargon.
- Be short and simple.
- Be grammatically correct.
- Not be biased or leading (e.g., "How satisfied are you with the timely response of school administrators?").
- Use the same scale for all questions if possible.
- Use consistent wording and leading phrases (e.g., "To what extent was your grading based on:
    - Homework
    - Quizzes
    - Papers
    - Exams").
- Not be double-barreled (e.g., "The principal is accessible and responsive").

5. Design the survey. A well-designed format will use at least a 10-point typeface on paper and have sufficient white space so that different sections and questions can be clearly differentiated by the respondents. Cramming a lot of questions on a page or computer screen is not recommended.

6. Develop directions. It is important to have clear instructions so that there is no ambiguity about how and where to respond, and what to do when completing the survey. It is best to give the directions at the beginning of the survey and each section with a different response scale, not in a cover memo or e-mail.

7. Develop a letter of transmittal. The letter of transmittal is crucial to obtaining a high response rate. The letter should be brief and professional in appearance. The following elements should be included:

- Credibility of the researcher and sponsoring institution or organization
- Purpose of the study
- Benefits of the study for the researcher, respondent, and profession
- Importance of a high response rate
- Protections related to anonymity and confidentiality
- Time limit for responding (typically, a few days to a week is fine)
- Request for cooperation and honesty
- Opportunity for respondents to receive results of the study

8. Pilot test. A critical step in survey research is to pilot-test a draft of the letter of transmittal and survey. This is typically accomplished with a sample of 15 to 20 individuals who are from the population to be sampled. In the pilot test the respondents should read the directions and complete the survey. When finished, they can comment on the clarity and format of the survey. The pilot helps the researcher know how long it will take to complete the survey. Often two pilots are conducted to be sure that there will not be surface problems or costly mistakes.

One of the most serious limitations of survey research is a low response rate. The smaller the response rate, the more likely the results will be biased. Response rates around 70% are considered adequate. If possible, nonrespondents should be analyzed to determine if they are different from the respondents. Response rate can be increased by doing the following:

- Use a well-designed, professional, attractive, and easy-to-complete survey.
- Use several contacts with the sample, including a prenotification, reminder, and reissuing of the survey.
- Use at first-class mail for paper surveys; certified mail and express mail are best for long surveys.
- If mailed, include return postage and a return envelope.
- Use a transmittal letter that clearly indicates the benefits of the survey.
- Use telephone follow-up.
- Use financial or other incentives.

Surveys are either given to one or more samples or populations at one time, or are given more than once to the same or similar subjects over a specified length of time. These differences have important implications for interpreting results and are discussed next as cross-sectional and longitudinal methods.

Cross-Sectional Survey Research

Cross-sectional: Subjects and variables studied at one time.

In a **cross-sectional** survey, information is collected from one or more samples or populations at one time. There are two types of cross-sectional surveys. One type simply studies a phenomenon as it occurs at one time, for example, political surveys and surveys that study an attitude or characteristic of a group. A good illustration is the Annual Gallup Poll of the Public's Attitudes Toward the Public Schools, published in *Phi Delta Kappan.* The purpose of this poll is to estimate the attitudes of the adult civilian population in the United States toward many aspects of schooling, including the perceived biggest problems facing public schools, inner-city schools, part-time work by high school students, length of the school year and day, and parental choice.

Another type of cross-sectional survey is intended to compare different age categories of subjects to investigate possible developmental differences or relationships. For example, if researchers are interested in changes in students' self-concepts between sixth and twelfth grades and factors that may affect self-concept at various ages, a cross-sectional survey could be designed in which samples of current sixth- through twelfth-grade students are selected and questioned. All subjects are asked the questions at about the same time (e.g., October 1990).

Cross-sectional surveys are convenient and allow some tentative conclusions about how individuals may change over time. However, caution is advised for two primary reasons. First, there may be important differences between the subjects who are sampled in each grade or in each age category. For instance, if the sampling is done within a school, an assumption is that the type of students attending the school has not changed. If current sixth-graders are different in important ways, besides age, from twelfth-graders, conclusions about changes over time are affected. Second, because the data are obtained at one time, what may show as a "difference" from sixth to twelfth grade may not represent a change. It could be that twelfth-graders did not, when in sixth grade, have the same responses of current sixth-graders.

Longitudinal Survey Research

Longitudinal: Same or similar subjects surveyed over time.

In a **longitudinal** survey, the same group of subjects is studied over a specified length of time. Thus, a longitudinal study of self-concept might begin in 2008 with sixth-graders and continue until 2011 for the same subjects. Data are collected at different times, often over several years. There are variations of longitudinal surveys, depending on the subjects who are sampled or used to make up the "same group." In what is called a *trend* study, a general population is studied over time, although the subjects are sampled from the population each year or time of data collection. Thus, the population changes somewhat over time. In a

USING EDUCATIONAL RESEARCH

Recent federal legislation has mandated that states use test scores to show that "adequate yearly progress" is being made by students. One way to approach this is longitudinal, examining the same students each year as they progress in school. Another approach is to compare the scores of one grade for different years. That is, what is the score of fifth-graders in 2009 compared to fifth-graders in 2010 and 2011? This approach introduces the *cohort effect,* because differences from year to year for the same grade will be related to the nature of the group of students each year. Controlling for these differences represents a challenge for both researchers and policy makers.

cohort longitudinal study, a specific population, such as the freshman class of 2010, is studied over time. A *panel* sample is a cohort study in which the same individuals are surveyed each time data are collected.

A longitudinal survey is typically much stronger than a cross-sectional one. However, a serious disadvantage may be loss of subjects, which occurs with studies that extend over a long period of time and with populations that are difficult to track (e.g., following high school or college graduates). Not only will the sample size sometimes become too small for adequate generalizations, but also there may be a systematic loss of certain types of subjects. For example, a longitudinal study of attitudes of high school students should consider the fact that some of the sample will drop out, leaving mainly those who in all probability have more positive attitudes.

It should be noted that the terms *longitudinal* and *cross-sectional* are also used to describe research that would not be thought of as a survey. The differences between longitudinal and cross-sectional studies are illustrated in Figure 7.6.

Internet-Based Surveys

The Internet has led to a dramatic increase in the number of electronic surveys. They are now commonplace, and are called e-surveys, e-mail surveys, Internet

FIGURE 7.6 **Cross-sectional and longitudinal designs.**

Cross-Sectional			May 2006 Samples of fourth-, fifth-, and sixth-grade students taken.
Longitudinal	May 2004 Sample of fourth-grade students taken.	May 2005 Sample of fifth-grade students taken.	May 2006 Sample of sixth-grade students taken.

surveys, or Web-based surveys. Their common feature is that the Internet is used to distribute the survey and gather responses.

Types of Internet-Based Surveys. There are essentially two types of Internet-based surveys: e-mail and Web-based. An e-mail survey is usually sent as an attachment, and it typically looks much like a paper survey. The Web-based survey, which is the most common type, directs the respondent to a specific website that contains the survey. Web-based surveys take full advantage of the electronic flexibility that is possible. The surveys are usually very attractive, using graphics and sometimes multimedia resources. Respondents often answer only a few questions on each screen, and then simply "click" to the next set of questions. They are very easy to complete.

Advantages and Disadvantages. The advantages of electronic surveys are obvious: reduced cost and time, easy access, quick responses, and ease of entering responses into a database. It can be used effectively as a follow-up to a written survey. Electronic surveys are most effective with targeted professional groups, with "in-house" groups, when they are short and simple, and when a password can be used to ensure anonymity. Disadvantages are also obvious. Samples are limited to those with access to the technology, both hardware and software, which may lead to bias. For example, there are large disparities by race and socioeconomic status with respect to Internet access. Even when access exists, the respondents need to feel comfortable with the procedures and Internet tools that are utilized. Perhaps the most serious limitation is that respondents may not believe that their answers will be confidential. Confidentiality and privacy issues are very important; many will be reluctant to be honest because, even with the use of passwords and assurances from the researcher, there is a lingering feeling that any electronic response can be traced to the individual. These advantages and disadvantages are summarized in Table 7.2.

It is clear that electronic surveys will be used with greater frequency. When the respondents are almost all Internet savvy (such as teachers, principals, college faculties and staff, and children and adolescents) and the nature of the topic is not personal, electronic surveys are excellent for conducting research.

Internet-Based Survey Design. Many of the suggestions about effective questionnaire and survey design previously summarized is applicable to Web-based surveys. There are some additional considerations related to technology. Essentially, a simple, clear layout with no clutter is needed for easy navigation. Some further suggestions include:

- Show only a few questions on each screen, unless a matrix of items with the same response scale.
- Show both question and response categories on the same screen.
- Avoid excess scrolling.
- Limit the use of matrix format questions.
- Direct respondents to simply click on their response to closed-end questions.

TABLE 7.2 Advantages and Disadvantages of Internet-Based Surveys

Advantages	Disadvantages
Costs less	Low response rate
Fast response	Response bias
Takes less time to distribute	Lack of confidentiality and privacy
Respondents enter answers directly for each question	Confidence that participant and not someone else answered the questions
Provides enhanced presentation through color and graphics (especially for children)	Potential information overload, such as too many questions
Immediate database construction	Participants must be skilled in computer usage
Convenient	Hardware compatibility
Increased accuracy of responses	Hard to inform participants about their ethical rights
Easy follow-up	Hard to provide incentives
Easy access to geographically diverse samples	Sampling limited to those with access to computers

- Use error messages that refer to the specific location needing attention.
- Use graphics, hypertext, and colors.
- Password-protect Web-based surveys.
- Indicate progress toward completing the survey.

Consumer-friendly software for constructing Internet-based surveys, such as SurveyMonkey and Inquisite, allows most anyone to construct and use these types of surveys (including children, most of whom are very comfortable with computers). There is typically an editor to help develop the survey and many different attractive formats so that answers are easy to record. In addition, the responses are automatically stored in a database and can be used to produce tables and graphs (including real-time compilations).

ANATOMY *of a* NONEXPERIMENTAL QUANTITATIVE RESEARCH STUDY

The following example of a published nonexperimental quantitative study is included to show you how such an investigation is designed and reported, and how it should be interpreted. This particular nonexperimental study is an example of comparative research.

ARTICLE 7.1

Causal Beliefs of Public School Students about Success and Failure in Music

Roy M. Legette
Shorter College

Student motivation and achievement in relation to Attribution Theory were examined in this study. Public school students (N = 1,114) were asked to respond to items on Asmus's Music Attribution Orientation Scale, indicating those causes that they attributed most to succeeding or failing in music. Results showed that, collectively, students placed more importance on ability and effort as causal attributions. Gender, school level, and school system were found to have significant effects on student response. Implications for teaching and future research are discussed.

Music educators have long been concerned with motivating students toward greater musical achievement. Although many studies involving this complex area have been conducted in educational psychology and related fields, few have specifically addressed issues in music education. In the present study, principles of Attribution Theory were applied to examine the causes that elementary and secondary public school students attribute most to succeeding or failing in music. According to Attribution Theory, motivation and achievement are influenced by students' beliefs about the causes of success or failure at given tasks, and future approaches to the same or similar tasks are influenced by these causal attributions (Weiner, 1972, 1972a). Four attributions commonly associated with this theory are ability, effort, task difficulty, and luck. These causal attributions are considered to be either internal (originating from the student) or external (not originating from the student). They are also viewed as stable (not perceived by the student to change with subsequent trials) or unstable (perceived by the student to change with repeated attempts). Thus, causal attributions of ability and effort are considered to be internal-stable and internal-unstable respectively, while task difficulty is considered external-stable and luck, external-unstable.

General research problem statement

Causal attributions have also been used to gain insight into affective reactions of students regarding future success or failure situations (Bar-Tal, 1978; Nicholls, 1976; Weiner, 1972). When students are successful and the reason is internal (e.g., ability, effort), they feel a sense of pride and accomplishment. Conversely, feelings of deep shame are experienced if students are unsuccessful. The external attributions of task difficulty and luck appear to produce considerably less pride. Whether students perceive an attribution as stable or unstable is important, because this perception affects their level of expectancy for accomplishing the same or similar tasks in the future. If students attribute the cause of success for a particular task to ability (internal-stable), there is a high probability that they will expect to be successful at this task in the future. Alternately, if students cite ability as a cause for being unsuccessful at a task, they will often expect to fail in future attempts. Should students attribute success or failure to effort (internal-unstable), varying results are often expected in subsequent trials.

As a result of extensive research conducted by Weiner (1972a, 1972b) demonstrating the importance of causal attributions in understanding student motivation and achievement, a substantial body of research has emerged. Much of it has to do with attributions made by students about their own successes and failures, and how these attributions influence future expectancies, affect, and subsequent achievement strivings.

Theoretical background

Medway and Lowe (1980) asked 122 children participating in crossage tutoring programs to cite causes they thought would influence successful or unsuccessful learning in a tutorial program. Whether attributions were measured prior to, during, or after tutoring, both tutors and tutees felt that tutorial learning was more dependent on effort than ability. Moreover, the tutees tended to attribute positive learning outcomes to their partners while attributing negative learning outcomes to themselves.

With the help of 176 students attending a junior high/high school for academically advanced students, Ames and Archer (1988) studied how motivation is related to mastery and performance goals in a classroom setting. Students were asked to respond to a questionnaire designed to ascertain their perceptions of classroom goals.

Review of literature

(continued)

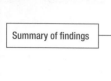

ARTICLE 7.1 (continued)

Summary of findings

Students who perceived an emphasis on mastery goals (e.g., students are given a chance to correct mistakes) in the classroom were reported as using their time more strategically, preferring challenging tasks, having a more positive attitude toward the class, and having a strong belief that success follows one's effort. Students who perceived an emphasis on performance goals (e.g., students feel bad when they do not do as well as others) tended to focus more on ability, attributing failure to the lack thereof. These findings suggest that causal attributions cited by students for success or failure affect how they approach various tasks in the classroom and that causal attributions are affected by students' perceptions of the classroom goals.

[Literature review continues.]

Literature most closely related to the research problem

In music education, Asmus (1986a) studied 143 undergraduate and graduate students enrolled in music education or music therapy programs. Attribution Theory was used to determine whether there was a relationship between students' perceived causes of success and failure when talking about themselves and their perceived causes of success and failure when talking about others. Results showed that success or failure was strongly attributed to task difficulty when students talked about themselves and to effort when they talked about others. Asmus (1985) also examined the views of sixth-grade general music students to gain a better understanding of why students think they succeed and fail in music. Again, principles of Attribution Theory were applied. Findings revealed that the majority of students selected the internal-stable attribution of ability and the internal-unstable attribution of effort as the major causes of their success or failure in music. Asmus (1986b) expanded the previous study by adding junior and high school students, greatly increasing the sample size. Students were asked to give free responses as to why some students are successful in music and others are unsuccessful. The major finding of this study was that 80% of reasons cited had to do with effort and ability. In addition, students tended to change their causal attributions with grade level. As the music students advanced in grade level, there was a gradual shift from effort attributions to ability attributions.

Summary of results

Summary of results

With the assistance of 105 instrumental music students, Austin and Vispoel (1992) investigated effects of failure, attribution feedback, and classroom goal structure on motivational response and decision making. Results showed that students attribute failure to the use of inappropriate strategies or insufficient efforts, rather than to lack of ability. Austin (1991) also demonstrated that positive achievement outcomes and success-oriented behaviors can be promoted if they are associated with a modifiable causal attribution such as effort.

Chandler, Chiarella, and Auria (1988) examined the motivations of 234 band-members by asking if they (1) had ever challenged for a chair position, (2) were happy with their current seat assignments, and (3) had performance-level expectations for the near future. Findings showed that if students view themselves as musically successful, they will challenge more and attribute success to internal factors, such as effort and musical ability. In failure situations, causes were attributed to external reasons (e.g., task difficulty, luck, and current level of performance).

Summary of results

Research conducted by Legette (1993) with 261 third- and fourth-grade students revealed that girls place more importance on effort as a causal attribution than do boys, and that significant differences in cited causal attributions tend to exist between grade levels. However, the study was somewhat limited in that it only used two grade levels, one school level, and two schools that were quite similar in terms of socioeconomic and ethnic makeup.

Analysis of previous research

The present investigation greatly expands the earlier study by including a broader spectrum of public school students from two neighboring school systems (city and county) that were demographically dissimilar in an attempt to determine whether demographic factors might have an effect on student causal attributions. In addition, previous research has shown that students tend to change their causal attributions with grade level, making a gradual shift from effort-related attributions to ability-related attributions with each advancing grade. The present investigation differs from previous research in that it examines student causal attributions due to school level rather than grade level and uses a much larger sample size. Considering

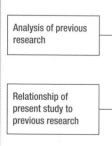

Relationship of present study to previous research

these differences, the purpose of the present study was to determine those causes to which elementary and secondary public school students most attribute success or failure in music. Four research questions were raised:

1. To what causes do elementary and secondary public school students most attribute their success or failure in music?
2. Do the genders differ significantly in their mean response as to the importance of each cause?
3. Does the importance of each attributed cause differ between students attending city schools and those attending county schools?
4. Do responses regarding the importance of each attributed cause differ by school level?

Causes as dependent variable
Gender as independent variable
Type of school as independent variable
School level as independent variable

METHOD

Subjects

Subjects were 1,114 elementary, middle, and high school students enrolled in music classes in two neighboring city and county public school systems in north Georgia (elementary school $n = 595$, middle school $n = 319$, high school $n = 199$). The music courses included instrumental, vocal, and general music subject areas. The sample consisted of 595 girls and 519 boys. Of the subjects in the city schools, 50% were black and 43% were white; in the county schools, 4% were black and 95% were white.

Convenience or available sample

Description of subjects

PROCEDURE

Subjects were administered Asmus's (1986c) Music Attribution Orientation Scale (MAOS) during their weekly music lessons. This scale was chosen because, unlike Weiner's (1972) model, it is germane to music and has a wider range of causal attributions. The MAOS is comprised of 35 items divided into five different subscales (effort, background, classroom environment, musical ability, and affect for music). There are seven questions corresponding to each subscale. Students were asked to indicate how important they thought each item was on a scale of 1 to 5 with 5 being "extremely important" and 1 being "not important at all." Points for the items in each subscale were summed (35 being the maximum number of possible points) and averaged, creating a single score for each subscale. No points were assigned for unanswered items. Asmus has determined reliabilities for each subscale as follows: effort (.824), background (.770), classroom environment (.764), musical ability (.774), and affect for music (.690). A cover sheet was attached to the MAOS by the researcher in order to obtain demographic information.

Probably internal consistency estimates

RESULTS

A *t*-test for two independent samples was used to test the research questions that dealt with differences in attributions due to school system and gender. Because inflation of the error rate was a concern due to multiple test comparisons, the initial alpha level of .01 was adjusted using the Bonferroni technique, resulting in a probability of .002. The first research question examined causes to which elementary and secondary public school students most attribute success or failure in music. Means and standard deviations respectively for all student responses within each subscale of the Music Attribution Orientation Scale are as follows: effort (4.04, 0.89), background (2.81, 0.94), class environment (3.85, 0.75), musical ability (4.12, 0.86), and affect for music (3.65, 0.87). As shown, musical ability, with a mean of 4.12, was the most important causal attribution cited, followed by effort, with a mean of 4.04.

(continued)

ARTICLE 7.1 (continued)

The second research question compared the students' mean response within each subscale by gender. Means and standard deviations are presented in Table 1.

Number of subjects

TABLE 1 Comparisons of Causal Attributions by Gender

Dependent variables

Variable	Males (n = 519) *M* (Mean)	*SD*	Females (n = 595) *M*	*SD* (Standard deviation)	*t* (Inferential statistic)
Effort	3.83	0.98	4.22	0.76	7.50*
Background	2.76	0.90	2.91	0.96	3.64*
Class environment	3.76	0.78	3.93	0.70	3.88*
Musical ability	3.95	0.95	4.27	0.75	6.22*
Affect for music	3.55	0.93	3.74	0.81	3.60*

* $p < .002$

Summary comparison of males to females

As indicated in Table 1, there were significant differences between males and females in their responses within each subscale ($p < .002$) with all female means being higher than those of males. Additionally, musical ability followed by effort were again cited as the leading causal attributions.

The third research question was concerned with whether causal attributions differed between students attending city schools and those attending county schools. Means and standard deviations are provided in Table 2.

Independent variable with two levels (dichotomous)

TABLE 2 Comparisons of Causal Attributions Between Students Attending City Schools and Those Attending County Schools

Dependent variables

Variable	City Students (n = 558) *M*	*SD*	County Students (n = 556) *M*	*SD*	*t* (Inferential statistic)
Effort	4.13	0.85	3.94	0.92	3.54*
Background	2.77	0.91	2.86	0.97	1.59
Class environment	3.72	0.74	3.99	0.73	6.07*
Musical ability	4.24	0.79	3.99	0.92	4.77*
Affect for music	3.62	0.83	3.68	0.91	1.13

*$p < .002$.

Findings shown in Table 2 reveal that subject responses within the two school systems differed significantly ($p < .002$) on three of the subscales, with students attending city schools placing more importance on effort and musical ability, and those attending county schools perceiving class environment as a more important causal attribution.

ANOVA is an inferential statistical procedure

One-way analyses of variance (ANOVAs) were used to compare cited causal attributions among the three different school levels. There were significant differences among the three school levels ($p < .002$) for the variables of effort, background, musical ability, and affect for music. No significant difference ($p > .002$) was found for class environment. Descriptive statistics are provided in Table 3.

Table 3 Means and Standard Deviations of Causal Attributions by School Level

	Elementary (n = 596)		Middle (n = 318)		High (n = 199)			
Variable	***M***	***SD***	***M***	***SD***	***M***	***SD***	***F***	***p***
Effort	3.83	0.95	4.16	0.82	4.43	0.59	43.24	.000*
Background	2.95	1.01	2.62	0.85	2.71	0.79	15.00	.000*
Class environment	3.90	0.77	3.79	0.74	3.83	0.67	2.39	.092
Musical ability	3.91	0.95	4.26	0.79	4.49	0.53	41.89	.000*
Affect for music	3.62	0.92	3.63	0.34	4.14	0.53	42.64	.000*

*$p < .002$

School level independent variable with three levels

Dependent variables

As shown in Table 3, music ability and effort were again listed as leading causal attributions with both variables increasing at each succeeding school level. Post-hoc means analysis using a Newman-Keuls multiple comparison procedure revealed that the mean responses by school level for the variables of effort, musical ability, and affect for music were significantly different from each other. As regards the background variable, scores were not significantly different between elementary and middle school students but were significantly different between high school students and the two remaining levels.

DISCUSSION

Summary of results

The results of this study indicate that students tend to place more importance on ability and effort as causal attributions for success or failure in music. This result is consistent with the findings of previous research (Asmus, 1988; Austin, 1991; Chandler, Chiarella, & Auria, 1988; Legette, 1993). In light of the fact that ability is often perceived by students as an internal-stable factor (Anderson & Dennis, 1978; Weiner, 1972), it is encouraging to see that students also place a great amount of importance on effort—a perceived internal-unstable causal attribution.

Relationship to previous research

Results showed that females perceived ability and effort as being more important than did males. This finding contradicts previous research, which has shown that females have a tendency to be more external—often attributing success or failure to task difficulty or luck (Bar-Tal, 1978).

Possible explanation for differences, between city and county

The school system attended (city versus county) significantly influenced how students responded on three of the attribution subscales: effort, class environment, and musical ability. Students in the city schools tended to place more importance on ability and effort, whereas students in the county schools perceived class environment as more important. The two school systems involved in the study were quite dissimilar in terms of ethnic makeup. Perhaps race was a contributing factor to the results.

Relationship to previous research

There were significant differences in attributed causes due to school level. It was interesting to note that not only were ability and effort the leading attributions cited, but they tended to increase as the school level increased. Previous research conducted by Asmus has shown that younger students tend to use more effort-related attributions and shift to ability-related attributions as they grow older. The results of this study are inconsistent with these findings and seem to indicate that younger students use more ability-related attributions and that both ability and effort attributions tend to increase concurrently as students move through school.

The fact that most subjects placed more importance on ability and effort as causal attributions for success and failure in music should be of interest to music educators. Attribution Theory states that student beliefs about the causes of their success or failure at a particular task will influence how they approach that task in the future. Success due to ability promotes a sense of pride, whereas failure due to ability promotes a sense of shame. It seems that ability as a causal attribution might constitute a double-edged sword. That is, if students who are successful attribute their success to ability, it is quite probable they will expect the same results in the future.

(continued)

ARTICLE 7.1 (continued)

However, should students fail and perceive ability as the cause, they might continually expect to fail in the future. Since effort has been shown to be perceived by students as a changeable attribution, students might believe that a subsequent attempt at the same task will yield a totally different outcome. For this reason, music educators might consider giving effort more (or at least the same) attention than they do ability. It appears that student perception, motivation and achievement are inextricably linked as the student progresses through the educational system. Obviously, much more research is warranted.

REFERENCES

Ames, C., & Archer, J. (1988). Achievement goals in the classroom: Students' learning strategies and motivation processes. *Journal of Educational Psychology, 80* (3), 260–267.

Anderson, C., & Jennings. D. (1980). When experiences of failure promote expectations of success: The impact of attributing-failure to ineffective strategies. *Journal of Personality, 48* (3), 293–407.

Asmus, E. (1985). Sixth graders' achievement motivation: Their views of success and failure in music. *Bulletin of the Council for Research in Music Education,* no. 85, 1–13.

[References continued].

STUDY QUESTIONS

1. What do researchers accomplish with nonexperimental studies?
2. In what ways can the characteristics of subjects affect the interpretation of descriptive and correlational studies?
3. How can graphs be used appropriately and inappropriately to summarize descriptive data?
4. Why should causation not be inferred from comparative or correlational designs?
5. Why is it important to examine the size of correlations as well as narrative conclusions about relationships?
6. What criteria would support a credible prediction study?
7. Give some examples of studies that would be classified as ex post facto and causal-comparative. What are some possible limitations in the designs?
8. What is the difference between cross-sectional and longitudinal surveys?
9. What are the advantages and disadvantages of using a cross-sectional rather than a longitudinal survey?
10. What are the advantages and disadvantages of using a written survey rather than a face-to-face interview?
11. Why is a pilot test an important step in designing a survey?
12. What are the advantages and disadvantages of using an electronic survey?

Chapter 8

Experimental Research Designs

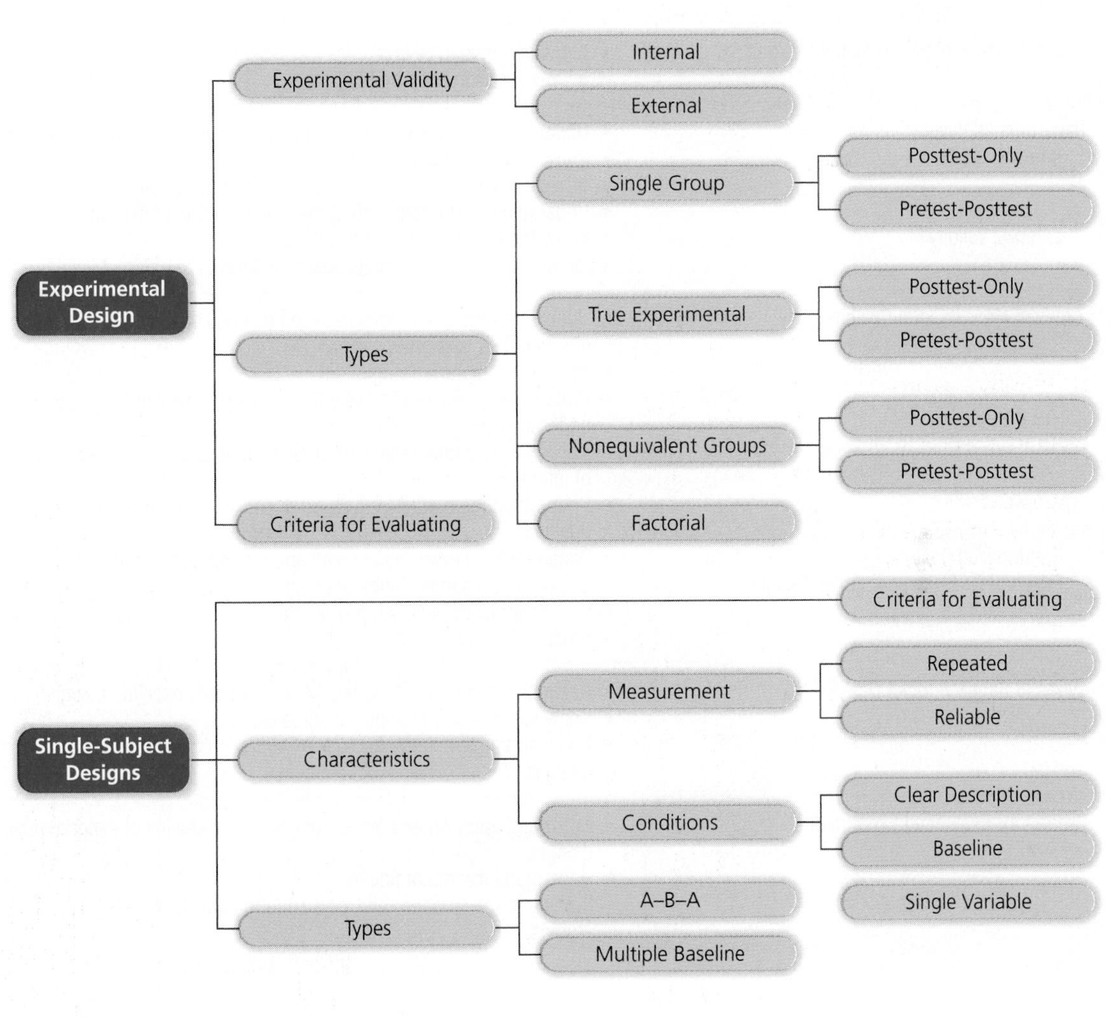

CHAPTER ROAD MAP

In the nonexperimental designs we have discussed, the researcher has no control over what has happened or what will happen to the subjects that may affect their responses to the dependent variable. We now turn to designs in which the researcher does have such control. These designs, experimental and single-subject, are the best approaches to investigating cause-and-effect relationships.

Chapter Outline	Learning Objectives
Characteristics of Experimental Designs	• Know and recognize in studies the essential design features that make an investigation experimental.
Experimental Validity Internal Validity	• Understand the concept of experimental validity and why it is important. • Know the threats to internal validity. • Be able to give examples of threats to internal validity. • Understand how threats affect the interpretation of results.
External Validity	• Know the threats to external validity. • Identify limitations to results based on threats to external validity.
Types of Experimental Designs	• Understand the differences between designs based on measures, interventions, and groups. • Be able to diagram designs. • Understand possible and likely threats to internal validity, depending on the design. • Recognize and understand factorial designs and the concept of interaction. • Understand the difference between control and comparison group designs.
Randomized Designs	• Distinguish between randomized and nonrandomized designs.
Pre- and Quasi-Experimental Designs	• Understand the importance of using a pretest. • Know conditions in which pre- and quasi-experimental designs can produce credible results.
Types of Single-Subject Designs	• Recognize and understand A–B–A and multiple baseline designs. • Know variations of multiple baseline designs. • Know and apply criteria for evaluating the credibility of single-subject designs.
Criteria for Evaluating Experimental Designs	• Know and apply criteria for evaluating the credibility of experimental designs. • Understand treatment fidelity. • Be able to read, understand, and critique published experimental studies.

CHARACTERISTICS *of* EXPERIMENTAL RESEARCH

There is one essential characteristic of all experimental research: direct control of an intervention. Direct control means that the researcher treats subjects in a planned way (hence, the term *treatment* that is used in experimental research). That is, the researcher decides on and carries out the specific intervention (or treatment) for one or more groups of subjects. Most educational experiments compare subjects who have received different interventions, in which the researcher must be able to "manipulate" the time during which these different interventions are received or experienced by the subjects. One simple intervention, for instance, is to give feedback to one group of subjects on their performance and compare their progress with subjects who received no feedback. The difference in the independent variable is receiving or not receiving feedback, and the researcher determines when the "experimental" subjects experience it. In educational research, the method of instruction, type of rewards given to students, curricula, type of grouping, amount of learning time, and assignments are common independent variables that become interventions in experiments.

It should be noted that my definition of experimental includes studies in which there is a single group that receives an intervention. Others may insist on having a control or comparison group, or the random assignment of subjects to different groups.

A second ubiquitous characteristic of experiments is control of extraneous and confounding variables. In an experiment, the researcher seeks to keep all conditions, events, and procedures the same, except the intervention. Keeping such factors constant eliminates them as explanations of the results. In other words, the effect, which is measured by differences on the dependent variable, should be produced only by the intervention. That is, control of extraneous variables is necessary to conclude that the intervention is causally related to the outcome. Though such control is relatively easy in contrived laboratory experiments, it is difficult in applied educational research.

Control is established by either eliminating a possible extraneous or confounding variable, or keeping the effect of such variables constant for all groups. Depending on the design, there may be extraneous or confounding variables that cannot be eliminated. For example, in an experiment designed to investigate which of two methods of instruction is most effective, teachers may be assigned to a particular method. This would mean that the explanation of results must include both teachers and interventions. The results may be because of the different interventions or because of different teachers.

A third characteristic that is critical in experiments in which two or more groups are compared is determining that there are no systematic differences between the individuals of one group and those of comparison groups. Differences could include achievement, gender, attitudes, backgrounds, and a host of other assigned variables. The goal is to have statistical "equivalence" of the groups. This is most effectively achieved with random assignment of a sufficient number of subjects to each group. The use of random assignment is so important that some researchers regard it as an essential characteristic, that a study should not be classified as an experiment without random assignment. My view is less strict—there are many good studies of interventions without random assignment, and for the purpose of critiquing and using results, it is helpful to think about them as experiments.

Author Reflection *I should point out that sometimes confusion exists about what an "experiment" is because of how science is taught. In some science "experiments" there is simply observation following an intervention or influence, such as mixing two chemicals. Other science "experiments" have a control or comparison group, more like educational experiments. Also, some sources on social science experiments maintain that an experiment must involve the random assignment of subjects. My take is that as long as there is control of the intervention, and you measure change, that qualifies as an experiment. There are different types of experiments, one of which includes random assignment.*

EXPERIMENTAL VALIDITY

The purpose of a research design is to provide answers to research questions that are credible. In the language and jargon of experimental research, two concepts are used to describe the level of credibility that results from the studies: *internal validity* and *external validity*. We will consider internal validity first since the primary purpose of experiments relates most closely to this concept.

Internal Validity

Internal validity: Control of confounding and extraneous variables.

Internal validity is the sine qua non of experiments. It refers to the extent to which the intervention, and not extraneous or confounding variables, produced the observed effect. A study is said to be strong in internal validity if extraneous and confounding variables have been controlled, and weak if one or more of these factors may have affected the dependent variable. That is, if something other than the intervention as defined was responsible for the effect, the study has weak internal validity. As we will see, there are many ways to design experiments, and each design controls for different extraneous/confounding variables. Therefore, some designs are relatively strong in internal validity, whereas other designs are comparatively weak.

Most possible extraneous/confounding variables fall into one of several major categories. These categories, often referred to as "threats" to internal validity, comprise factors that may weaken the argument that the intervention was solely responsible for the observed effects. We will discuss these threats briefly and then consider them within the context of different experimental designs. These factors represent the most important aspects of an experiment in interpreting the overall credibility of the research. When you read an experimental study, you should keep each threat in mind and ask: Is this a *plausible* threat to the internal validity of the study? The word *plausible* is key. To be a plausible threat to internal validity, two conditions must be met: (1) the factor must influence the dependent variable, and (2) the factor must be different in amount or intensity across levels of the independent variable. Thus, if a factor is present to the same extent at all levels of the independent variable, it is not a threat to internal validity, even if it does affect the dependent variable. Just because a potential threat is not "controlled," it is not automatically a threat to internal validity.

It is helpful in identifying plausible or likely threats to internal validity to first eliminate threats that are not even possible, or are very unlikely. These are typically determined by the specific design that is used, as we will see in considering each design. For threats that are possible or potential, and not controlled, it is then necessary to consider whether the threat is plausible or probable. This determination is made by examining how the study was carried out. In Figure 8.1 a decision tree is illustrated to help guide you through the process of determining threats to internal validity.

Keep in mind that the names of these various threats to internal validity should not be interpreted literally. Often the names have a broader meaning than the term may suggest at first. While some of the names are unique to this book, most were established many years ago by Campbell and Stanley (1963). Since that time some of the factors identified for both internal and external validity have been applied to nonexperimental studies as well.

Finally, it is most important to know what factors constitute plausible rival explanations, not which category of threats is correct.

History. In an experiment, some amount of time elapses between the onset of the intervention and the measurement of the dependent variable. Although this time is necessary for the independent variable to take effect and influence the participants , it allows for other events to occur that may also affect the dependent variable. **History** is the category of uncontrolled events that influence the dependent variable. If some event does occur during the study that is plausibly related to the dependent variable, it is difficult to know if the independent variable, the event, or some combination of the two produced the result. In this sense the event is confounded with the independent variable; the two cannot be separated.

History: Threat from uncontrolled events that affect the dependent variable.

History can occur "within" the study as participants are affected by something that happens during the intervention (internal history), or "outside" of the experimental setting (external history). For example, suppose a class is studying the Far East and the researchers are trying to determine what effect this unit has on multicultural attitudes. During the unit a major crisis occurs in China. If the students are affected by the crisis, which in turn influences the way they respond to a multicultural attitude questionnaire, this event, external to the experimental setting, constitutes a plausible history threat to the internal validity of the study.

History threats can also occur within an experimental setting. For example, a series of unexpected announcements that distracts a class receiving one method

FIGURE 8.1 Decision tree for determining threats to internal validity.

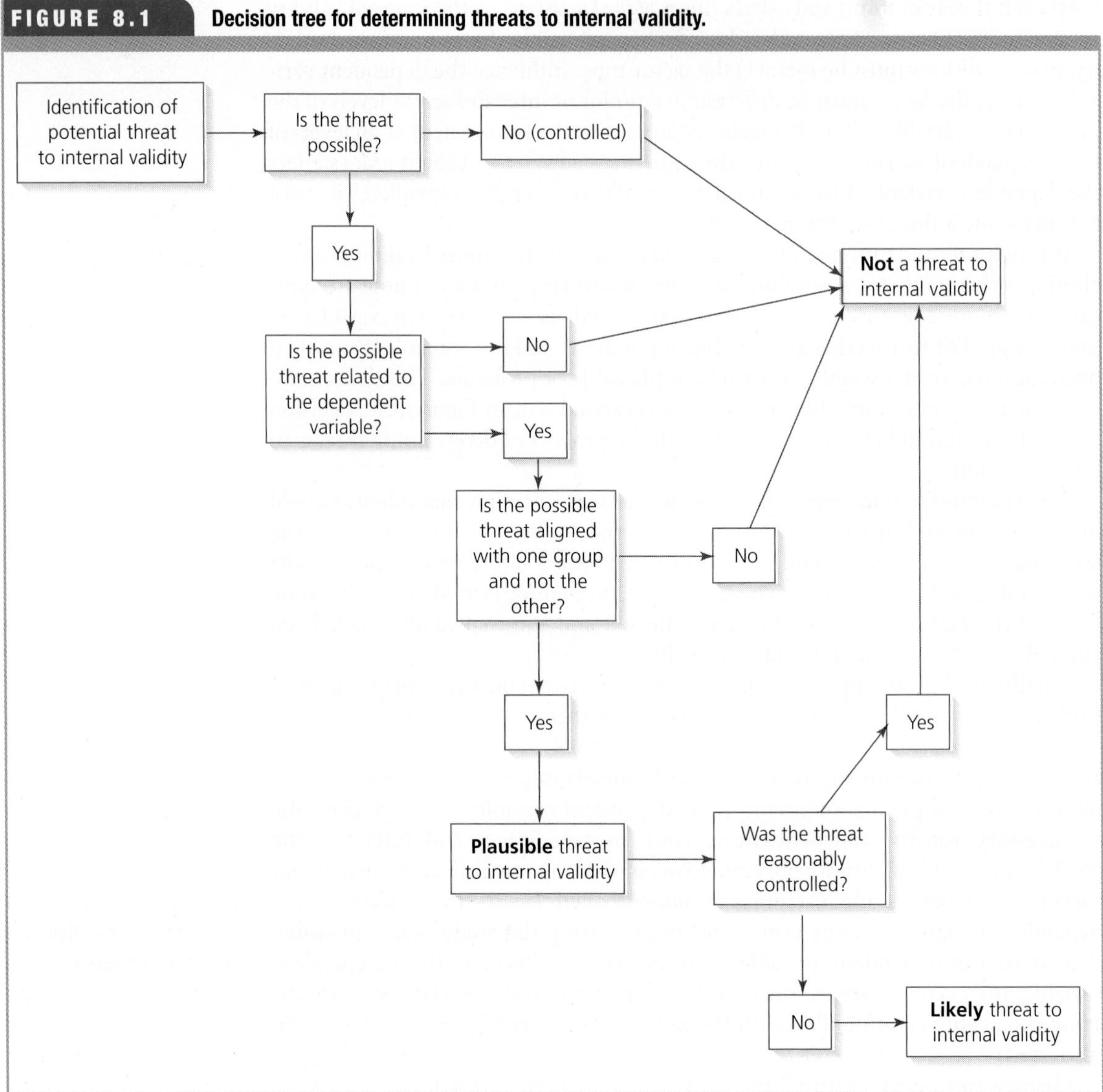

of instruction could adversely affect the influence of the lesson. Students in this class might score lower than other classes, but the researcher does not know if this result is caused by the distraction or the method of instruction. It should be noted, however, that if both groups had been distracted, there is less chance that history would be a plausible threat (see Figure 8.1). In general, if both groups in an experiment have the same experiences, history would probably not be a threat to internal validity.

FIGURE 8.2 **History threat to internal validity.**

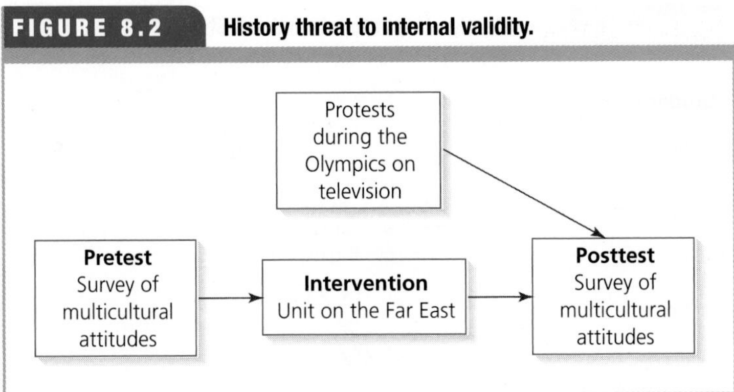

History also includes confounding variables that are associated with levels of the independent variable. For example, suppose an experiment compares two methods of instruction. One treatment is in the morning and the other is in the afternoon. A confounding variable, time of day, would constitute a threat to the internal validity of the study. Similarly, history is the category of threat in studies where different teachers are responsible for implementing each intervention. Figure 8.2 illustrates a history threat to internal validity for a single group study on the effect of a unit on the Far East on students' multicultural attitudes.

Selection. In most experiments two or more groups of participants are compared. One group receives one level of the independent variable, and the other groups receive other levels of the independent variable. In some experiments the participants are randomly assigned to levels of the independent variable. This procedure ensures that the different groups of participants are comparable on such characteristics as ability, socioeconomic status, motivation, attitudes, and interests. However, in some experiments the participants are not randomly assigned, and sometimes only a few participants are randomly assigned. In these circumstances it is possible that systematic differences will exist between the groups on characteristics of the participants. If these differences are related to the dependent variable, there is a threat of **selection** to internal validity (sometimes called *selection bias* or *differential selection*). For example, suppose one class is assigned to receive the blue health curriculum and another class receives the red health curriculum. The students are not randomly assigned to the classes; in fact, the students who have the blue curriculum are more capable academically than the students in the other class. At the end of the experiment the students who had the blue curriculum did better on a test of health concepts than the other class. Surprised? Obviously, the result is related to the initial differences between the classes, and the study would be judged to have very weak internal validity.

Selection: Threat from the characteristics of participants.

Selection is also a threat when the participants are selected in a way that affects the results. As previously discussed, volunteers may respond in ways that non-volunteers would not. Or suppose one group of participants had a choice in the

FIGURE 8.3 **Selection threat to internal validitiy.**

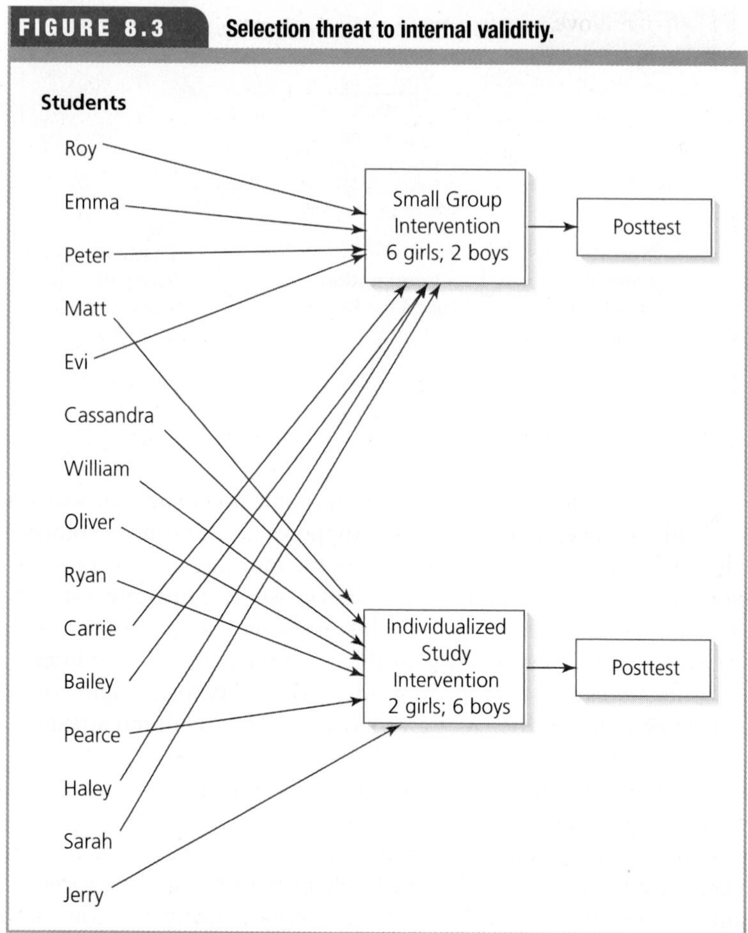

Source: Adapted from Creswell (2008), p. 304.

"treatment" experienced and another group had no choice. In such circumstances it is likely that the selection process will affect the findings.

Figure 8.3 shows why selection can be a threat to internal validity even with random assignment. The students in the class are randomly assigned to either the small group intervention or the individualized study intervention. While not likely, when the random assignment was completed, the small group intervention had many more girls than boys. Differences due to gender, then, would constitute a potential threat to internal validity.

Maturation: Threat from changes in participants over time.

Maturation. As stated earlier, there is some passage of time in an experiment. Just as events extraneous to the participants may affect the results (history), changes that may occur *within* the participants over time may also alter the results. These changes are called threats of **maturation.** People develop in naturally occurring ways that, over a sufficient period of time, can influence the dependent variable independent of a treatment condition. This can include physical, social, and mental development. For example, in an experiment on the effect of a new orientation course on the adjustment of college freshmen, the researcher may measure adjustment before college begins and then again at the end of the first year, after an orientation class. Although it would be desirable to attribute positive changes in adjustment to the orientation course, the researcher needs to consider the natural maturation process of 18- and 19-year-olds and how much adjustment will be influenced by this process.

Maturation also includes relatively short-term changes in people as they become tired, bored, hungry, or discouraged. Imagine that a researcher who needs to measure the attitudes of third-graders toward science, mathematics, reading, and art asks the children to answer questions for an hour to complete the questionnaire. What do you suppose the children are doing after the first 20 minutes or so?

Pretesting. A *pretest* is a measure of the dependent variable given before the treatment begins. When the pretest is used in an experiment, it is possible for the participants to act differently because they took the pretest. For example, if two groups are given a pretest measuring self-concept, the participants may be sensitized to issues concerning the development of self-concept because they took the pretest. While one group may receive an intervention to improve self-concept, those in another group may become motivated to do some outside reading that they otherwise would not have done; this reading would probably affect changes in their self-concept and the results of the study. This threat is termed **pretesting** or *testing*. Pretesting is also a threat when a single group of participants is given a pretest that influences responses on the posttest. In a study of changes of achievement, this is likely if there is a pretest of knowledge, a short lesson, then the same posttest. If an attitude questionnaire is used as a pretest, simply reading the questions might stimulate the subjects to think about the topic and even change their attitudes.

Pretesting: Threat from the effect of taking the pretest.

Instrumentation. The nature of the measurement used for the dependent variable can affect the results of research in several ways. **Instrumentation** refers to threats to internal validity because of changes or unreliability in measurement. Instrumentation also refers to changes in the measures or procedures for obtaining data. For example, if a researcher in an observational study has one set of observers for one group of participants and a second set of observers for another group, any differences between the groups may be due to the different sets of observers. Observers or interviewers can also become bored or tired or change in other ways that affect the results.

Instrumentation: Threat from unreliability or changes in measurement.

Treatment Replications. In an experiment the intervention (treatment) is supposed to be repeated so that each member of one group receives the same intervention separately and independently of the other members of the group. If the researcher is testing a new method of instruction with a class, there is really only one replication of the intervention; that is, the intervention is conducted once. Each class is a

Treatment replication: Threat from insufficient replications of treatments.

single participant, so several classes are needed to do the experiment properly. **Treatment replication** is a threat to internal validity to the extent that the reported number of participants in the study is not the same as the number of replications of the treatment. For example, a class could be shown a video, once to the entire group at the same time. This intervention would be completed once. However, if each student went to another room and viewed the video by him- or herself, the number of interventions would be equal to the number of students.

In Example 8.1 the authors describe how small groups of students, rather than individual students, are used as the number of replications.

EXAMPLE 8.1 | Appropriate Attention to Treatment Replication

Each group consisted of 3 participants, resulting in 15 control groups and 15 experimental groups. . . . All analyses . . . are based on the group level. Analysis on the group level was necessary because the individuals in a group were not independent of each other.

Source: Engelmann, T., Tergan, S., & Hesse, R. W. (2010). Evoking knowledge and information awareness for enhancing computer-supported collaborative problem solving. *The Journal of Experimental Education, 78,* 274, 282.

Subject attrition: Threat from loss of subjects.

Subject Attrition. **Subject attrition** (some researchers refer to this threat as *mortality* or *differential attrition*) occurs when participants systematically drop out of or are lost from the study and their absence affects the results. This is most likely to be a problem in longitudinal research that extends over a long period of time, but it can also be a threat to short experiments if one of the interventions causes more participants to drop out than does a comparison intervention. For example, if a study indicates that college seniors as a group are better critical thinkers than college freshmen, subject attrition is a possible extraneous variable since it is likely that students who are not good critical thinkers have dropped out of college and are not included in the senior sample. Suppose in a study of two interventions to effect weight loss the group with mandatory exercise has attrition of half of the subjects, while the group with a different diet experienced little attrition. In this example of differential attrition the groups are no longer comparable at the end of the study.

In Example 8.2 the researchers analyzed attrition since approximately 42% of the initial sample of college students were not available at the completion of the study.

EXAMPLE 8.2 | Analysis of Subject Attrition

We conducted attrition analyses to examine whether students who were not available at follow-up ($n = 403$) differed on variables of interest at baseline from those who remained in the study. We observed no significant differences between attriters and nonattriters on baseline alcohol use measures, but some differences did emerge on normative perceptions. . . .

> Cross-tabulation of attriters by treatment type revealed no evidence of experimental mortality. . . . 44% attriters in the SSNC condition and 45% in the ISNC condition.
>
> *Source:* Reilly, D. W., & Wood, M. D. (2008). A randomized test of a small-group interactive social norms intervention. *Journal of American College Health, 57*(1), 53.

Statistical regression: Threat from change of extreme scores to those closer to the mean.

Statistical Regression. **Statistical regression** (sometimes called *regression toward the mean regression effect*, or *regression artifact*) refers to the tendency of groups of participants who score extremely high or low on a pretest to score closer to the mean on the posttest, regardless of the effect of the interventions. That is, very low pretest scores are likely to be higher on the posttest and very high pretest scores are likely to be lower on the posttest (see Figure 8.4). Statistical regression is a result of measurement error and a function of mathematical probability. It is a threat when participants are selected for research *because* they have high or low scores. For example, in studies of programs to help low achievers or students with low self-concepts, the subjects are initially selected on the basis of low pretest scores. It would be expected that mathematically, without any influence of a treatment, the posttest scores of these students as a group, will be higher because of statistical regression.

FIGURE 8.4 Illustration of statistical regression.

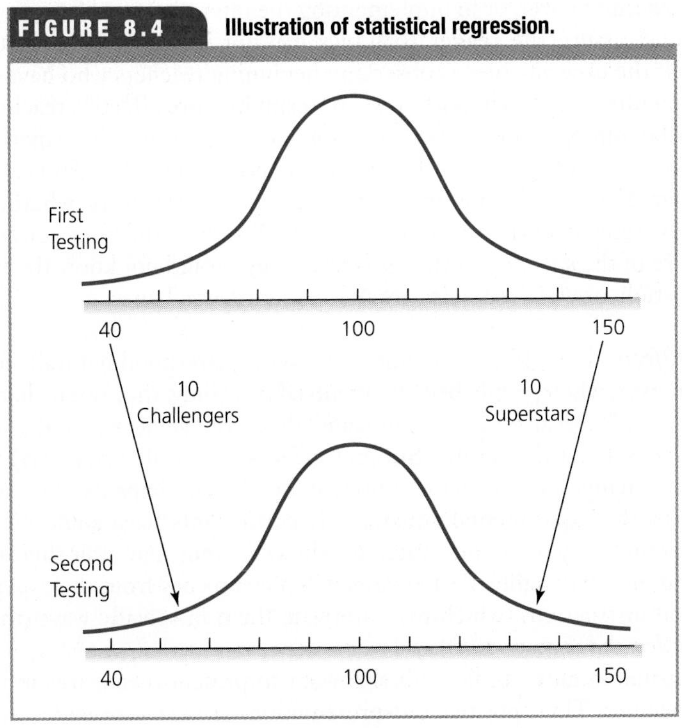

Diffusion of Treatment. In experiments with two or more groups that receive different interventions (treatments), it is best if the groups do not know about one another. If a control or comparison group does come into contact with a treatment group or knows what is happening to that group, the effects of the treatment could spread to both groups. **Diffusion of treatment** is the threat of any likelihood that an intervention given to one group affects other groups that do not receive the intervention. Suppose a researcher tests the effect of preschool on children by randomly assigning one twin from each family to a preschool. Diffusion of treatment is a threat because it is probable that any influence of the preschool is "diffused" to the other child when they are home together.

Diffusion of treatment: Threat from treatment effect on one group affecting other groups.

Experimenter effects: Threat from characteristics or expectations of the experimenter.

Experimenter Effects. **Experimenter effects** refers to attributes or expectations of the researcher that influence the results. In an ideal experiment, the investigators would have no effect on the responses of the participants; they would be detached and uninvolved. Attributes of the experimenter include such characteristics as age, sex, race, status, hostility, authoritarianism, and physical appearance. Participants may respond differently to certain characteristics. For example, studies suggest that female counselors are likely to elicit more self-disclosure from the client than male counselors are.

Experimenter expectancy refers to deliberate or unintentional effects of bias on the part of the experimenter, which is reflected in differential treatment of the participants, such as being more reassuring to the group the experimenter "wants" to do better. If the experimenter is involved in the research as an observer, as an interviewer, or in implementing the intervention, the procedures reported must assure the reader that bias has not influenced the results. For example, if the experimenter is observing beginning teachers who have been assigned a mentor, which is hypothesized to result in more effective teaching compared to beginning teachers who do not have a mentor, the experimenter's expectation may influence what he or she observes and records. In fact, this potential source of error is true for all observers and interviewers, whether or not they are the researchers conducting the study. Observers and interviewers should be unaware of the specifics of the research. They should not know the hypothesis of the study or which subjects are the "experimental" ones.

Subject Effects. In an ideal experiment the subjects respond naturally and honestly. However, when people become involved in a study, they often change their behavior simply because they understand they are "subjects," and sometimes these changes affect the results. **Subject effects** (also called *reactivity*) refers to participant changes in behavior, initiated by the participants themselves, in response to the experimental situation. If participants have some idea of the purpose of the study or are motivated to "do well," they may alter their behavior to respond more favorably. Participants will pick up cues from the experimental setting and instructions, which may motivate them in specific ways (these cues are called *demand characteristics*).

Subject effects: Threat from effects of awareness of being a subject.

Participants in most studies will also want to present themselves in the most positive manner. Thus, positive self-presentation, or *social desirability*, may affect the results. For instance, most people want to appear intelligent, competent, and emotionally stable, and they may resist interventions that they perceive as manipulating them in negative ways or they may fake responses to appear more positive. Some participants may increase positive or desirable behavior simply because they know they are receiving special treatment (this is termed the *Hawthorne effect*). Control group participants may try harder because they see themselves in competition with a treatment group or may be motivated because they did *not* get the treatment (this is termed the *John Henry effect* or *compensatory rivalry*). Other participants, when they realize that they were not selected for what they believe is a preferred treatment, may become demotivated (this is called *resentful demoralization*). Finally, many individuals will react positively, with increased motivation or participation, because they are doing something new and different (this is termed the *novelty effect*).

Whenever you read experimental research, you should keep these possible extraneous/confounding variables in mind. As we review some of the most frequently used experimental designs, you will see that some of these threats are of greater concern in some designs than in others. Other potential threats are related more to how contrived the study is, rather than to the design itself, and some threats are never completely controlled. In the end, internal validity is a matter of professional judgment about whether it is *reasonable* that *possible* threats are *likely* to affect the results. This kind of judgment is essential. In the words of Shulman (2005):

> Truth is, research is all about exercising judgment under conditions of uncertainty, and even experimental designs don't relieve us of the judgmental burdens. The acts of designing experiments themselves involve value judgments, and interpreting the results always demands careful judgment. (p. 48)

Table 8.1 lists the 11 types of threats to internal validity, with definitions and examples. While these names will help you remember specific kinds of threats, the bottom line is being able to recognize what might be messing up a study.

External Validity

The second concept that is used to describe the credibility of experiments and usefulness of findings is *external validity*. **External validity** refers to the extent to which the results can be generalized to other subjects, measures, interventions, procedures, and settings. Factors to consider in making appropriate generalizations are summarized in Table 8.2. To be able to make appropriate generalizations, you will need to attend carefully to the specific procedures for implementing an intervention, just as you need to know about the subjects' age, gender, socioeconomic status, and other characteristics to generalize appropriately to other individuals or groups. Like internal validity, external validity is described as weak or strong, depending on the specifics of the study's design. It is quite possible for a study to be strong in internal validity and weak in external validity. In fact, since the primary purpose of experiments is to control extraneous variables, external validity is often weak with these types of designs.

External validity: Generalizability of results.

Usually, external validity refers to generalizing *from* a sample *to* a population or other individuals. It may also be inappropriate to make generalizations *within*

TABLE 8.1 Summary of Threats to Internal Validity

Threat	Description	Example
History	Unplanned events that occur during the research	Fire drill occurs in the middle of a study on the effect of a computerized lesson.
Selection	Different characteristics of subjects in different groups	Students from a private school, who have strong parental support, are compared to students from a public school, who have weak parental support.
Maturation	Maturational or other natural changes in the subjects	Change in critical thinking of college students is attributed to a rigorous curriculum.
Pretesting	Taking a pretest affects subsequent behavior	Students take a pretest on their opinion toward creationism, read and discuss a book, then are posttested.
Instrumentation	Differences in results due to unreliability or changes in instruments, raters, or observers	One rater graded all the intervention group tests and a second rater graded all the control group tests.
Treatment Replications	Only a small number of independent, repeated treatments	A new method of instruction, using games, is administered in three classes.
Subject Attrition	Loss of subjects	More subjects drop out of the study from the intervention group, which was required to have strenuous exercise, than control subjects.
Statistical Regression	Scores of extreme groups of subjects moving closer to the mean on a second test	Students with the worst free throw–made percentage are used to test a new strategy for improving the accuracy of free throws.
Diffusion of Treatment	Treatment effects impact control or comparison groups	Fifth-grade students not able to participate in a new book club (control group) are resentful of the intervention group.
Experimenter Effects	Deliberate or unintended effects of the researcher	A teacher unconsciously helps experimental students get higher test scores.
Subject Effects	Changes in behavior generated by the subject by virtue of being in a study	Students give the professor high evaluations since they know he is up for tenure and their evaluations are key evidence.

the sample. Generalizing within the sample means that the researcher attributes the effects to subgroups of individuals in the sample rather than to the sample as a whole. For example, if a class of sixth-graders was used in an experiment and the class as a whole showed a positive gain in achievement, it may not be accurate to generalize the findings to subgroups such as the males or high-aptitude students, unless there is a specific analysis of these groups. In other words, what may be true for the class as a whole may not be true for a subgroup.

TABLE 8.2 Factors Affecting Generalizability

Factor	Description
Subjects	Characteristics of subjects such as socioeconomic status, age, gender, race, and ability. Whether and how subjects are selected from a larger population; conclusions based on group averages may be inappropriately assumed true for individuals or subgroups within the sample; subjects' awareness of the research.
Situation	Characteristics of the setting in which the information is collected, e.g., naturally occurring or contrived; time of day; surroundings.
Time	Some explanations change over time, e.g., years or decades.
Interventions (treatments)	Characteristics of the way in which an experimental intervention is conceptualized and administered.
Measures	Nature and type of measures used to collect information.

Review and Reflect *I have often suggested to my students that it would be helpful to put a list of the threats to validity on a card and then put that card on their bathroom mirror. The point is to memorize the threats so that it is easier to identify possible and likely factors that must be considered in evaluating results. Maybe you can come up with a clever mnemonic? Can you enumerate the lists and give original examples?*

TYPES *of* EXPERIMENTAL DESIGNS

We now turn our attention to six fundamental experimental designs. These designs will illustrate how some threats to internal validity are controlled by specific features of the design and how other threats are not controlled.

Aspects of experimental designs include interventions manipulated by the researcher, pretests and posttests, the number of groups in the study, and the presence or absence of random assignment. These aspects of the study will be represented in this chapter through the following notation system:

R	Random assignment
X	Intervention(s) (subscripts indicating different interventions)
O	Observation (pretest or posttest; subscripts indicating different tests)
A, B, C, D	Groups of participants

Single-Group Posttest-Only Design

This design and the next two are often called *preexperimental* because they usually have inadequate control of extraneous variables. In some circumstances one of these three designs can provide good information, but as we will see, this occurs only in special conditions.

In the single-group posttest-only design, the researcher identifies a group of participants, administers an intervention, and then makes a posttest observation of the dependent variable. It can be represented as follows:

Group		Intervention		Posttest
A	→	X_1	→	O_1

This is the weakest experimental design because without a pretest or another group of participants, there is nothing with which to compare the posttest result. Without such a comparison, there is no way to know if the intervention effected a change in the participants. This design is useful only when the researcher can be sure of the knowledge, skill, or attitude that will be changed before the treatment is implemented, and when no extraneous events occur at the same time as the treatment, that could affect the results. For example, suppose your research class instructor conducted an "experiment" by having you learn about threats to internal validity. It may be reasonable to assume that you had little knowledge about these concepts if this is your first research course, and it is unlikely that there would be any extraneous events or experiences that would also affect your knowledge of the concepts. In this circumstance the single-group posttest-only design can give you credible information.

Single-Group Pretest-Posttest Design

This design differs from the single-group posttest-only design by the addition of a pretest:

Group		Pretest		Intervention		Posttest
A	→	O_1	→	X_1	→	O_1

A single group of participants is given a pretest, then the intervention, then the posttest, which is the same as the pretest. The results are determined by comparing the pretest score to the posttest score. Although a change from pretest to posttest could be due to the intervention, there are many possible extraneous factors to be considered. Suppose an experiment is conducted to examine the effect of an in-service workshop on teachers' attitudes toward gifted education. An instrument measuring these attitudes is given to all teachers in a school division before two-day workshops are conducted and again after the workshops (one workshop for each school). What are some possible threats to the internal validity of this study?

First, because there are no control or comparison groups, we cannot be certain that extraneous events have not occurred, in addition to the workshop, that would change attitudes. Perhaps an article that appeared in the local paper during the two days of the workshop changed some attitudes, or maybe some of the teachers in some groups gave moving testimonials. Second, if the teachers began with negative attitudes for some reason, statistical regression would be a threat. Third, pretesting is a significant threat in this study because awareness due to completing the pretest questionnaire may affect attitudes. Fourth, attrition would be a problem if a significant number of teachers who do not like the workshop fail to show up for the posttest. Fifth, maturation is a potential threat if the teachers are tired at the end of the second day. Finally, experimenter and subject effects are definitely threats in this type of study if the teachers want to please the person conducting the workshop. With this number of plausible threats the study would be weak in internal validity.

The single-group pretest-posttest design will have more potential threats to internal validity as the time between the pretest and posttest increases and as the experimental situation becomes less controlled. The design can be good for studies in which subject effects will not influence the results, such as achievement tests, and when history threats can be reasonably dismissed. The design is strengthened if several pretest observations are possible, thereby providing an indication of the stability of the trait. If there is a sufficient number of both pretests and posttests, the study may be called an *abbreviated time series* design. In this design it is necessary to use multiple pretests and/or posttests with the same or very similar subjects.

Suppose you want to study a new technique for increasing attendance. It involves having teachers make targeted phone calls to the parents of students who tend to be absent. All teachers in the school participate. Attendance (O_1) is taken each week for four weeks prior to initiating the calls. After a week of calling, attendance is taken again. The study could be diagrammed as follows:

Group		Pretests (attendance)		Intervention (phone calls)		Posttest (attendance)
A	→	$O_1 O_1 O_1 O_1$	→	X_1	→	O_1

By having several "pretests," a stable pattern of attendance can be established so that it would be unlikely that a particularly "good" or "bad" week as a pretest would influence the results.

In the following example the authors describe both the name of the design and the nature of the analysis of results that illustrate a single-group pretest-posttest experiment. Note, too, the attention to design features intended to help rule out experimenter and subject threats.

EXAMPLE 8.3 | Single-Group Pretest-Posttest Design

The study utilized a single-group pretest/posttest design. In such a design, each participant serves as his or her own control. . . . All data (pre and post) were entered at the conclusion of the study to reduce potential experimenter and subject effects. . . . Pretest to posttest results were analyzed to determine whether the course content had a positive impact on school counselor trainees' perceptions of their readiness to implement the ASCA National Model. . . . Results indicate that participants' scores increased significantly.

Source: Wilkerson, K., & Eschbach, L. (2009). Transformed school conseling: The impact of a graduate course on trainees' perceived readiness to develop comprehensive, data-driven programs. *Professional School Counseling, 13*(1), 33.

Nonequivalent-Groups Posttest-Only Design

The third preexperimental design has a comparison or control group but no pretest:

Group		Intervention		Posttest
A	→	X_1	→	O_1
B		———————	→	O_1

One group of subjects (A) receives the treatment, while the other group (B) acts as a control, receiving no treatment. In some nonequivalent-groups posttest-only designs two or more groups receive different treatments:

Group		Intervention		Posttest
A	→	X_1	→	O_1
B	→	X_2	→	O_1
C	→	X_3	→	O_1

The crucial feature of this design is that the participants in each group may be different in ways that will differentially affect the dependent variable. That is, one group may be brighter, more motivated, better prepared, or in some other way different from the other groups on a trait that affects the dependent variable. Consequently, selection is the most serious threat to the internal validity of this design. Without a pretest it is difficult to control for such selection differences. For example, if teachers in one school received one type of form that will be used to evaluate their teaching during the year, and teachers in another school used a different type of evaluation form, you might conclude that if teachers in the first school were judged to be more effective, the forms were causally related to this difference in effectiveness. However, it may be that the teachers in the first school were *already* more effective! It is also possible that extraneous events in one school affected the results. This design is best employed when groups of participants are comparable and can be assumed to be about the same on the trait being measured before the treatments are given to the participants.

Author Reflection *I remember (now quite a few years ago) first learning about preexperimental designs as essentially useless, that at the very least one needed to use a quasi-experimental design. Now, I'm convinced that this was too dogmatic. Every experiment, regardless of design, has the potential to contribute important information. As long as the experimenter is sufficiently aware of and considers threats to internal validity, studies with preexperimental designs can be credible.*

Nonequivalent-Groups Pretest-Posttest Design

This design, which is often referred to as a *quasi-experimental* design (some contend that all experiments without random assignment are quasi-experimental) because it closely approximates the most desirable experimental designs, is commonly used in educational research. It is the same as the nonequivalent-groups posttest-only design, with the addition of a pretest:

Group	Pretest	Intervention	Posttest
A →	O_1 →	X_1 →	O_1
B →	O_1 ———	——— →	O_1

In this diagram there are two groups of participants (A and B). One group (A) takes the pretest (O_1), receives the intervention (X_1), and then takes the posttest (O_1); the other group (B) takes the pretest, receives no intervention, and takes the posttest. In this diagram group B is considered a "control" group because it does not receive any type of intervention. In other nonequivalent designs two or more different interventions may be compared, as indicated in the following diagram:

Group	Pretest	Intervention	Posttest
A →	O_1 →	X_1 →	O_1
B →	O_1 →	X_2 →	O_1

As a hypothetical illustration of this design, suppose Mr. Jones, a social studies teacher, wants to see if a new way of praising students is more effective than the method he uses now. Because it would be awkward to use different approaches in the same classroom, Mr. Jones decides to use the new type of praise in his morning class and to use an afternoon class as a comparison group. At the beginning of the same new unit on the Civil War, Mr. Jones gives his students a pretest of their knowledge. He then uses the new approach to praising students in the morning class and continues to use the same approach he has been using with his afternoon class. Both classes take the unit posttest at the same time.

The most serious threat to the internal validity of this design is selection. For example, Mr. Jones may find that students do better with the new type of praise, but this may be because the students in the morning class are brighter or more motivated than those in the afternoon class. Even though there is a pretest, which helps to reduce the threat of selection, differences in the subjects must be addressed. Often researchers will use measures of other characteristics of the subjects to show that even though the groups are not "equal," there are probably no significant differences between them.

The nonequivalent-groups pretest-posttest design is often used when participants are available in existing, or "intact," groups, such as classes. In the example with Mr. Jones, two intact classes were used. This procedure, using intact groups, creates problems other than selection. If the classes meet at different times of the day, as did Mr. Jones's classes, time of day is a confounding variable. In this example the same teacher conducted both interventions. Although in one respect this is a good method—because if different teachers were in each class, teachers would be a confounding variable—it also increases the potential for experimenter effects. Perhaps the most serious limitation is that the "intervention" is given only once to each class. In effect, there is only one replication of the intervention, so that other extraneous events associated with that one replication may affect the results. Thus, treatment replication is a potential threat to internal validity. Even though a pretest is used in this design, pretesting is not likely to be an extraneous variable since its effect is probably the same for both groups.

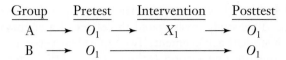

Example 8.4 shows how to summarize a nonequivalent-groups pretest-posttest design. This study investigated the effect of a cooperative learning intervention on student achievement. Two equivalent versions of a math test were given to students, one version as the pretest and the other version as the posttest.

EXAMPLE 8.4 | Nonequivalent-Groups Pretest-Posttest Design

The present study followed a nonequivalent pretest-posttest control group design involving three instructional conditions: (a) a treatment group with 12 sixth-grade dyads from four primary schools using CL [Cooperative Learning] instruction and practices based on a 2-year staff development CL program . . . (b) a control group with 6 sixth-grade dyads from two primary schools using CL instruction and practices based on a 1-year staff development CL program, . . . and (c) a control group with 6 sixth grade dyads from one primary school not using CL.

Source: Veenman, S., Denessen, E., van den Akker, A., & vander Rijt, J. (2005). Effects of a cooperative learning program on the elaborations of students during help seeking and help giving. *American Educational Research Journal, 42*(1), 120.

A strong indicator that groups are not significantly different, even though there is no random assignment, occurs when the groups are essentially equal on a pretest. That does not rule out other selection differences, but it does help in reducing the chance that selection is a plausible threat to internal validity. In the following excerpt, Example 8.5, the researchers compare pretest scores of two groups.

EXAMPLE 8.5 | Comparing Pretest Scores of Participants in Nonequivalent Groups

Our results indicated that prior to the beginning of the study no significant differences existed [between groups] in prior problem solving of procedural tasks between the two instructional approaches.

Source: Kramarski, B., & Gutman, M. (2006). How can self-regulated learning be supported in mathematical E-learning environments? *Journal of Computer Assisted Learning, 22*(1), 27

In Example 8.6 a nonequivalent pretest-posttest design was used to study the effects of a peer helping program. A diagram of the study would look like this:

Group	Pretests	Intervention	Posttests 1	Posttests 2
A →	$O_1 - O_5$ →	X_1 →	$O_1 - O_5$ →	$O_1 - O_5$
B →	$O_1 - O_5$ ———	——— →	$O_1 - O_5$ →	$O_1 - O_5$

EXAMPLE 8.6 **Nonequivalent Groups Pretest-Posttest Design with Multiple Dependent Variables**

A pretest, post-test experimental design, involving a treatment and control group, was carried out. . . . At the end of the training program, both the treatment and the waiting-list control group participants were administered the post-test instruments. . . . The follow-up-test instruments were administered to both groups six months later. . . . Results indicate that there was a significant difference between treatment and control groups in specific measures of empathic and reflection skills, but not in communication skills as a general measure. Significant improvements also were found in the treatment group participants' self-esteem and self-acceptance in regard to time.

Source: Aladag, M., & Tezer, E. (2009). Effects of a peer helping training program on helping skills and self-growth of peer helpers. *International Journal of Advanced Counseling, 31,* 255, 261.

Randomized-to-Groups Posttest-Only Design

This design and the one that follows are termed *true* (pure) experimental designs because they include comparison groups of participants that have been randomly assigned to different interventions or to an intervention and control condition. In the randomized-groups posttest-only design, participants are first randomly assigned to the different intervention or control conditions, given the intervention (or no intervention if control), and then given the posttest. The design, with a control group, is represented by the following diagram:

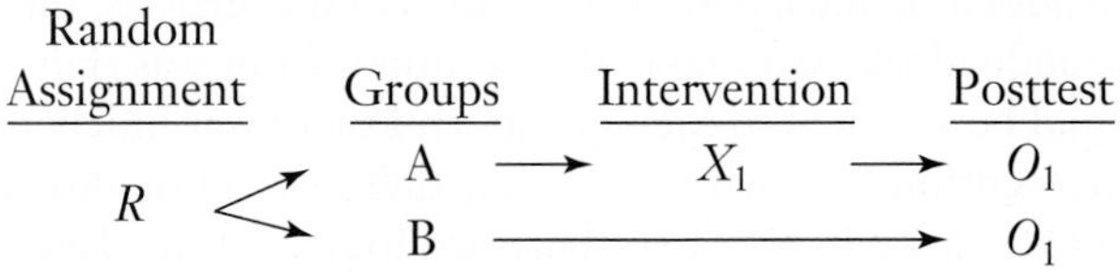

Random Assignment	Groups	Intervention	Posttest
R ↗	A →	X_1 →	O_1
↘	B →	→	O_1

If a comparison group is included, rather than a control group, the design looks like this:

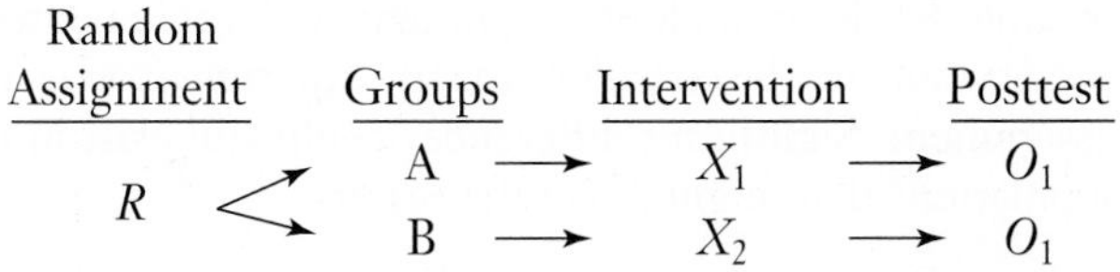

Random Assignment	Groups	Intervention	Posttest
R ↗	A →	X_1 →	O_1
↘	B →	X_2 →	O_1

In most educational experiments there is a comparison group rather than a control group because of limited resources and time to work with students.

Random assignment means that each participant has the same probability of being in either the intervention or comparison or control group. The purpose of random assignment is to equalize the characteristics of the participants in each group. This equalization can be assumed when a sufficient number of individuals is randomly assigned to each group (generally, 15 or more). The obvious strength of random assignment is the control of selection as a threat to internal validity. It is assumed that the participants in each group are essentially "equal" on any characteristics that may affect the dependent variable. Other threats, however, need to be considered that are not controlled by random assignment, including diffusion of treatment, experimenter effects, subject effects, treatment replication, and extraneous events within a group of subjects.

EXAMPLES 8.7–8.8 | Randomized-to-Groups Posttest-Only Design with a Single Independent Variable

Study 1 analyzed the effects of achievement feedback in a mathematical task on self-perceived verbal competence. Participants worked on a series of mathematical problems, after which they were given social comparison feedback information indicating that they had performed either better or worse than a comparison sample . . . participants were randomly assigned to conditions in a one-way design, with achievement feedback as the independent variable.

Source: Moller, J., & Koller, O. (2001). Dimensional comparisons: An experimental approach to the internal/external frame of reference model. *Journal of Educational Psychology, 93,* 827–828.

Participants were randomly assigned to one of three conditions; there were 35 participants in the control condition and 36 each in the reason and counterargue/rebut conditions.

Source: Borman, G. D., & Dowling, N. M. (2006). Longitudinal achievement effects of multi-year summer school. *Educational Evaluation and Policy Analysis, 28*(1), 25–48.

Careful attention needs to be paid to how "randomization" is carried out. If a researcher includes individual participant scores in the analysis, the "unit" of the analysis is the individual. As long as the randomization was done so that each participant could be assigned to each group, and there was independent replication of the intervention for each participant, then it is a randomized-to-groups design. In contrast, a study in which there are four existing classes of students, two of which are randomly assigned to the treatment and two to the control condition, is not a randomized-to-groups design. In this case randomly assigning only two cases to each group is not sufficient to be defined as a true experiment.

Note in Example 8.9 how random assignment was implemented by school. Consequently, this would not be considered a true experiment, even though there was random assignment. Significant differences could still exist in both student and teacher populations that might affect the results.

EXAMPLE 8.9 | Random Assignment by School

Four participating schools were matched and randomly assigned to intervention and control groups. . . . This longitudinal study consisted of a comparison of teacher change in effectiveness for teachers at schools that were matched and randomly selected to participate in the TPD program (Bryce and Zion) and for the control schools (Meadow and Hill).

Source: Johnson, C. C., & Fargo, J. D. (2010). Urban school reform enabled by transformative professional development: Impact on teacher change and student learning of science. *Urban Education, 45*(1), 4, 14.

Randomized-to-Groups Pretest-Posttest Design

This true experiment has both a pretest and a posttest. Otherwise, it is the same as the randomized-to-groups posttest-only design. A pretest is used to further equalize the groups statistically, in addition to what random assignment provides. Researchers use a pretest with random assignment when there may be small, subtle effects of different treatments, when differential subject attrition is possible, and when there is a need to analyze subgroups who differ on the pretest. Participants can be randomly assigned before or after the pretest. In some studies the pretest scores are used to match participant, and then one participant from each pair is randomly assigned to each group. The following, Example 8.10, describes a randomized two-group pretest-posttest experiment:

EXAMPLE 8.10 | Randomized-to-Groups Pretest-Posttest Design

Participants were 65 (boys and girls) ninth-grade students who were assigned randomly to two EL environments: EL+IMP and EL. Students in both environments studied the linear function unit for 5 weeks. . . . The study utilized two measures for the pre-test and post-test: mathematical test and SRL questionnaire.

Source: Kramarski, B., & Gutman, M. (2006). How can self-regulated learning be supported in mathematical E-learning environments? *Journal of Computer Assisted Learning, 22*(1), 27.

This study can be diagrammed as follows:

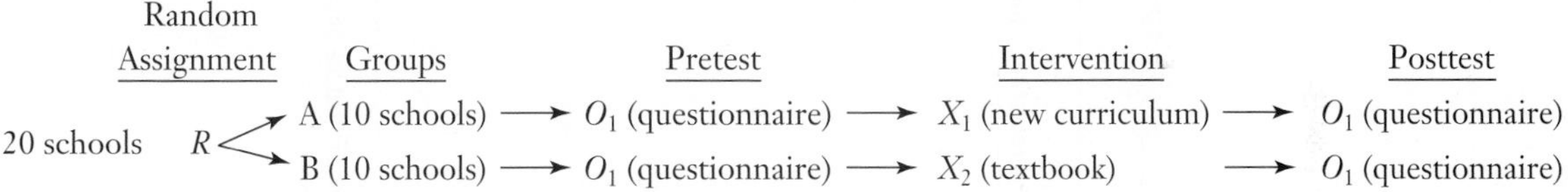

Table 8.3 summarizes threats to internal validity of the six designs. Although the "scoreboard" will give you a good start in evaluating the credibility of an experiment, each study must be judged individually. Overall, credibility is determined not so much by the particular design but by how well the researcher understands and controls for possible threats.

Factorial Designs

All of the designs we have considered in this chapter have one independent variable. Many experiments, as well as nonexperimental studies, will have two or more independent variables and employ what are called **factorial designs.** There are two primary purposes for using factorial designs. One is to see if the effects of a treatment are consistent across subject characteristics, such as age, gender, or aptitude. The second is to examine interactions, which are relationships that can only be investigated with designs that use two or more independent variables. If a study is testing the effect of two methods of instruction, for example,

Factorial designs: Containing two or more independent variables.

TABLE 8.3 **Internal Validity Scoreboard**

Design	Threats to Internal Validity										
	History	Selection	Maturation	Pretesting	Instrumentation	Treatment Replications	Subject Attrition	Statistical Regression	Diffusion of Treatment	Experimenter Effects	Subject Effects
Single-Group Posttest-Only	–	–	–	NA	?	?	?	–	NA	?	?
Single-Group Pretest-Posttest	?	?	–	–	?	?	?	–	NA	?	?
Nonequivalent-Groups Posttest-Only	?	–	?	NA	?	?	?	?	NA	?	?
Nonequivalent-Groups Pretest-Posttest	?	?	?	?	?	?	?	+	?	?	?
Randomized-to-Groups Posttest-Only	?	+	+	NA	?	?	?	+	?	?	?
Randomized-to-Groups Pretest-Posttest	?	+	+	?	?	?	?	+	?	?	?

In this table a minus sign indicates a definite weakness, a plus sign means that the threat is controlled, a question mark indicates a possible source of invalidity, and NA means that the threat is not applicable to the design.

computerized compared to traditional, it might be desirable to know if the effectiveness of the methods was the same for males as for females. Thus, such a study would have two independent variables, each with two levels. The study may be diagrammed in different ways, as illustrated in Figure 8.5. Figures 8.5b and c show that the students were first divided into groups of males and females and then randomly assigned to the two instructional methods. There is a numerical notation system used with factorial designs that tells you about the number of independent variables and the number of levels within each independent variable. In the previous example, the notation would be 2 × 2. Each number indicates a single independent variable with two levels. If a study has one independent variable with three levels and one with four levels, it would be designated as 3 × 4 (see Figure 8.6). If a third variable is added, with two levels, it would be 2 × 3 × 4.

FIGURE 8.5 Diagrams of 2 × 2 design.

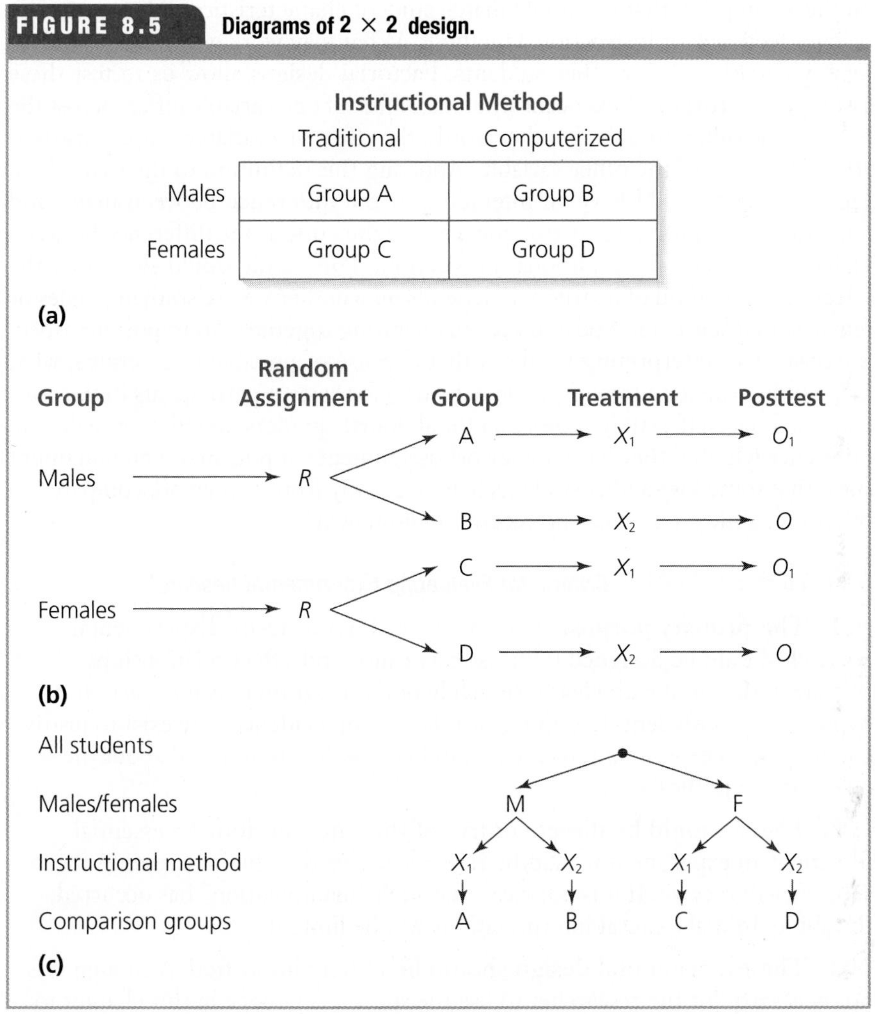

FIGURE 8.6 **Notation for a study of the effect of three types of teacher feedback in grades 2–5.**

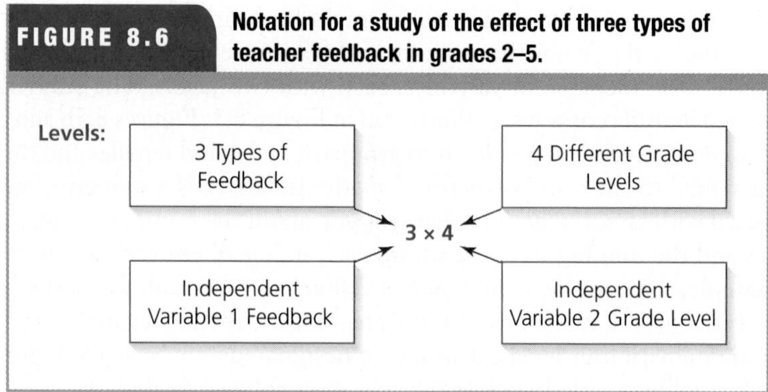

Interactions are very important since much of what we do in education is based on the assumption that we should match student characteristics with appropriate teacher feedback or instructional methods. What may work well for one student may not work well for other students. Factorial designs allow us to test these assumptions. **Interactions** occur when the effect of one variable differs across the levels of the other variable. In other words, the effect of a variable is not consistent across all levels of the other variable. Applying this definition to the example in Figure 8.5, we would have an interaction if the difference between males and females for computerized instruction was not the same as the difference between males and females for traditional instruction. This result would show that the effect of the method of instruction depends on whether we are studying males or females. In a sense, method and sex are operating together. An important aspect to consider in interpreting results is that because of possible interactions, what may not be true for a total group may be true for certain participants in the population. That is, if a study shows that for all fourth-graders, together, it makes no difference whether they have homework assignments or not, an interaction might show that some low-ability students benefit greatly from homework compared to other low-ability students who receive no homework.

Interactions: Effect of independent variables together.

CONSUMER TIPS: *Criteria for Evaluating Experimental Research*

1. The primary purpose is to test causal hypotheses. Experimental research should be designed to investigate cause-and-effect relationships that are anticipated with clear research hypotheses. If there is no research hypothesis, insufficient descriptive or relationship evidence may exist to justify conducting an experiment, or the researcher may be uninformed about the need for a hypothesis.

2. There should be direct control of the intervention. An essential feature of an experiment is that the researcher controls the intervention that subjects will receive. If it is not clear that such "manipulation" has occurred, the ability to make causal interpretations will be limited.

3. The experimental design should be clearly identified. Although it is not necessary for the researcher to use the specific language in this chapter to identify a design (e.g., randomized-to-groups posttest-only), it is important that sufficient details about the design are provided to enable you to understand what was done to which participants and the sequence of measurement and interventions. In fact, there should be enough detail so that you could replicate the study. As noted, the threats you need to focus on to evaluate the study depend to a certain extent on the design. If you cannot understand the design, the researcher may not have understood it either!

4. The design should provide maximum control of extraneous/confounded variables. The researcher should indicate how specific aspects of the design control possible extraneous and confounding variables. Obvious threats, such as selection in the nonequivalent-groups designs, need to be addressed. If obvious threats are not controlled by the design, the researcher should present a rationale for why a particular threat is not a plausible alternative explanation for the results. Failure to provide such a rationale may indicate that the researcher does not fully understand how such variables can influence results.

Use Table 8.4 to systematically evaluate the possibility and plausibility of threats to internal validity. For any given study or design, check first whether the threat is possible, then identify any of those that would be likely. Finally, depending on the specifics of the design, indicate whether any of the likely threats would be considered "fatal flaws."

5. The intervention should be described and implemented as planned. The key features of interventions and procedures need to be

TABLE 8.4 Evaluating Threats to Internal Validity

Threat	Possible?	Likely?	Fatal Flaw?
History			
Selection			
Maturation			
Pretesting			
Instrumentation			
Treatment replications			
Subject attrition			
Statistical regression			
Diffusion of treatment			
Experimenter effects			
Subject effects			

described in sufficient detail to allow other researchers to replicate the study and compare it to similar intervention studies, and to allow for research syntheses such as a meta-analysis. A complete description also allows you to connect the theory behind the intervention with what was implemented. Most interventions use labels that can be operationalized in different ways, in much the same way constructs are in measurement. For example, there are several ways of operationalizing "small class," "cooperative learning," "formative assessment strategies," and other interventions. You need enough detail to know what was actually done, not simply the label or general description. At the very least, the key features of the intervention should be completely described.

Intervention fidelity: Extent to which intervention occurred as intended.

In field studies it is important to document that the planned intervention was what was actually implemented. This can be called a *check on the intervention*, *adherence*, *treatment fidelity*, *treatment integrity*, *fidelity of implementation*, or *intervention fidelity*. **Intervention fidelity** is strong when evidence is presented that the *enacted* intervention is consistent with *intended* intervention. The evidence could consist of observations, surveys from participants, daily logs of activities, and/or interviews. In a study of the use of feedback to motivate students, observers in the classroom could determine if the nature of the feedback provided is consistent with what was planned. At the very least, it is important to document the completion of key features of the intervention. A more detailed study of the intervention helps researchers identify whether the level of intervention was constant or fluctuated across implementers. This analysis leads to a better understanding of the conditions in which the intervention is effective.

The following two examples show how researchers have addressed intervention fidelity. The first example is from a well-known experiment on class size. The second example is from the same study excerpted earlier on the effects of cooperative learning on elaboration.

EXAMPLES 8.11–8.12 | Fidelity of Intervention

In the STAR experiment, the primary treatment of interest is the manipulation of class size. The intent of the STAR experiment was to compare the achievement of students in small classes (13–17) with that of students in larger classes (22–26 students) and in larger classes with full-time aides. However, as in any field experiment, it is important to determine how well the treatment was implemented, because implementation is never perfect at all sites. Thus, in evaluating the STAR experiment, it is important to determine the actual size of the classes to see if the intent of the experimenters was realized.

Source: Nye, B., Hedges, L. V., & Konstantopoulos, S. (2000). The effects of small classes on academic achievement: The results of the Tennessee class size experiment. *American Educational Research Journal, 37,* 128.

The fidelity of the implementation of the 2-year CL staff development program that constituted part of the experimental condition was checked by observing the teachers in their classrooms on three occasions at approximately 11-month intervals; questionnaires were also administered to the teachers and students. The results of the implementation study showed that the teachers were able to implement those components required for successful CL.

Source: Veenman, S., Denessen, E., van den Akker, A., & vander Rijt, J. (2005). Effects of a cooperative learning program on the elaborations of students during help seeking and help giving. *American Educational Research Journal, 42*(1), 125.

6. The determination of *n* should be the same as independent replications of the interventions. In a classic experiment, each participant is randomly assigned to interventions and experiences the intervention independently from others. In some studies, participants are randomly assigned to groups and then all the subjects in each group receive one intervention together. Technically, each group in this situation is one "*n*." If each person experiences the intervention separately from the others, each person is one participant. However, if only one intervention is given to a group of people, the group should be identified as one "subject." In reading an experimental study, you should look for the number of times the program is replicated, which should be the same as the number of participants in the study. As we will see in Chapter 9, the statistical results of research are highly dependent on the number of participants.

7. The measure of the dependent variable must be sufficiently sensitive to capture the change caused by the intervention. The measurement of the dependent variable needs to be sensitive to change because of what has been implemented from the intervention. That is, it may be difficult to show change in scores on some standardized tests of ability or reasoning, or with relatively stable traits such as self-efficacy or cognitive style. For example, an intervention that focuses on critical thinking in a science class might not be detected by a broad measure of critical thinking that is not specific to science.

USING EDUCATIONAL RESEARCH

While recent federal legislation will increase the number of field experiments in education to demonstrate cause-and-effect relationships between educational interventions and student outcomes, an important experiment in Tennessee has examined the impact of class size on student achievement in early elementary grades. This four-year, large-scale randomized experiment, STAR, shows that class size effects are large enough to influence educational policy. The data show that small classes benefit all types of students in different kinds of schools.

SINGLE-SUBJECT DESIGNS

In the designs we have considered so far in this chapter, participants are studied in groups. By conducting experiments with groups, individual differences are pooled and the results can be generalized to other persons who are like the subjects. However, there are circumstances in which it may not be possible to administer an intervention to groups of participants. In these situations, researchers conduct their experiments with individuals through **single-subject** (or *single case*) **designs,** which use one or just a few participants to study the influence of a new procedure. The approach of the design is to repeat measures of the dependent variable before and after an intervention is implemented. The basis of comparison is the difference in behavior prior to and then after initiation of the intervention. Single-subject designs are used extensively in research with exceptional children and in counseling, where the focus of change is on individuals rather than on groups.

Single-subject design: Individual behavior recorded before and after an intervention.

Characteristics of Single-Subject Research

McMillan and Schumacher (2010) summarize five characteristics of single-subject research:

1. Reliable measurement: Since these designs involve multiple measures of behavior, it is important for the instrumentation to be reliable. Conditions for data collection, such as time of day and location, should be standardized, and observers need to be trained. Consistency in measurement is especially crucial in the transition before and after the intervention.

2. Repeated measurement: The same behavior is measured over and over again. This step is different from most experiments, in which the dependent variable is measured only once. Repeated measures are needed to obtain a clear pattern or consistency in the behavior over time. They control for the normal variation of behavior that is expected within short time intervals. This aspect of single-subject designs is similar to abbreviated time series studies, which investigate groups rather than individuals and do not provide for a return to conditions that were present before the intervention was implemented.

3. Description of conditions: A clear, detailed description of the conditions of measurement and the nature of the intervention is needed to strengthen internal and external validity.

4. Baseline and intervention conditions: Each single-subject study involves at least one baseline and one intervention condition. The **baseline** refers to a period of time in which the target behavior (dependent variable) is observed and recorded as it occurs without a special or new program or procedure. The baseline behavior provides the frame of reference against which future behavior is compared. The term *baseline* can also refer to a period of time following an intervention in which conditions match what was present in the original baseline. The intervention condition is a period of time during

Baseline: Measurement of behavior before the intervention.

which the experimental manipulation is introduced and the target behavior continues to be observed and recorded. Both the baseline and intervention phases of the study need to be long enough to achieve stability in the target behavior.

5. Single-variable rule: During a single-subject study, only one variable should be changed from baseline to intervention conditions. In some studies two variables are changed together during the same intervention condition. This is an interaction in single-subject research.

Types of Single-Subject Designs

Although some single-subject designs can be rather complex, most are easily recognized variations of an A–B–A or multiple-baseline design.

A–B–A *Design.* Single-subject designs use a notation system in which A refers to a baseline condition and B to a treatment condition. The order of the letters indicates the sequence of procedures in the study. Thus, in an A–B design there is one baseline and one intervention condition. In an A–B–A design the intervention condition is followed by another baseline, as indicated in the following diagram:

Baseline	Intervention (treatment)	Baseline

$$X_1X_1X_1X_1X_1X_1X_1X_1$$

$$O_1O_1O_1O_1O_1O_1O_1O_1O_1O_1O_1O_1O_1O_1O_1O_1O_1O_1O_1O_1O_1O_1O_1$$

Withdrawal design: Treatment removed after implementation.

This design is called an A–B–A **withdrawal design.** The intervention is introduced after a number of observations of the baseline behavior, and is stopped to return to the same condition that was present during the original baseline measurement. The design allows a strong causal inference if the pattern of behavior changes with the addition and withdrawal of the intervention. Without the second baseline phase (some single-subject studies use only an A–B design), extraneous events that occur at the same time as the intervention may influence the behavior. Extraneous events are well controlled when the pattern of behavior changes twice, or even more often in some designs (e.g., A–B–A–B). For example, suppose a teacher is interested in trying a new procedure to reinforce a student, Mary, to increase Mary's time on task (time actually engaged in studying and learning). The dependent variable is time on task. The teacher would observe the percentage of time Mary is on task for several days to establish a baseline. Then the teacher would introduce the new reinforcement technique and continue to record the percentage of Mary's time on task. After a few days of the new procedure (when the behavior is stable), the teacher would withdraw the new reinforcement technique and record the percentage of time on task for this second baseline period. Figure 8.7 shows how the results would be graphed and indicates evidence that the new technique is affecting Mary's time on task. Given the positive benefits of the new type of reinforcement, the teacher would want to reinstitute it.

FIGURE 8.7 Results of A–B–A single-subject design.

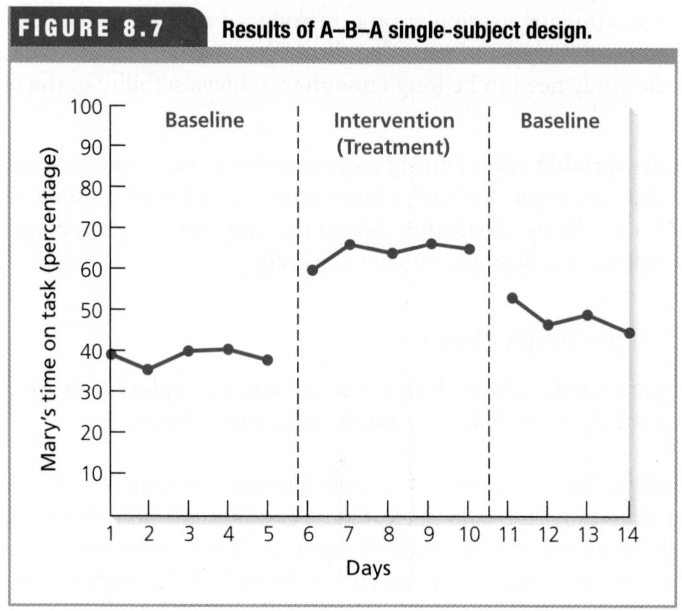

One limitation of the A–B–A design is the difficulty in interpreting a positive change that is not altered during the second baseline. In this situation the intervention may be so strong that its effect lasts a long time, or something else may have occurred with the intervention that affected the behavior and did not stop when the intervention did.

Multiple-baseline design: More than one subject, behavior, or setting.

Multiple-Baseline Designs. In a single-subject **multiple-baseline design,** observations are made on several subjects, different target behaviors of one or more subjects, or different situations. Thus, multiple baselines are conducted across subjects, behaviors, or settings. A design that has more than one subject may implement the intervention with each subject or use one or more subjects as a control condition. Different behaviors are studied when an intervention is applied to more than one target behavior. For example, the effectiveness of using time-out for institutionalized individuals with mental retardation can be observed for several types of behavior, including taking food from others and hitting others. If a study examines the effect of the same procedure on behaviors in several different settings or situations, such as different classes, a multiple-baseline across-settings design is employed. For instance, an investigator may be interested in whether a particular type of praise is as effective with an individual in math class as it is in science class.

Example 8.13 is from an article in which accuracy was examined across three subjects—spelling, mathematics, and reading comprehension—for six fourth-grade students. This resulted in three A–B analyses for each individual, with a follow-up that used two-week intervals.

EXAMPLE 8.13 | **Single-Subject Multiple Baseline Study Across Behaviors Design**

A multiple baseline design across behaviours was employed to evaluate the effects of a randomized group contingency program on students' homework accuracy rates. . . . Baseline data were collected for 3 weeks, the intervention was implemented for 6 weeks, and follow-up data were obtained for 8 weeks.

Source: Reinhardt, D., Theodore, L. A, Bray, M. A., & Kehle, T. J. (2009). Improving homework accuracy: Interdependent group contingencies and randomized components. *Psychology in the Schools, 46*(5), 474.

CONSUMER TIPS: *Criteria for Evaluating Single-Subject Research*

1. There should be reliable measurement of the target behavior. It is important for the measurement to be standardized and consistent. Evidence for reliability should be presented in the procedures section of the study. If more than one observer is used, interobserver reliability should be reported.

2. The target behavior should be clearly defined operationally. There should be a detailed definition of the dependent variable, described operationally in terms of how it is measured.

3. Sufficient measures are needed to establish stability in behavior. There should be enough measures to establish stability in the behavior that is measured. Typically, a minimum of three or four observations is needed in each phase of the study to provide measures that do not show more than a small degree of variability. This step is especially important for the baseline condition since this is the level of behavior against which behaviors occurring during the treatment are compared, but it is also necessary for the intervention condition. Usually, there is the same number of measures during each phase of the study.

4. Procedures, subjects, and settings should be fully described. Since the external validity of single-subject designs is relatively weak, the usefulness of the results depends to a great extent on the match between the procedures, characteristics of the subjects, and settings in the study with other subjects and settings. The best judgments of the extent of this match are made when there is a detailed description of what was done, to whom, and where.

5. A single, standardized intervention should be used. The procedures for administering the intervention should be standardized so that precisely the same procedure is given each time. Only one intervention or one combination of interventions should be changed from the baseline to treatment phases of the study.

6. Experimenter or observer effects should be controlled. Because of the heavy reliance on a single observer, who in many cases is the same person as the experimenter, it is important to indicate how bias is controlled, that is, how bias is not a potential threat to internal validity. Judging the credibility of the researcher may not be easy, although you will find hints of bias in many parts of the research report or article.

7. **Results should be practically significant.** The results of most single-subject studies are analyzed by inspecting their graphic presentation and judging whether the patterns of behavior in different phases of the study appear to be different. This judgment should be based on graphs that do not distort differences by artificially increasing the intervals used to describe the behaviors. Clear differences should be evident, and they should be significant in practical terms, showing enough of a difference to clearly affect the behavior of the subject. Some single-subject studies use a statistical analysis of the results, but a "statistically significant" difference still needs to be practically significant.

Author Reflection *Is it really worth it to conduct experimental research? Sometimes it seems that so many possible and plausible threats to the design exist that it would be nearly impossible to say that there is strong internal validity, especially for field experiments. My perspective on this issue is that yes, field experiments can be very helpful, even with limitations. As long as the researcher is aware of possible threats before conducting the experiment, the design can be sufficiently strong to be able to make valid causal conclusions. What is most problematic is when the results show no difference. Then it is hard to know whether some limitation in the design led to the result or whether, in fact, the intervention was not effective. We'll explore this aspect of research in the next chapter.*

ANATOMY *of an* EXPERIMENTAL RESEARCH STUDY

The following article is an example of how an experimental study is designed and reported. This particular investigation is quasi-experimental.

ARTICLE 8.1 **Using Tests as an Incentive to Motivate Procrastinators to Study**

Bruce W. Tuckman
Florida State University

Abstract. *The purposes of this study were to compare two approaches for enhancing the recall and understanding of text and to compare the effectiveness of the two approaches for students differing in procrastination tendency. The first approach was to provide incentive motivation by giving a test on each text chapter; the second approach was to provide a learning strategy by requiring students to outline each chapter as a homework assignment. Eighty-two students were classified by level of procrastination based on scores on the Procrastination Scale. Half of the students experienced the test condition; the other half experienced the homework condition. Although the test condition produced significantly higher scores overall on a final achievement examination than the outline condition did, a significant interaction between condition and student procrastination level reflected an almost 12% advantage for the test condition among high procrastinators. There was virtually no difference between conditions for medium and low procrastinators.*

MANY OF THE TASKS AND ENTERPRISES that individuals undertake are done voluntarily. Tuckman and Sexton (1990) labeled *self-regulated performance* acts that require the exercise of influence over one's own behavior, such as studying, dieting, or cleaning up after oneself. Self-regulated performance is particularly important in school. . . .

The absence of self-regulated performance has been labeled *procrastination*—the tendency to put off or avoid an activity under one's control (Tuckman & Sexton, 1989). Procrastination may result from a combination of (a) disbelieving in one's own capability to perform a task (Bandura, 1986), (b) being unable to postpone gratification, and (c) assigning blame for one's own "predicament" to external sources (Ellis & Knaus, 1977; Tuckman, 1989). To accurately measure and predict the tendency to procrastinate, Tuckman (1991) developed the Procrastination Scale.

As a student proceeds through school, the responsibility for controlling performance shifts progressively from parents and teachers to the student, reaching a high point during the college years. The inability to overcome procrastination tendencies may be related to problems encountered by many college students, leading some researchers to be on the lookout for effective strategies that may help such students regulate their own learning (see, e.g., Tuckman, 1990; Zimmerman, 1989). In the present study, I investigated one such strategy: using tests to motivate procrastinators to study on a timely basis.

Incentives, or goal objects that individuals desire to attain or avoid, have figured prominently in a number of theories of motivation (e.g., Atkinson, 1964; Rotter, Chance, & Phares, 1972; Vroom, 1964). In these theories, the degree to which the object is desired is referred to as its *incentive or reward value*. These incentive theories of motivation suggest that people will perform an act when its performance is likely to result in some outcome they desire. Behavior that is motivated or prompted by the desire to attain or avoid an incentive can be said to be the result of *incentive motivation* (Petri, 1996). Overmier and Lawry (1979) theorized that incentive motivation can be regarded as a mediator between the stimulus characteristics of a situation containing a goal object and the responses directed toward that object. . . .

Pintrich and Schrauben (1992) reviewed a large body of research that suggests that (a) the value of an outcome to a student affects that student's motivation and (b) motivation leads to cognitive engagement, with such engagement manifesting itself in the use or application of various learning strategies. . . . A technique for enhancing incentive value is to provide a situation that can be linked to performance incentives, or what Bandura (1986) referred to as *competency-contingent incentives*. Again, a test would seem to provide the very performance incentives that a procrastinator requires to overcome procrastination. . . .

In the present study, I compared two approaches for enhancing the recall and understanding of information. The *incentive approach* focused exclusively on will as a function of incentive motivation, and the *strategy approach* focused on skill, or effective strategy use. For the incentive approach, I used a semiweekly spot quiz on the information to be covered. I theorized that studying voluntarily on a semiweekly basis for the tests would reflect the desire to obtain a high grade or avoid a low one (the incentive), thus representing incentive motivation. The degree and nature of text processing would depend on the value of the incentive to the student. For the strategy approach, I used a text-processing homework assignment on that same information to ensure, at a minimum, a comparable degree of cognitive engagement across conditions. In the homework condition, processing of the text by the students would be guaranteed because it was assigned. It would not depend on motivation.

Tuckman (1996) showed that the incentive-motivation approach with spot quizzes has a greater impact on subsequent achievement than the homework approach does, particularly among college students with low grade point averages (GPAs). Based on that result, I hypothesized that the students in the test condition would outperform the students in the homework condition, primarily because the test condition would be more likely to motivate procrastinators to study on a timely basis.

METHOD

Eighty-two college juniors and seniors, preparing to be teachers, participated in the study. The average age of the students was 21, and two thirds of the group were women. They were enrolled in two sections of a 6-week, summer educational psychology course required for teacher certification. A comparison of the two classes on age, gender, and self-reports of scores on the combined verbal and mathematics portion of the College Level

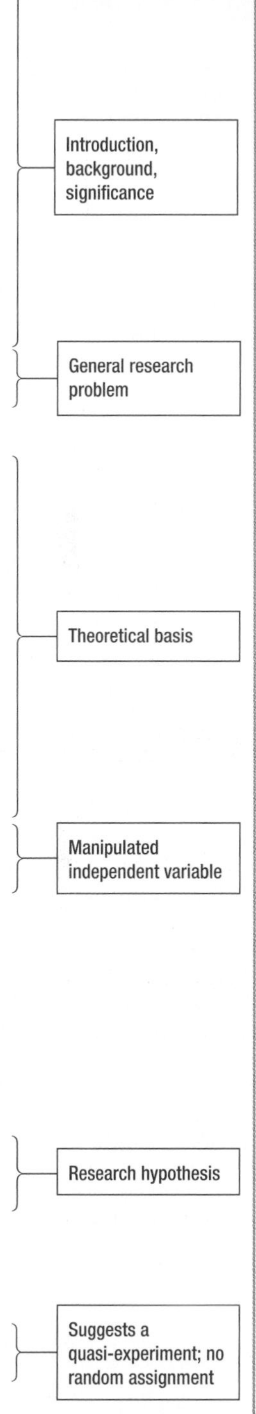

(continued)

ARTICLE 8.1 (continued)

Shows similarity between groups to rule out selection as a threat

Possible bias

Description of interventions

Academic Skills Test (CLAST), prior semester's GPA, and grade expectation showed them to be equivalent. Correlations between CLAST scores and achievement in this course have been found to be about .5 (Tuckman, 1993). Both sections met twice a week (at the same time of day), covered the same content (learning theories), and used the same textbook. The same instructor taught both courses.

At the beginning of each class period, one class was given a seven-completion item spot quiz (SQ) that covered the textbook chapter assigned for that week. The quiz was projected via an overhead projector. The instructor allowed 15 min. for its completion. At the time of the spot quiz, no instruction had yet been given on the chapter covered by the quiz. The only informational resource was the textbook itself. Following the spot quiz, the students exchanged papers and the instructor went over the answers so that the students could grade one another's tests. The students were informed that the average of their spot-quiz grades would count as much as the final achievement test toward their final grade.

Description of interventions

The other class was given the homework assignment of preparing an outline of the assigned chapter that was arranged hierarchically and that covered major terms and their meanings. This approach is considered to be a cognitive strategy for extracting meaning from text (Gagne, Weidemann, Bell, & Anders, 1984; King, 1992). The students turned in their outlines, were given written feedback comparable to the feedback given following the spot quizzes, and were graded on the quality of the outlines. These grades were averaged and counted as the equivalent of the final achievement test, the same as in the spot-quiz condition.

Measures of attribute independent variables

The students completed the 32-item Procrastination Scale (Tuckman, 1991) and were divided into high (≥67), medium (68–78), and low (≤67) groups. I selected cutoffs to produce groups of approximately equal size. Items on the scale include "I needlessly delay finishing jobs, even when they're important"; "I postpone starting in on things I don't like to do"; and "When I have a deadline, I wait till the last minute." The reliability of the scale (Cronbach's alpha) was .86. Construct validity was based on a correlation of −.54 between scores on the scale and performance on a voluntary task that reflected the motivational tendency to self-regulate (Tuckman, 1991). Concurrent validity was based on (a) a correlation between scores on the scale and on the General Self-Efficacy Scale of −.47 (Tuckman) and (b) a significant path coefficient linking scale scores and student ratings of course demands (Abry, 1997). The relative independence of the measure of procrastination from scores reflecting general achievement is shown by correlations of −.19 and −.22 between the procrastination scores and the students' self-reported expected grade and GPA, respectively (Abry).

Description of dependent variable

The final achievement test contained 65 multiple-choice items, most of which measured conceptual, rather than factual, knowledge. The general content domain of the test corresponded equally to the content domain of the spot quizzes and the outlines. However, the nature of the items on the test was quite different from the nature of those on the spot quizzes. The reliability of the test (Kuder-Richardson) was .77.

Check on the manipulation

The students were also required to keep a log of time spent either preparing for spot quizzes or completing outlines and to turn the log in on a weekly basis.

RESULTS

Two independent variables, one with two levels, the second with three levels.

I conducted a two-way analysis of variance (ANOVA) on scores on the final achievement test with condition (spot quiz vs. outline) and procrastination score (high, medium, low) as the independent variables. The results of the ANOVA are shown in Table 1, and the means and standard deviations are shown in Table 2. The main effect for condition was significant at the .01 level with the spot-quiz students outperforming the outline students on the achievement test (76.8% to 71.7%). The main effect of procrastination was not significant. The interaction of condition and procrastination level was significant at the .05 level. A comparison of means using the least significant difference approach revealed that although low and medium procrastinators differed only slightly on achievement across the two conditions (75.2% to 72.9% in favor of SQ for lows; 75.9% to 74.8% in favor of SQ for mediums), high procrastinators differed significantly in achievement across the two conditions, $t(26) = 3.54, p < .01$ (79.2% to 67.3% in favor of SQ). In other words, high procrastinators who took spot quizzes on each chapter obtained significantly higher achievement test scores on the final exam than those who completed outlines on each chapter did. No such advantage based on spot quizzes was found for low procrastinators.

Time-log scores for class preparation by the students in the two conditions showed no significant differences. The students in both conditions reported an average of approximately 2 hr of preparation time per week. The relative independence of procrastination, by itself, and achievement was reflected in a correlation of –.05.

DISCUSSION

In the present study, the students who were given spot quizzes on each chapter outperformed the students who completed chapter outlines on a test of achievement; the difference between the conditions was based primarily on the performance of procrastinators, who profited most from the quizzes. . . .

Summary of results

TABLE 1 ANOVA of Achievement Test Score, by Condition and Procrastination Level

Source	*df*	*SS*	*MS*	*F*
Condition	1	527.27	527.27	6.05**
Procrastination level	2	63.28	31.64	0.70
Interaction	2	540.50	270.25	3.10*
Error	76	6,625.53	87.18	

$^*p < .05$. $^{**}p < .01$.

TABLE 2 Mean Achievement Test Scores and Standard Deviations for the Two Intervention Groups, by Procrastination Level

	Procrastination Level			
Treatment	**Low**	**Middle**	**High**	**Combined**
Spot quiz				
M	75.2	75.9	79.2*	76.8*
SD	8.7	9.2	7.5	8.4
Outline				
M	72.9	74.8	67.3*	71.7*
SD	8.4	7.2	10.2	10.3
Combined				
M	74.0	75.3	72.8	
SD	8.5	8.1	12.3	

*Significantly different from mean for other intervention ($p < .01$).

(continued)

ARTICLE 8.1 (continued)

Explanation of results

Spot quizzes, as an instructional intervention, motivated procrastinators to study continually over an entire course. They induced students to study on a daily or weekly basis, rather than postponing studying until the middle or end of the course. Moreover, completing homework assignments did not have the same impact on procrastinators as weekly spot quizzes did, despite students' reports that they spent an equivalent amount of time completing assignments as studying for quizzes.

Relationship of results to theory

For procrastinators, incentive motivation may provide the needed inducement to self-regulate. Regular testing of assigned material appears to be a necessary stimulus for causing timely studying by procrastinators. Current thinking on instruction promotes the reduction of formal course requirements and the use of evaluation strategies other than testing, but teachers may be favoring the more motivated students by following that approach. Procrastinators may have difficulty acquiring new knowledge if steps are not taken to enhance their motivation. Frequent testing, therefore, may be thought of as a motivational "equalizer." Additional research should be undertaken to examine the long-term effects of this approach, especially in regard to transfer.

REFERENCES

Abry, D. (1997). *The relationships among procrastination, perceived course demands, and course satisfaction.* Unpublished manuscript, Florida State University, Tallahassee.

Atkinson, J. W. (1964). *An introduction to motivation.* Princeton, NJ: Van Nostrand.

Bandura, A. (1986). *Social foundations of thought and action: A social-cognitive theory.* Englewood Cliffs, NJ: Prentice-Hall.

Cook, L. K., & Mayer, R. E. (1983). Reading strategies training for meaningful learning from prose. In M. Pressley & J. R. Levin (Eds.), *Cognitive strategy research: Educational implications* (pp. 87–131). New York: Springer-Verlag.

Ellis, A., & Knaus, W. J. (1977). *Overcoming procrastination.* New York: New American Library.

Gagne, E. D., Weidemann, C., Bell, M. S., & Anders, T. D. (1984). Training thirteen-year-olds to elaborate while studying text. *Human Learning, 3,* 281–294.

King, A. (1992). Facilitating elaborate learning through guided student-generated questioning. *Educational Psychologist, 27,* 111–126.

Mayer, R. E. (1987). *Educational psychology: A cognitive approach.* Boston: Little, Brown.

Overmier, J. B., & Lawry, J. A. (1979). Conditioning and the mediation of behavior. In G. H. Bower (Ed.), *The psychology of learning and motivation* (Vol. 13, pp. 1–55). New York: Academic Press.

Petri, H. L. (1996). *Motivation: Theory, research, and applications* (4th ed.). Pacific Grove, CA: Brooks/Cole.

[References continue.]

STUDY QUESTIONS

1. What are the essential characteristics of experiments? How are experiments different from relationship studies?
2. Why is internal validity important in interpreting experiments?
3. Give an example of how extraneous events (history) can threaten the internal validity of an experiment.
4. In what experimental designs is selection a serious threat to internal validity? Why?

5. How is selection "controlled" in the nonequivalent-groups pretest-posttest design?
6. Under what circumstances are so-called pre-experimental designs valid?
7. What are potential threats to the internal validity of any type of experimental design? Why?
8. What does it mean to say that "the number of subjects in a study is equal to the number of replications of the intervention"?
9. Give an example of a factorial design.
10. Why is a factorial interaction important in research?
11. What characteristics would you look for in a good single-subject design?
12. What are the advantages of a multiple-baseline single-subject design?
13. How are the results of a single-subject design analyzed? What does it mean to have "practical" significance?

Chapter 9

Understanding Statistical Inferences

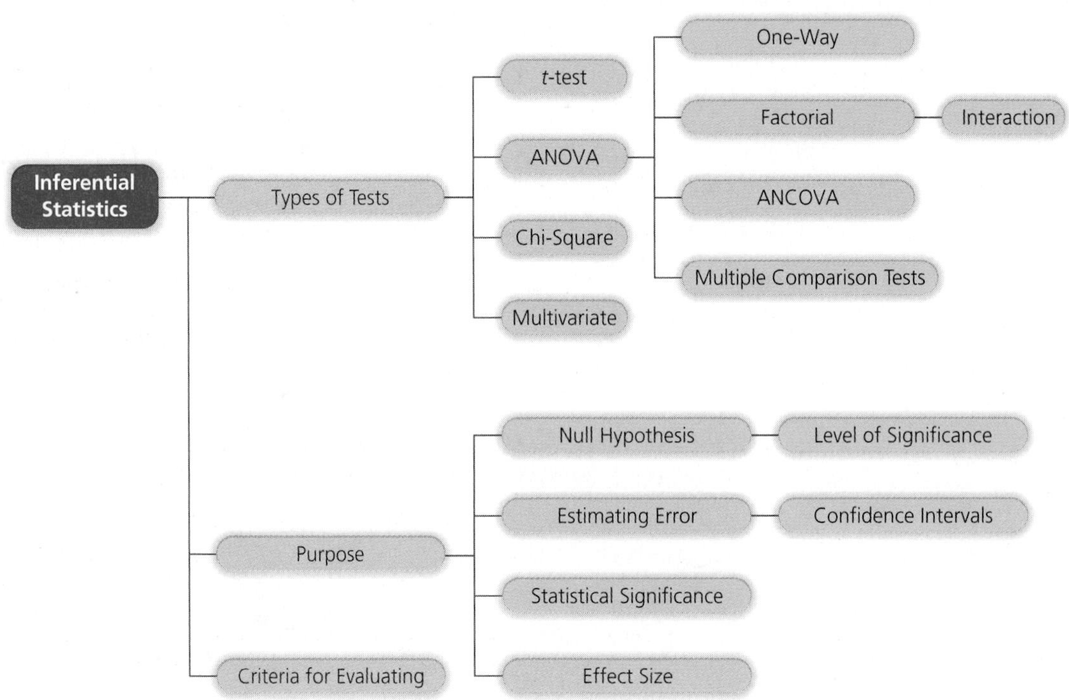

CHAPTER ROAD MAP

It may not be much of an understatement to say that you probably were not particularly eager to get to this chapter! There is usually a perception that complex mathematics are involved in understanding statistical principles and that the strange symbols and letters encountered are of little practical value. Although it is true that most statistical procedures require complex calculations, the computer handles these very efficiently. We will focus on the logic and meaning of the procedures, which will not require sophisticated mathematics, and on understanding and evaluating the use of the procedures in research reports and articles.

Chapter Outline	Learning Objectives
Purpose of Inferential Statistics	• Understand the concept of estimating errors in sampling and measurement. • Understand how characteristics of populations are inferred from sample statistics.
Hypothesis Testing	• Recognize null hypotheses and differentiate them from research hypotheses. • Understand level of significance and how it is used in hypothesis testing. • Understand the difference between Type 1 and Type 2 error in hypothesis testing. • Understand how confidence intervals are used to report probable results.
Effect Size	• Know why effect size, and other indicators of practical significance, are essential in communicating the results of studies. • Interpret the meaning of different effect size estimates.
Use and Interpret Specific Inferential Tests	• Know the difference between parametric and nonparametric tests.
t-Test	• Know when it is appropriate to use an independent samples or paired samples *t*-test. • Be able to interpret *t*-test results presented in studies.
Analysis of Variance (ANOVA)	• Know when it is appropriate to use simple and factorial analysis of variance. • Understand how multiple comparison procedures are used in interpreting ANOVA results. • Be able to interpret ANOVA results presented in studies.
Factorial Analysis of Variance	• Understand how two or more independent variables are combined in factorial ANOVAs. • Know how to describe factorial designs. • Understand why interactions are important. • Be able to interpret the main and interaction effects presented in studies.
Analysis of Covariance	• Understand why analysis of covariance is used. • Know how to interpret analysis of covariance results presented in studies.
Chi-Square	• Know when it is appropriate to use chi-square analyses. • Be able to interpret chi-square results presented in studies.
Multivariate Statistics	• Know when it is appropriate to use multivariate statistics.

The PURPOSE *and* NATURE *of* INFERENTIAL STATISTICS

As indicated in Chapter 5, statistics are mathematical procedures used to summarize and analyze numerical data. In this chapter we will concentrate on procedures that use descriptive statistics to estimate from a sample what is true for a population, or what is likely to be true given the inexact nature of measurement. These procedures, called **inferential statistics**, are necessary to understand the precise nature of descriptions, relationships, and differences based on the data collected in a study.

Inferential statistics: Infers characteristics of a population.

Degree of Uncertainty

It would be nice (not to mention profitable) if we could be certain about our predictions. How certain is a principal that a particular kind of evaluation procedure will provide credible information on which to base merit salary increases? Are you confident in your ability to predict who will win a race or an election? If we know that a small sample of sixth-graders will pass a minimum competency test, how certain can we be that all sixth-graders will pass it? The degree to which we can be certain in each of these circumstances, and in others, will vary. There is some degree of *uncertainty* in the questions addressed in educational research, and inferential statistics indicate in a precise way what we can, for the most part, be confident about. The degree of confidence depends on the amount of error in sampling and measurement.

Estimating Errors in Sampling and Measurement

Sampling was discussed in Chapter 4 as a procedure for studying a portion of a larger population. Subjects in the sample are measured to obtain *descriptive statistics for the sample*. Inferential statistics are then used to *infer* to the entire population (refer back to Figure 4.2). Suppose a researcher is interested in the attitudes of seventh-graders toward learning and school. The population is large, say, 1,000 seventh-graders, so a sample of 100 seventh-graders is selected randomly and these students respond to the attitude questionnaire. The researcher then uses the results from the sample to infer the attitudes of all 1,000 seventh-graders. Since there is some degree of error in sampling, this error must be taken into account in making the inference to the population. That is, even with a random sample, the mean attitude of the sample drawn is not likely to be the same as that for the entire population. A second or third random sample of 100 students would result in a somewhat different mean.

If a researcher does take three random samples, which one is most correct? Which one can we be most certain will provide the most accurate estimation of the population? The answer is that we do not know because we have not measured the entire population. But we can estimate, on the basis of one sample, the error that should be considered in inferring the attitudes of the population. So if the mean attitude of the sample was 25, on a scale of 10 to 35, and there was little error, we might estimate the population attitude to be somewhere between, say, 23 and 27. If there was a large error, the estimate might be between 21 and 29. We use inferential statistics to indicate the precise range in which the actual mean attitude for the 1,000 students lies.

Suppose a researcher uses the entire population. Would the measure be the "real" or "actual" value of the trait for the population? Although in this circumstance no sampling error exists, there is measurement error, which also needs to be taken into consideration. We infer a real or true value on a trait from imperfect measurement. Just as in sampling error, each time you measure a group, the result will be somewhat different, depending on the reliability of the scores. If the scores are highly reliable, there will be little error, but if the reliability is low, the results could vary considerably each time, especially for small samples. Thus, we take this error into account with inferential statistics by indicating the range in which true scores are likely to lie. The estimates of the true values of the population are then used to compare two or more values to see if significant differences exist between the groups that are being compared.

The Null Hypothesis

In a study that compares two groups on a measure of achievement, the question that is investigated is the likelihood that there is a difference between the groups. Since we know error exists, it is more accurate to conclude that there probably is or is not a real difference. In most social science and educational research, the procedure for making the decision about whether there is or is not a difference begins with a **null hypothesis.** As indicated in Chapter 2, the null hypothesis is a statement that no difference exists between the populations that are being compared. In a relationship study, the null hypothesis would indicate that there is no relationship. The researcher uses inferential statistics to determine the probability that the null hypothesis is untrue, or false. If the null is probably untrue, the researcher concludes that there probably *is* a relationship or difference between groups. Thus, if we reject the null hypothesis, the chances are good that we are not wrong in saying that there is a difference.

Null hypothesis: Statement of no difference or relationship.

The double and even triple negatives expressing interpretations of null hypotheses can be tricky. Here is a sequence of phrases that may help:

Null hypothesis: no difference (same)
Reject null hypothesis: difference (not the same)
Wrong in rejecting the null hypothesis: mistake to say there is a difference

Note in Example 9.1 how the authors expressed their null hypotheses. There are two independent variables in their study, one of which is experimental.

EXAMPLE 9.1 Null Hypothesis

Hence the present study was carried out to find the interaction effects of teacher quality, instructional strategy and performance in science. Arising from this, three null hypotheses were generated for testing at the 0.05 level of significance.

The hypotheses are:

Ho.I: There is no significant difference between the Biology mean scores of students taught by professional and non-professional teachers.
Ho.2: There is no significant difference between the Biology mean scores of students taught using concept mapping and guided discovery strategies.
Ho.3: There are no significant differences between the Biology mean scores of students taught by professional teachers using concept mapping and non-professional teachers using guided discovery strategies.

Source: Okoye, N. S., Momoh, S. O., Aigbomian, D. O., & Okecha,, R. E. (2008). Teachers' quality, instructional strategies, and students' performance in secondary school science. *Journal of Instructional Psychology, 35*(2), 206.

Level of Significance

Level of significance: Probability of being wrong in rejecting the null hypothesis.

Inferential statistics tell us the probability of being wrong in rejecting the null hypothesis. This probability is called the **level of significance,** which is indicated with the small letter p (probability) and is reported as $p = x$ or $p < x$ (e.g., the level of significance is .05 or less than .05). The value of p indicates how often the results would be obtained because of chance (rather than a "real" difference). Thus, if $p = .20$, there is a 20% probability that the difference is due to a chance variation, that is, error in sampling and measurement. This is too great a chance to accept in research. Typically, researchers will not conclude that there is an actual difference in the populations unless the probability of obtaining the difference by chance is equal to or less than 5% ($p \leq .05$). This is a convention that is translated to mean a "statistically significant" difference. If the level of significance is .001, there is only 1 chance out of 1,000 that the difference obtained is due to chance. This would be a more probable result than a p value of .01 (1 chance out of 100). What we have to know is whether the decision (to reject or not reject) is true. If the decision is to reject the null hypothesis when it is, in fact, true (no difference in the populations), the researcher has made what is called a **Type I error.** The probability of making this type of error is equal to the level of significance. It is also possible to fail to reject the null hypothesis when it is, in fact, not true and should have been rejected. This is called a **Type II error.**

Type I error: Rejecting the null hypothesis when it is true.

Type II error: Not rejecting the null hypothesis when it is not true.

In most studies the researcher will indicate the level of significance of rejecting each null hypothesis. In some studies the level of significance is set prior to data collection as a criterion for rejecting the null hypothesis. This value is called the *alpha level* (a). Since there is no absolute rule in what constitutes statistical significance, it is necessary to interpret summary narrative statements in the context of the actual p values. Sometimes a p value between .10 and .05 is called "marginally" significant. In exploratory studies a p value of .10 may be judged sufficient to conclude that a significant difference exists. In medicine, where the

FIGURE 9.1 **Determinants of level of significance.**

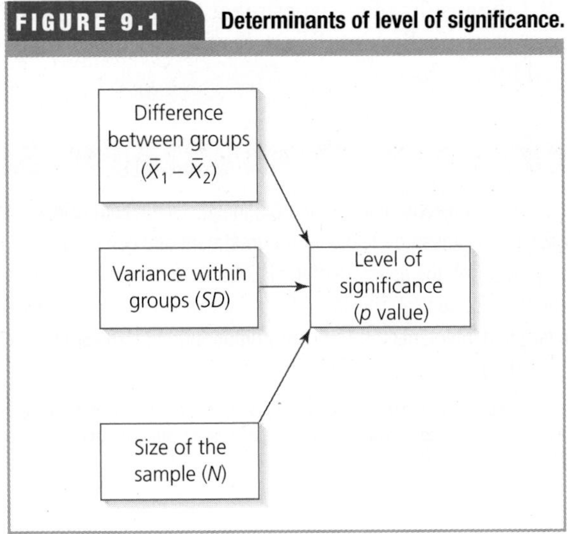

probability of being wrong has serious consequences, a significant difference may require a *p* value of .0001.

The level of significance is affected by three factors, as illustrated in Figure 9.1. The first is the difference between the groups being compared. The greater the difference, the smaller the *p* value. The second is the degree of sampling and measurement error. The lower the error, the smaller the *p* value. The third factor is the size of the sample. If a very large sample is used, the *p* value will be smaller than if the sample size is small. In fact, in some studies a seemingly small difference may be reported as "significant," because of the large number of subjects. (If you increase the sample size enough, almost any result will be "statistically significant.")

The level of significance helps us make a *statistical* decision related to the null hypothesis but it does not tell us anything about *why* there was a difference. When the null hypothesis is rejected, we examine the design of the study to see if there are extraneous variables that may explain the results. If the null hypothesis is not rejected, we are tempted to conclude that there is, in reality, no difference or no relationship. In a well-designed study, failure to reject the null hypothesis is just as important, scientifically, as rejecting it. The problem is that in many studies that find "no significant differences," there are usually factors in the design that may have contributed to the finding, for example, low reliability, sampling error, low number of subjects, diffusion of treatment, and other threats to internal validity. We simply do not know if there is really no difference or if the study as designed fails to show a difference that, in fact, exists.

In Example 9.2 the results of an experiment (notice "treatment" and "control group") lead to a statistically significant result. No more than three decimal places are needed for *p*-values.

EXAMPLE 9.2 | Reporting Level of Significance

For the sixth-grade spring [Group Reading and Diagnostic Evaluation] GRADE [normal curve equivalents] NCEs, the unadjusted means for the treatment and control groups are 31.0 and 29.8, respectively. However, the estimate of the HLM-adjusted means for spring NCEs is 30.0 for treatment and 27.2 for control. This indicates an estimated impact of 2.76. Sixth-grade students in the targeted intervention significantly outperformed sixth-grade students in the control group ($p = .034$).

Source: Cantrell, S. C., Almasi, J. F., Cater, J. C., Rintamaa, M., & Madden, A. (2010). The impact of a strategy-based intervention on the comprehension and strategy use of struggling adolescent readers. *Journal of Educational Psychology, 102*(2), 266.

BEYOND SIGNIFICANCE TESTING

There is a now long-standing debate among researchers about the value of null hypothesis statistical significance testing. Some have argued, in fact, that such tests should be banned (which might make your student life a little easier!). Essentially, many believe that making a simple dichotomous decision based on an arbitrary level of significance (e.g., the *magical* $p < .05$ is completely arbitrary) is fundamentally flawed. This is because in many studies assumptions for using a specific statistical test may not be met due to the heavy influence of sample size, and because rejecting the null hypothesis does not tell us anything about the importance of the result.

Of course, as you know from reading quantitative research articles and reports, null hypothesis testing is still ubiquitous. Clearly, it is not going away any time soon. However, it is important to understand the limitations of this kind of reasoning, and to supplement inferential significance testing with other analyses that can ameliorate these limitations. There are three primary ways of doing this: using (1) descriptive statistics, (2) confidence intervals, and (3) effect size. Descriptive statistics have already been presented. Simple descriptive statistics, in the same metric that was used in the measurement of variables, is absolutely essential to be able to understand a statistically significant result. Scatterplots and graphs are also very helpful. We'll consider the other two procedures here in greater detail.

Confidence Intervals

Confidence interval: Interval in which the true value of a trait lies.

Confidence intervals provide a range of values in which the population or "real" trait value lies with specific probabilities. It is calculated with the same data used for significance tests, but there is no *p* value or a specific cutoff point. This is how it works: Taking the sample data, the researcher calculates a measure of variability called the *standard error of the mean* ($SE_{\overline{X}}$). This value is then used to create intervals around the sample mean that correspond to the probability of obtaining a population value in that interval. For example, if a sample mean is 60, a researcher might have a 95% confidence interval of 48–72. This means that there is a 95% chance that the population or "true" mean is somewhere in this interval. By presenting confidence intervals, researchers utilize variability in reporting results. Without these intervals variance is used as part of the statistical test but is not reported separately. Confidence intervals are also used when comparing groups to show how much the intervals overlap. This gives you a sense of the likely difference(s) between two or more groups.

The use of confidence intervals is illustrated in the following, Example 9.3. This is a nonexperimental comparative design. The odds ratio is used, which is typical for a logistic regression. The true value of higher odds is between 1.21 and 5.98 for boys and between 1.32 and 6.37 for girls.

EXAMPLE 9.3 | Reporting Confidence Intervals

Multilevel logistic regression models revealed that boys at secondary level with a larger number of outdoor facilities at school had 2.69 times [95% confidence interval (CI) = 1.21–5.98] and girls 2.90 times (95% CI = 1.32–6.37) higher odds of being physically active compared with students in schools with fewer facilities.

Source: Haug, E., Torsheim, T., Sallis, J. F., & Samdal, O. (2010). The characteristics of the outdoor school environment associated with physical activity. *Health Education Research, 25*(2), 248.

Effect Size

Chapter 7 pointed out that there is an important difference between statistical significance and practical significance. Practical significance is related to the importance and usefulness of the results. The null hypothesis and level of significance refer *only* to statistical significance to provide a measure of chance variation. It is up to each consumer to judge the practical importance of what may be, "statistically significant." This judgment is made by examining the actual differences or relationships that are called statistically significant and considering the context in which the results are used. For example, a very small but statistically significant difference in the reading achievement of students may not justify changing the method of instruction if teachers' attitudes toward the new approach are negative. It is also possible that a large effect size accompanies statistical nonsignificance, which may suggest further study and consideration. That is, statistical significance is not needed to have important practical significance. In the end, only the reader can determine what is practical and meaningful in using the results. In this sense, your conclusions are more important than those stated by the researchers.

There are several procedures that are used to quantify the practical significance of results. In correlational studies, the correlation coefficient or coefficient of determination is used. In studies that compare different groups, as with

FIGURE 9.2 Effect size estimates.

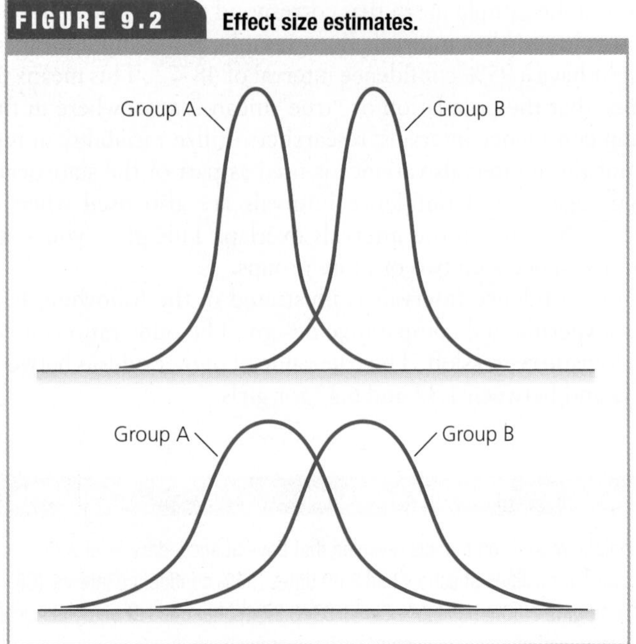

Effect size: Measure of practical significance.

experiments, a procedure called *effect size* is often reported. The **effect size** is a way of quantifying the degree of difference between two groups. Some researchers use effect size to refer to any of several procedures for determining the magnitude, importance, or practicality of a difference or relationship. Other terms that are used include *effect magnitude*, *magnitude effect*, or even *magnitude of effect*. For our purpose here, effect size will be restricted to the comparison of two groups.

The logic of effect size is that the difference between means is contextualized by including the variance. This point is illustrated in Figure 9.2. It shows how the means of two groups can be the same but the amount of overlap, or variance, is quite different. When there is little overlap, as illustrated in the top half of Figure 9.2, the effect size is greater or more significant.

A simple formula, called Cohen's *d*, is often used with two groups, where $\overline{X}_1$ is the mean of one group, $\overline{X}_2$ is the mean of a second group, and *SD* is a measure of variance (pooled from the groups or from the control group):

$$d = \frac{\overline{X}_1 - \overline{X}_2}{SD}$$

With this formula, *d* represents the difference between two groups as a function of variance. In other words, *d* expresses the difference in terms of standard deviation units. Thus, if the difference between the means is 3 and the standard deviation is 3, $d = 1$. If the difference is 2 and the standard deviation is 4, then $d = .5$. In the social sciences a rule of thumb has been used to label different values of *d* into "small," "moderate," and "large" effects. This general guideline is presented in Table 9.1, along with correlations that correspond to different effect sizes. An important guideline for education is what has been established by the What Works Clearinghouse. They label an effect size equal to or greater than .25 as "substantively significant." This is saying that a difference of one-quarter of a standard deviation shows practical significance. Effect size is best applied in situations when the effect can be stated as a measure that has direct practical application. For example, when an effect size of .33 is converted to percentile ranks for a group average, it's like saying one group's average is at the 50th percentile, the other at the 63rd percentile. This kind of difference would probably have important implications for high-stakes accountability testing. An effect size of 1.0 is one group at the 50th percentile and the second group at the 84th percentile. This is a very large increase and would clearly have practical value.

TABLE 9.1 Interpreting Cohen's *d* and Correlation Effect Sizes

	Cohen's *d*	Pearson *r*
Small	.20	.10
Moderate	.50	.50
Large	.80	.90

It is important to remember that the meaning of a specific effect size is ultimately a matter of professional judgment, depending on circumstances, context, costs, and benefits. For example, finding that a small group of students who fail a high-stakes test and participate in a new computerized individualized instructional approach, which increases the likelihood of their passing the retest by 30%, may be very important, even though the increase may not be statistically significant. Waiting to obtain a $p < .05$ result could be unfair to these students. The following two excerpts illustrate the use of effect size using two different statistics. In the first example Cohen's *d* is used. In the second example a statistic called *eta* is used. Eta is often used to indicate the effect size when more than two groups are compared.

In the following two examples effect size is used to indicate the magnitude of the results. In Example 9.4 effect size is used with a meta-analysis (see Chapter 3). The effect size in Example 9.5 is large, reported with the confidence interval.

EXAMPLES 9.4–9.5 | Reporting Effect Size

Research studies have implicated executive functions in reading difficulties (RD). But while some studies have found children with RD to be impaired on tasks of executive function other studies report unimpaired performance. A meta-analysis was carried out to determine whether these discrepant findings can be accounted for by differences in the tasks of executive function that are utilized. A total of 48 studies comparing the performance on tasks of executive function of children with RD with their typically developing peers were included in the meta-analysis, yielding 180 effect sizes. An overall effect size of 0.57 (SE 0.03) was obtained, indicating that children with RD have impairments on tasks of executive function. However, effect sizes varied considerably suggesting that the impairment is not uniform.

Source: Booth, J. N., Boyle, J. M., & Kelly, S. W. (2010). Do tasks make a difference? Accounting for heterogeneity of performance of children with reading difficulties on tasks of executive function: Findings from a meta-analysis. *British Journal of Developmental Psychology, 28*(1), 133.

All of the students (121) from an introductory course for statistics in dentistry were randomly assigned to use the tool with one of two 6-problem sets, known as types A and B. The primary endpoint was the grade difference obtained in the final exam, composed of two blocks of questions related to types A and B. The exam evaluator was masked to the intervention group. Results: We found that the effect of e-status on the student grade was an improvement of 0.48 points (95% CI: 0.10–0.86) on a ten-point scale. Among the 94 students who actually employed e-status, the effect size was 0.63 (95% CI: 0.17–1.10).

Source: Gonzalez, J. A., Lluis, J., Cobo, E., & Munoz, P. (2010). A web-based learning tool improves student performance in statistics: A randomized masked trial. *Computers & Education, 55*(2), 704.

Review and Reflect *Before moving on to specific inferential tests, it's a good idea if you become completely comfortable with the language and logic of hypothesis testing and levels of significance. A good test is to use different ways of stating what is being communicated. For example, how could you state in different words the following statement: There was a likelihood of being wrong one time out of a hundred. Try some of these with fellow students, friends, spouses, and partners (well, maybe not friends, spouses, and partners!).*

SOME SPECIFIC INFERENTIAL TESTS

Parametric: Statistical procedures based on certain assumptions.

Nonparametric: Used when assumptions for parametric tests are not met.

Inferential statistics are procedures used to obtain a level of significance for rejecting a null hypothesis. There are many different inferential procedures. Each is used to analyze the results of particular research designs. Thus, depending on the design, a specific statistical formula is used to obtain a level of significance appropriate to the null hypothesis. Most of the procedures you will read about are **parametric** statistics. These statistics are used when certain assumptions can be made about the data, such as having a population that is normally distributed, equal variances of each group, and interval-level measures. If these assumptions cannot be met, researchers use **nonparametric** statistics. The interpretation of the results is the same with both types of statistics, but parametric statistics have greater power to detect significant differences. The computational equations are different, but both test a null hypothesis and report a level of significance. Parametric tests are sometimes used even when all needed assumptions are not clearly met. We will consider commonly used parametric and nonparametric procedures.

The *t*-Test

***t*-test:** Compares two means.

The ***t*-test,** a parametric statistical equation, is most often used to test the null hypothesis that the means of two groups are the same. The *t*-test is also used to see if a correlation coefficient is significantly different from zero (no correlation) and to compare a mean to a set value. In comparing two means, the researcher uses the two sample means, the group variances, and the sample size with a formula that generates a number, called the *t* value or *t* statistic. This *t* value is then used to obtain a level of significance for rejecting the null hypothesis that the population means are the same. In most studies the researcher will report the *t* value for each *t*-test, with corresponding *p* values. The *t* values may be in a table or in the narrative of the results section. Often there will be a table of the means of each group, with accompanying *t*-values.

There are two forms of the *t*-test. One, the *independent-samples t*-test, is used in designs in which there are different subjects in each group, for example, two randomly assigned groups on a posttest of achievement (see Example 9.6). If the subjects in the groups are paired or matched in some way, a second form of the *t*-test is used. This may be called a *paired dependent-samples*, *correlated*, or *matched t*-test. It is most commonly used in the single-group pretest-posttest design when the same group of subjects is given both the pretest and posttest (see Example 9.7).

EXAMPLES 9.6–9.7 | Independent Samples and Paired *t*-Tests

Teachers who reported that their current teaching assignment was special education (n = 38) were compared to teachers who reported that their current teaching assignment was general education (n = 275). Only one of the measures' *p* values fell below .05: individual achievement tests (t = 2.24, df = 299, p = .026). Special education teachers rated individual achievements higher than general education teachers (M = 4.05, SD = 1.48 for general education teachers, M = 4.63, SD = 1.55 for special education teachers). However, with the large number of writing variables measured, a corrected alpha does not allow a positive determination of statistical significance to be made.

Source: Gansle, K. A., Gilbertson, D. N., & VanDerHeyden, A. M. (2006). *Practical Assessment, Research & Evaluation, 11*(5), retrieved July 2, 2010, from http://pareonline.net/pdf/v11n5.pdf.

There was not a significant difference between pre- and posttest scores on the Urban Teacher Selection Interview after completing a traditional internship experience at an urban high-poverty school. The mean pretest score for the 30 student interns was 34.50 (SD = 3.721), whereas the mean posttest score was 33.57 (SD = 4.629). This difference was not significant at the .05 level of probability when a paired-samples *t*-test was conducted (t = .322, df = 29, $p > .05$).

Source: McKinney, S. E., Haberman, M., Stafford-Johnson, D., & Robinson, J. (2008). Developing teachers for high-poverty schools: The role of the internship experience. *Urban Education, 43*(68), 76.

The *df* in the examples refers to "degrees of freedom." This number is used to calculate the level of significance and is approximately equal to the number of subjects in the study. It may be indicated in parentheses after the *t* without the letters *df*. In other articles the degrees of freedom may be implied or indicated in a table of results, not in the narrative.

Simple Analysis of Variance

Analysis of variance (ANOVA): Compares two or more means.

Analysis of variance (abbreviated **ANOVA**) is a parametric procedure that has the same basic purpose as the *t*-test: to compare group means to determine the probability of being wrong in rejecting the null hypothesis. Whereas the *t*-test compares two means, ANOVA compares two or more means. In effect, ANOVA is an extension of the *t*-test that allows the researcher to test the differences between more than two group means. In *simple* ANOVA (also called *one-way* ANOVA) a single independent variable is analyzed with a single dependent variable. For instance, if a researcher compares three types of students—high, medium, and low socioeconomic status (SES)—on a measure of locus of control, there are three levels of the independent variable. ANOVA would test the null hypothesis that there is no difference among the means of all three groups. It would be referred to as a 1 × 3 ANOVA (one independent variable with three levels). The ANOVA equation uses the variances of the groups to calculate a value, called the *F* statistic (or *F* ratio). The *F*, analogous to the *t* value, is a three- or four-digit number employed to obtain the level of significance that the researcher uses to reject or fail to reject the null hypothesis. If the *F* value is large enough, the null hypothesis can be rejected with confidence that at least two of the population means are not the same.

In the preceding example, let us assume that the locus of control means for each group are as follows: high SES, 30; medium SES, 23; low SES, 22. The null hypothesis that is tested is that 30 = 23 = 22. If the *F* statistic calculated with ANOVA is 4.76 and the *p* value is .01, the null would be rejected. However, this analysis does not indicate *which* pair or pairs of means are different. In some studies the results are such that the different pairs are obvious (as in this example), but in most studies there is a need for further statistical tests to indicate those means that are significantly different from other means. These tests are called **multiple comparison procedures** (or post hoc comparisons). There are several types of multiple comparison procedures, including Bonferroni, Fisher's LSD, Duncan's new multiple range test, the Newman-Keuls, Tukey's HSD, and Scheffe's test.

Multiple comparison procedures: Indicate which pairs of means are different.

The results of a simple 1 × 3 ANOVA are summarized in the following examples.

EXAMPLES 9.8–9.9 | One-Way ANOVA with Post Hoc Tests

To determine if there were significant differences in the composite mean scores among grade levels for teachers and for students, we conducted analyses of variance. . . . For students we found a significant grade-level difference science. . . . Tukey HSD post hoc analyses were then conducted to identify which grades differed. Of the six possible pairwise comparisons of grades, three were significant. The science composite mean score for grade 8 students was significantly higher than the scores for each of the other three grades, meaning that grade 8 students were more likely to report a greater emphasis on the science standards.

Source: Parke, C. S., & Lane, S. (2007). Student perceptions of a Maryland state performance assessment. *The Elementary School Journal, 107*(3), 317.

Education majors had the highest attitude score (*M* = 3.48, *SD* = .72) and Business Administration majors had the lowest attitude score (*M* = 2.95, *SD* = .92). Mathematics majors had a mean of 3.21 (*SD* = .67). The overall mean for all three majors was 3.35 (*SD* = .78). The ANOVA showed significant differences between groups (Table 4).

The Scheffe post hoc procedure was conducted to determine which groups differed. The results from the Scheffe procedure indicated that the difference between Education majors and Business Administration majors was statistically significant (*p* = .000). No other differences between groups were found. These results illustrate that Education students had a more positive attitude towards group work than Business Administration majors but there were neither differences between Education and Math majors, nor between Math and Business Administration majors.

TABLE 4 Analysis of Variance for Student Attitude

Source	*SS*	*df*	*MS*	*F*
Between Groups	**12.38**	**2**	**6.19**	10.77***
Within Groups	**163.92**	**285**	**.58**	
Total	176.31	287		

Note: N = 288. *** *p* <.001

Source: Gottschall, H., & Garcia-Bayonas, M. (2008). Student attitudes towards group work among undergraduates in business administration, education, and mathematics. *Educational Research Quarterly, 32*(1), 15.

Factorial Analysis of Variance

As indicated in Chapter 8, factorial designs have more than one independent variable and allow the investigation of interactions among the independent variables. The statistical analysis of such designs requires the use of **factorial analysis of variance.** The most common factorial ANOVA has two independent variables and is therefore referred to as a *two-way* ANOVA. In a two-way ANOVA three null hypotheses are tested: one for each independent variable and one for the interaction between the two independent variables. Consequently, there are three *F* ratios, one for each null hypothesis. The test for each independent variable, sometimes called a *main effect*, is similar to a one-way ANOVA for that variable by itself. Thus, there will be an *F* ratio and corresponding *p* value for each independent variable. If one variable in a factorial design has two levels and another variable has three levels, the analysis would be a 2 × 3 ANOVA. A 3 × 3 × 4 ANOVA would mean that there are three independent variables, two with three levels and one with four levels.

Factorial analysis of variance: Two or more independent variables analyzed together.

In interpreting factorial ANOVA studies, you will find that significant interactions are often presented in a graph. The graph is constructed to show

FIGURE 9.3 Graph of hypothetical 2 × 2 ANOVA and interaction.

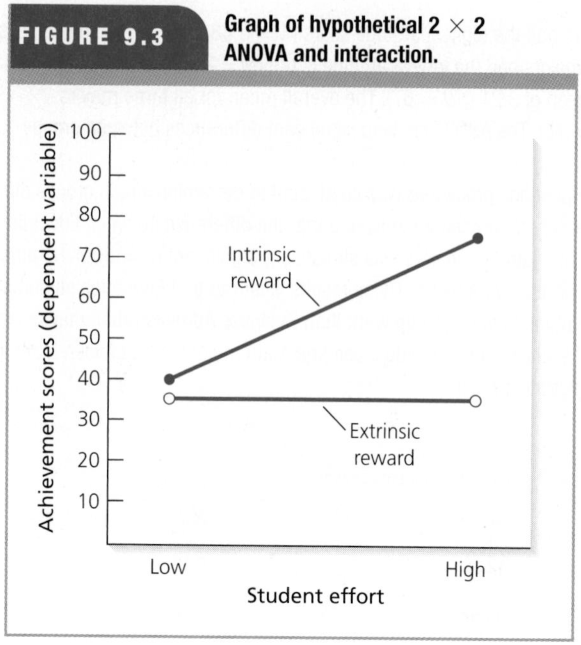

how the means of all the groups compare. The values of the dependent variable are placed along the vertical axis of the graph, and levels of one of the independent variables are on the horizontal axis. The means of all the groups are then indicated in the graph by reference to the second independent variable. For example, Figure 9.3 illustrates a significant interaction. The two independent variables are student effort (high or low) and type of reward (intrinsic or extrinsic). The results of the 2 × 2 ANOVA indicate that, overall, high-effort students did better on achievement, a main effect for effort, and that there was a significant interaction—high-effort students who received an intrinsic reward did better than high-effort students who received an extrinsic reward. For low-effort students it did not matter if they received intrinsic or extrinsic rewards. A 2 × 2 factorial design is illustrated in Example 9.10, and results from a 2 × 2 design are shown in Example 9.11.

EXAMPLE 9.10 | A 2 × 2 Factorial Design

Students from different German secondary schools ($N = 70$) participated in this experiment. . . . The students were randomly assigned to one condition of a 2 × 2 factorial design (see Fig. 1), where one factor was the provision of an informed prompting (with and without) and the other factor a provision of a learning-journal example (with and without).

FIGURE 1 The design of the study.

<table>
<tr><td colspan="2" rowspan="2"></td><td colspan="2">Informed prompting</td></tr>
<tr><td>Without</td><td>With</td></tr>
<tr><td rowspan="2">Learning-journal example</td><td>Without</td><td>Control condition
(n = 17)</td><td>Informed prompting condition
(n = 18)</td></tr>
<tr><td>With</td><td>Learning-journal example condition
(n = 17)</td><td>Informed prompting plus learning-journal example condition
(n = 18)</td></tr>
</table>

Source: Hubner, S. Nuckles, M., & Renkl, A. (2010). Writing learning journals: Instructional support to overcome learning-strategy deficits. *Learning and Instruction, 20,* 22.

There are many variations of factorial designs and many terms are used to describe specific types of analyses. You may read such terms as *split plot, randomized block, within subjects,* or *repeated measures* in the results sections of articles. Regardless of the language, the results are interpreted in basically the same manner. There is some type of null hypothesis that needs to be tested, and the F ratios are used to see whether there were statistically significant differences.

EXAMPLE 9.11 | Factorial Analysis of Variance

Results

Means, standard deviations, and sample sizes for the achievement and motivation levels by treatment group are reported in Table 1. The results of the ANOVA in which achievement level was the dependent variable and test anxiety and evaluative threat were the independent

TABLE 1 Means, Standard Deviations, and Sample Sizes of Achievement and Motivation Levels

	Threat of Evaluation								
	Low			High			Overall		
Treatment Group	*M*	*SD*	*n*	*M*	*SD*	*n*	*M*	*SD*	*n*
Achievement									
Low test anxiety	91.3	2.52	15	91.60	3.67	15	91.77	3.09	30
High text anxiety	92.20	3.95	15	87.94	3.86	16	90.00	4.40	31
Overall	92.07	3.26	30	89.71	4.14	31	90.87	3.89	61
Motivation									
Low text anxiety	17.33	1.99	15	17.00	2.27	15	17.17	2.10	30
High test anxiety	17.73	2.12	15	14.63	3.16	16	16.13	2.63	31
Overall	17.53	3.03	30	15.77	2.49	31	16.64	2.43	61

TABLE 2 2 × 2 Analysis of Variance of Effects of Test Anxiety and Threat of Evaluation on Achievement

Variable	*SS*	*df*	*MS*	*F*
Test anxiety (TA)	43.93	1	43.93	3.49
Threat of evaluation (TE)	80.46	1	80.16	6.39*
TA × TE	58.18	1	58.18	4.67*
Residual	717.871	57	12.59	

*$p < .05$.

variables are given in Table 2. The main effect for test anxiety was not significant. $F(1,57) = 3.49$. $p < .05$. Students with high test anxiety did not obtain a significantly lower mean score ($M = 90.00$, $SD = 4.40$) in achievement than did students with low test anxiety ($M = 91.77$, $SD = 3.09$). However, there was a significant main effect for evaluative threat, $F(1,57) = 6.39$, $p > .05$. Individuals in the high evaluative threat group demonstrated a significantly lower average level of achievement ($M = 89.71$, $SD = 4.14$) than did their peers in the low evaluative threat group ($M = 92.07$, $SD = 3.26$). The magnitude of difference or effect size between the high and low evaluative threat groups as calculated with Cohen's *d* (Hedges & Olkin, 1985) was 0.57.

Furthermore, there was a statistically significant interaction, $F(1, 57) = 4.67$, $p < .05$ (see Figure 1), revealing an effect on students' achievement of the combination of independent variables. Specifically, high test anxiety students in the high evaluative threat condition obtained a significantly lower mean score ($M = 87.94$, $SD = 3.86$) in achievement than did high test anxiety students in the low evaluative threat condition ($M = 92.20$, $SD = 3.95$; ($t = 3.04$, $p < .05$) and low test anxiety students in both the high evaluative threat condition ($M = 91.60$, $SD = 3.67$; $t = 2.71$, $p < .05$) and the low evaluative threat condition ($M = 91.93$, $SD = 2.52$, $t = 3.39$, $p < .05$).

Source: Hancock, D. R. (2001). Effects of text anxiety and evaluative threat on students' achievement and motivation. *The Journal of Educational Research, 94*(5), 287–288.

FIGURE 1 **Test anxiety (TA) and threat of evaluation on achievement.**

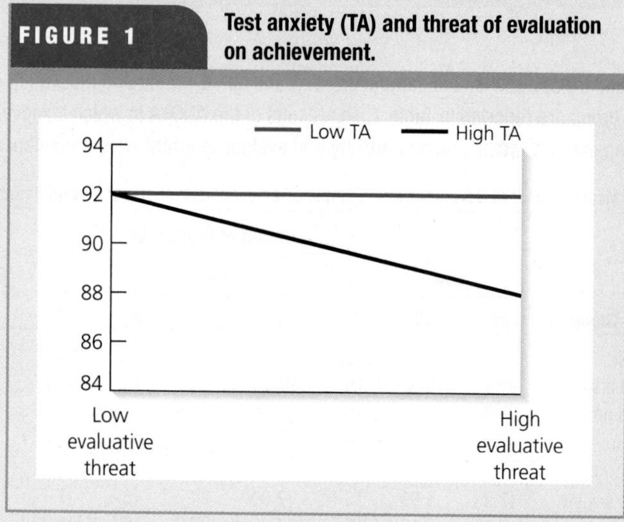

Analysis of Covariance

Analysis of covariance (ANCOVA): Adjusts for pretest differences between groups.

Analysis of covariance (ANCOVA) is a variation of ANOVA. It is used to adjust for pretest differences that may exist between two or more groups. For instance, suppose in an experiment that one group has a mean value on the pretest of 15 and the other group has a pretest mean of 18. ANCOVA is used to adjust the posttest scores statistically to compensate for the three-point difference between the groups. This adjustment results in more accurate posttest comparisons. The pretest used for the adjustment is called the *covariate.* Several other types of covariates can also be used in a study, such as socioeconomic status, aptitude, attitudes, and previous achievement. Sometimes a covariate other than the pretest is used with the pretest covariate, and sometimes covariates are used when there is no pretest in the design of the study. Covariates are helpful only if they are related to the dependent variable. ANCOVA is used with both one-way and factorial designs.

EXAMPLE 9.12 | Analysis of Covariance

Because prior research suggests that reading comprehension and vocabulary respond differently to summer reading interventions. . . we conducted an analysis of covariance (ANCOVA) on each of the three GMRT posttests with pretest scores serving as the covariate. . . . An ANCOVA on the total reading scores revealed a nonsignificant main effect of condition, $F(2, 307) = 0.40$, *ns*, suggesting that there was no difference in covariate-adjusted total reading scores among children in the three experimental conditions. When we analyzed treatment effects by subtests on the GMRT, we found no significant main effect in reading comprehension, $F(2, 309) = 0.35$, *ns*, or reading vocabulary, $F(2, 310) = 2.22$, *ns*. These findings suggest that opportunities solely to read 10 books or in combination with a family literacy intervention did not produce significant improvements in children's reading comprehension or vocabulary scores.

Source: Kim, J. S., & Guryan, J. (2010). The efficacy of a voluntary summer book reading intervention for low-income Latino children from language minority families. *Journal of Educational Psychology, 102*(1), 25.

Multivariate Statistics

Univariate: One dependent variable analyzed.

Multivariate: Two or more dependent variables analyzed together.

Each of the preceding parametric statistical procedures represents what is termed a **univariate** analysis because a single dependent variable is used. However, in many complex social settings, such as schools, there is often a need to study two or more dependent variables simultaneously. For example, a teacher may be interested in comparing two teaching methods on attitudes toward learning and school. A principal may want to determine the effect of a new homework policy on parent involvement, student confidence, and achievement in each of several different subject areas. In such situations it may be inappropriate to analyze each dependent variable separately, with a different ANOVA or *t*-test. Rather, a **multivariate** statistical procedure may be warranted. Multivariate statistics analyze all the dependent variables in a single procedure, which is important in accounting for the relationships between the dependent variables. For each of the univariate statistical procedures, there is a multivariate analog (e.g., Hotelling's *T* for the *t*-test, and MANCOVA for ANCOVA).

Multivariate procedures are now commonly reported in the literature. Although the computations and interpretation of multivariate tests are complex, they employ the same basic principles for rejecting the null hypotheses. It should also be pointed out that some researchers have a somewhat different definition of the term *multivariate*, which may refer to any study that has more than one variable, either independent or dependent. With this definition, multiple correlation would be considered a multivariate procedure. Note in Examples 9.13–9.14 that MANOVAs were used initially to analyze the results, and once significance was shown, additional analyses were needed to complete the statistical procedures.

EXAMPLES 9.13–9.14 | Multivariate Analysis of Variance

For each domain, a multivariate analysis of variance (MANOVA) was conducted with cluster membership as the independent variable and competency beliefs and achievement values as the dependent variables. When the results of an omnibus MANOVA were statistically significant, we used multivariate follow-up procedures to determine the source of significance.

Source: Buehl, M. M., & Alexander, P. A. (2005). Motivation and performance differences in students' domain-specific epistemological beliefs profiles. *American Educational Research Journal, 42*(4), 715.

We performed a multivariate analysis of variance on perceptions in four dependent variable domains: (a) quality of relationship with their supervising teacher, (b) knowledge of school policies and procedures, (c) perception of teaching ability, and (d) adequacy of time to prepare for profession. The independent variable was type of student-teaching experience, which consisted of two levels: extended year-long and traditional semester-long internship. With the use of Hotellings' criteria, the association between the combined dependent variables and the type of internship experience was statistically significant. . . . We conducted a series of independent t-tests to examine the nature of the relationship.

Source: Spooner, M., Flowers, C., Lamber, R., & Algozzine, B. (2008). Is more really better? Examining perceived benefits of an extended student teaching experience. *The Clearing House, 81*(6), 267.

Chi-Square

Chi-square: Tests frequency counts in different categories.

When researchers are interested in the number of responses or cases in different categories, they use a procedure called **chi-square** to analyze the results. The null hypothesis is that there is no difference between an observed number and an expected number of responses or cases that fall in each category. The expected number is usually that which would be expected by chance alone. Suppose an administrator wanted to see if there is a difference between the number of male and female students who take advanced placement courses. The expected number by chance alone would be an equal number of males and females in advanced placement courses. The administrator would use the chi-square test to determine if the actual number of male students taking advanced placement courses was significantly different from the number of female students taking advanced placement courses.

The chi-square test (represented by c²) can also examine questions of relationship between two independent variables that report frequencies of responses or cases. For example, a researcher may be interested in investigating the relationship between gender and choices of books for a book report. There may be several types of books, such as romantic, adventure, mystery, and biography. The researcher would count the number of males and females who choose each type of book and analyze the results with a chi-square to determine if the null hypothesis, that there is no relationship between gender and book choice, can be rejected. This type of chi-square may be referred to as a *contingency table*, in this example a 2 × 4 table. The result is often reported with a single measure of relationship called a *contingency coefficient*, which is interpreted in the same way as a correlation coefficient.

The results of a chi-square will usually be reported in a table that shows either the number and/or percentage of responses or cases in each category. If the number is less than five in any single category, the chi-square test needs to be "corrected" with what is called *Yates's correction*. This correction statistically adjusts the numbers to provide a more valid result. Another approach when a small number of observations is observed is to use a procedure called *Fisher's exact test*. The results will indicate the value of the chi-square (c²) and the level of significance with the c².

Note in Example 9.15 that percentages were compared, and nonsignificant results were reported.

EXAMPLE 9.15 | Chi-Square Test

Table 2 provides a national estimate of the migration destinations (i.e., changes in school location) music teachers traversed based on 2000–2001 TFS data. Results indicated that most music teachers were retained by the profession in schools located in the same state, district, and school they occupied in 1999–2000 (i.e., they did not move), yet 5.8% moved to schools in a different school district within the same state, whereas 3.3% moved to schools in the same school district. In general, migration destination results for music teachers were similar to those for non-music teachers, χ^2 (3, $n = 2{,}477$) = 1.56, $p > .05$.

TABLE 2 Q2000–2001 Natoional Estimates of School Location for Retained and Migrating Teachers

	Music Teachers		Non-Music Teachers	
Category	**National Estimate**	**Column (%)**	**National Estimate**	**Column (%)**
Same school	93.857	90.2	2,436,498	91.8
Different school, same district	3,433	3.3	98,902	3.7
Different district, same state	6,081	5.8	92,804	3.5
Different state	674	0.7	26,461	1.0

Note: The 4 × 2 chi-squre for this table was 1.56 (p > .05)

Source: Hancock, C. B. (2009). National estimates of retention, migration, and attrition: A multiyear comparison of music and non-music teachers. *Journal of Research in Music Education, 57*, 100.

TABLE 9.2 **Parametric and Analogous Nonparametric Procedures**

Parametric	Nonparametric
Pearson product-moment correlation coefficient	Spearman rank-order correlation coefficient
Independent samples *t*-test	Median test
	Mann–Whitney *U* test
Dependent samples *t*-test	Sign test
	Wilcoxon test
One-way ANOVA	Median test
	Kruskal–Wallis ANOVA

The chi-square is a nonparametric statistical procedure because the data that are analyzed are nominal-level data, and assumptions of normal distribution and equal variances may not be met. There are nonparametric analyses that can be used instead of a particular parametric analysis. Some of these are summarized in Table 9.2.

CONSUMER TIPS: *Criteria for Evaluating Inferential Statistics*

1. **Basic descriptive statistics are needed to evaluate the results of inferential statistics.** Remember that the results of an inferential test rely on the descriptive data that were gathered—the means, variances, frequencies, and percentages. Although inferential statistics provide important information about the probability that conclusions about populations, or "true" values, are correct, the interpretation of the results depends on the descriptive statistical results. It may be misleading to rely solely on the conclusions of the inferential test results. *You should always look at the more basic descriptive data to derive meaning from the results.*

2. **Inferential analyses refer to statistical, not practical significance.** It is easy to confuse statistical with practical significance. The results of inferential analyses should not be the sole criteria for conclusions about changing a practice or other decisions. The use of inferential tests should be kept in balance with other considerations relative to the use of the results.

3. **Inferential analyses do not indicate external validity.** Although we use inferential statistics to infer population values from sample values, generalizability to other subjects and settings depends on whether the subjects were randomly selected, the characteristics of the subjects, and the design of the study.

4. **Inferential analyses do not indicate internal validity.** The extent to which a result shows a causal relationship depends on how the data were gathered

and what happened to the subjects. The inferential test is used as the first and necessary step to conclude that an intervention caused a change in the dependent variable. Once the statistics show that there is a relationship or difference, you need to analyze the design and procedures to determine if there is adequate internal validity to derive a causal conclusion.

5. The results of inferential tests depend on the number of subjects. An important factor in determining the level of significance for a statistical test is the number of subjects. If there are many subjects, a very small difference or relationship can be statistically significant; if only a few subjects are used, what appears to be a large difference or relationship may not be statistically significant. This phenomenon is especially important in experimental studies in which there is a difference between the number of subjects and replications of the treatment. If a researcher uses number of subjects when it is clear that the number of independent replications of the treatment is much smaller, the inferential test that leads to a conclusion to reject the null hypothesis may be invalid.

6. The appropriate statistical test should be used. It is important for researchers to use a statistical test that is appropriate to the design and questions of a study. Most journal reviewers and editors evaluate studies to be certain that the appropriate tests were employed. However, it is likely that some studies are published that use the wrong statistical test. The most likely mistakes are to use a parametric procedure when the assumptions for using such a test are not met and to use many univariate tests when a multivariate test would be more appropriate.

7. The level of significance should be interpreted correctly. Remember that the level of significance indicates the probability that the difference or relationship is not due to chance. It is not a definitive statement that there either is or is not a difference or relationship. A high level of significance (e.g., .20 or .40) does not necessarily mean that there is no difference or relationship in the population or in reality. Nonsignificant findings may result from inadequate design and measurement.

8. Be wary of statistical tests with small numbers of subjects in one or more groups or categories. Whenever there is a small number of subjects in a group, there is a good chance that the statistical test may provide spurious results. When only a few numbers are used to calculate a mean or variance, one atypical number may significantly affect the results. It is best to have at least 10 subjects in each comparison group and 30 subjects in calculating a correlation. The results of studies that use a small number of subjects also have less generalizability.

Author Reflection *I hope that you will not be intimidated by inferential statistics. They are only used to make estimates about statistical significance. The more important information is provided by simple descriptive statistics and carefully constructed figures that represent score distributions. Further, there is far too much reliance on statistical significance and not enough emphasis on practical significance. While some journals require magnitude-of-effect statistics, the use of these estimates is spotty at best, with little discussion of what effect size statistics, such as Cohen's* d, *really mean. As with so many topics in this book, you, as an informed consumer, will need to make your own evaluations.*

STUDY QUESTIONS

1. Why is it necessary to use inferential statistics?
2. What is the relationship between inferential and descriptive statistics?
3. What is the difference between sampling error and measurement error?
4. How is the null hypothesis used in inferential statistics?
5. Why is it important to understand what "level of significance" means?
6. What is the difference between Type I and Type II errors?
7. Does it matter whether the null hypothesis is rejected?
8. Why is it important to distinguish between "statistical" and "practical" significance?
9. What is "effect size" used for?
10. Under what circumstances would it be appropriate to use nonparametric statistical tests?
11. Give an example of a study that would use an independent sample *t*-test.
12. Give an example of a study that would use simple ANOVA.
13. Give an example of a study that would use factorial ANOVA.
14. What does a factorial ANOVA tell us that a simple ANOVA does not?
15. Why would it be helpful to use ANCOVA rather than ANOVA?
16. Why are multivariate statistics used?
17. Give an example of a study that would use a chi-square statistical analysis.

Chapter 10

Qualitative Research Designs, Data Collection, *and* Analysis

CHAPTER ROAD MAP

This chapter is a rather abrupt change from the previous four, not only in research methods and data analysis but also philosophical assumptions about how it is best to understand what is being studied. We begin by reviewing characteristics that are common to most qualitative studies, then discuss in greater detail methods of four types of qualitative research that have different perspectives about how to gather and interpret the data. The chapter concludes with a discussion of criteria that should be used to judge the credibility of qualitative studies.

Chapter Outline	Learning Objectives
Characteristics of Qualitative Designs	• Be able to name and describe eight characteristics of qualitative research. • Know and recognize in studies the essential design features that make an investigation qualitative. • Compare and contrast qualitative with quantitative research.
Types of Qualitative Research Designs	• Be able to name and describe five major families of qualitative research designs. • Recognize qualitative research designs in published studies.
Obtaining Data from Observations	• Understand how different observer roles affect what data are gathered. • Recognize and evaluate the adequacy of field notes. • Understand why it is important to separate descriptive information from reflective information and observer comments.
Obtaining Data from Interviews	• Know different types of interviews and characteristics of each type. • Know what foci are typically used in interviews. • Understand when to use different types of interviews. • Know the differences between individual and focus group interviews.
Obtaining Data from Documents and Artifacts	• Know what constitutes documents and artifacts. • Know the difference between primary and secondary sources.
Data Analysis and Interpretation	• Understand how to code data. • Understand how codes are used to create categories and themes. • Know how patterns and models are developed and their purpose. • Be able to read and evaluate the quality of data collection and analyses.
Credibility and Quality of Qualitative Research	• Understand what credibility is and how it is established. • Understand and recognize triangulation, member checking, and other specific strategies for establishing credibility. • Be able to read qualitative research and identify procedures used for credibility.
Generalizability	• Know how generalizability in qualitative research is different from quantitative research. • Know and recognize the appropriate characteristics of transferability.

INTRODUCTION *to* QUALITATIVE RESEARCH

Although most empirical studies use quantitative techniques, you will also read qualitative research, which is based on a different set of assumptions and methods. It is important to remember that these methods are no less "scientific" than quantitative methods. Indeed, most qualitative researchers would maintain that their approach is scientific with respect to being systematic and rigorous. What is most different for qualitative studies are epistemological assumptions about the nature of the information that is needed to arrive at credible findings and conclusions. Researchers using a qualitative approach believe that there are multiple realities represented in participant perspectives, and that context is critical in providing an understanding of the phenomenon being investigated. In contrast, a quantitative study assumes that there is a single objective reality that can be measured. Qualitative approaches are characterized by the assumption that the researcher's biases and perspectives must be understood and included in interpreting findings, whereas in a quantitative study researcher bias is a threat to internal validity. One approach is not necessarily better than another. Each has advantages and disadvantages, strengths and weaknesses. Most educational researchers would agree that problems are best investigated by using whatever methods are most appropriate, separately or in combination; that is, we begin with a research question or problem and *then* select the methods that will provide the most credible answers.

CHARACTERISTICS *of* QUALITATIVE RESEARCH

In Chapter 1, qualitative research was described as a tradition of research techniques, as well as a philosophy of knowing. The term *qualitative* refers to a number of approaches that share some common characteristics. Before examining the four qualitative approaches covered in this chapter in greater detail, we will review these characteristics (summarized in Table 10.1). Finally, it is also helpful to remember that there are many terms associated with qualitative research, such as *field research*, *naturalistic*, *participant observation*, *ecological*, *constructivist*, *interpretivist*, *ethnomethodology*, and *case study*. The exact definition and use of these terms, as well as "qualitative," vary according to their disciplinary roots (anthropology, sociology, psychology, political science, and philosophy). Educational researchers are likely to use qualitative in a generic sense, as a methodology that has some or all of the following characteristics.

Natural Settings

A distinguishing characteristic of most qualitative research is that behavior is studied as it occurs naturally. There is no manipulation or control of behavior or settings, nor are there any externally imposed constraints. Rather, the setting for some qualitative research is an actual classroom, school, playground, clinic, or neighborhood. This is why qualitative research is often described as *field research;* much of it takes place out in the field or setting. For example, a qualitative

TABLE 10.1 Key Characteristics of Qualitative Research

Characteristic	Description
Natural setting	Study of behavior as it occurs naturally in specific contexts.
Direct data collection	Researcher collects data directly from source.
Rich narrative descriptions	Detailed narratives that provide in-depth understanding of contexts and behaviors.
Process orientation	Focus on why and how behaviors occur.
Inductive data analysis	Generalizations induced from synthesizing gathered information.
Participant perspectives	Focus on participants' understanding and meaning.
Socially constructed meaning	Knowledge is based on experience and social interactions with others.
Emergent research design	Research design evolves and changes as the study takes place.

approach to studying beginning teachers would be to conduct the research in a few schools and classrooms in which these individuals were teaching. In contrast, a quantitative approach might use a questionnaire to gather the perceptions, beliefs, and practices of a sample of beginning teachers. There are two reasons for conducting research in the field. Qualitative researchers believe that (1) behavior is best understood as it occurs without external constraints and control, and (2) the situational **context** is very important in understanding the behavior. The setting influences the way humans behave and, therefore, it is not possible to understand the behavior without taking into account the situational characteristics.

Context: Environment in which behavior occurs.

Direct Data Collection

In qualitative studies the investigator has a direct role in obtaining information, as either the interviewer, an observer, or as the person who studies artifacts and documents. Qualitative researchers want to obtain information directly from the source. They do this by spending a considerable amount of time in direct interaction with the settings, participants, and documents they are studying. They tend to be reluctant to use other observers or quantitative measuring techniques because the researchers are then not as "close" to the data as they need to be for a full understanding.

Rich Narrative Descriptions

Qualitative researchers approach a situation with the assumption that nothing is trivial or unimportant. Every detail that is recorded is thought to contribute to a better understanding of behavior. The descriptions are in the form of words or pictures rather than numbers, although simple numerical summaries are used in some qualitative studies and in investigations that use both qualitative and quantitative methods. The intent is to provide rich descriptions that cannot be achieved by reducing pages of narration to numbers. Rather, the descriptions capture what has been observed in the same form in which it occurred naturally. Nothing escapes scrutiny or is taken for granted. The detailed approach to description is necessary to obtain a complete understanding of the setting and to accurately reflect the complexity of human behavior. To accomplish these goals, the studies may extend over a long period of time and require intense involvement, and they typically culminate in extensive written reports.

Process Orientation

Qualitative researchers want to know how and why behavior occurs. In contrast with most quantitative studies, qualitative methods look for the *process* through which behavior occurs, not just the outcomes or products. For example, while quantitative research can document the effect of teachers' expectations on student achievement, qualitative studies would be appropriate for understanding *how* teachers' expectations affect students' achievement and behavior. The emphasis would be on how expectations are formed and how they are played out in the nature of teacher interactions with students. The emphasis on process allows for conclusions that explain the reasons for results. For instance, suppose a state is interested in how staff development affects student achievement. A quantitative approach would be to simply record student behavior following the staff development, whereas a qualitative inquiry would focus on how the teachers changed as a result of the staff development and how this change affected student achievement. This approach would provide a greater understanding of what it was about the staff development that was most important.

Inductive Data Analysis

Qualitative researchers do not formulate hypotheses and gather data to prove or disprove them (deduction). Rather, the data are gathered first and then synthesized inductively to generate generalizations, models, or frameworks. Conclusions are developed from the "ground up," or "bottom up," from the detailed particulars, rather than from the "top down." This approach is important because the qualitative researcher wants to be open to new ways of understanding. Predetermined hypotheses limit what data will be collected and may cause bias. The process of qualitative research is like an upside down funnel (see Figure 10.1). In the beginning, the data may seem unconnected and too extensive to make much sense, but as the researcher works with the data, progressively more specific findings are generated.

Participant Perspectives

Qualitative researchers try to reconstruct reality *as the participants they are studying see it.* They do not apply predetermined definitions or ideas about how people will think or react. For example, a quantitative researcher may assume that a

FIGURE 10.1 **Steps in inductive data analysis.**

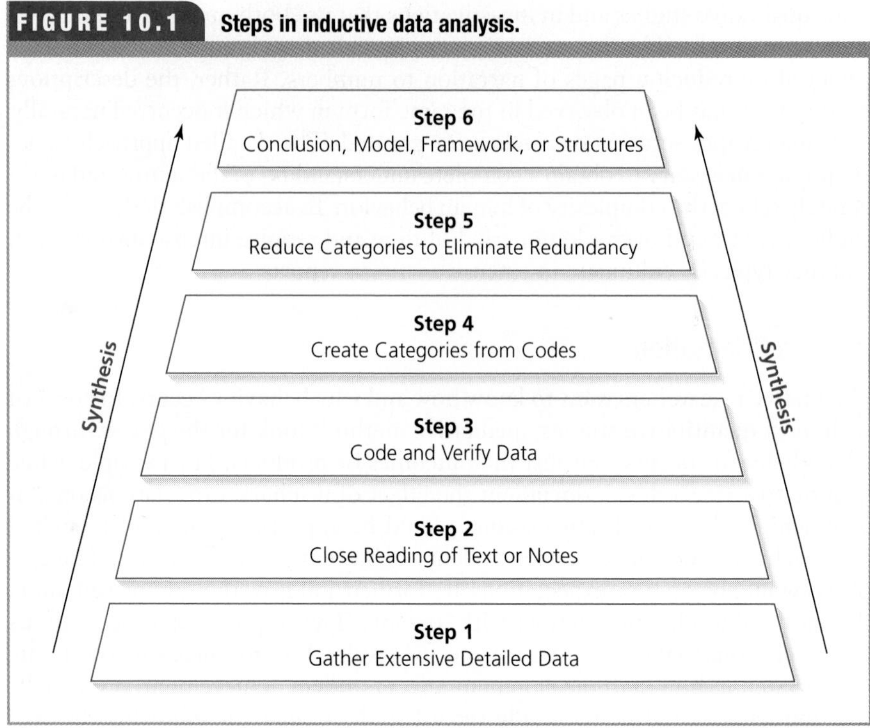

teacher's praise is interpreted by students in a certain way, whereas a qualitative researcher would be interested in how the participants (students) interpreted the praise. The goal in qualitative research is to understand participants from their point of view. In other words, the focus is on the *meaning* of events and actions as expressed by the participants. Thus, in a qualitative study of what motivates students, it would be important to focus on what the students said and did, to describe motivation using the words and actions of the students, not the researcher.

Socially Constructed Meaning

A key characteristic of qualitative research that is based on participant perspectives is the belief that participants actively construct their own reality. They develop meaning from their experiences and their own way of describing this meaning. Knowledge, then, for each individual, is built on their lived experiences and situation-specific interactions with others. Meaning is "socially constructed," arising from interactions with others. This suggests that there is no final truth or "reality" since meaning is individualistically constructed. Likewise, the meaning of different situations is individualized.

A theory of knowledge closely related to social constructivism is called interpretivisim. This theory lies at the heart of qualitative research and provides the fundamental notion of how qualitative research differs from quantitative research.

The following quote from a noted qualitative researcher describes this approach very nicely:

> Interpretivist theories are fat with the juice of human endeavor . . . with human contradiction, human emotion, human frailty. . . . [They] are derived from pure lived experience . . . replete with multiple levels of understanding; assembled from many "ingredients"; and patched together to form new patterns, new images, new languages, rather than extracting what are believed to be a priori patterns. (Lincoln, 2010, p. 6)

Emergent Research Design

As in quantitative research, qualitative researchers have a plan or design for conducting the research. The difference is that in a qualitative study researchers enter the investigation "as if they know very little about the people and places they will visit. They attempt to loosen themselves from their preconceptions" (Bogdan & Biklen, 2007, p. 54). Because of this perspective, they do not know enough to begin the study with a precise research design. As they learn about the setting, people, and other sources of information, they discover what needs to be done to fully describe and understand the phenomena being studied. Thus, a qualitative researcher will begin the study with *some* idea about what data will be collected and the procedures that will be employed, but a full account of the methods is given *retrospectively*, after all the data have been collected. The design is emergent in that it remains flexible and evolves during the study.

Before going on to more specific types of qualitative designs, I want to stress again that the above characteristics are typically present *to some degree* in any single qualitative investigation. The extent to which each characteristic is included depends on the particular design and the orientation of the researcher. In "pure" qualitative studies each of these characteristics is present, whereas in other qualitative studies only some of them are present.

We will now examine five specific qualitative approaches in greater detail. The nature of each approach has implications for the research design, types of data collection, and data analysis.

USING EDUCATIONAL RESEARCH

The highly influential *Scientific Research in Education* (Shavelson & Towne, 2002) makes a strong case for "evidence-based" policy that relies heavily on what could be considered traditional quantitative methods. It should also be pointed out, however, that the report does not distinguish between qualitative and quantitative forms of inquiry, preferring instead to contend that either method, when properly used, can contribute credible evidence on important topics and issues. What is most important is that researchers do a good job with whatever method is best matched with their question.

TYPES of QUALITATIVE RESEARCH

Ethnographic Studies

Ethnography: In-depth involvement in a culture to describe naturally occurring behavior.

An ethnographic qualitative study, or **ethnography,** is an in-depth description and interpretation of cultural patterns and meanings within a culture or social group. Ethnography has been the primary mode of study in anthropology for many years. Anthropologists have used ethnography to investigate primitive cultures, including such aspects of culture as religious beliefs, social relations, child rearing, marriage, and language. The approach to gathering data in these studies was to (1) observe the culture for weeks, months, even years; (2) interact with and interview members of the culture; and (3) analyze documents and artifacts. These three methods of gathering data—observation, interviews, and document analysis—remain the primary modes of data collection for ethnographic studies in education. Whatever the mode of data collection, the researcher engages in extensive work in the naturally occurring setting or context, the *field.* In education, this is typically the school or classroom. Only through prolonged experience in the field can the researcher obtain a complete understanding of the educational system, process, or phenomena.

A hallmark of an ethnographic study is its emphasis on culture. Culture can be defined as shared patterns of beliefs, normative expectations and behaviors, and meanings. The emphasis is on what is characteristic of a group. The key concept in culture is *shared.* What is individualistic, not repeated for others, is not culture. A group must adopt meanings and normative behaviors and expectations over time to be defined as having a culture. Though it is possible for a group to consist of two individuals, the minimum number is more typically 6–10. Regardless of how it is defined, the group must have interacted for a sufficient period of time to establish shared patterns of thinking and behavior. Of course, there is still individual variation in behavior and beliefs, but in an ethnographic study the main emphasis is on groups. For example, if observations and interviews of students at risk of failing identify common traits, such as the need for a social support system, this could be viewed as culture. A specific social support system, such as going to church, which may be true for only a few students, is not a cultural trait. In the end, educational ethnographers study specific cultural themes, such as the induction of beginning teachers, student–teacher relationships, persistence of athletes, and teacher decision making about classroom assessment and grading practices.

A description of an ethnography is illustrated in Example 10.1. In this study the groups were classrooms. Notice that there are many approaches to collecting data. This is a characteristic of ethnographic studies.

EXAMPLE 10.1 | Ethnographic Study

Our methodology is aligned with Goodall's (2000) notion of new ethnography, which deals more directly with the interpersonal aspect. . . . We used autoethnography to engage in reflexivity and interpret our respective roles as instructors (Goodall, 2000). As teachers attempted to engage students in CRP for the first time, student voices provided critical feedback. Analysis at the student level helped to authenticate whether or not the task was culturally relevant. Analysis at the teacher level allowed them to reflect and learn from their pedagogy. . . . Analysis at the teacher-researcher level allowed me to reflect upon my instruction in the professional development course. . . . This three-tiered process allowed us to describe the complexities of culturally relevant teaching in high school from the perspectives of student, teachers, and teacher research. . . . In addition to student and teacher artifacts, data sources included observations and field-notes of five of the eight teacher participants' instruction. . . . Data sources also included teachers' course reflection papers and log entries related to their CRP projects. . . . Other data sources included lesson plans, transcripts, and student artifacts.

Source: Leonard, J., Napp, C., & Adeleke, S. (2009). The complexities of culturally relevant pedagogy: A case study of two secondary mathematics teachers and their ESOL students. *The High School Journal, 93*(1), 9–10.

The first step in conducting an ethnographic study is to formulate the research problem statement. The foreshadowed questions, as discussed in Chapter 2, are initially general and are subject to change as the study is conducted. Once the research problem statement or question is established, the researcher designs data collection by determining the nature of the research site, how to enter the research site, how to select participants, how to obtain data, and how to analyze the data.

Case Studies

Case study: In-depth analysis of a single experience or entity.

A **case study** is an in-depth analysis of one or more events, settings, programs, social groups, communities, individuals, or other "bounded systems" in their natural context. The case study is an investigation of one entity, which is carefully defined and characterized by time and place. The single entity could be a single school, for example, which would be a *within-site* study, or a number of schools (*multisite*). Also, in a single study there may be one or multiple cases (collective case study).

Note in Example 10.2 how the researchers justified their use of a case study design of two student-initiated retention programs to meet the needs of underrepresented students of color.

EXAMPLE 10.2 | Instrumental Case Study

We chose case study as a research method for the obvious reason that we needed to develop a holistic understanding of SIRPs [Student Initiated Retention Project]. Yin (1989) described case study research as a flexible form of inquiry best suited for studying a particular phenomenon within its natural context. Such studies . . . through the use of interviews and observations, seek to develop "thick descriptions" of the setting or phenomenon in question. . . . Accordingly, we relied on formal structured interviews, informal interviews (with key informants), observations, and key documents.

Source: Maldonado, D. E. Z., Rhoads, R., & Buenavista, T. L. (2005). The student-initiated retention project: Theoretical contributions and role of self-empowerment. *American Educational Research Journal, 42*(4), 615.

In Example 10.3 a collective case study is described in which two teachers and their classrooms in two high schools in New Zealand were investigated. A multisite case study is illustrated in Example 10.4.

EXAMPLES 10.3–10.4 | Collective and Multisite Studies Case

An interpretivist-based methodology was used, and this comprised a multiple case study approach. . . . In the first case study a total of 12 one-hour lessons were observed . . . while in the second fewer lessons were observed. . . . A case study approach was used in order to facilitate a holistic, interpretive investigation of events in context with the potential to provide a more complete picture of the science curriculum students were experiencing compared to other modes of research. . . . The interpretive analysis concentrated on their [students'] perspectives of classroom reality.

Source: Hume, A., & Coll, R. K. (2009). Assessment of learning, for learning, and as learning: New Zealand case studies. *Assessment in Education: Principles*, Policy & Practice, *16*(3), 274.

This two-site, qualitative case study examined how the Chicago and Boston Public School Districts alternatively prepared new teachers through partnerships with private, nonprofit urban teacher residencies. . . . The study asked how the reform partners defined "teacher quality" and how the structure of their partnerships contributed to those meanings.

Source: Boggess, L. B. (2010). Tailoring new urban teaches for character and activism. *American Educational Research Journal*, *47*(1), 65.

Though the term *case study* has become identified as a type of qualitative research, this is typically because in-depth studies of a single entity use qualitative methods to gather data. Case studies can also be conducted with quantitative approaches. Often, both qualitative and quantitative methods are used in the same case study. In our discussion here, however, we will restrict usage of case study to qualitative research.

Once a researcher has decided on using a case study approach, the type of case study needs to be specified to determine appropriate research questions and methods. Table 10.2 summarizes several types of case studies. Each is targeted for a unique need.

Because the primary purpose of a case study is to obtain a detailed description and gain an understanding of the case, generalizability of the findings is a concern. Sometimes, researchers will try to identify a "typical" case to study. If so, they are concerned with at least some generalization to a larger group or other situations as traditionally defined. However, this is difficult in education since it is not very feasible to find a single exemplar that is representative of others. For example, doing a case study of a single classroom to investigate how a beginning teacher functions will provide in-depth descriptions of that classroom and teacher, but it is unlikely that other classrooms or teachers will be the same. The best to hope for is that the readers will come to their own conclusions regarding generalizability.

TABLE 10.2 Types of Case Studies

Type	Description
Historical organizational	Focus is on a specific organization over time, often tracing the organization's development.
Observational	Participant observation is the primary method of gathering data to study a particular entity or some aspect of the entity (such as a school or classes within a school).
Life history	A first-person narrative that is completed with one person; also referred to as an *oral history*.
Situation analysis	A specific event (e.g., how students deal with the death of a parent) is studied from different perspectives.
Multicase (collective)	Several different independent entities are studied.
Multisite	Many sites or participants are used to, in the main, develop theory.
Instrumental	Study of an entity, theme, or issue.

Research problem statements in case studies are written to focus on an in-depth description and understanding. Often there is a single central question, followed by several subquestions. For example, the questions in Example 10.5 were used in a study that examined how three middle school teachers integrated the use of laptop computers for instruction. Note how the authors emphasized the need to reconstruct the questions as the study was undertaken.

EXAMPLE 10.5 | Case Study Research Questions

Before we defined specific boundaries for the study, broad areas of investigation were identified with the understanding that they would serve as guidelines for collection of data about the school community and that research questions, along with their data collection strategies, would be developed over time. After several months, two questions emerged that we felt captured the complexity of how the teachers were learning to use laptop technology in the classrooms:

1. How do participants' personal histories and beliefs about learners and learning play out within the institutional culture to influence their technology-related instructional practices?
2. How do teachers construct technology-related norms and practices with peers and students through their participation in various activity settings?

Source: Winidschitl, M., Schendel, J. M., & Ulman, J. E. (2002). Tracing teachers' use of technology in a laptop computer school: The interplay of teacher beliefs, social dynamics, and institutional culture. *American Educational Research Journal, 39*(1), 172.

Phenomenological Studies

Phenomenological: Understanding the essence of experiences.

The purpose of conducting a **phenomenological** study is to describe and interpret the experiences of participants in order to understand the "essence" of the experience *as perceived by the participants.* The basis of phenomenology is that there are multiple ways of interpreting the same experience or event, and that the meaning of the experience to each participant is what is used as primary data. This is akin to the previously mentioned characteristic of *participant perspectives.* Though all qualitative studies have this orientation, a phenomenological study focuses much more on the consciousness of human experiences. Typically, there is a search for essential or invariant structure in the meanings given by the participants. The researcher needs to suspend, or "bracket," any preconceived ideas about the phenomenon to elicit and better understand the meanings given by the participants.

The research problem for a phenomenological study is focused on what is essential for the meaning of the event, episode, or interaction. It is also focused on understanding the participants' voice. This can be stated directly, as in "What is the essence of meaning behind student conferences with counselors?" or less directly, as in "What is the relationship between a school counselor and student really like?" Usually, there is a single, central question in the research. Several subquestions are used to orient the researcher in collecting data and framing the results.

The abstract from a phenomenological study is reproduced in Example 10.6. This study illustrates the focus on the lived, subjective experience of a small number of participants (in this case, four teachers). In the second example, Example 10.7, the excerpt describes the rationale for using phenomenology.

EXAMPLES 10.6–10.7 | Phenomenological Study

This report focuses on examining alternatively prepared high school matthematics teachers' perceptions of the connections and disconnects of their program experiences and the realities of urban classrooms. Using phenomenology as the framework, a storytelling approach is employed to capture the perceptions of the teachers' experiences. This approach allows the teachers to convey their understanding of the relationship between their alternative preparation and teaching in urban classrooms.

Source: Junor Clarke, P. A., & Thomas, C. D. (2009). Teachers' perceptions of connections and disconnects between their alternative preparation and teaching in uran classrooms. *Urban Education, 44*(2), 144.

This study used a phenomenological approach to investigate the recollections of participants of an out-of-school science program. Phenomenology seeks clarification and understanding of people's perceptions and experiences, especially the meanings they give to events, concepts, and issues. . . . This process examines the experience of each participant and recognizes that these experiences have a relationship with the phenomenon (in this case the out-of-school science experience).

Source: Knapp, K. (2007). A longitudinal analysis of an out-of-school science experience. *School Science and Mathematics, 107*(2), 46.

Grounded Theory Studies

Grounded theory: Theory generated from qualitative data.

The intent of a **grounded theory** study is to discover or generate theory that explains central phenomena from the data. The theory is essentially an abstract schema, or set of propositions, that pertains to a specific experience, situation, or setting. It is the context of the phenomenon being studied that provides the basis for a grounded theory study. In this sense, the theory is "grounded" or derived from data collected in the field.

Research problems in grounded theory studies are focused on what happened to individuals, why they believe it happened as it did, and what it means to them. The questions are broad and general, such as the following:

What did you experience when you worked with a gifted student?
What did you experience when you worked with a new teacher?
How did you decide to split up the work with the mainstreamed student?
How did you feel about working with a delinquent student?

This is usually followed by subquestions related to coding of the data. For example, a study of curriculum revision in private colleges could begin with questions such as "What theory explains the curriculum change process in private colleges?" and "How does the faculty participate in the curriculum change process?" and then include subquestions such as these:

How was the change process initiated?
What were the obstacles to success of the revision?
Who were the most important people to the success of the revision?
Why were they influential?
What was the final outcome of the revision process?

Creswell (2008) identifies three types of grounded theory designs: systematic, emerging, and constructivist. The systemic approach is used extensively in education. It involves the use of rigorous procedures and techniques with careful coding categorization. The coding of data is dependent on what is suggested by the data, rather than using preexisting categories. With an emerging design the coding and categorization are less structured and prescribed. There is more flexibility in determining codes, categorization, and themes. The constructivist design focuses on the perspectives of the participants, reflecting "active" codes that emphasize how participants have changed their perceptions and insights.

A grounded theory approach is explained in Example 10.8.

EXAMPLE 10.8 | Grounded Theory Study

In the present study we applied the principles of grounded theory to frame a set of factors that seem to set major challenges concerning both successful work in the school physics laboratory and also in the preparation of lessons that exploit practical work. The subject groups of the study were preservice and inservice physics teachers who participated in a school laboratory course. Our results derived from a detailed analysis of tutoring discussions between the instructor and the participants in the course, which revealed that the challenges in practical or laboratory work consisted of the limitations of the laboratory facilities, an insufficient knowledge of physics, problems in understanding instructional approaches, and the general organization of practical work. Based on these findings, we present our recommendations on the preparation of preservice and inservice teachers for the more effective use of practical work in school science and in school physics.

Source: Nivalainen, V., Asikainen, M. A., & Sormunen, K. (2010). Preservice and inservice teachers' challenges in the planning of practical work in physics. *Journal of Science Teacher Education, 21*(4), 393.

Critical Studies

Critical studies are distinguished by a researcher role as advocate to respond to the themes and issues of marginalized individuals. These studies are focused on systems of power and control, privilege, inequity, inequality, dominance, and influence based on race, gender, and socioeconomic class. The central issue that is studied is typically the struggle of targeted groups to enhance their power and influence, emancipating them from the more dominant culture. For example, a researcher might focus on the inequitable treatment of students with learning disabilities, or students whose primary language is not English. Data would be gathered to challenge the status quo and to initiate action to ameliorate injustices. Essentially, the researcher applies a critical "lens" through which data are gathered and analyzed (e.g., feminine, gender).

A critical study is used in Example 10.9. In this case, low socioeconomic, cultural, feminist lens were used to advocate more effective mother voices.

EXAMPLE 10.9 | Critical Study

This study's use of qualitative methods allowed mothers to define how they make meaning of their educational view, choices and experiences, and how these are shaped by socioeconomic and cultural factors. I also examined how the mothers perceive school contexts, policies, and other sociopolitical conditions as hindering or empowering them within an urban educational marketplace, and I learned how they used strategies to help empower themselves within this setting . . . in accordance with feminist methodological standards.

Source: Cooper, C. W. (2007). School choice as "motherwork": Valuing African-American women's educational advocacy and resistance. *International Journal of Qualitative Studies, in Education, 20*(5), 487–488.

Review and Reflect *Try identifying the key characteristics of each type of qualitative study, then give original examples of each. While knowing the different types is helpful in evaluating the quality of the research, it's most important to focus on the quality of data collection and analysis.*

TABLE 10.3 Comparison of Different Types of Qualitative Studies

	Purpose	Data Collection	Data Analysis	Reporting of Results
Ethnography	Describing a cultural group	Primarily observations and interviews	Description, analysis, interpretation	Description of cultural behavior
Case Study	In-depth analysis of single or multiple cases	Use of multiple sources of data	Descriptions, themes, assertions	In-depth description of case(s)
Phenomenology	Understanding the essence of experiences	Extended interviews with up to 10 participants	Statements, meanings, themes, general description	Description of essence of the experience from participants' perspectives
Grounded Theory	Developing a theory from field data	Interviews with 20–30 participants	Coding to constantly compare findings to themes	As a set of propositions, hypotheses, or theories
Critical Studies	Advocates for marginalized individuals	Use of multiple sources of data	Descriptions, themes, assertion, advocation	As assertions based on inequity or inequality

Source: Adapted from Creswell, 2008.

The five traditions or approaches to qualitative studies presented in this chapter are summarized and compared in Table 10.3. Remember that the different types of qualitative studies will overlap in many respects to some degree, and that the general characteristics summarized at the beginning of the chapter will apply to each type. We now move on to issues that are important in judging the quality of qualitative studies. For this purpose, all five will be considered together since the principles are pertinent to all types.

TYPES *of* DATA COLLECTION

Three major types of data collection techniques are used in qualitative research: observation, interview, and document and artifact review. Before any data collection, however, the researcher needs to identify the participants and sites, and gain entry into the field, as applicable. We'll consider briefly the identification of participants and sites, then discuss approaches for entering the field.

Identification of Sites and Sources of Data

The selection of sources of data, whether people, documents and artifacts, or events, is done purposefully. Selection of participants for qualitative studies was covered in Chapter 4. Essentially, purposeful samples (of people or documents and artifacts) are identified and used to provide the greatest amount and depth of information.

Consequently, key informants are identified and used in groups where all cannot be studied. Certain documents deserve more attention than others because they are richer and lead to greater depth of descriptions and understanding. It is better to select a few entries for in-depth results rather than a larger number that would result in more superficial information. Sites (where data are collected) are also selected purposefully to provide rich data. Characteristics of information-rich sites are gleaned from the literature, and these characteristics provide a description of what is needed.

Internal sampling: Selection of participants, times, and documents at a site.

For an ethnographic case study, the selection of participants would be completed after identifying the site and entering the field (**internal sampling**). Sites, like participants, are selected purposefully to provide the best information related to the initial or central question. This would include the setting, where the data will be collected, time frames, and events of interest. For example, observations may be planned for researching how students respond to a computer program to help them write. There would be a need to use the most informative settings (e.g., within a classroom or computer lab), when observations should be made (e.g., morning, afternoon, beginning of the school year, days of the week, etc.), and what students would be doing during the selected times at the designated locations (e.g., actively writing with the software or revising based on feedback).

In a case study, a "group" of participants is usually identified. The group is a collection of individuals who interact with each other, share the same space, and identify with each other. Typical groups in educational case studies would be students in a classroom, athletes on a team, teachers in the same grade level or department, and learning-disabled students in a mainstreamed class. One consideration in selecting the group is size. Other factors being equal, the smaller the group, the greater the chance that the researcher's presence will change their behavior. For example, in a case study of teenage same-sex friendships in which the researcher stayed with two or three pairs of participants, it is likely that the researcher's involvement would affect the friendships. A larger number of participants makes it easier to remain unobtrusive and relatively anonymous. Of course, a larger number of participants makes it more difficult to keep detailed records on everyone; depth is sacrificed for less intrusion.

Purposive sampling for a case study is illustrated in Example 10.10, a study that investigated economically disadvantaged, high achieving urban high school students.

EXAMPLE 10.10 | Purposive Sampling in a Case Study Investigation

For the purpose of this study, high ability students were defined as those demonstrating well above average potential as measured by a score above the 90th percentile using local norms on standardized intelligence or achievement tests during his or her school career. . . .
The participants were recommended by the high school's guidance counselors for the study as achievers when three of the following four criteria were met: (1) identified and enrolled in an academically gifted elementary or middle school program, (2) achieved at a superior level academically as evidence by high grades, (3) nominated for the study by a teacher/counselor and (4) received various academic awards and honors.

Source: Reis, S. M., Colbert, R. D., & Jebert, T. P. (2005). Understanding resilience in diverse, talented students in an urban high school. *Roeper Review, 27*(2), 113.

The participants in a phenomenological study are selected because they have lived the experiences being investigated, are willing to share their thoughts about their experiences, and can articulate their conscious experiences. Typically, between 5 and 25 individuals will be selected for study.

The sample of participants, documents, and artifacts for a grounded theory study is based on the ability of each to contribute to the development of theory. Often, a homogeneous sample is selected first, one in which each individual has had a similar experience. Once the theory is developed, a heterogeneous sample, individuals who have had different experiences, may be selected to confirm or disconfirm tenets of the theory.

In a critical theory study, sources of data are identified to provide the most convincing advocacy among the group, issue, and event being investigated. Stories of individuals who have been marginalized are especially powerful, so participants with such stories are selected.

Entry into the Field

Whether the researcher physically goes into field settings, such as schools, or figuratively by interviewing and collecting documents and artifacts, it is important to establish an appropriate role, obtain permission, and establish an appropriate rapport. The researcher role defines the position of the investigator and his or her relationships with others. At one extreme, the researcher is a *complete outsider*, totally detached from the naturally occurring behavior and activities of the participants. There is no involvement with what occurs in the setting. The researcher is detached—comes in, gathers data, and then leaves. A *complete insider*, on the other hand, is a researcher who has an established role in the setting in which data are collected, engaging in genuine and natural participation. In between these extremes, the researcher may be labeled *insider/outsider* or *partial participant*. In ethnographic studies, it is best if the researcher is a stranger to the site. Examples of different researcher roles are presented in Table 10.4.

Qualitative researchers often change their role as data are collected. The nature and duration of different roles are determined, in part, by the situation. As situations change, roles also change. When first entering a site, the researcher might take on primarily a complete outsider role. As the study progresses, more of an insider role could develop. In studies with a limited time frame, it is difficult for the researcher to be an insider, which is why in ethnographies extended time is needed to "walk in the shoes" of the participants.

Researcher roles will vary depending on the type of qualitative study. In many ethnographies, case studies, and grounded theory approaches, the interactions are widespread but the researcher is less intrusive in collecting data. In phenomenological studies, the interaction is more intrusive, close, and personal.

In obtaining initial permission, it is best if there is an agreement that permits access to all potentially helpful sources of data. This is important since the gathering of data evolves from initial approaches as the researchers learn from current data. It is also important to be clear about how confidentiality and anonymity will be maintained.

TABLE 10.4 Examples of Researcher Roles in Collecting Data

	Complete Insider	Partial Participant	Complete Outsider
Observation	Counselor observes students participating in small groups.	Researcher from outside the school helps counselors observe small groups.	Researcher from outside the school observes students in small groups.
Interview	Principal interviews teachers in his or her school.	Researcher from outside the school interviews teachers in their school.	Researcher from outside the school interviews teachers at a university.
Document and Artifact Review	Teacher reviews memorandums concerning formative assessment practices in his or her department.	Teacher from another department reviews memorandums.	Researchers from outside the school review memorandums.

Rapport with individuals in the research site is enhanced when the researcher takes time to understand others' perspectives and shows respect for different viewpoints and personalities. Favorites should be avoided, and the researcher needs to use honest, authentic, and sincere communication. Rapport is also enhanced when the researcher is able to participate in daily activities, establish common interests, and relax and act naturally.

Observation

By observing naturally occurring behavior over many hours or days, qualitative researchers hope to obtain a rich understanding of the phenomenon being studied. In an ethnography, observation is *comprehensive* in that it is continuous and total. The quality of the results in an ethnography is often directly related to the length of the observations. It is unlikely that valid and credible data will result for this type of study from a few hours of observation.

Participant observer: Observer involved as a participant.

An important aspect of the observation is the extent to which the researcher is an active participant with the subjects. If the researcher is a genuine participant in the activity being studied, he or she is called a **participant observer.** For example, to study the life of a college freshman, the participant observer would become a college freshman, directly experiencing everything other freshmen experience. This is essentially what an anthropologist would do in conducting ethnographic research on a culture. The anthropologist would virtually become a member of the group and live just as others in the group live.

In educational research, it is rare for the investigator literally to adopt the same role as the individuals who are being studied. There may be some participation in some of the activities, but it is usually limited. The researcher interacts with the participants to establish a rapport and a relationship but does not become a member of the group. When participation is limited, the researcher is called an *observer participant.*

TABLE 10.5 Roles of the Qualitative Observer

Passive Participation	Moderate Participation	Active Participation	Complete Participation
Complete observer: Observes without becoming a part of the process in any way.	Observer participant: Identified as a researcher and does not take on the role of the participants.	Participant observer: Participates as a member of the group but is known as a researcher.	Complete participant: Participates as a member of the group and is not known as a researcher.

As illustrated in Table 10.5, you can think of the degree of participation and involvement as a continuum, ranging from a *complete participant* on one end to a *complete observer* on the other end. A **complete observer** is totally detached from the behavior of the participants who are being studied. Of course, the mere presence of an observer, whether involved or detached, may affect the behavior of those observed.

Complete observer: Observer detached from participants.

The extent of participation by an observer often changes during a study. In the beginning, the researcher may limit participation to become accepted. As the group being studied becomes comfortable with the researcher, participation increases. Another variable that affects the extent of participation is the nature of the research question. If, for example, the study is focused on the perspectives of students, then it makes sense to participate more with the students than with the teacher. On the other hand, if teacher perceptions are the focus of the study, then the researcher should take on more of an observer role.

The more the researcher is actively involved with the participants, the greater the chance that this involvement will significantly alter what occurs. Any degree of participant involvement is likely to affect the interpretation of what is observed. As a consumer, you need to look for clues indicating that researcher participation may have been an important influence on the results (e.g., emotional involvement or bias in the interpretation of what is recorded). The researcher should indicate a sensitivity for this effect and should take precautions to ensure that his or her participation does not significantly distort the observations. Some researchers will indicate their biases and personal beliefs at the outset of the study, thereby demonstrating an explicit concern with compensating for them.

Observers usually record observations as brief notes while they are observing. These brief notes are then expanded to become what are called *field notes*. **Field notes** are detailed written descriptions of what was observed, as well as the researcher's interpretations. They constitute the raw data that the researcher analyzes to address the research problem. The assumption is that nothing is trivial, so whatever is seen, heard, or experienced is recorded and considered. Observation sessions will typically last one to two hours. Longer sessions make it difficult to keep an in-depth recording of what is observed simply because there is too much data. Good observation is hard work and requires excellent listening skills.

Field notes: Detailed recordings of observed behavior.

Field notes include two kinds of information. The first type is *descriptive*. The purpose of the description is to use pictures, words, drawings, maps, and diagrams that capture the details of what has occurred. The field notes usually include a description of the setting, what people looked like, what they said, and how they acted. The date, place, and time are recorded, as well as a description of the activities in which people were involved. Portraits of the participants are written, including their dress, mannerisms, and physical appearance. Often a description of the researcher and his or her dress and actions is included. As much detail as possible is recorded, including direct quotes or close approximations of what was said. In the description, interpretations are avoided. Thus, rather than using words such as *angry* or *effective*, the researcher would describe the specific behaviors observed. The observation is *unstructured* in the sense that there are no predetermined categories or checklists. Whatever is observed is recorded in a form that captures the perspectives of the individuals being studied.

The second kind of information in the field notes is *reflective*. These are researcher speculations, feelings, interpretations, ideas, hunches, and impressions—subjective notions related to the research. Reflections include thoughts about emerging themes and patterns, thoughts about methodological problems or issues, considerations of ethical concerns, and introspective discussions about researcher opinions, attitudes, and prejudices. It is important to keep these reflections separate from the descriptive information. In the field notes, they are often identified as *observer comments*.

Most observations result in notes about *who*, *what*, *where*, *how*, and *why* something happened. Examples of how each of these dimensions manifests itself in studies are presented in Table 10.6.

TABLE 10.6 Dimensions of Observation Foci

Observation	Description
Who is in the group?	How many students are present? What race or ethnicity is represented? What are the ages of the students? How long have they been in the school?
What is happening?	In what activities are the students involved? How long are the activities? How are students communicating? How long is the duration of their involvement? What topics are commonly discussed? Who talks and who listens? How do students behave with each other and the teacher?
Where is the class located?	What are the physical dimensions of the setting? What technology is available? Where is the class located in the school?
When does the class meet?	How long and how often do students meet to engage in the activity? When during the day do students typically engage in the activity?
Why does the class engage in the activity?	Do students agree on why the activity is important? What reasons are given for the activity? What meanings do students give the activity?

It is critical for the field notes to be accurate and extensive. You will be able to judge the level of detail provided by the excerpts the researcher uses to illustrate conclusions, and the overall amount of data analyzed.

The following example of field notes, Example 10.11, will give you some idea of the detail that is recorded. These field notes were collected as part of a study on mainstreaming learning-disabled high school students. What is reproduced here represents about *one-tenth* of the notes for an observation period of 1.5 hours. O.C. stands for observer comment.

EXAMPLE 10.11 | Field Notes

I walked into Marge's class and she was standing in front of the room with more people than I had ever seen in the room save for her homeroom which is right after second period. She looked like she was talking to the class or was just about to start. She was dressed as she had been on my other visits—clean, neat, well-dressed but casual. Today she had on a striped blazer, a white blouse and dark slacks. She looked up at me, smiled and said: "Oh, I have a lot more people here now than the last time."

O.C.: This was in reference to my other visits during other periods where there are only a few students. She seems self-conscious about having such a small group of students to be responsible for. Perhaps she compares herself with the regular teachers who have classes of thirty or so.

There were two women in their late twenties sitting in the room. There was only one chair left. Marge said to me something like: "We have two visitors from the central office today. One is a vocational counselor and the other is a physical therapist," but I don't remember if those were the words. I felt embarrassed coming in late. I sat down in the only chair available next to one of the women from the central office. They had on skirts and carried their pocketbooks, much more dressed up than the teachers I've seen. They sat there and observed. . . .

I looked around the room noting the dress of some of the students. Maxine had on a black t-shirt that had some iron-on lettering on it. It was very well-done iron-on and the shirt looked expensive. She had on Levi jeans and Nike jogging sneakers. Mark is about 5'9" or 5'10". He had on a long-sleeve jersey with an alligator on the front, very stylish but his pants were wrinkled and he had on old muddy black basketball sneakers with both laces broken, one in two places. Pam had on a lilac-colored velour sweater over a button-down striped shirt. Her hair looked very well-kept and looked like she had had it styled at an expensive hair place. Jeff sat next to her in his wheelchair. He had one foot up without a shoe on it as if it were sprained.

Source: Bogdan, R. C., & Biklen, S. K. (2007). *Qualitative research for education: An introduction to theories and methods* (5th ed.). Boston: Allyn & Bacon, 261–263.

Interviewing

Interviews were described in Chapter 6 as a data collection technique, ranging from structured to unstructured formats. In qualitative research, interviews are perhaps the most widely used method of collecting data. Typically, the qualitative interview is *in-depth* and either semi-structured or unstructured. An in-depth interview uses a few open-response, relatively general questions with some probes to obtain more detail. In qualitative studies, interviews can be unscheduled, consisting of informal conversations with participants, but are more typically scheduled with a specific purpose. They can be done in person, by telephone, over the Internet, with individuals or small groups. The most commonly used format is in person, individually, or with small groups. Within these variations in format, there are specific types of qualitative interviews.

Types of Qualitative Interviewing. Qualitative interviews can be classified according to whether they are individual or small group, and by whether they are relatively structured or unstructured.

In a relatively unstructured general interview, the researcher begins with a general idea of what needs to be asked, but does not have a list of prespecified questions with precise wording. A general direction is established with the respondent and then specific questions are formulated based on what the respondent says. The respondent controls the interview, not the interviewer, and does most of the talking. The interviewer needs to be flexible and allow the respondent to control the flow of information but at the same time keep the overall focus on the research problem being investigated.

In an *informal conversational interview*, the questions emerge from the immediate context and are asked in the natural course of events spontaneously; there is no predetermination of questions, topics or phrasing, and nothing is planned ahead. For example, a researcher may meet a student in the hallway and have a conversation from which data are derived. In the *interview guide approach*, topics are selected in advance, but the researcher decides the sequence and wording of the questions during the interview, and may use preestablished prompts. For both individual and small group interviews, this approach is most common. It allows for important topics to be covered but also gives respondents freedom to emphasize other areas. One variation of the interview guide approach has a preestablished set of questions and prompts that are asked in order. Thus, all participants get the same questions in the same order. This assures extensive comments on each area, but may constrain and limit the naturalness and relevancy of the responses. This kind of interview tends to be less engaging and more formal, and reduces interviewer flexibility to probe in new and potentially important ways. Good qualitative interviewing has probes and pauses. Establishing trust, being genuine, maintaining eye contact, dressing appropriately, and connecting with the respondent are important.

One way good qualitative researchers keep the interview going with rich information is to *not ask* questions that can be answered dichotomously (e.g., yes or no). Notice how the following dichotomously answered questions can be rephrased to be more effective:

Did the teachers have difficulty in the seminar?	What did you expect teachers to have difficulties with in the seminar?
Did the teachers change?	How did the teachers change?
Did you learn anything from the workshop?	What did you learn about the teaching strategies presented in the workshop?
Were any problems identified at the committee meeting?	What problems were identified at the committee meeting?

One type of individual interview, the **key informant interview,** is used extensively in ethnographic studies. It is based on the assumption that in-depth interviews with a few "key" participants, individuals who are particularly knowledgeable and articulate, will provide insights and understandings about the problem. For example, certain students may be best able to provide information on the effect of working part-time while participating in sports. The assistant principal responsible for instruction would probably be a key informant in a study of how a new curriculum is being integrated.

Key informant interview: Interview of a few particularly knowledgeable participants.

However, the qualities that make key informants valuable also make them unrepresentative of the group. Thus, the researcher should carefully describe key informants and address the question of representativeness. Key informants should be selected after the researcher has become familiar with the setting to increase the probability that they will provide needed information truthfully. Informant bias may occur because of a person's position or values. Selecting key informants to represent the diversity of perspectives present in the setting lessens the potential for bias. As with all interviews, the skill of the interviewer is critical to gathering valid data. As a general rule, skill is directly related to training and experience—the more training and experience, the greater the skill.

In a second type of individual interview, the **life-history interview,** the researcher is interested in learning about the subject's life. The data from life histories are helpful in obtaining a historical perspective or a broad perspective on how an individual has developed. Life histories in educational research can provide insights into career development. Note in the following example how qualitative interviews were used to examine how women in athletic training positions balance work and family.

Life-history interview: Information about what has occurred throughout the participant's life.

EXAMPLE 10.12 | Life-History Interviews

Using a qualitative research approach, in-depth interviews were conducted with eight female athletic trainers who are mothers. A purposeful sampling strategy was used to select participants based on consultation with the Athletic Training Women's Taskforce. A one-on-one, open-ended, semi-structured format was used, allowing time for the researcher to develop rapport and trust with the participant.

Source: Rice, L., Gilbert, W., & Bloom, G. (2001). Strategies used by division I female athletic trainers to balance family and career demands. *Journal of Athletic Training, 36*(2 Suppl), S-73.

A group interview technique that is used extensively is the **focus group interview.** A focus group is typically a 1- to 2-hour interview of 8 to 12 persons that is designed to promote interaction among the individuals and lead to a richer understanding of whatever is being studied because of what is generated in the discussion. Focus groups have been used to evaluate products in marketing research for many years. A moderator guides the discussion, based on a topic guide

Focus group interview: Group interview about a particular topic or problem.

that has been prepared in advance. The focus group technique is most useful for encouraging subjects, through their interaction with one another, to offer insights and opinions about a concept, idea, value, or other aspects of their lives about which they are knowledgeable.

Some so-called focus groups are little more than a small group discussion. To be effective, focus groups need to be conducted by someone with skill in interviewing and group dynamics. The group should be homogeneous with respect to important participant characteristics. For example, in learning about a vision for a school of education, it would be more effective to have untenured professors in one group and tenured professors in another group, alumni in a separate group, and students in a separate group. This assures that the voice of each group is clear and well-represented. If the group is mixed, one perspective may dominate, or the session may turn out to be a series of individual responses in a group setting. Typically, the session is tape-recorded and notes may be taken by a second researcher (it's difficult to conduct the interview and take notes at the same time!). My experience in conducting both individual and group interviews is that the participants don't have a concern with tape-recording, and having a verbatim record is very important for data analysis.

A focus group strategy for collecting data is illustrated in Examples 10.13 and 10.14.

EXAMPLES 10.13–10.14 | Focus Group Interviews

Three student focus groups represented Praire High's diverse student population, but the groups selected by faculty and staff were stratified by race. The "at risk" group was comprised entirely of African American and newcomer Latino students. . . . The "average" students focus group was equally divided among African American, Latino, and white students. The "honors" group was all white.

Source: Patterson, J. A., Hale, D., & Stessman, M. (2007). Cultural contradictions and school leaving: A case study of an urban high school. *High School Journal, 91*(2), 7.

The present study employed focus groups as the principal means of data collection. Focus groups are an effective method for obtaining in-depth information about a concept or issue and learning about people's experiences. . . . Instead of being directed by predetermined hypotheses or controlled by existing measures, focus groups enable participants to express themselves in their own words in an open and flexible process. . . . An experienced professional moderator facilitated all focus groups using a question route developed by the research team. The question route consisted of opening comments about the topic of stress, introductory questions to engage the participants in the topic, transition questions related to evaluations of stress, key questions on the causes of stress and coping strategies, and ending questions to summarize the discussion and confirm main points.

Source: Iwasaki, Y., & Mactavish, J. B. (2005). Ubiquitous yet unique: Perspectives of people with disabilities on stress. *Rehabilitation Counseling Bulletin, 48* (4), 196 .

Review and Reflect *Observation and interviewing are by far the most used types of data collection in qualitative research. Compare the strengths and weaknesses of each and match these to different types of qualitative studies. Are grounded theory studies stronger if they use more observation? What approach is best for critical studies? Can ethnographies be completed* without *observation? Try some interviews and observations. What makes them difficult? What skills are needed to do them well?*

Document and Artifact Analysis

The third primary method of collecting data for ethnographic studies is by reviewing documents and artifacts. **Documents** are written records. They can be virtually anything written or printed, such as yearbooks, school budgets, dropout rates, committee minutes, memos, letters, newspapers, diaries, test scores, and books. Nonprint materials, such as pictures, videotapes, memorabilia, and films, can also be used. If the documents provide firsthand information, they are *primary* sources. In a primary source the document is written in first person. It is written by someone who has had direct experience with the phenomenon, organization, or group being studied. *Secondary* sources are secondhand documents, such as descriptions of an event on the basis of what is heard from others, or a summary of more extensive primary information.

Documents: Written records.

Artifacts are archival sources that are different from documents. This would include comments in student files; record of testing results; statistical data; objects such as athletic letters, trophies, posters, and awarded plaques; bulletin boards; photographs, videos; art objects; film; physical trace evidence (e.g., wearing on the floor); e-mails; ritual objects; and sounds, smells, and tastes.

Artifacts: Archival sources different from documents.

Table 10.7 (on page 296) summarizes the strengths and weaknesses of observations, interviews, and document and artifact analysis.

The most common use of documents is to verify or support data obtained from interviews or observations. For example, teacher notes taken at the end of the school day that reflect on the successes and obstacles in using a new curriculum could be used to supplement researcher observations about implementing the new curriculum. Student essays could also be examined if written as part of the curriculum. The researcher usually finds existing documents and artifacts that have been produced, but occasionally, a researcher will ask participants to keep records or narratives as a way of producing documents. It should be clear, however, that a document is written or created as a natural outgrowth of the situation, and not in response to some kind of predetermined structure imposed by the researcher.

DATA ANALYSIS *and* INTERPRETATION

Observation, interview, and document and artifact analysis techniques result in a great amount of data that must be summarized and interpreted. Pages of field notes or interview transcripts must be critically examined and synthesized. The analysis is done during data collection as well as after all the data have been gathered. In many qualitative studies data collection and analysis are

TABLE 10.7 Strengths and Weaknesses of Different Types of Qualitative Data Collection

Type	Strengths	Weaknesses
Observation	• Can observe behavior in natural settings. • Observer is able to see behavior firsthand as it occurs. • Enhances understanding of the context. • Useful for gauging engagement, interest, and attitudes. • Unintended behavior can be observed. • Allows an understanding of sensitive areas that individuals may not want to discuss.	• Observer can change the behavior of the participants. • Limited to when observations are made. • Observer bias or expectations may influence what is recorded and how it is interpreted. • Labor- and resource-intensive. • May be difficult to record important behavior that occurs quickly.
Interview	• Allows researcher to control the conversation and obtain the information needed. • Facilitates verbatim transcriptions as raw data. • Good backup if observations are not possible or are impractical. • Direct interaction allows recording of nonverbal behavior that accompanies answers to questions. • Participants are able to provide historical perspective.	• Information is indirect, not naturally occurring. • Skill, biases, and expectations of the interviewer may affect results. • It may be difficult to establish rapport to obtain in-depth and authentic responses. • Participants may be uncomfortable, inarticulate, or uncooperative. • Anonymity cannot be assured, which may affect the disclosure of sensitive information.
Document and Artifact Analysis	• If unobtrusive, it will not be affected by participant awareness. • Audio-visual data provide creative sources of information. • Allows participants to share their perspectives in unique ways. • Provides data for which participants have had significant and thoughtful input. • Relatively inexpensive with fewer needed resources. • Provides alternative sources for triangulation. • Accessible when convenient for the researcher. • Provides detailed participant language and wording.	• Is not naturally occurring behavior. • Does not allow probing for additional information. • Sources may not be accurate or complete. • Data may be difficult to understand and code. • Medium may be disruptive and unnatural. • May provide incomplete or partial information.

FIGURE 10.2 Steps in qualitative data analysis and interpretation.

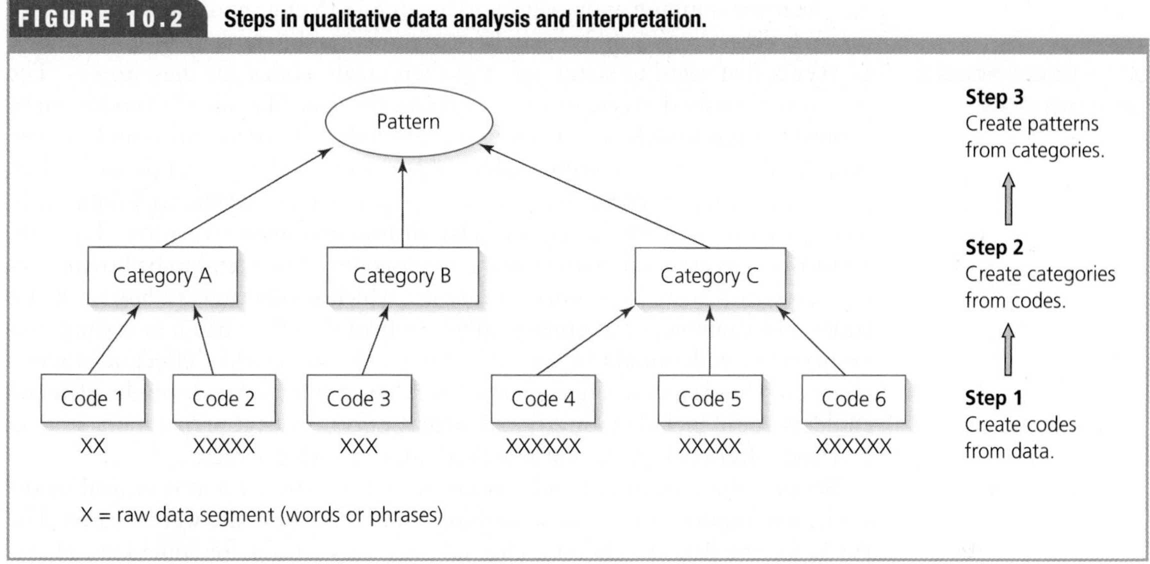

interwoven, influencing one another. The goal of the analysis is to discover patterns, ideas, explanations, and "understandings." Specific data elements have to be organized and then synthesized to derive the patterns and ideas that will form the basis of the conclusions. A thorough analysis requires three steps: organization of the data, summarizing the data as codes, and then interpreting the data to search for patterns. These steps are illustrated in Figure 10.2.

Data Organization

The first step in data analysis is to organize the data, separating it into workable units or segments. With many pages of data, simply organizing the data is quite a task. Fortunately, several computer software programs are available to record and analyze the data more efficiently.

Emic: Participant wording.

Etic: Researcher representations of emic data.

Most studies organize the data according to their source. **Emic** data contain information provided by the participants, in their own words. By capturing language, actions, expressions, terms, and explanations as communicated by the participants, the richness and depth of the findings can be summarized. **Etic** data are representations of the researcher. These representations are the researcher's interpretation of emic data. This is usually illustrated with themes or conclusions that explain trends and findings. For example, in a study of teachers' reasons for using particular grading practices, the participants might say something like "I use objective tests to show parents how grades were determined" and "I use tests that have the same type of items as the high-stakes test given at the end of the semester." These statements represent emic data. The researcher might synthesize these and call them "external pressures," which would be etic data.

Codes: Words or phrases to signify units of data.

The most common approach to organizing both emic and etic data is to read through the narratives and researcher comments and to look for words, phrases, or events that seem to stand out, and then create **codes** for these topics. The codes are then used as categories to organize the data. "Families" of codes can be applied to most studies. The families include codes related to setting and context, subjects' definitions of a setting, subjects' perspectives about other people and aspects of a setting, process changes over time, activities, events, techniques subjects use to accomplish things, and relationships and social structures. Typically, 30 to 50 codes are used. Some may be *major* codes, which tend to be broad, general categories, while others may be *subcodes*, which are divisions among the major codes. For example, in an ethnographic study of the effect of a new testing program, major codes might be time of testing, effect on teacher, effect on student, effect on school climate, effect on teacher relationships. Subcodes under effect on students could include motivational effects, effort, student preparation, student reactions after testing, student reactions after receiving scores.

Because the creation of codes is up to each researcher and is critical to the study, it is important to know something about how the codes were created. The key is for the data to suggest codes, not vice versa. Look for some kind of systematic process in the development of the codes, such as using general research questions that are stated prior to the research and that are generated during the study. Regular review of field notes to plan next steps keeps a researcher close to the data and familiar with major themes. Qualitative researchers need to write many observer comments as they are interviewing or observing or reviewing documents because these comments form the basis of important insights and categories. Sometimes playing with analogies and metaphors will provide an overview of organization of ideas.

An example of coded field notes is illustrated in Figure 10.3.

Data Summary

Organized data then need to be summarized into a much smaller number of categories or themes. This step can be arduous. Before computers, it would not be unusual to have each piece of information written on cards and sorted into piles according to different codes. Imagine a room with 30 piles of cards, each pile having 10 to 50 data elements. For example, in the aforementioned study on the effect of testing, one code is effect on students. In this pile there would be many cards that indicate observations or interview responses pertaining to effect on students. This could be something as simple as "The students moaned when testing was mentioned" to more complicated entries such as "One student came up after class and asked the teacher for more details about the testing. The student wanted to know about the difficulty of the test in comparison to classroom tests, and whether it would help to study for the test." The researcher's job in summarizing is to examine all the entries that have the same code and write a sentence or two that captures the essence of the information.

FIGURE 10.3 Example of coded field notes.

Code	Field notes
teachers' work	Then I went down to the teachers' lounge to see if anybody might happen to be there. I was in luck. Jill Martin sat at the first table, correcting papers; Kathy Thomas was also there, walking around and smoking. I said, "Hi Jill, hi Kathy. Okay if I join you?" "Sure," Jill said. "You and your husband have been to China, right?" I said, "Yes. Why?" Jill then turned to Kathy and said, "Have you studied China yet? Sari has slides that she can show."
authority	Kathy said to me that she was going to study world communities, even though "they" had taken them out of the sixth-grade social studies curriculum. "Now can you tell me who 'they' are?" I asked her. She said, "You know, 'them': 'they.'"
autonomy	Both Jill and Kathy were upset at how "they" had mandated what the teachers could teach in their rooms. "They" turned out to be the central office who had communicated the state's revised sixth-grade social studies curriculum. The state has "taken out all the things that we think are important" from the curriculum and have substituted the theme of "economic geography" for the sixth-graders to study.
doing your own thing	Both Jill and Kathy think that "sixth-graders can't comprehend economic geography well," and think world communities of Africa and Asia are more important. They said they planned to teach what they wanted to anyway. Kathy said, "They'll come around one of these days." "Oh, Kathy, are you a rebel?" I asked. "No," she replied, "I'm just doing my own thing."
parents	After we chatted for a little while, Jill turned to me: "You're interested in what concerns us. I guess one thing is parents." She proceeded to describe a parent conference she had participated in yesterday
parents	afternoon with a child's parents and a child's psychiatrist. She said, "What really upsets me is how much responsibility they placed on me to change the child's behavior." They seemed to give lip service, she reported, to have "controls" come from the child when they said, "It's so difficult for parents to see that kids need to take responsibility for their actions."

Source: Bogdan, Robert C. and Biklen, Sari Knopp (2007). Qualitative research for education: An introduction to theories and methods (5th ed., p. 188). Published by Allyn and Bacon, Boston, MA.

A **category,** then, is formed from coded data as a more general and abstract idea that represents the meaning of similarly coded information. Some codes will be used in more than one category.

Category: Idea that represents coded data.

When the researcher is engaged in forming categories, a very important process occurs. This could be described as *recursive*. The recursive process involves the repeated application of a category to fit codes and data segments. This is sometimes called constant comparison, in which the researcher is continually searching for both supporting and contrary evidence about the meaning of the category. The recursive process is usually reported as part of data analysis. The recursive process is shown in Example 10.15.

EXAMPLE 10.15 | Recursive Analysis

Moreover, iterative methods were used to identify themes in the participant narratives. I fully transcribed each interview and read through the transcripts several times to pinpoint salient themes, patterns and relationships. . . . I coded the transcripts while reading them, and I repeatedly reevaluated my coding scheme. I looked for consistency and contradictions with and across the mother's narratives. Furthermore, I drafted three sets of memos that captured my preliminary analysis of the individual, school-based and cross-participant findings. Once I was confident of the trustworthiness and usefulness of my coding scheme, I clustered my data by code and did a final review. Inductive analytical methods were used to confirm or disconfirm the salience of my theoretical framework.

Source: Cooper, C. W. (2008). School choice as "motherwork": Valuing African-American women's educational advocacy and resistance. *International Journal of Qualitative Studies in Education, 20*(5), 498.

As with many data analysis procedures, computer software programs are available for qualitative data storage and analysis. A good source to compare the programs is a book by Ann Lewins and Christia Silver, Using Software for Qualitative Data Analysis: A Step-by-Step Guide (Thousand Oaks, CA: SAGE, 2007). The primary advantage of such software is that it is much easier to store and organize a large amount of data, and to search for and locate segments that are similar. This is similar to content analysis, where single words or like phrases can be pulled together with a click of the mouse. It is also possible to combine text with audio and visual components, and some programs provide a mapping of relationships among codes and categories.

Author Reflection *Like quantitative software, qualitative software is becoming more available and easier to use. I have done qualitative analyses both with and without a software program, and I'm partial to not relying too much on the computer to do my work. There is something to be said about reading transcripts all the way through, from the beginning to end of a single interview, to capture the essence of what is being said. Sometimes coding and categorizing too quickly make it difficult to understand the whole from the parts. Try doing qualitative analysis both ways—see what you think and compare your conclusions with others.*

Data Interpretation

Once the data have been coded and summarized, the researcher looks for relationships among the categories and patterns that suggest generalizations, models, and conclusions. At this point the researcher interprets the findings inductively, synthesizes the information, and draws inferences. The researcher essentially reveals what he or she has found and what it means. Because so much of the analysis depends on the researcher, it is best to know the researcher's perspectives, background, and theoretical orientation. For each major finding and interpretation, it is common for the researcher to use actual quotes from participants, field notes, or documents to illustrate the point and enliven the results. It also gives the reader an opportunity to see how the researcher has been thinking and the basis for conclusions.

A study of adult self-disclosure about having a learning disability presented five themes to organize the interview data the researchers obtained. Example 10.16 is an excerpt from one theme to show how exact quotes are used. The second excerpt, Example 10.17, is from a study on the use of higher-level thinking to enhance student self-regulation. Interviews were conducted with seven teachers.

EXAMPLES 10.16–10.17 | Use of Participant Quotes

In fact, 15 of the 18 interviewees offered responses that specifically referred to the stigma of their disability. For example, one adult said, "you feel terrible stupid. . . . I'm hesitant . . . the word *disability* . . . there's so many stigmas out there." A second explained, "It [disclosed learning disability] can be damaging to you." A third told us "The biggest thing I'm afraid of is people thinking I'm stupid and treating me differently, like my boyfriend's family does."

Source: Price, L. A., Gerber, P. J., Mulligan, R., & Williams, P. (2005). To be or not to be learning disabled: A preliminary report on self-disclosure and adults with learning disabilities. *Thalamus, 23*(2), 22.

Six of seven teachers interviewed for the study found writing higher-order thinking questions for reading assignments and quizzes to be initially challenging in that they had been used to prepare questions on the literal level of comprehension. As one teacher noted, "The greatest challenge I faced was maintaining the higher-order thinking skills notion when writing the questions. We've become so accustomed to asking literal questions and emphasizing the meaning of certain vocabulary words." Teachers regress just as well as students. Since students are more successful and comfortable with the literal interpretation of readings, teachers have become comfortable in asking literal questions.

Source: Cooper, J. E., Horn, S., & Strahan, D. B. (2005). If only they would do their homework: Promoting self-regulation in high school classes. *High School Journal, 88*(3), 19.

The process of pattern-seeking begins with the researcher's informed hunches and ideas as data are being collected and interpreted. Once tentative patterns are identified, additional data are examined to determine if they are consistent with that pattern. It is also common to have different researchers independently review data to see if they come up with the same patterns. This is a more deductive process, one in which there is a search for negative or discrepant data that would not support the pattern. Such a finding modifies the pattern. Pattern-seeking is also characterized by enlarging, combining, subsuming, and creating new categories that make sense logically. It is not uncommon to derive overarching models that show the relationships among several patterns in the findings visually, in the form of a diagram or chart. For example, a qualitative study of teachers' classroom assessment and grading decision making found that there were six major categories with subcategories that explained the data. Figure 10.4 identifies some of the data, codes, and categories from this study. Note how some data are used in more than one category.

FIGURE 10.4 A model of teacher assessment in decision making.

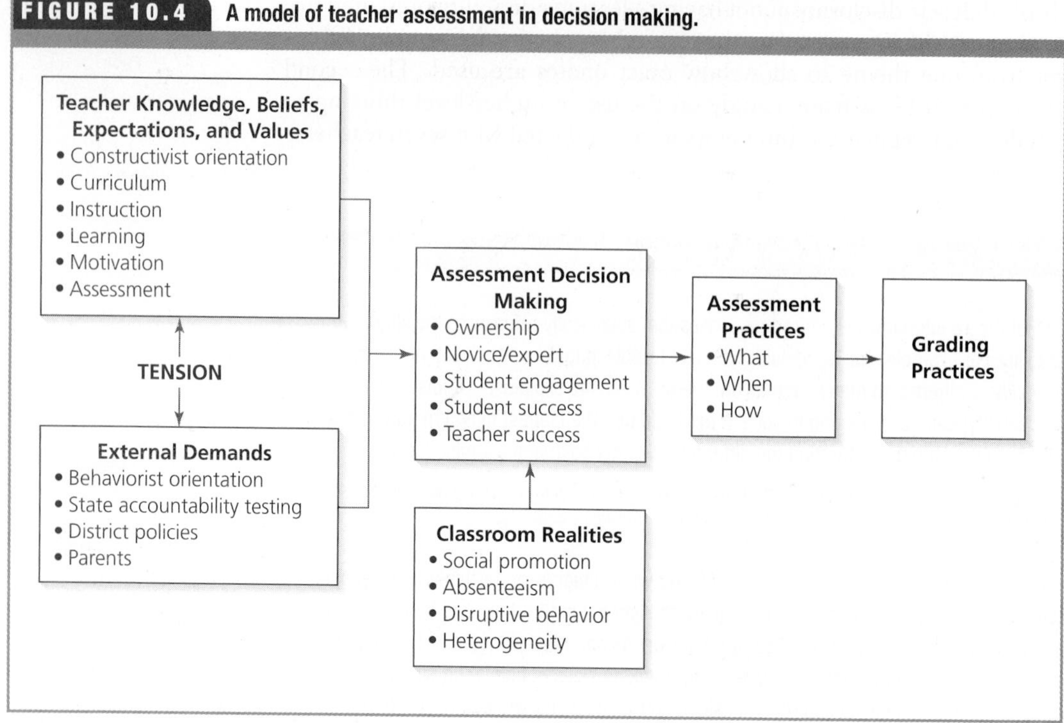

Source: Adapted from McMillan (2002).

CREDIBILITY

In quantitative research the criteria for credibility are based primarily on the validity and reliability of scores and on internal validity. In qualitative research somewhat different criteria are necessary because its approach, design, and data are different.

The primary criterion for evaluating qualitative studies is the *credibility* of the study. (Some qualitative researchers will use the terms *validity* or *internal validity* to refer to credibility—others won't use these quantitatively oriented terms.) **Credibility** is defined as the extent to which the data, data analysis, and conclusions are accurate and trustworthy. Are the themes and the patterns that emerge from the data plausible? Are they accurate, consistent, and meaningful? Are they authentic? How much confidence do you have in the results and conclusions?

Credibility: Accuracy and trustworthiness.

Qualitative researchers judge the credibility of a study from a holistic perspective. Creswell (2009) suggests eight procedures that can be used to enhance credibility in qualitative studies:

1. *Prolonged Engagement.* It is important for the researcher to be closely engaged with the participants and the setting to provide details for the narrative that presents the results. This suggests a need to have extensive experience and close involvement. There needs to be sufficient engagement

so that additional time in the setting or with the participants would not change the results. Think of prolonged engagement resulting in saturation—where additional observations or interviews or document review would not add new findings.

2. *Member Checking*. **Member checking** is completed when the researcher asks the participants to review interpretations and conclusions, and the participants confirm the findings. This could be accomplished by having participants review interviewer or observer conclusions about what was said or done if there is no recorded transcript. For example, an interviewer can summarize his or her notes at the end of the interview to see if the notes accurately reflect the point of view of the participants, if they are accurate. More important, the researcher can check with the participants about codes, categories, themes, patterns, and other findings to see if these are viewed by the participants as fair, reasonable, accurate, and complete. This can be accomplished by sharing drafts of final products, in writing or by interviews, and allowing participants opportunities to make comments (see Example 10.19).

Member checking: Participant review of data.

3. *Triangulation*. **Triangulation** is a technique that seeks convergence of findings, cross-validation, among different sources and methods of data collection. That is, data are collected from different individuals at different times or in different places, or several sources of data are used to see if the results are consistent. For example, if researchers are studying student engagement in a class, they could observe the students, interview the students, and ask the teacher for his or her opinion. Or the effectiveness of staff development could be judged by observing workshops and interviewing the participating teachers. If the results from each source of data point to the same conclusion, then the researcher has *triangulated* the findings (doesn't need three or more sources of data; can be done with two).

   Triangulation is perhaps the most widely used technique to establish credible findings. In Examples 10.18 and 10.19, the researchers used triangulation in their studies.

Triangulation: Compares the findings of different techniques.

EXAMPLES 10.18–10.19 | Triangulation

The credibility of the findings was verified through data triangulation . . . by using several sources: field notes by two persons, verbatim transcripts, multiple raters, moderator, observer, second rater, member checks the accuracy of notes, and stakeholder reviews.

Source: Gallagher, P. A., Rhodes, C. A., & Darling, S. M. (2004). Parents as professionals in early intervention: A parent educator model. *Topics in Early Childhood Special Education, 24*(1), 9.

Trustworthiness was established by first triangulating the data using multiple data sources, including teacher questionnaires, teacher interviews, and student interviews. Second, the teachers reviewed the transcribed interviews. This member-checking procedure (Creswell & Miller, 2000) permitted teachers to verify the content of the interviews and offer any clarification of points, if needed. . . . Finally, the data were examined by and discussed with a peer debriefer trained in qualitative research.

Source: Xiang, P., Solomon, M. A., & McBride, R. E. (2006). Teachers' and students' conceptions of ability in elementary physical education. *Research Quarterly for Exercise and Sport, 77*(2), 190.

4. *Negative Case Analysis.* Actively looking for findings that present discrepant information is needed to reflect the reality that not all data will provide the same result, and to change results when justified. Presenting negative cases enhances the credibility of the study because it shows that the researchers are examining the cases in detail. In other words, it's not only fine, it's good for the researchers to present information that contradicts themes, patterns, and overall results.
5. *Peer Debriefing.* Peer debriefing is completed by asking a colleague or another person to review the study for credibility and determine if the results seem to follow from the data. Someone who is knowledgeable about the topic and qualitative analyses, but sufficiently detached to provide a fresh perspective, is preferred. That person's own biases should be reflected in his or her evaluation, which gives feedback about the selection and meaning of categories, themes, patterns, and study conclusions.
6. *External Audit.* An external audit is similar to peer debriefing. An external auditor, however, is unfamiliar with the project and provides a more objective review. Like a peer debriefer, the external auditor examines all aspects of the study to look for coherence, reasonableness, accuracy, data analysis, interpretation, and conclusions, and points out weaknesses or "threats" to credibility.
7. *Researcher Reflection.* The researcher's self-reflection of possible biases, background, and values supports the credibility of the study. It is important to know that the researcher understands how his or her own perspectives, shaped by gender, socioeconomic status, or position, will influence his or her expectations, interpretations, and conclusions. Good qualitative researchers know that their subjectivity may influence results, and direct examination of this subjectivity, through reflection, adds to credibility. This is reflected in the excerpt in Example 10.20.

EXAMPLE 10.20 | Researcher Reflection

My social positionality as a Caucasian, able-bodied male may have detracted from the study because of my culturally- and socially-imposed blinders to the realities of other peoples' experiences different from my own—which may have been manifested in the classroom to an important extent without my even knowing it. Using the strategy of progressive subjectivity (Guba and Lincoln, 1989) to record my initial and on-going expectations of how I thought authority would be negotiated in the classroom, however, helped assure that I moved beyond my initial preconceptions and effectively derived the finds from the actual words and actions of participants.

Source: Brubaker, N. D. (2009). Negotiating authority in an undergraduate teacher education course: A qualitative investigation. *Teacher Education Quarterly, 36*(4), 104.

8. *Thick Descriptions.* Credible qualitative studies use detailed, in-depth, thorough, and extensive descriptions, what is sometimes described as "thick" and/or "rich." That is, there is abundant use of detail. This enhances credibility because it indicates extensive engagement with the data and an appreciation of how all information is valuable. It enables the reader to understand the complexity and realism of the site and participants. For example, a rich, detailed description of a college student commons may be needed to understand the dynamics of students meeting there for discussions with faculty. Thick descriptions include presenting verbatim language from participants and detailed field notes. The research procedures should also be described in detail.

Note in the following example how multiple methods of data collection are utilized to ensure trustworthiness and reliability (accuracy). This study took three years to complete, which surely meets the criteria of having sufficient length!

EXAMPLE 10.21 | Establishing Credibility

In this study, the accuracy of the observations and the trustworthiness of this investigation were enhanced by the use of tape-recorded interviews and field notes that enabled the researcher to examine and clarify information; photography that was used to document and study specific situations and/or settings that required more than a single view; triangulation between methods; depth of detail; and continuous cross-checking for accuracy. The methods, procedures, and strategies used to ensure accuracy included: observations of informants in various settings; interviews with informants, teachers, relatives, and others; document review; and photography.

Source: Reis, S. M., Colbert, R. D., & Jebert, T. P. (2005). Understanding resilience in diverse, talented students in an urban high school. *Roeper Review, 27* (2), 113.

GENERALIZABILITY

Generalizability in qualitative studies is very different from what is used for quantitative studies. In qualitative studies, there is no intent to generalize to other participants, settings, instruments, interventions, or procedures. There is little or no emphasis on replications, except with some case study research. Qualitative researchers use the term *transferability* to get at generalizability. **Transferability** refers to the appropriateness of applying the results to other contexts and settings. It is enhanced by a thick description of the site, participants, and procedures used to collect data. This makes it easier for the person wanting to apply the results to his or her setting to know whether or not there is a good fit, if it makes sense to generalize. In qualitative research the person who wants to use findings from one study in their context, rather than the researcher of the original study, is responsible for determining generalizability.

Transferability: Application of findings to similar contexts.

If the contextual, participant, and procedural details match, the user has greater confidence that it is appropriate to generalize the findings.

CONSUMER TIPS: *Criteria for Evaluating Qualitative Research*

1. **The researcher's background, interests, and expectations should be clear.** Because a qualitative study is influenced greatly by the researcher's perspective, it is necessary to know the researcher's background—previous experiences, motivations for the research, and characteristics that may affect the recording or interpretation of data. Good qualitative researchers acknowledge how their expectations and preconceived ideas affect what they observe, interpret, and conclude.

2. **The conceptual and theoretical frameworks for the study should be clear.** The frameworks selected by the researcher guide the study and affect the results. You should look for an explanation of such frameworks early in the study, along with other thoughts and perceptions of the researcher.

3. **The method of selecting participants should be clear.** Qualitative studies often investigate a few persons in depth rather than many subjects more superficially. Consequently, the choice of subjects is critical to the results of the study. The researcher should indicate how and why the participants were selected and the extent to which they are representative of others in the setting.

4. **Field notes should contain detailed objective descriptions of just about everything.** This goal may seem impossible, but it is one for which qualitative researchers strive. They should give detailed descriptions of behaviors and indicate the place, time, date, and physical setting of the observations. The descriptions should avoid using interpretive words such as *effective*, *positive attitude*, and *hostile*. Field notes that are not detailed suggest that the researcher may have missed important behaviors or may have biases that anticipated the results.

5. **Researchers should be trained to conduct data collection.** Because the researchers are directly involved in collecting data, either as observers, interviewers, or reviewers of documents and artifacts, they should be trained in the procedures they use. Although adequate training is not easy to determine, you should look for some indication of previous experience that has been checked for adequacy. Untrained researchers are tempted to conduct qualitative research because it sounds so promising and interesting (and does not involve statistics). What often occurs is that there is usually a cursory level of involvement.

6. **The credibility of the research should be addressed.** Researchers should summarize their procedures to enhance the credibility of the findings (e.g., triangulation, member checking, thick descriptions).

7. **Descriptions should be separate from interpretations.** In the core of a qualitative article you will find specific and general descriptions of what was observed or recorded and interpretations of the data. The descriptions are the basis for the researcher's analyses and interpretations. If these descriptions

are not clearly separate from the analyses and interpretations, it is difficult for you to judge the reasonableness of the researcher's claims (e.g., if there was selective presentation of data or if inductive processes seem reasonable on the basis of the data presented). It is also difficult to know if the researcher was objective in recording or observing behavior.

8. The researcher should use multiple methods of data collection. The quality of qualitative research is greatly enhanced by multiple methods of collecting data. If only one method is used, the findings may be significantly influenced by the limitations of the technique. Multiple methods allow for triangulation, which is the strongest type of evidence for the credibility of the findings. If the study is limited to one method, its limitations should be addressed.

9. The study must be long enough. Accurate and credible qualitative research requires the researcher to become intimately involved with what is being studied, to know it completely. It usually takes a long time to achieve this intense level of involvement. It cannot be done in interviews of 20 minutes or observations that last a few hours. You need to know how much time the researcher spent with the participants. Sufficient time will be reflected in the detailed data and in the researcher's depth of understanding.

ANATOMY *of a* QUALITATIVE RESEARCH STUDY

The following case study uses a variety of ethnographic techniques to collect qualitative data.

ARTICLE 10.1 Learning on the Job: An Analysis of the Aquisition of a Teacher's Knowledge

Paul G. Schempp
The University of Georgia

This study analyzed the criteria used by an experienced teacher to acquire the knowledge necessary to teach. An interpretive analytic framework and case study methodology were used in this yearlong project with a midcareer high school teacher. Data were collected using a variety of ethnographic techniques including: nonparticipant observations, artifact and document analysis, stimulated recall from videotapes, and formal and informal interviews. Data analysis followed the conventions described by Glaser and Strauss (1967). Five distinct knowledge categories were identified each with unique selection criteria. These knowledge forms included: class organization and operation, teaching behavior, subject matter, pedagogical content knowledge (Shulman, 1986), and external conditions. In matters of class organization and operation, Bob (the teacher) looked to his experience for those things that worked (i.e., insured classroom order). The acquisition of instructional behavior came largely from observations of other teachers (e.g., cooperating teacher, peers) or from experience. Bob selected subject matter knowledge based upon previous knowledge, current personal interests, resource availability, and student interest. Pedagogical content knowledge was comprised in three phases: demonstrations, drills, and activities. External conditions were influences outside the classroom (e.g., laws, school policy). Years of occupational service have left Bob with a well developed set of criteria upon which he acquires the knowledge to teach.

Case study of a single teacher

ARTICLE 10.1 (continued)

A distinguishing characteristic of any profession is the body of knowledge for practicing that profession. Professionals are called into service because they bring a unique undestanding and critical insight to a situation that is inaccessible to the uninitiated. It is the body of professional knowledge that explains what those in a particular occupation do and why (Schon, 1983). The body of knowledge currently used in a profession is, therefore, of major concern to those practicing the profession and preparing future practitioners. . . .

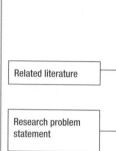

Related literature

Within the last decade, educational researchers have studied rules and principles used in teacher thinking (Elbaz, 1983), teachers' classroom images (Clandinin, 1985), the experience of classroom cycles and rhythms (Clandinin & Connelly, 1986), subject matter expertise (Leinhardt & Smith, 1985), and pedagogical content knowledge (Grossman 1989; Gudmundsdottir & Kristjansdottir, 1989). These studies, and other similar work, represent the start of a growing trend in research into what teachers know and how they use that knowledge in their classrooms. This study continues that line of inquiry by offering a glimpse into the world of an experienced high school teacher. Specifically, this case study examines the criteria one teacher employed in acquiring the knowledge he found necessary for his professional practice.

Research problem statement

METHOD

Teacher

Detailed description of the teacher

Robert Halstop has taught high school physical education for the past 14 years at Hillcrest High School (HHS). Over those years, Bob has coached many sports and been involved in numerous school clubs, groups, and projects. At the time of this study, he was coaching the girls' varsity basketball team. Besides teaching and coaching, he performed normal student counseling activities and other school duties assigned by the administrators. Bob worked at a local lumber mill during the summers, but did not work outside the school during the academic year. Bob's school day officially began at 7:30 a.m. and ended at 3:30 p.m., but he was usually in school much earlier and it was common for him to stay later. There were seven instructional periods in the day. Bob was assigned six classes, one planning period, and had a 30-minute lunch break. . . .

Setting

Description of context

Hillcrest is a small, rural community in the Pacific Northwest. Education was held in high esteem as evidenced by the town having one of the highest tax bases in the state. Hillcrest High School enrolled approximately 470 students. Two years before this study, HHS received an educational excellence award from the United States Department of Education. All first-year students were required to take physical education for one year and could elect physical education after that. The freshman physical education classes were separated by gender and were taught as a survey course to cover many subject areas. The other physical education classes were coeducational and defined by student interest (e.g., recreational sports, weight training). HHS had two physical education teachers: one for boys (Bob) and one for girls (Kathy).

Data Collection

Data were collected and analyzed using a variety of qualitative techniques. Among these techniques were nonparticipant observation, artifact and document analyses, stimulated recall using videotaped classes, and both formal and informal interviews. Besides Bob, Kathy and other school personnel (e.g., students, teachers, administrators) were also interviewed. Field notes were recorded during and after observations and a summary statement was made off site after each day of data collection. Data collection began 2 days before the start of school and officially ended just before the Christmas break. I was present in the school on a daily basis for the first month of the study and made field trips twice a week on average after that.

Data Analyses

Data analysis began on the first day of the study and ended approximately l year later. Concurrently collecting and analyzing data allowed me to develop data summary themes and check the emerging themes against recurring field activities. Analyzing data during the study also allowed data collection techniques to be tailored to gather data that were amenable to testing and understanding the emerging themes. Specific strategies employed to insure data trustworthiness included triangulation of methods, member checks (particularly the use of key informants and the constant use of follow-up interviews to check consistency of responses), disconfirming case analyses (the investigation of responses and/or occurrences that were incompatible with emerging themes), and cultivating reactions from the case-study teacher to the themes, categories, and events to be included in the final report.

My key informant was Bob's teaching colleague, Kathy. At the time of this study, Kathy and Bob had been teaching physical education together at Hillcrest for 3 years. Kathy was particularly helpful in cross-checking stories and events described by Bob. In cases where discrepant information occurred (e.g., differences between what Bob told me and what I observed) Kathy often provided valuable insights.

Data analysis involved summarizing data into themes and categories using procedures recommended by Miles and Huberman (1984), Goetz and LeCompte (1984), and Patton (1980). The construction of these categories was influenced by Shulman's (1987) theory of a knowledge base for teaching. He identified seven categories of teachers' knowledge: subject matter, general pedagogical, curriculum, pedagogical content, learners, contexts, and purposes. As themes emerged and clustered into categories, these categories were checked against Shulman's propositions. Four of Shulman's seven categories were ultimately used to describe the forms of knowledge Bob acquired in pursuit of his professional practice: subject matter, general pedagogical (renamed teaching behavior), pedagogical content, and context (renamed external conditions). Classroom organization and operation was a category constructed independent of Shulman's theory as it appeared to better describe a dominant form of Bob's knowledge.

The themes and categories identified forms of knowledge as well as the criteria Bob used in acquiring pedagogical knowledge. The categories allowed the data to be summarized and reported in a succinct, yet accurate, manner. The first step was to review the collected data to determine tentative categories. Next, the data were coded using the tentative scheme. The category scheme underwent revisions until the data were able to be classified within the scheme with no redundancy of categories. The constant comparison method of analysis (Glaser & Strauss, 1967) was used to identify these patterns and relationships.

The final step of the analytic procedure was to present a copy of the report to Bob for his comments and reactions. The findings were brought back to the case study teacher so that he could: (a) check the accuracy of the data (reliability), and (b) validate the findings of the report. This procedure was considered a critical component for establishing the validity and trustworthiness of the study's findings (Lather, 1916). Additional revisions were then made based on the responses and reactions from the teacher. Events contained in the report seen by Bob as either inaccurate or threatening to confidentiality were rechecked and eliminated where appropriate. Bob's comments and additional supporting evidence were incorporated into the final draft of the report to lend strength to the propositions put forth.

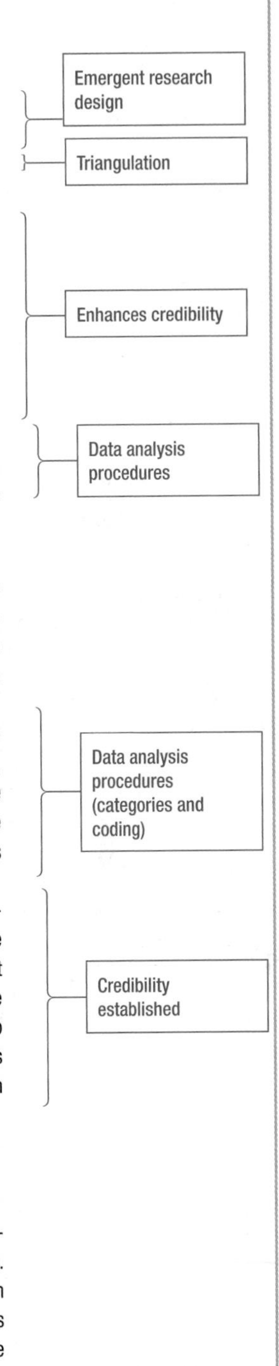

FINDINGS

From years of contact with many sources of occupationally useful information, Bob had constructed a comfortable set of criteria for evaluating and selecting knowledge necessary for his day-to-day classroom operation. He seemed to have a clear sense of both the expectations others held for him and his own purpose for being in the school. These criteria formed a screen through which all potential pedagogical knowledge passed. Bob's knowledge acquisition represented an intersection between the demands of his day-to-day practice and the

(continued)

ARTICLE 10.1 (continued)

knowledge available to meet those demands. Thus, Bob appropriated knowledge based upon his perception of the power and quality of its source, and his perception of its potential to solve a recurring problem or improve a current practice.

Categories emerged from the data

In analyzing the data, five knowledge categories emerged: (a) classroom organization and operation, (b) teaching behavior, (c) subject matter, (d) pedagogical content knowledge, and (e) external conditions. Each category was unique in terms of the problems it addressed, the sources from which it came, and the criteria that determined knowledge selection and rejection.

Class Organization and Operation

Like many teachers (West, 1975; Yinger, 1980), classroom order and control were predominant concerns for Bob. The concern for classroom organization and controlled operation rose from Bob's belief that, if order was not established and the classroom not operated in the manner he needed, little could be accomplished. In his own words,

Direct quote to illustrate findings

> I'm going to get across more to kids in a structured setting. Otherwise kids are pretty much allowed to go where they want to and pick and choose what they want to take and what they don't want to take. . . . I have more kids working at a higher level than I would otherwise.

Relationship to literature

. . . Bob, like many teachers (Clandinin, 1985; Clandinin & Connelly, 1986), relied on practical rules and principles, routines, and habits to guide classroom operation rather than inflexible standards or absolute rules.

Bob perceived the ability to organize and operate a class to be a fundamental and critical responsibility of a teacher. When asked "What would you look for in a high school teacher to determine if they were a good teacher?" he responded with a list of criteria heavily skewed toward organizational and operational concerns. His list included: (a) the kids are paying attention; (b) gives directions clearly and the kids respond to directions showing that they heard; (c) what he said made good sense; (d) organized drills, organized calisthenics, lesson didn't get bogged down; (e) didn't let a few kids take over the lesson; and (f) didn't get distracted from where he wanted to go.
[Discussion of findings continues.]

Teaching Behavior

A significant portion of Bob's everyday actions and activities were devoted to the task of instructing students. Knowledge for meeting these demands was classified by Shulman (1987) as general pedagogical knowledge, for this knowledge transcended a particular subject content. Much of Bob's teaching behavior was characterized by well-rehearsed, time-worn rituals. Every class began with student-led exercises while Bob took attendance. Then Bob informed the students of the day's activities. A brief skill demonstration or explanation was followed by a drill. Most classes closed with a game or culminating activity. Sometimes, a game was played for the entire class period. The practices that defined Bob's teaching behavior were largely composed of comfortable habits and familiar routines. In crafting a teaching style, comfort does not appear to be an uncommon criterion among teachers (Lange & Burroughs-Lange, 1994; Russell & Johnston, 1988).

Importance of participant perspectives

Bob did not actively pursue knowledge that directly affected his instructional practices. The roots of this perspective can be traced to his undergraduate days. "When I was going through college," he said, "they didn't have any methods classes. None. Zero." The fundamental criterion used to determine the success of a lesson was, therefore, not so much what students learned, but rather their level of enjoyment. During one interview Bob told me that "they really seem to enjoy it (the activity). They develop certain skills. The more skill they develop, the more they seem to enjoy it."
[Discussion of findings continues.]

Although student learning was a concern in Bob's occupational activity, it was not the driving force behind his pedagogical practices. He harbored a stronger concern for maintaining control over the collective social behavior of the students. He showed far greater frustration when there was a breach of order than when students failed to make significant learning gains. The concern for classroom control over educational substance has been a consistent finding in research on physical education teachers' conceptions of their occupational duties and responsibilities (Placek, 1983; Schempp, 1985, 1986).

Relationship to literature

The immediate and multiple demands placed on Bob's time in school often relegated the learning of his approximately 130 students to the back burner of his priorities. During one observation, Bob and I were in his office between classes and I remarked, "I can't believe all the things you have to attend to." His comment was

> Yeah, there's a lot going on. Right now I'm trying to get a test set up, get the equipment I need for that, worry about the two kids who are on their way to the counselors' office to drop the class, answer kids' questions about what we're doing today, think about that indoor soccer ball for next period, I have two home counseling visits coming up, remember to read the announcements this period, and I have an executive school meeting.

Illustrative quote

He rose out of his chair, picked up his roster book, glanced over a tardy note pushed into his hand by a late student, and was on his way to take roll and begin another class.

Detailed observation

Subject Matter

The content of Bob's classes was described and detailed in a curriculum guide he had compiled. Objectives for each program were identified and the policies used to conduct the program were also described. The largest portion of the guide was composed of the specific subject-matter units. When asked about the resources used to complete the guide, Bob told me that most of the units came from an undergraduate curriculum course assignment. He has added to the guide materials and resources gathered at in-service programs.

Although the guide was a 148-page document and included an outline of each subject taught, it was used sparingly. Over the course of my time with Bob, I observed him using the guide perhaps a half dozen times, mostly to review teaching points for an upcoming lesson or remind himself of game rules. The guide did not hold the majority of subject matter Bob taught, for experience has taught him that he must "keep most of the (subject matter) knowledge organized in my head and I can't write it down because everything is situation specific."

In-depth anecdotal observation

Bob acquired new subject-matter knowledge based upon these criteria: (a) perceptions of his own competence in teaching the subject, (b) personal interest in the subject matter, (c) perceptions of student interest, (d) actual student demand as demonstrated by elective class enrollments, (e) time investment necessary to teach or prepare to teach the subject, (f) the novelty of the subject, and (g) facility and equipment constraints.

Bob reported that gymnastics and outdoor education were two content areas recently dropped. Gymnastics was no longer offered because Bob did not like teaching it and had a concern for liability. Outdoor education was no longer part of the curriculum because the individual who taught the course had left the school and Bob did not want to give up his weekends for the activities. Weight training was a new subject added to the course offerings because of student demand, Bob's personal interest in teaching the subject, and the availability of an adequate facility. Personal understanding and meaning of subject matter plays an important role in Bob's acquisition and use of content knowledge. Teachers in other subject areas also appear to rely on personal understanding in selecting content (Wilson & Wineburg, 1988).

Importance of detailed description

By his own admission, Bob is not an expert in many of the areas he teaches. Rather, he knows enough to teach a 10-day unit in the selected subject. He would draw from the subject areas in which he had expertise to bolster areas that were unfamiliar. For example, soccer drills were structured very much like basketball drills. Bob was required to teach over 23 different units in any given year. It would be difficult for any teacher to be knowledgeable in so many different subjects.

[Discussion of findings continues.]

(continued)

ARTICLE 10.1 (continued)

Pedagogical Content Knowledge

Shulman (1986) defines pedagogical content knowledge as content knowledge "which goes beyond knowledge of subject matter per se to the dimension of subject matter for teaching" (p. 9). Years of experience have forged a mode of operation, a routine, which frames the knowledge Bob imparts to his students. Bob seeks curricular content that fits his teaching style. In pedagogical practice, he teaches an activity in terms of its essential skills by giving brief explanations and sometimes demonstrations, then has students practice these skills through drills, and after varying amounts of practice the students are then given the rules and play the game. These procedures have been used for years by Bob with all varieties of subject matter. He is, therefore, more inclined to select new activities that fit his mode of operation than he is to look for new ways to teach old subject matter. Further, Bob was less likely to teach subject matter in depth and more likely to teach many activities at the introductory level. The more new information conveniently fits into familiar routines, the more likely it would be incorporated.

Findings compared to literature

Bob's content knowledge appeared to not only influence what he teaches, but how he teaches. Activities, particularly skill drills, were borrowed from better-known subject lessons and adapted and applied in lesser-known subject areas. In concept explanations, metaphors and images were drawn from parallel concepts in better-known subjects and used to help explain subject concepts that he did not know well. Bob does not appear unique in this regard. Teachers of mathematics (Leinhardt & Smith, 1985; Marks, 1990), social studies (Gudmundsdottir & Shulman, 1987), and English (Grossman, 1989, 1990; Gudmundsdottir, 1991) all seem to follow this process in acquiring and developing pedagogical content knowledge.

Importance of participant's wording of explanations

As Bob screened new content knowledge for his pedagogical practice, he used the term practical to identify acceptable pedagogical content knowledge. For example, in explaining why he takes few university courses, he stated he had "a great deal of difficulty finding coursework of relevance for a teacher in my situation. A lot of philosophy, theory, etc., but not many practical, time-proven methods which I can use in my class." Another time, he identified coaching clinics as more worthwhile than teaching workshops because the clinics "offer practical information that can be directly implemented into our program." Content that could be incorporated into the existing classroom routines and rituals was highly valued. Previous research reveals that Bob is not alone in his regard for knowledge that is easily imported into existing classroom practices (Alexander, Muir, & Chant, 1992; Elbaz, 1983).

External Conditions

Conditions originating outside the classroom, and removed from Bob's immediate control, came to bear on several pedagogical decisions. These conditions include local regulations and requirements that were imposed by the administration and school board as well as regulations and laws handed down from state and federal agencies. Therefore, the wishes and demands of administrators, students, parents, and state agencies factored into Bob's procurement of knowledge. The influence of administrators, parents, and students on Bob's knowledge was discussed above. School and state regulations also influenced him, but to a far lesser degree.
[Discussion of findings continues.]

CONCLUSION

After years of service, Bob had a well developed set of criteria to guide his acquisition of occupational knowledge. These criteria allowed Bob to identify gaps in his knowledge and to assess new knowledge in light of its potential contribution to his teaching. Contrary to the belief of many students, administrators, and colleagues, Bob continually reviewed and screened new information and then made attempts to integrate this knowledge into his professional practice. Because the criteria used in acquiring new knowledge were primarily comprised of experiences, interests, values, beliefs, and orientations, Bob's professional knowledge appeared personal and idiosyncratic (Carter, 1990); Zeichner, Tabachnick, & Densmore, 1987). Bob was, by his own admission, set in his ways. Therefore, the changes and alterations he did make were neither dramatic nor overtly visible. In short, little changed in the observable practices of Bob's day-to-day activities as a teacher and he became fairly predictable in his course of action.

Classroom order and operation held the highest priority in Bob's pedagogical knowledge. Subject matter that fit his personal interests, workplace conditions, and would result in student enjoyment had the greatest chance of penetrating the curriculum. New knowledge that conformed to his well-worn classroom practices passed Bob's test of valued professional knowledge. He acknowledged a lack of information regarding effective teaching behavior, and given his workplace conditions, this situation appears to have little chance to change. Will Bob ever change? He is, in fact, always changing as new information comes to him and is incorporated into his professional knowledge base. In the final analysis, however, Bob's time in service has made him well aware of who he is, what he does, why he does it, and what knowledge is required for him to meet the demands of teaching in a public school.

REFERENCES

Alexander, D., Muir, D., & Chant, D. (1992). Interrogating stories: How teachers think they learn to teach. *Teaching and Teacher Education, 8,* 59–68.

Carter, K. (1990). Teachers' knowledge and learning to teach. In W. R. Houston (Ed.) *Handbook of Research on Teacher Education* (pp. 291–330). New York: Macmillan.

Clandinin, D. J. (1985). Personal practical knowledge: A study of teachers' classroom images. *Curriculum Inquiry, 15,* 361–385.

Clandinin, D. J., & Connelly, F. M. (1986). Rhythms in teaching: The narrative study of teachers' personal practical knowledge of classrooms. *Teaching and Teacher Education, 2,* 377–387.

Doyle, W. (1986). Classroom organization and management (pp. 392–431). In M. Wittrock (Ed.) *Handbook of Research on Teaching* (3rd ed.). New York: Macmillan.

[References continue.]

Author Reflection *Heed this warning if you want to do qualitative research: Patience and extensive periods of time are needed for gathering, analyzing, synthesizing, and interpreting the data. The amount of time needed to do good qualitative research almost always surprises people. At first it seems so simple—just do some interviewing or observation—but if it remains simple, so will the results. I learned this lesson well in one of the first qualitative studies I directed, on the resilience of at-risk students. I continually miscalculated the amount of time needed to do the study, always thinking that it should take less time than it did. Plan accordingly when carrying out (or reading) qualitative studies so you won't be frustrated in this electronic age of immediacy. You will likely be rewarded with a depth of understanding that will have lasting and positive impacts.*

STUDY QUESTIONS

1. What are the major characteristics of qualitative research?
2. What is the difference between qualitative research and ethnography?
3. How are participants usually selected for a qualitative study?
4. What types of roles may a qualitative observer assume in a study?
5. Why is it necessary to have detailed field notes?
6. What are different ways to conduct qualitative interviews?
7. How are ethnographic and case study data analyzed?
8. What is the fundamental difference between ethnographies and case studies, phenomenological studies, and grounded theory?
9. What is the relationship between codes, categories, and patterns?
10. What are some approaches for establishing the credibility of qualitative studies?
11. How is qualitative research generalized to other settings and people?

Chapter 11

Mixed-Method Designs

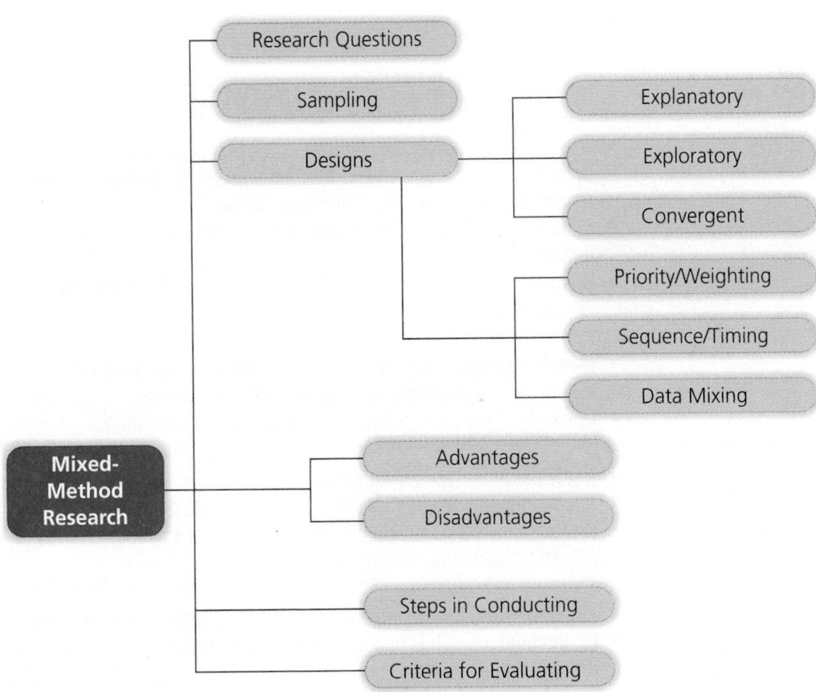

With the assistance of Gina Pannozzo for the Fifth Edition

CHAPTER ROAD MAP

In contrast to the research designs presented in previous chapters, this chapter examines those that involve combining quantitative and qualitative methods in a single study. Mixed-method designs are grounded in the idea that despite having different philosophical assumptions about how research problems can best be understood, as well as different purposes and procedures, researchers can (and sometimes should) capitalize on the strengths of each method. Rather than thinking in terms of interpreting research problems from one or the other perspective, which often leaves out important pieces of the puzzle, mixed-method designs allow us to put together the pieces to form a more complete picture.

Chapter Outline	Learning Objectives
Characteristics of Mixed-Method Studies	• Understand the essential characteristics of mixed-method studies. • Be able to explain why mixed-method studies can provide stronger results than studies using either quantitative or qualitative methods. • Be able to identify the advantages and disadvantages of mixed-method designs. • Be able to describe situations in which mixed-method designs would be appropriate.
Research Questions	• Be able to identify key components of research questions for explanatory, exploratory, and convergent-type studies. • Understand the logic communicated in research questions.
Sampling	• Know common types of sampling for mixed-method studies. • Know unique types of sampling for mixed-method studies. • Understand how sampling in one phase of a mixed-method study influences sampling in another phase.
Mixed-Method Designs	• Know the logic of explanatory, exploratory, and triangulation designs. • Understand when it is appropriate to use explanatory, exploratory, and triangulation designs. • Be able to recognize and generate examples of explanatory, exploratory, and convergent designs.
Conducting Mixed-Method Studies	• Understand how priority/weighting and sequence/timing are important considerations in planning a mixed-method study. • Know when it is appropriate to use data mixing. • Know the steps that are appropriate in conducting a mixed-method study.
Evaluating Mixed-Method Studies	• Know the criteria for evaluating mixed-method studies. • Apply the criteria for evaluating mixed-method studies to a published example. • Be able to read, understand, and critique a mixed-method study.

WHY MIXED-METHOD STUDIES?

First there was quantitative, then qualitative approaches to research. Now there is a third: mixed-method. Why do we have this third kind of study? Why is it needed given the acceptance of both quantitative and qualitative methods? The answer rests in part on the limitations of each of these two traditions, and the realization that sometimes the best approach to answering important research questions is to use both qualitative and quantitative methods in the same study. This is especially the case when the goal or purpose of the research is to obtain an understanding of both product and process, or outcomes and explanations of outcomes. For example, evidence gathered from teacher surveys might help a school administrator understand how teachers think and feel about the implementation of a new policy, but it may not adequately explain the barriers or resistance teachers perceive that make it difficult for them to implement the new policy. Mixed-method designs are also useful when the results of quantitative data collection and analysis do not adequately explain the outcomes and additional data is needed to help interpret the findings. This is particularly useful when there are individuals or a small group of individuals whose outcomes differ in significant ways from the pattern of outcomes for the majority of the sample (e.g., outliers) or from our expectations. Finally, researchers might also choose to use mixed-method designs when they first need to identify variables, key concepts, and themes through qualitative data collection in advance of using quantitative techniques to further investigate a problem. In these situations, the qualitative data collection and analysis provide useful information to the researcher by highlighting the important factors and relevant questions that become the focus of subsequent quantitative investigation. Note in Example 11.1 how the authors delineate their justification for using a mixed-method study.

EXAMPLE 11.1 | Justification for a Mixed-Method Design

The present investigation was based on a longitudinal mixed-methodology case study of a large, high poverty district's experiences during a decade of accountability-focused reform efforts. A mixed-method design was chosen in a pragmatic effort to capture the widest range of effects of accountability efforts (the what and so what of reform efforts together with a range of participants' perspectives of how and why various reforms were attempted.

Source: Stringfield, S. C., & Yakimouwski-Srebnick, M. E. (2005). Promise, progress, problems, and paradoxes of three phases of accountability: A longitudinal case study of the Baltimore City Public Schools. *American Educational Research Journal, 42*(1).

Consider investigating whether there is a relationship between high-stakes testing results and the dropout rate. On the surface, this question lends itself nicely to a nonexperimental, quantitative study in which characteristics of students can be entered into a regression model, including scores on high-stakes tests, to determine if performance on the tests predicts dropping out once other variables have been controlled. On a deeper level, it would also be helpful to understand why students did not perform better on the tests and how having failed to pass high-stakes tests affects students' motivation to graduate. These issues could be studied most effectively with qualitative data gathered from student and teacher interviews. By combining the qualitative data with quantitative data, a more complete understanding of the relationship between the variables can be obtained, and incomplete, inconsistent, or unexplained findings can be clarified and resolved.

The idea of mixing methods, however, is not like making bouillabaisse or a stew! It's not as if the methods are changed. It's more a matter of using more than one method in a single study. Other terms are sometimes used interchangeably with mixed-method, including *mixed methodology*, *multiple methods*, *blended research*, *triangulated studies*, *hybrid*, and *integrative research*. In reading research literature, you will find that different ideas exist about what constitutes mixed-method, and that there is a trend toward using the term rather liberally to include any study that has some degree of both quantitative and qualitative methods. Does this mean that if a survey is created to ask open-ended questions and content analysis procedures are used to analyze these responses, mixed-method applies? Or, if in an experiment the researcher observes the intervention and notes anything important in what is occurring, does this mean it's mixed-method? In these situations the use of the open-ended questions and observations is simply a way of supplementing the main purpose of quantitative studies, and they would not be considered mixed-method.

For an investigation to be mixed-method, there needs to be an integrative approach in which different paradigms are used in the same study. Thus, it is more than using both quantitative and qualitative methods of gathering, analyzing, and reporting data separately. Rather, there needs to be a convergence of philosophies, traditions, methods, logic, and principles of adequacy. This is what makes mixed-method studies unique and results in enhancement, insight, clarification, and explanation that would not be possible if either method was used without the other.

ADVANTAGES *and* DISADVANTAGES *of* USING MIXED-METHOD DESIGNS

There are several advantages to using mixed-method designs when conducting research (Table 11.1). Of these, the two biggest advantages are (1) the ability to provide more a thorough understanding of a research problem because of the opportunity to examine multiple forms of data that are more comprehensive than data that might be collected via either quantitative or qualitative methods alone; and (2) the ability to answer complex research questions that cannot be addressed through the use of quantitative or qualitative methods alone. In addition, the use of mixed methods allows researchers to capitalize on what are viewed as the strengths of one method in a way that compensates for what have typically been viewed as the weaknesses of the other. These are particularly relevant given the nature and complexity of most educational settings. Focusing on an outcome (e.g., student achievement) doesn't necessarily help us understand how we "get

TABLE 11.1 Advantages and Disadvantages of Mixed-Method Research

Advantages	Disadvantages
Provides more comprehensive data	Researcher needs an ability to conduct and interpret results from both quantitative and qualitative designs
Includes multiple approaches to compensate for disadvantages with using a single method	May require more extensive data collection
Allows investigation of different types of questions in a single study	May require more time and resources
Allows examination of complex research questions	Difficult to combine approaches when writing reports and forming conclusions
Includes triangulation to enhance credibility of the findings	

there"; similarly, sometimes we focus so much on process that we lose sight of where we're going. Mixing methods allows us to keep both in the forefront.

There are also some distinct disadvantages to using mixed-method designs. First and foremost, the ability to successfully implement a mixed-method study requires the researcher to have a level of expertise and comfort with both quantitative and qualitative methods. A passing or rudimentary level of understanding of procedures and data analysis techniques is not sufficient enough to allow you to present credible findings. Gaining the required level of expertise requires study and practical application of each method. Second, mixed-method research typically involve data collection (and subsequent analysis) that is more extensive and labor intensive, takes more time, and requires more resources than might be required of a study employing either quantitative or qualitative methods alone. As a result, researchers who wish to use mixed methods may choose to collaborate in partnerships to which each brings a different methodological expertise.

Finally, as you may have experienced in reading various research articles, the writing style and format used to report the results of quantitative and qualitative studies are different. These differences can make it challenging to report the results of a mixed-method study in a way that balances the writing style and format of each individual method, and at the same time integrates findings to present a coherent report rather than reading as though two separate studies have been combined into a single report.

RESEARCH QUESTIONS *for* MIXED-METHOD STUDIES

As emphasized in Chapter 2, good research begins with clear research questions that are then matched to methodology. Since in mixed-method studies there are quantitative and qualitative methods, both quantitative and qualitative questions are appropriate. These questions will usually indicate the logic of the design. If both types of data are collected at about the same time, the design may focus on convergence of the information resulting from each method, giving equal emphasis to each. This may be called a *convergent* or *triangulation* type of study, with all questions stated together. If the logic of the design is *explanatory*, to explain obtained quantitative results, there will be quantitative questions, followed by qualitative questions. An example of research questions with this type of design is illustrated in Example 11.2.

EXAMPLES 11.2 | Explanatory Research Questions

The following research questions were addressed in this study:

1. To what extent do scores on an institutional ESL placement test . . . predict international graduate students' academic performance and their language difficulties in content courses during the first semester of their graduate education?
2. To what extent and in what ways do qualitative interviews with students and faculty members serve to contribute to a more comprehensive and nuanced understanding of this predictive relationship?

Source: Lee, Y., & Greene, J. (2007). The predictive validity of an ESL placement test. *Journal of Mixed Methods Research, 1*(4), 369.

The sequence of questions is the opposite for what is called an *exploratory* design. With this type of design qualitative data are gathered first. Often this type of design is used to develop a survey, as shown in the following example:

EXAMPLE 11.3 | Exploratory Research Questions

This study was designed to examine kindergarten teachers' perceptions of retention as an intervention. The following research questions guided the structure of the study:

1. What are kindergarten teachers' perceptions on kindergarten retention as an intervention?
2. Does a significant relationship exist between teachers' certification status and their perception of kindergarten retention?
3. Is there a significant relationship between teachers, teaching experience and their perception of kindergarten retention?

Source: Okpala, C. O. (2007). The perceptions of kindergarten teachers on retention. *Journal of Research in Childhood Education, 21*(4), 402.

Another example of exploratory questions could come from a study of the failure of political ads to engage college students in the campaign. Focus groups could be used initially, followed by a quantitative content analysis of political ads.

Further examples of these three major types of research questions are presented in Table 11.2.

EXAMPLE 11.4 | Exploratory Research Questions

Qualitative focus groups of college students examined how young voters interpret the salience of political advertising to them, and a quantitative content analysis of more than 100 ads from the 2004 presidential race focus[es] on why group participants felt so alienated by political advertising. . . . Three questions . . . are addressed:

- How does the interaction between audience-level and media-based framing contribute to college students' interpretations of the messages found in political advertising?
- To what extent do those interpretations match the framing found in the ads from the 2004 U.S. presidential election?
- How can political ads be framed to better engage college students?

Source: Parmelee, J. H., Perkins, S. C., & Sayre, J. J. (2007). Applying qualitative and quantitative methods to uncover how political ads alienate college students. *Journal of Mixed Methods Research, 1*(2), 186.

TABLE 11.2 **Types of Mixed-Method Research Questions**

		Example	
Type	**Definition**	**Method**	**Questions**
Explanatory	Findings from quantitative methods are followed by qualitative methods to provide explanations for the findings.	Teacher survey about grading practices is followed by teacher interviews to explain why zeros are used extensively in grading students.	What are teachers' grading practices? Why do teachers use zeros in grading students?
Exploratory	Qualitative methods are used to generate information that is utilized in conducting the quantitative phase of the study.	Teacher interviews about grading practices are used to develop a survey that is given to a large sample of teachers.	What factors do teachers use in grading students? What is the extent to which these factors are used with middle school teachers?
Convergent	Quantitative and qualitative data are collected at about the same time to allow triangulation of the findings.	Concurrent interviews and surveys of both teachers and students.	To what extent is effort used in grading students? To what extent is grading used to motivate students?

SAMPLING *in* MIXED-METHOD RESEARCH

Sampling for mixed-method research was discussed in Chapter 4. For the quantitative phase the sample is selected using either probability or nonprobability procedures, and of course for the qualitative part some type of purposeful sampling is used. This results in a great number of combinations of different kinds of sampling that can be found in a single study (e.g., snowball, extreme case, typical case, maximum variation for the qualitative phase; stratified, convenience, cluster, systematic for the quantitative phase). Typically, like research questions, sampling follows the logic of the design. Thus, for explanatory studies some kind of probability or convenience sample could be used to generate the quantitative findings, followed by some kind of qualitative sampling for the qualitative part of the study.

An exploratory study may begin with extreme case sampling and then use a probability sampling procedure for the quantitative part of the study. A triangulation design uses sampling that will allow a synthesis of findings from each group of participants. That is, the samples are typically very similar in a triangulation design so that it makes sense to combine data from separate components.

What is unique for some mixed-method studies is that the sampling for each phase of the study can be connected. Thus, the participants who are interviewed in an explanatory study may be identified by their responses to the survey. For example, in studying grading practices, a survey could be given to a random sample of teachers, and of these teachers those showing the most extreme practices could be selected for the interviews.

In some mixed-method studies, though, the samples could be completely independent. An illustration of this type of sampling is given in Example 11.5. This study was focused on teacher attitudes about teaching in urban, low-income schools. The quantitative data were obtained from an existing database, and qualitative data from a completely separate study of 12 elementary teachers.

EXAMPLE 11.5 | Independent Mixed-Method Sampling

We use quantitative methods and longitudinal data from a nationally representative sample of children attending low-income public schools. . . . Our second source of data, which we analyze with qualitative methods, is composed of an intense ethnographic study in six low-income schools in three cities. . . . Our analyses draw primarily on our interviews with the teachers in these classrooms.

Source: Halvorsen, A. L., Lee, V. E., & Andrade, F. H. (2009). A mixed-method study of teachers' attitudes about teaching in urban and low-income schools. *Urban Education, 44*(2), 187–188.

TYPES *of* MIXED-METHOD DESIGNS

Mixed-method designs can vary considerably, depending on the weight given to each approach and when each method is used. Although there are many different designs, the three designs presented here are the most commonly discussed in the literature.

Notation

To assist readers in identifying the type of design employed, Creswell, 2008 and Creswell & Plano Clark, 2011, suggest incorporating the following notation system in combination with visual diagrams to illustrate the design for readers:

- Uppercase letters (e.g., *QUAN* or *QUAL*) to indicate the method given *priority* (primary method used) in the study

- Lowercase letters (e.g., *qual* or *quan*) to indicate if a method was given a lower priority (less emphasis) in the study
- Arrows (→) to indicate that methods occur in a sequence
- Pluses (+) to indicate that methods occur concurrently

This notation allows for diagrams that show the logic of the design. The diagrams help clarify three important characteristics of the design:

1. Which component of the design, if any, is dominant (all caps)? Or, do the components have equal status?
2. Are the components sequential, one following the other, or concurrent?
3. In sequential designs, which component occurs first?

We will consider three mixed-method study designs, using the logic that has already been used (explanatory, exploratory, convergent). Many more variations exist, especially when there is more than one quantitative and/or qualitative component, but these are ones that are most commonly used and recognized.

Sequential Explanatory Design

In a **sequential explanatory design** there are two phases or components, qualitative following quantitative, with the primary emphasis on quantitative methods. Initially, quantitative data are collected and analyzed. In the second phase qualitative data are collected and analyzed. The design is represented as follows:

Sequential explanatory design: Quantitative, then qualitative.

QUAN ⟶ qual

Explanatory designs are used when the purpose of the study is to elucidate, elaborate on, or explain quantitative findings. Often qualitative data are used to analyze outliers or other extreme cases.

A two-stage study by McMillan (2000) is a good example of an explanatory design. In this study a large sample of teachers (850) was surveyed to determine the extent to which different factors were used in classroom assessment and grading. This provided a general overview of the teachers' practices. In the second phase teachers were selected who represented extremely high or low scores on the factors in the survey. These teachers were interviewed using a qualitative method to determine reasons why certain practices were used. Thus, the qualitative phase was used to augment the statistical data to provide explanations for the practices.

This same approach was taken by another study that examined the impact of teacher preparation programs on teaching competence. As illustrated in Example 11.6, the researchers first gathered survey data from a large number of teachers over four years, then employed interviews and observations.

EXAMPLE 11.6 | Sequential Explanatory Design

In this study, we sought not only descriptions but also explanations of results, in this case teacher education outcomes. . . . The challenge in deciding on the design of the study was to reduce the complexity of the research object without . . . unjustifiable simplifications. . . . We faced the "breadth-depth" problem. . . . Written questionnaires were the chief instruments used to survey the whole sample. . . . We selected from all of the respondents a smaller number to form a representative subset . . . which was studied by . . . qualitative methods.

Source: Browwer, N., & Korthagen, F. (2005). Can teacher education make a difference? *American Educational Research Journal, 42*(1), 167, 171.

In Example 11.7 a sequential explanatory design was used to investigate how instructions influence readers' personal reading intentions, goals, text processing, and memory. In this case, an experiment was completed, followed by interviews.

EXAMPLE 11.7 | Sequential Explanatory Design with Random Assignment

Undergraduates were randomly assigned to one of three pre-reading relevance instruction conditions. . . . Results showed that information was read more slowly and remembered better when it was relevant. Post-reading interviews were analyzed to explain these reading differences. . . . The data sets were complimentary: the quantitative data indicated differences in reading time and recall, and the qualitative data allowed us to explain why these differences occurred.

Source: McCrudden, M. T., Magliano, J. P. , & Schraw, G. (2010). Exploring how relevance instructions affect personal reading intentions, reading goals and text processing: A mixed methods study. *Contemporary Educational Psychology 35*(4), 229.

Sequential Exploratory Design

Sequential exploratory design: Qualitative then quantitative.

A **sequential exploratory design** is another two-phase design in which the qualitative data are gathered first, followed by a quantitative phase. In these designs, results from the qualitative data analysis are used to help determine the focus and type of data collection in the quantitative phase. The purpose of this design is typically to use the initial qualitative phase with a few individuals to identify themes, ideas, perspectives, and beliefs for the larger-scale quantitative part of the study. The premise is that exploration is needed because 1) "measures or instruments are not available, 2) the variables are unknown, or 3) there is no guiding framework or theory" (Creswell & Plano Clark, 2011, p. 86).

Often, this kind of design is used to develop a survey. By first using a qualitative component, researchers are able to use the language and emphasis of the subjects in the wording of items for the survey. This increases the validity of the scores because they are well matched to how the subjects, rather than the researchers, think about, conceptualize, and respond to the phenomena being studied. It could be represented as follows:

Qual ⟶ QUAN

For example, in a study by Rue, Dingley, and Bush (2002), the researchers utilized qualitative interviews and language from many participants with varied chronic health conditions to develop an instrument to measure "inner strength." This study relied heavily on participant language and experiences with chronic conditions to develop items for a survey that could then be used to quantitatively assess inner strength. Here the major emphasis is the quantitative measure, and qualitative interviews helped to form the survey. If the quantitative portion of the study was used to confirm, determine, or expand on qualitative findings, the qualitative part of the study will be emphasized:

QUAL ⟶ Quan

A sequential exploratory design is explained in Example 11.8. You will see that the authors make it clear that the quantitative component of the study followed the qualitative part.

EXAMPLE 11.8 | Sequential Exploratory Design

The design began with a framing theory-based qualitative exploration of how college students interpret political ads, followed by quantitative investigation of the hypotheses that were generated as part of the qualitative study.

Source: Parmelee, J. H., Perkins, S. C., & Sayre, J. J. (2007). Applying qualitative and quantitative methods to uncover how political ads alienate college students. *Journal of Mixed Methods Research, 1*(2), 186.

Concurrent Convergent Design

In the **concurrent convergent design** the researcher simultaneously implements both quantitative and qualitative methods—collecting and analyzing data concurrently. At each stage of research, the researcher employs the most appropriate quantitative or qualitative techniques, merging together results to facilitate a single interpretation. Sometimes researchers may choose to transform qualitative data to a more quantitative format to facilitate merging data and interpretation. Triangulation designs are typically used when researchers are interested in validating and expanding on the quantitative findings through the use of qualitative methods. The purpose is to develop a more thorough understanding of a single phenomenon. A special subtype of triangulation designs, called *nested designs*, involves using different methods to gather information from individuals or groups at different levels within a system (Tashakkori & Teddlie, 1998). For example, a researcher might use observations of students, interviews with teachers,

Concurrent convergent design: Quantitative and qualitative at the same time.

surveys with administrators, and focus groups with parents. The general purpose is the same, but the interest is in gaining multiple perspectives from individuals or groups who have different roles within a system. Approximately equal emphasis is given to each method, even though one can follow the other:

QUAL → QUAN or QUAN → QUAL

If conducted at the same time, the study could be represented by

QUAN		QUAL
+	or	+
QUAL		QUAN

To illustrate a concurrent convergent design, consider this hypothetical study on school culture. A quantitative school culture survey could be used in conjunction with some focus groups of students, teachers, and administrators. To the extent that that survey results match focus group results, the greater is the validity of the conclusion that a certain type of culture exists in the school. The advantage of the survey is that a large number of students, teachers, and administrators can be represented, while the focus group would provide descriptions in voices specific to each group. In the following excerpt the researcher explains how both quantitative and qualitative data are obtained. In this study, Example 11.9, a survey was used prior to selecting the students for interviews, and then an additional survey and interviews were conducted.

EXAMPLE 11.9 | Concurrent Convergent Design

The participants responded to a prestudy measurement of their attitude toward computers. . . . I used the Sense of Classroom Community Index (SCCI) . . . to evaluate the sense of classroom community. . . . To collect qualitative data, I used semistructured interviews with follow-up questions to probe for additional information.

Source: Wighting, M.J. (2006). Effects of computer use on high school students' sense of community. *Journal of Educational Research, 99*(6), 373–374.

Review and Reflect *See if you can come up with at least one hypothetical example of each of the three main types of mixed-method designs. Think about what it would take to actually conduct the studies. Do they seem feasible? Do they reflect the advantages of doing mixed-method studies? Search ERIC using the term "mixed-method" and see what is identified over the past 10 years. Are there more studies in more recent years? What kind of journals publish mixed-method studies? What types of designs are most prevalent?*

The advantages and challenges of each type of design are presented in Table 11.3.

TABLE 11.3 Advantages and Challenges of Different Mixed-Method Designs

Type of Design	Advantages	Challenges
Explanatory	• The two-phase structure makes its implementation straightforward. • The two-phase structure makes writing the report straightforward because it can be completed in two phases. • The focus on quantitative methods in the first phase often appeals to researchers whose primary expertise is quantitative methods.	• The two-phase structure requires additional time for implementation and data collection. • Researchers need to make a decision whether to collect data from the individuals, the same sample, or separate samples from the same population in both phases. • Because the researcher cannot identify how participants will be selected for the qualitative phase until after initial quantitative results have been explored, it can be more difficult to obtain institutional review board (IRB) approval.
Exploratory	• Separate phases make implementation straightforward. • The inclusion of the quantitative component in a design that generally emphasizes qualitative methods is likely to make this design attractive to researchers whose primary expertise is quantitative method.	• The two-phase structure requires additional time for implementation and data collection. • Researchers need to make a decision whether the same individuals will serve as participants in both phases. • It is difficult to specify the quantitative procedures to be implemented. • Prior analysis of qualitative data can create issues with obtaining institutional review boards (IRBs).
Convergent	• In terms of time for implementation data collection, it is an efficient design as both types of data are collected and analyzed at the same time. • Because the quantitative and qualitative data can be collected and analyzed independently of one another, these designs are well-suited to collaborations or research teams.	• Because of the concurrent nature of data collection, additional effort and expertise in each method are required if researchers are working alone on a study. • Researchers may encounter situations in which the results of the quantitative and qualitative data analyses diverge (do not agree or appear to tell different "stories"). • This may require additional data collection to determine the nature of the inconsistencies.

Source: Adapted from McMillan (2010) and Creswell & Plano Clark (2011).

DESIGN CONSIDERATIONS

Regardless of the research questions and type of design chosen, all mixed-method studies should include: an explicit rationale for the type of design chosen and both quantitative and qualitative types of data, discussions of priority/weighting, an indication of sequence/timing, and whether there is data mixing.

Rationale

It is important to clearly identify and explain your reasons for mixing quantitative and qualitative methods. Readers should have enough information about why you have chosen a mixed-method design to be able to determine for themselves if your methods are justified. Creswell and Plano Clark (2011) suggest that researchers devote a paragraph at the start of the methods section to an overview of the study design that includes four topics: (1) identification of the type of design, (2) defining characteristics of the design, (3) the overall purpose or reason for using the type of design (this is distinct from the study's stated purpose), and (4) references to mixed-method literature.

Priority/Weighting

Priority refers to the weight or emphasis the quantitative and qualitative methods receive within a study (Creswell, 2008). Depending on the type of design and purpose for the study, researchers have three choices in terms of weighting: (1) quantitative and qualitative data can be given equal weight (i.e., triangulation designs); (2) qualitative data can be weighted more heavily than quantitative data (i.e., exploratory designs); or (3) quantitative data can be weighted more heavily than qualitative data (i.e., explanatory designs). As previously indicated, in terms of notation, priority/weighting is depicted by upper- or lowercase letters.

Choosing how to weight the quantitative and qualitative methods in a study is dependent primarily on the purpose of the study; and which data collection and analysis methods are most well-suited to answering the research questions. Additional considerations include the availability of resources and time constraints, relative expertise of the researcher(s) in implementing quantitative and qualitative methods, and the intended audience. Limitations in terms of time and resources may force the researcher to prioritize and focus more on one method than the other. If researchers are uncomfortable or lack the expertise to implement either quantitative or qualitative methods effectively, they may rely more on methods that are within their realm of expertise. Finally, if the intended audience is more familiar with or expects a certain method to be employed, researchers may choose to emphasize that method.

Sequence/Timing

Sequence refers to the both the timing of implementation of the quantitative and qualitative methods and the order in which data are used (Creswell & Plano Clark, 2011). Concurrent studies are those in which both the quantitative and qualitative methods are implemented simultaneously (i.e., triangulation designs). Sequential studies are those in which either the quantitative methods are implemented before the qualitative methods (i.e., explanatory), or the qualitative methods are implemented before the quantitative methods (i.e., exploratory). In terms of notation, sequence is indicated by (+) for concurrent designs or (→) for sequential designs.

Data Mixing

Data mixing refers to how the quantitative and qualitative data are combined and the types of data that are mixed (Creswell & Plano Clark, 2011). Researchers can employ different strategies to mix data during research studies. One involves merging the two types of data into a single dataset, usually during the interpretation phase (discussion). In this case, quantitative and qualitative data are analyzed and reported separately within the results section. Researchers might also choose to merge datasets during analysis by transforming data of one type into another. Convergent designs typically employ this strategy and involve a single phase. Another option is to connect data of one type to data of another type by using the analysis of one type of data to inform the data collection of the other type. Explanatory and exploratory designs employ this strategy. In explanatory designs, the quantitative data analyses influence the qualitative data that are collected; for exploratory designs, the qualitative data analyses influence the quantitative data that are collected.

Table 11.4 presents some examples of types of data collection procedures and their uses, broken down by each type of design, as well as the sequence of implementation.

TABLE 11.4 Data Collection, Design, and Analytic Procedures in Mixed-Method Studies

Sequence of Data Collection	Priority and Sequence	Examples
Concurrent (QUAN and QUAL data collected simultaneously)	Triangulation QUAN + QUAL	• Quantifying qualitative data: Code qualitative data, assign numbers to codes, and record the number of times codes appear as numeric data. Descriptively analyze quantitative data for frequency of occurrence. Compare the two datasets. • Qualifying quantitative data: Factor-analyze the quantitative data from questionnaires. These factors then become themes. Compare these themes to themes analyzed from qualitative data. • Comparing results: Directly compare the results from qualitative data collection to the results from quantitative data collection. Support statistical trends by qualitative themes or vice versa. • Consolidating data: Combine qualitative and quantitative data to form new variables. Compare original quantitative variables to qualitative themes to form new quantitative variables.
	Nested (QUAN and QUAL data collected from participants at multiple levels at the same time)	• Examining multilevels: Conduct a survey at the student level. Gather qualitative data through interviews at the class level. Survey the entire school at the school level. Collect qualitative data at the district level. Information from each level builds to the next level.
Sequential	Explanatory (QUAN followed by qual) QUAN ⟶ qual	• Following up on outliers or extreme cases: Gather quantitative data and identify outlier or residual cases. Collect qualitative data to explore the characteristics of these cases. • Explaining results: Conduct a quantitative survey to identify how two or more groups compare on a variable. Follow up with qualitative interviews to explore the reasons why these differences were found. • Using a typology: Conduct a quantitative survey and develop factors through a factor analysis. Use these factors as a typology to identify themes in qualitative data, such as observations or interviews.
	Exploratory (QUAL followed by quan) QUAL ⟶ quan	• Locating an instrument: Collect qualitative data and identify themes. Use these themes as a basis for locating instruments that use parallel concepts to the qualitative themes.

(continued)

TABLE 11.4 (Continued)

Sequence of Data Collection	Priority and Sequence	Examples
		• Developing an instrument: Obtain themes and specific statements from individuals that support the themes. During the next phase, use these themes and statements to create scales and items in a questionnaire. Alternatively, look for existing instruments that can be modified to fit the themes and statements found in the qualitative exploratory phase of the study. After developing the instrument, test it out with a sample of a population. • Forming categorical data: Site-level characteristics (e.g., different ethnic groups) gathered in an ethnography during the first phase of a study become a categorical variable during a second-phase correlational or regression study. • Using extreme qualitative cases: Qualitative data cases that are extreme in a comparative analysis are followed by quantitative surveys during a second phase.

Source: Adapted from Creswell et al. (2003) and Creswell (2008).

STEPS *in* CONDUCTING *a* MIXED-METHOD STUDY

Creswell (2008) has identified seven steps to conducting mixed-method studies, regardless of their design specifications (see Figure 11.1).

1. Determine the feasibility of conducting a mixed-method study. Feasibility is a function of the level of training and expertise of the researcher(s) or team, and resources and time available for data collection and analysis. If any of these are less than adequate, the likelihood of successfully implementing a mixed-method design is reduced.

2. Identify the rationale. As previously discussed, it is important to identify the reasons for conducting a mixed-method study prior to the actual start of the research. If you are unable to clearly identify why you are conducting a mixed-method study, you are unlikely to be able to clearly justify your purpose to readers.

FIGURE 11.1 **Steps in conducting mixed-method studies.**

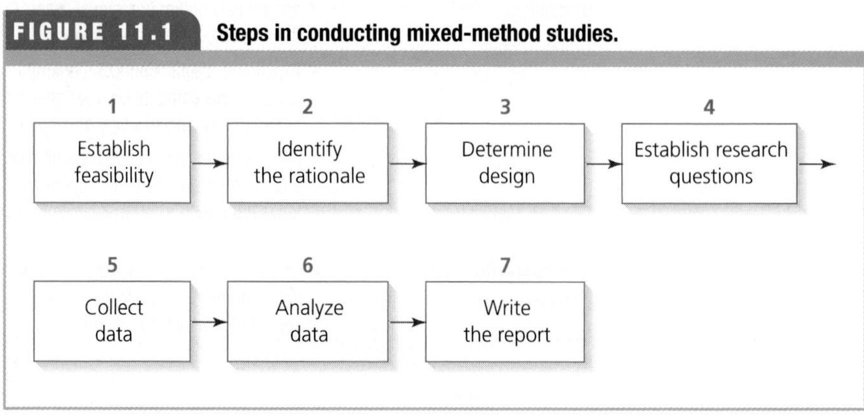

3. Determine the design, types of data, and a strategy for how you will collect data. Determining the type of mixed-method design (triangulation, explanatory, or exploratory), the priority and sequence of data collection, and the specific forms of information to be gathered is essential to planning the specific procedures to be followed. It is also useful at this point to map out the design using the notation system and diagramming methods presented earlier in the chapter.

4. Establish specific quantitative and qualitative research questions. Although Creswell suggests identifying questions at this step, I would argue that research questions need to be established in advance in order to determine whether a mixed-method study is warranted. At this stage questions should be refined to ensure they clearly reflect the design and can be answered by the identified data collection methods. In the case of explanatory designs, it may be difficult to define the qualitative questions prior to analysis of the quantitative data. Typically, researchers develop separate quantitative and qualitative research questions to incorporate into a single study. In developing your research questions, be sure to follow the guidelines for each type of research question presented earlier in the text.

5. Collect the data. The sequence of data analysis should already be identified by the type of design that was chosen. In terms of the research process, this stage is likely to be lengthy and time-consuming. It is important that conventional procedures for each type of data are followed to ensure the appropriateness of data collection.

6. Analyze the data. Depending on the type of design, quantitative and qualitative data will be analyzed separately and independently; or, less likely, might involve the integration of quantitative and qualitative data into single analytic strategy.

7. Write the report. As with many aspects of mixed-method studies, writing up the results of a study in a research report will depend on the type of design employed. Regardless of the design, though, the procedures employed in both the quantitative and qualitative components of the study need to be clearly explained in detail, and are usually reported separately within the method section of the report. In explanatory and exploratory designs, results for quantitative and qualitative analyses may be reported in a separate section for each phase of the study. In contrast, reports of triangulation designs are most likely to integrate the quantitative and qualitative results structured around the research questions in a single results section of the report.

CONSUMER TIPS: *Evaluating Mixed-Method Studies*

As we have seen, not all research studies are created equal. In critically evaluating mixed-method research studies, there are several considerations that must be considered in addition to the criteria used to evaluate entirely quantitative or qualitative studies. First and foremost, what sets mixed-method studies apart from other research designs is the intentional and substantial collection of both quantitative and qualitative data. This is the primary way to evaluate the rigor of mixed-method designs. For example, a study that collected data via quantitative surveys employing Likert scales and that included a few open-ended questions at the end of the survey, as the "qualitative" component, is not a true mixed-method design. Similarly, a study that employs random sampling as the only quantitative component of the study is not a mixed-method design because of insufficient use of quantitative methods. For the most part, mixed-method studies should be able to "hold their own weight" with regard to standards of rigor and quality checks for both quantitative and qualitative methods.

Mertens (2010, p. 305–306) presents eight questions that can be applied to the evaluation of mixed-method studies:

1. What are the multiple purposes and questions that justify the use of a mixed-method design?
2. Has the researcher matched the purposed and questions to appropriate methods?
3. To what extent has the researcher adhered to the criteria that define quality for the quantitative portion of the study?
4. To what extent has the researcher adhered to the criteria that define quality for the qualitative portion of the study?
5. How has the researcher addressed the tension between potentially conflicting demands of paradigms in the design and implementation of the study?
6. Has the researcher appropriately acknowledged the limitations associated with data that were collected to supplement the main data collection of the study?
7. How has the researcher integrated the results from the mixed methods? If necessary, how has the researcher explained conflicting findings that resulted from different methods?
8. What evidence is there that the researcher developed the design to be responsive to the practical and cultural needs of specific subgroups on the basis of such dimensions as disability, culture, language, reading levels, gender, class, and race or ethnicity?

See Leech et al. (2010) for additional considerations in evaluating mixed-method studies. They describe a validation framework that can be used to evaluate the credibility of the research, and provide three examples from published studies.

ANATOMY *of a* MIXED-METHOD STUDY

The following article is an example of how a mixed-method study is designed and reported. This particular study involves a convergent design.

ARTICLE 11.1 Student Perceptions of the Transition from Elementary to Middle School

Patrick Akos
University of North Carolina

Transitions are often a difficult time of life. The stress and challenge inherent in adjustment can create developmental crises for even the heartiest individuals. Helping students in transition is similarly challenging. To facilitate successful transitions, helping professionals such as school counselors should consider the developmental tasks of various stages, the coping abilities and flexibility of individuals, and the potent systemic and contextual factors of influence.

General research problem

School personnel recognize the difficult transition students undertake when moving from one level of schooling to another. The transition from elementary to middle school may be especially challenging because it often involves significant school and personal change. One consideration is that most middle school environments differ significantly from the elementary environment (Perkins & Gelfer, 1995). Contextual transitions commonly include additional and unfamiliar students and school staff, and multiple sets of behavioral and classroom rules and expectations.

This contextual change during the transition to middle school is heightened by personal change. Physical, emotional, and social changes that occur in puberty have been associated with heightened emotionality, conflict, and defiance of adults (Berk, 1993). Although pubertal changes have been viewed more as an opportunity than a crisis (Papalia, Olds, & Feldman, 2001), the varied timing of preadolescent development is difficult for students (Berk, 1993). Pubertal changes occur at different times and at different rates for students in the same grade. Therefore, as students transition to middle school, they confront both external contextual changes and internal pubertal changes.

Research has highlighted the developmental and academic difficulties often associated with the transition from elementary to middle school. Both boys and girls show a significant increase in psychological distress across the transition to middle school (Chung, Elias, & Schneider, 1998; Crockett et al., 1989). Even though declines in achievement and increased distress are not gender exclusive, boys tend to show a significant drop in academic achievement, while girls seem to experience a greater level of psychological distress after the transition (Chung et al., 1998). Also, during the transition, girls find peer relationships most stressful, whereas boys find peer relationships, conflict with authority, and academic pressures as equal stressors (Elias, Ubriaco, Reese, Gars, Rothbaum, & Haviland, 1992).

Along with psychological and academic outcomes, studies have shown that student motivation and attitudes toward school tend to decline during the transition to middle school (Anderman, 1996; Harter, 1981; Simmons & Blyth, 1987). Eccles et al. (1993) used "stage-environment fit" to describe the poor fit between the developmental needs of preadolescents and the environment of middle school or junior high school (e.g., academic tracking, increasing competition, and awareness of personal peer group status). Declining student motivation and attitude were highlighted by Simmons and Blyth, who found more negative consequences for students in the transition from elementary to middle school as compared to students making the same grade transition in K–8 schools.

Review of literature

While most of the research describes the negative outcomes associated with the transition to middle school, several authors also suggested interventions to reduce negative outcomes. Schumacher (1998) identified social, organizational, and motivational factors as important aspects of successful interventions. Eccles et al. (1993) suggested strategies designed to create a school context appropriate to developmental levels of preadolescents. These included building smaller communities within the school, using teaming and cooperative learning, eliminating tracking, empowering teachers, and improving student/teacher relationships. Similarly, Felner et al. (1993) found teaching teams and advisory programs as important preventative interventions for students in transition.

Analysis of literature

Although much of the research has either noted the detrimental effects of the school transition or suggested interventions, few investigations have sought student perceptions during the transition to middle school. Arowosafe and Irvin (1992) interviewed students about the transition at the end of the sixth-grade year. They asked students about stressors, school safety, perceptions of school, and what people told them about middle school. Students reported heightened levels of stress related to safety concerns in the school. They also noted that students report friends and the information they received from others as critical factors that affect the transition experience.

Review of literature

(continued)

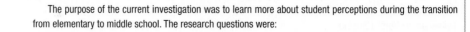

ARTICLE 11.1 (continued)

The purpose of the current investigation was to learn more about student perceptions during the transition from elementary to middle school. The research questions were:

Specific research questions

- What questions do students have about middle school?
- What specific concerns do students have about middle school?
- What aspects of middle school do students see as positive?
- What do students think middle school will be like?
- Whom do students turn to for help during the transition into middle school?
- What is important for students to know about coming to middle school?

METHOD

Participants

Description of sample

The research was conducted in four phases. For phases I and II, participants included all 331 fifth-grade students in a large, rural, Southeastern public school district. Participants included students from three different elementary schools that were scheduled to enter one large middle school (sixth to eighth grade). The mean age was 11.8 years, with a range of 10 to 13 years old. Racial composition of the participants included 59% white students (n = 195), 37% black students (n = 122), and 4% other (n = 14). There were 175 females (53%) and 156 males (47%). Approximately 45% (n = 149) were on free or reduced lunch during the fifth-grade year.

Random selection (quantitative)

Purposeful sampling (qualitative)

Rationale for qualitative methods

At the start of the sixth-grade year (phase III), 103 students (four home-base classrooms) were randomly selected from the 331 fifth-grade students. Demographic information mirrored that of the first sample. Phase IV included a purposeful sample of participants (n = 97), again from the 331 fifth-grade students, who experienced success at the middle school. The sample was selected in December of the sixth-grade year. Success was defined by average or better grades (no grade lower than a C), appropriate behavior (no more than one behavior referral), and regular attendance (no more than two unexcused absences) during the first academic marking period (9 weeks) of sixth grade. The researcher felt that perceptions and insight from students with generally positive records, rather than a random or complete sample, would be valuable for understanding student perceptions of the transition. The phase IV sample included students with similar demographics as compared to the participants for the earlier phases.

Setting

Importance of context

Due to the contextual influence on this research (i.e., the significance of elementary school and middle school context), it is important to provide data about the setting. In the participating elementary schools, students attend neighborhood schools that use self-contained classrooms. This middle school is centrally located in the large rural county. The middle school uses teaching teams, four teachers per team that cover primary subjects, and each student has one of those teachers for a home base. As with most middle schools, students move between four to six teachers and are introduced to lockers, showering in gym class, and more responsibility than in elementary school. Students from this district can also travel for up to one and one-half hours each way on a bus to and from their middle school. Although middle school students commute to school on a bus with students from similar geographic areas, students also ride with all students in grades 6 to 12 in the school district.

Procedure

A longitudinal analysis of student perceptions occurred in four phases, starting in January of fifth grade and concluded in December of sixth grade. In phase I (January of the fifth-grade year), the participants submitted questions about middle school. In phase II (May of the fifth-grade year), the participants completed a questionnaire designed to discover more information about student perspectives. In phase III (in August—the start of the sixth-grade year in middle school), students completed a questionnaire similar to the one used in phase II. The phase III questionnaire was administered in home base at the conclusion of the first two weeks of school. In the last phase, phase IV (December of the sixth-grade year), a purposeful sample of selected successful students completed a questionnaire that repeated questions from phases II and III. The phase IV questionnaire was administered at a meeting of selected students led by the school counselor to assist in planning for the upcoming year.

Data Collection

One writing assignment and three questionnaires were used to elicit student perspectives during the transition. In phase I, participants were asked to write any questions they had about middle school. In phase II, the participants completed a five-item questionnaire. One item of the questionnaire asked students to select concerns from a list of 13 themes. A second item consisting of the same 13 themes, asked students to select positive aspects. The checklist items were generated from themes written by students in phase I, and each checklist included an open-ended response. The checklists were identical and included items such as changing classes, using your locker, getting good grades, older students, and making friends. The questionnaire also assessed general feelings about coming to middle school. One question asked students to indicate how they feel about coming to middle school (worried, a little worried, a little excited, or excited). Additionally, an open-ended question was included to assess perceptions of what middle school would be like. Finally, one question asked students to select the person or persons they felt were most helpful to them during the transition to middle school (teachers, counselors, parents, friends, or someone else).

Questionnaires that include both quantitative and qualitative questions

During phase III, students completed a second questionnaire in home base. This seven-item questionnaire inquired about academic strategies and goals for sixth grade. Included in the questionnaire were items replicated from previous phases. Students were asked what, if any, questions they had about middle school and what concerns they had about middle school.

The third questionnaire again replicated previous questions. This six-item questionnaire included open-ended questions about concerns and best aspects of middle school. The questionnaire also replicated the question about the person or persons who helped students during the transition to middle school. These questions were worded as reflections over the past transition year (e.g., "What were the best aspects about coming to middle school?"). The questionnaire also included an open-ended question to seek students' recommendations for helping fifth-grade students in the transition to middle school for the next academic year. Finally, the questionnaire concluded with one question about class schedule and one about team membership.

Data Analysis

The open-ended writing assignment and series of questionnaire responses were analyzed for content and qualitative themes concerning the transition. Data were subjected to content analysis to identify emergent themes in the responses. Because categories in a content analysis should be completely exhaustive and mutually exclusive, a step classification system (Holsti, 1969) was used. First, each participant's response was categorized into a meaning unit. Meaning units are described as perceived shifts in attitude or a shift in the emotional quality of a response (Giorgo, 1985). These units are not meant to be independent, but rather expressions of aspects of the whole response. For the writing assignment, each question listed by students was coded as a meaning unit. In questionnaires, individual question responses were also coded as meaning units. Open-ended questions on the questionnaires were analyzed for meaning shifts and coded accordingly. For example, a response such as "both scary and fun" would be coded as two separate meaning units. The data, divided into meaning units, describe meaningful aspects of the response, with minimal inferences from the researcher (Seidman, 1991).

Shows qualitative emphasis

After meaning units were coded and tabulated for all data, the researcher examined the coding for their thematic meaning and collapsed coded content into larger themes. Larger themes were identified from the most

(continued)

ARTICLE 11.1 (continued)

frequent responses emerging from the initial coding. For example, one student wrote eight separate questions. Although all eight questions were distinct meaning units, the first five focused on rules and procedures, while the last three listed concerns about bullies and older students. Additionally, several responses did not collapse into larger categories and were judged atypical. These responses represented less than 3% of the total responses.

Researcher and Researcher Bias

Possible threat to internal validity

The researcher is a white male who at the time of the study was a practicing school counselor at the middle school. Although student perceptions formed the base of all conclusions, the researcher also had assumptions that may have influenced the results. As a school counselor, research bias included an increased focus on personal/social adjustment during the transition. The researcher also assumed a level of anxiety concerning the transition to middle school.

RESULTS

Phase I—January of Fifth-Grade Year

What questions do students have about going to middle school? Three hundred thirty-one participants submitted a total of 555 questions. Most students submitted 3 to 5 questions, with a range from 1 to 15. Twenty-eight percent ($n = 156$) of the questions focused on rules and procedures (e.g., "What's the consequence for being late?"), 16% ($n = 90$) on class schedules in sixth grade (e.g., "Do sixth graders get to do chorus?"), 11% ($n = 60$) on PE or gym class (e.g., "Do you get to play basketball in gym class?"), 9% ($n = 52$) on expectations for sixth graders (e.g., "Do you have a lot of work to do?"), and 9% ($n = 52$) on lunch (e.g., "if you have last lunch, do you always have pizza?"). The remaining questions (27%) addressed topics (each one comprised less than 5% of the total) that included lockers, extracurricular programs, recess, teachers, and sports. Of particular note and consistent with current events in schools today, a few of the questions concerned school violence or safety. For example, two questions included "What happens if you threaten to hurt a teacher?" and "Do people kill people in middle school?"

Phase II—May of Fifth-Grade Year

What specific concerns do students have about coming to middle school? A total of 735 concerns were selected by the 331 participants. The frequency of selected concerns was spread somewhat evenly over the 13 choices provided in the questionnaire. In fact, no one response comprised more than 15% of the total selections. The most frequent responses included older students, 14% ($n = 102$); homework, 13% ($n = 98$); using one's locker, 12% ($n = 88$); and getting good grades, 12% ($n = 85$). Only lunchroom, bathrooms, and the open-ended choice received little attention (comprised less than 1%).

Which aspects of middle school do students see as positive? A total of 808 items were selected by the 331 participants. Parallel to the worries of fifth-grade students, students selected a variety of potential positive aspects of middle school. The most mentioned aspects included making friends, 16% ($n = 130$); gym/PE class, 15% ($n = 124$); using your locker, 11% ($n = 90$); and both changing classes and getting good grades, 10% ($n = 82$ for each). Only the open choice received less than 1% ($n = 10$).

Mix of quantitative and qualitative data

What do students think middle school will be like? A total of 329 meaning units were coded from the responses by the 331 participants. Forty-five percent of the responses listed that middle school will be "fun" ($n = 148$), 14% of the responses mentioned that middle school will be "exciting" ($n = 46$), 11% of responses suggested it will be "cool" ($n = 36$), while 9% of the responses listed "hard" or "scary" ($n = 31$). A variety of other responses (each category represented less than 5% of the total) included "weird," "tight," "good," "awesome," and "like a maze."

Whom do students turn to for help during the transition to middle school? A total of 480 choices were selected by the 331 participants. Thirty-five percent of the responses specified friends (n = 166), 22% parents (n = 105), 21% teachers (n = 103), 14% school counselor (n = 68), while 8% mentioned other sources including "cousins," "siblings," and "other family" (n = 38).

Phase III—August of the Sixth-Grade Year

Mix of quantitative and qualitative data

What questions do students have about middle school? A total of 91 responses were reported by 103 randomly selected participants from phases I and II. Thirty-four percent of the responses indicated no questions about middle school (n = 31), 16% of responses centered on rules and procedures (n = 15; e.g., "Can I have one more minute extra to change classes?"), 15% of the responses focused on homework (n = 14; e.g., "How much homework do we get?"), and 7% of the responses focused on classes (n = 6; e.g., "Do I have to take an elective?"). The remaining responses (n = 31) were varied, and each category accounted for less than 5% of the total.

What specific concerns do students have about middle school? A total of 115 responses were tabulated from the 103 randomly selected participants from phases I and II. Twenty-four percent of the responses focused on bullies or older students (n = 28; e.g., "Being picked on on the bus with the older kids"), 19% about getting lost in the building (n = 22; e.g., "Getting lost"), and 19% about doing well in classes (n = 22; e.g., "I am worried that I might not do as well as I have in the past years"). Fourteen percent of the responses suggested there were no concerns (n = 16) and 7% of the responses centered on being tardy to class (n = 8; e.g., "What happens if I am a minute late to class?"). The remaining responses (n = 27) were varied, and each category accounted for less than 5% of the total responses.

Phase IV-December of Sixth-Grade Year

What were the most difficult aspects of middle school? A total of 152 responses were listed by the 97 participants from a purposeful sample of successful students in phases I and II. Twenty-six percent of the responses focused on getting lost (n = 40; e.g., "Fear of getting lost"), 13% on making friends (n = 19; e.g., "Getting to know people"), 11% on learning the class schedule (n = 17; e.g., "Knowing how to change classes"), 10% on lockers (n = 16; e.g., "Opening your locker"), 8% on getting to class on time (n = 12; e.g., "Tardies, all of them you can get"), and 5% of responses indicated there were no difficulties. The remaining responses (n = 50) were varied, and no category accounted for more than 5% of the total.

What were the best aspects of being in middle school? A total of 118 responses were reported from 97 participants of a purposeful sample of successful students from phases I and II. Forty-three percent centered on freedom/choices (n = 51; e.g., "You get more freedom, like not having to walk in lines"), 18% focused on friends (n = 21; e.g., "Get more time to talk to friends"), 16% on classes (n = 19; e.g., "Different and better classes"), and 13% on lockers (n = 15; e.g., "You get your own space and can put stuff in your locker"). The remaining responses (n = 12) were varied, and each category accounted for less than 5% of the total.

Who helped students the most with the transition to middle school? A total of 131 choices represented the people most helpful to the 97 participants. Forty percent of the responses selected friends (n = 52), 23% chose teachers (n = 30), 19% selected parents (n = 25), 11% selected other family ((n = 14); e.g., "brothers," "cousins"), while 8% selected the school counselor (n = 10).

What is important to tell fifth-grade students about coming to middle school? Of the 158 responses from the 97 participants, 23% felt it was most important to tell fifth-grade students about rules (n = 36; e.g., "You can't chew gum"), 18% reported expectations/responsibilities (n = 29; e.g., "You have to do your homework to go to incentive day"), 10% where classes and other items are located (n = 16; e.g., "Art is on the eighth-grade hall"), 9% that it is fun (n = 14; e.g., "It is more fun than elementary school"), 8% there are nice teachers (n = 12; e.g., "Teachers are pretty nice"), and 6% that it is not hard (n = 9; e.g., "Most of the classes are easy, except social studies"). The remaining responses (n = 69) accounted for categories represented by less than 5% of the total.

(continued)

ARTICLE 11.1 (continued)

DISCUSSION

Students' questions about middle school were dominated by rules and procedures throughout the transition from fifth to sixth grade. Although school rules may be a typical part of orientation programs, being explicit and thorough about rules and procedures seems crucial. The data suggest that students are keenly aware of the contextual change in the transition. Although sixth-grade students at times may exhibit adolescent characteristics, it seems important to remember that these students need an "elementary" orientation concerning rules and procedures. Rules such as walking in the halls or keeping one's hands to oneself, or procedures such as reporting to class before the tardy bell seem simplistic, but these rules and procedures are what students asked about the most. In fact, students 9 weeks into the sixth grade still reflected that expectations and responsibilities were most important to tell fifth-grade students. Although class scheduling is often the start and focus of the orientation process for students in fifth grade, these data suggest that rules/procedures and expectations are most important to students.

Current study related to literature

Student worries about middle school include a wide variety of topics. Although orientation programming attempts to minimize these concerns, these data indicate that it is important to address a variety of worries involved in the transition. In fact, the spread and frequency of reported worries suggest that there is a generalized or overall persistent level of worry for most students in transition. This conclusion is similar to research suggesting the difficulty of school transitions (Chung et al., 1998; Crockett et al., 1989).

It is also noteworthy both in the fifth grade and at the start of the sixth-grade year that older students or bullies were a particular concern. This echoes findings from Arowosafe and Irvin's (1992) study in which students reported safety as a concern because of rumors about older students. Orientation programming could address this persistent concern by including older students as tour guides or peer mentors in the school to ease the transition. Alternatively, schoolwide bullying programs may help alleviate student concerns about school safety. It is also important to note that homework and doing well in classes seem to be of particular concern to students in both fifth grade and the start of sixth grade. Students' academic concerns may suggest that it is important to build students' confidence in the "classroom by teaching homework and study skills. In light of research (Anderman, 1996; Harter, 1981; Simmons & Blyth, 1987) that suggests academic and motivational declines in the transition, addressing these concerns seems especially important. Additionally, getting lost in middle school is a main concern of students upon reflection in December of the sixth-grade year. This fear could be addressed by providing school tours or comprehensive class schedule-based orientations.

Implication of results

Although intervention or orientation programming can be useful to address questions and worries, designing orientation programs that facilitate and build upon student enthusiasm and confidence might provide encouragement to overcome worries and build motivation during the transition. Students recorded more entries for positive aspects than concerns and indicated excitement about a variety of aspects of middle school. In fact, 70% of the student responses were positive to the open-ended question, "What will middle school be like?" During the transition, orientation leaders should highlight aspects of middle school that students seem to enjoy, including increased freedom and choices, the opportunity to change classes, and having their own lockers. Also, it is important to note that students mentioned friends as the top source of help during the transition. This finding supports the need to include peers in transition interventions and orientation programming. Upon reflecting about the transition, sixth-grade students suggest it is important to tell fifth graders that middle school is fun and there are nice teachers.

Implication

Although a few studies have found students that thrive in the transition (Crockett et al., 1989; Hirsch & Rapkin, 1987), these data contradict most of the previous research reporting the transition as a rather negative event for students (Anderman, 1996; Chung et al., 1998; Crockett et al., 1989; Elias, Gara, & Ubriaco, 1985; Harter, 1981; Simmons & Blyth, 1987). This study suggests that there are equal, if not more positive, aspects related to the transition to middle school from the student perspective.

Conclusion

This study revealed the importance of including a variety of people in the transition or orientation program. Although school counselors are often responsible for transition planning, students reported that friends, parents, and teachers are all sources of help in the transition. Again, friends and peers are reported as the most frequent resource for students in transition. However, some peers may not provide accurate or helpful information. In this way, it may be useful to identify role-model students who exhibit a desire and skill set that would make them good candidates to help students in transition. An ambassador or peer-helping program may be extremely helpful in the transition (Arowosafe & Irvin, 1992). In fact, Mittman and Packer (1982) found that students attribute a good start frequently to the presence of old friends and the making of new friends. This type of peer support has a strong relationship with adolescent mental health (Hirsch & DeBois, 1992).

Similarly, including teachers and parents in programming is important. Although teachers often provide an orientation to their individual classrooms, integrating teachers in a systemic way may be useful. For example, teachers may have unique classroom rules of procedures, but perhaps a combined orientation can be presented by teachers about general topics such as hall passes or discipline referrals. Arowosafe and Irvin (1992) suggested that teachers can be integrated in advisor/advisee activities. Similarly, although parents are included in open house and class scheduling in most cases, it seems important that parents are informed about rules/proceedings and expectations in the middle school.

Implication for Practice

Arowosafe and Irvin (1992) also suggested it is important to provide parent consultation on the transition to middle school, as they found most parents tended to provide warnings rather than positive information about middle school. In this way, parent orientation can strengthen and support student orientation to the middle school. Students look for help from parents during the fifth-grade year, while teachers replace parents to become more important during the sixth-grade year. This shift in adult influence fits developmentally as preadolescents struggle to form an identity independent of family. Interestingly, students still continue to desire adult assistance throughout the transition.

Limitations

With only one primary researcher, qualitative data coding is limited. No researcher can enter into a study without bias (Rowan, 1981). With only one researcher involved with data analysis and only one school district, this study requires replication. Interviews, rather than questionnaires, with students may also elicit richer information about difficulties and positive aspects of the transition. All of the data are self-report, which has inherent limitations.

Limitations

IMPLICATIONS FOR SCHOOL COUNSELORS

Data from this research and the research to date (e.g., Arowosafe & Irvin, 1992; Crockett et al., 1989; Eccles & Midgley, 1989) on school transition suggest that preventive or proactive programming is needed to assist students with the elementary to middle school transition. The transition provides both a challenge and opportunity for school counselors. This research suggests the following guidelines for school counselors coordinating transition programs: (a) rules, expectations, and responsibilities are the primary concern of students and should be presented early in fifth grade and infused throughout the transition year (this is also an excellent opportunity to include administrators and teachers in transition programming), (b) school counselors have an opportunity both to address concerns and stressors and to promote positive aspects of the transition to middle school, (c) transition programs should include peers, family, and teachers as students look to significant others for help, and (d) transition programs should evolve throughout the transition year as student perceptions and needs change.

REFERENCES

Anderman, L. (1996). The middle school experience: Effects on the math and science achievment of adolescents with L. D. *Journal of Learning Disabilities, 31*, 128–138.

Arowosafe, D., & Irvin, J. (1992). Transition to a middle level school: What kids say. *Middle School Journal, 24*(2), 15–19.

Berk, L. (1993). *Infants, children, and adolescents.* Needham Heights, MA: Allyn & Bacon.

Chung, H., Elias, M., & Schneider, K. (1998). Patterns of individual adjustment changes during the middle school transition. *Journal of School Psychology, 36,* 83–101.

Crockett, L., Peterson, A., Graber, J., Schulenburg. J., & Ebata, A. (1989). School transitions and adjustment during early adolescence. *Journal of Early Adolescence, 9,* 181–210.

Eccles, J., & Midgley, C. (1989). Stage/environment fit: Developmentally appropriate classrooms for early adolescents. In R. Ames & C. Ames (Eds.), *Research on motivation in education* (Vol. 3, pp. 139–186). New York: Academic.

Eccles, J., Wigfield, A., Midgley, C., Reuman, D., MacIver, D., & Feldlaufer, H. (1993). Negative effects of traditional middle schools on students' motivation. *The Elementary School Journal, 93,* 553–574.

Elias, M., Gara, M., & Ubriaco, M. (1985). Sources of stress and support in children's transition to middle school: An empirical analysis. *Journal of Clinical Child Psychology, 14,* 112–118.

Elias, M., Ubriaco, M., Reese, A., Gara, M., Rothbaum, P., & Haviland, M. (1992). A measure of adaptation to problematic academic and interpersonal tasks of middle school. *Journal of School Psychology, 30,* 41–57.

Felner, R., Brand, S., Adan, A., Mulhall, P., Flowers, N., Sartain, H., & DuBois, D. (1993). Restructuring the ecology of the school as an approach to prevention during school transitions: Longitudinal follow-ups and extensions of the School Transition Environment Project (STEP). *Prevention in Human Services, 10*(2), 103–136.

Giorgo, A. (1985). *Phenomenology and psychological research.* Pittsburgh. PA: Duquesne University.

Harter, S. (1981). A new self-report scale of intrinsic versus extrinsic orientation in the classroom: Motivational and informational components. *Developmental Psychology, 17,* 300–312.

Hirsch, B., & DuBois, D. (1992). The relation of peer support and psychological symptomatology during the transition to junior high school: A two-year longitudinal analysis. *American Journal of Community Psychology, 20,* 333–347.

Hirsch, B., & Rapkin, B. (1987). The transition to junior high school: A longitudinal study of self-esteem, psychological symptomatology, school life, and social support. *Child Development, 58,* 1235–1243.

Holsti, O. (1969). *Content analysis for the social sciences and humanities.* Reading, MA: Addison-Wesley.

Mittman, A., & Packer, M. (1982). Concerns of seventh graders about their transition to junior high school. *Journal of Early Adolescence,* 2, 319–338.

Papalia, D., Olds, S., & Feldman, R. (2001). *Human development* (8th ed.). New York: McGraw-Hill.

Perkins, P., & Gelfer, J. (1995). Elementary to middle school: Planning for transition. *The Clearing House, 68,* 171–173.

Rowan, J. (1981). A dialectical paradigm for research. In P. Reason & J. Rowan (Eds.), *Human inquiry* (pp. 93–112). New York: John Wiley.

Schumacher, D. (1998). *The transition to middle school* (Report No. EDO-PS-98-6). Washington, DC: Clearinghouse on Elementary and Early Childhood Education. (ERIC Document Reproduction Service No. ED 422 119)

Seidman, I. (1991). *Interviewing as qualitative research: A guide for researchers in education and the social sciences.* New York: Columbia Teachers Press.

Simmons, R., & Blyth, D. (1987). *Moving into adolescence: The impact of pubertal change and school context.* Hawthorne, NY: Aldine de Gruyter.

Acknowledgment: This research was sponsored by the American School Counselor Association Practitioner Grant.

STUDY QUESTIONS

1. What is mixed-method research, and how is it distinguished from other types of research?
2. What are the advantages and disadvantages of mixed-method research designs?
3. When are mixed-method designs useful?
4. How do explanatory, exploratory, and convergent designs differ in purpose and procedure?
5. What are the key advantages and disadvantages of each type of mixed-method design?
6. Why is it important for researchers to clearly explain their rationale for conducting a mixed-method study?
7. What is the difference between *priority* and *sequence* in mixed-methods designs?
8. How do explanatory, exploratory, and convergent designs differ in priority and sequence?
9. What are some key considerations in evaluating mixed-method studies?

Chapter 12

Action Research

with
LISA ABRAMS

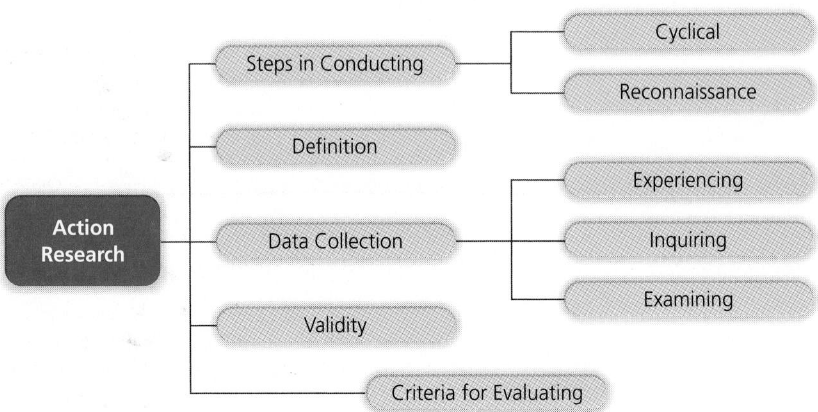

CHAPTER ROAD MAP

OK, now it's time to plan and conduct your own study! This will be accomplished with what is called *action research*. **Action research** is a systematic investigation conducted by practitioners to provide information to immediately improve teaching and learning. The emphasis is on teachers, counselors, and administrators designing, carrying out, and using the results of a study in their immediate work environment.

Action research: Conducted by and for practitioners.

Chapter Outline	Learning Objectives
What Is Action Research?	• Know the characteristics of action research. • Know how action research is different from more traditional types of research.
Why Action Research?	• Understand how action research can be used to enhance practice.
Conducting Action Research	• Know the steps that are used to conduct action research.
Selecting a Topic	• Know how to come up with a researchable topic. • Apply reconnaissance to establish an area of focus. • Be able to establish specific research questions.
Determine Design and Data Collection	• Describe interventions. • Identify measures that will be used to collect data. • Be able to identify common quantitative and qualitative data collection techniques. • Know the differences between examining, experiencing, and enquiring. • Understand how triangulation can improve results. • Know ethical guidelines that should be used to implement the study.
Summarize and Interpret Data	• Understand which descriptive data are most important and how to present the data.
Using Action Research	• Know how to draw conclusions from the data. • Understand how different types of validity are used to establish credibility of the conclusions.
Evaluating Action Research	• Know the criteria for evaluating the quality of action research. • Apply the criteria for evaluating action research to an actual action research study.

WHAT *is* ACTION RESEARCH?

With the recent emphasis on best practice, evidence-based practice, and data-driven decision making in schools, the field of practitioner research and inquiry continues to grow. These studies have become commonplace and very important in schools. The emphasis of this chapter is on one form of practitioner inquiry—action research. This form of research is exciting because it brings together characteristics of systematic inquiry and practice, making it highly relevant and useful.

Action research is an area that is gaining increased attention and recognition in the field of educational research. The term *action research* was first used by Kurt Lewin, a social psychologist, in the 1930s (Mills, 2007). Lewin recognized how specific social problems could be addressed through group discussions (Creswell, 2005). According to Creswell (2005), Lewin's group process included four stages: planning, acting, observing, and reflecting. This approach was the basis for the current approaches and models of action research that emphasize a clear systematic process, participation of various stakeholders, collaboration, and a focus on social change. The emphasis of action research is on practical value, not publication in journals (though many action research studies are published). The following are several definitions of action research that are related to Lewin's original intent:

- An investigation conducted by the person or the people empowered to action concerning their own actions, for the purpose of improving their future actions (Sagor, 2005, p. 4).
- A constructive inquiry, during which the researcher constructs his or her knowledge of specific issues through planning, acting, evaluating, refining, and learning from the experiences . . . a continuous learning process in which the researcher learns and also shares the newly generated knowledge with those who may benefit from it (Koshy, 2005, p. 9).
- Any systematic inquiry conducted by teachers, researchers, principals, school counselors, or other stakeholders in the teaching/learning environment to gather information about how their particular schools operate, how they teach, and how well their students learn. . . . [It] is done by teachers for themselves (Mills, 2007, p. 5).
- Collaborations among school-based teachers, and other educators, university-based colleagues, and sometimes parents and community activists. The efforts of action research center on altering curriculum, challenging common school practices, and working for social change by engaging in a continuous process of problem posing, data gathering, analysis, and action (Cochran-Smith & Lytle, 2009, p. 40).

Clearly, the word *action* signifies a significant departure from traditional research. The intent is to do something different in teaching, to change instruction or other practices, based on more than personal experience or suggestions from others. There is an application of systematic inquiry into a teacher's classroom. By being directly relevant and because of the investment of effort, the results are often very persuasive. Knowledge is generated from within the school, rather than from outside sources.

Because so much of the emphasis of action research is on teachers, you may find the terms *teacher researchers* or *teachers-as-researchers* in such studies. Other terms used to indicate a type of action research include *classroom research*, *teacher research*, *teacher action research*, *classroom action research*, *school research*, *school action research*, and *collaborative action research*.

BENEFITS *of* ACTION RESEARCH

Action research has a number of benefits. In the process of conducting action research, teachers, counselors, and administrators collaborate with others and reflect meaningfully on why the results were obtained and what the results mean as related to their teaching or counseling. This not only empowers teachers, it also helps them understand the benefits of existing literature in an area as well as evidence-based systematic inquiry. Action research engages individuals and acts as a powerful professional development activity. It models a way of thinking for students, and changes the professional dispositions of teachers. Finally, action research changes the climate of a school to a more open atmosphere in which it is standard practice to openly ponder teaching methods, take risks, and depend on others to design studies and to understand the usefulness of results. Glanz (2003, p. 19) lists the following benefits of action research:

- Creates a systemwide mind-set for school improvement—a professional problem-solving ethos.
- Enhances decision making—provides greater feelings of competence in solving problems and making instructional decisions. In other words, action research provides for an intelligent way of making decisions.
- Promotes reflection and self-assessment.
- Instills a commitment to continuous improvement.
- Creates a more positive school climate in which teaching and learning are foremost concerns.
- Impacts directly on practice.
- Empowers those who participate in the process. For instance, educational leaders who undertake action research may no longer uncritically accept theories, innovations, and programs at face value.

There is one additional benefit that we think is very important. Implementing action research gives practitioners the tools to think more systematically about the effectiveness of the practices. The tools are principles of research, such as how to present and summarize data, construct graphs, and consider threats to internal validity. Through the process of action research, these skills are strengthened and subsequently applied to reading published studies and critically analyzing conclusions. The approach to learning about research is relevant and meaningful, something that may be missing in a class or workshop on traditional research.

Action research differs from traditional research in several ways. As discussed in this chapter, action research has a practical focus and can be conducted in a participatory or collaborative manner. The practical aspect of action research situates the focus of the investigation within a specific context such as a classroom or school. The results of the research are intended to inform a plan of action related to instructional decisions, curricular changes, or school policies, for example. As such, the sampling, data collection methods, analysis, and dissemination reflect this emphasis on practical and local problem solving. The results of action research studies are not intended to be broadly applicable beyond the specific context or problem which is the focus of the study. Action research encourages teachers and administrators to engage in reflective practice and is considered a form of professional development. These characteristics clearly distinguish action research from traditional research. Table 12.1 summarizes the differences between the two. The reader should keep in mind, however, that there can be significant variability in the extent to which characteristics of traditional research are used in action research.

TABLE 12.1 Characteristics of Action Research Versus Traditional Research

Characteristic	Action Research	Traditional Research
Goal	New knowledge relevant to the local setting	New knowledge that contributes to the field of study
Who determines the research question and carries out the study?	Practitioners: teachers, principals, counselors	Trained researchers: university professors, scholars, graduate students
Setting in which research is carried out	Schools and classrooms where the practice is implemented	Any setting in which appropriate control is achieved
Literature review	Brief, with a focus on secondary sources	Extensive, with an emphasis on primary sources
Instrumentation	Measures are often locally developed and are convenient and easy to administer and score	Measures typically off-the-shelf, selected on the basis of technical adequacy
Sampling	Convenience, purposeful sampling of teachers and students in the targeted setting	Tends to be random or representative
Design	Tends to be nonexperimental or quasi-experimental	Whatever design is needed
Data analysis	Descriptive	Descriptive and inferential
Dissemination of results	To specific individual or school	To the field through presentations and publications

CONDUCTING ACTION RESEARCH

As illustrated in Figure 12.1, the steps in conducting action research are cyclical, indicating an ongoing series of studies to address a research problem, coupled

FIGURE 12.1 Steps in conducting action research.

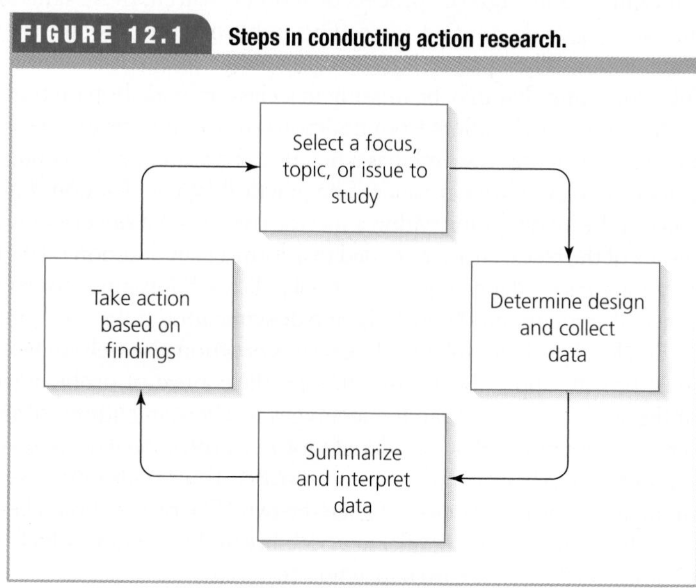

with action and critical reflection. As such, it is an emergent process that modifies research based on the results of action. This is important because it increases the relevance and application of the results, promotes collaboration, and stresses the recursive nature of the process. Essentially, it is a continuing process of research → action → reflection → research → action → reflection → research → action → reflection. Note in Example 12.1 the reference to this cyclical process.

EXAMPLE 12.1 | Cyclical Process in Action Research

This study was conducted in three phases over a two-year period and involved students and staff from three faculties. . . . An action research process based on cycles of action and reflection . . . was used to develop peer assessment procedures that were responsive to the student and staff needs and concerns. This process was participatory, collaborative, and reflexive.

Source: Ballantyne, R., Highes, K., & Mylonas, A. (2002). Developing procedures for implementing peer assessment in large classes using an action research process. *Assessment and Evaluation in Higher Education, 27*(5), 427.

Selecting a Focus, Topic, or Issue to Study

Selecting a focus area is the initial step in any kind of research. Most importantly, you need to identify a practical problem that can be systematically investigated. There are five criteria to use to when identifying an area. The area of study should:

1. Involve some aspect of teaching/learning.
2. Be something that is a part of your own teaching, classroom, or school.
3. Be something that you can control or have influence on.
4. Be something that you can change or improve.
5. Be something you feel passionate about, something that you are motivated to learn more about.

Usually, the experiences of the practitioner are used to identify topics for action research. School-based action research topics may address individual students, classrooms, group work, instruction, curriculum, or school improvement issues. Generally, the focus of action research among teachers and administrations include areas that concern improving teaching, learning, and the overall school atmosphere or functioning. Research is often suggested to address educational issues in an effort to gain understanding or solve problems. Once topics are identified, researchable questions need to be formulated to determine the appropriate methods of data collection. Example 12.2 describes an elementary science resource teacher's investigation of the effectiveness of an instructional unit on student learning. The researchable question that guided this action research project was, "What are the students' conceptions of the specific life science topics and how are they influenced by the teaching of a unit on crayfish adaptations?" (Endreny, 2006). This question informed the selection and use of several different data collection methods, including interviews, observations, and written assessments.

EXAMPLE 12.2 | Action Research Questions and Process

In this paper, I describe the action research I conducted in my third-grade science classrooms over the course of two years. In order to gain an understanding of my third-grade students' ideas about animal adaptations and how the teaching of a unit on crayfish influenced these ideas, I used clinical interviews, observations, and written assessments. I did this research while working as a science resource teacher in a suburban elementary school. Their first year, I piloted the unit myself and then made changes to the unit based upon my findings. During the second year, the entire third-grade team taught the unit, and I co-taught with one of these third-grade classroom teachers. I found that students' ideas are developing and the connections to other parts of the science curriculum such as habitats, gases, and plants were necessary yet lacking. Teachers should be prepared to understand these connections themselves and to highlight them to students. Teachers should recognize that elementary students will not develop an understanding of adaptations from merely working with and observing animals in their habitats. Further research in needed to see if the students need specific lessons on adaptations, an understanding of evolution, and/or more experience and maturity in order to truly understand the concept of adaptation.

Source: Endreny, A. (2006). Children's ideas about animal adaptations: An action research project. *Journal of Elementary Science Education, (18)*1, 33–43.

Reconnaissance: Self-reflection of focus

Once an area is identified, it is helpful to reflect on the area through a process termed *reconnaissance*. **Reconnaissance** occurs as you take time to self-reflect on the area from the perspective of your own beliefs and from the context of the classroom or school. This time of self-reflection allows you to enhance your understanding of the area from the perspective of theories, values, beliefs, knowledge, the larger context of your school, and relevant historical contexts. Essentially, reconnaissance is self-reflection that solidifies the significance of your area of focus.

There are several practical approaches to take in identifying the area of focus. One technique is to write down some reflections about what has and has not worked in your area of interest, or to keep a journal of thoughts. Note in the following example how this teacher simply lets her thoughts flow, without trying to identify a specific area.

EXAMPLE 12.3 | Teacher Written Self-Reflection

Teaching social studies to eighth-graders had become such a battle for me. Over the years, I became used to seeing the same pattern: My students came to class on Day 1 expecting to hate it. They saw no purpose in studying government and were sure that this was going to be the most boring material they would ever have to endure. . . . What was even worse was dealing with their cynicism. Truthfully, I was starting to dread the start of each new class. I once read where at the beginning of each term, the students and the teacher negotiate a treaty.

Source: Sagor, R. (2005). *The action research guidebook: A four-step process for educators and school teams.* Thousand Oaks, CA: SAGE, 13.

Eventually, you will want to focus on *who*, *what*, *where*, and *when*. Answering these questions will help you identify more specific research questions from a general area of focus. For example, a teacher could ask the following about the general area of teaching grammar:

- Which students are having the most difficulty with grammar?
- What is the nature of the evidence used to confirm that this is, indeed, a problem?
- Are students having difficulty during class or with homework?
- How much time do students spend on grammar in class and with homework?

Addressing these questions, the teacher might decide to focus on grammar homework and identify students who are having the most difficulty. Alternatively, the teacher could decide to use a new instructional approach in her classroom that purportedly maintains better student engagement and motivation.

Another approach to reconnaissance is to simply talk with others. Not only will your own thoughts be clarified by articulating them to others, but through the discussions you will get different perspectives, ideas, and suggestions about the nature of interventions, measurement of variables, and data analysis. Involving others helps establish a team mentality and keeps individual perspectives in context. Administrators need to talk with teachers, and teachers need to talk with administrators.

It is always helpful to do some reading on the topic. This can be accomplished through a brief review of literature, which is easily done by accessing ERIC on the Internet. The Internet can be searched more generally as well. Chances are very good that other practitioners have written and thought about the same topic. Professional journals that come to the school can be reviewed, and professional organizations have many good ideas and resources. The important part of doing a literature review is to *keep it brief.* There is so much out there that it's easy to keep reading and reading. Action research is primarily intended to inform practice, so the literature needs to be reviewed with that purpose in mind. Practitioners have limited time, which is why secondary sources are excellent. Trying to understand primary studies may simply take too long for this type of research. That being said, it is always helpful to read the literature!

As a result of reconnaissance, specific research questions can be generated. If data collection involves quantitative methods, independent and dependent variables should be identified. If qualitative, then the questions will be more general. At this point it's also helpful to indicate if there is a need for descriptive, comparative, relationship, or causal conclusions. This will help direct the nature of the design for collecting data.

Notice in Example 12.4 the informal, conversational tone of the author describing how the area of focus was identified for her study. This style of writing is typical.

EXAMPLE 12.4 | Identifying an Area of Focus

While I was teaching, I was concurrently enrolled in a master's degree program where I learned new strategies for middle school students and involved them in action research pilot projects. I experienced some success in my classroom and offered to share the approached I'd learned with Lydia and Jane. . . . I just wanted to help struggling students and teachers. . . . I came to realize that changing just a few aspects of the reading program would not be enough; the entire program needed to be overhauled.

Source: Ahrens, B. C. (2005). Finding a new way: Reinventing a sixth-grade reading program. *Journal of Adolescent and Adult Literacy, 48*(8), 645.

Determine Design and Data Collection

The second step in doing action research is to determine what kind of design will be employed, the nature of the data that need to be gathered, and how that data will be collected. Decisions need to be made about whether the design is qualitative, experimental, or nonexperimental; what type or types of data need to be collected; and the sample from which the data will be collected. Initially, both quantitative and qualitative methods should be considered. Using both approaches and a variety of data collection strategies strengthens the study by providing multiple perspectives.

Using multiple types of data collection from different sources to strengthen studies is also known as *triangulation*. Table 12.2 illustrates the concept of triangulation in action research. As shown, there are multiple data sources for each of the three questions that are the focus of the action research study. Note that the data collection methods include both quantitative and qualitative approaches. For example, the second research question asks, "What changes occurred with our priority achievement targets?" To answer this question, the researcher collected quantitative measures of student achievement such as grades (i.e., data source 1) and qualitative observational notes and examples of student work or artifacts.

TABLE 12.2 Triangulation in Action Research

Research Question	Data Source 1	Data Source 2	Data Source 3
What did we actually do?	• Lesson plan book	• Attendance record	• Joann's portfolio of daily work
What changes occurred with our priority achievement targets?	• Grade book (quizzes, homework, journals, reflection papers, projects tests, weekly assessments)	• Observational notes • Comments on her tests and papers	• Joann's portfolio of daily work • Joann's self-assessments
What was the relationship between the actions taken and changes in performance on the achievement targets?	• Contrast lesson plans with performance data from grade book	• Correlate lesson plans with observation notes • Correlate lesson plans with comments on papers	• Correlate lesson plans with material in Joann's portfolio • Correlate lesson plans with Joann's self-assessments.

Adapted from Sagor, R. (2005). *The Action research guidebook: A four-step process for educators and school teams.* Thousand Oaks, CA: Corwin Press, p. 98.

With the emphasis on *action* in action research, it is often recommended that teachers do a small-scale experiment by using an intervention and then seeing the effect of it on student outcomes such as achievement and attitudes. With these experiments it is difficult, to say the least, to have a within-class control or comparison group, and to randomly assign students to an intervention and control group. This means that most experimental action research is, at best, quasi-experimental. Often it is a simple pretest-posttest design in which students complete a pretest, experience an intervention, and then take the posttest. Here, the most significant threat to internal validity is history, but that can usually be addressed because the teacher is intimately involved in the situation and will know what other influences have occurred. It's as though the teacher is an anthropologist, from a qualitative perspective, in knowing very well what has transpired during the experiment. As explained earlier in Chapter 8, this is a great supplement to an experiment.

The most typical qualitative design is a case study. When there is a need to understand something within the context of a specific class or school, it is essentially a signal entity that is studied. The nature of the case is defined as a single group of students in the case of a classroom, or teachers if the focus is on the school. The purpose is to gain a detailed description and understanding of the area of focus. The research question is general, rather than specific. The results are used to determine possible actions in the setting, rather than to study the effect of an intervention *as* action. Different qualitative data collection techniques can be used, with the greatest emphasis on interviewing and observation.

The sample is usually a given—whoever is in the class or school being studied. What you need to think about is which students or teachers in the school should be included in data collection. Sometimes it is best to use all students in a class, especially when the inquiry has clear implications for all of them. Sometimes it's better to select a sample from a larger group, as when investigating certain types of students or when conducting a small-scale experiment in which there is a control or comparison group.

A factor in determining the sample as well as the study design will be what is needed for human subjects' protection. Depending on the school or school district policies, this might mean obtaining permission from parents (i.e., parental consent) to conduct research with their children, and quite possibly obtaining permission from the students. This permission process allows parents and students to carefully consider participation in the study. Sometimes this type of active consent process results in a smaller sample than anticipated, so you will need to be careful about bias in the sample. Regardless, priority should be placed on clearly communicating to parents and students what participation in the study involves and allowing for voluntary participation. In action research, the dual role of teacher and researcher presents unique and complex ethical considerations.

A recently completed study illustrates sampling by targeting specific students. The area of focus is on the motivation of high-ability students, and a single-subject design is used, much like an experiment with only two subjects.

In selecting measurement tools and approaches, it's a challenge to select the right one or ones, primarily because there is so much to choose from

EXAMPLE 12.5 | Purposeful Sampling in Action Research

After nearly a full year in the second-grade class, both students have shown varying degrees of interest in learning and self-discipline. There was an apparent discrepancy between their scores on standardized tests their actual performance on daily work in the classroom. They quite often seemed to coast and attempt to get by with the barest minimum of effort.

Source: Hargrove, K. (2005). What's a teacher to do? *Gifted Child Today, 28*(4), 38.

(see Figure 12.2). A good starting point is to decide whether quantitative or qualitative measures will be used by themselves or in some combination. Whatever the approach, measures typically are locally developed and targeted to the class or school, rather than being standardized. The quality of the measures, then, depends heavily on judgments of items and instruments related to reliability and validity. Here, individuals need to have others review intended measures for clarity and credibility, making sure that researcher bias is minimized. Another important principle about instrumentation for action research is to use more than one measure of the dependent variable or outcome of interest. This allows for triangulation to support credibility and trustworthiness.

Mills (2007) suggests that it is helpful to think about qualitative data collection techniques in one of three categories: experiencing, enquiring, or examining. These categories are especially relevant to the nature of action research. *Experiencing* refers

FIGURE 12.2 Examples of different types of action research.

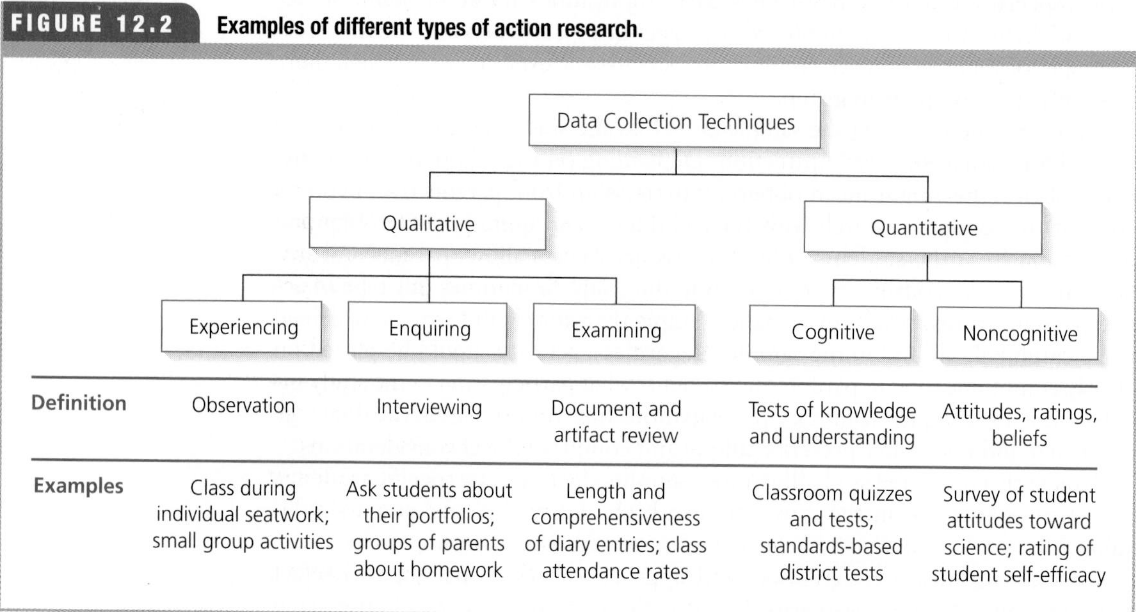

to the use of direct observation of participants. Teachers constantly observe, so it is relatively easy and convenient for them to formalize their observations to be more systematic and rigorous. As an active participant in the class, the teacher often takes on the role of *participant observer*. With this role in qualitative data collection, the teacher needs to find a way to record what is or has occurred. Since teaching requires full immersion, the recording of observations needs to be somewhat formal. This can be done by allowing a few minutes after a lesson or classroom activity to write notes, at the end of the day, and at breaks during the day. Discipline is required! From a qualitative perspective you might want to record "everything" going on, but it is more realistic to try to be more focused. Keep your recording of what has happened separate from your opinions about what it means. That helps to control personal bias and allows others to more easily check what might be inferred.

Enquiring in qualitative approaches means interviewing students, teachers, parents, or whoever would be most appropriate, to obtain information. It is best to have a semistructured format so that, as in observing, there is some degree of focus. A completely unstructured interview is simply too broad and has less probability of eliciting important information. Also, unstructured interviews require greater training. By asking a few questions to prompt open-ended responses, you will have the best chance of getting the data you need. Plan on taking notes during the interview, whether it is with an individual or with a small group. Notes should be brief and completed as soon as possible after the interview. While recording interviews can be very helpful, it can be time-consuming to listen and/or do written transcriptions.

There are two key features of successful interviews in action research. The first is to make sure that you are interviewing the right students or parents. Interviews are effective as a way to gather in-depth data from just a few individuals, so those selected to be interviewed are critical. You want to select individuals who (1) will answer the questions with more than just a few words, and (2) will not be influenced by their "subordinate" position to you. This second issue is a difficult one. If you don't get honest, thoughtful answers, the study will not be productive. Ensuring confidentiality is helpful, but most important is your ability to set participants at ease and take the time necessary to establish a positive relationship in the interview. Often a combination of small group and individual interviews is effective, though in some groups there might be a reluctance for participants to be honest and/or for a few participants to dominate. Again, the best approach is to use more than one method of collecting information so that you are not entirely dependent on what is obtained from the interview.

Examining refers to the use of existing documents, records, and other artifacts that are already available or will become available. Examples include minutes of meetings, archival data, attendance, discipline referrals, test scores, and student participation in co-curricular activities. Student journals and responses to open-ended questions and prompts can also be used. For example, if you did a study to enhance students' interest in reading, an artifact that could be used would be the number of books taken from the school library. In Example 12.6 the authors used student written and verbal reactions related to assignments to better understand how students acted on them.

EXAMPLE 12.6 | Qualitative Data Collection

Because we were interested in how students understood and acted on these assignments, we focused considerable attention on each student's verbal and written reactions to the social and community inquiry assignments. Using standard qualitative data analysis techniques for developing themes through coding, we examined these data sources to learn how our students understood broad systems of oppression and how that understanding was in turn associated with their role as teachers.

Source: Hyland, E., & Noffke, S. E. (2005). Understanding diversity through social and community inquiry: An action-research study. *Journal of Teacher Education, 56*(4), 372.

Quantitative data collection can be divided into tests, quizzes, papers, and projects designed to assess student knowledge and understanding (cognitive) and questionnaires that measure student or teacher perceptions. Teacher-made tests are used most frequently, though in our current climate of accountability there are often district tests that can provide a more "external" assessment of knowledge, understanding, and skills. It is very important for teachers to have colleagues review tests, both before giving them and after students' open-ended answers and products, such as papers, projects, and presentations, are graded. These judgments will provide validity evidence to support the accuracy of the evaluations. While "objective" tests reduce the potential influence of researcher bias, remember that professional judgments are involved in both the development of questions and scoring of responses.

Noncognitive quantitative assessment occurs as students self-report their attitudes, values, and beliefs on questionnaires. These instruments are very helpful, especially if they can be administered in a way that ensures students' anonymity. It is best to use short questionnaires, and better to use several short ones rather than a long one. Questionnaires are relatively easy to prepare, administer, and score, and provide a very helpful supplement to qualitative methods.

Summarizing and Interpreting Data

When quantitative measures are used, the best kind of summary and interpretation is descriptive, using calculations such as mean, range, and standard deviation. The data need to be cleaned to remove any outliers or any obviously inaccurate numbers. The summary presents what you found; the interpretation focuses on what the summary means, how it should be interpreted. Graphs of results are commonly used, including bar graphs and histograms, and provide an effective summary. Descriptive statistics should be interpreted on the basis of practical, not statistical, significance. With the small number of subjects used in action research, it is very difficult to obtain statistical significance, and many teachers are not well versed in what statistical significance means. What is most important is a descriptive summary that best informs the practice of education within the specific context.

VALIDITY *in* ACTION RESEARCH

Making a determination about the validity or credibility of the conclusions drawn from action research is dependent on the research design and data collection methods that were employed to conduct the investigation. As such, researchers should use the recommendations for ensuring the validity of interpretations of results that have been discussed in previous chapters of this book. In addition to these recommendations, Anderson, Herr, and Nihlen (1994) suggested that action research required a unique system for judging the integrity or quality of the study. This system is based on five criteria: *democratic validity*, *outcome validity*, *process validity*, *catalytic validity*, and *dialogic validity*.

Democratic validity is concerned with representation of the stakeholders in either the process of conducting the action research or as data sources. For example, in an effort to ensure democratic validity, a researcher would want to gather multiple perspectives on an issue from the relevant groups that have a stake in the problem, such as students, other teachers, parents, and administrators. Also, researchers may want to put together a collaborative research team that includes members from these various stakeholder groups. *Outcome validity* refers to the extent to which the action plan that emerges from the study is viable and effective. For example, researchers would want to ask, "Does the action plan address the problem?" *Process validity* is related to concepts of internal validity in quantitative research, and models of credibility (Maxwell, 1992) and trustworthiness (Guba, 1981) in qualitative research. Process validity is concerned with the way in which the action research study was conducted. According to Mills (2007), "Process validity requires that a study has been conducted in a 'dependable' and 'competent' manner" (p. 91). Enhancing process validity requires that action researchers take measures to ensure that their data collection methods are effective and appropriate for obtaining the information needed to answer the questions guiding the study. *Catalytic validity* is based on the "action" component of action research. This concept of validity addresses the extent to which participants are compelled to "take action," such as changing instruction, modifying curriculum, or implementing new or altering existing school policies on the basis of the study findings. The final criteria, according to Anderson et al. (1994), *dialogic validity* is related to the dissemination of the study findings. Sharing the results of the action research investigation involves having a "conversation" or dialogue with colleagues through some type of public medium, such as peer-reviewed journals, conferences, district-level professional development sessions, or websites.

CONSUMER TIPS: *Criteria for Evaluating Action Research*

1. Determine the motivation and involvement of the researcher. Good action research is conducted by individuals who have a vested interest in the study, but at the same time this motivation should not result in experimenter bias. The more the researcher is involved in doing an intervention and obtaining information, the greater the opportunity for experimenter bias.

2. Look for consistency between the research question and your methodology. Action research uses whatever methodology is most appropriate, so the determining factor is nature of the question. Much, if not most, action research has some kind of qualitative component. That approach is best when the emphasis is on deeper understanding of a practice or effect on learning.

3. Look for whether multiple methods of data collection have been utilized. There are many advantages to using multiple methods of data collection, especially in action research where there may not be sophisticated psychometric properties of the measures.

4. Confirm that there has been an emergent, cyclical process of research—action—reflection. The cyclical nature of action research is essential to being effective. It's not simply a matter of doing a single study; there needs to be a continual spiral of action based on research that is reflected on and followed by more research, action, and reflection.

5. Is there any external monitoring or feedback? In the best of circumstances teachers and administrators who are conducting action research receive some kind of "external" review of their methodology, results, and reflection. This can be accomplished by another professional in the school or district. It's an important step to maintain quality control and give feedback that will facilitate further good research, which provides credible information that can be used to change practice.

ANATOMY OF AN ACTION RESEARCH STUDY

The following article is an example of how action research is conducted and reported.

ARTICLE 12.1 Improving Student Understanding and Motivation of Multiplication Facts

Fourth-grade teacher (teacher-researcher)

Alyson Maryland

Abstract

This action research project focuses on promoting student understanding and motivation while teaching the basic multiplication facts (0–9). The study examined the effectiveness of teaching methods with an emphasis on rote memorization, compared to those focusing on problem solving. Research advocates the use of problem solving when introducing and teaching basic facts, and holding off on drill and practice methods until after they've developed an understanding. The participants in the study consist of thirty-five fourth-grade students. The students participated in lessons on arrays and multiplication games, and they discussed efficient versus inefficient counting strategies. Data were collected from their old timed tests, state math scores, interviews, and worksheets. The results of the study suggest a positive relationship between balancing conceptual understanding and procedural skills, and student success with basic facts. The results also show a positive relationship between playing games and student motivation for studying the basic facts.

INTRODUCTION

Research problem focused on instructional strategies

Research suggests that for every time you do something wrong, you have to do it right seventeen times before your brain gets used to doing it correctly. These findings are startling when you consider the vast amount of drill and practice methods used in the classroom to teach students their basic math facts. The purpose of my action research project was to seek out and examine effective and efficient methods for teaching the basic facts. My second objective for this project was to develop effective strategies for increasing student motivation in terms of studying their multiplication facts. Students are often frustrated and bored studying things they don't understand, or when using tedious study methods.

BACKGROUND

Review of literature

According to the 2004–2005 Oregon State Standards, by the end of fourth grade students are expected to have developed efficient strategies for solving multiplication problems. They should be fluent with these strategies and able to solve all basic fact problems mentally within three seconds. Unfortunately, researchers have found that an alarming number of eighth grade students still resort to finger counting and other inefficient strategies when solving simple problems (Isaacs, Carroll, & Bell, 2001). These strategies are inefficient because they take too much time and are not done mentally.

One promising practice is to reduce the use of drill and practice methods (Jones, 1995). These methods include timed tests, flash cards, and worksheets with rows of basic facts. One reason researchers advise educators to stay away from drill and practice methods is because they don't aid in students' conceptual understanding of multiplication. These methods provide students with procedural skills that they are taught to mimic. Teaching in this way makes it hard for students to apply multiplication concepts to word problems or real-life situations.

Significance

Effective strategies for teaching basic facts include balancing procedural skills and conceptual knowledge. Teaching with balance includes the use of word problems, arrays, and open-ended problem-solving assignments. Isaacs et al. (2001) recommend practicing multiplication in a variety of contexts and situations to increase the students' ability to transfer the skill/concept.

Other promising practices suggest three components to use when teaching basic facts. The first component is developing a strong understanding of the operations of number relationships. The second focuses on trading inefficient strategies for efficient ones, and the third component is providing students with drill and practice assignments. Van de Walle (2003) stresses the importance of not moving to step three until after the students have developed efficient strategies. If you introduce drill before the students have mastered one or more efficient strategies, the practice will only reinforce the inefficient strategies. Inefficient strategies include counting on fingers, adding the numbers instead of multiplying them, using manipulatives, drawing pictures, etc. Inefficient methods are inefficient because they take a long time and cannot be done mentally. Efficient methods include skip counting, simplifying the problem, and ultimately, memorization.

INTERVENTION

Suggests experimental study

My planned intervention to address students' understanding of, and motivation to learn, basic number facts included the following:

Note informal first person style of writing

- Lessons focused on building students' conceptual understanding of the multiplication process.
- Teaching students efficient strategies for solving basic facts.
- Introducing students to fun games they could play while studying their basic number facts.

DATA COLLECTION

The data collection tools I used were:

1. Students' scores on state math tests
2. Results of timed tests
3. Informal interviews
4. Students' written work

Very brief; suggests mixed-methods.

(continued)

ARTICLE 12.1 (continued)

DATA ANALYSIS

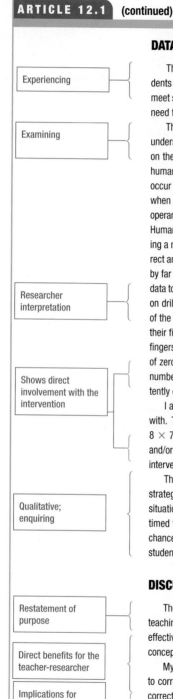

Experiencing

The data I collected from the students' state math test was surprising. I was shocked to find that eleven students (about thirty-five percent of the class) did not meet the state standards in math. The students who did not meet state standards were consistent with the students who were not passing their timed tests. I decided I would need to spend some extra time working with these eleven students.

Examining

The data I collected from students' timed tests were by far the most helpful in planning my intervention and understanding where students were having the most trouble. The data I collected from the timed tests focused on the types of errors students were making. Edelman, Abdit, and Valentin (1995) describe four types of errors humans make when multiplying; they include operand, table, operation, and non-table errors. Operand errors occur when the incorrect answer given is correct for another problem that shares an operand (e.g., $4 \times 2 = 16$, when 16 is the correct answer for 4×4). Table errors occur when the incorrect answer given does not share an operand with the correct answer, but the answer given does reside in the multiplication table (e.g., $6 \times 9 = 56$). Humans make operation errors when they perform a different operation, such as adding or subtracting, when solving a multiplication problem (e.g., $9 \times 0 = 9$). The final error is a non-table error, and it occurs when the incorrect answer is not an answer to any problem in the multiplication table (e.g., $5 \times 6 = 31$). Operand errors were by far the most common error made by the students, They accounted for fifty-five percent of the error total. This data told me that students were associating the incorrect answer with one of the operands, and the early emphasis on drill and practice has reinforced these wrong answers. Non-table errors accounted for twenty-three percent of the errors. I believe students are making a high amount of non-table errors, because they are miscounting on their fingers. Solving 6×7 on your fingers is both hard and confusing, so I assumed students who rely on their fingers make the majority of the table errors. Operation errors occur mostly in problems containing an operand of zero or one. The students often switch to addition and solve the problem by adding zero or one to the other number. This error occurs mostly when the zero or one is on the bottom. I didn't feel the error occurred consistently enough to be considered a problem, so I decided not to focus on it during my intervention.

Researcher interpretation

Shows direct involvement with the intervention

I also used the students' timed tests to identify which multiplication facts they were having the most trouble with. The problems I found gave students the most trouble were 6×7, 7×6, 7×4, 7×7, 8×8, 8×7, 6×6, 8×6, and 6×8. In general, though, any problem including an operand of six, seven, eight, and/or nine was answered incorrectly by the majority of students. This data was especially helpful in adjusting my interventions, because it allowed me to focus on the problems with which students were having the most trouble.

Qualitative; enquiring

The informal interviews provided me with insight into what the students thought about timed tests, what strategies they used to solve basic fact problems, and how well they could transfer their skills to real-world situations. I was surprised to find that very student answered "yes" to the question about whether or not they felt timed tests were helpful. The majority of students supported their answer stating that timed tests gave them a chance to practice their multiplication facts. The interviews also allowed me to discover which strategy each student relied on when solving multiplication facts.

DISCUSSION

Restatement of purpose

The purpose of my action research project was to seek out and examine effective and efficient methods for teaching basic math facts. Upon completion of my action research project, I feel confident that I will be able to effectively and efficiently teach basic facts to any grade, first through sixth. I am now aware of the common misconceptions regarding rote memorization and the premature use of timed tests.

Direct benefits for the teacher-researcher

Implications for others

My results tell me that timed tests can be beneficial when used as a form of practice. Students should be able to correct their own tests, allowing for immediate feedback on which problems they got wrong and what the correct answer should have been. Teachers should also consider not grading the tests so students can focus on improving their skills and not on a grade.

From my research, experience, and results I was also able to infer that effective teaching strategies center around balancing conceptual understanding and procedural skills. To provide this balance, educators should emphasize problem-solving strategies at an early age. Problem-solving methods provide students with flexibility in their learning, making it easier for them to transfer their knowledge to various math problems and real-life situations. Also, teachers should teach one concept at a time, and teach it to master before moving on.

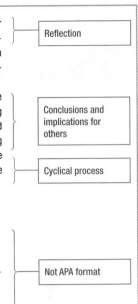

Reflection

To motivate their students, educators must first develop their understanding of the multiplication procedure and concept. This understanding will boost the students' self-esteem, giving them confidence and motivating them intrinsically. The second step in motivating students is introducing fun ways for them to learn, study, and memorize the basic facts. In my experience, students preferred competitive games, especially when playing against the teacher. The participants in my study were really excited about having a "multiplication bowl," where the two fourth-grade classes would face off in a multiplication competition. I am excited to continue to test these teaching strategies in the next cycle of my action research journey.

Conclusions and implications for others

Cyclical process

REFERENCES

Edelman, B., Abdit, H., & Valentin, D. (1995). Multiplication number facts: Modeling human performance with connections networks. *Psychologica Belgica.* 1–23.

Isaacs, A., Carroll, W., & Bell, M. (2001). UCSMP everyday mathematics curriculum. *Everyday Mathematics.* 2–5.

Jones, S. C. (1995). Review of cognitive research. *Educational Memory Aids.* 57–60.

Van de Walle, J. A. (2003). Elementary and middle school mathematics: Teaching developmentally. *Pearson.* 156–176.

Not APA format

STUDY QUESTIONS

1. What makes action research more relevant to practitioners than other types of research?
2. Why does action research use both qualitative and quantitative methods?
3. How does triangulation strengthen the design of an action research study?
4. How does the concept of validity differ in action research compared to other forms of education research?
5. How is the credibility of action research determined?

Chapter 13

Discussion *and* Conclusions

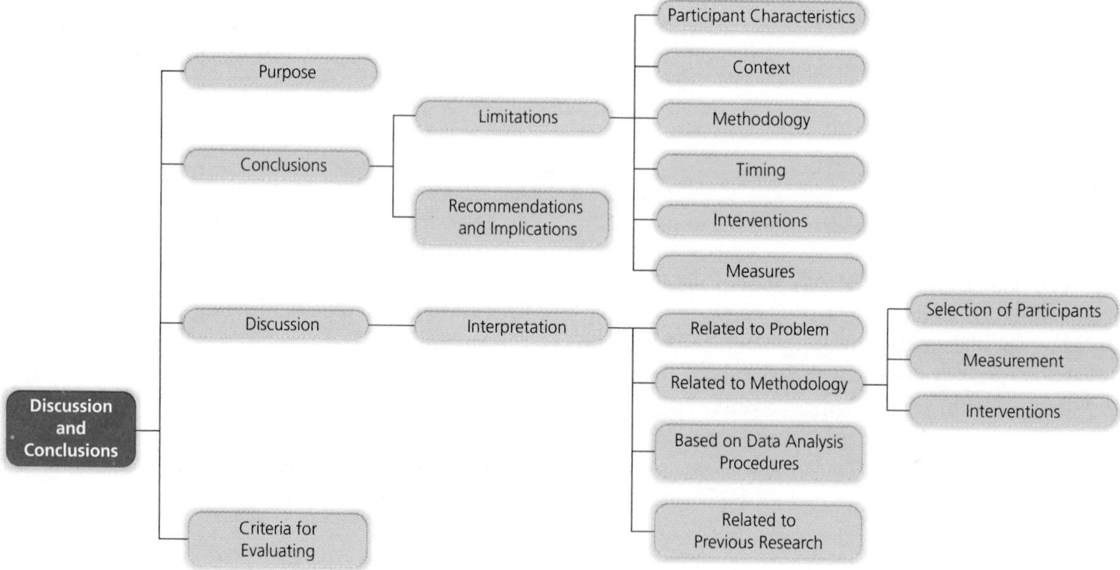

CHAPTER ROAD MAP

We have come to the final section of research reports. Once the results of a study have been summarized, the researcher will present a nontechnical discussion of their meaning. This section of an article may be identified as *Conclusions*, *Conclusions and Recommendations*, *Discussion*, *Summary*, or *Discussion and Conclusions*.

We will first consider why interpretations of the results are needed and the nature of interpretations, then turn to conclusions.

Chapter Outline	Learning Objectives
Discussion	• Know the purpose and format of the discussion section.
Interpretation	• Be able to identify author interpretations of results based on the research problem, previous research, methodology, and statistical procedures. • Understand how interpretations help clarify the meaning of the results.
Conclusions	• Know the difference between results and conclusions. • Be able to identify conclusions. • Understand the limitations of conclusions based on participant characteristics, context, methodology, and time frame.
Recommendations	• Be able to identify and understand author recommendations and implications for further research.

PURPOSE *and* NATURE *of the* DISCUSSION

The purpose of the discussion is to present an interpretation of the results, the conclusions, and recommendations for further study. Authors use the discussion to explain the meaning of the results and to speculate about their implications. The discussion is more than a restatement of the results; it is a more general summary of findings and an evaluation of the methodology and results to help readers understand what the results mean and how they can be used. It is essentially a synthesis of the study reflecting the professional judgment of the researcher. The synthesis integrates the research problem and review of literature with the results, and explains *why* the results were obtained and what the results *mean*. The professional judgment of the researcher is reflected in the nature of the synthesis and the implications suggested in the form of conclusions and recommendations, framed by the significance of the study.

You will find that discussion sections are the least structured parts of an article and that authors differ about content and organization. Some authors begin the discussion with conclusions and then analyze the conclusions, whereas others will explain why they obtained the results, the limitations of the study, and then present the conclusions. Some authors may even combine results with discussion and conclusions. We will consider each of the major aspects of the discussion section, even though the order in which these are found in articles will vary.

INTERPRETATION *of the* RESULTS

Once the results are presented, it is necessary to analyze and interpret them. This analysis consists of reasoned speculation to answer these kinds of questions:

Why did the results turn out as they did?
What may have affected the results?
Are there any limitations that should be noted?
To what extent were hypotheses supported?
What is the meaning of the findings?
How do the results relate to previous research findings?

Interpretation of the results may be related to the research problem and/or hypothesis, theory, statistical procedures, the methodology of the study, and previous research on the problem.

Interpretation Related to the Problem and/or Hypothesis

Discussion sections often begin with a restatement of the problem or hypothesis, followed by some indication of the answer to the problem or degree of support for the hypothesis. There may be an evaluation that the findings provided a strong or clear answer or the hypothesis was strongly or marginally supported. Unexpected findings may be summarized as surprising. In this type of interpretation, the authors indicate their professional opinion about how well the data answer the questions. It is important when reading these interpretations to think about how researcher bias may have influenced the opinions that are expressed. Your judgment about the relationship between the questions and the findings may be quite different from that of the researcher. Sometimes researchers will focus only on findings that support their expectations.

Interpretation Based on Theory

When research has a clear theoretical basis, it is helpful to interpret results in light of that theory. Sometimes competing theories are examined, which would also result in a discussion of how the results are related to the contradictory theories and the extent to which the study contributed to a resolution. Note in Example 13.1 how the authors address theoretical implications of their findings.

EXAMPLE 13.1 | Interpretation Based on Theory

Theoretically, the results generally support instructional practices based on a dual coding theory of reading (Sadoski & Paivio, 2001, 2004), and specifically the VV program of Bell (1986) designed to develop reading comprehension consistent with dual coding theory principles. . . . Other aspects of the LBLP program that are consistent with dual coding theory . . . also received support.

Source: Sadoski, M., & Willson, V. L. (2006). Effects of a theoretically based large-scale reading intervention in a multicultural urban school district. *American Educational Research Journal, 43*(1), 151.

Interpretation Related to Methodology

As stressed throughout this book, methodology is very important in understanding and analyzing results. Often methods are used as a reason for obtaining certain results and also suggest specific limitations. Consequently, when researchers interpret the results, they refer to specific aspects of the methodology. Even if the researchers don't do this, you should! You may find significant weaknesses that are not addressed by the researcher in explaining the results.

For quantitative studies, interpretations related to methodology focus on whether the methods affect internal validity. For experiments, the researcher examines the results to see if there are any methodological factors that could constitute plausible rival hypotheses. For nonexperimental quantitative studies, the focus is on measurement and subject selection. Limitations based on methodology in quantitative investigations are emphasized more with results that fail to show statistical significance.

In qualitative studies, interpretations based on methodology emphasize the researcher's role in gathering and analyzing the data. There is less emphasis on the "limitations" of the methods and more emphasis on the meaning of the results as influenced by methodology.

Interpretation Related to Selection of Participants. One aspect of the methodology that may affect the results is the selection of participants. As noted in Chapter 4, volunteer and available samples may give unique and limited results. Often there is a tendency to ignore the effects of specially selected participants. In the following example, the authors appropriately point out limitations in the results because of sampling.

EXAMPLE 13.2 | Interpretation Based on the Sample

This study has several limitations. Therefore, these limitations should be considered when results are interpreted. First of all, sample size seems too small. Although the current study is titled as Turkish mothers, results should not be generalized to all Turkish mothers or culture. . . . Secondly, almost all participant mothers had little education and all were housewives. This aspect should be carefully taken into account while interpreting the results.

Source: Diken, I. H. (2006). Turkish mothers' interpretations of the disability of their children with mental retardation. *International Journal of Special Education, 21*(2), 16.

For Quantitative and Mixed-Method Studies: Interpretation Related to Measurement of Variables. A second type of interpretation is to examine how the measurement of variables may affect the results. Many of the points in Chapters 5 and 6 are relevant:

- Instruments should show evidence of validity and reliability.
- Procedures for administering an instrument can be important.
- Possible effects of observers and interviewers need to be documented.

- There is the possibility of response set and faking in noncognitive measurement.
- Norms may not be appropriate.

Authors may also point out advantages of using certain measures, as illustrated in Example 13.3.

EXAMPLE 13.3 | Interpretation Based on Measurement of Variables

Certainly, the present results confirm the value of independent assessment of both intrinsic and extrinsic motivations. Our modified version of Harter's (1980, 1981) scale is an initial step toward this end. Indeed, intrinsic and extrinsic motivations were assessed independently in the present with instruments that have been shown to be both reliable and valid. . . . Thus, our decomposed version of Harter's original scale provides the first independent measure of extrinsic motivation for elementary and middle school children. . . . A second advantage of our measures of intrinsic and extrinsic motivation related to the removal of several items from Harter's original scale that were either psychometrically or conceptually problematic in the new format.

Source: Lepper, M. R., Corpus, J. H., & Iyengar, S. S. (2005). Intrinsic and extrinsic motivational orientations in the classroom: Age differences and academic correlates. *Journal of Educational Psychology, 97*(2), 191.

For Quantitative and Mixed-Method Studies: Interpretation Related to the Intervention. A third category of factors in interpreting results concerns experimental intervention. The specific nature of some aspect of an intervention or the manner in which treatments are administered may influence the results (see Examples 13.4 and 13.5).

Note in Example 13.4 how the researchers appropriately addressed an "unexpected" finding.

EXAMPLES 13.4–13.5 | Interpretation Based on the Nature of the Intervention

An unexpected finding was that students in the comparison condition received lower scores on their posttest measures of quality and on the development of their claims than they did at pretest. The most plausible reason for this finding appears to be based on the limitation in the study, noted by the American history professor and high school history teacher, that the posttest materials were slightly harder than those presented at pretest. We believe that students in the experimental group were better equipped to deal with these more difficult materials, after learning the historical reasoning and writing strategies, and their performance was not negatively impacted. In contrast, students in the comparison group had engaged in group discussions that emphasized understanding of specific historical content rather than strategic processes that could be transferred to new learning situations (i.e., different source materials). Hence, their performance suffered when asked to read more difficult materials, and to respond in writing to an historical essay prompt at posttest.

Source: De La Paz, S., & Felton, M. K. (2010). Reading and writing from multiple source documents in history: Effects of strategy instruction with low to average high school writers. *Contemporary Educational Psychology, 35,* 189.

Another potential limitation of the study is the use of only one manipulation of grade distributions and one of grading procedures. In actuality, students' perceptions of distributive fairness may be influenced not only by comparison between their grades and expectations, but also by comparisons between their grades and others' grades.

Source: Tata, J. (1999). Grade distributions, grading procedures, and students' evaluations of instructors: A justice perspective. *The Journal of Psychology, 133*(3), 268.

Interpretation Based on Procedures for Analyzing Data

For quantitative studies, an important factor in a discussion is an analysis of the statistical procedures used in the study. Although a complete discussion of statistical problems is beyond the scope of this book, a few basic statistical principles need to be considered.

The first thing a reader should do is check for any apparent errors in reporting statistical results. This is done by looking for consistency and agreement between numbers reported in tables and graphs and the statements written in narrative form in the article. Errors will inevitably appear despite proofreading because of the frequent transfer of data (from answer sheets to coding sheets to computers to manuscript to typeset copy).

A second concern is whether statistical procedures have violated important assumptions. A *t*-test or analysis of variance, for instance, assumes a population that has a normal distribution, about the same variance for each group, and interval-level measurement. In studies in which violation of the assumptions could have important implications, the researcher should indicate whether the assumptions have been met. In many educational studies there is a question about the appropriate unit of analysis. Because students influence each other in a class and treatments given to classes are not replicated for each individual student, most statisticians believe that the classroom, not the individual student, is the appropriate unit of analysis (the unit of analysis determines the level of significance of the statistical test).

Some researchers assume that the failure to find a statistically significant difference should be interpreted to mean that there is in reality no difference. As noted in Chapter 9, there are many reasons why researchers fail to find a significant difference or relationship, only one of which is that there exists no difference or relationship. Researchers also confuse statistical differences with practical or meaningful differences. That is, there is confusion between what is statistically significant and what is educationally significant. Meaningfulness should be judged by examining the difference between means, or the correlation coefficient, and by considering the specifics of the situation in which the results will be used. Often, what are summarized as significant differences turn out to be very small actual differences with little practical value.

With the increasing use of effect size statistics, researchers often include this measure of the practicality of the findings in the interpretation part of the article. Good examples are in Examples 13.6 and 13.7.

EXAMPLES 13.6–13.7 | Interpretation Based on Effect Size

To evaluate the practical importance of the $4\frac{1}{2}$-year findings, we compared the effect sizes that were associated with child care with effects associated with two other well-recognized influences on young children's development: parenting quality and poverty. The obtained quantity effects on caregivers' reports of child behavior problems were larger than the effects on behavior problems that were associated with parenting ($d = .38$ versus .23) and almost as large as the effects associated with poverty ($d = .43$ versus .47).

Source: NICHD Early Child Care Research Network. (2002). Early child care and children's development prior to school entry: Results from the NICHD study of early child care. *American Educational Research Journal, 39*(1), 157.

Moderate to large effect sizes were also found for many components when analyzed by ability level and subject matter. Clear patterns emerged with ability level of the class, indicating that this is an important variable related to assessment and grading practices and cognitive levels of assessments. This is illustrated by the magnitude of positive relationships among ability level of the class and use of academic achievement ($d = .78$), use of constructed-response assessments ($d = .41$), and assessment of higher-order thinking (.89).

Source: McMillan, J. H. (2001, April). *Teachers' classroom assessment and grading practices decision making.* Paper presented at the Annual Meeting of the National Council of Measurement in Education, New Orleans, 31.

In qualitative research, the approaches used to code, categorize, and develop themes are important in synthesizing the data. There may not be specific statistical methods, but the data still have to be analyzed. The manner in which codes were identified and applied can affect the results. For example, if a researcher has not checked preliminary coding or engaged in constant comparison of categories as data are collected, this may result in significant limitations related to analysis. Different qualitative software programs may use different criteria for coding and categorizing, which could affect the results. There may be something about the manner in which qualitative researchers assess their role in a study that affects the results. If documents were analyzed, how, specifically, was that accomplished? Would a different approach to document review provide different results?

Example 13.8 shows how researchers went about data analysis for their qualitative study. They use "bracketing" and "data extraction" and identify "essential structures," but how, specifically, were these processes completed? Did each researcher do this independently? Could different approaches result in different findings?

EXAMPLE 13.8 | Qualitative Data Analysis

We bracketed the transcribed teachers' stories. Through this process, we were able to dissect the stories in searching for essential structures. Data were extracted from the teachers' stories about their experiences in the alternative teacher preparation program and the realities of their urban classrooms. . . . The characteristics of a high-quality mathematics teacher were also extracted from their stories.

Source: Junor Clarke, P., & Thomas, C. D. (2009). Teachers' perceptions of connections and disconnects between their alternative preparation and teaching in urban classrooms *Urban Education, 44*(2), 149.

Interpretation Related to Previous Research

The purpose of a review of previous research is to place the study in the context of other investigations. Once the study is completed, the results should be discussed in light of the reviewed literature to help explain the reasons for the results and the meaningfulness of the study. Although the style of relating results to previous studies will vary, there is usually an indication of whether the current findings are consistent or inconsistent with previous research. When the results are inconsistent or contradictory, the authors should provide explanations.

In Example 13.9 the authors discuss how their study was different from previous investigations of the same intervention, extending and expanding the significance of the results.

EXAMPLE 13.9 | Interpretation Based on Previous Research

Like other studies focused on teaching students comprehensive sets of strategies (e.g., Brown et al., 1996; Dole, Brown, & Trathen, 1996; Palinscar & Brown, 1984; Paris et al., 1984; Paris & Jacobs, 1984; Paris & Oka, 1986) and those conducted specifically on the LSC (e.g., Clark et al., 1984; Lenz & Hughes, 1990; Woodruff et al., 2002), these findings suggest that the strategies instruction had an effect on comprehension and use of metacognitive strategies, particularly for sixth graders. However, findings from the present study differ from the aforementioned studies in several important ways. First, like Anderson's (1992) study of transactional strategies instruction and Westra and Moore's (1995) study of reciprocal teaching, the present study yielded significant findings with sixth-grade adolescent struggling readers. Second, this study was conducted with a much larger sample across a much longer period of time than previous studies of strategies instruction, suggesting that sixth-grade struggling readers were beginning to internalize the strategic processing routines that would enable transfer to occur. Finally, findings from this study were examined using a randomized controlled field trial and analyzed using multilevel modeling techniques that heretofore had not been used in studies of the impact of strategies instruction on long-term comprehension and strategy use. In light of Slavin et al.'s (2008) synthesis of research on reading programs in middle and high schools and their plea for more rigorous studies, these findings are particularly critical.

Source: Cantrell, S. C., Almasi, J. F., Carter, J. C., Rintamaa, M., & Madden, A. (2010). The impact of a strategy-based intervention on the comprehension and strategy use of struggling adolescent readers. *Journal of Educational Psychology, 102*(2), 270.

Interpretation as related to previous studies and other literature is the most common feature of discussion sections. Such an interpretation is important because it places the results more directly and explicitly in the context of other research, thereby enhancing the contribution of the new research to a recognized body of knowledge. It also demonstrates that the authors have a good understanding of the literature, which increases their credibility.

The following are examples of how results are interpreted by relating them to other studies or literature.

EXAMPLES 13.10–13.12 | Interpretation Based on Previous Research

The results of the analyses, consistent with earlier research by Brookhart (1994) and Cizek et al. (1995), show that most elementary teachers use a multitude of factors in grading students. The hodgepodge of factors considered when grading appear to be organized into six distinct components. Academic performance is clearly the most important factor in grading students, as also reported by Stiggins and Conklin (1992), but the results of the present study show that nontest performance and behavior, such as effort, participation, and extra credit work, also are very important for many teachers, consistent with the Gullickson (1985) study.

Source: McMillan, J. H., Myran, S., & Workman, D. (2002). Elementary teachers' classroom assessment and grading practices. *The Journal of Educational Research, 95*(4), 211.

The results suggest that children are more self-regulated learners in small-group and seat work. However, the results do not imply that teacher-directed instruction is not *an effective means of teaching.* On the contrary, we agree with Weinert and Helmke (1995) that some strategies are more effectively taught and enhanced through *teachers' direct instruction* and modeling. Teachers' direct or explicit instruction of learning strategies can promote children's regulatory performance (Cardell-Elawar, 1992; King, 1991; Meloth & Derring, 1994). However, in order for children to truly become self-regulated learners, the classroom should include all three contexts to provide direct instruction, independent practice, and the opportunity to practice metacognitive skills in a social situation.

Source: Stright, A. D., & Supplee, L. H. (2002). Children's self-regulatory behaviors during teacher-directed seatwork and small-group instructional contexts. *The Journal of Education Research, 95*(4), 242.

As in previous research (DiBattista et al., 2004; Epstein & Brosvic, 2002), students had favorable responses to the IFAT, with more than three quarters indicating that they would like to use the IFAT in all of their courses having multiple-choice tests. It is not surprising that almost all students liked having the opportunity to obtain partial credit on multiple-choice items . . . students may also prefer the IFAT because they believe that it is fairer than other types of multiple-choice response techniques, lets them learn more, and makes the test feel a bit like a game (DiBattista et al.). . . . Our findings agree with previous research that has consistently shown test anxiety to be inversely related to test performance in a variety of settings (Clark et al., 1998; Hembree, 1988; Musch & Bröder, 1999; Powers, 2001). We found inverse associations among RTAS scores and various measures of test performance, including overall test scores and scores on the multiple-choice and nonmultiple-choice portions of the test. In contrast, trait anxiety was not associated with any of these measures of test performance, and, furthermore, the associations between RTAS scores and test performance were not statistically significantly diminished when trait anxiety was statistically controlled. These findings are consistent with the notion that test anxiety is related to, yet distinct from, trait anxiety (Spielberger et al., 1978).

Source: DiBattista, D., & Gosse, L. (2006). Test anxiety and the immediate feedback assessment technique. *The Journal of Experimental Education 74*(4), 309.

CONCLUSIONS

One of the final parts of a research article is a statement of the conclusions. Conclusions are summary statements of the results as they pertain to the research problem, often presented as answers to the questions, hypotheses, or purposes of the research. Sometimes conclusions simply repeat a technical, statistical presentation of the results in short summary sentences in nontechnical language. In other studies, the conclusions will be based on the interpretation of the results, reflecting the professional judgment of the investigators. Usually, the major or most significant findings are summarized as conclusions.

Conclusions may be stated at the beginning or at the end of the discussion section and may precede or follow interpretations of the results. A common approach is to begin the discussion with the purpose or research problem, state the major findings, and then interpret the findings. If there are several major findings, one may be presented and discussed, followed by another. The term *conclusion* may or may not be used. By beginning the discussion with conclusions, the author provides a succinct overview of the most important findings, which helps to orient the reader to the discussion that follows. Often, conclusions are stated succinctly in the abstract of an article, as in the following example.

EXAMPLE 13.13 | Conclusion Within an Abstract

The findings of this study demonstrated stereotypical feelings of the culturally diverse and educationally disadvantaged students from the local teachers are prevailing, but that there are some differences in cultural diversity awareness between the East and West.

Source: Yeung, A. S. W. (2006). Teachers' conceptions of borderless—A cross-cultural study on multicultural sensitivity of the Chinese teachers. *Educational Research for Policy and Practice, 5*(1), 33.

Researchers should indicate *why* the conclusions are supported. The following examples show how the authors begin their discussion of the results with a qualified conclusion, then go on to explain why such conclusions need to be interpreted with caution.

EXAMPLES 13.14–13.15 | Conclusion Statement

Overall faculty/staff perceptions of the KASA portfolio system indicated that the system was flexible and could satisfy a variety of purposes in the education of future speech-language pathologists. The potential for improved learning was evident throughout the investigation. Although disadvantages were noted, the faculty and staff were largely open to moving forward with the KASA portfolio system and revising the system to make it more manageable.

Source: McNamara, T. L., & Bailey, R. L. (2006). Faculty/staff perceptions of a standards-based exit portfolio system for graduate students. *Innovative Higher Education, 31*(2), 140.

These results appear to indicate that cooperating teachers trained in the general principles and practices of mentoring and supervision with a specific framework to guide interactions have a more positive impact on prospective teacher development than do those with no training. However, upon looking more closely at the results, one notices areas within the framework (specific criteria) where mentoring alone (group effect) does not appear to be the factor that is primarily responsible for discrepancies. Although in each specific criterion the group effect is positive, some results indicate that differences were, at least in part, caused by individual differences at pretest.

Source: Giebelhaus, C. R., & Bowman, C. L. (2002). Teaching mentors: Is it worth the effort? *The Journal of Educational Research, 95*(4), 246.

Limitations

An important aspect of the discussion is to indicate any limitations to the conclusions. Authors will often point out that the results or conclusions are limited to subjects with certain characteristics, to features of the design, or to particular settings. This is essentially a way for the researcher to address the generalizability, translatability, or comparability of the findings. Beyond the particulars of a research setting, you need to consider whether it is reasonable to expect the results to represent a general pattern that would occur again and again. This consideration can be directly addressed from the researcher's perspective in the article, but it is also necessary for you to judge the extent to which the conclusions are useful in contexts. For this reason, it is helpful for you to think about the following factors that may limit the results.

USING EDUCATIONAL RESEARCH

Sometimes different researchers will reach conflicting conclusions about important topics. A good contemporary issue that illustrates this nicely is the debate in the literature about whether certification for new teachers results in more effective teaching and student learning. In the summer 2000 issue of *Educational Evaluation and Policy Analysis,* two researchers claimed that teacher certification has little bearing on student achievement. In a 2001 issue of the same journal, three researchers critiqued the 2000 study and reached far different conclusions. The 2000 authors also provided a rejoinder to the 2001 critique, in the same 2001 issue, concluding that there is insufficient evidence about the impact of teacher certification. Reading the discussion and conclusion sections of the three articles is interesting and shows the importance of appropriate interpretations of data.

Limitations Related to Participant Characteristics. The participants in a study have certain characteristics, such as age, race, ability, and socioeconomic status. Strictly speaking, results and conclusions are limited to other individuals who have the same, or at least very similar, characteristics. In research jargon, this factor is referred to as **population validity.**

Population validity: Generalizability to other individuals.

There are two ways in which limitations related to subject characteristics affect the use of the results. The first concerns generalizing from a sample, or the subjects used in a study, to a larger population or to other individuals. For example, if a study of fourth-grade students shows that cooperative learning strategies are better than individualized approaches, the results are limited to other fourth-graders with similar characteristics. Similarly, research conducted with high school students is limited to other high school students; research done with males should not be generalized to females; what may be true for one type of student may not be true for other types of students; and so forth.

One key to understanding the extent to which results should be limited to subject characteristics is to know the characteristics. That may seem rather obvious, but you will find in some studies that the subjects are not described adequately enough to allow you to judge generalizability, translatability, or comparability. An important aspect of a quantitative study is whether probability sampling was used. If representative sampling was used, then the limitations apply to the population rather than to the sample. If available samples were used, you need to examine the procedures to see if limitations are suggested, for example, as with paid or volunteer samples.

A second limitation is to be careful not to generalize what is true for a group of subjects to individuals or subgroups. For example, if you determine that teachers' expectations of students seem to be affected by reviewing test scores from the previous year, the overall finding is true for the group as a whole and may not be true for any individual teacher or for certain groups of teachers. In other words, expectations may be influenced in some types of teachers but not in other types of teachers, even though when all types of teachers are analyzed together, there are significant results. It is similar to saying that although in the entire group of twelfth-grade students there is a positive relationship between attendance and achievement, the relationship may be more or less positive for particular groups of twelfth-graders.

The following examples show how results may be limited because of how paticipants were selected.

EXAMPLES 13.16–13.19 | Limitations Based on Participant Selection

In fact, generalizing the present study's findings to younger or less-advanced music students should be done with caution. The musicians who served as subjects in this study are in many ways quite different than the learners who populate school music programs. It is possible that the acquisition of expressive performance skills is best accomplished by other means (not reflected in this report), depending on the learners' developmental level. Additional research with younger musicians would provide needed insight into this.

Source: Woody, R. H. (2006). The effect of various instructional conditions on expressive music performance, *Journal of Research in Music Education, 54*(1), 34.

We designed this study to test relations among improvements in reading rate and other aspects of reading. Because all of our students were slow readers for their grade level, we cannot expect the relations found for these poor readers in Grades 2 and 4 to generalize to average-reader populations.

Source: O'Connor, R. E., Swanson, H. L., & Geraghty, C. (2010). Improvement in reading rate under independent and difficult text levels: Influences on work and comprehension skills. *Journal of Educational Psychology, 102*(1), 16.

Finally, it should be noted that this article has focused on a single urban school district. While there are many advantages to evaluating a population of students within a single, large urban school district, it is possible that different results and interpretations may be found in other school districts of varying urbanicity. The results, thus, could be compared to those using data from additional urban districts in order to arrive at multi-district conclusions.

Source: Gottfried, M. A. (2010). Evaluating the relationship between student attendance and achievement in urban elementary and middle schools: An instrumental variables approach. *American Educational Research Journal, 27*(2), 460.

The present results may not be generalized to all teachers working in multicultural classrooms in the Netherlands due to the possibility of a sample selection bias. Participation in the present study was voluntary, and many teachers refused to participate, mostly due to time constraints. Those teachers who were willing to participate may therefore not be fully comparable to those teachers who refused to participate, which makes our sample less than completely representative of the population of elementary school teachers working in multicultural classrooms in the Netherlands.

Source: van den Bergh, L., Denessen, E. Hornstra, L., Voeten, M., & Holland, R. W. (2010). The implicit prejudiced attitudes of teachers: Relations to teacher expectations and the ethnic achievement gap. *American Educational Research Journal, 47*(2), 522.

Limitations Related to Contextual Characteristics. Contextual characteristics are specifics of the setting and context in which the study is conducted. They include the place of the study—whether in a classroom, laboratory, playground, home, and so on—and what is present in this setting—for example, the type of equipment in a playground or the objects in a classroom. If research on prosocial behavior is studied in a day-care center, for example, the results may not be generalizable to unstructured play in a neighborhood. What may occur in one school may not occur in another because of differences in their structure and specific features. Limitations because of settings are part of the conditions of conducting the research. (Other conditions are considered below.) Together, they may be referred to as factors affecting the **ecological validity** of the research. Ecological validity is strong when the results can be generalized to different settings. This is obviously a limitation in studies that occur in a single classroom or school. As with subject characteristics, your judgment of generalizability will depend on how well the setting is described. If your situation is similar in most respects, the findings may be useful. On the other hand, if your situation is quite different, for example, an inner-city school compared to a suburban school, the results may not be useful.

Ecological validity: Generalizability to other settings, times, treatments, and measures.

Limitations Related to Methodology. One of the most common limitations is related to the nature of the methodology that was used. Often nonexperimental studies that examine relationships will indicate that causal conclusions should not be reached. Similarly, caution is often suggested in making causal conclusions for quasi-experiments or for studies in which internal validity is weak. Notice in the first example, Example 13.20, how the researcher makes it very clear that causal conclusions are not appropriate.

EXAMPLES 13.20–13.21 | Limitation Based on Methodology

Because this was an observational study, it cannot prove causality. It does, however, add to our knowledge of the differences between schools and classrooms whose students are attaining higher than expected levels of literacy achievement, and those who are not, across a very diverse range of schools and student populations.

Source: Langer, J. A. (2001). Beating the odds: Teaching middle and high school students to read and write well. *American Educational Research Journal, 38*(4), 877.

The present study is of course not without limitations. Principal among these is the fact that it employed a retrospective, cross-sectional design. With this type of design, the participants' pretransition recollections could have been influenced either by their post-transition experiences or by forgetting given that they were surveyed in October, approximately two months after the students had entered their new school.

Source: Akos, P., & Galassi, J. P. (2004). Middle and high school transitions as viewed by students, parents, and teachers. *Professional School Counseling, 7*(4), 218.

Limitations Related to When the Research Is Conducted. There are several ways in which time is related to limitations. The first is that interventions may be effective at one time but not at another. What may work in the morning may not work in the afternoon, and what may be effective in the fall may be ineffective in the winter. Responses of subjects to treatments and measures also vary according to time. Students' responses may be much more accurate in the morning than in late afternoon. Measures of self-concept will be affected by when the students respond, as will attitudinal measures. From a broader perspective, the sociohistorical context in which the research is carried out may limit the findings. That is, how students respond will be affected by the cultural values at the time the research is conducted.

EXAMPLE 13.22 | Limitations Based on Timing

An additional limitation in terms of the research design is that we report assessments of outcomes relatively close to the implementation of the intervention. Intervention activities ceased in March; data collection to assess the effect on students began for student and teacher surveys 6 to 8 weeks following the last intervention activity. Follow-up data that include longer-term assessments of intervention effects, specifically, beyond the year of intervention and once students no longer have the intervention teacher, are currently being collected.

Source: Hamm, J. V., Farmer, T. W., Robertson, D., Dadisman, K. A., Murray, A., & Meece, J. L. (2010). Effects of a developmentally based intervention with teachers on native American and white early adolescents' schooling adjustment in rural settings. *The Journal of Experimental Education, 78,* 371.

Limitations Related to Interventions. In experimental research generalizability is limited by the nature of the intervention. It is necessary to know how an intervention is defined and carried out to know whether it will be useful to you in your situation. For example, there has been a great amount of research recently on what is termed "active teaching or instruction," but its definition may vary from study to study. The same would be true for such practices as cooperative learning, homogeneous and heterogeneous grouping, individualization, praise, and reinforcement. You need to look at what is sometimes the fine print in the methodology section to know precisely how an intervention is defined and implemented. Results and conclusions are, of course, limited to this operational definition and the procedures for implementing the treatment.

Limitations Related to Measures. Quantitative research is limited by the manner in which the variables, independent or dependent, are measured. For example, an independent variable may be "on-task behavior" and the dependent variable "attitudes toward learning." Both of these variables can be measured in several ways. Results of research are generalized to other situations in which the variables are measured, or at least conceptualized, in the same manner. Thus, it is necessary to understand in some detail how the variables are defined and measured.

EXAMPLES 13.23–13.25 | Limitations Related to Measures

In spite of our attempt to model all the channels for a class size effect, a caveat is in order: The curriculum and instructional measures available in the TIMSS are very crude. The number of math topics taught indicates the breadth but not the depth of the curriculum. In TIMSS, there are many variables on teacher-reported instructional practices. Virtually all indicate how often teachers use certain instructional methods. Clearly, to use a method more or less does not necessarily tell us how well teachers use a particular method.

Source: Pong, S., & Pallas, A. (2001). Class size and eighth-grade math achievement in the United States and abroad. *Educational Evaluation and Policy Analysis, 23*(3), 269.

Another factor to consider in these analyses is the limitations created by other measures used in our studies. For example, reliabilities for the social desirability scale were lower than we would have liked.

Source: Polan, S. A., & Aguilar, T. E. (2001). Measuring educator's beliefs about diversity in personal and professional context. *American Educational Research Journal, 38*(1), 175.

Although this study offers some unique insights regarding the relationship between prosody (stress) and the different components of reading over time, it does have some limitations. For instance, only one aspect of prosody was measured at Time 1: stress. The speech rhythm measure used in this study was selected because it measures stress, it has good internal reliability, and recent studies have found that performance on this task is significantly related to children's reading development independently of phonological awareness (Holliman et al., 2008, in press). It was also found to be the best prosodic task (from a selected battery) for discriminating between poor reading and chronological-age and reading-age matched controls (Holliman et al., 2009). However, "It is possible that different aspects of prosody may be linked to different aspects of the reading process" (Miller & Schwanenflugel, 2008, p. 339). . . . Therefore, prosody certainly encompasses other components (e.g., timing, pausing, and tone) that were not explicitly assessed in the prosodic measure included this study, and therefore the findings should perhaps be treated with caution.

Source: Holliman, A. J., Wood, C., & Sheehy, K. (2010). Does speech rhythm sensitivity predict children's reading ability 1 year later? *Journal of Educational Psychology, 102*(2), 364.

Reasonable Limitations. There is a tendency to be too strict in analyzing the limitations of research. If we are overly strict, the results of studies would be useful only in a few situations and to other individuals who are just like those in the study. It is better to use our best, reasonable, professional judgment. The situation may be somewhat different, as may be the measures or subjects, but the differences may not be great enough to affect the usefulness of the findings. For example, suppose you read a study that examines the effect of advance organizers on a lesson (advance organizers are broad conceptual frameworks to structure and organize the material). The study is conducted with a biology unit, using seventh-graders as subjects, and finds that students who use advance organizers show better learning and retention. Your class is sixth grade and you need to teach a social studies unit. Should you simply dismiss the implications of the study because your situation is not exactly the same? In a case like this the limitations of the study may suggest some caution in using advance organizers in your class, but overall there is sufficient overlap to conclude that what worked in the study would probably work for your social studies unit as well.

Recommendations and Implications

Toward the end of the discussion section you will often find statements that suggest future research or practice as a result of the study. These statements are called *recommendations* and *implications.* In journals primarily intended for other researchers, the recommendations tend to be oriented toward changes in specific methods in the study, such as instruments, sampling, or procedures. Recommendations and implications in journals that consumers are likely to read tend to be related to practice. It is important for researchers to be specific in their recommendations and implications. It is inadequate for researchers to say, simply, "Further research is needed in this area." What is needed is an indication of what types of research are necessary.

Following are examples of recommendations and implications that have adequate specificity.

EXAMPLES 13.26–13.27 | Recommendations for Further Research

Findings from the regression analyses highlight several directions for future research. First, children's pretest vocabulary scores and English language proficiency at the end of fourth grade explained over 50% of the variance in reading posttest scores. These results suggest that future intervention studies might couple efforts to improve vocabulary instruction and

English language proficiency in an effort to prevent summer reading loss among low-income Latino children from language minority families.

Source: Kim, J. S., & Guryan, J. (2010). The efficacy of a voluntary summer book reading intervention for low-income Latino children from language minority families. *Journal of Educational Psychology, 102*(1), 29.

Future studies should consider the extent to which other aspects of language besides vocabulary can be increased (e.g., syntax, phonological processing). In addition, more work is needed to understand the factors that affect the degree to which Head Start teachers implement language-enhancing strategies in their classrooms.

Source: Wasik, B. A., Bond, M. A., & Hindman, A. (2006). The effects of a language and literacy intervention on head start children and teachers. *Journal of Educational Psychology, 98*(1), 72–73.

EXAMPLES 13.28–13.29 | Implications for Practice

Findings like these could suggest to teachers where their practices might inadvertently steer students towards some genres and not others. The findings can also inform teachers about what students may feel more familiar and comfortable with in their writing and therefore which genres offer more of a challenge for them. It would allow teachers to choose the examples of novel openings with gender representations in mind and plan discussion that considers this.

Source: Murphy, P., & Ivinson, G. (2005). Gender, assessment and students' literacy learning: Implications for formative assessment. *Teacher Development, 9*(2), 198.

Our results indicate that policy designations of economic risk should include parent education information, at a minimum, and that cutting educational funding may block low-income mothers with the most at-risk children from a pathway of action that likely has the most payoff.

Source: Crosnoe, R., & Cooper, C. E. (2010). Economically disadvantaged children's transitions into elementary school: Linking family processes, school contexts, and educational policy. *American Educational Research Journal, 47*(2), 283.

CONSUMER TIPS: *Criteria for Evaluating Discussion and Conclusion Sections*

1. The results should be interpreted. It is important that the researcher do more than repeat the major findings of the study. The discussion should include interpretations of the research problem, methodology, and previous research. It should include a detailed analysis of how imperfections in the design and extraneous variables may have affected the results and how the results are integrated with other literature on the topic. All major findings should be addressed in the discussion, including those that are unexpected, surprising, and conflicting. There should not be an analysis of every specific result, but important findings should not be ignored or overlooked.

2. Conclusions should answer research problems. Each problem or research question should be clearly answered by the conclusions. The answers should accurately reflect the results and interpretations of the data.

3. Conclusions should be limited by participant characteristics and selection. The discussion should include an analysis of how the characteristics of the participants, such as age, gender, and socioeconomic status, limit the generalizability of the conclusions. Researchers should not overgeneralize either in terms of these characteristics or by suggesting that what may be true for the group as a whole is true for individuals or subgroups.

4. Conclusions should be limited by the nature of interventions and measures. Researchers should indicate how specific aspects of interventions and measures should be considered in interpreting conclusions. They should point out, when appropriate, how different operational definitions of treatments and measures might lead to different conclusions.

5. Statistical significance should not be confused with practical significance. Researchers should not interpret statistically significant results to mean that they have practical value or importance. Statistical significance does not necessarily mean that the results will have important practical implications.

6. Failure to show statistical significance does not necessarily mean that there is no relationship or difference. Researchers need to be careful in interpreting results that fail to show statistical significance. Most studies do not provide an adequate test of whether the statistical insignificance reflects no relationship, nor whether weaknesses in the design account for the findings.

7. Limitations of findings should be reasonable. Researchers should find a middle ground between being overly strict or too confining and completely ignoring obviously important limitations. There are shortcomings to all research, but there is no need to dwell on every possible specific limitation. Important limitations should be mentioned even though the results support a hypothesis.

8. Recommendations and implications should be specific. Recommendations and implications for future research should be included in the discussion and should specifically describe the changes in methodology that would be desirable in subsequent studies. Recommendations and implications for practice should be made only when the data and design support such inferences.

Author Reflection *Now that you have read some research articles, have you noticed how many qualifiers are used to limit, restrict, or otherwise provide a basis for caution? While on the one hand, it seems like such language simply allows the researchers to avoid stating in clear terms what was found, it also is very much needed to help consumers of research draw accurate conclusions so that possible influences on practice are not overgeneralized. In my experience, in fact, most authors do not give sufficient attention to limitations and often reach untenable conclusions. Also, when you write up a study, you will find that the interpretation section is quite challenging because of the need to incorporate previous studies when explaining why the results were obtained. While there is a need for analysis of the results, in light of different kinds of limitations, it is also important to bring in other studies to shed light on the interpretations, conclusions, and implications and recommendations.*

STUDY QUESTIONS

1. What is the purpose of a discussion section in an article?
2. What are the major components of a discussion section?
3. Why is it important to relate findings to previous research?
4. What aspects of the methodology of a study may have implications in interpreting the results?
5. Give an example of a specific feature of the design of a study that would be important in interpretation.
6. What is the purpose of the conclusions?
7. What is the difference between limitations based on generalizing to other people and generalizing to individual subjects?
8. In what ways should conclusions be limited to the timing of the research and to the nature of interventions, measures, and data analysis?
9. What is wrong with recommending simply that "further studies need to be done"?
10. How do quantitative and quantitative discussion sections differ?

Chapter 14

The *Intelligent* Consumer: Putting It All Together

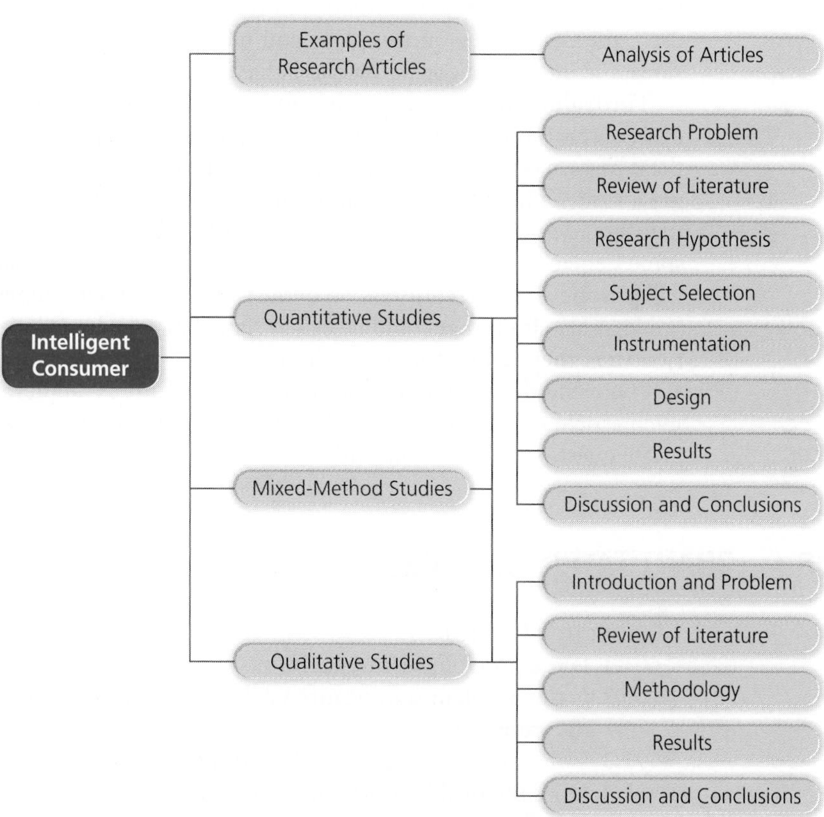

Our aim in this book has been to present and explain fundamental principles of educational research that you will be able to use in evaluating research. As a consumer of educational research, you need to be able to locate, read, critically analyze, and then use, when appropriate, the results of research to enhance teaching and learning. Throughout the book there has been an emphasis on how knowledge derived from research can enhance your role as a professional who will constantly make decisions and judgments.

Research on educational problems can provide information that will improve your judgments, but the quality of published research varies greatly. In fact, there is evidence that a substantial percentage of published studies have serious flaws. Thus, it is essential that you have the knowledge and skills to evaluate critically the research you read. A consumer of educational research may use the information provided in studies, but you must be an *intelligent* consumer. Intelligent consumers can make their own judgments about the credibility and usefulness of research. By being able to understand the researcher's intent, the type of design used, the deficiencies in sampling and measuring, the results, and the conclusions, the intelligent consumer can judge the quality and usefulness of the study.

Throughout the book key points for analyzing and evaluating different aspects of research reports have been summarized as Consumer Tips. In this chapter these tips are rephrased as questions that you will want to ask yourself when reading a study. The intent is to gather, in one place, the most important questions that should guide your evaluation. If you remember that every study will contain some deficiencies, the answers to these questions, when considered as a whole, will provide an overall impression of the credibility and usefulness of the findings. You may also find what could be called "fatal flaws." These deficiencies are so serious that they render the results useless.

Following the outlines of questions there are three complete research studies. Each article is critically analyzed on the book website by answering the appropriate questions in these outlines.

QUESTIONS *for* QUANTITATIVE STUDIES

1.0 Research Problem
- **1.1** Is the problem researchable?
- **1.2** Is the problem significant? Will the results have practical or theoretical importance?
- **1.3** Is the problem stated clearly and succinctly?
- **1.4** Does the problem communicate whether the study is descriptive, experimental, or nonexperimental?
- **1.5** Does the problem indicate the variables and population studied?

2.0 Review of the Literature
- **2.1** Does the review of literature seem comprehensive? Are all important previous studies included?
- **2.2** Are primary sources emphasized?

- **2.3** Is the review up-to-date?
- **2.4** Have studies been critically reviewed, and flaws noted, and have the results been summarized?
- **2.5** Does the review emphasize studies directly related to the problem?
- **2.6** Does the review explicitly relate previous studies to the problem?
- **2.7** If appropriate, does the review establish a basis for research hypotheses?
- **2.8** Does the review establish a theoretical framework for the significance of the study?
- **2.9** Is the review well organized?

3.0 Research Hypothesis

- **3.1** Is the hypothesis stated in declarative form?
- **3.2** Does the hypothesis follow from the literature?
- **3.3** Does the hypothesis state expected relationships or differences?
- **3.4** Is the hypothesis testable?
- **3.5** Is the hypothesis clear and concise?

4.0 Selection of Participants

- **4.1** Are the subjects clearly described?
- **4.2** Is the population clearly defined?
- **4.3** Is the method of sampling clearly described?
- **4.4** Is probability sampling used? If so, is it proportional or disproportional?
- **4.5** What is the return rate in a survey study?
- **4.6** Are volunteers used?
- **4.7** Is there an adequate number of participants?

5.0 Instrumentation

- **5.1** Is evidence for validity and reliability clearly stated and adequate? Is the instrument appropriate for the subjects?
- **5.2** Are the instruments clearly described? If an instrument is designed for a study by the researchers, is there a description of its development?
- **5.3** Are the procedures for gathering data clearly described?
- **5.4** Do the scores distort the reality of the findings?
- **5.5** Does response set or faking influence the results?
- **5.6** Are observers and interviewers adequately trained?
- **5.7** Are there observer or interviewer effects?

6.0 Design

- **6.1** Nonexperimental
  - **6.1a** If descriptive, are relationships inferred?
  - **6.1b** If comparative, are criteria for identifying different groups clear?
  - **6.1c** Are causal conclusions reached from correlational findings?
  - **6.1d** Is the correlation affected by restriction in the range and reliability of the instruments?
  - **6.1e** If causal-comparative, has the causal condition already occurred? How comparable are the subjects in the groups being compared?

6.2 Experimental

6.2a Is there direct manipulation of an independent variable?

6.2b Are the design and procedure clearly described?

6.2c What extraneous/confounding variables are not controlled in the design?

6.2d Is each replication of the intervention independent of other replications? Is the number of subjects equal to the number of intervention replications?

6.3 Single-Subject

6.3a Is the measurement of the target behavior reliable?

6.3b Is the target behavior clearly defined?

6.3c Are there enough measures of the behavior to establish stability?

6.3d Are procedures, subjects, and settings described in detail?

6.3e Is there a single intervention?

6.3f Are there experimenter or observer effects?

7.0 Results and Analysis

7.1 Is there an appropriate descriptive statistical summary?

7.2 Is statistical significance confused with practical significance?

7.3 Is statistical significance confused with internal or external validity?

7.4 Are appropriate statistical tests used?

7.5 Are levels of significance interpreted correctly?

7.6 How clearly are the results presented?

7.7 Are data clearly and accurately presented in graphs and tables?

8.0 Discussion and Conclusions

8.1 Is interpretation of the results separate from reporting of the results?

8.2 Are the results discussed in relation to previous research, methodology, and the research problem?

8.3 Do the conclusions follow from the interpretation of the results?

8.4 Are the conclusions appropriately limited by the nature of the participants, treatments, and measures?

8.5 Is lack of statistical significance properly interpreted?

8.6 Are the limitations of the findings reasonable?

8.7 Are the recommendations and implications specific?

QUESTIONS *for* QUALITATIVE STUDIES

1.0 Introduction and Problem

1.1 Are the researcher's background, interests, and potential biases clear from the outset?

1.2 Does the researcher have the skill and training needed to conduct the study?

- **1.3** Is the problem feasible?
- **1.4** Is the problem significant?
- **1.5** Is there a clear conceptual and theoretical framework for the problem?
- **1.6** Does the introduction include an overview of the design of the study?
- **1.7** Is the purpose of the study clearly stated?

2.0 Review of the Literature

- **2.1** Is the review preliminary? Does it indicate that the researcher is knowledgeable about previous work in the area?
- **2.2** Is the review up-to-date?
- **2.3** Does the review establish an adequate background and theoretical framework for the study?
- **2.4** Is the review well organized?
- **2.5** Is the literature analyzed as well as summarized?

3.0 Methodology

- **3.1** Is the method of selecting participants clear?
- **3.2** Is the selection of participants biased?
- **3.3** Will the participants selected provide a credible answer to the research question?
- **3.4** How involved is the researcher in the setting? Will the researcher's involvement affect the findings?
- **3.5** Are data collectors trained?
- **3.6** Are multiple methods of data collection used?

4.0 Results and Analysis

- **4.1** Is there adequate detail in presenting results?
- **4.2** Are direct quotes from participants?
- **4.3** Is there adequate immersion in the field to develop a deep understanding of what is being studied?
- **4.4** Is there an analysis of triangulation?
- **4.5** Is there consideration of researcher bias or perspective in interpreting the results?

5.0 Discussion and Conclusions

- **5.1** Are descriptions clearly separate from interpretations and researchers' opinions?
- **5.2** Is the credibility of the findings addressed in terms of reliability, credibility, and trustworthiness?
- **5.3** Are the results discussed in relation to previous research?
- **5.4** Do the conclusions follow from the interpretation of the results? Are the conclusions consistent with what is known from previous research?
- **5.5** Are appropriate limitations indicated?
- **5.6** Are appropriate recommendations and implications indicated?

QUESTIONS *for* MIXED-METHOD STUDIES

1.0 Introduction and Problem
- **1.1** Is the problem feasible and researchable?
- **1.2** Is the problem significant? Will it have practical and/or theoretical importance?
- **1.3** Is the problem stated clearly and succinctly?
- **1.4** Are separate research questions asked for the quantitative and qualitative aspects of the study?
- **1.5** Is it clear if the study is primarily quantitative or primarily qualitative?
- **1.6** Does the quantitative research question indicate the variables, population, and logic of the design?
- **1.7** If there is a research hypothesis, is it clear, concise, and testable? Does it follow from the literature?

2.0 Review of the Literature
- **2.1** Is the review primarily preliminary or comprehensive?
- **2.2** Are primary sources emphasized?
- **2.3** Is the review up-to-date?
- **2.4** Are studies analyzed as well as summarized, and related to the research questions?
- **2.5** Does the review establish an adequate background and theoretical framework for the study?
- **2.6** Is the review well organized?

3.0 Selection of Participants
- **3.1** Is the selection of the participants clear?
- **3.2** Are the participants well described?
- **3.3** Is it likely that the participants will provide credible data?
- **3.4** Are the participants likely to be biased?
- **3.5** If sampling was used, what was the return rate? Is it adequate?

4.0 Instrumentation
- **4.1** Is there adequate evidence of reliability and validity?
- **4.2** Are instruments clearly described?
- **4.3** Are procedures for data collection clearly described and adequate?
- **4.4** Are interviewers and/or observers adequately trained?
- **4.5** Is there likely to be bias from participants, interviewers, and/or observers?
- **4.6** Are multiple methods of data collection used?

5.0 Design
- **5.1** Is the design explanatory, exploratory, or a triangulation?
- **5.2** If nonexperimental quantitative, is the study descriptive, comparative, causal-comparative, ex post facto, or correlational?

- **5.3** If experimental, is the intervention clearly described?
- **5.4** If experimental, are possible extraneous/confounding variables accounted for?
- **5.5** Is it clear how the researcher gained entry into the field and the role of the researcher in data collection?
- **5.6** Are there multiple settings and contexts from which data are gathered?
- **5.7** Is the design likely to provide credible information to answer the research questions?

6.0 Results

- **6.1** Are data clearly and adequately described, including the use of tables and figures?
- **6.2** Is there adequate discussion of practical significance? Is it distinguished from statistical significance?
- **6.3** Are field notes and interviewer notes adequately detailed?
- **6.4** Are verbatim transcriptions and quotations used?
- **6.5** Is there triangulation?
- **6.6** Are codes and categories adequately described?
- **6.7** Are results clearly separate from researcher opinion?

7.0 Discussion and Conclusions

- **7.1** Are the results discussed in terms of previous research, methodology, and research question?
- **7.2** Is the credibility of the results addressed in terms of reliability, internal validity, credibility, and trustworthiness?
- **7.3** Are there conclusions? Do they follow logically from the results and interpretation?
- **7.4** Are limitations to the findings indicated?
- **7.5** Are appropriate recommendations and limitations indicated?

EXAMPLES *of* RESEARCH ARTICLES

ARTICLE 14.1 How Elementary School Counselors Can Meet the Needs of Students with Disabilities

Helen Nicole Frye

ABSTRACT

This article presents the results of an ethnographic study that examined how three elementary school counselors meet the personal/social needs of students with disabilities. For this study, the term "students with disabilities" included any student with a disability who was receiving special education services in each counselor's school. Counselor strategies, reliance on theories, and use of the ASCA National Model[R] are explored. Critical themes to emerge out of this study included the influence of the ASCA National Model, advocacy, the

(continued)

ARTICLE 14.1 (continued)

variety of counseling strategies, collaboration and teaming, and leadership. Implications for school counselors are presented.

In 1993, the American School Counselor Association (ASCA) issued position statements on school counselor involvement with students with disabilities and suggested the following school counselor roles in working with students with disabilities: (a) advocacy, (b) transition planning, (c) behavior modification, (d) counseling parents, (e) making referrals to specialists, (f) improving self-esteem, (g) working as part of the school multidisciplinary team, (h) teaching social skills, and (i) serving as consultants to parents and school staff (ASCA, 1993). The most recent education and counseling reform movements—No Child Left Behind (U.S. Department of Education, 2002), the ASCA National Standards (ASCA, 2003), and the ASCA National Model (ASCA, 2003)—have further increased the focus of meeting the needs of all students, including students with disabilities (ASCA, 1993, 2003; Baumberger & Harper, 1999; Milsom, 2002; U.S. Department of Education). These new national standards call for school counselors to "change their emphasis from service-centered for some of the students, to program-centered for every student" (ASCA, 2003, p. 18).

School counselors do not have much training in working with students with disabilities, despite the fact that reform movements call for increasing their involvement with these students (Astigarra & McEachern, 2000; Deck, Scarborough, Sferrazza, & Estill, 1999; Helms & Katsiyannis, 1992; Milsom, 2002). With pressure to change their role in schools to ensure that all students' needs are being met, school counselors will quickly need to focus their efforts on changing the services they provide to all students, including those with disabilities, and to provide evidence and data to support that their school counseling activities are effective.

PERSONAL/SOCIAL DEVELOPMENT

Many young children with disabilities have unique personal/social needs in addition to academic issues related to their disability. Current research suggests a number of personal/social difficulties that come with a diagnosis of a physical disability, emotional disorder, or learning disability. Some of these issues include higher levels of stress and anxiety (Margalit, 1992), poor social skills (Okolo & Sitlington, 1986; Voeller, 1993), and learned helplessness and low self-esteem (Barton & Fuhrmann, 1994; Bender & Wall, 1994; Bowen & Glenn, 1998; Glenn & Smith, 1998). Students with disabilities often have negative school experiences (Kottman, Robert, & Baker, 1995), maintain an external locus of control (Bender & Wall; Omizo & Omizo, 1994; Tabassam & Grainger, 2002), and demonstrate ineffective anger management strategies (Baker, 2000; Garcia, Krankowski, & Jones, 1998).

There is also an increased risk of suffering from depression, conduct disorders, and substance abuse, related to a diagnosis of a disability (Brumback & Weinberg, 1990; Larson, 1998; Rodis, Garrod, & Boscardin, 2001; Spreen, 1988). It now appears that students with disabilities develop low self-concepts in more areas than just academics alone (Kloomok & Cosden, 1994). Kish (1991) maintained that students with disabilities become more handicapped by their lack of personal/social skills than by their academic skill deficits, and research indicates that strong personal/social skills are necessary for future success as an adult and that these skills can be learned (Schumaker, 1992).

PURPOSE OF THE STUDY

This study examined how three elementary school counselors meet the personal/social needs of students with disabilities, through the use of the ethnographic interview method of qualitative inquiry (Spradley, 1979). Qualitative methodology was chosen to obtain an in-depth account of the experience of elementary school counselors working with students with disabilities. The following questions were the main focus of this study: (a) Are these three professional school counselors using the ASCA National Model to guide them in their work with students with disabilities? (b) What strategies do these three professional school counselors use in their work with students with disabilities and how are they implemented? (c) What theories guide these three professional school counselors in their work with students with disabilities? And, (d) how do these three professional school counselors make a difference in the lives of students with disabilities? These four subquestions help to answer the main research question of the study, "How do these three professional school counselors meet the personal/social needs of students with disabilities?"

METHODS

Participants

The three school counselor participants all worked in a large metropolitan school system on the East Coast of the United States. There were two female participants who described themselves as Caucasian and one male who described himself as African American. Each of the school counselors had been a school counselor for at least 4 years and only one counselor had worked in the field of education before becoming a school counselor. Each of the school counselors held a master's degree and one was enrolled part-time in a doctoral program. All of the school counselors had a minimum of 440 students on their caseload, which included students with a variety of disabilities. None of their students was diagnosed with traumatic brain injury and that was the only disability qualifying for special education that was not represented among their students.

Procedure

Because of the newness of the ASCA National Model, it was important to choose a school system where school counselors had already received some training in using it as a guide. The three school counselor participants were chosen by reputational case selection through a joint decision between two of their county supervisors of guidance. Patton (1990) has described this type of sampling as sampling extreme or deviant cases to shed light on an issue, and Merriam (1998) has described this as the best approach to use when the sample is of interest because it is so unique or different. The supervisors had been informed of the purpose of the study and chose these school counselors because they felt they were actively involved in meeting the needs of students with disabilities, they were fully licensed school counselors, and they had received ASCA National Model training, thus meeting the criteria for involvement in the study. Dunn, Wood, and Baker (2002) indicated that not all school counselors actively work with students with disabilities, so it was very important for this study to examine school counselors who actively worked with students with disabilities.

The ethnographic interview method was employed over a 12-week period at the start of the school year and focused on gathering information from each school counselor through the use of an open-ended survey with vignette, three in-depth interviews, and journals that allowed the school counselor to reflect upon and provide important, relevant examples of issues (Spradley, 1979). This procedure allowed the collection of rich data to gain an understanding of how school counselors meet the personal/social needs of students with disabilities and how they view their involvement with these students. Survey and interview questions were developed after a literature review as a multistep process and originally piloted with school counselors working in another school system before this study took place. Following the pilot study, an additional literature review was conducted; at this time, questions regarding the ASCA National Model were incorporated into the interviews and survey.

Data Measures

The school counselor survey was conducted along with the first interview in September at the start of the school year. The survey included demographic information from the school counselors along with information

(continued)

ARTICLE 14.1 (continued)

regarding their training and counseling activities and required a response to a vignette that focused on how they would work with a student diagnosed with Asperger syndrome (considered a higher-functioning form of autism) who was having difficulty at school.

Interviews were held during the 1st, 6th, and 12th week of the 12-week study. They were recorded and transcribed verbatim, which allowed for documentation and reflection upon the school counselor's native language (using the exact terminology that the school counselors used to describe their experience) (Spradley, 1979). Multiple reviews of the tapes ensured that transcripts were correct. School counselors were encouraged to provide a "full and accurate report that gave detailed, concrete material, rather than generalizations" (Weiss, 1994, p. 212). They were reminded of the purpose of the study before each interview and were given final copies of the product, per Spradley's recommendations for ethnographic interviewing. A definition of a "student with a disability" and a copy of the Executive Summary of the ASCA National Model were given to the school counselors to assist in answering questions and to ensure that all involved in the study would share a common understanding of terms discussed.

Following Spradley's (1979) research recommendations, the interviews asked descriptive, structural, and contrast questions to discover the cultural themes and native language (counseling terminology, such as using the term "personal/social skills" versus "social-emotional skills") that the school counselors used. Spradley has provided a "Taxonomy of Ethnographic Questions" (p. 223), which was used to develop the interview questions throughout the research process. An example of descriptive questions from the interview was, "Can you tell me about the last time you worked with a student with a disability? What kind of issues did they present? Describe for me what the counseling process looked like?" The following structural question was asked in one interview: "What words would school counselors use to describe these students?" Contrast questions were the last type of question and an example from the interview was, "Special educators often try to meet the personal/social needs of students with disabilities by giving them work from a social skills training program. How do school counselors meet the personal/social needs of students with disabilities?"

The counselors' journals provided additional data during the weeks that there were no interviews and they provided a way to triangulate the data that school counselors described in the survey and interviews. Writing down their thoughts and experiences during the weeks they were not interviewed assisted the school counselors in recalling counseling activities for upcoming interviews, and this reflection helped to provide more in-depth answers to interview questions (LeCompte & Pressle, 1993). The school counselors recorded their work with students with disabilities in journals each week; the journal was an opportunity to document their work and reflect upon their effectiveness and was an outlet for discussing frustrations and expectations as well as brainstorming new ideas.

Data Analysis and Interpretation

Each of the interviews was transcribed, coded, and then merged using a qualitative data analysis software program, NVivo (QSR International, 2003), which assisted with the development of themes and categories. The comparison and analysis of survey, interview, and journal data was ongoing to identify themes and patterns and to create additional questions per Spradley's (1979) guidelines for ethnographic inquiry, and coding matrices were developed and refined through ongoing interaction with the data. The constant comparative method of data analysis (Glaser & Strauss, 1967) was used in this study to review all data sources and to systematically code examples into as many categories as possible.

Through ongoing interaction with the data, additional categories were developed and defined. Developing codes were analyzed to determine how the data relate to one another. The analysis of information was "issue focused," to describe what has been learned from all of the respondents about people in their situation and to achieve both local and inclusive integration (Weiss, 1994, p. 153). Categorical examples and non-examples also were analyzed and interpreted, and the researcher checked for alternative explanations and negative evidence and compared the results with existing theory. The researcher also shared the results with the school counselors in the study and with experts in the field. These methods enabled the researcher to effectively deal with the major validity threats to the study, which included bias in the selection of counselors and self-report bias.

RESULTS

As found in prior research, these school counselors all described personal/social difficulties in their students with disabilities that included difficulties with social skills (Okolo & Sitlington, 1986: Voeller, 1993), behavior (Bender & Wall, 1994; Garcia et al., 1998; Omizo, Cubberly, & Longano, 1984; Tabassam & Grainger, 2002), and low self-esteem (Barton & Fuhrmann, 1994; Bender & Wall, 1994; Bowen & Glenn, 1998; Glenn & Smith, 1998). The school counselors in this study found similar difficulties in their students in the areas of high stress and anxiety levels and ineffective anger management skills (Garcia et al., 1998; Margalit, 1992). School counselors observed how the deficits these students had in social skills resulted in rejection from their peers and less involvement in social activities (Gresham, 1992; LaGreca & Vaughn, 1992; Schumaker, 1992; Swanson & Malone, 1992; Tabassam & Grainger, 2002; Vaughn & Hager, 1994).

Previous research indicated that there was great variation in whether students with disabilities received counseling services (Deck et al., 1999; Helms & Katsiyannis, 1992) or whether school counselors had time to focus on the personal/social difficulties of students with disabilities (Dunn et al., 2002). However, the school counselors in this study considered students with disabilities "on their caseload" and actively sought out ways that these students could participate in counseling activities that would be helpful to them. Unlike Grigsby's (1990) evaluation of school counselors as having limited involvement and desire to work with students with disabilities, these school counselors felt they were important in meeting the personal/social needs of students with disabilities. The school counselors in this study did not defer the responsibility of meeting the personal/social needs of students with disabilities to other school personnel, as has been indicated by previous research studies (Deck et al.; Glenn, 1998).

Influence of the ASCA National Model

In the review of the data obtained from this study, several themes related to the ASCA National Model emerged (ASCA, 2003). Findings revealed that school counselors felt they were doing many of the things suggested by the ASCA National Model and were encouraging other school counselors to utilize the model. Themes that emerged from this study included the influence of the ASCA National Model, advocacy, the variety of counseling strategies, collaboration and teaming, and leadership. While this study examined school counselors' work toward meeting the personal/social needs of students with disabilities, it was apparent that the three school counselors were focusing on activities that supported all three domains suggested by the Foundation portion of the ASCA National Model (ASCA, 2003, pp. 27–37). School counselors were using collaboration with other school staff to meet students' personal/social needs. They reflected on their efforts in working with students with disabilities to constantly monitor what was working, and they also were trying to find the best ways to collect and use data to monitor students' progress.

Under the Delivery System component of the ASCA National Model, school counselors were teaching the guidance curriculum, planning individually with and for students, providing responsive services, and using consultation and collaboration with others (ASCA, 2003, pp. 3944). The Management System portion of the ASCA National Model was used by the school counselors as they were monitoring student progress and using data to support action plans (ASCA, 2003, pp. 45–58). The school counselors felt they were being held more accountable for their work with students and they used data to demonstrate their success, although each one had his or her own way of documenting successes. They also had a few suggestions on ways to use data to demonstrate progress. Some of the ways they demonstrated success were using journals to record their work, gaining

(continued)

ARTICLE 14.1 (continued)

pre- and post-measures of skills, having students complete self-report measures, and using parent and/or teacher feedback forms.

The county school system currently is reviewing the Accountability portion of the ASCA National Model (ASCA, 2003, pp. 59–66). The school counselors have been collecting their own information, knowing that they are held more accountable than they were in the past, to demonstrate to their county supervisors the work they are doing with students. At this point, however, the school system has not told counselors what to collect and they are just collecting data on their own. The school counselors feel that they are holding themselves more accountable to all of their students, and their conscious effort to meet the needs of students with disabilities is more a result of holding themselves accountable than of having a supervisor tell them they are accountable.

These particular counselors have been collecting data to measure their own effectiveness. They felt that the biggest areas of change since the ASCA National Model have involved measuring effectiveness and collecting data. One of the counselors described the model as an "extra focus on what they are already doing." The counselor further explained that they already used data to demonstrate that their activities were effective, instead of using data solely to demonstrate how often they did a particular counseling activity. Now they would be sharing their data with their supervisors instead of using it for their own self-reflection. They felt they were prepared to demonstrate their effectiveness to others because they were already measuring it for themselves through their self-evaluations, counselor checklists, observations, and parent/teacher checklists or interviews.

After the data were examined, it was apparent that school counselors were beginning to feel the influence of the ASCA National Model in their work with students with disabilities. While many of the different aspects of the ASCA National Model have not taken full effect in their school system (e.g., a change in the evaluation of school counselors, the management system, and a mandated school system-level collection of specific data), the school counselors seemed to agree that there is an increased demand for demonstrating effectiveness and using data and that they are held more accountable for their work with all students than they were in the past.

Advocacy

The next theme that emerged from the study was advocacy. Advocacy is one of the ASCA National Model's main themes and the use of advocacy was indicated as a strategy that counselors employ to meet the personal/social needs of their students with disabilities. Advocacy was demonstrated when the school counselors focused on looking at the individual needs of students with disabilities and used individual planning to create personal goals to meet their needs. Therefore, school counselors viewed students with disabilities as individuals and as part of the larger school group. Advocacy also was demonstrated when counselors made sure to include students with disabilities in all of their counseling program activities, not just ones they created for groups of students with disabilities. Counselors also made certain that students with disabilities were included in school-wide activities, not just those activities that were counselor created.

Counselors were proactive in that they were very cognizant of the unique personal/social needs of these students and they watched out for areas of concern. They sought out ways they could collaborate with other professionals to increase their own training to better work with these students and they actively found additional school staff and professionals to assist them in meeting the needs of their students with disabilities. These counselors reinforced the belief that it was their job to meet the personal/social needs of students with disabilities and they encouraged other school counselors to focus on meeting the personal/social needs of their students with disabilities.

Variety of Counseling Strategies

All data sources provided examples of counseling strategies that the three school counselors used to meet the personal/social needs of students with disabilities. These strategies included (a) individual planning and individual counseling; (b) goal setting for students; (c) actively making sure students with disabilities are included in activities; (d) refusing to accept the "duplication of services" idea (the idea that students with disabilities already get help from special education, so they are not on a counselor's caseload); (e) modifying classroom guidance lessons; (f) developing behavior management plans; (g) providing specific skills training (e.g., social skills, behavior management, anger management); (h) collaborative counseling; (i) counseling with art, books, and play; (j) counseling with social stories; (k) leading groups (e.g., social skills, anger management, coping with divorce, lunch bunches for friendship); (l) developing connections with students; (m) doing active collaboration; (n) training parents and teachers; and (o) participating in Independent Evaluation Plan meetings.

While the school counselors seemed to have an eclectic approach to choosing strategies for working with students with disabilities, each of the three counselors provided examples in which they (a) served as an advocate, (b) provided training, (c) collaborated, (d) used group counseling, and (e) communicated with others. Each of the school counselors indicated that he or she worked with students with disabilities every week through classroom guidance, group counseling, or individual counseling when necessary. It is important to note that none of these counseling strategies or activities was specifically designed to be used only with students with disabilities. The counselors all explained that whether or not they would implement the strategies was based on their personal exposure to, experience with, and ease of comfort in using each of the strategies.

The school counselors all described learning and using more strategies the longer they were a school counselor. The counselors learned two of the strategies (sensory box and social stories) from collaborating with other school personnel (occupational therapist and special education teacher). The sensory box was a school box that had been filled with items (gel bags, rice bags, silly-putty, etc.) that students could use that may help them reduce overstimulation from the classroom environment and calm down. Social stories, which often are used with students with autism, are easy-to-read stories that help students to learn routines or deal with upsetting situations.

Counseling Theories

All of the school counselors had difficulty responding to questions regarding how counseling theories influenced their choice of activities with students with disabilities, for two reasons: (a) They were not looking at theories specifically for students with disabilities, and (b) they tended to look at specific counseling strategies in their work with students rather than relying on specific counseling theories to guide their practice. During the first round of interviews, school counselors made comments such as, "There may be theories guiding it, but it would be subconsciously," and, "I wouldn't have a clue as to what a counseling theory regarding counseling special ed students would even entail." When struggling to find helpful activities for a student with a disability, they would collaborate with other school personnel or "use trial and error."

The counselors indicated that they could pull activities from any of the counseling theories, such as Adlerian/play (Corey, 1996; Seligman, 2001), brief/solution focused (Amatea, 1989; Thompson & Littrell, 1998), person-centered (Goor, McKnab, & Davison-Aviles, 1995; Williams & Lair, 1991), or reality choice theories (Garcia et al., 1998), but they maintained that they were choosing counseling activities based on the activity, and not based on reliance on a particular counseling theory. The school counselors each advocated using an eclectic approach when working with students with disabilities.

(continued)

ARTICLE 14.1 (continued)

Collaboration and Teaming

Collaboration and teaming is an important theme in the ASCA National Model and one that was demonstrated in each of the data measures in this study. The school counselors collaborated with other school counselors and staff to plan, participate in collaborative counseling, and obtain new ideas and strategies. They communicated with doctors and outside therapists to coordinate services for their students and connected parents who needed assistance to outside sources. When asked to describe their work with students with disabilities, one counselor said, "Collaborative, because almost nothing you do with special ed kids are you doing on your own. There are a lot of other professionals helping, so you have to keep the lines of communication open. So it's a collaborative process." Each of the school counselors described collaboration as "very effective" at meeting the needs of students with disabilities, especially in developing goals for students and in monitoring student progress.

The following is a list of individuals with whom the school counselors could collaborate: (a) regular education teacher, (b) special education teacher, (c) gifted education teacher, (d) parents, (e) other school counselors, (f) behavior specialist, (g) special education counselor, (h) supervisor of counseling, (i) school administrator, (j) occupational therapist, (k) speech teacher, (l) physical therapist, and (m) school psychologist.

As the school counselors spoke about the need for collaboration, they mentioned that collaboration was the best advice they could give to other counselors who were interested in developing their skills in working with students with disabilities. These counselors suggested collaborating to develop their own support system for the following reasons: (a) "It is very difficult working with students with disabilities, because you don't always see the positive results and sometimes they are hard to find"; (b) "there will always be things or issues that come up that you don't know how to help and the important thing to do is to keep trying until you find the fight person to ask"; and (c) collaboration helps one to "continue to grow professionally."

One counselor described how her initial attempts to collaborate have led to increased collaboration with school staff as they hear about her collaborative efforts. She suggested collaboration with special education teachers to learn more strategies for counseling students with disabilities and gave the example of using social stories with nondisabled students:

> All the different special ed strategies, you can use in all aspects of your job. You can use them in a group that nobody has labeled special ed, but [where] they could all benefit from a social story, especially kindergarteners. They don't have to have Asperger's to benefit, because it's pictures. And that is what is going to work for any kindergartener who is trying to learn a routine.

In the review of the information obtained from the school counselors, collaboration served two purposes. Collaboration helped to better meet the personal/social needs of students with disabilities, through having other staff brainstorm and work on the same goals. Collaboration also served to provide school counselors with additional strategies they could use in working with their students.

Leadership

The last theme that emerged from this study, leadership, is yet another theme encompassed in the ASCA National Model. These school counselors were chosen to participate in this study based on their reputation of leadership, of actively working to meet the personal/social needs of students with disabilities in their schools when not all school counselors focus on working with these students. These school counselors described working with students with disabilities as challenging and unclear, and even though they felt undertrained, they continued to focus on working with these students and took the initiative to learn more about the students and their disabilities.

The fact that these school counselors have been moving their counseling programs toward an increased focus on students with diverse needs demonstrates in itself the excellent leadership skills of the school counselors. These counselors also have been taking steps to implement the recommendations of the ASCA National Model into their counseling programs even though they had not been mandated to do so, had not received much training on the ASCA National Model, and had not been given specifics on how to do this at the time.

These school counselors have been serving in leadership roles within their schools. They actively made certain that students with disabilities were included in all school activities, not just in counseling activities. They went against the status quo and attempted to make improvements in how these students' needs were best served. They assisted in training school staff and parents in how to work with these students. Through the influence of their data collection and reflection, they consistently tried to improve their school's counseling programs.

Additional Factors That Influence Working with Students with Disabilities

Several issues that surfaced during the study illustrated additional challenges faced by school counselors working with students with disabilities. One major issue was in counselors describing how some school principals place a greater emphasis on the school counselor working on academic improvement over personal/social issues in students. If a school counselor was working for a principal who was more focused on academic success, it may be more difficult for that counselor to spend time focusing on the personal/social needs of students.

Another issue discussed in the study was time. School counselors found it difficult to schedule groups around guidance counseling activities because students with disabilities were already being pulled out of the classroom for additional supportive services such as speech and occupational therapies.

The overabundance of reform initiatives was the next issue. At the time of this study, the state was in the process of creating its own set of guidance standards. Counselors were distracted by the recent development of the state guidance standards that were currently in draft form. While these were closely aligned with the ASCA National Model, the counselors had to remind themselves which one they were talking about during the study because they were receiving information on both at the same time, along with information on No Child Left Behind. School counselors seemed to be inundated with new guidelines and materials at this time as the school system was attempting to sort out the school counselor's role in working with students and in response to recent legislation.

The fourth issue of "duplication of services" was described by the school counselors as an issue that they reject but one that many counselors consider. The idea of "duplication of services" suggests that students with disabilities who are involved in counseling activities are getting double services, once from special education and another time from the counselor. One counselor mentioned that some school counselors make it a point not to actively counsel students with disabilities because they feel that they are already getting services from special education and that special education students are not on their caseload. While the counselors involved in this study disagreed with this idea, they felt that some students may not be served if their counselor agrees with the idea of "duplication of services."

DISCUSSION

The ASCA National Model asks school counselors to examine "how students are different because of school counseling" (ASCA, 2003, p. 17). The school counselors involved in this study stated that students with disabilities are different because of school counseling for several reasons. These students make a connection with the school counselor and have someone who will advocate for them when necessary to make sure that the student is included and involved in all school activities. Students with disabilities can better deal with their personal/

(continued)

ARTICLE 14.1 (continued)

social difficulties because they are learning coping skills, such as improving self-esteem and behavior, from the school counselor. They learn to feel comfortable in who they are and to not see their disability as a limitation. Classroom guidance helps students with disabilities because it focuses on treating others with respect, fairness, and dignity and it incorporates anti-bullying lessons.

In summary, these school counselors meet the personal/social needs of students with disabilities through an eclectic counseling approach. They use classroom guidance and both individual and group counseling activities that focus on teaching students how to improve behavior and social skills and increase their self-esteem. These counselors help students by going against the status quo, providing activities that help the students feel better about themselves, and teaching students coping skills.

It is important to note that the school counselors do not see the counseling strategies they use as strategies that are specific to working only with students with disabilities, but rather as strategies that they have added to their repertoire for all students. This is advantageous for those who are concerned about becoming more skilled in working with students with disabilities. These school counselors are adapting their current counseling activities to meet the needs of these students, not having to acquire numerous new techniques and training that requires years of experience to develop skills. They are building on their professional expertise with other educational staff present in their own schools. They have found that through their desire to learn more about disabilities and through collaboration with other school professionals, they have gained additional counseling strategies that could be used with a variety of students.

Despite the newness of the ASCA National Model, it was interesting to note that many of the activities described by these school counselors as part of their repertoire of working with students with disabilities are those same activities encouraged and recommended by the model as part of ASCA's vision of successful and effective counseling and guidance programs.

Limitations

Limitations to this study include the small number of participants and the fact that the ethnographic interview method is designed only to provide information as to how these individual elementary school counselors meet the needs of the students with disabilities at their schools. The fact that these school counselors were chosen based on purposeful sampling and reputational case selection indicates that they were considered exemplary for their work with students with disabilities and that they do things differently than other school counselors. Therefore, these results most likely do not represent what other school counselors are doing to meet the needs of students with disabilities. The school counselor survey is another limitation as it was created by the researcher and is not a standardized measurement based on psychometrics. This study is unique and there is limited research on the ASCA National Model from which to compare this study's results.

The study and survey also could be criticized for looking at students with various disabilities, rather than looking at specific counseling strategies for particular disabilities. Another limitation comes from the use of self-report measures in the journal, vignette, survey, and interview questions. While efforts were made to triangulate the data through asking questions in different formats—that is, survey, journal, interview—and with different phrasing, the researcher was not present in any counseling session and did not observe the events that school counselors described.

Researcher bias is also a possible limitation to this study. While the researcher has experience with collaborative counseling and is enrolled in a counseling program, this researcher is a special educator. Efforts to control for this possible bias included receiving input from dissertation committee members on survey, interview, vignette, and journal question formats, including member checks throughout the process, and asking descriptive and contrast questions throughout the interviews. In fact, interview questions clearly focused on this issue and asked school counselors to describe their role compared to the roles of other school personnel in working with students with disabilities.

Implications for Practice

The school counselors in this study felt there was still more they would like to learn in regards to working with this population. Therefore, in-service training could be developed that would provide school counselors with counseling recommendations so they don't have to generate counseling strategies on their own. School counselors could develop in-service training to help principals and school staff better understand the counselor's role in working with all students, including those with disabilities, and assist in making certain their counselors had training in working with this population.

School counselor preparation programs could incorporate counseling internships that include more exposure to working with students with disabilities, specific counseling strategies and materials that are successful with students with disabilities, and strategies that encourage collaboration with other school personnel. An increased effort could be made within these courses to link counseling strategies for students with disabilities to specific counseling theories. In this way, school counselors could feel more comfortable in relation to counseling theory and their chosen interventions as well as be certain they were using counseling strategies that were supported by research.

Examining the existing beliefs and attitudes of school staff as well as counselor beliefs about their roles would be important in making certain that all involved in meeting the personal/social needs of students with disabilities were performing and doing so with specific awareness of their unique roles in meeting these needs. Additional training on the ASCA National Model and in strategies for working with students with disabilities also would help school counselors reluctant to work with students with disabilities to understand that these students are part of their caseload, thus refuting the "duplication of services" idea.

CONCLUSION

This study demonstrated that school counselors are providing activities to students with disabilities to meet their personal/social needs and that the activities they use with these students are in accordance with the ASCA National Model (ASCA, 2003). In order for schools to best meet all the needs of their students with disabilities, the academic, career, and personal/social needs of students with disabilities must be better recognized and addressed. When school counselors work with students with disabilities, they are following the ASCA National Model's guidelines for meeting the diverse needs of all of their students. The work that school counselors do to meet the needs of students with disabilities (collaboration, serving in leadership roles, advocating for students, and using a variety of strategies) is not a supplemental or discrete task required of school counselors. Rather, it is an example of school counselors using the ASCA National Model as it was intended—to guide forward the tasks of the counselor and to serve as a framework to help all students experience success.

REFERENCES

Amatea, E. S. (1989). *Brief strategic intervention for school problems.* San Francisco: Jossey-Bass.

American School Counselor Association. (1993). *Position statement: Students with disabilities.* Alexandria, VA: Author.

American School Counselor Association. (2003). *The ASCA national model: A framework for school counseling programs.* Alexandria, VA: Author.

Astigarra, J., & McEachern, A. G. (2000). Not broken, just different: Helping teachers work with children with attention-deficit/hyperactivity disorders. *CACD Journal, 20,* 27–33.

Baker, S. B. (2000). *School counseling for the 21st century.* Englewood Cliffs, NJ: Merrill.

(continued)

ARTICLE 14.1 (continued)

Barton, S., & Fuhrmann, B. (1994). Counseling and psychotherapy for adults with learning disabilities. In P. Gerber & H. Reiff (Eds.), *Learning disabilities in adulthood: Persisting problems and evolving issues* (pp. 82–92). Boston: Andover Medical.

Baumberger, J. P., & Harper, R. E. (1999). *Assisting students with disabilities. What school counselors can and must do.* Thousand Oaks, CA: Corwin Press.

Bender, W. N., & Wall, M. E. (1994). Social-emotional development of students with learning disabilities. *Learning Disability Quarterly, 17,* 323–341.

Bowen, M. L., & Glenn, E. E. (1998). Counseling interventions for students who have mild disabilities. *Professional School Counseling, 2,* 16–25.

Brumback, R., & Weinberg, W. (1990). Pediatric behavioral neurology: An update on the neurological aspects of depression, hyperactivity, and learning disabilities. *Pediatric Neurology, 8,* 677–703.

Corey, G. (1996). *Theory and practice of counseling and psychotherapy* (5th ed.). Pacific Grove, CA: Brooks/Cole.

Deck, M., Scarborough, J. L., Sferrazza, M. S., & Estill, D. M. (1999). Serving students with disabilities: Perspectives of three school counselors. *Intervention in School and Clinic, 34,* 150–153.

Dunn, N., Wood, A., & Baker, S. A. (2002). Readiness to serve students with disabilities: A survey of elementary school counselors. *Professional School Counseling, 5,* 277–284.

Garcia, J. G., Krankowski, T., & Jones, L. L. (1998). Collaborative interventions for assisting students with acquired brain injuries in school. *Professional School Counseling, 2,* 33–39.

Glaser, B. B., & Strauss, A. L. (1967). *The discovery of grounded theory: Strategies for qualitative research.* Chicago: Aldine.

Glenn, E. E. (1998). Counseling children and adolescents with disabilities. *Professional School Counseling, 2,* iii–iv.

Glenn, E. E., & Smith, T. T. (1998). Building self-esteem of children and adolescents with communication disorders. *Professional School Counseling, 2,* 39–47.

Goor, M. B., McKnab, P. A., & Davison-Aviles, R. (1995). Counseling individuals with learning disabilities. In. A. F. Rotatori, J. O. Schween, & F. W. Litton (Eds.), *Advances in special education: Counseling in special populations: Research and practice perspectives* (Vol. 9, pp. 98–118). Greenwich, CT: JAI Press.

Gresham, F. M. (1992). Social skills and learning disabilities: Casual, concomitant, or correlational? *School Psychology Review, 21,* 348–360.

Grigsby, D. A. (1990). Dialogue: Cross cultural counseling for exceptional individuals and their families. *National Forum of Special Education Journal, 1,* 67–69.

Helms, N. E., & Katsiyannis, A. (1992). Counselors in elementary schools: Making it work for students with disabilities. *The School Counselor, 39,* 232–237.

Kish, M. (1991). Counseling adolescents with LD. *Intervention in School and Clinic, 27,* 20–24.

Kloomok, S., & Cosden, M. (1994). Self-concept in children with learning disabilities. The relationship between global self-concept, academic discounting, nonacademic self-concept, and perceived social support. *Learning Disability Quarterly, 17,* 104–153.

Kottman, T., Robert, R., & Baker, D. (1995). Parental perspectives on attention-deficit/hyperactivity disorder: How school counselors can help. *The School Counselor, 43,* 142–150.

Larson, K. A. (1998). A research review and alternative hypothesis explaining the link between learning disability and delinquency. *Journal of Learning Disabilities, 21,* 357–369.

LaGreca, A. M., & Vaughn, S. (1992). Social functioning of individuals with learning disabilities. *School Psychology Review, 21,* 423–427.

LeCompte, M. D., & Pressle, J. (1993). *Ethnography and qualitative design in educational research* (2nd ed.). San Diego, CA: Academic Press.

Margalit, M. (1992). Sense of coherence and families with a learning-disabled child. In B. Wong (Ed.), *Contemporary intervention research in learning disabilities* (pp. 134–145). New York: Springer-Verlag.

Merriam, S. B. (1998). *Qualitative research and case study applications in education.* San Francisco: John Wiley & Sons.

Milsom, A. (2002). Students with disabilities: School counselor involvement and preparation. *Professional School Counseling, 5,* 331–338.

Okolo, C. M., & Sitlington, R. (1986). The role of special education in LD adolescents' transition from school to work. *Learning Disability Quarterly, 9,* 141–155.

Omizo, M. M., Cubberly, W. E., & Longano, D. M. (1984). The effects of group counseling on self-concept and locus of control among learning disabled children. *Humanistic Education and Development, 23,* 69–79.

Omizo, M. M., & Omizo, S. A. (1994). Group counseling's effects on self-concept and social behavior among children with learning disabilities. *Journal of Humanistic Education and Development, 26,* 109–117.

Patton, M. Q. (1990). *Qualitative evaluation and research methods* (2nd ed.). Newbury Park, CA: Sage.

QSR International. (2003). *NVivo: New generation software for qualitative data analysis.* Doncaster Victoria, Australia: Author.

Rodis, P., Garrod, A., & Boscardin, M. L. (2001). *Learning disabilities and life stories.* Boston: Allyn and Bacon.

Schumaker, J. B. (1992). Social performance of individuals with learning disabilities: Through the looking glass of KUIRLD research. *School Psychology Review, 21,* 387–399.

Seligman, L. (2001). *Systems, strategies, and skills of counseling and psychotherapy.* Upper Saddle, NJ: Prentice Hall.

Spradley, J. P. (1979). *The ethnographic interview.* Orlando, FL: Harcourt.

Spreen, O. (1998). *Learning disabled children growing up: A follow-up into adulthood.* New York: Oxford University Press.

Swanson, H. L., & Malone, S. (1992). Social skills and learning disabilities: A meta-analysis of the literature. *School Psychology Review, 21,* 427–442.

Tabassam, W., & Grainger, J. (2002). Self-concept, attributional style, and self-efficacy beliefs of students with learning disabilities with and without attention deficit hyperactivity disorder. *Learning Disability Quarterly, 25,* 141–151.

Thompson, R., & Littrell, J. M. (1998). Brief counseling for students with learning disabilities. *Professional School Counseling, 2,* 60–68.

U.S. Department of Education. (2002). *No Child Left Behind.* Retrieved April 26, 2003, from http://www.ed.gov/nclb/landing.jhtml

Vaughn, S., & Hager, D. (1994). Social competence as a multifaceted construct: How do students with learning disabilities fare? *Learning Disability Quarterly, 17,* 253–266.

Voeller, K. (1993). Techniques for measuring social competence in children. In G. Lyon (Ed.), *Frames of reference for the assessment of learning disabilities* (pp. 523–554). Baltimore: Brookes.

Weiss, R. S. (1994). *Learning from strangers: The art and method of qualitative interview studies.* New York: First Free Press.

Williams, W. C., & Lair, G. S. (1991). Using a person-centered approach with children who have a disability. *Elementary School Guidance and Counseling, 25,* 194–204.

ARTICLE 14.2 The Effect of Reciprocal Peer Counseling in the Enhancement of Self-Concept Among Adolescents

E. O. Egbochuku J. J. Obiunu

INTRODUCTION

The desire for a positive evaluation of self affects a person's feelings, actions, and aspirations throughout life. School experiences play an important role in the development of self-perceptions in the course of childhood and adolescence and this can have powerful long-term effects on an individual's self concept; yet most proposals for school improvement and reform emphasize either teachers, administrators, parents, or class size, overlooking one of the most crucial change agents—the students. All of this is contrary to the peer principle, which believes that deep, lasting changes, individually and structurally, must ultimately come from sharing with like individuals.

The effectiveness of the use of peer counsellors within the school system has been well documented in foreign literature (Hsiao-Chen, 2003; Ladyshewsky 2001; Hoffman and Warner, 1976). Gartner and Riessman (1998) in their study proposed the application of the peer counseling principle in schools since research has shown that peer counselling and other peer support programmes are effective in improving attitudes and behavior and even have a ripple effect on the schools' overall dynamics. Shechtman (2002) reviewed the outcome of research on group psychotherapy with children and found a consensus on its effectiveness. Shechtman's review also found that in order to improve achievement, the social and emotional dimensions along with academic need must be addressed. Peer counsellors fall under the general rubric of paraprofessionals—that is those without professional training who are selected from the group to be served, trained and given on-going supervision to perform some key functions generally performed by professionals. Peer group counselling provides a non-judgemental acceptance, care and support; provides opportunities to give and receive from others and creates a non-competitive, empowering environment.

In the Nigerian society, the child in school is expected to receive instruction and guidance from the adults in the school. There is no evidence in literature about the use of peers as counsellors in Nigerian secondary schools. However, it is critical to note that young people are far more influenced by their peers than by parents, teachers or other adults (Gartner and Riessman, 1998). Peers have a profound effect on each other's fashions, social attitudes and decisions. For better or for worse, they model themselves on other young people. While there may be unquestionably much negativity in peer influence, there are lots of young people who are dedicated to their own advancement and that of their mates. These students, if trained can form the core of the peer counselling programmes, the essential idea being that people are influenced and can be helped best by others who share their problems or conditions.

Brigman and Campbell (2003) opined that one of the most promising interventions for school counsellors interested in making their impact felt on students' achievement and behaviour is peer group counselling. Peer group counselling is a mode of counselling which involves a relationship among three or more persons of relatively same age and status in which all mutually seek the goal of bringing about positive behavioural changes in group members. One of them acts as the facilitator. A modification of this mode of counselling is the reciprocal peer group counselling in which group members act as facilitators in turns. Such developmental programmes are proactive and preventive, helping students acquire the attitudes necessary for successful mastery of normal developmental tasks. But do our educational administrators understand fully the potentials and significance of peer programmes? Do they understand that peer influence can be positive? If a child is given the opportunity to participate in peer counselling as a counsellor having the opportunity to share a valuable and worthwhile experience, will he or she not gain in self worth? Will the experience not motivate him/her to reach out to others and to perfect his or her skills? In the same vein, if a child is a client to a peer counsellor after whom he or she can model himself or herself, will his or her feeling of self worth not be enhanced because he or she has a counsellor who truly understands? Will the similarity in experience not enhance the self-concept of both counselor and client?

It is therefore hoped that the results of the present study will draw the attention of school counsellors, educational planners, and administrators to the significance of the peer principle in relation to self-concept enhancement that will invariably influence the school improvement and reforms.

Hypotheses

The following null hypotheses were formulated to guide the study.

1. There will be no significant difference in the self-concept of adolescent students in the experimental and control group at post-test.
2. There will be no significant difference in the self-concept of males and females in the treatment groups.

Methodology

This study is experimental in nature. A pre-test/post-test control design was employed. The impetus of the study was to observe the effects of peer counselling on self-concept. The variables were peer counselling verse control (manipulated variables), and sex (intervening variable) on enhancement self-concept (criterion variable). The population of the study was all the senior secondary schools in Benin City, Edo State. There are about thirty-four senior secondary schools in Benin City. These are single sex and co-educational schools with population ranging from 5002,500 students. The choice of Benin City is based on its metropolitan nature. It is the state capital consisting of three out of the eighteen local government areas in the state. The inhabitants are of diverse socioeconomic status.

Stratified random sampling was employed to select three schools from the strata—Boys', Girls', and co-educational schools. The sample consisted of sixty-eight senior secondary school II students (males and females) from the three schools randomly selected. Simple random sampling was used to select one intact class each from the SS II classes in the three schools. The choice of SS II students for the study was made because SS I students are new in the senior secondary school system and are still settling down while SS III is the certificate class, preparing for an external examination.

The initial concept of the study was to select only subjects with low self-concept scores: However, on administration of the instrument (pre-test), it was found that there were no students with low self-concept. This could be as a result of parental involvement with the African child. Students were therefore randomly assigned to the treatment and control groups. The final selection of subjects was carried out at the point of analysis of data collected. Subjects with very high self-concept at the pre-test were dropped.

A 40-item self-concept scale was constructed, validated and used to measure the variable, self-concept. Peer counselling was employed to effect self-concept modification in the subjects, while a control group of students also received a non-specific treatment. Sixty-eight senior secondary school two students were involved in this study. One instrument was used in the study. The instrument, an Adolescent Self Concept Inventory (ASCI) was adapted from the Akinboye (1977) adolescent personal data inventory (self concept scale). The original version of the scale was made up of 30-items. Some items on the scale were modified in language and ten new items were added to make the present instrument a 40-item scale. In Akinboye (1977), APDI a nine-point scale ranging from least "like me" to "most like me" was used to rate each item, while the present instrument used a 5-point Likert scale ranging from "completely true of me" to "completely untrue of me."

(continued)

ARTICLE 14.2 (continued)

Treatment Programs

The treatment programmes for the study included pre-treatment, treatment and post treatment sessions. There were two groups of subjects, the treatment and control groups. The treatment programme for the treatment group was designed to enhance the self-concept of the subjects. The treatment programme for the control group consisted of lessons in English language on the topic-spoken English, which was taught by the English teachers in the three schools.

The pre-treatment for all the subjects, involved, first, a pre-test of the instrument, and secondly, random assignment of subjects into the treatment groups. For the treatment group, besides the pre-test and random assignment of subjects into the group, peer counsellors were randomly selected and trained; research assistants were also trained. Eleven sessions were used for the training of the ten peer counsellor (on a one-to-one basis) and research assistants in each of the schools. The treatment programme involved 10 one (1) hour sessions in which the subjects in a peer group counselling encounter focussed on the topics: Leadership skills, self esteem, good study habits, skills for effective study habits, preparing for examinations, self awareness, self worth, body image, self acceptance and being yourself. For the control group, the treatment programme involved English lessons on spoken English, which focussed on consonant sounds. This also lasted for 10 sessions.

RESULTS

To determine the effects of treatment on the self-concept of the subjects, the following hypothesis was tested at .05 level of significances.

There will be no significant difference in the self-concept of adolescent students in the various treatment groups at post-test.

The data displayed on Table 1, reveal that the mean score for peer counseling ($M = 164.71$) is significantly higher than that of the control group ($M = 132.82$). This indicates a significant difference in the self-concept of adolescent students who participated in the various treatment programmes. Further analysis was carried out to determine if the mean score for the peer-counselling group was significantly higher than that of the control group.

TABLE 1 Distribution of Post-Test Mean Scores for Self-Concept

Groups	*N*	Mean	*SD*
Peer counselling	34	164.71	13.44
Control	34	132.82	26.63

Analysis on Table 2 reveals that the calculated *t*-value of 6.58 is greater than the critical *t*-value of 1.96 with $df = 66$ and alpha level of .05. The null hypothesis is therefore rejected at $p < .05$ and conclusion is reached that there is a significant difference in the self-concept of subjects in the treatment groups at post-test.

TABLE 2 Mean, Standard Deviation, and *t*-Test Data on the Effects of Treatment on Post-Test Self-Concept of Subjects

Treatment	*N*	$\bar{X}$	*SD*	Mean Difference	*t*
Peer-counselling	34	164.71	13.45		
Control	34	132.82	24.86	31.88	6.58*

*Significant at .05 level.

There will be no significant difference in the self-concept of male and females in the treatment groups at post-test.

Figures in parentheses represent number of subjects in the subgroups.

The data displayed in Table 3 reveals that the mean score for males in the treatment groups as (M = 148.25) is not significantly different from the mean score for female (M = 149.36). Further analysis of the data shown on Table 4, also reveals that the calculated t-value of .17 is less than the critical t-value of 1.96 with degree of freedom, 66 and at level of .05.

TABLE 3 Distribution of Mean Post-Test Scores of Treatment Groups by Sex

	Treatment		
Sex	**Peer Counselling**	**Control**	**Total**
Male	165.5 (18)	132.8 (20)	148.28 (38)
Female	163.81 (16)	132.85 (14)	149.36 (30)
Total	164.71 (34)	132.82 (34)	68

Figures in parentheses represent number of subjects in the subgroups.

TABLE 4 Mean, Standard Deviation, and t-Test Data on the Effects of Sex on the Post-Test Self-Concept of Subjects

Sex	N	$\bar{X}$	SD	Mean Difference	t
Female	30	149.37	26.62		
Male	38	148.29	24.96	1.08	.17*

*Not significant at $p > 0.05$.

The null hypothesis which states no significant difference in self-concept between male and female is therefore accepted at $p > 0.05$.

Discussion

The finding of this study indicates that reciprocal peer counselling has a significant positive effect on the self-concept of the adolescent students. This finding lend credence to the assertion made by (Hoffman and Warner 1976; Divers-Starnes 1991; and Ladyshewsky 2001; Hsiao-Chen, 2003) among others, that paraprofessionals, particularly peers can be as effective as professionals in counselling when given the required training. The findings are also in agreement with those of Oladele (2000) who reported positive effect in programme participants' self efficiency and behaviour as well as increased self-esteem, self-awareness and capacity for empathy. The researchers of the present study are not surprised at the outcome of the study. Peers have a profound influence on one another and peer-oriented interventions are designed to capitalize on the potentially positive influence of peers in bringing about improvement in behaviour (Choudhury, 2001). Generally, studies have shown that children have certain advantages over adults in helping their peers. They understand their problems better because they are cognitively closer and this fact makes the peer counsellor present the issue in terms the group members will understand (Nwagwu and Nwaneri, 2002). The peer counsellors can effectively model study skills and habits, ask and answer questions posed by group members. It was based on the above assumptions that the present study set out to improve the self concept of adolescents through reciprocal peer group counselling in which many of the children had the opportunity of being models to others and these enhanced the self-concept of the students. As Patwardhan (2002) noted in his study, the similarity between model and learner increases with the influence of modelling. The findings of this study therefore give support to the use of peers in bringing about fundamental positive changes in students' behaviour, both academic and general.

(continued)

ARTICLE 14.2 (continued)

The findings of the study indicate that there is no significant effect of sex on the self-concept of the students involved in the study. These findings are at variance with the findings of Fontana, (1981), and Obidigbo (2002) who reported that girls had a lower self-concept than boys. A possible explanation for this is that in the last few decades, women's career choices and social relations have been diversified and the distinction between jobs for men and women are becoming hazy. This has resulted in Nigerian adolescents, perceiving themselves positively irrespective of sex, age or socio-economic status. Moreover, models exist for both sexes in all spheres of life encouraging both sexes in all spheres of life encouraging both sexes to aspire high. The findings of the study are in consonance with those of Egbochuku, (1997) and Nwagwu and Nwaneri (2002) who studied the demographic difference in adolescent self-concept, and made findings, which indicated no significant difference in the way, Nigerian boys and girls perceive themselves.

CONCLUSION

The results of the study reveal that reciprocal peer counselling is effective in enhancing the self-concept of individuals; sex has no effect on the self-concept of the adolescents. It can be concluded that peer influence can be positive and that the peer group counselling encounter can be psychologically rewarding. Also there was no significant difference in the way males and females perceive themselves in the study. This shows that peer counselling is a technique that can be used for the enhancement of self-concept for both sexes. Since Reciprocal peer counselling therapy proved effective in the enhancement of self-concept, it follows therefore that the result of this study is valuable to the Nigerian educational system. The implementation of the results of this study will to a large extent bring about a change both to the individuals and the school and the society at large, which could lead to a reduction in cult activities; and wastage rates in the school system.

REFERENCES

Akinboye, J. O. (1977), Adolescent personal data inventory (self-concept scale), University Press Limited Ibadan.

Brigman, G., and Campbell, C. (2003) "Helping students improve academic achievement and school success behaviour". Professional school counselling. Dec. 2003. American School Counsellor Association.

Choudhury, I. (2001). Use of reciprocal peer tutoring technique in an environmental control systems course at an undergraduate level. ASC proceedings of the 37th Annual Conference, University of Denver, Colorado.

Diver-Starnes, A. C. (1991) "Assessing the effectiveness of an inner-city high school peer counselling program." *Urban Education 26,* 269–284.

Egbochuku, E. O. (1997). "Differential effectiveness of three guidance techniques to fostering maturity among secondary school adolescents." Unpublished Ph.D. Thesis. University of Benin-Benin City, Nigeria Coppersmith.

Fontana, D. (1981). *Psychology for teachers.* British Psychological Society and Macmillan Publishers, Ltd.

Hoffman, A. M., and Warner, R. M. (1976). "Paraprofessionals effectiveness." *Personnel and Guidance Journal, 54*(10).

Hsiao-Chen, H. (2003). "A research on career self concept and its relevant factors of high school students from single-parent family."

Ladyshewsky, R. (2001). *Reciprocal peer coaching: A strategy for training and development in professional discipline.* Jamison, ACT, Australia: Higher Education Research and Development Society of Australia Inc.

Nwagwu H. and Nwaneri, C. (2002). "The demographic differences on adolescent self-concept." *Nigerian Journal of Clinical and Counselling, 8*(2), 44–166.

Obidegbo, G. C. (2002). "The relationship between self concept and academic performance of Nigerian Students." *IFE Psychologia, 10*(2).

Oladele, J. O. (2000). *Fundamentals of guidance and counselling. A functional approach.* Johns-Lad Publishers. Lagos.

Patwardhan, V. (2002). Self-concept of Eritrean Students: Exploring self-concept of students' links with gender grade and future identity.

Shechtman, Z. (2002). "Child group psychotherapy in the school at the threshold of a new millennium." *Journal of Counselling and Development, 50,* 293–299.

Sisco, P. (2000). "Peer Counselling: An Overview." Independent Liong Institute Canada.

REFERENCES

American Educational Research Association. (2008). *Definition of scientifically based research*. Washington, DC: American Educational Research Association. Available at http://www.aera.net/Default.aspx?id=6790&terms=definition+of+scientifically+based+research.

Anderson, G., Herr, K., & Nihlen, A. (1994). *Studying your own school: An educator's guide to qualitative practitioner research*. Thousands Oaks, CA: Corwin Press.

Balli, S. J. (1998). When mom and dad help: Student reflections on parent involvement with homework. *Journal of Research and Development in Education, 31*, 142–147.

Bogdan, R. C., & Biklen, S. K. (2007). *Qualitative research in education: An introduction to theory and methods* (5th ed.). Boston: Allyn & Bacon.

Borich, G. D., & Madden, S. K. (1977). *Evaluating classroom instruction: A sourcebook of instruments.* Reading, MA: Addison-Wesley.

Borman, G. D., & Dowling, N. M. (2006). Longitudinal achievement effects of multiyear summer school: Evidence from the teach Baltimore randomized field trial. *Educational Evaluation and Policy Analysis, 28*(1), 25–48.

Bryman, A. (2006). Integrating quantitative and qualitative research: How is it done? *Qualitative Research, 6*(1), 97–113.

Calhoun, E. M. (1994). *How to use research in the self-renewing school.* Alexandria, VA: Association for Supervision and Curriculum Development.

Campbell, D. T., and Stanley, J. C. (1963). Experimental and quasi-experimental designs for research on teaching. In N. L. Gage (Ed.), *Handbook of research on teaching.* (pp.171–246), Washington: American Educational Research Association (printed by Rand-McNally).

Case, R. E. (2004). Forging ahead into new social networks and looking back to past social identities: A case study of a foreign-born English as a second language teacher in the United States. *Urban Education, 39*(2), 125–148.

Certo, J., Cauley, K. M., & Chafin, C. (2002). *Students' perspectives on their high school experience.* Paper presented at the Annual Meeting of the American Educational Research Association, April, New Orleans.

Choi, H., & Heckenlaible–Gotto, M. J. (1998). Classroom-based social skills training: Impact on peer acceptance of first-grade students. *Journal of Educational Research, 91*, 209–214.

Chun, K. T., Cobb, S., & French, J. R. P., Jr. (1974). *Measures for psychological assessment: A guide to 3,000 original sources and their applications.* Ann Arbor: Institute for Social Research, University of Michigan.

Comrey, A. L., Backer, T. E., & Glaser, E. M. (1973). *A sourcebook of mental health measures.* Los Angeles: Human Interaction Research Institute.

Conger, D. (2005). Within-school segregation in an urban school district. *Educational Evaluation and Policy Analysis, 27*(3), 225–244.

Creswell, J. W. (2008). *Educational research: Planning, conducting, and evaluating quantitative and qualitative research* (3rd ed.). Upper Saddle River, NJ: Pearson Education.

Creswell, J. W. (2009). *Research design: Qualitative, quantitative, and mixed methods approaches* (3rd ed.). Thousand Oaks, CA: Sage.

Creswell, J. W., & Plano Clark, V. L. (2011). *Designing and conducting mixed methods research* (2nd ed.). Thousand Oaks, CA: Sage.

Endreny, A. (2006). Children's ideas about animal adaptations: An action research project. *Journal of Elementary Science Education, 18*(1), 33–43.

Fabiano, E. (1989). *Index to tests used in educational dissertations.* Phoenix, AZ: Oryx Press.

Gall, M. D., Borg, W. R., & Gall, J. P. (2003). *Educational research: An introduction* (7th ed.). New York: Longman.

Gall, M. D., Gall, J. P., & Borg, W. R. (2007). *Educational research: An introduction* (8th ed.). Boston: Allyn & Bacon.

Giebelhaus, C. R., & Bowman, C. L. (2002). Teaching mentors: Is it worth the effort? *The Journal of Educational Research, 95*, 246–254.

Glanz, J. (2003). *Action research: An educational leader's guide to school improvement* (2nd ed.). Norwood, MA: Christopher-Gordon.

Goldman, B., & Mitchell, D. (2007). *Directory of unpublished experimental mental measures* (Vol. 9). Washington, DC: American Psychological Association.

Goodwin, W. L., & Driscoll, L. (1980). *Handbook for measurement and evaluation in early childhood education: Issues, measures, and methods.* San Francisco: Jossey-Bass.

Greene, J. C., Caracelli, V. J., & Graham, W. F. (1989). Toward a conceptual framework for mixed-method evaluation designs. *Educational Evaluation and Policy Analysis, 11*(3), 255–274.

Guba, E. (1981). Criteria for assessing the trustworthiness of naturalistic inquiries. *Educational Communication and Technology, 29*(2), 75–91.

Hammill, D. D., Brown, L., & Bryant, B. (1992). *A consumer's guide to tests in print* (2nd ed.). Austin, TX: Pro-Ed.

Hanson, W. E., Creswell, J. W., Plano Clark, V. L., Petska, K. S., & Creswell, D. J. (2005). Mixed methods research designs in counseling psychology. *Journal of Counseling Psychology, 52*(2), 224–235.

Heck, R. H., & Crislip, M. (2001). Direct and indirect writing assessments: Examining issues of equity and utility. *Educational Evaluation and Policy Analysis, 23,* 19–36.

Henry, G. T., Gordon, C. S., & Rickman, D. K. (2006). Early education policy alternatives: Comparing quality and outcomes of head start and state prekindergarten. *Educational Evaluation and Policy Analysis, 28*(1), 77–99.

Herndon, M. K., & Hirt, J. B. (2004). Black students and their families: What leads to success in college. *Journal of Black Studies, 34*(4), 489–513.

Johnson, B., & Christensen, L. (2008). *Educational research: Quantitative, qualitative, and mixed approaches.* Thousand Oaks, CA: Sage.

Johnson, L. B., & Onwuegbuzie, A. J. (2004). Mixed methods research: A paradigm whose time has come. *Educational Researcher, 33*(7), 14–26.

Johnson, O. G. (1976). *Tests and measurements in child development: Handbook I and II.* San Francisco: Jossey-Bass.

Juhler, S. M., Rech, J. F., From, S. G., & Brogan, M. M. (1998). The effect of optional retesting on college students' achievement in an individualized algebra course. *Journal of Experimental Education, 66,* 125–137.

Keyser, D. J., & Sweetland, R. C. (Eds.). (1984, 1994). *Test critiques* (Vols. 1–10). Kansas City, MO: Test Corporation of America.

Koshy, V. (2005). *Action research for improving practice: A practical guide.* Thousand Oaks, CA: Sage.

Langer, J. A. (2001) Beating the odds: Teaching middle and high school students to read and write well. *American Educational Research Journal, 38*(4), 837–880.

LaParo, K. M., & Pianta, R. C. (2000). Predicting children's competence in the early school years: A meta-analytic review. *Review of Educational Research, 70,* 443–484.

Leech, N. L., Dellinger, A. B., Brannagan, K. B., & Tanaka, H. (2010). Evaluating mixed research studies: A mixed methods approach. *Journal of Mixed Methods Research, 4*(1), 17–31.

Lewis, A. E. (2001). There is not "race" in the school-yard: Color-blind ideology in an (almost) all-white school. *American Educational Research Journal, 38,* 781–811.

Lincoln, Y. S. (2010). "What a long, strange trip it's been . . .": Twenty-five years of qualitative and new paradigm research. *Qualitative Inquiry, 16*(1), 3–9.

Lustberg, R. S., Motta, R., & Naccari, N. (1990). A model using the WISC-R to predict success in programs for gifted children. *Psychology in the Schools, 21,* 126–131.

Maddox, T. (2002). *Tests: A comprehensive reference for assessments in psychology, education, and business* (5th ed.). Kansas City, MO: Test Corporation of America.

Marsh, H. W., Koller, O., & Baumert, J. (2001). Reunification of East and West German school systems: Longitudinal multi level modeling study of the big-fish-little-pond effect on academic self-concept. *American Educational Research Journal, 38,* 321–350.

Mathes, P. G., Torgensen, J. K., & Allor, J. H. (2001). The effects of peer-assisted literacy strategies for first-grade readers with and without additional computer-assisted instruction in phonological awareness. *American Educational Research Journal, 38,* 371–410.

Maxwell, J. (1992). Understanding and validity in qualitative research. *Harvard Educational Review, 62*(3), 279–300.

McCardle, P., & Chhabra, V. (Eds.) (2004). *The voice of evidence in reading research.* Baltimore, MD: Paul H. Brookes.

McLendon, M. K., Hearn, J. C., & Deaton, R. (2006). Called to account: Analyzing the origins and spread of state performance-accountability policies for higher education. *Educational Evaluation and Policy Analysis, 28*(1), 1–24.

McMillan, J. H. (2000). *Teachers' classroom assessment and grading practices decision making.* Paper presented at the Annual Meeting of the National Council of Measurement in Education, New Orleans.

McMillan, J. H. (2001). Secondary teachers' classroom assessment and grading practices. *Educational Measurement: Issues and Practice, 20,* 20–32.

McMillan, J. H. (2002). *The impact of high-stakes external testing on classroom assessment decision making.* Paper presented at the Annual Meeting of the American Educational Research Association, New Orleans.

McMillan, J. H., Myran, S., & Workman, D. (2002). Elementary teachers' classroom assessment and grading practices. *The Journal of Educational Research, 95*(4), 203–214.

McMillan, J. H., & Reed, D. F. (1994). At-risk students and resiliency: Factors contributing to academic success. *Clearing House, 67,* 137–140.

McMillan, J. H., & Schumacher, S. (2010). *Research in education: A conceptual introduction* (7th ed.). Boston: Allyn & Bacon.

Mertens, D. M. (2010). *Research and evaluation in education and psychology: Integrating diversity with quantitative, qualitative, and mixed methods* (3rd ed.). Thousand Oaks, CA: Sage.

Miller, D. C., & Salkind, N. J. (2002). *Handbook of research design and social measurement* (6th ed.). Thousand Oaks, CA: Sage.

Miller, M. D., Linn, R. L., & Grouland. N. (2008). *Measurement and assessment in teaching* (10th ed.). Upper Saddle River, NJ; Columbus, OH: Pearson, Merrill, Prentice-Hall.

Mills, G. E. (2007). *Action research: A guide for the teacher researcher.* Upper Saddle River, NJ: Merrill/Prentice Hall.

National Research Council. (2002). *Scientific research in education.* Washington, DC: National Academy Press.

Onwuegbuzie, A. J., & Slate, J. R. (2006). *Conducting mixed methods data analyses: A step-by-step guide.* Presentation materials from a professional development course at the Annual Meeting of the American Educational Research Association, San Francisco.

Robinson, J. P., & Shaver, P. R. (1973). *Measures of social psychological attitudes.* Ann Arbor: University of Michigan, Institute for Social Research.

Rue, G., Dingley, C., & Bush, H. (2002). Inner strength in women: metasynthesis of qualitative findings and theory development. *Journal of Theory Construction and Testing, 4*(2), 36–39.

Sagor, R. (2005). *The action research guidebook: A four-step process for educators and school teams.* Thousand Oaks, CA: Corwin Press.

Shavelson, R. J., & Towne, L. (2000). *Scientific research in education*. Washington, DC: National Academy Press.

Shulman, L. S. (2005, June 8). Seek simplicity . . . and distrust it. *Education Week*, p. 45.

Simon, A., & Boyer, E. G. (1974). *Mirrors for behavior III: An anthology of observation instruments*. Wyncote, PA: Communications Materials Center.

Stake, R. E. (1995). *The art of case study research.* Thousand Oaks, CA: Sage.

Tashakkori, A., & Teddlie, C. (1998). *Mixed methodology: Combining qualitative and quantitative approaches.* Thousand Oaks, CA: Sage.

Tashakkori, A., & Teddlie, C. (2003). *Handbook of mixed methods in social and behavioral research.* Thousand Oaks, CA: Sage.

Teddlie, C., & Yu, F. (2007). Mixed methods sampling: A typology with examples. *Journal of Mixed Methods Research, 1*(1), 77–100.

Touliatos, J., Perlmutter, B. F., Straus, M. A., & Holden, G. W. (2001). *Handbook of family measurement techniques.* Thousand Oaks, CA: Sage.

Walker, D. K. (1973). *Socioemotional measures for preschool and kindergarten children: A handbook*. San Francisco: Jossey-Bass.

Wilcox, B., Williams, L., & Reutzel, D. R. (1997). Effects of task roles on participation and productivity in the intermediate grades. *Journal of Educational Research, 39*, 165–205.

CREDITS

Article 1.1: David P. Shepardson and Edward L. Pizzini. "Gender, achievement, and perception toward science activities". *School Science and Mathematics, 94*(4), 188–93, 1994. Reprinted with the permission of the publishers.

Article 7.1: Roy M. Legette, "Causal Beliefs of Public School Students about Success and Failure in Music" from *Journal of Research in Music Education 46*(1) (1998). Copyright © 1998 by Music Educators National Conference. Reprinted with the permission of the publishers.

Article 8.1: Bruce W. Tuckman, "Using Tests as Incentive to Motivate Procrastinators to Study" from *Journal of Experimental Educational Foundation, 66*(2), 141–147, 1998. Reprinted with permission of the Helen Dwight Reid Educational Foundation. Published by Heldref Publications, 1319 Eighteenth St., NW, Washington, DC 20036-1802. Copyright © 1998.

Article 10.1: Paul G. Schempp, "Learning on the Job: An Analysis of the Acquisition of a Teacher's Knowledge" from *Journal of Research and Development in Education 28* (1995). Copyright © 1995 by Eastern Educational Research Association. Reprinted with the permission of the University of Georgia.

Article 11.1: P. Akos, "Student Perceptions of the Transition from Elementary to Middle School." *Professional School Counseling, 5* (2002), 339–345. Reprinted by permission from Professional School Counseling, published by the American School Counselor Association.

Article 12.1: A. Maryland, "Improving Student Understanding and Motivation of Multiplication Facts." In Geoffrey E. Mills (Ed.), *Action Research: A Guide for the Teacher Researcher* (2007), 81–83. Upper Saddle River, NJ: Prentice-Hall. Adapted by permission of Pearson Education, Inc., Upper Saddle River, NJ.

Article 14.1: Helen Nicole Frye, "How Elementary School Counselors Can Meet the Needs of Students with Disabilities." *Professional School Counseling, 8*(5), 442–451, 2005. Reprinted by permission of the publisher.

Article 14.2: E. O. Egbochuku and J. J. Obiunu, "The Effect of Reciprocal Peer Counseling in the Enhancement of Self-Concept among Adolescents." *Education, 12*(3) 2006, 504–512. Reprinted by permission of the publisher.

INDEX